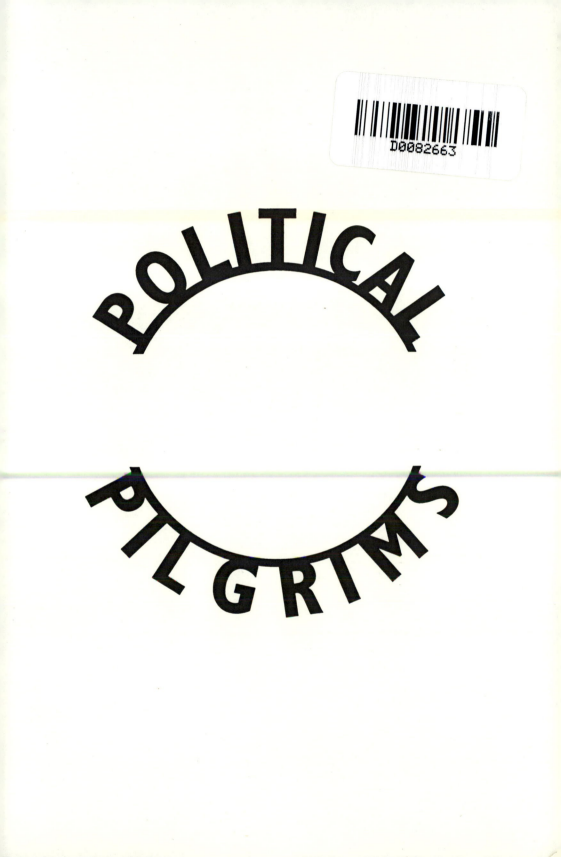

POLITICAL

PILGRIMS

FOURTH EDITION

**with a new introduction
by the author**

POLITICAL

Western Intellectuals in
Search of the Good Society

PILGRIMS

PAUL HOLLANDER

Transaction Publishers
New Brunswick (U.S.A.) and London (U.K.)

Eleventh printing 2009

New material this edition copyright © 1998 by Transaction Publishers, New Brunswick, New Jersey, www.transactionpub.com

Originally published in 1981 by Oxford University Press. Preface to the 1982 edition originally published by Oxford University Press. Preface to the 1990 edition originally published by University Press of America.

Library of Congress Catalog Number: 97-7925
ISBN: 978-1-56000-954-2
Printed in the United States of America

Library of Congress Cataloging-in-Publication Data

Hollander, Paul, 1932-
    Political Pilgrims : Western intellectuals in search of the good society / Paul Hollander ; with a new introduction by the author.
        p. cm.
    Originally published: New York : Harper Colophon Books, 1981.
    Includes bibliographical references and index.
    ISBN 1-56000-954-3
        1. Communist countries—Foreign public opinion. 2. Intellectuals—Journeys—Communist countries. 3. Intellectuals—Political activity— History—20th century. 4. Intellectuals—Attitudes—History—20th century. 5. Public opinion.

D850.H65 1997
306.2—dc21   97-7925

This book is dedicated
to the memory of my father,
Jenö Hollander

Contents

Introduction to the Transaction Edition: The Durable Significance of the Political Pilgrimage

> Wishful thinking has always figured in human affairs. When the imagination finds no satisfaction in existing reality, it seeks refuge in wishfully constructed places and periods . . . travel romances have been continually changing expressions of that which was lacking in actual life.
>
> KARL MANNHEIM, *Ideology and Utopia*

Political Pilgrims was first published in hardcover by Oxford University Press in 1981; it was followed by a paperback edition by Harper & Row in 1983 and another soft cover edition by the University Press of America in 1990. Each of these printings (far from huge) were sold out.

Much has changed not only since the first but even since the most recent edition. In 1989 (when the preface for the 1990 edition was written) there was already advanced decay and turmoil in communist systems, but few predicted how close their collapse was, symbolized by the tearing down of the Berlin Wall later in the same year. Nor did I anticipate in 1989 that one year later the leftist government in Nicaragua would allow itself to be voted out of power and thereby deprive political tourists from their prime destination during the 1980s. In Ethiopia the civil war culminated in the overthrow of the exceptionally brutal Soviet- and Cuban-supported regime in 1991. The pro-Soviet regimes in Angola and Mozambique sought to make peace with the anti-Communist guerillas who controlled much of these countries. The Communist regime in Afghanistan was likewise overthrown by the anti-Soviet guerillas as Gorbachev withdrew the Soviet troops supporting it.

I noted in the 1990 preface that

> for the most part the estranged, adversarial intellectuals and quasi-intellectuals in the West averted their eyes from these developments, from the resounding moral and material failures of these socialist countries. They were especially disinclined to detect any connection between the ideas and ideals of Marxism-Leninism and the sorry states of the societies that sought to implement these ideas. (p. x, 1990 preface)

This still remains the case.

By the time the Soviet Union itself fell apart in 1991 few countries remained to inspire significant amounts of political pilgrimages. Of the countries which used to be the major destinations of the pilgrims or, as I also called them, the political tourists (a more applicable term with the rise of such mass tourism, and especially in the context of Nicaragua),[1] few remain. The entire Soviet bloc disappeared by 1991; Nicaragua ceased to inspire political tourism in the absence of a leftist government; China has increasingly allowed foreign capitalists to penetrate its economy and encouraged private entrepreneurship and consumption (although the political monopoly of the party has been retained); similar trends developed in Vietnam. Given the anti-capitalist convictions of those inclined to political tourism, their interest in these countries was bound to decline.

Cambodia under Pol Pot lost credibility back in the 1970s as soon as the Vietnamese Communist regime went to war with it. The conflict made acceptable even on the far-left the criticism of the Pol Pot regime for the massacres which were earlier doubted, or outright denied. In this context it will be instructive to recall Noam Chomsky's erstwhile remarks on this matter as he remains a sterling example, indeed archetype of the bitterly estranged Western intellectual, for now without an alternative land of social justice to promote. His last enthusiasm was Sandinista Nicaragua.[2]

The political system of Cuba remains largely unchanged, though more impoverished, with the disintegration of the Soviet bloc and the vanishing of its steady support. What I wrote in the 1990 preface is still valid:

> Cuba under Castro has retained a fair amount of support . . . though it has remained one of the most repressive, intolerant, militaristic and economically mismanaged of the Communist systems. It has also been a country 10% of its population preferred to leave. . . . Such matters were overlooked by the sympathizers, perhaps in part precisely because the Cuban regime, personified by Castro, never lost its outward self-assurance and never failed to claim moral superiority over the United States and other capitalist systems. (p. xii, 1990 preface)

Regardless of what happened to the actual pilgrimages (and whatever survives of them will be examined below), what is probably of greater significance is the mind-set which gave rise to them and which by no means has disappeared especially in the United States. It is in that direction that the justification for reprinting this study lies: *Political Pilgrims* may still be read with some profit (and occasional amusement) as a parable of durable alienation, or what an English sociologist called "middle class radicalism."[3]

Regardless of the current, far more limited availability of countries upon which longings for a better world may be projected, it remains to be better understood (notwithstanding the efforts of this author) why in the first place so many Western intellectuals had been so irresistibly drawn to repressive and mendacious totalitarian systems and movements, and how they succeeded for long periods of time to overlook or downplay their morally debilitating flaws and misdeeds. Doris Lessing was among the few also preoccupied with this question and critical of the double standards associated with it. In 1987 when the Soviet Union sought to subdue Afghanistan with great brutality, she wrote:

> There is a reluctance to criticize the Soviet Union. After all that has happened, all the information we have had . . . an inhibition persists . . .
>
> . . . if the Soviet Union, at Chernobyl, releases radioactivity that poisons its own water and soil and will cause the deaths of no one yet knows how many of is citizens . . . then in no time at all we will be reading and hearing Chernobyl and Three Mile Island equated—Three Mile Island which killed no one, and did not poison food, animals and soil. It means that if the Soviet Union shoots down a civilian airliner . . . almost at once this will be in some way proved to be the fault of the U.S. . . .
>
> How . . . did it come about that the most brutal, cynical regime of its time was so much admired, excused, by people describing themselves as humanists, humanitarians, and long after its true nature was thoroughly exposed?[4]

As far as Chernobyl was concerned it may be worth noting here that an American "peace activist," John Mack, M.D. (professor of psychiatry at the Harvard Medical School) managed to find a benign interpretation for the withholding of information about the disaster as part of the "tendency on the part of Soviet authorities to downplay catastrophes and instead offer reassurance to the Soviet people so as to prevent emotional distress."[5] This was the same Professor Mack who more recently expressed his firm belief in extraterrestrial visitors harassing American women.[6] Perhaps his assessment of the therapeutic value of Soviet censorship prepared him to subscribe to his belief in visitors from outer space.

It may also be recalled here that while the Soviet political system had ceased to be an object of admiration for Western intellectuals a long time ago, since the late 1960s the prevailing view on the left was by no means totally negative; as a former charter member of the New Left summed it up:

> The Soviet Union was not a very appealing country. . . . Rather, my comrades and I regarded the USSR in the same way one might regard a brainless bully who happens to be in your corner during the street fight. The Soviet Union was, we thought, the ultimate guarantor of world revolution . . . the USSR . . . stood behind . . . Havana and Hanoi where we believed utopia was being born.[7]

Questions Doris Lessing raised are very similar to those addressed in this book and reexamined in the introductions to its successive editions. Of late, Daniel Bell asked essentially the same: "why did not the young zealots read and learn about the history of revolutions, and why . . . did one and does one, see the continual 'process of enchantment,' the aching need to embrace revolutionary romanticism which recurs time and again?"[8] Martin Malia, the Russian historian too raised the baffling question: "How could the Soviets get away for so long . . . with what turned out to have been from the start a world-historical fraud?"[9] Malcolm Muggeridge in 1934 had an answer, limited as it was at the time, to the Soviet case:

> The answer . . . is terribly simple. . . . You are indulgent towards the dictatorship of the proletariat because. . . . You are frustrated revolutionaries, and the spectacle of a revolutionary government in actual existence so intoxicates you that you fall on your knees . . . in awed worship. . . . The dictatorship of the proletariat is all-powerful and mouths your aspirations; and you, who have for so long had to be content with spinning your ideas into words, see in it the possibility of translating them suddenly into deeds.[10]

More recently Todd Gitlin, himself a former 1960s radical made reference to a similar mentality: "They were so eager to see the future work; they were hungry to believe that somewhere out there, preferably on the dusky side of the globe where people looked exotic, some decency was under construction."[11]

To this writer it did not cease to be deeply puzzling how and why so many Western intellectuals could lose, at certain periods of time, the capacity to differentiate, to note important distinctions between various social-political systems, countries, amounts of repression, corruption, social injustice, organized lying, and so forth. Such an impaired capacity to make pivotal moral and historical distinctions underlies the phenomenon of the political pilgrimage and the attitudes supporting it. This impaired capacity to make important moral and political distinctions appears to be a major legacy of the 1960s, its rhetoric, its impatient anti-intellectual, anti-rationalist mind-set, its radical revolutionary romanticism.

A more recent observation of Doris Lessing sheds further light on the mentality that, as I also argue in the book, is crucial to the pilgrimages and continues to show vitality:

> [these attitudes] . . . can only come out of some belief, one so deep it is out of sight, that a promise of some kind had been made and betrayed. Perhaps it was the French Revolution? Or the American Revolution which made the pursuit of happiness a right with the implication that . . . [it] is to be had as easily as taking cakes off a supermarket counter? Millions of people in our times behave as if they have been made a promise . . . that life must get freer, more honest, more comfortable always better.[12]

This introduction is as an attempt—within the obvious limitations of space—to update the volume as a whole. I will first discuss the new settings or destinations for such pilgrimages; second, I will examine the extent to which the countries (and their political systems) discussed in the book have remained attractive to Westerners, and especially Americans, in search of alternatives to their own political system and culture. Finally, I will also take this opportunity to make amends for past omissions either in regard to places of pilgrimage, particular techniques of hospitality used, or important pilgrims overlooked.

As some readers may note this edition comes with a different subtitle. While the original one properly described what the book was about ("Travels of Western intellectuals to the Soviet Union, China, and Cuba"), the new subtitle, "Western Intellectuals in Search of the Good Society," reaches further and reminds the reader that the political pilgrimages are a part of a broader and more timeless quest.

In the following I will also further develop the argument that the attitudes and impulses which led to the pilgrimages of the past persist, as indicated by their substitutes or functional equivalents which emerged in American society over the past decades.[13]

New Destinations?

The new post-apartheid South Africa held a promise to become a destination for political pilgrims if only it had moved into a more radical, or vigorously socialist-revolutionary direction. This, however, has not happened under the moderate and conciliatory policies Nelson Mandela pursued. Social-political change has not been revolutionary but incremental and reformist and as such prosaic—nothing to fire the imagination of Westerners yearning for a new attempt aimed at the radical transformation of the human condition. Even those far to the left of Mandela, as for instance Joe Slovo, chairman of the South African Communist party, embraced moderation and engaged in a certain amount of rethinking. Slovo's recent response to the question "how could an intelligent man could have spent as much time as he did in Moscow and its satellite capitals without seeing that his surroundings were repressive, hypocritical and corrupt?" also helps to understand the mentality this study sought to grasp:

> "If you've ever been part of an official delegation, you learn less about a country than sitting in the British Museum and reading about it.... You don't meet the people. You don't actually see the conditions ... people said there were gulags and millions of people incarcerated there, and we were assured

that there was no such thing. We didn't go to these areas. We didn't have opportunities to actually check."

Even so, Mr. Slovo confesses that he began to have deep doubts about his communist patrons in the 1960s but suppressed them. To speak out against, say the crushing of dissent in Czechoslovakia . . . would have meant his ostracism from the Communist Party. . . . "The choice that you face is that you either continue to be able to make a contribution to the struggle or not."[14]

Although Slovo differed from the typical political pilgrims or tourists by virtue of his life-long involvement with the communist movement, he apparently shared with them both the ignorance of the most disturbing aspects of the communist systems (e.g., the camps) and the predisposition to doubt that they existed.

Iraq and Iran, because of their intransigently anti-Western policies and rhetoric, had a potential attraction for those deeply estranged from Western society and comfortable in the presence of its critics. On the other hand, Islamic Fundamentalism was hard to swallow, especially for Americans, except for the likes of Mr. Farrakhan who paid a supportive visit to the most radical Islamic states (Iran, Libya, Sudan, and Iraq) in February 1996.[15]

Iraq, less Islamic than repressive, has been a special case as the apparent victim of the West and its technology (in the Gulf War). On the other hand, Saddam Hussein lacked Castro's charm and charisma and the socialist rhetoric of his regime was insufficient to overcome its other liabilities. Even so even Iraq had its Western champions, (such as Ramsey Clark) always ready to feel a sense of solidarity with those hostile to the United States.[16] A group of 600 Western Europeans who visited Libya in 1989 belonged to organizations such as "'Women Against Military Madness' . . . West Germans from the Libya Committee of Bochum, [they were] members of various Green organizations and other collections of leftist and pacifists. Black Americans from the Nation of Islam came too."[17]

More significant than the actual number of American or European visitors to militant Islamic countries has been the attitude of American academic intellectuals specializing in Middle Eastern studies. It is from their ranks that the staunchest Western champions of present-day radical Middle Eastern political systems have risen; their sympathies emanate less from travelogues and more from scholarly (or putatively scholarly) studies and papers.

I learned since the earlier editions of the book that the popularity of Middle Eastern studies among the fiercest critics of the United States and the West is comparable to that of Latin America among scholars similarly disposed. It may be argued that it was the study of these areas which made the critics aware of American and Western iniquities, or one may surmise that people who gravitate to such area studies already harbor a strong animus toward the United States and the West as a whole. What has been called the "Arabization" of Middle Eastern studies lends plausibility to the latter.[18] As two recent observers (themselves specialists in the Middle East) noted, "contempt for traditional America permeates much of the scholarly writing on the Middle East. It disproportionately blames the woes of that region on the United States. It conjures up an American 'warrior culture.'"[19] In a similar spirit the United States has been held responsible for the ills of Latin America by many Latin Americanists.

Richard Falk (a venerable critic of American society and U.S. foreign policy whose name appears in the book)[20] noted that American society is "shaped by the commercialization of violence . . . and [is] a culture shaped by rising crime, official corruption and pervasive fear." In his opinion it was the inherently aggressive traits of American culture which led to the Gulf War.[21] Symptomatic of the attitudes permeating Middle Eastern studies, one of the rare books (*Cruelty and Silence* by Kana Makiya) written by a native of the region and critical of Hussein's Iraq and its domestic terror was viciously attacked by Eqbal Ahmad, a professor at Hampshire College in Amherst, Massachusetts.[22] Ahmad, like Falk, has a long and distinguished record of vehement criticism of the United States and the West.

It may be noted here that Saddam Hussein's Iraq found defenders among the Swedish literati as well. Jan Guillou, a prominent journalist, believed that his regime was "clearly popular," that there was "widespread confidence in the leadership," and that allegations of political violence in Iraq was a "racist fantasy." He also joined the ranks of Westerners who had something good to say about the prisons of police states:

> In Iraqi prisons . . . people learned to read and write. Prisoners did not escape, despite guards being conspicuously few in number. There are no isolation cells because this is "a barbaric form of punishment." The cells have air conditioning, radio and television. There is "absolutely no doubt" about conditions there being superior, for example, to the Osteraker prison in Sweden.[23]

Among the Islamic states here mentioned, Iran, like the communist states discussed in the book, developed at least one model prison for the benefit of foreign visitors. Behzad Naziri, like the Polish Jerzy Gliksman six decades earlier in the former Soviet Union (see pp. 154–56), had been both member of a delegation to whom the prison was shown, and subsequently an inmate in the same prison. On the former occasion the prison warden "explained that Evin was not really a prison but a university to introduce 'deceived' youngsters to the true teachings of Islam. Hundreds of 'inmates' sitting in orderly

rows, described humane conditions and warm treatment buy the guards."
Four months later Naziri (who worked for a French press agency) was arrested. "This time, the prison authorities wasted little time introducing me to
the unspeakable cruelties behind closed doors. I immediately ran into some
familiar faces—those 'prisoners' I had interviewed before. They were prison
guards."[24] Substituting prison employees for inmates too had precedent in
the former Soviet Union which probably pioneered this technique (see p.
159).

There has also been sympathy on the part of the World Council of Churches
toward militant Islamic states; its general secretary "[Konrad] Raiser defended
the WCC's dialogue with Islamist extremists who have persecuted Christian
minorities. . . . The WCC is not attempting to criticize militant Islam, Raiser
pledged, but to 'understand' it."[25] As the reader will see the WCC took a
highly sympathetic view of the destinations of several major pilgrimages discussed below.

A promising new destination for political tourists has been the state of
Chiapas in Mexico where in the winter of 1994 a peasant uprising broke out.
It was quickly put down, but the rebels withdrew to appropriately remote and
scenic jungles and mountains and a stalemate developed between them and
the government. They were led by a highly articulate, voluble, and romantic
figure, who wore a ski mask and called himself Subcomandante Marcos, and
excelled in making long statements for the media. Once more a revolutionary
social movement emerged promising to bring together downtrodden peasants and "brigades of young radicals" or "Marxist missionaries"[26] from urban
areas. Subcomandante Marcos was the latest incarnation of the revolutionary
intellectual who closed the gap between ideals and actions, intellectuals, and
the authentic masses. His intellectual credentials were displayed as he regaled visitors with "labyrinthian discussion of the work of Julio Cortazar,
Borges, Garcia Marquez and other notables."[27]

The movement, fiercely anti-capitalist and anti-American, called itself "The
Zapatista Army of National Liberation" (thereby also making use of an older
authentic revolutionary hero) and initially attracted much attention in as well
as outside Mexico. As one sympathizers wrote "The designation of the
Zapatistas as the first post-modern Latin guerilla formation has been confirmed by the intellectual greats and near greats . . . [their] armed audacity
and poetic vision have won them an international constituency."[28]

Visitors of the guerillas included Hollywood celebrities such as filmmaker
Oliver Stone and actor Edward James Olmos; they were followed by the
former French first lady Danielle Mitterand (also a great friend of Castro, see
p. xxxii) and Regis Debray, an old admirer of Latin American guerillas (un-

less they were anti-Communist contras).[29] On the television program "60 Minutes" Marcos was compared to Robin Hood. He was one of "a group of young Marxist philosophy and sociology professors at the Autonomous Metropolitan University of Mexico . . . [who] moved to the Chiapas" in the 1980s. Reportedly Benetton "offered Marcos a juicy modelling contract" which he turned down.[30]

Oliver Stone's visit got particular attention:

> Oliver Stone is skipping tonight's awards ceremony [the Oscars] to meet with leftist guerillas in southern Mexico. . . . Stone said he wanted to see the conditions that prompted an Indian uprising two years ago. The rebels, many of them wearing straw hats and black wool ponchos, greeted Stone with a five-piece mariachi band. "I am here because I believe in their struggle," Stone said after meeting with 23 leaders of the Zapatista National Liberation army. "We are coming on a fact-finding mission. . . . to see with our own eyes the situation."[31]

While American sympathizers of the zapatistas allowed that "ours is a time of actually nonexisting socialism," they were nonetheless encouraged "to see a promise of what a democratic revolutionary movement might look like and sound like."[32]

The Latin American Studies Association (a steady supporter of Castro's Cuba and Sandinista Nicaragua) passed a resolution in support of the Zapatista rebels. On the same occasion its members voted down a proposal critical of Cuban humans rights violations.[33]

North Korea

North Korea was one of the few Communist countries which, as far as I knew, had inspired little political tourism. Nor apparently did it try to stimulate conducted tours; "American tourists are almost never granted visas," a journalist noted.[34] Gus Hall, head of the Communist party of the United States had no such problems and recommended North Korea both as a vacation spot and exemplar of socialism.[35] Western leftists were largely indifferent toward a country which preserved intact its Stalinist institutions and policies—a country where according to one of the rare Western visitors "everything was either forbidden or compulsory."[36]

More recently there has been an increase of Western visitors connected with the regime's desire to attract foreign capital and events such as the 1996 Sports and Cultural Festival; however, the regimentation of visitors sometimes interfered with their appreciation of the political system. The sites shown on one of these tours were typical of all such tours: in the capital, Pyongyang, they included the Great People's Study Hall, a cement factory, the house where the Great Leader (Kim Il Sung) was born, the Victorious Fatherland Liberation War Museum, and the Martyr's Cemetery (where tourists were required to buy flowers with U.S. dollars). At the opening ceremonies of the International Sports and Cultural Festival, "Muhammad Ali was a guest of honor." Not only was the tour hectic and regimented, but the "guides used virtually every exchange with us as an opportunity to vilify America."[37]

A few years ago I had the good fortune to come across a highly informative book that received all too little attention in this country written by a British psychiatrist who specialized in visiting unusual and not too inviting parts of the world. From his book I learned that occasionally Western tourists did make an appearance in North Korea and were bestowed forms of hospitality that were remarkable even in comparison with the corresponding efforts of other Communist governments described in this book. The year was 1989 when the winds of change, as the saying goes, were blowing all over the Soviet empire. Anthony Daniels, the author of this book, managed to get into North Korea as a member of the British delegation attending the Soviet financed World Festival of Youth and Students held in Pyongyang that year. Before departing Daniels met members of the delegation in London:

> I first met my fellow delegates . . . a couple of weeks before departure. . . . I soon found myself having to explain, somewhat shamefacedly, that I represented no one but myself: to be a mere individual when everyone else represented, or claimed to represent, the downtrodden, the disadvantaged, or the dispossessed was tantamount to class treachery. . . . our journey to Pyongyang . . . was uneventful though even by the time we reached Moscow airport a certain strain had begun to make itself felt. A temporary but enforced association of left-wing activists, each with his or her cause to promote, and each utterly convinced of his or her own righteousness, is not necessarily a recipe for social cohesion. . . . To be a member of a victimised group was a vocation and destiny that obviated the need for consideration of others . . . the majority of the delegates considered themselves persecuted whether as women, members of splinter communist parties, vegetarians, homosexuals, Irish by descent, proletarians, immigrants or any combination of these.[38]

As these remarks make clear his group consisted of people who held their own society in great contempt, estranged enough to extend sympathy to virtually any political systems they perceived as being opposed to their own.

Throughout the visit, these tourists preserved their credulousness, which was probably bolstered by the special treatment they received. For example, their buses had a police escort with sirens and flashing lights on the six lane highway leading from the airport to the city which had absolutely no traffic in either direction. . . . The police escort . . . transformed a group of unimportant young discontents into people of consequence. This form of flattery exactly suited the psychology of at least some of them, convinced as they were that the country from which they had come unjustly failed to recognise . . . their manifest talents.[39]

As will be further discussed in the book, I am not suggesting that the political pilgrims and tourists were predominantly people feeling insufficiently recognized, or of lower status in their own countries. On the contrary most of those appearing on these pages were well known and widely respected. At the same time the types described by Daniels were also represented.

Daniels' companions were utterly lacking in scepticism toward the displays produced by the official hospitality:

[As their] bus passed through the streets of Pyongyang, the pedestrians stood still and waved to us, and the faithful waved back happily, thinking they were expressing international proletarian solidarity. But for those who cared to observe, the waving of the pedestrians had an odd quality. . . . They waved stiffly, like automata; as soon as the bus passed their upraised arms dropped like stones to their sides and they walked on. This was friendliness by decree.

At a model secondary school with no students in evidence, with blackboards never written upon and blackboard dusters never used, one of the tourists commented

"Only socialism can do this" . . . he did not ask whether the school, even if real, was typical, though if he were shown anything good in his own country would immediately retort that it was exceptional. . . . Here critical thought dissolved at the first sight of the marble entrance hall; far from unintelligent he was a true political pilgrim . . . for whom this preposterous charade was staged.

Likewise in the model Maternity Hospital: "No patients, no staff, no trolleys cluttered the corridors, which echoed to no sound except that of our praises."[40]

A unique feature of the North Korean attempt to impress foreigners was the total absence of mentally retarded or otherwise handicapped people in the capital: "it appears that the Government has exiled disabled people . . . for fear that foreigners might see them and get a bad impression. North Korean officials deny this, saying that disabled people have voluntarily moved to other parts of the country."[41] Daniels reported that "whenever they were asked about the complete absence from Pyongyang of disabled people, our guides replied with ominous decisiveness: 'This problem has been solved.'"[42]

The disposition of these political tourists was most strikingly revealed at the official opening of the festival in a stadium holding 150,000 people, when the great leader arrived and was greeted by the well-orchestrated frenzy. Daniels recalled:

> To my horror, the people around me [the British and other foreign delegations—P.H.] joined in this mindless activity. . . . What were they cheering, what were they celebrating, what emotion, or rather, pseudo-emotion were they feeling? . . . There was no external compulsion for these people to behave as they did, to abandon their critical faculties, to lose their identity, to be united in a pseudo-mystical communion with a hundred thousand people of whom they knew nothing. . . . Yet they could not wait to do so; in fact they rejoiced on doing it, and they felt fulfilled afterwards.[43]

These visitors were not offended by the grotesque cult of Kim Il Sung that was in evidence everywhere and by the omnipresent assault of propaganda: "My companions . . . did not pause to wonder why or how was it that every person in North Korea without exception wore a badge with a portrait of the great leader. If they had considered it at all, they would have said it was simply because of his popularity."[44]

Perhaps the most remarkable example of the techniques of hospitality was the Department Store No. 1. in Pyongyang. My examination of the techniques of hospitality extended by various Communist states failed to turn up anything quite like it, although there were, in other Communist states too, model institutions (especially model prisons), set up, almost entirely for the benefit of the foreign visitors. The magnitude of investment in this and other installations of similar purpose in North Korea suggests that there were apparently more such visitors than I had thought.[45]

During his two week visit Daniels paid several visits to the Pyongyang Department Store No. 1.:

> It didn't take long to discover that this was no ordinary department store. It was filled with thousands of people, going up and down the escalator . . . going in and out of the front entrance in a constant stream . . . yet nothing was being bought or sold. I checked this by standing at the entrance for half an hour. The people coming out were carrying no more than the people entering. . . . In some cases I recognised people coming out as those who had gone in a few minutes before. . . . And I watched a hardware counter for fifteen minutes. There were perhaps twenty people standing at it; there were two assistants behind the counter, but they paid no attention to the "customers". . . .
>
> I decided to buy something—a fountain pen. I went to the counter where pens were displayed . . . no more for sale than the Eiffel Tower. As I handed over my money, a crowd gathered around, for once showing signs of animation. I knew . . . that I could not be refused: if I were, the game would be given away completely. And so the crowd watched goggle-eyed and disbelieving as this astonishing transaction took place: I handed the assistant a piece of paper and she gave me a pen.[46]

In one of its rare dispatches from North Korea, the *New York Times* provided corroborations for the account of Daniels regarding the preparations for the same youth festival in 1989:

> For a year, factory workers have been struggling with special classes in the basics of English, and everything paintable is gleaming under a fresh coat. Farm trucks are washed before they are allowed on the main roads. Koreans on the street scrutinize oncoming cars and wave whenever they see a foreigner go by. . . .
>
> Ordinary people . . . seem happy to talk to foreigners. . . . But conversations often sound exceedingly stilted, and it is rare for a minute to pass without a Korean offering praise to the 77-year-old "great leader" . . . or the 47-year-old "dear leader," the President's son and heir. . . .
>
> More than 1000 Mercedes-Benzes have been imported to take guests around.

The dispatch of the *New York Times* correspondent also suggested that some American visitors had motifs similar to those in the British delegation described by Daniels and their level of information about North Korea was also similar. "I am taking a look at student struggles throughout the world," a student leader from the City College of New York explained. "I want to make contact with people fighting for social and economic justice all over the world."[47]

There are further, occasional glimpses of the attitudes of Western visitors to North Korea, few as their numbers might have been. They bear striking resemblance to the deluded Western visitors to the Soviet Union in the 1930s, to Mao's China in the 1960s and to Cuba all along, as will be shown in this book. Walter Russell Mead of the New School for Social Research who visited North Korea on a recent relief mission wrote: "Like Castro, Kim [Il Sung] built a political base by raising miserable living standards. . . . Both countries saw a vast expansion of health and educational facilities. . . . The sons and daughters of illiterate peasants received university educations; landlords were ejected from the vast, prerevolutionary estates." He also observed that North Korea "engaged in behavior that appalled and astonished outsiders" (referring to the seizure of the U.S. ship Pueblo and the brutal murder of two American soldiers in the demilitarized zone in 1976, among others), but, as the wording suggests, he distanced himself from those "appalled." He did not wish to be judgmental of this political system. He merely allowed that North Korea was "prickly . . . and liable to lash out if provoked."[48]

The case of Reverend John Swomley, a retired United Methodist professor of ethics and founder of the American Committee on Korea is almost too good to be true, as far as the typology of political pilgrims is concerned. (To fully appreciate the following the reader is advised to consult chapter 8, "The Techniques of Hospitality.") Apparently moved by his concern with peace (if there were other reasons we cannot learn from his account) Rev. Swomley visited North Korea in 1994 as a guest of the government in the company of "two Korean Americans . . . who had been there before and were fluent in the Korean language" (he does not reveal who they were, how he met them, and what, if any, connections these two had with the North Korean authorities).

The sightseeing tour included all the standard sights which were regarded by the Communist authorities as incontrovertible evidence of the superiority of their system. The reverend was taken to "three large hospitals" in one of which he was "permitted to watch open heart surgery on a video screen and . . . the removal of a tumor in the brain." There was more to follow:

> In Pyongyang we visited the Children's Palace. . . . We saw calligraphy and embroidery classes . . . we witnessed a most remarkable stage performance . . . massed children's choirs . . . large orchestras of children, male and female singers, acrobats and dancers and 13 accordion players in perfect unison, all of them very young children.
> At the end of the performance, my interpreter . . . said to me: "Don't let Americans destroy these children."

Then came Kim Il Sung University with its 14 faculties and 10 research institutes and a collective farm complete with "day care nursery, hospital, agricultural college, theater . . . barbers, hairdressers and shops and an experimental research station." In addition

> My colleagues and I also visited a huge automated cement factory, workers' apartments, a University of National Economy . . . [and] a small Roman Catholic Church built in 1986 by its members with an interest-free loan from the government . . . [and] a much larger Protestant church. Afterward we met with the pastor. . . . He expressed great concern about US troops in South Korea and urged that they be withdrawn.

There was also a meeting with the Anti-Nuclear Peace Committee followed by a banquet in honor of Rev. Swomley.

> [As for] Kim Il Sung whom we did not meet though he sent personal greetings to us [it] seems clear . . . that he was no Stalinist. He seemed friendly to religion, regularly visited farms, factories, schools, and was frequently in touch with ordinary people. I was told that there is no death penalty in North Korea and no liquidation of opponents but there are "re-educational labor camps" which I was unable to see.
> Some of those with whom we talked [not clear who they were—P.H.] did not like the use of the word *dictator*. Others interpreted him as benevolent . . . more like a patriarchal father who makes final decisions. . . .
> It is apparent that Kim Il Sung was respected, admired even venerated. From everything I could gather in my limited contacts, the people liked and believed in him.

As has been the case with other visitors of a similar disposition Rev. Swonley found support for his beliefs not only in what he had seen but also in what he did not: "[on the way to the demilitarised zone] . . . [we] saw no tanks, armored vehicles or fortifications. . . . Nowhere along that stretch of road [by the DMZ] did we see any evidence of the million man army which the CIA has reported is there."

By contrast on the South Korean side he saw the troops and fortifications guarding the border. He was especially indignant about "the huge concrete wall initiated by the US military" he compared unfavorably to the Berlin Wall which at least permitted cross border visits while the wall in Korea did not! In contrast to the South Korean militarization of the border area, in the North, he saw "unarmed uniformed soldiers helping farmers to plant rice." Moreover, "Other public employees expected to assist farmers on Friday with planting and hundreds of them were also walking from Pyongyang three to eight miles to work in the fields. All appeared well nourished or they would have been unable to walk that distance and work all day in the fields."[49]

Rev. Swomley, needless to say, was blissfully unaware of the chronic mismanagement and inefficiency of agriculture in Communist states and the resulting need to supplement the regular labor force with city dwellers; nor could he imagine that such extra work was not entirely voluntary. His sojourn makes clear that the old-style pilgrim, carefully chaperoned, totally duped and favorably impressed even by an exceptionally repressive police state is not yet fully extinct.

Further indications of how thoroughly North Korea controls what foreigners are allowed to see come from two dispatches of *New York Times* correspondents. One noted that "when foreigners are permitted to travel in North Korea they are usually booked on night trains so that they cannot see the . . . countryside." Some day trains are permitted on certain lines "but a wall has been built along the tracks so that passengers cannot see anything."[50] Another correspondent noted that when he engaged a native in conversation, "no fewer than five security agents listened intently." Not surprisingly the interviewee assured him of the excellence of the food supplies. The appearance of foreigners on other occasions led to the flight of the natives at a train station and not even children showed any interest in rarely seen foreigners. And "when Mr. Han, the factory worker was asked if he would allow a visitor to see his home, a security agent immediately went to look inside without Mr. Han's permission, came back and indicated that a visit would not be allowed."[51]

The 1994 visit of former president Carter to North Korea on a self-styled peace and goodwill mission was another astonishing demonstration of the

implausible persistence (or revival?) of attitudes this book has documented
and sought to explain. He was, among other things, favorably impressed by
the great leader and unaware of, or unbothered by, his grotesque cult of personality. According to a press report, "Mr. Carter heaped praise on Kim Il
Sung. . . . 'I found him to be vigorous, intelligent . . . well informed . . . and
in charge of decisions about his country.'" Carter also succeeded in the course
of his short visit to note "the reverence with which they [the North Korean
people] look upon their leader."[52] Reportedly he also observed that,
"Pyongyang is full of pep—its shops remind him of the 'Wal-Mart in Americus
Georgia' and at night the neon lights remind him of Times Square."[53]

Perhaps stimulated by the Carter visit and hopes that a neglected and much
maligned socialist paradise may be found in North Korea in 1994, "38 prominent US citizens . . . formed a new national organization The American Committee on Korea." Its goals included, "to inform and arouse the conscience of
US citizens about the US occupation of Korea."[54] Its members included both
Ramsey Clark and William Sloane Coffin, two prominent political pilgrims
of earlier times whom the reader will repeatedly encounter in this volume.
As Daniels noted, "Perhaps in the 1930s there was some slight excuse for
intellectuals who were taken in. . . . inasmuch it was then something the
world had never previously experienced. But what excuse was there nearly
60 years later . . . ?"[55]

After his return from North Korea Daniels met in England "a professor of
medicine, a man of wide culture sand learning" to whom he described "the
ceaseless, ubiquitous and inescapable propaganda" he had experienced there.
His response was, "'but have you considered how much power Rupert
Murdoch wields in this country?'" Daniels continued:

> This was not untypical of the response of liberal intellectuals to my unflatter-
> ing descriptions of life in the communist countries I had visited. If one were
> to respond to a description of the horrors of Nazism by remarking on the
> prevalence in one's own country of domestic violence or cruelty to animals,
> one would be regarded (rightly) as a moral idiot; yet when one responds to the
> horrors of communism by making fatuous comparisons with the imperfec-
> tions of representative democracy, one still considers oneself to be, in some
> unspecified way, on the side of angels. And this long after the Soviet Union
> has admitted that what for nearly seventy years it called anti-Soviet propa-
> ganda was actually the truth.[56]

If there is no moral or intellectual excuse for these attitudes, there are psychological and cultural explanations which this book seeks to provide. It may
suffice to say here that in the 1990s as in the 1930s, 1960s, 1970s or 1980s,
the underlying factors were largely similar: foremost among them a diffuse

sense of moral indignation and discontent with the character of Western (and especially American) society, that predisposed to give every benefit of doubt to political systems which were diametrically opposed to the Western or American, and succeeded in impressing these individuals with their good intentions in the pursuit of social justice.

The occasional visitors to North Korea who appeared since the earlier editions of the book deserve to be remembered not because their perceptions and judgements were widespread but because of their exceptionally outlandish character, which illuminate the outer limits of credulousness, of the will to believe.

Latin America

The peaceful ouster of the Sandinista government in Nicaragua in the 1990 elections abruptly eliminated the last major destination of political pilgrims and tourists. (The pilgrimage to Nicaragua was dealt with in the preface to the 1990 edition of the book and at greater length in the author's *Anti-Americanism*.)[57] However, the attractions of Sandinista Nicaragua lingered and some of the former pilgrims found it difficult to distance themselves from their earlier experiences and attitudes even after the 1990 elections and in the aftermath of the global decay of communist systems.

John Brentlinger's massive volume on Nicaragua appeared in 1995 and deserves discussion as a fine example, indeed case study in the mind-set of the political pilgrim as preserved in the post-communist era.[58] Brentlinger, a professor of philosophy at the University of Massachusetts at Amherst was robustly and proudly alienated from American society and culture, his conviction of the uniquely evil and corrupt character of this society (and capitalism) unquestioned; in preserving these beliefs he has probably benefited from living amidst like-minded people in what has been jestingly called "the people's republic of Amherst, Mass." Brentlinger had also visited Cuba and found that "everyone has enough to eat and they have the best health care, the best education in Latin America."[59]

Brentlinger's heart went out to Communist Nicaragua because it was a plausible victim of American capitalism and imperialism and, at the same time, it promised to build the kind of society Brentlinger dreamed of: egalitarian, communitarian, permeated by a sense of justice and brotherhood. Also, it was a largely pre-industrial, pre-modern society, inhabited by seemingly uncorrupted peasants pursuing the simple, authentic way of life in harmony with nature, or so he believed. As the reader will see, these were visions which captivated each generation of political pilgrims, in almost every setting they visited. Brentlinger further resembled other pilgrims in suspending his capacity for critical thinking once he set foot in Nicaragua. It is clear from the beginning of his book that he was haunted by the desire of "being part of something larger and redeeming." He went to Nicaragua "to see what a society in revolution was like. . . . There was a vision there I wanted to hold on to, to bring back and transplant." He found

> a deeply spiritual country trying to become independent and build a new version of socialism. I felt the need and opportunity to learn and respond.
>
> What could be more important for us in the United States to experience than a people who rejected the inhumane order based on individual greed, who reignited the hope for a new order, a nurturant community. . . . Now after the Sandinistas have lost the election and the rule of greed is restored in Nicaragua, we need more than ever to renew this hope.[60]

He looked at the revolution as "a spiritual journey of a people." Everything he found in Nicaragua was transformed and uplifted, as it were, by this revolution:

> My experiences of the Nicaraguan revolution are always physical experiences—being blown, soaked, dried, burned, shaken, scratched, cut, chilled, touched, caressed by wind, sun and rain. There is constant physical exchange. It is sometimes hard . . . sometimes it is incredibly sweet, smooth and languid . . . gradually I come to feel a constant, vital metabolism, a direct, conscious and deeply energetic connection. . . . Nature in Nicaragua, does not appear to be subdued and exhausted.[61]

Clearly, wind, sun, and rain in the United States did not have similar effects on him. As was the case with other pilgrims, it was the context that transformed everything (including nature), no matter how mundane or ordinary (for examples of similar visions in the book, see pp. 108–109, 131, 138, 311, 312).

Even the police appeared benign and unthreatening: "Except for the weapons, it felt like they were college students hanging out in their dormitory." He also found that "political demonstrations in Nicaragua have more spirit and more fun than any I've ever seen. . . . Everyone is excited. People are chanting, singing, dancing and drumming. Helicopters drop candy from East Germany." It is not hard to imagine that if helicopters dropped candy at an American political rally during the election campaign, Brentlinger would have construed it as a repellent, dehumanized technological intrusion and a crude attempt to bribe the masses. The "Sandinistas" he met "seemed dedicated, intense . . . willing to admit mistakes and limitations, but were insistent concerning their good intentions and the progress the revolution was making."[62]

As so many pilgrims at other times and other places (see pp. 154–160, 339–344), Brentlinger was taken to a model prison, "a prison farm, a new initiative of the Ministry of Interior . . . there were no fences and the guards were unarmed. . . . The program was geared toward rehabilitation. . . . Here the system assumes personal growth instead of punishment. I love the ideas that a prison should be a productive and healthy environment."

A power plant shown to him "was so attractive that it could have been designed by an artist." In a child care center, "the children played games, sang, drew, and did crafts. . . . There was no political education, but they had begun to learn about their history and revolution," which he succeeded in perceiving as bereft of political content![63]

In Nicaragua he met other "internationalists," foreign supporters of the regime who were also "obviously happy and excited to be involved. It was the happiness of being part of the revolution, the sense of change, of possibility. . . It gives people a new energy; the blood flows more rapidly; it's like being in love." In the United States such happiness eluded him and the other sympathizers:

> in the States I often have the sense of floating in a huge becalmed ocean. Most people don't believe in change. The privileged minority is complacent and self-indulgent. The poor, disenfranchised minorities seem despairing. The left is small and fragmented. It was shocking to come back and see again the wide highways crowded with . . . vehicles, the supermarkets and malls, the clean, middle-class order of the community where I live.[64]

Brentlinger knew that "many Nicaraguans who voted [in 1990] for UNO [the opposition] were still Sandinistas in their hearts." Nonetheless at the end of the book he muses over the mistakes of the government and relates some critical comments of the natives which suggest that his earlier perceptions were incorrect—a conclusion he himself manages to avoid. The book ends with reflections about "socialism and the sacred" and calls for a "new conception of the sacred" as Brentlinger's quasi-religious urges make a final, barely concealed appearance.[65]

The end of the guerilla war in El Salvador in the early 1990s deprived Westerners of a revolutionary movement with the proper credentials (the attractions of the Salvadoran guerillas is discussed in the 1990 preface, pp. xviii–xix; also, in the 1981 preface, pp. xxx–xxxii).

There was still the Shining Path guerilla movement in Peru, an exceptionally violent group which seemed to have fewer supporters in the United States than in Western Europe. The *New York Times* reported that, "From Berkeley to London to Stockholm, solidarity groups have formed to support a group [Shining Path] that one human rights advocate called . . . 'the most brutal guerilla group that ever has appeared in the Western Hemisphere.'"[66] The late William Kunstler and John Gerassi were among the supporters of the Berkeley-based "Committee to Support the Revolution in Peru" that was especially concerned with the fate of Abiamel Guzman, the leader of the group captured by the government.[67]

More recently another Peruvian guerilla movement, the Tupac Amaru gained attention in connection with the imprisonment of Lori Berenson, its American supporter. She was not an ordinary political pilgrim or tourist. Her involvement with exotic revolutionary movements was more serious; she was no mere spectator. Her case is interesting on several counts. In the first place it shows that 1960s-style radicalism and enthusiasm for guerilla movements abroad are not totally extinct among those deeply estranged from American society. Lori Berenson fits the stereotypical image of the idealistic 1960s radical in search of a cause, as she moved from El Salvador to Nicaragua and then to Peru, embracing in each case a far left revolutionary movement. She was described "as someone not sure about what to do with her life" and later "as a woman who discovered a sense of purpose in the struggles in Latin America,"[68] as well as "a romantic dreamer" and a "hyper-egalitarian" who "walked everywhere [this was in El Salvador, and recalled by one of the former commanders of the Salvadorian guerillas—P.H.] instead of taking the bus to show solidarity with those who couldn't afford bus fare."[69] She had dropped out of MIT to work for CISPES (Committee in Solidarity with the People of El Salvador). She came from a New York liberal, middle-class family and during her teens displayed an uncommon idealism serving food in soup kitchens and later studied anthropology (at MIT) where she became interested in Central America. It is easy to imagine her as a serious young woman, full of moral indignation about the evils of American society. More difficult to know is how she made the leap from innocent "activism" to deadly political involvements caught as she was with the Tupac Amaru guerillas in Peru who were planning to kidnap members of the Peruvian Congress. She also displayed the sense of self-righteousness and invulnerability associated with a secure and privileged American middle-class background that was reminiscent of some of the 1960s radicals who also ended up in prison, as for example Cathy Boudin.[70] In the Peruvian court Berenson declared "at the top of her lungs" her solidarity with her Tupac Amaru comrades. Her parents believed she was "full of goodness" and incapable of hurting anybody.[71] She "found herself chasing the tail of history, increasingly committed to the ideal of revolutionary victory at a time when it was no longer on the agenda."[72]

The case of Guatemala deserves mention here not because it had a putatively socialist or revolutionary government but on the contrary, because it emerged as the counterpoint to systems which certain Westerners, including Americans, admired. One could visit Guatemala to pinpoint evil, and display, in some fashion, solidarity with the oppressed and exploited and occasionally with their supposed champions, the leftist guerillas of that country. Such visitors

> used Guatemala as a kind of psychotherapy, but not to achieve self-knowledge; rather, the country was for them a Disneyland of horror, where the attraction was not delight but moral outrage. Problems at home—with marriages, with crime on the streets, with the meaninglessness that material comfort brings—were insoluble, but here in Guatemala, at least it was possible to be on the side of the angels.[73]

Anthony Daniels (who spent eight months in Guatemala practicing as a doctor) found these visitors "people who used Guatemala . . . to assuage their self-important need for righteousness and guilt." They included "guerilophiles who so abound in Western Europe," vicarious revolutionaries, "romantic[s] seeing in the Indians all that was missing from . . . [their] own life: a sense of continuity, oneness with Nature and the like," who often entertained images of the uncorrupted peasants as "people as blank sheets of paper on which the most beautiful characters can be written."[74]

Cuba

Of all the pilgrimage sites Cuba has maintained the most credibility and popularity which is not to say that political tourism to Cuba in the 1990s approaches the 1960s–1970s levels. Latter-day political tourists still believe that something noble and desirable began in Cuba but it has been undermined by the intrigues of the United States and the collapse of the Soviet bloc. In their eyes Castro's Cuba still deserves support, hence the popularity of challenging the U.S. government embargo and sending various forms of assistance. Few among the people who are concerned about shortages in Cuba worry about, say, the needy in Bolivia or Honduras or El Salvador because they are unimpressed by the political system under which *they* live. Sending medical and other humanitarian supplies to Cuba is a predominantly political, rather than merely humanitarian gesture.[75]

Nobody knows (except some officials in Cuba) how many grass-roots organizations in North America continue to support Cuba and organize trips to it, bearing gifts, such as the group of women calling themselves "hermanas" (sisters) in Princeton, New Jersey. Reading their enthusiastic account nobody could guess that its subject was one of the last Marxist-Leninist police states that stifles even the most trivial criticism and has been chronically mismanaged by an aged, megalomaniac dictator unwilling to relinquish his grip on power. Their account, among many others, suggests that all would be well in Cuba except for the American trade embargo.[76]

Edward T. Walsh, a former chaplain at North Carolina State University and member of the Ecumenical Project for International Cooperation as well as the Baptist Peace Fellowship was "the first American to be approved by Cuba's Ministry of Higher Education and the Cuban Communist Party to teach" at Matanzas University—an approval in which he apparently took great pride. He was among those arguing with great passion against the embargo and holding responsible the United States for most of the ills of present-day Cuban society. His incomprehension of the character of that society and its political system was so profound that when a Cuban student visited him and said, "Professor I probably won't be back to see you again . . . we Cubans must be careful about getting a bad reputation by hanging around with foreigners especially those with U.S. dollars," he explained the reticence by "the sensitive situation created by the fact that some Cubans . . . are able to buy products with U.S. dollars that most Cubans cannot afford." As if the student was concerned with the disapproval of other Cubans and not the attention of the authorities who strongly discourage unauthorized and unsupervised contact with foreigners.[77]

Some of the old admirers of the Castro regime such as Carol Brightman (quoted in the book) still find much to their liking in Cuba in the 1990s, including Castro's efforts to devise a "different kind of socialism"; she was also thrilled about getting him to autograph a baseball cap for her 14-year-old son. Likewise Benjamin Spock, the venerable critic of American society, found much to admire and nothing to criticize in Cuba as of 1994.[78] Ted Turner, on good terms with Castro at least since his 1982 duck-hunting visit, claimed that, "The Cuba visit didn't really change my philosophy. . . . It gave me some tolerance of the Socialist system that I didn't have before. After seeing it face to face, I didn't see anything that made me afraid."[79]

The impressions of an academic delegation to Cuba (sponsored by the left-of-center Institute of Policy Studies in Washington, DC) reflected the durability of the favorable stereotypes during the late 1980s (a period not covered in my book). Bettina Horner, member of the delegation and president of Radcliffe College at the time, was greatly impressed by, among other things, Castro's concern with public health and his willingness to give up cigar smoking to set a good example. She (as the rest of the delegation) took the position that "human rights begin with access to food, literacy and health care," although there was also a perfunctory reference to "the lack of political and civil rights . . . an issue that deeply concerned members of the American delegation." If it had, the report failed to reflect it since it was highly laudatory:

> The delegation did not have the disquieting feeling of being in a police state. The atmosphere did not seem oppressive, nor did the Cubans seem to be uncomfortable talking with visitors about problems, said Horner. . . . Fidel seems to travel about without a large security retinue. . . . The Americans were told that frequently Fidel drops by the university for a pickup game of basketball with the students.
>
> At this stage of the revolution, Fidel now feels secure enough to invite criticism, Horner said. His policy of rectification, a kind of Cuban version of glasnost, encourages criticism.[80]

It is quite unlikely that Huber had the faintest idea about the number of people held in Cuban prisons precisely for the criticism of the regime, or of the conditions that prevailed in the prisons, or the reasons why a dictator in an established police state may seem to move about without a lot of bodyguards.[81]

If Bettina Huber, without expertise in Latin American affairs had some excuse for her views of Cuba under Castro, the consistently pro-Castro utterances and policies of the Latin American Studies Association had no such explanation. The LASA, or those who speak in its name, have a long, unbroken record of leftist political partisanship that has endured into the mid-1990s. The association, ready and willing to criticize violations of human rights and academic freedom anywhere in the hemisphere, steadfastly refused to do so regarding Cuba (or Sandinista Nicaragua) while warmly championing cultural relations with the Castro regime.[82]

Even in the 1990s it is safe to say that Susan Eckstein's approach was typical of American academics studying Cuba. While not wholly uncritical of Castro's system she credits it with great accomplishments (in health and welfare, the reduction of rural/urban and class inequities and the position of women and dark-skinned citizens) without examining the price paid for them (if indeed these achievements are what is being claimed)—the totalitarian dictatorship of Castro. While she makes occasional, abstract references to repression, the book does not have a single chapter on (or sustained discussion of) the massive, institutionalized human rights violations, the regimentation of cultural life or the historically unprecedented exodus of over 10 percent of the population. She treats Castro's reign as a largely successful effort in social engineering aimed at modernization and greater social justice, marred only by the cessation of Soviet bloc assistance and the recalcitrance of human nature. She disbelieves that the Committees for the Defense of the Revolution are neighborhood level informers and prefers to emphasize their more benign activities such as recycling and voluntary labor.[83] She does not reflect on how labor, or anything else, can be voluntary in a police state such as Cuba.

The continued indifference of many prominent American intellectuals toward political repression in Cuba has further illustrations. Kate Millett, the well-known feminist author, managed to write a book about contemporary political imprisonment around the world without mentioning Cuba although the book claims to cover Latin America! Her political sympathies are further evidenced by devoting six chapters (out of a total of eleven) to the evils of Western colonialism and one third of a chapter to Mao's China.[84] Also of some interest here is that the use of psychiatric methods against political prisoners in Cuba (unlike in the former Soviet Union) remains virtually unknown in the United States.[85]

As of 1991 American public television still presented what a television critic called, "A portrait of Cuba without the warts," emphasizing "the benefits brought by Cuban Communism, especially schools, hospitals and guaranteed job. The claim that everybody can read is given more attention than what one is permitted to read." Those who wrote the script of this program "like other observers with a soft spot for totalitarians of the left . . . seem[ed] torn between the evidence of 30 years of political suppression and economic failure and an enduring will to believe."[86] Organizers of recent New York Film Festivals apparently had a similar soft spot making sure that no films critical of Cuba were shown. According to a Cuban émigré filmmaker they were motivated both by their political sympathies and "fear of offending the Cuban film officials who invite them each December to the Havana Film Festival." Not only the New York Film Festival organizers but Hollywood celebrities (including Oliver Stone) too shared these sympathies and the pleasure of visiting Cuba.[87]

The favorable American (and Western European) perceptions of the Cuban political system are closely associated with, and dependent on, Castro's durability and manipulative skills. He clings with considerable success to the vestiges of his revolutionary credentials and charisma and remains a source of legitimacy for the foreign sympathizers and especially intellectuals, notwithstanding his unwavering intolerance of free expression. Moreover, Castro, among the remaining Communist leaders, has been the least willing to compromise his stern anti-capitalist principles, which also earned him good points among Western intellectuals who take pride in being on the left and their aversion to capitalism. For his European admirers in particular Castro has "the appeal of the underdog" confronting the might of the United States. This appeal is reflected, among other things, in the radical chic of trendy bars named after him in London "with walls smothered in revolutionary memorabilia," while in other establishments of similar kind, "Che Guevara remains a pin-up rivaled only by James Dean."[88]

Castro's 1995 state reception in France by President Mitterand was probably the high watermark of the favorable reputation he has enjoyed abroad. Mrs. Mitterand, an unabashed admirer of his (who has visited Cuba several times), believes that Castro is "nothing like a dictator" and his government accomplished "the summit of what socialism could do."[89]

Castro continues to be capable of "dazzling" visitors, especially those already favorably disposed, such as "a group of visiting Americans that includes East Hampton matrons, a cadre from Hollywood and a handful of Red Club types" observed by a reporter of *Vanity* magazine, herself greatly impressed by his "awesome vigor" and "legendary gallantry," among other things."[90] Saul Landau (of late more restrained in his affections for his regime) confessed: "As Fidel talked I allowed myself to listen closely and feel that peculiar sensation that I experience in his presence, as if I am meeting with a force of nature, a man so filled with the energy of historical mission that he is almost of a different species. Power radiates from him."[91] Another memorable assessment comes from the International Affairs Secretary of the Swedish Social Democratic party, Pierre Schori, who considered Castro "one of the greatest figures in contemporary history. . . . He is an encylopaedist and has virtually the characteristics of a Renaissance Prince."[92]

Castro's five-day visit to New York in 1995 on the 50th anniversary of the United Nations further highlighted his continued immunity from serious criticism. Robert Torricelli, then a U.S. representative from New Jersey (now a senator), concerned with human rights violations in Cuba wrote:

> It is hard to know what is more disturbing—the thought of business leaders like David Rockefeller sitting down to a lunch with Fidel Castro or the sight of hundreds of people at the Abyssinian Baptist Church in Harlem cheering the fatigue-wearing Cuban revolutionary. . . .
>
> Of all things, a civil rights leader, Representative Charles Rangel, who once led the fight for economic sanctions against the apartheid regime in South Africa put himself on the church dais with a dictator who has jailed more political dissidents than any other leader in this hemisphere.[93]

There was during this visit "tremendous media coverage with not a single tough question asked . . . the feel-good gossipy aspect of the Shaw interview [Bernard Shaw of CNN] was a landmark television disgrace." Castro was "courted by David Rockefeller, Lee Iacocca, Mort Zuckerman, the Council on Foreign Relations, the luxury magazine *Cigar Aficionado*, businessmen hungry for a shot at the Cuban market . . . and an eager press."[94] On the same occasion Castro also met for two hours with a group of about 100 mostly

Protestant religious leaders, apparently eager to commune with him; one may presume (on the basis of past utterances from the clergy) that they did not complain about human rights violations by the Cuban authorities.[95]

While the profit-motivated courtship of Castro by businessmen is not to be confused with the effusions of intellectuals and political tourists, nonetheless the attitudes of the businessmen and the media reflect a climate of opinion that has remained largely uncritical of, if not totally positive toward, Castro and his regime. In contrast to political systems which had been found abhorrent and hence to be boycotted (such as the former South Africa), trade and cultural exchanges with Cuba carry no moral stigma among businessmen, journalists, academics, or show business celebrities,[96] although Castro made it clear that trade will not be allowed to lead to political reform.[97]

The views of Wayne Smith, a former American diplomat in Cuba, are probably representative of the liberal-left consensus on Castro and his system. Mr. Wayne, also described as "the dean of Fidel Castro's American apologists,"[98] had no doubt of Castro's popularity in Cuba, notwithstanding the well-known difficulties of reaching such conclusions in a police state where unflattering public remarks about the ruler can lead to serious difficulties. He also proposed with little to support it that "Cubans" were horrified by the developments on the Soviet Union and Eastern Europe and "are determined not to let that happen in Cuba," instead of suggesting that *Castro* was so determined. Even more astounding is Mr. Wayne's claim that "since the mid 1970s, Cubans have been able to vote in fair and democratic municipal elections." He believes that Castro has been unfairly "demonized" (in the United States) and is sceptical about allegations that he is "a bloody tyrant and murderer with the worst human rights record in the world." In a footnote Mr. Wayne tells the reader that his appraisals are based on "hundreds of interviews and conversations" he had with Cubans over the past few years.[99] He does not reveal how these Cubans were chosen or under what circumstances the conversations took place, with or without the presence of Cuban officials or interpreters. Jacobo Timmerman's sobering observations are relevant here:

> in Cuba, where everything one says or asks can be compromising . . . Cubans are verbally immobilized. Frozen. . . . They have internalized their fear of the regime. . . . At present the boundary that Cubans do not cross is the territory occupied by El Comandante and his regime. . . . It is impossible to maintain surveillance over every Cuban, but all Cubans feel as though they are being watched and controlled.[100]

Timmerman was also among the handful of visitors who had some reservations about the accomplishment of literacy, one of the major claims to legitimacy of the regime. He wrote: "If it is true that every Cuban knows how to read and write, it is likewise true that every Cuban has nothing to read and must be very cautious about what he writes." Timerman wondered, "whether it would not be preferable to be subjected to subliminal pressures so as to be a consumer of a particular toothpaste rather than forcibly plunged into the collective misery described as a happy, victorious society."[101]

Wayne Smith was not alone in making questionable assertions about Castro's popularity and the legitimacy of his political system. A correspondent of the *New York Times* managed in the course of a 17-hour drive to establish to his own satisfaction "that support for Mr. Castro and his revolution . . . remains strong in the Cuban countryside."[102]

It is possible that Cuba, no longer a protégé of the Soviet Union, has become an even more appropriate candidate for the role of the victim of the United States—an essential ingredient in the choice of countries upon which the pilgrims bestowed their affections. Mark Falcoff wrote:

> even now the Castro regime exercises a residual hold on the loyalties of our cultural elite . . . all of a sudden . . . many books, policy studies and op-ed pieces are urging us to provide for Cuba . . . a "soft landing." Could it be that a precipitous collapse threatens to reveal the real bases of its power, and in so doing, sweep away the last of the illusions that have nourished the socialist idea in the West . . . ?[103]

Saul Landau, perhaps the most persistent among the American admirers of Cuba (see pp. 223, 239), was convinced (as of 1989) that "Fidel's brand of socialism, not glasnost or perestroika, has wide popular backing." At the same time he modified his earlier views significantly:

> Like other foreigners who visited Cuba in the early revolutionary years, I discovered there wonderful possibilities that Jean-Paul Sartre and C. Wright Mills popularized for the European and American New Left. . . .
>
> But in 1989, Cuba's problems are no longer excusable or attributable to CIA subversion and the U.S. economic embargo. . . .
>
> Fidel's unwillingness to embrace Soviet style change springs from his conviction that social justice and relative equality cannot be achieved in an atmosphere of material incentives. . . . The work that remains in perfecting Cuban society, in Fidel's view, is not to adapt his model to the Cuban citizenry, but to perfect the citizenry to adapt to the model. "Socialism still has many defects and shortcomings," Fidel told a Mexican reporter in 1985, "but these deficiencies are not in the system, they're in the people."

Unlike most visitors and political tourists Landau recognized at last that Cuba was not just a poor but proud egalitarian society: "While inefficiency is demoralizing, outright corruption has even more insidious effects. Several old guerilla comrades appointed by Fidel . . . have used their positions to engage in what Cubans call *la dolce vita*. Others have allowed corruption to spread to their ministries."[104]

The late Maurice Halperin also used to be a supporter of the Castro regime and lived in Cuba between 1962 and 1968 teaching at the University of Havana and working in the ministry of foreign trade. Revisiting Cuba in 1989 he recalled that huge inequalities and elite privileges existed even in the early days of the revolution, as for instance when during an elaborate dinner at the home of a cabinet minister, "my host took me aside and told me with an impish twinkle in his eyes: 'As we all know, when Cuba reaches the stage of communism, there will be a great abundance of everything. What we have here is an experiment in adapting to the joys of communism. We are getting prepared for the future.'"

Halperin, familiar with a "confidential public opinion poll made by the Communist Party in . . . 1987" about public health conditions in Holguin province, provides a far less rosy picture of the vaunted health care system than one can find in much of the literature on Cuba under Castro. Of those polled (over ten thousand) 87 percent had unfavorable views of the health care they received. Most of the complaints "as summed up in the report concerned 'lack of attention, negligence and abuse of patients.'" There were also many complaints "about the chronic absenteeism of both doctors and nurses and about favoritism in the treatment of well-connected patients."

Unlike most visitors, Halperin was not charmed by Castro whom he regarded as suffering of "an uncontrollable compulsion to lead and dominate" (a compulsion bordering on a personality disorder), and found him "projecting sincerity while concealing cunning calculations."[105]

Anthony Daniels was another of the rare Western visitors who cast a sceptical eye on Castro observing that, "Thirty years of sycophantic audiences had rendered him incapable of concision, of saying anything in two words when a hundred would express the same thought. His fascination with his own personality was such that his merest whim was law for him." Researching the available reading material for the newly literate Cubans he found book shops filled with pre-glasnost Soviet propaganda (in Spanish) including a children's book entitled "*Felix significa felix*, [or] Felix Means Happy—Felix being none other than Felix Dzherzhinsky, the first chief of the Soviet secret police." Daniels took note of the stultifying abundance of political propaganda:

> To compensate for the lack of goods there was a wealth of exhortatory propaganda. . . .
> . . . little quotations everywhere: "*To create is to be victorious*" in the post office, where the clerks behind the counter moved resentfully as though strug-

gling through glue; *"Men come in two types, those who love and construct and those who hate and destroy"*, on the crumbling walls of dilapidated buildings; *"Art is life itself, art knows nothing of death,"* in the entrance to an art gallery so little visited that it had the atmosphere of a morgue.

Daniels met one of the few "foreign philo-Fidelistas living in Cuba," an English woman who "failed to notice the dissolution in Cuba of the distinction between what was voluntary and what was compulsory, one of the hallmarks of a totalitarian dictatorship"—a disposition widespread among political tourists and helpful for understanding why they so readily conflated public displays of support with a genuine endorsement of the system.

At last Daniels addressed the recurring theme of legitimation in the accounts of the sympathizers: "Did medical care and a bare sufficiency of rice and beans render freedom superfluous? Was I wrong to conclude from the fact that no refugees ever sought asylum in Cuba that whatever its achievements, Cuban socialism was not what anybody wanted if offered a choice?"[106]

Cambodia, Vietnam, and China

The Western popularity of Communist Cambodia (Kampuchia) was short-lived and limited, a spin off, one might say, of the Vietnam War (references to Cambodia may be found on pp. 68–69, 349, and 370). Following its losing war with Vietnam (another Communist state), the Pol Pot regime became discredited, its critique acceptable on the left. But while the mass murders in Cambodia were going on, Doris Lessing pointed out, "no one demonstrated for them [the victims], the humanitarians were not protesting. . . . But then they were murdered by a communist dictator . . . so the automatic inhibition came into action: rather bad taste, really to mention it."[107] This has been an attitude the late William Kunstler made explicit when he said that, "I do not believe in public attacks on socialist countries where violations of human rights may occur."[108]

At this point it is of more than historical interest to recall the observations of Noam Chomsky and Edward S. Herman who, in 1977, regarded the truly genocidal massacres of Pol Pot as "tales of Communist atrocities" and did their best to discredit reports of them, and those reporting them, both the refugees and Western observers. What is significant is not so much that a prominent academic intellectual supported the most murderous political system since Nazi Germany and the Soviet Union under Stalin (and to this day failed to apologize or otherwise engage in any soul searching over this fact), but that he has not been thoroughly discredited in the academic-intellectual community as a result.

To recall, in Chomsky's (and his collaborator's) opinion the allegations of mass murders were based on "extremely unreliable refugee reports" and were to be treated "with great caution" since "refugees questioned by Western reporters or Thais have a vested interest in reporting atrocities on the part of the Cambodian revolutionaries, an obvious fact that no serious reporter will fail to take into account."[109] In their 1978 book (*not* discussed in *Political Pilgrims*) Chomsky and Herman developed the same argument at far greater length and in a seemingly more scholarly manner. A distinctive feature of Chomsky's style has been the couching of the highly inflammatory and outlandish statements in a language generously sprinkled with phrases which suggest detachment and objectivity.[110]

In the book Chomsky and Herman argued that those giving credence to the testimony of refugees wished "to defame the regime"; they compared the Cambodian massacres to those in "France after liberation where a minimum of 30–40,000 people were massacred within a few months with far less motive for revenge." Chomsky doubted the high estimates of the Cambodian victims on the ground that if so many people had been killed "one would expect if not a rebellion than at least unwillingness to fight for the Paris educated fanatics at the top." Moreover, it was unfair to blame the Khmer Rouge for the deaths due to "malnutrition and disease." He quoted with approval from an account of Richard Dudman, "an experienced foreign correspondent with excellent credentials" (!), who, while admitting that the visit "amounted to a conducted tour," nonetheless had no hesitation to communicate his favorable impressions and "did not find the grim picture painted by thousands of refugees who couldn't take the new order." Dudman (quoted by Chomsky) also noted, among the signs of popular satisfaction that farm workers

> appeared to be reasonably relaxed at the height of the busy harvest season. They sometimes leaned on their hoes like farm workers everywhere. And they often . . . waved. . . . There were no signs of government cadres giving orders or armed guards enforcing the working hours, although individuals seemed to know what was expected.

Chomsky, thus aided by Dudman, reached the conclusion that

> the peasant population probably did not regard "the austere standard of hard manual labor" . . . as an onerous imposition of the regime. . . . one might reach the conclusion that much of the population may well have supported the regime, particularly if it is true, as Dudman was informed . . . that "decisions were taken collectively" in the cooperatives and even the army.

As for the massacres,

> there has been extensive fabrication of evidence. . . .

It is surely not in doubt [!] that it was U.S. intervention that inflamed a simmering civil struggle . . . Gareth Porter,[111] who had exposed earlier bloodbath lies . . . also raised doubts about the evidence offered in connection with Cambodia. . . .

It is a truism, obvious to anyone who has ever dealt with refugees . . . or simply uses common sense [!] that "accounts of refugees are indeed to be used with great care." . . .

It is quite evident [!] that to understand events in the aftermath of the war it is necessary to pay attention to the historical background of the peasant revolution, which was further inflamed and deeply embittered by the U.S. attack culminating in the bombing of 1973. . . .

. . . While many questions remain open about Cambodia during the 1975–78 period . . . on another question . . . we feel that the facts are clear and overwhelming. . . . [!] It is a fair generalization [!] that the more extreme the condemnation of Cambodia, the more confident the claim that "Communism" lies at the root of the present travail. . . .

. . . where evidence [of the massacres, that is-P.H.] is subject to some independent check it repeatedly and with remarkable consistency [!] turns out to be fabricated. . . .

We stress again that . . . as all observers of even moderate seriousness agree [!], what happened in Cambodia in the 1975–78 period under review, whatever it may have been, lay beyond our control. . . .[112]

Such and other statements, as indeed the whole volume reflects Chomsky's unshakable conviction that no evil committed anywhere in the world could possibly measure up to the evils he ascribes to the United States, the target of his relentless hostility; thus, the enemies of his enemies become his friends.

Two years after Chomsky's defense of the Pol Pot regime, the late Alex Carey, an Australian academic, also attempted to discredit the refugee reports and "the picture of a satanic, pointlessly repressive Khmer Rouge regime" that emerged from them.[113] Another Australian apologist, Ben Kiernan who recently taught at Yale wrote, among other things that, "There is ample evidence . . . that the Khmer Rouge movement is not the monster that the press have recently made it out to be"; "Photographs of alleged atrocities [are] fake. . . . The Western press have more of an interest in a 'bloodbath' in Cambodia than the Communists do."[114]

The Pol Pot's regime was defended not only by American authors such as Chomsky, Herman, and Gareth Porter but also by some prominent Swedish intellectuals. Birgitta Dahl, a recent speaker of the Swedish Parliament, (earlier minister of the Environment and Energy as well as chairman of the Swedish Committee on Vietnam, Laos, and Cambodia) was one of them. Like Chomsky she regarded the reports of the Cambodian massacres as "lies or conjecture" and had no difficulty to justify the forced evacuation of Phnom Penh by the Khmer Rouge: "The evacuation of Phnom Penh was absolutely necessary. . .

. Food production had to be started quickly, and his was bound to require great sacrifices from the population."[115] P. O. Enquist, a writer well known (in Sweden) regarded the same evacuation as a form of huge house cleaning, to get rid of the "degradation" imposed on the residents by Western influences: "The brothel having been evacuated, cleaning is in progress. This is something which only pimps can regret."[116]

Vietnam which has long ceased to be a destination for political tourists has nonetheless occasionally inspired feelings similar to those entertained by the earlier generation of war protestors and sympathizers (see also pp. xi–xii in the 1990 preface). Susan Brownmiller, better known as a radical feminist from the late 1960s and the 1970s, visited Vietnam in 1992 on assignment for *Travel & Leisure* magazine. According to a reviewer of her book she appeared confident, "that she knows the situation of these Vietnamese better than they do"; her "lack of inquisitiveness is startling." The latter was revealed, among other things, in her conversation with English-speaking monks near Hue

> who seemed ready to talk about their experiences under the Communist Government's repressive policy toward religion. But nothing in her account suggests that Ms. Brownmiller sought to find out anything from them. Instead, as she describes the encounter, *she* informed *them* about the current status of the issue: "I think you're home free . . . you are now an important tourist attraction. The Government needs you."

The reviewer's conclusion applies to countless similar travelogues: "Full of sympathy and good will for the Vietnamese, Ms. Brownmiller nevertheless reveals a self-centeredness that is all too American. Coming from a prosperous society, we tend to travel the world, like Ms. Brownmiller, with answers, not questions."[117]

Another American visitor, Lewis Lapham, who was taken to the house where Ho Chi Minh used to live and run the war against the United States had this to say:

> The simplicity of Ho's military headquarters conforms to a perception of the Vietnam War that turned a generation of Americans against their own government. On one side a few small men, poor and thinly clothed, seated among flowering trees; on the other side the technological splendor of the Pentagon and a regiment of generals decorated with goldbraid, talking to themselves in air conditioned rooms.[118]

The author of these observations leaves the impression that this *was* a correct perception (of the war) and thereby perpetuates the questionable and highly romanticized view of the Vietnam War as one of David vs. Goliath, when in fact the Communist guerillas were perfectly well provided for the purposes of a guerilla war even if lacking in air conditioned conference rooms (see also pp. 267–74).

At last it is worth noting for the record a fact missing from the original edition of this book, namely, Chomsky's visit to Hanoi on April 14, 1970, from where he sent his greetings to the 1970 "Spring Offensive" of the American peace movement. In his speech—monitored by the U.S. Foreign Broadcast Information Service and thus preserved for posterity—he said:

> The people of Vietnam will win . . . because your cause is the cause of humanity as it moves forward toward liberty and justice, toward the socialist society in which free, creative man control their own destiny.
>
> . . . We are deeply grateful to you that you permit us to be part of your brave and historical struggle. We hope that there will continue to be strong bonds between the people of Vietnam and many Americans who wish you success and who detest with all of their being the hateful activities of the American government.

In the same speech he referred to the United States as an "empire, that has no place in the 20th century, that has only the capacity to repress, and murder and destroy."[119]

China, as noted earlier, has been largely abandoned by Westerners in search of revolutionary purity and idealism since it embraced private enterprise and consumerism. The apparent exceptions have been the handful of aged American and European Maoists who had actually moved to China decades ago and, understandably enough, made valiant and pathetic efforts to protect their lifelong emotional-ideological investment. One of them was Joan Hinton, "cling[ing] to political beliefs that most Chinese abandoned years ago" and retaining a "devotion to Maoist ideals." She said that, "'Mao started the Cultural Revolution to cure the disparity between the few and the many. . . . How could that be wrong?'"[120]

At the present time defenders of China in the United States are more likely to be businessmen seeking lucrative trade and unconcerned with China's long record of human rights violations. A representative of American companies manufacturing oil refinery equipment chided Warren Christopher and other American officials for meeting (or trying to meet) Chinese dissidents and for criticizing China for its continued political repression. As in the old days (as the reader will see) he points out that in China there is little crime, nobody sleeps on the streets and everybody is well provided with essentials—highly questionable claims in the mid-1990s. He assures us that "when people are ready [in China] they will change their system with no need for help from the United States as big brother."[121]

It is possible that self-interest of another kind (permission to stay in China?) accounts for the interpretation of the June 1989 Tienanmen Square massacres offered by a Maryknoll missioner who at the time taught at a Chinese university and claimed that he "had lived and worked in China before June (1989) and I am still here trying to make some modest contribution to the Chinese people's struggle for reform, development and modernization." He also wrote:

> The Communist leaders of China have committed their lives unconditionally and sacrificed everything even at mortal risk to advance China. For them, the road to reform and development still means revolutionary change and dialectical materialism. The events of May and June . . . [in 1989] were perceived by them as anarchical threats to the Government, the Communist Party and the socialist system. They reacted to preserve national security.[122]

The reverend did not seem to be aware of the numerous other historical occasions when rulers of various dictatorships in our times felt similarly threatened by something or other, and used their "perception" of such a threat to justify the murder or imprisonment of those personifying the threat.

In the 1990s a rare public defender of the "great" Cultural Revolution in the United States could still be found. She was a 1971 pilgrim who also edited *The New China* magazine, presumably an organ of propaganda. In her view,

> during the Cultural Revolution . . . new social relations were being forged . . . the Chinese I saw were characterised by dignity and optimism. . . . It is no wonder that in this centennial year of the birth of Mao Zedong, many in China as well as around the world are looking at the experience of Maoist years not only with nostalgia, but also for lessons for the future.[123]

In another reading of the lessons of history Professor Chase-Dunn of Johns Hopkins University offered reassurance that, "The revolutions in the Soviet Union and the People's Republic of China have increased our collective knowledge of how to build socialism despite their only partial successes."[124]

Further Details of Hospitality

Recent perusal of Victor Serge's memoirs (a foreign-born supporter of the Russian Revolution of 1917) reminded me how far back into the past the tradition of political hospitality extends. Discussing the years 1919–1920 Serge (who at the time lived in Russia) noted that

> The only city foreign delegates never got to know (and their incuriosity in this respect disturbed me) was the real, living Moscow, with its starvation-rations, its arrests, its sordid prison-episodes, its backstage racketeering.

Sumptuously fed amidst universal misery . . . shepherded from museums to model nurseries, the representatives of international Socialism seemed to react like holiday-makers or tourists. . . . The words "dictatorship of the proletariat" functioned as a magical explanation for them without it ever occurring to them to ask where this dictator of a proletariat was, what it thought, felt and did.[125]

More recently an English journalist recalled his impression during the Brezhnev era:

I do not forget the first evening I spent in the company of Russians, in the sunken gloom of the Brezhnev era. A journalist on assignment, I was escorted by three or four "guides" ostensibly from the Intourist Agency, to see "a typical family" in a highrise building. . . . An evening of tormented silence was broken . . . by the exchange of platitudes. . . .

A complex and protracted system of visas and prepaid vouchers for hotels and restaurants ensured that a foreigner could never escape supervision.[126]

Since the book only dealt with the Soviet political pilgrimages before Stalin's death, it is of some interest to note here that during the late 1970s and 1980s political tourism to the Soviet Union, stimulated by the peace movement, revived. In this period well-meaning American "peace activists" visited not so much in search for a superior social system but to find support for their conviction that the United States rather than the Soviet Union was responsible for the cold war and the threat of nuclear annihilation; they were also anxious to discover that "ordinary" Soviet people were just like ordinary Americans and equally averse to nuclear incineration. Advertisements of such tours during this period could be found in *The Nation* magazine, among other places. Participants often were aged "old leftists" who would

tell you how wonderful the Soviet Union was: Pensions were huge, housing was cheap and they practically paid you to get medical care. . . . These were people who believed everything about the Soviet Union was perfect but they were bringing their own toilet paper. . . . [They] spent most of every day talking . . . not making observations. What they were doing was agreeing with each other. . . . On Reagan, the weapons freeze, on the badness of Israel, on the dangers of war, on the need for peace, they agreed.[127]

East German political hospitality followed the Soviet model and when the visitors were suitably predisposed, achieved its objectives. For example, when the editor-in-chief (Theo Sommer) of the West German newspaper *Die Zeit* visited in 1986 with a delegation of nationally known opinion makers, the DDR (German Democratic Republic, as it was officially called), his hosts,

conducted [the group] around showplaces and introduced [them] to leading personalities. Everything passed off without a hitch. Sommer thanked politburo members for allowing him to perceive that DDR politicians, unlike those at home, meant what they said. The series of articles which Die Zeit ran . . . was ecstatic. . . . Sommer rhapsodized about the lack of anxiety which he had detected, the plentiful supply of goods, growing rates of production, the protection of the environment and the fresh scope for artists.[128]

Such reports could not have been written and published without a climate of opinion dominated by West German intellectuals alienated enough from their own society and hence ready to give the benefit of doubt even to East Germany.

A rare report of political hospitality in the former Communist Czechoslovakia was provided by one of 90 foreign students of Slavonic studies. All standard techniques were noted: the students were far better fed than the natives; they were given "a generous amount of pocket money"; they "were made to feel rather important"; they were photographed and interviewed; they were shown movies that Czechs could not see; they were taken to collective farms, museums, and monuments while the hosts seized "every opportunity for self-congratulation," characterizing "ordinary utilitarian installations" as singular achievements of the regime. There was also constant praise of and thankfulness to the Soviet Union.[129]

In Bucharest under Ceausescu a department store was set up (along the lines of the North Korean model discussed earlier). It was inspired by Macy's in New York, which Ceausescu discovered during his American visit. As reported by a former high ranking Romanian official:

On the day of its inauguration by Ceausescu himself the store was chock full of merchandise. . . . A few days later the shelves were virtually empty. Periodically the store was "prepared" for visits by high-level foreigners or by Ceausescu himself. It would be closed off to the public and stuffed with merchandise. For his part, Ceausescu has never really believed that Macy's was not especially stocked for his visit.[130]

A critical examination of the techniques of hospitality in Communist China in the 1950s not mentioned in my book was written by Richard L. Walker. Among other things he noted that, "Many tourists visit Mao's birthplace and talk to an uncle of his (one correspondent refers to 'uncles' working in shifts)"[131]—one among the numerous illustrations of the Chinese efforts to excel in political hospitality.

At last it is worth recalling that sometimes political hospitality was also extended to distinguished Soviet citizens who lived abroad and whom the regime wished to impress favorably in order to persuade them to return. The cases in point are Maxim Gorky, the writer, and Sergei Prokofiev, the composer. The task was given by Stalin to Genrikh Yahoda, head of the political police (GPU) at the time:

> Beginning in 1928 Gorky, in Sorrento [Italy], was inundated with telegrams and letters from his homeland, in which workers' groups, prompted by the GPU, told him how they missed their bard.
>
> In the same year, the Boss had organized celebrations in honor of Gorky's sixtieth birthday, the likes of which had never been seen. Through Yahoda's emissaries, the Boss offered Gorky the post of spiritual leader. . . .
>
> He agreed to visit the USSR. . . .
>
> When Gorky returned, Yahoda was his inseparable companion. "Yagodka" ("Little Berry") was Gorky's affectionate name for the secret police. "Little Berry" took him on a tour around the GPU camps. Gorky was shown former thieves and prostitutes who had become shock workers (those who set new productivity standards). . . . In the camps Gorky was touched by the successes of reeducation. Moved to tears he sang the praise of the GPU. He would return to the Soviet Union.

Prokofiev was another famous artist to be brought back to add his presence to the luster of Stalin's Soviet Union:

> Negotiations were going on with another celebrity . . . the composer Sergei Prokofiev. The enticement of Prokofiev was also a GPU operation. In January 1927 . . . Prokofiev decided to visit. . . .
>
> As soon as . . . [he] arrived . . . "a certain Zucker" was attached to him as his "constant companion" . . . [he] was of course a GPU agent.
>
> Prokofiev was taken to the best hotel, the Metropole . . . "Zucker spent the whole journey enthusiastically explaining the beneficial activities of his Party. It proved very interesting . . ." [Prokofiev wrote in his diary]
>
> The process continued. Prokofiev was taken to a "special restaurant," where the meal was "exceptionally tasty" and the service just as good. There were "grouse, marvelous whipped cream" and "in general a host of forgotten Russian things." When he entered the Conservatoire the orchestra welcomed him with a triumphal march. . . .
>
> Zucker finally decided to show complete confidence in Prokofiev by taking him along "as a guest" to the Kremlin. The company chosen for this occasion was as "intellectual" as could be arranged. . . . Prokofiev like what he saw. He paid several subsequent visits to the USSR and eventually resettled there. Yahoda had succeeded.[132]

Forgotten Pilgrims

Lincoln Steffens provides an early example of the triumph of predisposition over information. U.S. Ambassador Bullit seeking information about Soviet conditions from Lincoln Steffens (one of the earliest of all pilgrims) found him of little use "since Steffens seldom left his room in Moscow"—a circum-

stance which did not prevent him from becoming an early authority on the
Soviet Union in the United States. Moreover, according to Bullit, "Steffens
thought up the famous phrase in which he later characterized his impressions
of the Soviet regime . . . [i.e.] 'I have seen the future and it works!' on the
train to Stockholm, long before he entered Russia."[133]

The historical record can be further strengthened by other materials I was
unaware of, or did not exist when the book was written. Thus, I learned that
the famous French intellectual (and critic of the "Treason for intellectuals")
Julien Benda visited Communist Hungary in 1949 shortly after the execution
of Laszlo Rajk and others, victims of the major Hungarian show trial. His
visit was recalled by a Hungarian writer, George Faludy, who had known
Benda earlier in France:

> We met in the lobby of Hotel Bristol, the official accommodation for Western
> visitors. . . . Benda began by pointing out that he inspected Budapest thor-
> oughly, including manufacturing plants, and was greatly impressed by the ac-
> complishments of the People's Democracy.[134] He mentioned, as evidence, the
> excellent food at Bristol and his visit to the Csepel Steelworks; he spoke with
> the workers and all expressed satisfaction with their lives. . . . When he was
> taken into one of the workshops he went to the first workbench (which he found
> remarkably clean) and asked the worker using it how much he made . . . he
> made 3600 forint per month [a very high income for the period—P.H.], owned
> a small villa and car . . . the car was also shown. . . .
>
> "You see" he said "when will the French worker able to have such a car and
> income?" . . .
>
> I smiled, as did the interpreter who accompanied Benda . . . we both knew
> that in the great assembly plant of the Csepel Works there was a workbench at
> the entrance occupied not by a worker but an employee of AVO [the Hungar-
> ian State Security] for the benefit of visitors touring the plant. The AVO man
> did not work and was at the workbench only when a visitor appeared, which is
> why it was so clean. As an employee of the AVO he indeed earned 3600
> forint, had free accommodation and owned a car. . . .
>
> Subsequently Benda explained his visit; he came because of the Rajk af-
> fair. He related that in France there were still some people who believed that
> Rajk was innocent. . . . But he wanted to learn the truths about the case on the
> spot. . . .
>
> In Budapest he spoke with many trustworthy individuals, writers, legal
> scholars, historians and politicians . . . they all insisted that there was no
> doubt Rajk was a treacherous conspirator . . . intent on bringing back the days
> of fascism to Hungary. . . . Benda was grateful to Mathias Rakosi [head of the
> ruling Communist party at the time-P.H.] for inviting him and providing ev-
> ery assistance to get to the bottom of this matter. . . .
>
> . . . I would have liked to tell him that our lives would be more bearable if
> we did not have to suffer the visit of such well intentioned but feeble minded
> Western visitors such as Benda or Andersen Nexo or Paul Eluard . . . let alone
> Lion Feuchtwanger and Jean Paul Sartre.[135]

Hungarian writers themselves fell victim to the attitudes and techniques which trapped Benda during the same period. Two among them, who a few years later became the leading critics of the regime, and played a part in the 1956 Revolution, described (much later) their own pilgrimage to the Soviet Union in 1950 as members of a writers' delegation:

> The writers were deeply moved as they crossed the border; they got off the train inspired. Here at last was the fulfillment of their fondest dreams: they set foot on the soil of the land of socialism. Their heart overflowed with affection and gratitude toward the great liberating friend and exemplar. The rooms in the hotel were comfortable (though not especially well heated); the food was excellent (but the service slow) and the performances at the Stanislavski theatre were fascinating; on the other hand people on the street seemed somewhat poorly dressed. They inspected museums, factories and schools but unfortunately (despite their request) they did not manage to visit the apartments of ordinary citizens of Moscow. Never mind, they quickly got over the deficiencies and requests unmet and talked at length and enthusiastically of all that met their expectations. They were moved and anxiously curious as they stood in the department stores displaying shabby merchandise and later reported to one another of all the wonders they had seen. No, they did not lie. They were good communists who wished to see the Soviet Union as the land of marvels and succeeded in doing so.[136]

Another important and well-known Western intellectual I failed to include in the book was Graham Greene, though I discussed him elsewhere as a prominent anti-American.[137] Grahams' favorite countries were Castro's Cuba, Sandinista Nicaragua, and, more peculiarly, Panama under General Omar Torrijos. His fluctuating admiration for these countries had its roots in his largely negative attitude toward his own society, supplemented by an English upper-class anti-Americanism. He wrote in 1967: "If I had to choose between life in the Soviet Union and life in the United States I would certainly choose the Soviet Union, just as I would choose life in Cuba to life in those southern American republics . . . dominated by their northern neighbor, or life in North Vietnam to life in South Vietnam."[138] His hero worship of General Torrijos of Panama (which inspired an entire book) was a more idiosyncratic expression of the same disposition fuelled by the conflict between Panama and the United States. According to Michael Korda, his American editor, Graham "was always trying to discover sainthood in secular figures; he prized in others simplicity and an innocence that he had been denied, and his later works are a kind of pilgrimage in search of a different kind of faith."[139] Greene was, in Korda's words, "a sentimental leftist" with a soft spot for countries which seemed to challenge the West and the United States in particular and which, he believed, were victims of the West. (There is much discussion of this mentality in the book especially in chapters 1, 2, and 9).

An interest and idealization of Panama was also apparent in a recent article of John Le Carre (better known for his spy stories conceived in the spirit of moral equivalence between the United States and the Soviet Union), which also exemplified the link between such idealizations and rejection of one's own society. Le Carre wrote:

> Panama is like no other Latin American country, in that its people possess a mysterious self-righting mechanism. . . . Panama has a new dawn ahead of it . . . I wish I could say the same for England. . . .
> When I sat in the Club Union and watched the antics of Panama's filthy rich, I might as well have been sitting in some yuppie luncheon hell in the City of London. Same faces . . . same appetites, same ethic—except that what might just be pardonable in a country that had been systematically corrupted by colonization was a lot less attractive in a country that had colonized a third of the world.[140]

Here we have again the paradigmatic conception of the West spreading corruption among the otherwise uncorrupted, a theme in the pilgrimages which involve non-Western societies.

Another famous English intellectual and playwright, Harold Pinter, is also missing from the previous editions of *Political Pilgrims*. He has been, at least since the early 1980s a vigorous critic of his own society, and apparently as a result, an uncritical admirer of the political system idealized at the time by leftist intellectuals, namely, Sandinista Nicaragua. Pinter was among the founders of a newsletter called "Samizdat" to protest repression in England; presumably the name was supposed to remind one of the "moral equivalence" between East and West while seeking to capitalize on the prestige of the genuinely repressed Soviet dissenters of the time. Pinter compared Soviet intervention in Czechoslovakia in 1968 to the American intervention in Nicaragua: rulers of the United States were motivated by the fear that since the Sandinistas "set out to establish a stable and decent society" they would set a precedent to the people in Central America that had to be "crushed."[141] Chomsky shared this belief: "If peasants starving to death in Honduras can look across the borders and see health clinics, land reform, literacy programs . . . the rot may spread still farther, perhaps even to the United States. . . . It is necessary to destroy the rotten apple before the rot spreads through the barrel."[142]

Gunter Grass, the famous German writer has been another archetypal pilgrim and fierce critic of the United States and the West missing from the original edition of the book. (I made numerous references to him in *Anti-Americanism*, cited earlier.) Grass was one of those Western intellectuals for whom "every revolution, however remote . . . personified the ideals which their nations lacked . . . who descend on the precarious countries of the Third

World and later return to their comfortable cities with four hundred or so pages about that world, pages written in ignorance, or even falsified in the name of hope"—an observation made by Heberto Padilla, the exiled (and formerly imprisoned) Cuban writer.[143] More recently it was noted that Grass has remained Germany's "last unreconstructed leftist, a staunch critic of the West and defender of Fidel Castro." In his latest novel, the hero who appears to be his alter ego views post-unification East Germany as "a land that was once happy but has been raped by ruthless Western tycoons."[144]

Earlier Grass' estrangement led him to the admiration of Sandinista Nicaragua and Castro's Cuba. Grass, as an important visitor, was escorted around Nicaragua by Tomas Borges, the head of the state security, and taken to one of the model prisons. Suitably impressed he concluded that "in this tiny, sparsely populated land . . . Christ's words are taken literally."[145]

Another important figure (who could be called a "resident pilgrim") given all too little attention in the book was Walter Duranty. He was, for many years, a Moscow correspondent of the *New York Times*, providing exceptionally distorted and upbeat reports of Stalin's Soviet Union which probably contributed to the favorable expectations and delusions of many American visitors. It was he who coined the famous phrase "you can't make an omelette without breaking eggs" to deflate moral indignation over the sufferings inflicted by the Soviet system on its people. For his efforts he earned the praise of Stalin himself who said to him, "You have done a good job in your reporting the USSR . . . you try to tell the truth about our country and to understand it and to explain it to your readers. I might say that you bet on our horse to win."[146]

Also of interest in the context of reevaluating the pilgrims and pilgrimages is that in 1989 a prominent American journalist, Tom Wicker (himself briefly a latter-day pilgrim to Communist Mozambique—see pp. 276–77), sought to defend the reputation of the late Owen Lattimore (see pp. 102, 153, 156, 157) who went on a high-level conducted tour (with Henry Wallace) to the Soviet Union in 1944 and whose misperceptions of the Soviet system were among the most bizarre and surrealistic. In his article entitled "Smearing the Dead" Wicker displayed no awareness of Lattimore's fulsome praise for the Soviet labor camps he visited and their commander who was his host, or other foolish statements of his Soviet experiences. Apparently Wicker was also unfamiliar with Lattimore's subsequent cocky defense and rationalization of his misguided statements (see p. 158). Wicker insisted that Lattimore "was not a fellow traveler, nor a pro-Communist in any shape or form."[147]

The credulousness of the political pilgrims and tourists is better understood if we recall that even shrewd Western politicians succumbed to illusions about the nature of Communist systems and especially their leaders. I made no mention in the earlier editions of Franklin Delano Roosevelt who exemplified these attitudes regarding the Soviet Union and Stalin. Robert Nisbet wrote:

> After his return from Yalta in February 1945, he [Roosevelt] described Stalin to his cabinet as having "something else in his being besides this revolutionist, Bolshevik thing." The President went on to tell his rapt audience that this might have something to do with Stalin's early training for the "priesthood." He added: "I think that something entered into his nature of the way in which a Christian gentleman should behave."

Roosevelt's naivete allowed him to express confidence that in the Baltic states the Soviet Union had occupied, "the people would vote to join the Soviet Union." According to Nisbet, "Roosevelt saw in Stalin's Russia, equality, social justice and social democracy growing underneath the top dressing of force necessary to repulse capitalists and other enemies of the Soviet Union." To be sure, "in his credulity toward Stalin and . . . Russian Communism Roosevelt was not alone. In academic, journalistic, entertainment and other circles there was wide-eyed adulation of Stalin after the Nazis invaded Russia."[148] That adulation has been extensively documented in *Political Pilgrims*.

More recently A. M. Rosenthal of the *New York Times* argued that American politicians and segments of the educated public show a highly patterned capacity to benignly misinterpret the policies and behavior of dictators. For instance,

> Fidel Castro: again and again he says that he will not ease political terrorism against Cubans, even if it could end the American embargo tomorrow. No Gorbachevian sucker he, says el comandante.
> However often he says it, hordes of Americans, Canadians, Europeans return from Cuban pilgrimages to announce that if the embargo is lifted he will allow elections, a free press, public debate and similar steps he understandably believes will be fatal to his Communist regime.[149]

The Roots and Durable Significance of the Pilgrimages

There was an insight that eluded me earlier regarding certain motives of the American pilgrims and tourists. I made no reference to the long-standing aversion of Americans toward traditional autocracies and their corresponding greater tolerance for those which appear "progressive." (I have written about this elsewhere.) Jeane Kirkpatrick pointed out that: "traditional autocracies are . . . deeply offensive to modern American sensibilities. The notion that public affairs should be ordered on the basis of kinship, friendship and other personal relations rather than on the basis of objective, 'rational' standards violates our conception of justice and efficiency." By contrast modern socialist systems often appeared rational, efficient, and egalitarian.[150] But these systems also had a less than fully rational appeal, offering, as they seemed, a route to greater moral perfection, here, if not now. As Martin Malia observed, "socialism is not a historical or social-science term at all, but ultimately a messianic, indeed quasi-magical term."[151]

In the final analysis it is not altogether surprising that the disintegration of communist systems between 1989 and 1991 had a only modest impact on the attitudes here discussed.[152] The political pilgrimages and tours are significant as symptoms of other, more deeply entrenched and durable attitudes. I labelled these attitudes variously as alienation, estrangement, reflexive rejection, or an adversarial disposition; they appear to survive regardless of the availability of suitable pilgrimage sites, regardless of the unravelling and resounding discreditation of communist systems around the world.

Since the late 1970s when this book was written the sources of estrangement from and discontent with Western societies had remained fairly stable. If socialism as such is no longer the name given to the longings and impulses associated with political tourism, the fundamental reasons which made the idea of socialism attractive are still there, in particular the "quest for community," or, "group solidarity and its regulation by common purposes," or, in the words of F. A. Hayek, "an atavistic longing after the life of the noble savage . . . the main source of the collectivistic tradition."[153] The yearning for equality (which socialism promises to gratify) is less a yearning for social justice than for wholeness, brotherhood, and community. Peter Berger referred to the same attitudes as "counter-modernizing" impulses.[154]

There would be no political pilgrims and tourists (and more recently, no "multiculturalists") unless groups of people, and especially the intellectuals among them, did not feel, to varying degrees, a strong aversion to their own society and its culture, that is Western culture. This hostility, as I argued more explicitly in *Anti-Americanism*, is, in the final analysis, a product of an unease and discomfort with life in modern, secular, affluent technologically advanced and pluralistic societies, lacking a collective sense of purpose. We may define contemporary Western intellectuals (in addition to innumerable other ways) as those among the educated and leisured strata who are most unhappy with the experience of living in such societies and are best capable of articulating such discontent. There are many other people of some education, leisure, and high living standards who share this distaste without qualifying as "intellectuals"—portions of the clergy, many journalists, some politicians, celebrities in entertainment, those among the guilty rich.

Hence, the breeding ground of an aversion to the status quo, or the potentials for what Malia calls "the maximalist temptation," remain. Even if the pilgrimages have greatly diminished, the impulses behind them are still with us as are the enclaves of what I called earlier the adversary culture, especially in and around colleges and universities.[155] In these settings many of the values, attitudes, and impulses which animated the pilgrims have become institutionalized, entrenched, even routinized. They are genuine subcultures with their basic, taken for granted assumptions.

One enduring conclusion that may be drawn from the phenomena here considered—including the bizarre misperceptions of particular political systems and the misplaced idealistic impulses which led to them—is that intellectuals, and highly educated people in general, are not well protected either by their education or cognitive intelligence from major errors of judgement. To put it more simply, emotional dispositions prove to be overpowering, an observation far from original, but resoundingly confirmed in the pages which follow. It is especially striking to behold these emotional forces in apparent control of highly trained, often otherwise brilliant minds. Here again Anthony Daniels, a fellow student of these matters, observed that there is "the kind of nonsense to which only intelligent people can give their assent, since it requires a vast and intricate intellectual edifice to do so."[156] This is a point of view shared by Orwell and connected to the familiar observation that intellectuals suffer from a deficit of common sense due to their insulation from certain prosaic, practical realities, or perhaps due to their reflective disposition and readiness to entertain abstractions (see especially pp. 411–15). To the extent that more and more intellectuals are academic intellectuals, this insulation deepens, as academic enclaves provide a sanctum from many of the experiences, problems, and irritations of the world outside; many of their inhabitants quite self-consciously seek such insulation from the "mainstream" of the population they hold in some contempt, especially in the United States. These circumstances also help to explain the persisting popularity (of versions) of Marxism among academic intellectuals in the West and other academic trends (even more strikingly removed from the observable realities of the world) which emerged since this book was written, including postmodernism and deconstructionism. The latter not only represent new heights of cognitive and moral relativism, but are conveyed in language and terminology incomprehensible for those outside academia and even to many within. Many academic intellectuals attracted to these ideas make no pretense of seeking to reach audiences outside their peers in the academic enclaves. Jeffrey Herf appropriately designated these endeavors as "the counter-Enlightenment project" and pointed out that, "the postmodernist blurring between fact and fiction, and its assumption that all knowledge is the product of power, weakens the discipline of history as such"—and not only history. He also recalled that both Nazism and communism "attacked notions of objectivity, common standards and rules of evidence in favor of forms of what have been called identity politics."[157]

As I briefly noted in the 1990 preface (and at far greater length in *Anti-Americanism*), since the late 1980s the major expression of discontent with Western culture and societies found expression in the ideology and educational reforms associated with "multiculturalism" or "cultural diversity," two terms which, as commonly used, are highly inaccurate and misleading. Ostensibly an effort to reflect the cultural diversity and interests of demographic groups (foremost among them blacks and Hispanics) in the United States, "diversity" has also become a new justification and codeword for the preferential treatment of some of them.

Although multiculturalism (or cultural diversity) has been championed by different groups (blacks, Hispanics, radical feminists, homosexuals, lesbians, etc.) they have in common an intense hostility toward Western traditions, ideas, values, social arrangements, and even science.[158] To be a multiculturalist critic of the United States (or other Western societies) it is not necessary to visit other, putatively superior social systems or cultures. Academic enclaves are sufficient for the incubation and propagation of these views and attitudes. Flights into an imaginary and idealized past also substitute for pointing to existing, superior societies—an approach especially preferred by Afrocentrists, who would find it difficult to point to an example of an actually existing African country that would inspire admiration or emulation, let alone pilgrimages. While originating and well entrenched on the campuses, multiculturalism has also exerted strong influence over school systems all over the country as well as a variety of other institutions from museums to symphony orchestras.

There are other phenomena which are characteristic of the current cultural landscape in the United States and feed into, or reflect, the adversarial currents noted. Among them has been the proliferation of accredited or aspiring victims groups over the past decades, each representing further proof of the inequities of the system.[159] Moral and material factors alike have stimulated this process. Christopher Lasch remarked on the attraction of "a cult of the victim in which entitlements are based on the display of accumulated injuries inflicted by an uncaring society."[160]

Another trend also linked to multiculturalism has been the propagation of self-esteem as a key to group and individual uplift. While it has become an implicit cultural maxim that self-esteem must be raised regardless of what

the "self" achieves, personal and group failure are ascribed to social conditions and structures. There is at last the phenomenon of identity politics,
intertwined with both multiculturalism and the battle for self-esteem. Identity politics assumes that some basic attribute such as race, sex, ethnicity, or
sexual preference is the single determinant and source of one's true identity
and all political interests. Again Christopher Lasch pointed out that, "The
same benefits misleadingly associated with religion—security, spiritual comfort, dogmatic relief from doubt—are thought to flow from a therapeutic politics of identity. In effect, identity politics has come to serve as a substitute for
religion."[161] The reader will undoubtedly note the relevance of these comments as the argument in this book unfolds regarding the religious or quasi-
religious underpinnings of the political pilgrimage.

The so-called revisionist historiography of the Soviet Union and of the
cold war remains another symptom of the attitudes among groups of American intellectuals which are far from irrelevant to the topic of this book. While
it is easier to understand why some of the historians who came of age during
the 1960s felt uncomfortable with blaming the Soviet Union for the cold war,
or with the concept of totalitarianism, it is more perplexing why some felt
compelled even to reinterpret the Purges of the 1930s and the mass murders
under Stalin, endeavors reminiscent of the Holocaust revisionism. An un-
stated commitment to the image of the United States as the most malevolent
force in contemporary (or all) history helps to understand the eagerness and
energy some of these historians put into their attempts to humanize the Soviet
system, even in its Stalinist incarnation.[162] Most recently, one of them, Robert
Thurston, even managed to produce a book that seeks to rehabilitate Stalin.[163]

Another academic trend that too reflects some of the attitudes here discussed is found in the concern of American historians with "the affairs of
ordinary people: what is usually called 'history from below'" and various
forms of "revisionism" which usually seek to show that American history is
far fuller of disgraceful episodes than had been thought earlier. This type of
history, a form of retroactive social criticism, strikes out in several ideological directions. On the one hand, it avoids and ignores the conventional elite
groups who used to get the lions' share of historical attention; on the other
hand, it idealizes the seemingly forgotten masses, the poor, the non-elites. As
Gerald Straus (himself a historian) observed, "it is hard to do popular history
. . . without feeling, that in some small measure, you are enlisted in the cause
of justice." These endeavors also seek to highlight, and bring attention to
aspects of American or Western history which further and retroactively justify the critics' aversion to the society to which they so ambivalently belong.
Gerald Straus wrote: "As we try to come to terms with past realities, we are

vulnerable to powerful interventionist incentives. . . . Unable to do much to improve the world, but with strong convictions about how this might be accomplished, we make of the past our field of action, seeing it as the site where, belatedly we rectify wrongs, where retroactive justice is done."[164]

It may be concluded that the most general as well as the most durable explanation of the phenomena here discussed—especially the meaning-seeking impulses which lead both to angry rejections and naive quests—are connected to modernity. Here, it hardly needs to be said, I am not referring to computers or telecommunications but to the most corrosive of all qualities of modernity that Christopher Lasch captured describing the United States today as "a society in which nothing is sacred and therefore, nothing is forbidden."[165] Such a society remains a fertile ground for alienation, vague longings, and discontents, all of which lead to the phenomena that this volume explores.

Paul Hollander
Northampton, Massachusetts
April 1997

Notes

1. On the "pilgrim" vs. "tourist" distinction see p. xiv of the 1990 preface.

2. A sampling of Chomsky's praise for Sandinista Nicaragua may be found, among other places, in Paul Hollander, *Anti-Americanism* (New York: Oxford University Press 1992, and New Brunswick: Transaction Publishers, 1995), 290, 291, 293.

3. See Frank Parkin, *Middle Class Radicalism: The Social Bases of the British Campaign for Nuclear Disarmament* (Manchester: Manchester University Press, 1968).

4. Doris Lessing, *The Wind Blows Away Our Words* (New York: Vintage, 1987), 165–66.

5. E. Chivian and J. E. Mack, "Soviet Minds Sheltered from Catastrophes," letter, *New York Times*, May 15, 1986.

6. John Mack, *Abduction: Human Encounters with Aliens* (New York: Scribner, 1994).

7. Peter Collier and David Horowitz, *Deconstructing the Left* (Lanham, MD: Second Thoughts Books, 1991), 116.

8. Daniel Bell, "Another Question," letter, *Dissent* (Spring 1995).

9. Martin Malia, *The Soviet Tragedy: A History of Socialism in Russia 1917–1991* (New York: Free Press, 1994), 15.

10. Malcolm Muggeridge, *Things Past* (London: Collins, 1978), 31–32.

11. Todd Gitlin, "Lost Cause: Why Intellectuals of the Left Miss Communism," *Los Angeles Times*, January 14, 1996, M3.

12. Doris Lessing, *Under My Skin* (New York: HarperCollins, 1994), 15–16.

13. Norman Podhoretz observed that while these beliefs have been

> discredited in [their] original forms . . . [they] mutated into insidious new shapes and thereby acquired a new lease on life, especially in the universities, where the assault on the traditions and values of this society comes disguised, under the name of multiculturalism, as an innocent effort to give the belated due to previously excluded ethnic and sexual minorities.

Norman Podhoretz, "Neoconservativism: A Eulogy," *Commentary* (March 1996), 26.

14. Bill Keller, "Conversations/Joe Slovo," *New York Times* (*News of the Week*), December 4, 1994.

15. See, for example, Kevin Merida, "In Farrakhan's Footsteps," *Washington Post* (Weekly Edition), March 4–6, 1996. Farrakhan also visited Cuba in September 1996. See M. Radu, "Cracks in the Wall," *Cuba Watch* (Philadelphia: Foreign Policy Research Institute, 1996).

16. See Paul Hollander, "New Antiwar Movement, Old Social Criticism," in *Decline and Discontent* (New Brunswick: Transaction Publishers, 1992), 273–87.

17. Alan Cowell, "The Innocents from Abroad Hail Qaddafi," *New York Times*, September 3, 1989.

18. Norwell B. D. Atkine and Daniel Pipes, "Middle Eastern Studies: What Went Wrong?" *Academic Questions* (Winter 1995–96): 70.

19. Atkine and Pipes, "Middle Eastern Studies," 66.

20. Whenever reference is made to the "book" it is of course this volume.

21. Quoted in Atkine and Pipes, "Middle Eastern Studies," 67.

22. Ahmad accused Makiya of "rationalizations . . . ill-founded hates and self-absorption" and of being a disloyal Arab, among other things (ibid., 62–63).

23. Quoted in Per Ahlmark, "Tyranny and the Left: A Summary" (Stockholm: Timbro, 1995), 20. This pamphlet is based on a book of the same title published in Swedish in 1994.

24. Bezzad Naziri, "Iran's Prisons, From Inside and Out," *New York Times*, op-ed, January 22, 1990.

25. Mark Tooley, "More World Than Church?" *Faith and Freedom* (Summer 1996): 9.

26. *Shadows of Tender Fury: The Letters and Communiques of Subcomandante Marcos and the Zapatista Army of National Liberation*, Introduction by John Ross, Afterword by Frank Bardacke (New York: Monthly Review Press, 1995), 11; hereafter cited as *Marcos*. For further information on Marcos, see Andres Oppenheimer, Bordering on Chaos (Boston: Little, Brown and Company, 1996).

27. *Marcos*, 14.

28. Ibid., 15.

29. Paul Berman put his finger on the difference between such attitudes toward the contras, as opposed to various Marxist guerillas, on the part of intellectuals such as Debray:

> in Mexico the Zapatistas were led by a clever philosophy professor, Subcomandante Marcos, who knew how to speak . . . for a certain kind of intellectual. But there were no professors in Nicaragua's 3–80 Northern Front [i.e., on the side of the contras-P.H.] and no elaborate doctrines to bathe the uprising in a golden light—just guns and farmers, burning with hatred and fear. ("In Search of Ben Linder's Killers," *New Yorker*, September 23, 1996, 73)

30. Andres Oppenheimer, "Guerillas in the Mist," *New Republic* (17 June 1996): 22.

31. Associated Press, "Oliver Stone Visits Mexican Rebels," *Daily Hampshire Gazette*, March 25, 1996.

32. *Marcos*, 259, 264.

33. *LASA* (Latin American Studies Association) *Forum*, No. 3., Fall 1995. See also Alfred G. Cuzan, "Turning a Blind Eye on Cuba," *Washington Times*, op-ed, November 8, 1995.

34. Sheila Melvin, "Culture Clash in Pyongyang," *New York Times* (Travel Section), February 4, 1996.

35. A. Stanley, "A Lament by America's Top Communist," *New York Times*, August 31, 1991.

36. Anthony Daniels, *Utopias Elsewhere: Journeys in a Vanishing World* (New York: Crown Publishers, 1991), 75.

37. Melvin, "Culture Clash."

38. Daniels, *Utopias Elsewhere*, 38–39.

39. Ibid., 40.

40. Ibid., 48, 49–50, 51.

41. Nicholas D. Kristof, "North Korea: What We Do Know," *New York Times* (News of the Week), July 17, 1994, 6.

42. Anthony Daniels, "People's Democratic Revue," *National Review*, September 1, 1989, 20.

43. Daniels, *Utopias Elsewhere*, 57–58.

44. Ibid., 56. Another visitor, professor James A. Gregor of the University of California, Berkeley, also noted that citizens of Pyongyang "pin an enameled portrait of the Great Leader . . . to their breast every morning before departing to work," *Korea Herald*, August 1, 1991.

45. Daniels noted for instance that at one of the sites of the conducted tour, the so-called Juche tower (supposedly symbolizing Kim Il Sung's philosophy called juche), there were "marble plaques attesting to the appreciation by foreign disciples. . . . In design the plaques are exactly like those one finds at the tomb of a miracle-working Catholic saint . . . there were plaques from India and Senegal, Paraguay and New Zealand, indeed from every country of the world" (p. 42).

46. Ibid., 53–54.

47. Nicholas D. Kristof, "North Korea Bids Hello to the World," *New York Times*, July 1, 1989, 3.

48. Walter Russell Mead, "More Method Than Madness in North Korea," *New York Times Magazine*, September 15, 1996, 51–52.

49. John M. Swomley, "The Human Face of North Korea," *Christian Social Action*, September 1994, 25, 27, 28, 26.

50. N. Kristof, "North Korea."

51. Andrew Pollack, "The Real North Korea: The Bustle of a Mausoleum," *New York Times*, September 23, 1996.

52. David E. Sanger, "Two Koreas Agree to Summit Meeting on Nuclear Issue," *New York Times*, June 19, 1994, 12.

53. Quoted in George Will, "Carter Misreads North Korea's Kim," *Daily Hampshire Gazette*, June 24, 1994.

54. "American Committee on Korea Formed," *Christian Social Action* (March 1994): 26.

55. Daniels, *Utopias Elsewhere*, 50.

56. Daniels, *Utopias Elsewhere*, 193.

57. Hollander, "The Pilgrimage to Nicaragua," in *Anti-Americanism*, 259–306.

58. John Brentlinger, *The Best of What We Are: Reflections on the Nicaraguan Revolution* (Amherst: University of Massachusetts Press, 1995). An earlier writing of Brentlinger on the same subject is cited on p. xvi of the 1990 preface.

59. Ibid., 42.

60. Ibid., 2, 3, 4, 68.

61. Ibid., 6, 9.

62. Ibid., 20, 26, 36.

63. Ibid., 37, 38, 54.

64. Ibid., 56, 67.

65. Ibid., 286, 348.

66. James Brooke, "Shining Path Supporters Abroad Anger Peru," *New York Times*, December 18, 1991.

67. "Who Speaks for the Victims," *Hemisphere* (Fall 1991): 18.

68. Ronald Radosh, "The Radical Delusion," *Newsday*, April 29, 1996.

69. "The Hidden Life of Lori Berenson," *Village Voice*, February 27, 1996.

70. For an examination of the Boudin case and the attitudes alluded to, see Hollander, *Anti-Americanism*, 44–46.

71. Eric Breindel, "The World-Saver," *New York Post*, January 18, 1996; see also Lizette Alvarez, "Gramercy Park Woman is Held as a Rebel in Peru," *New York Times*, December 6, 1995.

72. "The Hidden Life," *Village Voice*.

73. Anthony Daniels, *Sweet Waist of America* (London: Hutchinson, 1990), 242–43.

74. Ibid., 170, 171, 173, 180.

75. The same may apply to North Korea. In the spring of 1996, following reports of starvation, the National Council of Churches decided that North Korea needed urgent assistance. The donors were not to be allowed to monitor the distribution of the food and there was reason to believe that the donations would benefit primarily those the regime regards as the most important and loyal groups, including the military, a consideration that failed to impress the Council. Once more it seemed that the National Council of Churches was as much motivated by making a political statement as by aiding the needy. (See Alan Wisdom, "Aid to North Korea: Dilemma of Charity," *Faith and Freedom* [Spring 1996]). The political sympathies of the National Council of Churches are discussed at some length in *Anti-Americanism* by this author.

76. M. A. Stone, "Delegation to Cuba Finds Economic Upswing," *Princeton Packet*, April 26, 1996, 17A.

77. E. T. Walsh, "An Embargo's Devastating Impact on Higher Education in Cuba," *Chronicle of Higher Education* (March 22, 1996).

78. Quoted in Paul Mulshine, "The Unbearable Lightness of Being in Cuba," *Heterodoxy* (May-June 1994): 15; Spock Letter in the *New York Times*, September 4, 1994. More recently Brightman vigorously attacked a report of Cuba which was critical of the system as "distortions of the Torricelli-Helms-Mas Canosa troika." Cf. her letter in the *New York Times*, November 9, 1995.

79. "Giving the Globe a Nudge," an interview with Ted Turner in *Vis a Vis* (August 1988): 58 (this is a United Airlines publication distributed on the flights).

80. Aida K. Press, "President Horner Visits Cuba," *Radcliffe Quarterly* (March 1988): 3.

81. One of the former Black Panthers who hijacked a plane to Cuba described Cuban jail conditions to Elaine Brown (another former Black Panther):

> There had been no light and water. Laughing in retrospect, he told how he had longed for the days . . . in San Quentin, for the arguments with guards over television hours or library books. There had been not even a piece of paper or the hope of a book in Havana. Havana was a place where carrying a knife was punished with five years in prison . . . where hijackers were automatically imprisoned.

Elain Brown, *A Taste of Power* (New York: Pantheon, 1992), 378.

82. Alfred G. Cuzan, "The Latin American Studies Association vs. the U.S.," *Academic Questions* (Summer 1994). See also his 1995 conference paper, "Dictatorships and Double Standards: The Latin American Studies Association on Cuba," published by the Endowment for Cuban American Studies, Miami, Florida.

83. Susan Eva Eckstein, *Back from the Future: Cuba Under Castro* (Princeton: Princeton University Press, 1994), 22. The casual, taken for granted attribution of superior accomplishments in education and public health has been so often made and remains so widespread that even an article devoted to Cuban dancing in the Styles section of the *New York Times* would note in passing that the Cuban system "created the best medical and educational system in the third world." See Martin Cruz Smith, "Havana Rumba," *New York Times*, November 24, 1996, 47.

84. Michael Scammel's review of *Kate Millett: The Politics of Cruelty: An Essay on Political Imprisonment*, *New Republic*, May 16, 1994.

85. For a thorough documentation of psychiatric repression, see Charles J. Brown and Armando M. Lago, *The Politics of Psychiatry in Revolutionary Cuba* (New Brunswick: Transaction Publishers, 1991).

86. Walter Goodman, "A Portrait of Cuba Without the Warts," *New York Times*, April 6, 1991.

87. David Gonzales, "Cuban Exile Says Festival Capped Lens," *New York Times*, October 2, 1996; Clark Norton and Steve Faigrenbaum, "Hollywood Hits Havana," *Mother Jones* (June 1988).

88. Bella Thomas, "For Europeans Cuba Hasn't Lost Its Magic," *New York Times*, News of the Week, July 28, 1996, 32.

89. Craig R. Whitney, "Castro Given Big Welcome By Mitterand," *New York Times*, March 14, 1995.

90. Ann Louise Bardach, "Conversations with Castro," *Vanity* (March 1994): 130, 133.

91. Saul Landau, "After Castro," *Mother Jones* (July/August 1989): 48.

92. Quoted in Ahlmark, "Tyranny and the Left," 28.

93. Robert G. Torricelli, "Applause for Castro? Why?" *New York Times*, op-ed, October 25, 1995.

94. Barbara Probst Solomon, "Fidel in Manhattan," *Dissent* (Winter 1996): 88, 86.

95. Lizette Alvarez, "Giuliani? He Wouldn't Get Castro's Vote," *New York Times*, October 26, 1996.

96. See, for example, Merle Linda Wolin, "Hollywood Goes to Havana," *New Republic*, April 16, 1990.

97. A. M. Rosenthal, "Believing Dictators," *New York Times*, op-ed, April 5, 1996.

98. Charles Lane, "Fidel and Mr. Smith," *New Republic*, March 25, 1996, 6.

99. Wayne S. Smith, "Cuba's Long Reform," *Foreign Affairs* (March/April 1996): 104, 106, 107, 108.

100. Jacobo Timerman, *Cuba: A Journey* (New York: Knopf, 1990), 64, 74–75, 107. Timerman, better known as a victim and critic of the Argentinian military regime, is one of the rare left-liberal critics of Castro. He was allowed to travel in Cuba unescorted, having been regarded friendly by the Cuban authorities; he grew up in Argentina, hence for all practical purposes a native speaker of Spanish.

101. Timerman, *Cuba*, 30, 100.

102. William C. Rhoden, "17 Hours Across Rural Cuba: The Revolution Lives," *New York Times*, August 18, 1991, 1.

103. Mark Falcoff, "Is Cuba Next?" *Commentary* (November 1992): 46.

104. Landau, "After Castro," 22, 24, 46.

105. Maurice Halperin, *Return to Havana* (Nashville: Vanderbilt University Press, 1994), 60–61, 126–27, 186.

106. Daniels, *Utopias Elsewhere*, 157, 162, 163, 167, 189, 192.

107. Doris Lessing, *The Wind Blows Away Our Words* (New York: Vintage, 1987), 169.

108. Quoted by Nat Hentoff in *Village Voice*, May 28, 1979.

109. Noam Chomsky and Edward S. Herman, "Distortions at Fourth Hand," *The Nation*, June 25, 1977, 789, 791. For further quotes from and discussion of the article, see pp. 448–450 of the book.

110. Outlandish propositions are often prefaced or larded with expressions such as: "it is surely not in doubt . . ."; "assuming then that facts matter . . ."; "it is an obvious truism that . . ."; "observers of evident bias and low credibility . . ." (i.e., those Chomsky disagrees with, as opposed to people "with [unspecified] excellent credentials" cited with approval); "the available facts lead to one clear conclusion . . ." (i.e., lead *him* to one clear conclusion); "this communication from what seems a credible source . . ." (to whom?); "evidence from sources that seem to deserve a hearing. . . ." Views Chomsky dismisses are never "subject to possible verification."

A simulacrum of detachment is offered before attacking with gusto a book by saying that it "deserves more careful study and critical analysis" (p. 253), which however will not be forthcoming. Elsewhere Chomsky sententiously advises that an author he dismisses "might have troubled to inquire into the source of the allegations." As to the massacres as a whole, "evidence is slight and unreliable and informed opinion ranges over quite a wide spectrum" (p. 290). Noam Chomsky and Edward S. Herman, *After the Cataclysm: Postwar Indochina and the Reconstruction of Imperial Ideology* (Boston: South End Press, 1978). On Chomsky's methodology, see also Werner Cohn, "The Hidden Alliances of Noam Chomsky," pamphlet (n.d.), esp. p. 2.

111. This was the same Gareth Porter who described the atrocities of the Pol Pot regime "as the policy of self-defense . . . carried so far that it has imposed unnecessary costs on the population of Cambodia." See p. 449 in *Political Pilgrims*.

112. Chomsky and Herman, *After the Cataclysm*, 147, 149, 156, 162, 207, 208, 209, 136, 137, 141, 225, 287, 292, 293.

113. Quoted in William Maley, "Misconceiving Democracy," *Quadrant* (Australia) (October 1995): 86.

114. Quoted in Peter W. Rodman, "Grantsmanship and the Killing Fields," *Commentary* (March 1996): 52. For another critique of Kiernan and a reminder that "when the Khmer Rouge were in power, he was one of their more active apologists, attacking and impugning the motives of writers who charged them with mass killing," see William Shawcross, "Tragedy in Cambodia," *New York Review of Books*, November 14, 1996, p. 42.

115. Per Ahlmark, "Tyranny and the Left," 26. In a book of the same title published in Swedish in 1994 Ahlmark examines and documents in detail the attitudes of the Swedish left toward various communist dictatorships.

116. In Ahlmark, "Tyranny and the Left," 17.

117. Arnold R. Isaacs, "Why was She in Vietnam?" *New York Times*, Books Review Section, May 15, 1994.

118. Lewis H. Lapham, "Notebook: Vietnam Diary," *Harpers* (May 1989): 13.

119. Quoted in Rael Jean Isaac, "On 'historical revisionism,'" letter, *Chronicle* (July 1989): 4.

120. Seth Faison, "History's Fellow Travelers Cling to Maos' Road," *New York Times*, August 28, 1996.

121. Paul J. C. Yang, "China Tired of Kowtowing," *Seattle Post-Intelligencer*, March 8, 1994.

122. Reverend Lawrence Flynn, "Time to Seek Reconciliation with China," letter, *New York Times*, October 16, 1989.

123. Lou Greenberg, "Is China Taking a Great Leap Backward?" letter, *New York Times*, January 2, 1994.

124. Quoted in Louis Kriesberg and David S. Segal, eds., *The Transformation of European Communist Societies* (Greenwich, CT: JAL Press, 1992), 182

125. Victor Serge, *Memoirs of a Revolutionary 1901–1941* (London: Oxford University Press, 1963), 103.

126. David Pryce-Jones, *The Strange Death of the Soviet Empire* (New York: Henry Holt, 1995), 15–16.

127. P. J. O'Rourke, "Ship of Fools," in *Republican Party Reptile* (Boston: Little Brown, 1987), 45, 63. See also "America's Vogue for Things Russian," *New York Times*, October 19, 1988.

128. Pryce-Jones, *The Strange Death*, 354

129. Nicholas Simon, "Political Tourists," letter, *Encounter* (March 1988): 79–80.

130. Ion Mihai Pacepa, *Red Horizons* (Washington, DC: Regnery, 1987), 78.

131. Richard L. Walker, "Guided Tourism in China," *New Leader*, November 18, 1957, 12–13.

132. Edward Radzinski, Stalin (New York: Doubleday, 1996), 260–61, 229–30.

133. Quoted in John M. Thompson, *Russia, Bolshevism and the Versailles Peace* (Princeton: Princeton University Press, 1966), 175, 176. This source and the quotes were brought to my attention by Professor Richard Hamilton of Ohio State University.

134. "Peoples' Democracy" was the official designation of the type of political systems established after World War II in Soviet-controlled Eastern Europe.

135. Gyorgy Faludi, *Pokolbeli Vig Napjaim* (My Happy Days in Hell) (Budapest: Magyar Vilag, 1989), 313–15.

136. Tibor Aczel and Tibor Meray, *Tisztito Vihar* (Purifying Storm) (Munich: Griff, 1978), 128–29.

137. Hollander, *Anti-Americanism*, 375–77.

138. Graham Greene, "The Writers Engage in Battle," letter, *Times* (London) September 4, 1967.

139. Michael Korda, "The Third Man," *New Yorker*, March 25, 1996, 50.

140. John le Carre, "Quel Panama!" *New York Times Magazine*, October 13, 1996, 55.

141. Neal Kozodoy, "The All-Too-Revealing Non-Silences of Harold Pinter," *Contentions* (New York) (September 1990): 1–2.

142. Quoted in Collier and Horowitz, *Deconstructing the Left*, 237; see also Noam Chomsky, *On Power and Ideology: Managua Lectures* (Boston: South End Press, 1987), 38–39.

143. Heberto Padilla, *Heroes are Grazing in My Garden* (New York: Farrar, Straus, Giroux, 1984), 122.

144. Stephen Kinzer, "Gunter Grass: Germany's Last Heretic," *New York Times Book Review*, October 22, 1995, 47.

145. Quoted in Martin Diskin, ed., *Trouble in Our Backyard* (New York: Pantheon, 1983), 247.

146. Quoted in S. J. Taylor, *Stalin's Apologist* (New York: Oxford University Press, 1990), 185, 192. The omelette metaphor came from a poem entitled "Red Square," which Duranty wrote and published in the *New York Times* in 1932. Here are the relevant lines: "Russians may be hungry and short of clothes and comfort/ But you can't make an omelette without breaking an egg." The expression also appeared in a *New York Times* dispatch when Duranty was discussing food shortages in 1933 (ibid., 207).

147. Tom Wicker, "Smearing the Dead," *New York Times*, op-ed, July 11, 1989.

148. Robert Nisbet, *The Failed Friendship* (Washington, DC: Regnery, 1988), 11, 12, 26, 46.

149. Rosenthal, "Believing Dictators."

150. Jean Kirkpatrick, *Dictatorship and Double Standards* (New York: Simon and Schuster, 1982), 49–50.

151. Malia, *The Soviet Tragedy*.

152. See chapter 11 in Hollander, *Anti-Americanism*; also by same author, Introduction and chapter 14 in *Decline and Discontent*.

153. *The Quest for Community* is the title of a book by Robert Nisbet published in 1953. The other quotes come from Jeffrey Paul, "Up From Serfdom," *Orbis* (Summer 1989): 423.

154. Peter L. Berger, "The Myth of Socialism," *Public Interest* (Summer 1976).

155. Hollander, *Anti-Americanism*, and the new introduction to its second edition are follow-up explorations of the nature and persistence of the adversary culture, which since the 1960s has been a major breeding ground of political tourism. In two more recent articles I continued to assess the viability and persistence of this "culture": "'Imagined Tyranny?' Political Correctness Reconsidered," *Academic Questions* (Fall 1994); and "Reassessing the Adversary Culture," *Academic Questions* (Spring 1996).

156. Daniels, *Utopias Elsewhere*, 170.

157. Jeffrey Herf, "How Culture Wars Matter: Liberal Historiography, German History and the Jewish Catastrophe," in Michael Berube and Cury Nelson, eds., *Higher Education Under Fire* (New York: Routledge, 1995), 157.

158. Paul Gross and Norman Levitt, *Higher Superstition: The Academic Left and Its Quarrel with Science* (Baltimore: Johns Hopkins University Press, 1994).

159. See, for example, Shelby Steele, *The Content of Our Character* (New York: St.Martin's, 1990); Robert Hughes, *The Culture of Complaint* (New York: Oxford University Press, 1993); Charles J. Sykes, *A Nation of Victims* (New York: St Martin's, 1992); David Rieff, "Victims All?" *Harpers* (October 1991).

160. Christopher Lasch, *The Revolt of the Elites* (New York: Norton, 1995), 210.

161. Ibid., 17.

162. For example, A. J. Getty, *The Origin of the Great Purges* (New York: Cambridge University Press, 1985); A. J. Getty and Roberta Manning, eds., *Stalinist Terror: New Perspectives* (Cambridge: Cambridge University Press, 1993). For a critique, see Paul Hollander, "Soviet Terror, American Amnesia," *National Review*, May 2, 1994.

163. Robert Thurston, *Life and Terror in Stalin's Russia 1934–1941* (New Haven: Yale University Press, 1996).

164. Gerald Straus, "The Dilemma of Popular History," *Past and Present* (August 1991): 147, 148.

165. Lasch, *The Revolt of the Elites*, 222.

Preface to the 1990 Edition:
An End to the Political Pilgrimage?

Political Pilgrims was first published in 1981 by Oxford University Press in New York. It was widely and, for the most part, favorably reviewed though numerous reservations were also voiced (see the preface to the paperback edition, pp. lxxix–xci). Well over a hundred reviews appeared not only in the United States, but also in Great Britain, Canada, Australia, Hong Kong, India, Holland, Denmark, Sweden, Finland, Germany, Switzerland, Italy, and France. After Oxford University Press sold out its hardcover edition, Harper and Row published a paperback in 1983. By 1988 that also sold out but no further printings were contemplated. (Neither of these two printings amounted to much, perhaps a total of 15,000-20,000 copies, over a period of eight years.) At that point the Ethics and Public Policy Center kindly undertook the search for another publisher to keep the book in print and University Press of America obliged.

A Spanish translation of the book was published in two separate volumes in Madrid by Editorial Playor in 1986 and 1987 respectively, and an Italian edition by the Mulino Publishing Company in Bologna in 1988 (The Italian edition was enriched by the addition of a new chapter by an Italian scholar, Loreto Di Nucci, on "The Political Pilgrimages of Italian Intellectuals.")

Excerpts from the book appeared in the English monthly *Encounter* in 1981 and 1982; in the Mexican monthly *Dialogos* in 1982, and in *Pensamientos Centroamericanos*, published in Costa Rica, in 1988. The Hungarian translation of an excerpt is underway for an underground journal in Budapest.

While the book received more attention than most academic or semi-academic volumes, its impact was circumscribed. Comparing, for example, the attention the book received to that lavished upon another recent and more demanding academic volume (*The Decline of Great Powers*), by Paul Kennedy, is illuminating. The latter elicited a lengthy article in the *New York Times Magazine*, many talk-show appearances by Kennedy, and thorough coverage in relevant publications. Obviously Kennedy's suggestion that excessive military spending will hasten the decline of the United States (as it had of other great powers) struck a far more responsive cord than my cautionary tale of intellectual gullibility and Utopia-seeking.

Despite the fairly large number of reviews, *Political Pilgrims* was ignored by many important American journals and magazines including the *New York Review of Books*, *The New Yorker*, *Atlantic*, *Harpers*, *The Nation*, *Dissent*, the *Wall Street Journal*, and others. Talk-show hosts, with the exception of William F. Buckley, were not interested. The most hostile and dismissive reviews came from the professional journals of the two academic disciplines I have been most closely associated with (either by virtue of my training or because of the nature of my published work): *Contemporary Sociology* (the review journal of the American Sociological Association) and the *American Political Science Review*, the journal of the American Political Science Association.

All in all, it would be fair to say that the book had an ambivalently favorable, or mixed reception. Most reviewers quite readily accepted its historical account, namely that many Western intellectuals, distinguished and less distinguished, were deceived and self-deceived about various Communist countries. Visiting the countries (being "on-the-spot"), made matters worse, not better. On the other hand, reviewers seemed to be irritated by the suggestion that the susceptibility of the intellectuals was directly proportional to their estrangement from their own society. Heightened criticism of the United States (or other Western countries) could be combined with near total suspension of critical faculties while on the conducted tours and under the influence of political preferences and predispositions.

What of the phenomenon a decade later? Are political pilgrimages only a matter of historical interest or have they survived? If so, in what form? Some reference to this question has been made in the preface to the paperback edition. History, however, has not stood still and further reflections are in order in light of relatively recent developments in what used to be called the "Socialist Commonwealth," or the Soviet bloc. There are good reasons for a new look not merely at the pilgrimage itself, but at the attitude that underlies it.

The most striking political-intellectual phenomenon of the last few years is the growing imbalance between ideological uncertainty and turmoil inside the Communist bloc, *and* the persistence of certain Western political attitudes among those who have traditionally been drawn to political tourism. I referred to this phenomenon recently as "the survival of the adversary culture."[1] In *Political Pilgrims* I argued at length that it has always been the adversarial attitude—the estranged sensibility—that moved the pilgrims to look for glorious alternatives to their own flawed society. These attitudes have survived intact while developments in the socialist countries made it increasingly difficult to perceive them as alternatives to Western corruption and decline. The impulse to embark on new pilgrimages is still there but the number of available destinations has become much smaller.

By the mid-1980s the pace of change—especially the volume of self-critical disclosures—within the Communist bloc greatly increased. Most importantly, from the standpoint of potential pilgrims, internal scrutiny and soul-searching, now officially authorized, has sharpened. As a result, neither in China nor anywhere in the Eastern bloc, including the Soviet Union, was much left of the outward assurance and self-congratulatory disposition that had earlier impressed visitors in search of political rectitude, sense of purpose, and collectivized transcendence.

The new openness meant that critiques of these systems, earlier suppressed, could now be voiced and widely disseminated both in the official media and in new semi-official sources. These new revelations made mockery of what used to be the major appeal of these systems. By the mid-1980s, not even the most determined or visionary pilgrim (or potential pilgrim) could find the sense of purpose, warm social bonds, social justice, egalitarianism, let alone the spectacular material progress that had in the past exercised such a powerful attraction.

It was no longer merely the poor record of these societies regarding civil liberties and free expression that made idealization difficult. The new Gorbachev-era revelations made clear that these systems faced serious domestic crises and their claims of great material progress—formerly the justification for the lack of personal freedom—were unfounded. Social problems thought to be peculiar to capitalism abounded: crime, alcoholism, corruption, pollution, poor public health, disintegration of family, shortages of food and basic commodities, declining living standards, and old-fashioned poverty—the socialist countries had them all and they were getting worse not better.[2] Under state socialism, alienation held in its grip not only idealistic intellectuals with high expectations (as is more commonly the case in the West), but the masses of ordinary people as well. A new sense of stagnation and decline, even decomposition, not a sense of purpose or optimism, became the hallmark of these countries.

While Western intellectuals continued to lament the ravages and injustices of capitalism, socialist systems increasingly acknowledged the failures of the state control of the economy, massive inefficiency and the lack of productivity, and inability to meet human needs. Their leaders cautiously sought to reintroduce private enterprise.

There was massive irony in all this. In the West, Marxism continued to bask in the reverence of academic intellectuals. In the countries where it has been the centerpiece of the official value system, a guide to practice and major source of legitimacy, Marxism became a discredited doctrine not only for the masses (who never embraced or understood it), but even for the intelligentsia.

For the most part the estranged, adversarial intellectuals and quasi-intellectuals in the West averted their eyes from these developments, from the resounding moral and material failures of these socialist countries. They were especially disinclined to detect any connection between the ideas and ideals of Marxism-Leninism and the sorry states of the societies that sought to implement these ideas.

The persistence of Marxist belief in the West can most readily be ascribed to the institutionalization of the values of the protest movements of the 1960s giving rise to the adversary culture.[3] The survival of these political and cultural values is hard to miss. Witness the candidacy of Jesse Jackson in both the 1984 and 1988 presidential campaigns and the support he received not only among blacks, but among the white, liberal-left strata of the population (especially the academic community). Support for Jackson in these circles was proof of belonging to the right-thinking, enlightened sections of American society; of being an upholder of a critical worldview and a "caring" attitude.

Another example of the influence of the adversary culture has been the successful frustration of the efforts of the Reagan administration to sustain the anti-Communist guerrillas of Nicaragua.

A third indication of the spread of the adversarial outlook has been the triumph of the moral-equivalence school in public discourse: the belief that there are no moral distinctions worth making between the American and Soviet political systems and that both deserve to be viewed with equal cynicism (on closer inspection the upholders of this theory turned out to be far more critical of the United States than of the Soviet Union).

A fourth, tangible manifestation of the persistence of these attitudes may be found in the continued growth and entrenchment of demographic-municipal enclaves of the adversary culture, towns dominated by radical-left groups, usually campus towns such as Berkeley, Santa Cruz, and Santa Monica in California; Ann Arbor, Michigan; Madison, Wisconsin; Burlington, Vermont; and Amherst, Massachusetts, etc.

The recent movement to reform the curriculum in the colleges and universities so as to enhance its "non-Western" elements may also be a reflection of the mind-set discussed here. "Multicultural" courses and curricula generally consist of materials conveying criticism of Western values and institutions from a Marxist, Third-World, or militant-feminist perspective. While all this was already available in many courses, the new programs make it mandatory for everybody to study.[4]

How did these developments affect the political pilgrimage? While the Western pilgrims to the Soviet Union dwindled after World War II, in the last few years a new generation of Westerners has visited the Soviet Union in growing numbers. In the 1980s, it has been primarily the longing for peace and the hope that human contacts at the grassroots level will help to avert a nuclear holocaust, rather than the pursuit of political Utopia that brought well-meaning Westerners, and especially Americans, to the Soviet Union. (Others, in smaller numbers, went in pursuit of lucrative business, but revealingly trade was often justified less as a profit-making activity than as a device for promoting peace and understanding.) Whether such hopes were more realistic than those that inspired the earlier generation of pilgrims is debatable.

China, since the death of Mao, lost much of its political attraction as stories of its embrace of capitalism flooded the American media. Sympathizers could no longer thrill at its high-minded totalitarian morality or the egalitarian fervor of the Cultural Revolution.[5]

While Communist Vietnam (formerly North Vietnam) had its champions during the war and played host to many prominent Western, especially American, visitors (see below, pp. 268-75), it never attracted large numbers of pilgrims, remaining quite inaccessible due to distance and political controls. (The phenomenon of the boat people also made it more difficult to be publicly supportive of the Vietnamese regime.) Occasional Western delegations in the 1980s were given the usual treatment. Among them an American church group (composed of members of the Church World Service and United Methodist Committee on Relief) was profoundly impressed by a model "reeducation camp,"[6] under circumstances reminiscent of the well-organized visits to Soviet, Chinese, Cuban, and Nicaraguan model prisons (see below, pp. 140-60 and 335-46).

Cuba under Castro has retained a fair amount of support in the "adversarial" circles, though it has remained one of the most repressive, intolerant, militaristic, and economically mismanaged of Communist systems. It has also been a country 10 per cent of its population preferred to leave (often under difficult and risky conditions) for reasons that were both economic and political. Such matters were overlooked by the sympathizers, perhaps in part precisely because the Cuban regime, personified by Castro, never lost its outward self-assurance and never failed to claim moral superiority over the United States and other capitalist systems. Presumably Castro's charisma and durability played a part in keeping the loyalties of foreign admirers: here was an original revolutionary hero, still at the helm and unwilling to dilute the revolutionary purity and idealism of this system by concessions either to "bourgeois freedoms" or capitalistic greed.

Thus, it never became quite acceptable to express moral indignation toward Cuba among American or Western-European intellectuals on the left. As Reinaldo Arenas, the exiled Cuban writer, observed, "It is not fashionable to attack Fidel Castro; that would not be progressive. ... It is difficult [in the West] to get ahead as an enemy of a regime like Cuba. ... I encounter this in academic circles everywhere. At Harvard I was asked not to talk about politics during a lecture. In the meantime Communist writers like Cintio Vitier and Miguel Barnet were given free reign to talk of nothing else."[7]

Jesse Jackson is among the friends of Cuba. As journalist Fred Barnes has noted, his attitude toward Cuba is "similar to Shirley MacLaine's toward China in the 1970s, or the Webbs' toward the Soviet Union in the 1930s. ... Jackson visits the schools on the Island of Youth and finds them 'creative'. In truth they are the essence of totalitarianism, where Cuban children are leached of what a pro-Castro American tells me are their 'backward attitudes.' "[8] On his visit to Cuba Jackson also toured a renovated prison and inspected prisoners who were made to play baseball (in new baseball uniforms issued for the occasion).[9]

Church delegations were prominent among the last-ditch supporters of Cuba. A spokesman for some Methodists saw "a country where the great majority of people believe that they are the masters and beneficiaries of a new society. . . . Cubans are characterized by . . . a burning desire for the rest of humanity to gain the freedom that Cubans have so recently won."[10] Methodist bishops were persuaded that in Cuba people are imprisoned who oppose policies designed to remove inequalities. They found these grounds for imprisonment far superior to those in countries like Chile or Brazil where—they averred—those in favor of social justice are sent to jail.[11]

A National Council of Churches study guide praised the Cuban educational system: "Permeating Cuban educational practice is the concept that a new type of society will develop a new type of human being . . . [who] regards work at the creative center of life and is bound to others by solidarity, comradeship, and love."[12] Another publication of the National Council of Churches concluded that "at home Cubans have found a new dignity. . . . Internationally, the island nation . . . has been adopted as a symbol of revolutionary hope and courage by the Third World." Further south, the archbishop of São Paulo assured Castro on the thirtieth anniversary of the revolution that he was "present daily in [his] prayers," and that "Christian faith discovers in the achievements of the revolution signs of the Kingdom of God."[13]

The enduring support of Cuba also found expression in the sympathetic (though not uncritical) report of a delegation organized by the Institute for Policy Studies to assess prison conditions there. The participants "encountered a very strong sense of mission in most prison officials. They expressed great faith in their system and . . . seemed determined to work increasingly on their plan for reeducation and for incorporation of the penal population into work and free society. . . . The regular prison facilities we saw were all clean and hygenic, and we heard no serious complaints in this regard. We heard no complaints about the use of instruments of torture, . . . neither did we find any policy of extrajudicial executions or disappearances."[14] Such statements call to mind the Webbs in the Soviet Union during the 1930s, who noted that "the [prison] administration is well-spoken of and is now as free from physical cruelty as any prison in any country is ever likely to be." (see pp. 144-45) Debra Evenson, a professor at the law school of DePaul University in Chicago, could not stomach even such restrained criticism of Cuban prisons as was presented (in the *New York Review of Books*) by Aryeh Neier, and in a vigorous rejoinder assured readers of their superiority over American prisons.[15]

These exchanges and the prison report appeared just a few months before the Americas Watch Committee report, which offered renewed evidence of the human rights violations and overall repressiveness of the Cuban system.[16]

No matter how devoted the remaining supporters of Cuba have been, by the 1980s, the major setting of the pilgrimages and political tours shifted to Nicaragua. (To be sure, those supportive of Cuba were also sympathetic toward Nicaragua, and vice versa.) Political tourism may better describe the new phenomenon since visits to Nicaragua have been for the most part highly standardized group tours, rather than journeys of discovery by single, distinguished individuals accompanied by an entourage of guides and interpreters—a type of travel more properly described as a pilgrimage.

A new feature of the visits to Nicaragua is volunteering for various projects such as picking coffee beans or miscellaneous construction. (This has few precedents in the Soviet Union or China and was modelled on the Venceremos Brigade in Cuba, which brought in sympathizers to cut sugar cane.) Some Americans and Westerners also live more or less permanently in Nicaragua, while others are content to spend a few weeks on various projects.

An estimated 1500 Americans are "living and working in Nicaragua. . . . Since the Sandinistas came to power in 1979, about 40,000 Americans have gone to Nicaragua for humanitarian or political work."[17] The motives of the participants was summed up by a member of a women's brigade intent on building a school: "Going to Nicaragua is a direct act of conscience in opposition to our government's aggression and in solidarity with the Nicaraguan people.[18] The attraction to Nicaragua was also associated with a "renewal of belief in the possibility of a revolution not foreordained to be the cat's-paw of either superpower rivalry or homegrown despotism."[19] In other words, Nicaragua was the new antidote to the loss of illusions following the 1960s.

In a single year, according to a Nicaraguan government official, 100,000 foreigners visited Nicaragua, of whom 40 per cent were Americans. As the article quoting these figures pointed out, most of them did not come "to see natural beauty, but to get a look at the Sandinista revolution. Most of them . . . are connected with churches, unions, and universities; groups generally sympathetic to the Sandinistas."[20]

Sympathy toward the Nicaraguan Marxist-Leninist government had other manifestations as well. The Boston City Council proclaimed November 3, 1988, "Ernesto Cardenal Day" in honor of the Sandinista minister of culture, also a poet and priest.[21] Burlington, Vermont and Berkeley, California became sister cities of Managua. Across the nation support groups, especially those connected with churches, collected substantial amounts of money and supplies. In 1987 a national campaign aimed at collecting $60 million on top of another $40 million already raised in 1986.[22] At the anti-inauguration concert held in Washington, D.C., protesting the Bush presidency, Kris Kristofferson sang an ode to the Sandinistas that included the lines, "You have lived up to your name. . . . May your spirit never die! Hold a candle to the darkness! You're the keeper of the flame!"[23]

Daniel Ortega, on his visit to New York City, was honored at a reception at the Riverside Church (then presided over by the Reverend William Sloan Coffin, himself a pilgrim to both North Vietnam and Nicaragua (see pp. 268 and 273), basked in the admiration of the assembled celebrities, who included Morley Safer, Betty Freidan, Eugene McCarthy, Bianca Jagger, and Bernardine Dohrn, the former Weather Underground activist. Ortega also addressed the congregation of the Park Slope Methodist Church in Brooklyn.[24]

The misconceptions of, and the praise for the Nicaraguan political system and its representatives were impressive both on account of their repetitiveness, and because of the extraordinary resemblance they bore to earlier praises of other Communist systems, chronicled in this book. There was a willful, cheerful determination to overlook both the conflicting evidence of the nature of the political system and the lessons of history readily available by 1980. The reader of this book will undoubtedly observe that the tours of Nicaragua and the accounts written of them have reproduced with an almost improbable fidelity every illusion, idealization, projection and misperception that has been displayed in the earlier travelogues of the 1930s, 60s or 70s.

Salman Rushdie, the now very famous British writer, (courtesy of the Ayatollah Khomeni of Iran) made no secret of his favorable predisposition toward Nicaragua stimulated by his antipathy toward the policies of the United States: "When the Reagan administration began its war against Nicaragua, I recognized a deeper affinity with that small country. . . . I did not go as a wholly neutral observer. I was not a blank slate." Indeed he was not. His visit to Nicaragua had all the hallmarks of the earlier trips of other famous Western intellectuals described in this volume. He was taken on a splendidly organized conducted tour that featured both sumptious feasts (the "delicacies" included turtle meat "Which had been unexpectedly dense and rich, like a cross between beef and venison") and humble but all the more hospitable peasant meals, colorful fiestas, poetry readings, peasant cooperatives and speedboat rides in picturesque lagoons. The top leaders were always available and often kept him company on his tours of inspection; they turned out to be congenial intellectuals, more than that, fellow writers and poets whose only concern was to uplift the poor and retain the independence of the country. He "couldn't think of a Western politician who could have spoken so intimately" to a crowd and could not imagine Reagan or Thatcher "agreeing to submit themselves to a monthly grilling by members of the public" while failing to notice that these open and spontaneous leaders had no intention of ever leaving office, intending to carry out the mandate of history that fell upon them. Nor did he seem to have noticed the divergence between their life styles and those of the masses they sought to serve although he noticed (for intance) the "wonderfully kept tropical gardens" of foreign minister Miguel d'Escoto that was his "other great love", besides his collection of Nicaraguan art.

Rushdie confessed that "For the first time in my life . . . I had come across the government I could support." He also found Nicaragua's constitution "amount[ing] to a Bill of Rights that I couldn't have minded having on the statute book in Britain." Most importantly the country and its way of life was unlike the contemptible "West stuffed with money, power and things"[25]; instead there was a sense of purpose and community. There was also poverty and not a lot of material progress but it could be blamed on the past, the United States and the contras. Censorship caused him fleeting unease but that too was due to the hard times. Most importantly the system was dedicated to social justice and the people were simple and authentic. As a reviewer summed it up "Mr Rushdie appears to have set out on his pilgrimage, first to affirm his belief in what he would like Nicaragua to be, and by extension what he himself sorely feels he has failed to practice in his own life."[26] He was only one among a huge number of pilgrims and political tourists ready to discover and praise the new socialist virtues of Nicaragua.

According to Alice Walker, the American writer, Nicaragua "is a writer's paradise."[27] For a professor of philosophy at the University of Massachusetts at Amherst (and a frequent visitor) the Nicaraguan government was "honestly committed to the poor and could be a model to other Latin American countries . . ."[28]. A writer in the *Village Voice* reported that visitors to Nicaragua experience "a renewal of faith . . . what Nicaragua gives back to the Internationals [the volunteer workers] is hope . . ."[29] A retired Presbyterian minister from Atlanta found that the Sandinistas "have done some things that as a Christian I value very highly. They conducted one of the most sensational literacy campaigns in history . . . it is consistent with Christian values to spread health care to rural areas. They have given land to peasants. As a Christian I applaud that."[30] Even *Vanity Fair* found much to praise in Nicaragua including its first family. Rosario Murillo, spouse of Daniel Ortega was said to possess "the charm of a revolution peopled by the young, the brave and the good looking . . ." (the reader may juxtapose this observation to those of Julian Huxley on the forthcoming pages who paid similar tribute to the "fine physique" of the Russian people he observed: apparently all "solid, robust, healthy" and approximating the Greek Ideal of bodily perfection (pp. 134 below). But there was more than charm to Ms Murillo—"the dreamy poetess who oversees her fiefdom with an unyielding eye; the egalitarian revolutionary who revels in Ralph Lauren, the First Lady of a modest little country . . ." She was also characterised as "halfway between La Pasionaria [the Spanish Stalinist communist of the 1930s] and Bianca Jagger."[31]

Recent political tourists were just as certain as those of earlier generations that the citizens of the countries they held in high esteem cheerfully accepted all hardships in the joyous expectation of a better future and because of their appreciation of the good intentions of their leaders. A Labor Member of the British parliament wrote: ". . . the Nicaraguans accept all these hardships . . . because . . . most citizens realise that their government is doing its best in exceptionally difficult circumstances, that hardships and shortages are fairly shared."[32] How did Mr Kaufman know? As others before him, presumably he too relied on the information he was provided by his hosts who undoubtedly spared him of comparisons between *their* diet, housing, and means of transportation and those of the general population.

These curious perceptions of life in Nicaragua had much to do with the determination of the visitors (as was the case in the pilgrimages past) to accent the positive. A director of a theological seminary in California advised that it was desirable to try ". . . to discard our U.S. ideological lenses . . . and enter into networks of trust." He apparently was successful since he concluded that "Nicaragua has achieved more freedom, justice and grass roots democracy than any of its neighbors (with the exception of Costa Rica) has achieved in five hundred years."[33]

The churches were in the forefront of the support for Nicaragua and in organizing tour groups. In particular the Quakers, and their activist arm, the American Friends Service Committee, (their offshoot, the Witness for Peace), the National Council of Churches as whole and the Methodists in particular, the Catholic Maryknoll and the Sojourners (a leftist evangelical group) were the most dedicated to these efforts.

If the Reagan presidency (and the distaste it inspired in the left-of-center citizenry) helped nurture the sympathy toward Nicaragua presumably the Bush presidency will continue to have a similar, though perhaps milder effect of the same kind. Continued disenchantment with domestic conditions is likely to remain the major source of the susceptibility toward political systems that make impressive idealistic claims and also gain the goodwill of the domestic social critics for being critical of the United States.

It remains to be seen what if any long term effect of the cessation of the guerilla war in Nicaragua may have on the sympathizers and supporters. While in progress it provided the most satisfactory explanations (and excuses) of both the dire economic conditions and the political repression that prevailed. (After all, war was raging so the authorities were justified in restricting civil liberties. As to the economy, it was destroyed by contra sabotage and drained by the diversion of resources to the war effort.) Since the fighting stopped economic conditions continued to decline precipitously and civil rights barely improved either—conditions which may yet have some impact on the continued idealization of the system. The end of the guerilla war has also made it more difficult to blame the United States for its interference in Nicaraguan affairs and by the same token absolve the Nicaraguan authorities of responsibility for the conditions in the country.

These reflections seem to imply that the favorable attitudes toward Nicaragua have important rational components and when those weaken the admiration will subside. Unfortunately the record of past pilgrimages casts doubt on such speculations. For example, the fervent support for the Soviet system peaked at a time when the country lived under its worst totalitarian conditions, with Stalin's terror in full swing, the show trials in progress and millions starving. Likewise the veneration of communist China was most intense during Mao's insane campaigns, including the Cultural Revolution which exacted a huge price, human as well as material. In neither case were objective conditions a significant factor in shaping attitudes toward the countries and their political systems.

It may be predicted that if the Sandinistas' appeal becomes tarnished with the passage of time, or the craving for novelty overpowers old loyalties, there will be other political systems or movements to be idealised (on similar grounds), possibly the radical-leftist guerillas in El Salvador, in or out of power. Already they have attracted a vocal and well organized following that includes Hollywood actors such as Edward Asner who hopes that they will win power and who has it on good authority that "the rebel forces are now the most effective institution in El Salvador committed to health delivery."[32]

The continued outpouring of favorable sentiment toward the authorities in Nicaragua (and assorted anti-Western guerilla movements elsewhere) suggests that time has stood still within the adversary culture—the complex of beliefs, attitudes and values which entail suspicion, aversion, or hostility toward American society, its major values and institutions. Its adherents have not reexamined their ideals and pondered their alienation in the light of the changes taking place in the socialist world in the 1980s and especially since 1985, when Gorbachev came into power. They have managed to ignore not only the rising tide of revelations about the general malfunctioning of these systems and their intractable social problems but also the truly systemic failings of socialist economies.

Yet there is a limit to both self-deception and the impact of the skillful, organised deception Marxist-Leninist systems practised (see "political hospitality" below) for the benefit of those predisposed to admire them.

It has taken several decades for the facts to sink in about the nature of the Soviet system among those estranged from Western societies. It may take even longer for the more general, and (for them) far more disturbing idea to sink in that political systems inspired by Marxism-Leninism are incapable of realizing the dreams of the Western seekers of justice, social harmony and personal fulfillment.

> Paul Hollander
> Northampton, Mass.
> March 1989

Notes

1. Paul Hollander: *The Survival of the Adversary Culture: Social Criticism and Political Escapism in American Society*, New Brunswick: Transaction Books, 1988.

2. For a sampling of the Soviet coverage of some of these problems see T. Anthony Jones ed. "Social Deviance and Social Problems", *Soviet Sociology*, 1989, Vol. 27., No. 4.

3. For a discussion of the origins of the concept see Hollander cited pp. 10-13.

4. For example Thomas Short: " 'Diversity' and 'Breaking the Disciplines' " *Academic Questions*, Summer 1988.

5. But if China no longer stimulated rhapsodic reports nor was the general public necessarily well informed about the continuation of its repressive policies. Huge gaps of information remained as for instance about the violence in Tibet on March 5, 1988 when ". . . hundreds of Chinese police had rampaged through these sacred corridors [of Jokang Temple, the "holiest shrine of contemporary Chinese Buddhism"] clubbing and shooting to death thirty monks in retaliation for an unarmed, pro-independence demonstration. Hundreds of monks and lay Tibetans . . . were arrested and taken away to local prisons in Lhasa where they endured days of savage beatings . . ." J. Michael Luhan: "How the Chinee Rule Tibet", *Dissent*, Winter 1989, p. 21.

6. "Joint Statement by Dr Cleary and Ms Meinertz" quoted in *Time for Candor: Mainline Churches and Radical Social Witness*, Institute for Religion and Democracy, Washington, DC 1983, pp. 63-67.

7. Octavio Roca: "An Exile's Home Away from Home", *Insight*, October 10, 1988 p. 61.

8. Fred Barnes: "The Jackson Tour", *New Republic*, July 30, 1984, p. 21.

9. See for example S.L. Nall: "Prisoners Say Cubans Fooled Jackson on Jail", *Washington Times*, July 2, 1984.

10. Rusty Davenport: "Cuba: A Land of Contrast", *Common Ground*, Summer 1981; quoted in *A Time for Candor* cited p. 85.

11. *Time for Candor* cited p. 81.

12. Quoted in Joshua Muravchik: "Pliant Protestants", *New Republic*, June 13, 1983.

13. *Time For Candor* cited, p. 90; Alan Riding: "Brazil Cardinal's Praise of Castro Stirs Protest", *NY Times*, February 5, 1989 p. 20.

14. "Cuban Prisons: A Preliminary Report", Institute for Policy Studies, *Social Justice*, Summer 1988, p. 58, 59.

15. Debra Evenson: " 'In Cuban Prisons': An Exchange" *NY Review of Books*, September 29, 1988.

16. Joseph B. Treaster: "Rights Group Reports Continued Abuses in Cuba" *NY Times*, January 29, 1988.

17. Cheryl Sullivan: "U.S. Volunteers head for Nicaragua" *Christian Science Monitor*, June 2, 1987 pp. 3-4.

18. Margaret Lobenstein: "Brigada Companeras builds hope" *Valley Womens Voice*, February 1987.

19. Tom Carson: "The Long Way Back" *Village Voice*, May 12, 1987 p. 5, 7.

20. Marjorie Miller: "Nicaragua's Tourism Up Despite War", *Los Angeles Times*, March 12, 1986.

21. "Sandinista Holiday" *New Republic*, November 21, 1988.

22. Sullivan *cited*, p. 3.

23. Alex Heard: "Inaugural Anthropology", *New Republic*, February 13, 1989 p. 14.

24. Jim Motavalli: "Ortega Takes Manhattan", *Valley Advocate*, November 6, 1985; "Sandinista Makes His Case On a Brooklyn Church Visit", *NY Times*, July 28.

25. Salman Rushdie: *The Jaguar Smile: A Nicaraguan Journey*, New York: Viking, 1987, pp. 12, 32, 36, 63, 70, 96, 119, 170.

26. James LeMoyne: "Three Weeks in Managua", *NY Times Book Review*, March 18, 1987.

27. Harriet Rohmer: "Managua's First Book Fair", *Publisher's Weekly*, September 4, 1987 p. 19.

28. John Brentlinger: "Needed: a clear impression", *The Collegian*, November 7, 1985.

29. Carson *cited*, p. 28.

30. Steven Donziger: "The Nicaragua Connection", *Atlanta*, February 1988 p. 99.

31. Lloyd Grove: "Rosario's Revolution", *Vanity Fair*, July 1986 p. 58, 98.

32. Gerald Kaufman: "A makeshift toast to Nicaragua Libre", *New Statesman*, September 11, 1987, p. 16.

33. Ross F. Kinsler: "Observing Nicaragua Through Different Lenses", *Monday Morning* (a magazine for Presbyterian ministers) March 10, 1986, p. 16, 17.

34. "TV actors attack U.S. over Salvadorian policy" (Associated Press), *Daily Hampshire Gazette*, February 16, 1982 p. 11.

Preface to the 1982 Edition: Political Pilgrims and Estrangement Today

One of the benefits of having a second edition of one's book is that it allows for making either revisions* in the light of new information and critical comment or some additional reflections in a new preface.

I had two major reactions to the reviews received so far. One was pleasure over the critical attention and its largely favorable tone; the other was regret that the reviews tended to address, for the most part, only a narrow range of issues and topics dealt with in the book. At the expense of numerous other issues, the reviewers as a rule focused most of their attention on the colorful misperceptions of the countries intellectuals had idealized. Thus, for example, few reviewers had much to say about the substance of *what* these intellectuals found appealing (although I went to considerable length to discuss these matters) or about the mechanisms and processes involved in switching from social criticism at home to credulousness and affirming enthusiasm abroad. The sources of the alienation of Western intellectuals—also given much space in the book, since they provided the background and precondition of the pilgrimages—were also generally ignored; so was the social criticism Western intellectuals directed at their own society, a striking counterpart to the praise heaped upon the romanticized alternatives abroad. My analysis of the social position of intellectuals in the West, which helped to explain the evolution of their political attitudes, also attracted little critical attention, even though some reviewers thought that there was insuffi-

* The present edition has not been revised since it is being published only a year and a half after the original hardcover edition.

cient explanation of how such smart people could have displayed such poor judgment. Correspondingly little interest was shown in the comparison and examination of the social–historical and cultural conditions in the 1930s and 1960s and 70s in the United States and Western Europe. The point I am making here is not that such and other parts of the book were unfairly treated by the critics, but that they were simply bypassed with little (or no) comment. The reviewers were preoccupied with the gullibility of intellectuals, often in isolation from other matters, and with the techniques of hospitality used to influence the perceptions and judgments of the countries the visitors had toured. To be sure, some of these techniques and the situations created by them were not without their humorous aspects, unintended by hosts and guests alike.

While some reviewers considered *Political Pilgrims* a controversial book, contrary to the predictions of one of them, I have not, so far at any rate, been "denounced as a McCarthyist neo-jingoist," nor have I become "the target of an academic lynching party."[1] Along these lines it may be of some interest that neither the unfriendly critics nor readers questioned my overall assessment of the countries the pilgrims idealized. While this does not mean that these countries have no Western admirers left, it suggests that the public assertion of such admiration has become less respectable.

I expected that the publication of *Political Pilgrims* in hardcover (Oxford University Press, 1981) would provoke more controversy and hostility than it actually did. While *Political Pilgrims* has been widely reviewed, only a few reviews were negative or unfriendly. This surprised me, given the major thrust of the book: a criticism of many influential Western intellectuals, including famous writers, well-known academics, journalists, artists. I wrote in the Preface of the hardcover edition that ". . . much of the information collected, the outlooks documented and the conclusions reached in this volume still go against the grain of certain basic attitudes of quite large segments of the American (and Western European) intellectual community." While I still believe this to be the case, these attitudes rarely surfaced in the reviews. Apparently one part of the message of the book was quite readily accepted—and became the focus of critical attention: many Western intellectuals were p... ~ to be deceived on these trips. But while the political delusions of these intellectuals were readily grasped and accepted, far less attention was paid to the other side of the coin: their estrangement from their own societies, which had been the fundamental precondition of the pilgrimages and the attendant misperceptions. Few reviewers noted the importance of this alienation looming in the background, let alone asked how justified the intense rejection of Western societies had been and what the sources were of the social criticism and estrangement displayed. How much were these attitudes due to the observable defects of social institutions, and how much to the frustration over the lack of meaning and community in Western societies?

Political Pilgrims is critical of many intellectuals not only because of their pilgrimages and their outlandish statements about Stalin's Soviet Union or Mao's China. It also probes critically the whole phenomenon of estrangement. I think it was this aspect of the book that either was ignored or, when noted, provoked animosity. Thus, from the reception of the book so far, it appears that, while it has become more widely accepted in Western intellectual circles that in the past intellectuals misjudged societies which claimed to be socialist, it remains more difficult to face the fact that the propensity for such misjudgments is still with us because an underlying sense of alienation still creates a susceptibility to the claims of certain countries and their political systems.

The major and sporadically recurring criticism of the book, as formulated by Arthur Schlesinger, Jr., was that I had unfairly generalized from the attitude of a small, unrepresentative group of intellectuals, to all intellectuals; that I "[took] a part for the whole" and, "even more reckless[ly]," made it my thesis that "all intellectuals are lusting after a secular equivalent of religion." Professor Schlesinger also suggested that it was my purpose "to defame intellectuals as a class."[2] In addition, he faulted me for suggesting that exaggerated social criticism (what I called the continuous reflexive disparagement of society) could have undesirable cumulative effects, a point of view that he interpreted as opposition to social criticism in general. I responded in a letter to the book review section of the *New York Times*, which may be worth quoting:

> It was far from unusual on my part to define modern intellectuals with reference to their antagonism toward the society in which they live....
> As to overgeneralizing or "taking a part for the whole," it was not my purpose "to inquire into the varieties of intellectual experience." Instead I was intent on looking at the relationship between alienation and utopia-seeking and the fluctuation of the critical and uncritical impulses among certain groups of intellectuals. My argument was that "a significant portion of Western intellectuals, and especially the more famous and influential among them, displayed at one time or another signs of political estrangement from their society in combination with hopeful, affirming attitudes toward certain ... revolutionary societies. In all probability such intellectuals form a minority of those who may be called 'Western

intellectuals,' but certainly an important and vocal minority" (p. ix). . . .

The purpose of my undertaking was not "to defame intellectuals as a class" but to revise some prevailing ideas about them. I was critical not because of their attacks on authority but because of their suspension of critical faculties, their indifference to the benefits of political pluralism and especially intellectual freedom. I observed—following Emile Durkheim's remark that "a society . . . above all is the idea it forms of itself"—that such ideas in this country have been all too negative for some time, that this is a problematic situation, and many intellectuals contributed to it. This view is not incompatible with the criticism of injustice in one's own society. There is something between the celebration of society and its reflexive disparagement.

It was my intention in the book as a whole to make some contribution "to improving the capacity of some Western intellectuals for a better understanding of the virtues and vices of various political systems by recalling the conspicuously failed political judgments of the past.[3]

Professor Schlesinger also pointed out, as did some other reviewers, that I failed to pay attention to those intellectuals who were not gullible and whose visits to the Soviet Union led to the criticism of the Soviet system, such as André Gide, Bertrand Russell, or Malcolm Muggeridge. I was very much aware of the voices of these intellectuals and had quoted them in various contexts. But they were a small minority most visitors did not react negatively, or only with much delay, years later and in conjunction with a general reappraisal of the Soviet (or other communist) system. This, however, still does not take care of the question that other reviewers have also raised, namely, why were some intellectuals more likely to become political pilgrims than others?

I did not seek an answer to this question. The book was based on the premise that the phenomenon described was sufficiently widespread at certain periods of time, and the intellectuals involved did not constitute a bizarre, deviant minority whose behavior required special explanation by contrasting it with that of the more sober majority. Moreover, I dealt only with those intellectuals who had written about their experiences; certainly there might have been many others who visited the countries concerned and returned with fewer illusions but did not bother to put into writing either their illusions or the loss of them. We have no way of knowing how many such people there might have been. One thing is, however, reasonably certain: for every André Gide there were ten G. B. Shaws, if not more. It would certainly be interesting to find out why some Western intellectuals in the 1930s avoided becoming pro-Soviet and why others in the 1960s retained the use of their critical faculties as far as Cuba, China, and North Vietnam were concerned. Such intellectuals not caught up in the prevailing sympathy (or at least benefit-of-doubt attitude) toward these countries were, I believe, once more a minority or possibly a "silent majority." We have no way of knowing, since we can only judge these attitudes from their public and, especially, written expression.* The tone of the times and the climate of opinion in regard to these countries were set by the vocal "pilgrims," actual or potential, whether or not many of them ceased to admire these countries later on.

The only answer one may hazard to the question of why some became pilgrims but not others is that the more estranged a Western intellectual was from his society, the more likely he would end up admiring other social-political systems representing a counterpoint to his own. This, of course, raises another question: Why are some intellectuals more alienated than others, and why are some not alienated at all (if indeed that is compatible with the notion of what a true intellectual is)? *Political Pilgrims* did not try to answer this question. It did, however, proceed from the obvious observation that many are estranged (to different degrees and for different durations) and that such a disposition often leads to the idealization of other social systems.

Another critic thought that not only was my sample of intellectuals unrepresentative, but that many of those quoted were not intellectuals at all.[4] He also argued that people of "indisputably first rank intelligence" avoided the misjudgments I had attributed to them. While this was obviously incorrect (as much of the book has shown), I cannot dispute the fact that my roster of intellectuals included some less distinguished examples. Certainly Jean-Paul Sartre, Simon de Beauvoir, Pablo Neruda, Julian Huxley, George Bernard Shaw, Edmund Wilson, or Noam Chomsky are more impressive and creative intellectuals and had greater impact on our thinking than, say, Daniel Berrigan, Howard Bruce Franklin, Tom Hayden, Huey Newton, William Kunstler, or Staughton Lynd. Nonetheless, whatever one may think about the quality of thought or creative accomplishments of the latter group, they still are intellectuals according to criteria generally used (and discussed at some length in the book). Admittedly, I also quoted on occasion a few marginal or quasi-intellectuals (such as Jerry Rubin, members of the Venceremos Brigade, or Jane Fonda), but in each case there was an explanation for referring to their views. In any event, I could have purified my sources by removing all

---

* Opinion surveys could in theory shed light on these matters, but I am unaware of any directed specifically at "intellectuals" (as distinct from, say, academics or various professions), especially surveys that probed attitudes toward the Soviet Union in the 1930s and toward Cuba, China, and North Vietnam in the 1960s or 70s.

such questionable or marginal sources without any damage to the substance of the book and the propositions put forward. Correspondingly, it would present no problem to substitute other intellectuals with impeccable credentials voicing similar opinions and displaying similar attitudes.

An otherwise friendly critic, Leonard Schapiro, thought that I neglected to take into consideration "sheer dishonesty" in the motivation of some of the travelers[5] who knew better than their fulsome praise would allow one to guess. I do not think that this was often the case and in any event it is hard to know when it was. But even if this occurred in some instances, I suspect that underneath such falsification still loomed a perverted idealism; the Soviet Union (or China or Cuba, etc.) were seen as superior societies whose "warts" and "blemishes" should not detract from this "basic" or "essential" superiority.

On the whole it was my impression that *some* of the criticisms of *Political Pilgrims* stemmed from the feeling that it was the kind of book bound to give aid and comfort to reactionaries, right-wingers, old or neo-conservatives. That, of course, may well be true, yet trying to soften the message to avoid such possibilities would have put me in exactly the same position I criticized in the case of many fellow travelers and pilgrims who, as it turned out later, refrained from telling the truth for fear of giving comfort to or being associated with certain discredited political groups.

One of the most thought-provoking comments came from the critic Richard Grenier,[6] who drew attention to the contrasting behavior of the pilgrims of the 1930s on the one hand and those of the more recent generation of the 1960s and early 70s. Whereas many of the former seekers (people like Howard Fast, Gide, Koestler, Malraux, Silone, etc.) who became disillusioned subsequently engaged in serious reflection and soul-searching over their failure to grasp the nature of the Soviet system, most of the admirers of Cuba, China, or communist Vietnam engaged in no comparable intellectual exercises. ("Today's political pilgrims acknowledge no accountability for their earlier follies.") Whatever self-criticism has taken place has been qualified, cautious, and, in any event, rare.[7]

Since I did not pause to speculate about this significant contrast earlier, I take this opportunity to suggest some reasons for it. To begin with, I think that the pro-Soviet enthusiasts who had radically revised their views were confronted over time with such massive accumulation of evidence discrediting the Soviet regime that their earlier attitudes seemed especially shameful and embarrassing, creating strong pressures to revise them. Comparable quantities of disillusioning information are not yet widely available about the countries more recently idealized, although they are rapidly accumulating. This, however, is not a good enough explanation, since some admirers of the Soviet Union managed to resist successive waves of disillusioning revelation.[8] New evidence does not by itself explain either when and why minds change, or the willingness (or reluctance) to publicly reveal such changes. I think that, in the United States at any rate, the major obstacle to such public soul-searching in regard to communist Cuba, China, and Vietnam has been the persisting discomfort at the possibility of being tarred with the brush of anti-communism. If nothing else, Joseph McCarthy has succeeded in giving anti-communism an almost ineradicably bad name among intellectuals. Thus, such soul-searching in our times has become distasteful for many intellectuals, particularly since, in what I called the subculture of alienation, criticism of communist regimes is hardly a requirement and mistakes about their assessment are easily forgiven. Such mistakes merely show that the sympathizers' hearts were in the right place or they were carried away by their idealism. The adversary culture is concerned with the defects of its own society, hence criticism of other countries is unimportant. Few reputations seem to have been damaged by even the most outlandish statements made about China, Cuba, Vietnam, or the Third World. It is excusable in many circles to be "soft" on these regimes but not to be "soft" on the United States.* Thus what exempts many of the latter-day pilgrims from the need for self-criticism is the redemptive quality, or the moral absolution, that is conferred on them by their alienation, that is, the measure of rectitude demonstrated by the rejection of their own society to which the misjudgment of other societies is irrelevant.

Most reviewers seemed reluctant to ponder what, if any, lessons may be learned from the pilgrimages. This, as our Soviet friends like to say, was not an accident. Once we start thinking about such lessons, we must discuss estrangement—some degree or variety of which is still a required (and willingly assumed) posture of many Western intellectuals. Few critics asked, Could this happen again? How can intellectuals safeguard the integrity of their critical faculties "as the apple of their eye" (which

---

*This was exemplified by the hostile reception Susan Sontag got for her soul-searching *and* by her ritualistic denunciation of American foreign policy and the Reagan administration before she felt she could attend to the business on hand: the criticism of communist societies in the context of Poland.[9]

Stalin compared in importance to the unity of the Party)? What conditions must be met, or be averted, to spare intellectuals similar cognitive and ethical embarrassments, indeed disasters? Little was said and few speculations offered about this because of the delicacy of the topic: the links between alienation on the one hand and double standards and the crumbling of critical faculties on the other. There has been little discussion of why intellectuals learned so little from history that some two decades after the by then discredited pilgrimages to the Soviet Union they could embark on new ones, in almost identical spirit, to Cuba, China, and Vietnam. Even more astonishingly, upon the heels of this second wave of pilgrims we already have yet another group flocking to Nicaragua or to the embrace of various Marxist–Leninist guerrillas in Central America and other Third World countries.

Intense alienation is the single major factor that produced the pilgrimages and the attendant suspension of critical faculties in each period; and as long as alienation persists, emotion will continue to overpower intellect. This is so because intense rejection of one's society leads to (or entails) such anger, despair, and hostility that it becomes imperative to find alternatives to the social system the critic lives under—hence the growing susceptibility to the claims of other social systems opposed to that which he so despises.

It appears that today the political affections of Western intellectuals estranged from their own societies are more widely dispersed.[10] For one thing, the undifferentiated entity called "the Third World" continues to attract a certain vague reverence mainly because it is viewed by these intellectuals as a victim of the West, that is, their own societies. Yet, on the whole, these diffuse political sympathies are lacking in the degree and type of intensity and fervor that had characterized past devotion to the Soviet Union and China, or to Cuba during its more authentic revolutionary periods.

Besides the generalized and somewhat shallow reverence for the Third World, Nicaragua and the guerrillas in El Salvador have emerged as the prime foci of current political devotions and objects of wishful idealization (". . . there has to be at least one approved insurgent movement on the Left at any given time and at this time that movement was located in El Salvador," or, as Walter Goodman put it, ". . . the faithful do seem to need a place to which their faith can attach itself"[11]). The guerrillas of El Salvador are all the more appealing as they still represent the revolutionary promise and possibility short of fulfillment and are untarnished by contact with the reality of established power. As far as Nicaragua is concerned, it has become (as I have written in the original Preface) "an especially strong contender in the marketplace of revolutionary promise and purity." Thus, for example, Ramsey Clark, who in 1974 could detect no internal conflict in North Vietnam and felt "a unity of spirit" during his visit, reported from Nicaragua that "You will not find a revolutionary movement in our epoch in which there has been such a high commitment to human rights."[12] Other sympathetic observers eagerly rationalized the reluctance of the new rulers of Nicaragua to hold elections,[13] while a veteran admirer of Cuba, Saul Landau, helped to prepare a laudatory television program on public television about it.[14] Not only have many American intellectuals and students rallied to this latest embodiment of revolutionary promise, "Managua today is being occupied by a fresh-faced army of backpacking youth in shorts and hiking boots. They are left-wing students on holiday from Europe, here to see the revolution firsthand."[15] A New York *Times* reporter entitled his sympathetic article "Nicaragua's Revolution Breaks the Mold."[16]

Both the guerrillas of El Salvador and their victorious cousins in Nicaragua rekindled memories, images, and associations of Vietnam. Like the Vietcong, the Central American guerrillas were seen as heroic, popular, altruistic; idealists of the highest order, fighting evil, corrupt, unpopular regimes. There were certainly parallels with Vietnam, although not necessarily those the supporters of the Salvadoran guerrillas perceived and stressed. In the 1960s as in the early 1980s, the protest against United States involvement stemmed not only from aversion to the United States getting "bogged down" in a distant part of the world "where we had no business to be" (after all, El Salvador was a good deal closer than Indochina), but from sympathy toward the guerrillas. Their supporters, as those of the Vietcong, wanted them to win. In the early 1980s as in the late 1960s, almost any movement or regime opposed to American foreign policy and influence was regarded with warmth and supported by estranged intellectuals, including not only the government of Nicaragua and the Salvadoran guerrillas but also the PLO and Iran under Khomeini.[17]

There were also parallels in the sympathetic treatment by the media of the guerrillas of Central America and those of Indochina. Generous publicity was given to the atrocities committed by the forces opposing them, but meager was the information provided about guerrilla atrocities. More recently, as in the past, claims of foreign assistance were dismissed and ridiculed: The guerrillas in Central America were entirely independent and autonomous; Cuban or Soviet help was nonexistent or overblown, a

State Department invention just as North Vietnamese help of the Vietcong (and Soviet and Chinese help of North Vietnam) used to be dismissed or relegated to insignificance.

Whatever the exact nature of such similarities, the major continuities
in the history of political pilgrimages are to be found not in the usually
transient sympathy toward particular countries or political movements
abroad, but in the persistence of estrangement, which inspires the pilgrimages in the first place. Of late, it may be argued, alienation and
social criticism has once more intensified in the United States due to the
Republican Administration and its various domestic and foreign policies.
One may also explain, at least in part, the recent upsurge of the anti-
nuclear movement (or nuclear freeze movement) as a protest against and
rejection of the policies and values of the Reagan administration as much
as a protest against the dangers of nuclear holocaust per se. Alienation
from the prevailing social order is reflected in the ultimate assumptions
of many adherents of the new anti-nuclear movement in the revival of
the "better red than dead" sentiment.*

In contrast to the mistrust many freeze adherents display toward their
own society is the almost benign, benefit-of-doubt attitude shown toward
the Soviet Union that many protestors seem to regard as more sincere
about disarmament and less threatening despite all its nuclear and conventional armaments. Western European disarmament movements in
particular have shown hardly any apprehension about the Soviet medi-
um-range missiles already installed and aimed at their countries, yet rise
to a fevered pitch of concern about the American missiles yet to be
introduced into the areas.[18] It has also been suggested that "Perhaps the
current revival of mass-unilateralism, so reminiscent of the radical religious crowd-movements of the Middle Ages, should be seen as a spiritual
holding operation, pending the emergence of a new totalitarian
messiah."[19]

I believe that just as the Vietnam antiwar movement tapped preexist-
ing or latent reservoirs of alienation and social criticism, the protest
against U.S. aid to the Salvadoran regime (even under its moderate
Christian Democratic leader, Duarte) and the protest against primarily
Western nuclear arms stem from similar sources.

There have been similarities and continuities, not only between the

---

*Related expressions of alienation could also be found in the "instant celebrity" con-
ferred by the media and anti-draft organizations, upon the first person indicted for evad-
ing draft registration (see "Draft Evader Wins Indictment and Celebrity," *New York
Times*, July 14, 1982.)

general predispositions and attitudes of estrangement behind the protests and pilgrimages, but also between the specifics of political tourism, their organization, and, sometimes, impact as well. In other words, political tourism still flourishes and its organizers still anticipate results. Guardian Tours of New York (associated with the radical weekly *The Guardian*) organizes tours to Cuba, Vietnam, Grenada, and Nicaragua, which from their published descriptions fit exactly into the patterns I had discussed in *Political Pilgrims*.[20] *Nation* magazine cosponsored tours to the USSR that encouraged the traveler to "Find out for yourself what's going on in the Soviet Union . . . nightly dialogue with leading Soviet and American experts . . . relax in comfort and fellowship . . . visit Lenin's birthplace . . ."[21] Trips to Cuba promoted for the benefit of college students likewise promised: "Cuba trip allows one to see for self" and offered to combine the joys of the Caribbean with visits to the Museum of the Literacy Campaign and meetings with African students on the Isle of Youth.[22]

The most remarkable recent example of the manipulation of the visitor's experience, yielding particularly rich results for the hosts, was provided by the visit of the Reverend Billy Graham to the Soviet Union in May 1982. His visit offers a number of striking similarities to those of a long line of clergymen, intellectuals, and politicians who made brief forays into the USSR either for idealistic motives or with a pragmatic political purpose in mind. Like others before him, Billy Graham appeared to be under the impression that whatever his hosts' intention in using him for their purposes, he too used them for his own. ("I know I may be used for propaganda . . . but I believe my propaganda—the Gospel of Christ—is stronger.") In the same spirit, he also observed with satisfaction upon his return that while the visit created controversy, it "helped increase the size of the crowds" in the United States. And, as had been so often the case, his compliant attitude toward the Soviet government was also motivated by the desire to return ("his aides said the evangelist was circumspect in the hope of returning to the Soviet Union someday").[23]

The most striking, and perhaps the only major, difference between the visits and statements of the dignitaries of the past and those of the Reverend Billy Graham is that those lending themselves to Soviet propaganda in the past usually arrived in the USSR with a markedly favorable predisposition (like, for example, Hewlett Johnson, the Dean of Canterbury, or Sherwood Eddy, the American Protestant leader among the clergymen) rather than with the anti-communist credentials of Billy Graham.

The major similarity between Billy Graham's statements and those of past luminaries has been the total lack of restraint in generalizing from startlingly limited and highly manipulated experiences (Billy Graham had seen "no evidence of religious repression"—did he expect to be taken on a tour of prison camps where Baptists are held?), not unlike George Bernard Shaw, who had seen no evidence of food shortages in 1931 in the first-class restaurant he was taken to by his considerate hosts. There is special poignancy to this parallel since Billy Graham also commented in a similar spirit on the provisions he had received: "The meals I had are among the best I have ever eaten"; and elsewhere: "In the United States you have to be a millionaire to have caviar, but I had caviar with almost every meal" (while in the Soviet Union).[24]

The remark suggests yet another similarity in the pattern of responses to the VIP treatment, past and present. Evidently, the techniques of hospitality (including the regular and ample supply of caviar and other high-quality provisions) work in many if not all cases. The Reverend was clearly impressed by his treatment as a major dignitary and respected guest, and presumably those daily portions of caviar contributed to the favorable impressions he so readily shared with his hosts and the world outside. Most important, he was eager to associate himself, without reservation, with the one-sided and partisan "peace" propaganda campaign conducted by the Soviet Union. His hosts also succeeded in inducing him to exonerate the Soviet regime of any antireligious policy or offense; he even made favorable comparisons between religious freedom and participation in the United States and the USSR.[25] These were remarkable accomplishments on the part of the Soviet hosts, especially since Billy Graham, being a Baptist, might have been particularly concerned with, or at the least interested in, the fate of the same religious group in the USSR which suffered most severely in recent years. In the final analysis, it is hard to decide what blend of ignorance, vanity, opportunism, and willful denial of reality produced the attitudes and embarrassingly uninformed statements that made this visit of the Reverend Billy Graham both memorable and discouraging.

The case of Billy Graham is more an illustration of the power of the techniques of hospitality and political opportunism than of the pursuit of political ideals in a distant, mysteriously attractive country. As noted before, the more genuine political pilgrims of recent times avoid the Soviet Union; they head for the Third World. But what matters is not where these people go, but that the impulse for political tourism, for political pilgrimages, is still there. Their enthusiasm toward such countries, short-lived or not, is the counterpoint to their disenchantment and bitterness toward their own society. For many such intellectuals, the role of social critic at home has become a prime source of personal, professional, and ethical identity, one that can confer a sense of virtue and rectitude. The more one is aware of the surrounding corruption and injustice, the better one feels for not being a part of it; pointing the finger at evil is not only a social function, it is also a source of great personal gratification. It has been a paradox of our time that for many intellectuals these attitudes and activities have remained so persistently localized and one-sided.

While a better knowledge of the distant countries the pilgrims idealize could, and occasionally does, erase their appeal, such information—even after it becomes widely available—tends to become neutralized by the intimately known and strongly felt flaws of their own society. Intellectuals, like most people, can only become truly disappointed with what they know. This simple observation continues to explain the persistent interplay between the political disenchantment and political daydreams of Western intellectuals.

Northampton, Mass.   P.H.
July 1982

Preface to the 1981 Edition

It was in the late 1960s that I first considered writing something about totalitarian societies on the basis of the reports of foreign visitors. Such travel reports, I thought, could be an interesting source material about generally secretive, "closed" societies that offer little reliable information about themselves. It did not take long to realize that travel writings describing these societies tended to reveal more about their observers than about the countries observed. Gradually my interests shifted to the social roles and political attitudes of Western intellectuals, many of whom were among the authors of such travelogues. At last these interests became fused and crystallized in a desire to better understand the varied relationships between Western intellectuals, politics, and morality.

The phenomenon of the political pilgrimage—that is to say, the reverential tour of politically appealing countries, which had become highly patterned in our century—made it possible to combine and explore these interests in a coherent conceptual framework. I chose the half-century between 1928 and 1978, which provided a broad enough vista to observe the rise and fall of various pilgrimages and the underlying enthusiasm toward different political systems inspiring such journeys. At the beginning of the chronological spectrum in the late 1920s was the upsurge of interest in the Soviet Union; at the other end, half a century later, by the late 1970s, the corresponding interest waned in China, the most recently popular target of political pilgrimages.

Although my preoccupation with this topic dates back to the late 1960s, it was only in 1973 that I began to work on this book. Over the years it has become—perhaps inevitably so, given its subject matter—a combination of intellectual history, social psychology, and the exploration of the sociological roots of ideas. Other than this volume I had only published one piece on the subject, an article in 1973 entitled "The Ideological Pilgrim—Then and Now."

It seems to me that much of the information collected, the outlooks documented, and the conclusions reached in this volume still go against the grain of certain basic attitudes of quite large segments of the American (and Western European) intellectual community. Moreover, I cited critically the views of specific individuals, many of them well-known public figures with established reputations, who cannot be expected to applaud the vivid recalling of utterances they probably prefer to forget. And those who retain their enthusiasms for their pilgrimages have still better reason to object. Thus, it is fair to assume that most of the former pilgrims, whatever their destinations had been, will not treat the appearance of this book as an opportunity to publicly reexamine their past commitments and to join the author in probing the political and psychological roots of their beliefs. It is, of course, only human not to dwell on past error and to be reluctant to lightly discard values and judgments that represent prolonged and substantial investments of psychic and intellectual energy.

At the same time people do not invariably refuse to reexamine their past commitments or persist at all costs in their political beliefs disregarding all new evidence and experience. Many "pilgrims" mentioned in this book have probably ceased to admire the societies they had earlier revered, though they prefer to withhold from the public the specifics of their change of heart. Other former enthusiasts, it may be surmised, have retained their core beliefs and sympathies toward the political systems concerned but turned more reticent in voicing them. It is probably the smallest group that engaged in some public soul-searching and measured self-criticism with respect to their former beliefs. One of them, Susan Sontag, alluded in a recent interview to her "illusions and misconceptions about what was possible in the rest of the world." Reviewing her politics in the 60s, she added: "It was not so clear to many of us as we talked about American imperialism how few options many of these countries had except for Soviet imperialism which was maybe worse. . . . When I was in Cuba and North Vietnam, it was not clear to me then that they would become Soviet satellites, but history has been very cruel. . . ."[1] Mary McCarthy too expressed unhappiness with the developments in Vietnam:

As for my current views on Vietnam, it's all rather daunting. I've several times contemplated writing a real letter to Pham Van Dong (I get a Christmas card from him every year) asking him can't you stop this, how is it possible for men like you to permit what's going on? . . . I've never written that letter, though. . . . I might have signed the Joan Baez protest about the boat people, but I was never asked.

Well, socialism with a human face is still my ideal. Living under such a system would require quite an adjustment, but it would be so exciting that I hope one would be willing to sacrifice the comforts of life that one has become extremely used to. I think that the excitement would make all the difference. . . .[2]

Among those who acknowledged in print their former illusions about Mao's China, Orville Schell and Jonathan Mirsky may be noted. Mirsky wrote in 1979 of his attitudes in 1972: "Throughout our trip . . . we sheathed the critical faculties which had been directed at our own Government and . . . humbly helped to insert the rings in our own noses." He quoted one of his former guides, whom he met again in 1979: "*We* wanted to deceive you. But *you* wanted to be deceived."[3] There were others too, of course, who in earlier decades had lost the corresponding enthusiasm for the Soviet system.

It may be argued that perhaps I have overestimated the depth of alienation among Western intellectuals both in the earlier (1930s) and more recent periods (1960s and 1970s) under consideration. Admittedly, I did not attempt a quantitative analysis of the political attitudes of Western intellectuals. What I proposed, however, did not require such numerical underpinnings. I argued that a significant portion of Western intellectuals, and especially the more famous and influential among them, displayed at one time or another signs of political estrangement from their society in combination with hopeful, affirming attitudes toward certain putatively or genuinely revolutionary societies. In all probability such individuals form a minority of those who may be called "Western intellectuals," but certainly an important and vocal minority which in large measure set the tone of the times and shaped the established forms of social criticism.

An alternative objection to the views expressed in this book might be that whatever left-leaning attitudes prevailed among Western intellectuals in the past—that is, in the 1930s and 1960s—have become increasingly unrepresentative of the intellectual community by the mid- and late 1970s, and are especially atypical in the early 1980s. If this were true, this study could claim only a historical interest.

As I see it, the characteristic predispositions examined in the context of the pilgrimages have survived among Western intellectuals regardless of their disillusionment with particular formerly idealized societies and despite changes in the general political climate signalled by events such as the Republican electoral victories in the United States in 1980 and those of the Conservatives in England in 1978. Thus I doubt that the phenomenon that is the principal subject of this book—that is, the amalgam of alienation and utopia-seeking peculiar to many Western intellectuals—has run its course. To be sure, there is now in the United States a well-defined and vocal corps of intellectuals designated as "neo-conservatives" and there are in France the "new philosophers," both groups much opposed to the attitudes and beliefs associated with the political pilgrims and their supportive audiences. It is also indisputable that the pilgrimages to the Soviet Union are a thing of the past and the enthusiasm for China subsided almost as fast as it arose, although Cuba remains for some Western intellectuals an only mildly tarnished symbol of the good revolution.

As we enter the 1980s no country in the world occupies the place of honor and reverence that used to be reserved for the USSR in the 1930s, China in the early 1970s, and Cuba in the late 1950s and early 60s. At the same time, it must not pass unnoticed that on a smaller scale the old scenario has revived and is replayed in other parts of the world. For some, as noted above, the place remains Cuba; for other small groups it may be Mozambique, Albania, or Angola.[4] Thus, for example, a British visitor detected similarities between the atmosphere of present-day Angola and revolutionary Petrograd of 1917 as well as Barcelona of the Spanish Civil War and was led to conclude that ". . . the Angolan revolution has a real chance to confound its enemies. . . ." In a somewhat similar spirit, New York *Times* correspondent Anthony Lewis urged the American government in a series of four sympathetic articles to extend diplomatic recognition to Angola and promote trade.[5] Nicaragua too has become an especially strong contender in the marketplace of revolutionary promise and purity.[6] Guardian Tours of New York, an agency associated with the radical newsweekly *The Guardian,* is evidently confident that political tourism is here to stay and specializes in tours for "Travelers with an affinity for politics" of a certain kind, one may add, who are offered "tours to Nicaragua, Grenada, Vietnam and Cuba." The visitors to Nicaragua (as others before them in other places) will have "On the itinerary . . . meetings with literacy workers, women's organizations and the Sandinista Defense Committee as well as stops at an agricultural cooperative, a school and a factory." In Vietnam, "On the itinerary: a farming cooperative, a new economic zone, a school, factories and the tomb of Ho Chi Minh."[7]

More important than such forms of resurgent if isolated enthusiasm for the latest embodiments of social justice and revolutionary zeal is that the decline in the idealization of distant societies has not been accompanied, on the part of large segments of Western intellectuals, by any significant alteration in their attitudes toward their own societies. There remain in the United States and elsewhere, powerful intellectual groupings, lobbies, institutes, and publications whose major mode of relating to their society remains suspiciousness and hostility.[8] Many Western intellectuals continue to believe that the United States and other Western countries are lacking in any moral mandate in the world and hence should stand by while the Soviet Union and its surrogates and allies impose their conception of a desirable social order, from Afghanistan to Angola, from Nicaragua to Indochina.

Most Western nations cheerfully continue trading with the Soviet Union and turn a blind eye to the transfer of technology that greatly benefits the Soviet military establishment. Western businessmen, living up to the old stereotype, are indeed willing "to sell the rope" (which is supposed to be used to hang them) as Lenin had confidently predicted.[9] And even if the Soviet invasion of Afghanistan was an eye-opener to former President Carter, resulting in the grain embargo and U.S. boycott of the Moscow Olympics, there is little foundation to the received wisdom that the Soviet Union "paid a high price" for extending "the Socialist Commonwealth" to Afghanistan. It is all too easy to predict that a Soviet invasion of Poland would not elicit significantly different reactions either, although the level of sorrowful verbiage (over further injury to "détente") may temporarily rise.

Whether or not one should seek a connection between the low levels of collective self-esteem that seem to prevail in the West and the attitudes and expressions of estrangement on the part of Western intellectuals is of course an open and contentious question but one that, at least by implication, links this study to the political dramas and dilemmas of our times.

It is not easy to say, beyond certain generalities, what the author of such a study expects to accomplish. I certainly hope that some lessons may be learned from what might be called an inquiry into half a century of political daydreaming. It would be especially gratifying if I contributed in whatever measure to improving the capacity of some Western intellectuals for a better understanding of the virtues and vices of various political systems by recalling the conspicuously failed political judgments of the past. Of course, the most heartening outcome would be a strengthening of the critical faculties, which would ultimately lead to the curbing of the impulses and fantasies out of which the political pilgrimages arise.

Northampton, Mass.   P.H.
February 1981

Acknowledgments

A variety of individuals of different generations, academic disciplines, political philosophies, and intellectual outlook read the manuscript (or parts of it) and commented in writing or verbally. Several of them read the entire manuscript and gave me helpful written comments, which invariably led to some improvements. They are Peter Berger of Boston College; Guenter Lewy, my colleague at the University of Massachusetts in Amherst; Charles Page, my former teacher and colleague; Stanley Milgram of the Graduate Center, City University of New York; Alan Sica of the University of Kansas; and Adam Ulam and Richard Pipes of Harvard University. I am especially grateful for the detailed and lengthy written responses I received from Charles Page, Guenter Lewy, and Alan Sica. Mina Harrison, my wife, also read the entire manuscript and registered many useful criticisms, both stylistic and substantive.

In attempting to limit the imposition on people's time, I asked other scholars and friends to read only individual chapters, selected on the basis of their interest and expertise. Thus, Peter Kenez, a Soviet historian at the University of California in Santa Cruz, read the parts having to do with the Soviet Union; Jorge Dominguez of Harvard and Olga Mandel (both natives of Cuba) read the chapter on Cuba, as did Julius Lester (of the University of Massachusetts), who was among the early visitors of Castro's Cuba, and Stanley Rothman of Smith College (who was not). The chapter on China benefited from the lengthy written comments of such eminent specialists as Ezra Vogel of Harvard and Martin Whyte of the University of Michigan at Ann Arbor, and the verbal reactions of

Stephen Goldstein of Smith College. I also had stimulating conversations on the pilgrimages to China and the techniques of hospitality with Jerome Alan Cohen and Ross Terrill of Harvard and Lucian Pye of the Massachusetts Institute of Technology. In turn, my understanding of intellectual and political life in the United States in the 1930s was improved by a long conversation with Archibald MacLeish. I received thoughtful responses to the concluding chapter from my departmental colleagues Christopher Hurn and Randall Stokes, and also from Bennett Berger of the University of California at San Diego and Janet Vaillant of Harvard. Sheldon Meyer, senior vice president of Oxford University Press, also read the entire manuscript and made many helpful written comments. He is a welcome symbol of continuity, whose assistance I had already enjoyed in the early 1970s when Oxford published my *Soviet and American Society*. Vicky Bijur of Oxford furnished skillful editorial assistance. Ilva Funke of Northampton provided the most thoughtful, expert, and conscientious typing services I have ever had, which resulted in the final manuscript.

I was awarded a Guggenheim Fellowship for the 1974–75 academic year for the purpose of undertaking this study. Even if it did not see me through all the years it took to complete *Political Pilgrims*, the fellowship was a much appreciated form of support and encouragement, which made it possible to get started full time on the project. The University of Massachusetts at Amherst also helped with a fully paid sabbatical semester in the fall of 1976 and with a faculty research grant in 1978, which covered most of the typing and Xeroxing expenses. The Russian Research Center of Harvard University, with which I have been associated in various ways since 1963, provided me with private office space between 1974 fall and 1977 spring. Other benefits of such association included the use of Harvard libraries and the company of many stimulating and knowledgeable scholars.

I also benefited from exposing the ideas of this book during the different stages of research to various audiences at Harvard (at the Russian Research Center, the Department of Sociology, and the East Asia Legal Study Center), the Five College Faculty Seminar on Slavic Studies in Northampton, Massachusetts, the Center for Russian and East European Studies at Stanford University, and the Department of Sociology of the University of California, San Diego, at La Jolla.

Political Pilgrims

1

Themes

A world purified of all evil and in which history is to find its consummation—these ancient imaginings are with us still.   NORMAN COHN[1]

A great deal of intelligence can be invested in ignorance when the need for illusion is deep.   SAUL BELLOW[2]

The Political Judgment of Intellectuals—
A Point of Departure

Although much has been written about Western intellectuals, the relationship between their critical and uncritical attitudes—or, between estrangement and affirmation—remains to be more fully explored and much better understood.

My interest in this matter was sparked initially by the political judgments of contemporary Western intellectuals, both distinguished and less distinguished. For many years prior to conceiving of this book, I harbored misgivings about their ability to make what I considered sound political judgments. It seemed that they had a tendency for a selective preoccupation with various historical and social events and issues while allowing others to bypass them completely. I was struck by a puzzling juxtaposition of insight and blindness, sensitivity and indifference. As time went by, I came to discern a pattern. It appeared to me that most of these intellectuals tended to be rather harsh on their own societies, and surprisingly indulgent of as well as uninformed about others, unless the defects of these societies were somehow linked to their own.

My misgivings gradually broadened into an interest in the political values, cultural beliefs, and deeper apprehensions of intellectuals about the social world they inhabited. As the signs of psychic and political discomfort multiplied among Western intellectuals during the 1960s and early 70s, I became increasingly eager to comprehend better their attitudes and the less self-evident sources thereof. It appeared that the broader ramifications of this study were associated with the ambiguous

3

position of intellectuals in contemporary Western societies and with their contradictory attitudes toward power and powerlessness, belief and disbelief, social order and disorder. Intellectuals in Western societies at once articulate, occasionally attempt to solve, and sometimes themselves create certain social problems and conflicts. Their self-images too are often ambiguous, replete with paradox as they combine self-doubt with a sense of entitlement to influence, assertions of powerlessness with claims on power, humility with self-righteousness. Many Western intellectuals view themselves as the true elite of our times, especially in their capacity as opinion makers, and there are those among them who would feel comfortable with the appellation "engineers of the soul."[3]

I came to believe that the most distinctive trait of a large segment of contemporary Western intellectuals has been the fluctuation in their attitudes between estrangement and affirmation. Moreover, I felt that a more systematic examination of the relationship between the two could lead not only to a better understanding of these intellectuals but also of certain socio-cultural problems in contemporary Western societies.

I discovered that there is a body of literature that could provide much of the information required to examine the connections between estrangement and affirmation and between belief and disbelief: the reports of intellectuals on their visits to societies they found appealing. Such writings contained both lengthy statements about the attractions of the countries visited and detailed criticisms of the social system of their own countries. These books and articles offered more than an outline of the political values of a sizable group of Western intellectuals: they contained their notions of good *and* bad society, social justice *and* injustice. Almost invariably they contrasted the defects of their own societies with the virtues of those visited. Not surprisingly, these writings revealed more about their authors—and about the societies which nurtured them, if that is the right word—than about the countries ostensibly depicted.

The phenomenon of such political tourism, and the accounts written about it, provided an excellent opportunity for an inquiry into the grasp of reality, common sense, and political "instinct" of these tourists. Moreover, an examination of the politically purposeful travelers was bound to intersect with the broader issue of the relationship between alienation and utopian impulses in contemporary Western societies.

In recent times intellectuals in pursuit of political utopia have been particularly interested in four countries. Naturally enough, following the October Revolution of 1917, the Soviet Union was the first focus of attention, although many of the visits only took place after the mid-1920s, and the greatest number of such visitors arrived there in the early and mid-1930s. Less numerous but propelled by similar motives were the trips undertaken to Cuba, especially in the first years after the 1958 revolution, and to North Vietnam in the mid- and late 60s.* Interest in China among American intellectuals intensified after the diplomatic initiatives in 1972 which also allowed for the spectacular expansion of visits. Western European intellectuals visited China in more substantial numbers during the 1950s and 1960s.

Those political tours and pilgrimages are significant in several ways. In the first place they provide documents that can aid in understanding the values, aspirations, longings, and revulsions of an important and influential segment of Western intellectuals. The reports of the travelers have also molded our conceptions of the societies they described, and of those from which they have become estranged. At a minimum, the surge of favorable assessments of these societies contributed to the drowning out of voices more critical (or reduced their credibility) and certainly neutralized the expression of many skeptical viewpoints. By sheer repetition certain seemingly unassailable platitudes and axioms have evolved, gained footholds, and acquired plausibility.†

The travel reports also offer some startling illustrations of selective perception and the associated capacity for selective moral indignation and compassion—attitudes which were among the principal concerns of this study.

Why was it that sensitive, insightful, and critical intellectuals found societies like that of the USSR under Stalin, China under Mao, and Cuba under Castro so appealing—their defects so easy to ignore (or, if observed, to excuse)—and so strikingly superior to their own societies? How was it possible for many of them to have visited these societies often at their most oppressive historical moments (as was clearly the

---

* Trips to North Vietnam were unusual insofar as it was a country in a state of undeclared war with the United States. At the same time the American bombing of North Vietnam was a major cause of the sympathy that country evoked among many American intellectuals who often were more opposed to the American policy in Vietnam than in favor of the political system prevailing in North Vietnam.

† Edward Shils, for example, has stated that "Among the collectivistic liberals of the West, the exhilaration which accompanied the early years of the Soviet Union has expired. Nonetheless, a certain image of the institutions and practices of the Soviet system has over four decades become imprinted in the minds of Western intellectuals; it comprises 'public ownership' of the instruments of production, social security from the cradle to the grave, 'no unemployment,' the avoidance of inflation, the extirpation of the 'acquisitive instinct,' or the 'profit motive,' social equality and the solution of the 'ethnic problem.' "[4]

case of the USSR in the 1930s and China during the Cultural Revolution) and yet *not* notice their oppressiveness? Or, if they did, what psychological and ideological mechanisms enabled them to take a tolerant view?* One's sense of bewilderment deepens, since it is usually taken for granted that a key attribute of intellectuals is a keenly critical mind, fine tuned to every contradiction, injustice, and flaw of the social world.

Intellectuals critical of their own society proved highly susceptible to the claims put forward by the leaders and spokesmen of the societies they inspected in the course of these travels. They were inclined to give every benefit of doubt to these social systems and were successful in screening out qualities that might have detracted from their positive vision. How could such contradictory attitudes coexist and be reconciled with one another in such a highly patterned way? How do intensely critical (even suspicious) frames of mind blend with highly impressionable and uncritical mental postures? Do such opposing mental postures form some sort of a "dialectical" unity? Are they mutually supportive and made possible by one another, or do they represent compartmentalized contradictions?[6] Or is it perhaps possible that what appears at first a merciless, but realistic, critical impulse—exhibited by these intellectuals toward their own society—is *also* distorted because they are predisposed to attribute the worst to the social setting with which they are familiar and systematically to ignore its positive characteristics? To what extent were the favorable perceptions and judgments induced by the way the hosts controlled and manipulated the impressions and experiences of the visitors?

While the manipulations of the visitors' experiences—or as I call them, the techniques of hospitality—doubtless influenced the judgments—both by exposing them to reality selectively and by the highly flattering personal attentions they showed them—I do not believe that these techniques were decisive. What was decisive was the predisposition of the intellectuals themselves. And this leads us back once more to the crucial question: under what circumstances and for what motives do "critical

---

* Hans Magnus Enzensberger, the radical German social critic, posed essentially the same question when he wrote: "such an analysis [of these attitudes] would have to go beyond individual idiosyncrasies and search out the historically determined elements of the wishful thinking and their blindness to reality and their corruption. The point is not to discover that 'man is evil', but why professed socialists let themselves be politically blackmailed, morally bribed and theoretically blinded, and not just a few individuals, but in droves. . . . the 'Tourism' of the Revolutionaries' . . . is only one of the symptoms."[5]

intellectuals" become uncritical ones? What pressures lead to the apparent suspension of critical judgment in certain situations? How can sensitivity to social injustice and indignation over the abuses of political power so abruptly give way to the cheerful acceptance, or denial, of comparable flaws in other social systems?

The answer to these questions lies in the realization that intellectuals, like most other people, use double standards and that the direction of their moral indignation and compassion is set and guided by their ideologies and partisan commitments.

I hope that this study may contribute to a reexamination of certain widely held views about intellectuals. It will, if nothing else, show that their political attitudes and moral commitments are more contradictory and complex than has generally been envisaged. It will also show that their critical impulses are neither infallible nor consistent—above all, that being of a critical disposition per se may not be the major defining characteristic of Western intellectuals but instead an attribute of their ideal, or rather idealized, image.

Alienation, Utopia Seeking, and Choosing the Model Societies

The most striking paradox in the political judgment of intellectuals involves the contrast between their views of their own society and of those they designate—from time to time—as lands of promise or historical fulfillment. Correspondingly, in the interstices and interconnections of these two attitudes—estrangement and affirmation—lie the cherished values of Western intellectuals, their conceptions of good and evil in politics and history.

Not surprisingly, my inquiry found that alienation from one's own society and susceptibility to the attractions, real or imagined, of others are very closely linked. The late 1920s and early 1930s provide an excellent example. Then, as in the 1960s and early 1970s, Western intellectuals responded to the crises and problems of their society with intensified criticism and a surging interest in alternatives. The Soviet case offered the most hopeful alternative to the economic and social chaos of the first period. In more recent times the problems of Western societies were less economic and more spiritual and political in nature. In the 1960s and early 70s the putative emptiness of affluence and material comforts provided the broad background against which specific causes for discontent and social criticism came to be projected: Vietnam, race relations, corporate capitalism, consumerism, or the bureaucratization of life. More generally, I contend that in recent times the increasing strains of secularization played an important part in predisposing many intellectuals to admire such societies as China under Mao or Cuba under Castro. These were social systems which exuded a sense of purpose and appeared to have provided meaningful lives for their citizens. Evidently social criticism must rest on a vision of alternatives. Hence, estrangement from one's society invariably precedes or accompanies the projection of hope and affirmation upon other ones. This reciprocal process is enhanced by the circumstance that the societies these Western intellectuals tend to idealize in turn attack Western societies—through their spokesmen and mass media—on almost exactly the same grounds as the estranged intellectuals. Kindred voices are raised, it would seem, across the various geographical and ideological boundaries, which denounce capitalistic greed and wastefulness, excessive military expenditures, racism, poverty, unemployment, the impoverishment of human relationships, the lack of community, the vulgar noises of advertising, the crudeness of commercial transactions—practically everything that is intensely disliked by the Western intellectual. How could he fail to find some sense of affinity with those who seemingly share his values, his likes and dislikes?

The remarks of Tom Hayden and Staughton Lynd are illustrative of these attitudes:

> . . . we also discovered that we felt empathy for those more fully "other" members of the other side, spokesmen for the Communist world in Prague and Moscow, Peking and Hanoi. After all, we call ourselves in some sense revolutionaries. So do they. After all, we identify with the poor and oppressed. So do they.[7]

Thus a favorable predisposition toward these societies was based in part on the belief that they stood for the values the intellectuals cherished. Moreover, their very existence meant that Western intellectuals did not have to retreat to purely utopian alternatives to the evils they deplored. Intellectuals critical of their society must believe that social institutions superior to those in their own society can be created. They must be in a position to point, at least tentatively, to the actualization of their ideals in some existing society in order to lend strength to their social criticism at home. If other societies are no better than the one they know best how can they rise to intense moral indignation about the defects of their own society? While it is possible to reject one's society without becoming favorable toward another, it is psychologically difficult and rare to do so, for it generates a sense of hopelessness. Much of the literature we examined shows that most people estranged from their own society tend to drift to the idealization of others—or, rather, they cannot idealize others without a previous alienation from their own. The admission or realization that other social systems represent little or no improvement over one's own dilutes moral outrage; if social injustices and defects are endemic and discernible even in "new" revolutionary societies, it becomes difficult to sustain an impassioned criticism of one's own. Most of us are not capable of vehement and prolonged criticism about such ills which are widespread, seem to resist eradication, and appear determined more by impersonal forces than by identifiable human beings. By contrast, when particular defects of a society are seen as easily remediable, and when specific societies can be pointed to as illustrative of such improvements, a new and vastly superior basis for the critique of one's society is created.

It was precisely this need for new alternatives—along with certain historical facts and new information increasingly difficult to ignore—that explains why the Western intellectuals' attachment to the Soviet model-exemplar was relinquished with the passage of time. Since the late 1950s there has been not only an impressive accumulation of information concerning the departure of Soviet society from its revolutionary origins and ideals, but also the emergence of new and seemingly more authentic revolutionary societies—such as Cuba, China and North Vietnam—which could absorb sentiments and sympathies which had earlier been reserved for the Soviet Union.* H. Stuart Hughes's comment about the late J. P. Sartre (one of the few older intellectuals whose political attitudes and commitments formed a bridge between two periods and generations, having shifted from pro-Soviet to pro-Cuban and other more diffuse "Third World" sympathies) is readily applicable to many New Left radicals of the 1960s in search of new models of political rectitude: "Like Lenin before him, Sartre discovered the underdeveloped world when he needed it most to buttress a faith that seemed increasingly inapplicable to European conditions."[9]

The importance of unfamiliarity as a component of the appeal of distant societies and their leaders was also noted by Hannah Arendt in her comment on the popularity of Mao, Castro, Che Guevara, and Ho Chi Minh as compared with the lack of interest in and enthusiasm for the

---

* Once more one could witness what James Hitchcock, the historian, called "the obscure process by which people in a declining and weakening culture come to admire the vitality and self-assertiveness of a culture seemingly on the rise."[8]

much more accessible Yugoslav system and its leader, Tito.[10] It should be stressed, however, that geographical distance as such is not the decisive criterion in endowing countries with some sense of mystery, promise, or exotic attraction. The recently emerged popularity of Albania among Western European radicals shows that geographic proximity can be compatible with political appeal *if* little is known about the country in question. Thus, for example:

> A recent visitor to a Scandinavian university, after a heated debate with a group of students who had complained bitterly about the lack of freedom in their own countries and in the West in general, asked which country in the world they most admired. The answer was Albania. None of the students were familiar with conditions in Albania, none had been there or had the faintest wish to go, but Albania was nevertheless the name of their utopia.[11]

George Kennan reported a similar experience:

> I asked a Norwegian student recently what it was that the radical students at the University of Oslo most admired—what did they look up to as an example of a hopeful civilization? After considerable brooding and thought-taking, he said it was . . . Albania! Can anyone think of anything more miserable than the regime of Albania? Obviously there is not one shred of reality in this view—no interest at all in the objective truth about Albania. Albania is picked up simply because it seems to be a club with a particularly sharp nail at the end of it with which to beat one's own society, one's own traditions, one's own parents. . . . Apparently the criterion of their affections is the degree of hatred . . . for the West, and especially for their own societies.[12]

Indisputably the solution of these Scandinavian students is extreme but in some ways very consistent: the selection of a totally unknown country such as Albania confirms the symbolic nature of the quest for a model of a perfected social order.

There is another option for intellectuals who are reluctant to project their hopes on or invest their sympathies in known, existing political systems because of the lessons or history or common sense. It is to idealize abortive revolutions or social movements which were not given a chance to go stale or become oppressive. A recent example is the French student rebellion of 1968, which an American social critic considered "the most significant event in Western politics in a generation."[13] Admiring defeated revolutions has the same advantages as worshipping from a distance a beautiful woman (or man) whose charms have never been tested by sharing a bed, bathroom, or kitchen.

Apparently the appeals of political systems, revolutionary or other, are determined not by the volume of information that is available about them, nor by their actual accomplishments, nor by the degree of personal access to them. It is at least plausible to suggest that the needs of the observer—as the case of Albania's admirers suggests—frequently take precedence over the evaluation of social-political realities. The Soviet Union enjoyed the greatest prestige among Western intellectuals at the times when it was most savagely repressive, most severely plagued by material shortages, and subject to Stalin's personal dictatorship—that is, during the early and mid-1930s. By the time it had shed some of its most unattractive features—that is, after Stalin's death and under Khrushchev— the USSR no longer enjoyed the interest and endorsement of Western intellectuals. To be sure, following the death of Stalin more information became available about Soviet society, much of it unflattering. Yet the shift in attitudes cannot be explained merely as a rational response to more information. Nor can it be argued that in the 1930s, the time when the Soviet Union was so popular among Western intellectuals, there was no information at all about the Purges and other unappealing products of the Soviet system. Such information was available (for example, through Trotsky and his followers), but neither was it widely enough disseminated nor were intellectuals so receptive toward it, while much counter-information (or rather, misinformation or propaganda) was disseminated to neutralize it by the Soviet Union and its supporters abroad.

Adam Ulam's explanation for the waning popularity of the Soviet system among Western intellectuals is the most persuasive:

> . . . an intellectual often finds a certain morbid fascination in the puritanic and repressive aspects of the Soviet regime and also in its enormous outward self-assurance, which contrasts so saliently with the apologetic, hesitant self-image of the democratic world. When this facade of self-assurance began to collapse, first after the revelations about Stalin in 1956, and then as a consequence of the split in the communist camp, many Western intellectuals began to shed their loyalty to the one-time idol, now certainly more humane than it had been under Stalin.[14]

The same process is apparently taking place in regard to the attitudes toward China since the death of Mao. As in the Soviet case following the death of Stalin, the outward self-assurance and image of monolithic unity of the Chinese regime has been seriously hurt by the power struggle resulting from the elimination of what came to be called the "Gang of Four," who had earlier been major repositories of power and authority. Mao's death and the instability associated with it also allowed the revelation of many shortcomings of the Chinese regime, partly as a result of the desire of the present leadership to discredit the defeated competitors for power, partly as an unintended consequence of a somewhat loosened grip on power. Also, as in the Soviet case in the post-Stalin period, the waning popularity of the Chinese regime among Western intellectuals has coincided with its becoming less, not more, repressive.

A more general aversion toward modern, highly bureaucratized industrial societies (of which the USSR is one) elaborated by Marcuse and his followers further explains why the Soviet system can no longer inspire the majority of Western intellectuals. Indeed, these generalized reservations on the part of intellectuals about industrial society are among the major differences between the sensibilities of the 1960s and 1930s.

Thus both the popularity and unpopularity of the Soviet Union among Western intellectuals have more to do with the state of Western societies than with that of the Soviet. Admiration of the Soviet system peaked not when its performance was the most impressive or its policies most humane, but at the time when a severe economic crisis buffeted the Western world (in the 1930s), which helped create a perception of the Soviet Union as an island of stability, order, economic rationality, and social justice. Likewise the attractions of China, Cuba, and North Vietnam emerged and intensified during the 1960s when, once more, a crisis of confidence shook the United States (this time on account of Vietnam and racial conflict), and when both in the United States and in Western Europe rising non-material aspirations were unmet by new spiritual resources. Clearly it is possible to admire countries when one knows little about them; political systems can also be detested when there is scanty knowledge about them. *

While the amount of information may not be important or decisive in shaping opinion, there are other factors which play a greater part in the process of attitude formation—namely, the extent to which the informa-

---

* Thus, for instance, the U.S. has become a symbol of evil and a global scapegoat in the eyes of many Third World intellectuals who know little about it. A study of anti-Americanism and the reasons why the U.S. has become a near universal scapegoat symbol today would be no less fascinating than the one pursued here. Such attitudes represent the other side of the coin, as it were: uncritical, unreflective rejection rather than unreflective acceptance. Four attributes of the U.S. seem to invite, in my view, such worldwide animosity: 1. affluence; 2. a pervasive global *cultural* presence and appeal; 3. the combination of power with the weakened will to use it, or the image of the cowardly bully that can finally be taunted and abused with relative impunity; 4. at last, the American propensity for guilt and self-criticism, since people do not think well of those who think poorly of themselves.[15]

tion is visual, vivid, and dramatic. Arthur Koestler noted: "A dog run over by a car upsets our emotional balance . . . three million Jews killed in Poland cause but a moderate uneasiness. Statistics don't bleed; it is the detail which counts."[16]

As far as such "details which count" are concerned, there is a striking imbalance between the unavailability of unflattering visual information about the most repressive police states (and especially those with a left-wing one-party system*) and the abundance of such information about the unattractive features of American and other Western societies. This is significant, since the availability or absence of vivid, visual information relating to various social-political issues is a major factor in the creation of stereotypes, both negative and positive. The unappealing features of Western societies and particularly the United States can be seen and have indeed been depicted on television, in movies, magazines, and newspapers with considerable regularity.[17] Western, and again pre-eminently American, audiences have been provided, for some time, by the mass media of their countries with vivid images of the worst aspects of their societies. We have all seen them: ethnic slums, street corner gangs, welfare clients and the unemployed in line, angry strikers, political protesters on the campuses or streets, dilapidated schools, over-crowded hospitals, bleak prisons, policemen dispersing demonstrators, the grief of families who lost their sons in Vietnam, scenes of bloodshed and violence in Vietnam (and elsewhere in the West), photogenic extremists and bigots of many varieties, farmers destroying food, the ravaged physical environment, garbage-strewn city-scapes, scenes of crime, distress, waste, destruction and brutality—the list is endless. We do have a richly documented pictorial inventory of the ills of our society.

What of the other side? It is hardly news that police states, among them the Soviet Union, China, Cuba, North Vietnam, North Korea, Cambodia, Albania (and many others), are not in the habit of this kind of critical self-exposure, or of allowing outsiders to produce critical photographic inventories. They do not invite foreign cameramen to make

* I emphasize the unavailability of such information on left-wing police states, since right-wing dictatorships, or more precisely those of a non-Leninist persuasion, tend to be more negligent about the control of the mass media and communications in general. Since they are not quite as serious about treating ideas as weapons, their systems of propaganda and censorship tend to be less refined. Several unflattering newsreels and documentary movies have been made in and of the South African regime, various Latin American dictatorships, former Western colonies, South Vietnam, Franco's Spain, etc. It would be hard to come by such documentaries or even isolated photographs of this kind about the USSR, China, Cuba, North Vietnam, Albania, etc.

visual records of the seamier sides of their life, though they will occasionally allow them to make a record of their accomplishments. Western audiences have not seen many (if any) pictures of what Soviet, Chinese, or Cuban prisons look like; of people in those countries lining up for food; of scenes of heavy, demeaning, and fatiguing manual labor performed by women,* of substandard housing, crowded public transportation, house searches, early morning arrests, deportations (or relocations of segments of the population), factories with few safety devices, rotting crops which do not get harvested, industrial equipment left to rust in the open, shoddily built housing complexes, and empty stores. Likewise, they had few glimpses of the officials riding in curtained limousines or of the private retreats (or second homes) of members of the elite groups. Nor have Western audiences been treated to interviews with ordinary citizens of Cuba, China, or the USSR who would express criticism of any aspect of the system under which they lived.

Until recently, not only visual information and images but even graphic descriptions of the less attractive sides of life in such countries were not available or scarce.† The importance of such information is illustrated by the impact of Solzhenitsyn's artistry and power of description which for millions around the world made it possible to grasp the concept of Soviet concentration camps, if not necessarily to visualize.

What I wrote almost a decade ago contrasting American and Soviet attitudes toward publicity and societal self-exposure can be extended to other "closed" societies discussed here, such as Cuba, China, or North

---

* An exception to this are the occasional photographs of women cleaning the streets in the Soviet Union. Such picture-taking is much disapproved of in the USSR but not always prevented.

† For example, a recent survey of human rights around the globe had this to say about China: "So little is known about what goes on in Asia's largest nation, China, that outsiders can only guess at the state of human rights there."[18] Such a bland assessment reflects not only the actual paucity of information but a somewhat strained benefit-of-doubt posture. If Mr. Gwertzman had said that not enough is known to make specific assessments about the *magnitude* of the violation of human rights, one may leave it at that. But to suggest that there is so little known that *nothing* can be said (that one can only make guesses) is going too far. In any event this quote and the associated attitudes illustrate the point that was made above. Many Western intellectuals or public figures require mountains of evidence about the unappealing aspects of left-wing dictatorships before they abandon their benefit-of-doubt attitudes. There is in fact a discernible parallel here between the Soviet and Chinese cases. There was just as little disposition in the 1930s among Western intellectuals and opinion leaders to believe in the existence of Soviet concentration camps as there is today to believe in Chinese violations of human rights. And in neither period was information quite as scarce, or evidence so unsubstantiated, as the benefit-of-doubters would have us believe.

Vietnam. By the same token, a good deal of what was said about the American attitudes toward publicity applies, with some qualifications, to other Western societies and their mass media. Thus it may be said that the images of all the societies discussed in this book are influenced by contrasting levels of censorship, political constraints as well as cultural differences toward publicity and collective self-exposure. (However, cultural factors become subordinated to political requirements if they offer resistance to the policies of revolutionary systems.)* This is what I wrote about the contrast between American and Soviet society in regard to publicity:

> . . . The United States is an immensely publicity-conscious, publicity-oriented society. A more limited sense of personal privacy has its counterpart in the public realm, slanted toward sensationalism and exposure. Much of the indigenous publicity in the United States concerning American society might be described as scandal-minded, or on a more serious level, problem-oriented. The commercialism of the mass media and their quest for the eye-catching and sensational supply some of the motivation for this. Other motives are provided by the long standing tradition of social criticism. American society and its domestic . . . critics do, as a rule, a far better job at exposing its defects than the most venomous foreign critics. . . . Indeed a large proportion of Soviet (and other foreign) critiques of American society rely on American sources.† By contrast Soviet society is not publicity oriented except in a narrow, programmed sense. . . . These differences affect profoundly the images of the two societies throughout the world . . . it is a gap of particular importance in a comparative assessment of the images of American and Soviet society. Poverty, oppression, urban decay and rural stagnation, abuses of public office, political dissatisfaction and social conflicts are not recorded by reporters

---

* The primacy of the political over the cultural factors in such matters is well illustrated by the fact that, contrary to what one might expect by focusing on certain Latin American cultural stereotypes or traits—e.g., openness, expressiveness, volubility, etc.—Cuban censorship is not noticeably different from the Soviet one, and the Cuban mass media hardly more lively or apt to reveal the less appealing aspects of Cuban life than the Soviet.

† Which are often permeated by a breast-beating quality. An advertisement in the N.Y. *Times* exemplifies this: ". . . We, the American people—We: Affluent, corrupt, dehumanized, brutalized, chauvinistic, racist, white America—who share guilt for U.S. policy and for the atrocities. . . ."[19]

A European writer who arrived in the 1960s, commenting on these propensities, noted that social protest ". . . is a new industry, a new way of making money and accumulating affluence. Three things are necessary to start this business: a pen, a guitar, and a free society as one's professional space. Written protest brings decent livings, vocal protest brings millions. One who knows how effectively to exhibit his social misery and anguish rapidly becomes a millionaire."[20]

(domestic or foreign) in the Soviet Union; nor are they depicted in photographs, films or television tapes . . . whatever disturbs the Soviet citizen . . . is not conveyed to worldwide (or domestic) audiences as is the case with the ills of American society. This . . . helps to explain not only certain Soviet perceptions of American society but also in part the worldwide phenomenon of anti-Americanism, coupled with a comparatively mild or neutral position toward Soviet society. . . . The highly unfavorable [collective] self-images disseminated by the American mass media may also account for the paradox pointed out by Jacques Barzun: "As a nation whose citizens seek popularity more than any other kind of success it is galling (and inexplicable) that we, the United States, are so extensively unpopular." ("The Man in the American Mask," *Foreign Affairs*, April 1965, p. 427.) Ideas are weapons, as generations of Soviet leaders have believed. The control of the mass media and publicity is more than an irrational reflex of a sensitive political system. In the final analysis the finer points of the freedom of expression and criticism score less than the visible portraits of misery, injustice and despair.[21]

Even when the quality of information available about political regimes carries considerable weight in the making of political judgments, ultimately such judgments are the products of deeply held values.

While intellectuals are especially critical of their society in periods of crisis, turmoil, and collective self-doubt (which they voice most eloquently and which they sometimes magnify), idealistic men and women need no such upheavals to become sensitized to the defects of their society. Even during periods of relative tranquility, many intellectuals find reason for disenchantment with a social environment* which offers them few spiritual challenges and no relief from the burdens of the human condition.

The Techniques of Hospitality

Although it is my belief that the intellectuals' predisposition played a greater part than the actual travel experience in their assessments of the countries concerned, the nature of the visits also deserves close attention. On the one hand, without some measure of favorable predisposition the conducted tour aspects would have been ineffectual and possibly

---

* Many critically disposed intellectuals are distinctly unhappy in quiescent periods when the absence of social turmoil or political crisis reduces the resonance of and receptivity to their social criticism; hence, the increasing retrospective denunciation since the mid-1960s of the "complacent," "smug," and quiescent 1950s in the United States. But even during the period itself many intellectuals were visibly pained by its tranquility.

counter-productive. On the other hand, the particular manifestations of hospitality were important in swaying those who came with a neutral or benefit-of-doubt attitude rather than outright enthusiastic anticipation. And even in the cases of those who went on the journey with the most favorable expectations, the actual travel experience had a positive function because it confirmed these expectations. Thus, no matter what the attitudes of the visitors, the actual travel experience (with very few exceptions) rarely led to disillusionment. Those with favorable predispositions emerged from the experience with these attitudes strengthened and vindicated, while the wavering were moved to more sympathetic positions.

Later, I will offer a detailed examination and examples of the techniques of hospitality in individual countries. Here I want to note that these techniques divide into two complementary parts. The first has to do with the personal treatment of the visitor, his comfort and welfare, and the measures taken to make him feel important, appreciated, well liked. The goal (and usually also the result) of these measures is to make it psychologically difficult for the visitor to develop and express negative sentiments or critical thoughts toward his hosts and toward the society they represent. It *is* difficult to be critical of people who are kind to us, attentive to our personal comfort, take an interest in our personality, and appreciate our work. It is also difficult to be critical of the broader social setting in which all these agreeable personal attentions are received. An American scholar writing about the Soviet treatment of foreign visitors observed: "Thus we have a picture of lavish entertainment of foreigners, including many who (in their own opinion) had been underrated and ignored at home. Every individual was made to feel important. How could one criticize a host who contributed to one's sense of dignity and expended the valuable time of important top officials in this endeavor?"[22] Naturally, the quality of such treatment varied with the importance of the visitor, or groups of visitors, and with the particular objectives pursued by the various regimes concerned at certain periods.

The second major component in the techniques of hospitality is the selective presentation of "reality," which accounts for the highly organized and planned nature of the tours. The probability of gaining positive impressions is obviously enhanced when a visitor is systematically and purposefully exposed only to the attractive features of a country: good food and accommodations, comfortable travel, politeness and attentiveness at every turn, pleasant, interesting, or inspiring sights. (Which is not to say that the appropriate agencies of the host country always accomplish these objectives satisfactorily. They do, however, strive to attain them and do so with a good measure of success, again in part depending on the perceived importance of the visitor.) Under such conditions, even if the visitor harbors any abstract or generalized notions about the possibilities of social injustice, material scarcity, or institutional malfunctioning (and few come with such expectations), the visible, tangible realities he comes in contact with powerfully counteract his apprehensions. The visitors are shielded from unappealing aspects of life, and they are not allowed to intrude on those selected by the hosts and calculated to make favorable impressions. Moreover, for the most part what the visitors see is real:* there are in these (as in most) countries enough feats of engineering, impressive cultural institutions, natural wonders, historical monuments, and attractive individuals that are appealing and interesting. What the visitors are in no position to know is *how typical* or how characteristic such sights and impressions are, or how adequately they convey the flavor of life in the country at large.

It is the cumulative impact rather than the specific details of the hospitality that matters. Warm reception on arrival, comfortable accommodations, pleasant travel arrangements, fine food, interesting sights, encounters with important and busy political figures—all add up to a set of experiences calculated to make the visitor feel receptive to the messages his hosts intended to convey. Thus, given the combination of (various degrees of) favorable predispositions, personal flattery, physical comforts, and carefully screened sights and contrived personal encounters, it would be surprising if the visitors did not leave the countries concerned with their favorable predispositions strengthened and with a new fund of enthusiastic observations and judgments.

Even if most visitors would (and did) agree that their hosts were anxious to make a good impression, there would be less agreement about the results of all the attentions received. Surely, most travelers would argue that they were not bribed or blinded by any manifestation of hospitality. Nor can it be proven that such was the case. All one can say is that the hosts were intent on making a good impression, and in

---

* I said "for the most part" because there are also instances of total deception, things built or specially arranged for visitors which have no independent existence, or justification apart from being a showpiece or showplace of some kind. Specific examples of such sights and arrangements, modern "Potemkin villages," will be given later on.

most instances the visitors did depart with such impressions as reflected in the written accounts of their trips.

In regard to the Soviet Union, it has been clearly established that the visitors in the 1930s had been deceived, not necessarily by staged events, fake settings, or the unrepresentative sampling of the sights, but by the overall image of Soviet life and society conveyed to them. The Soviet case at any rate makes clear that "being on the spot" and "seeing things for oneself" are not a guarantee or sufficient condition for assessing accurately the nature of a country and its social system.

More generally speaking, it is one of the paradoxes of our times that greater physical mobility and potential access to new places and their inhabitants do not necessarily broaden or deepen our understanding of these places and peoples—a phenomenon also illustrated by the millions of non-political tourists who manage to visit many diverse parts of the world without learning anything of importance about them. Of course, most non-political tourists do not go abroad in order to enlarge their knowledge of the world: they merely wish that a *somewhat unfamiliar* setting provide them with familiar pleasures.[23] At best, they are interested in a handful of the most stereotyped features of the "strange lands" they visit, those which had been made familiar to them by the mass media and tourist advertising (gondolas in Venice, the Eiffel Tower in Paris, changing of the Guard in London, calypso music in the West Indies, etc.). Thus "being on the spot" may mean a very small spot indeed, and what one may "see for oneself" may not always be worth seeing.

Or, as a visitor in China pointed out, tongue-in-cheek:

> Some years ago, on the basis of careful research, I announced a theorem, which slightly simplified reads: anything that can be learned by travel, can be learned faster, cheaper, and better in a good library. The accumulation of evidence supporting the travel theorem is now overwhelming. What, then, can one report about China on the basis · of a 19-day visit? Very little from the travel itself. . . .[24]

While this may be an overstatement, the point of view deserves a hearing, since the perceptions of the travelers, and the often sweeping conclusions drawn from what they had seen, rest on exactly the opposite premise: namely, that what they had seen represents a fair, typical, and informative sampling of the social institutions and aspects of life in the country they visited. If the idea crossed their mind that they might have been exposed to carefully pre-selected sights, events, or groups, such doubts were usually brushed aside. For the most part our intellectuals succeeded in believing or in gradually convincing themselves that what they were shown was neither unusual nor exceptional. It is for that reason that they felt free to generalize: about health care in the country as a whole on the basis of one or two hospitals; about the system of education after seeing a handful of classrooms; about attitudes toward the political system after conversing with a few citizens selected by their hosts, and so on. They rarely confronted the self-evident limitations of their experience and its implications for generalizing about all they had not and could not have seen. Among these limitations was the fact that most of the visitors did not speak the language of the countries visited, and therefore most of their contacts with the "natives" were limited to communications through interpreters (occasionally they spoke to individuals other than the interpreters who knew the visitors' language, but these were hardly chance encounters). Characteristically they traveled in groups and were escorted by guide-interpreters. As a rule, even those traveling alone had a guide assigned to them. Frequently the visitors were either guests of the government (or some official organization or agency) or were given a significant reduction in their travel expenses. (Sometimes some organization of their own country footed the bill or made contributions to it.) In most instances the visitors had never been in the country before, and, generally speaking (though with some notable exceptions), their knowledge of the country and its history and culture was limited.

For the most part, people who had given indication of a critical attitude toward the countries involved were not invited or encouraged to go on such trips; sometimes they were refused entry if intending to do so.

Although there were many similarities between the techniques of hospitality used in all four societies and in both periods, this by itself does not prove that visitors to China, Cuba, and North Vietnam were misled in the manner their predecessors had been in the Soviet Union in the years of Stalin.*

There are, however, grounds for suspecting that in the more recent instances too the gap between the selected sights the tourist was allowed to see and what he had no opportunity to see was considerable, and consequently such a tour was conducive to the serious misapprehension of the character of the political systems concerned. The lesson of

---

* Both before Stalin's rise to power and after his death travelers could learn more about Soviet realities.

the Soviet conducted tours is that such techniques of hospitality, combined with a favorable predisposition on the part of the visitors, can lead to bizarre misperceptions of a political and social system. The post-Mao revelations in China, both official and unofficial, lend support to the suspicion that visitors to China too were given a distinctly unrepresentative and misleading impression which contributed significantly to their misjudgments and admiration of that society.

A definitive assessment of the contributions of the techniques of hospitality to the positive visions of China, Cuba, and North Vietnam must await the further accumulation of reliable information about these societies. In the meantime, we can only make guesses as to the magnitude of the gap between their idealized images and their more mundane and unattractive aspects.

The Source Materials: Their Sampling and Context

The sources to be used in this study were more or less ready-made. Since I was interested in the views and professed values of contemporary intellectuals of some distinction, I turned to their writings, in particular to their writings about their visits to the countries selected. Possibly these interests could also have been pursued through interviews with many of the authors still alive. However, written accounts were preferable because they were intended for a wider public, and therefore their authors invested more care and energy in them than they would have in an interview (assuming that they would have granted an interview). Interviews, in any event, are by necessity short and may reflect more about the interviewer—through his questions—than about the respondent. It would have been also of limited usefulness to interview people years or decades after their travel experiences. Over time opinions and attitudes get revised, impressions fade, memories become extinct. I was interested in the written testimonies of the travelers because they were for the record, because they are fuller, richer, more detailed, and more accurately reflective of the attitudes and experiences of the authors at the time of the visit than interviews could have been.

The travel writings proved to be excellent source material because they contained detailed inventories of *both* the alienated aspects and attitudes of intellectuals (or, of their critical sides) *and* their affirming, enthusiastic, and supportive ones. Taken together, these accounts afforded considerable insight into the values which sustained their authors. It became apparent very soon that the choice of politically attractive countries on the part of intellectuals was highly patterned. First, they had to be relatively distant and/or poorly known. Second, they had to be revolutionary or post-revolutionary societies, seemingly dedicated to some semi-utopian goals, to radical social transformation. Third, and in connection with the second criterion, such countries had to be claimants of some variety of the Marxist ideological legacy.* Fourth, they had to be and were hostile to the United States and most Western countries. Fifth, and perhaps most important, was the victimized, underdog image. (This image sometimes endured well beyond the time when any rational, objective, or historical basis could be found for it. Victim and victimizer were frozen permanently in the minds of many observers.) Each country at the time of the visits was seen as a victim of the West or a particular Western power: Russia, many times invaded by Western countries in its history; China, exploited by the colonial powers and much maligned after World War II by the American mass media; Cuba, the victim of American economic imperialism; North Vietnam, destroyed by American air power. Correspondingly, the appeal of the Soviet Union declined by the mid-1950s, partly because it became rather difficult to cast it in the role of the underdog once it had become the second major industrial and military superpower in the world. On the other hand, it should also be noted that the image of the former underdog combined with that of an emergent and avenging power—the process of the weak becoming strong—had its own fascination. Thus, many Western intellectuals were able to find the military muscle of revolutionary societies thrilling while they abominated militarism at home.

Finally, there was the appeal of underdevelopment per se as distinct from that associated with the victimized status. All four countries chosen were technologically and industrially underdeveloped at the time of their greatest popularity—although the Soviet Union in the 1930s had already made much progress in closing the gap, and the other countries too were undergoing development in various ways. Yet the fact remains that, at the time of the most enthusiastic travel reports, none were highly de-

---

* The tenacious "leftism" of Western intellectuals and the continued (or periodically resurgent) hold of (some version of) Marxism on them was one of the interesting findings of this study. So was the attraction exercised by almost any set of claims, slogans, and terminology vaguely Marxist. As will be further discussed below, Old and New Left were united—despite many differences—in being drawn emotionally to some variety of Marxism or some elements of Marxism. This author often wondered as did Saul Bellow: "why it should rend people's hearts to give up their Marxism. What does it take to extinguish the hopes raised by the October Revolution? How much more do intellectuals need to learn about the USSR?"[25]

veloped industrial societies and each partook of the virtues—real or imagined—of the amorphous entity that came to be known as the Third World. Certainly, the appeal China, Cuba, and North Vietnam had in the eyes of many Western intellectuals was part of the more general appeal of the Third World. Underdevelopment, in the eyes of such beholders, is somewhat like innocence. The underdeveloped is uncorrupted, untouched by the evils of industrialization and urbanization, by the complexities of modern life, the taint of trade, commerce, and industry. Thus, underdevelopment and Third World status are, like childhood, easily associated or confused with freshness, limitless possibilities, and wholesome simplicity.* Sympathetic visitors usually did not fully grasp the contradiction that, although largely untouched by the original sin of industrialization at the time of their visits, the countries in question were furiously trying to expand their industries. In any event, admirers of these countries maintained that they learned the lesson and were not going to repeat the disruptions and vices of Western-style industrialization. It is the centerpiece of the myth of socialism that it promises to combine modernization with social cohesion and sustaining community.[27]

The two groups of intellectuals who journeyed to the various countries in the 1930s on the one hand and in the 1960s and 1970s on the other belonged, with few exceptions, to different generations and were in some ways of different political persuasion. As noted before, one of the most obvious differences between them was that by the 1960s alienated Western intellectuals were no longer looking to the Soviet Union (or Soviet bloc countries) for inspiration.† Nor, as a rule, were the alienated

---

* As Peter Berger put it, "Perhaps what is at work here is an archaic mythic motif, that of simpler and purer lands far away, from which some healing secret might be learned."[26]

† There were a few odd exceptions. For instance, Angela Davis visited and lauded the Soviet Union in 1973 very much in the style of the 1930s and was given the appropriate VIP treatment, which included the publication of a sixty-page pamphlet about her visit, printed in 45,000 copies. An explanation of her untimely affection for the Soviet Union may lie not only in her membership in the pro-Soviet Communist party of the U.S. but perhaps also in her being one of those Western intellectuals who cannot help sympathizing with every authoritarian regime which bestows the "socialist" title upon itself. (She has also written with much enthusiasm about her visit to Cuba in her autobiography.) An equally curious (and probably transitory) enthusiasm was provoked in Dr. Ralph Abernathy, the civil rights activist, by East Germany, one of the most oppressive of the Soviet-type regimes. At the end of his two-day visit he said: "Every minute of my stay in your wonderful country was filled with joy and valuable political experience. I go back to my country richer for having learned to know and appreciate the German Democratic Republic." In turn, Scott Nearing, the American social critic, on his visit found that East Germany was governed wholly without coercion.[28]

Western intellectuals of the 1960s adherents, members, or fellow travelers of the pro-Soviet Communist parties in their own countries. Thus, a comparison of the two groups or generations also amounts to a comparison of the Old and New Left, and especially of the social criticism these generations had formulated.

The differences between these two generations were more sharply defined in the case of the Americans. There seemed to be a greater number of estranged American intellectuals in the 1960s than in the 1930s, and they also appeared more intensely estranged than their predecessors. The more recent generation of critical American intellectuals also seemed more alienated in comparison with their English, French, German, or Scandinavian counterparts. If such impressions are correct, Vietnam and the American racial conflict—problems without equivalent in Western Europe—may provide the explanation.

The apparent growth of alienation* in the United States might have also been a reflection of the growing number of people ready to claim intellectual status and the stances associated with it. In the United States, perhaps more than other Western societies, some degree of proclaimed estrangement from the major values and institutions of society became an informal norm or expectation during the 1960s among intellectuals and aspiring intellectuals. Perhaps for the first time in history, during these years the lone voices of beleaguered intellectuals forming a small, isolated, critical vanguard were replaced—in the United States at any rate—by a vast, well-orchestrated chorus of standardized nay-saying emanating from what may be described as a massive subculture of alienation, or establishment of estrangement. By the end of the 1960s it ceased to be clear which attitudes represented conformity or nonconformity: the traditional support for existing social institutions and values or their reflexive disparagements. The spread of higher education was doubtless related to this phenomenon:

> The enormous expansion in higher education . . . means that we now have a large class of people . . . who though lacking in intellectual distinction (and frequently even intellectual competence) nevertheless

* Various aspects of alienation will be discussed in the next chapter. The essential psychological component of this concept, as I see it, is the feeling that there is little if anything of value and worthy of respect in society, combined with profound pessimism as to the chances of improvement. Two trends and traditions often interwoven might be discerned in contemporary discussions of alienation. One is the Marxist, the other the Weberian. Both account for alienation, largely with reference to the loss of tradition; the former stresses economic factors, the latter the process of secularization and bureaucratization.[29]

believe themselves to be intellectuals. . . . in a country like America today [there are] . . . several million "intellectuals" who are looking at their society in a highly critical way and are quick to adopt an adversary posture toward it.[30]

Certain qualitative changes in the attitudes of estranged American intellectuals (and to some degree those in Western Europe too) also had a bearing both on the character of their social criticism and on their susceptibility to the appeals of other societies. I am referring here primarily to the "revolution of rising expectations" which, contrary to popular belief, has been much more a Western than "Third World" phenomenon.* Clearly, the growth of individualistic expectations and their corollary— the unwillingness to accept scarcity or deprivations of any sort—have contributed to the intensification of social criticism both on the part of intellectuals and the social groups for whom they strive to be spokesmen.

The spread of such attitudes has been related not only to the greater accessibility of higher education, but also to the changes in its quality and content. Specific trends, innovations, and movements in American education have done much to encourage the belief in the limitless potential and unique personal qualities and needs of every individual. Such beliefs have, of course, always been part of American culture rich in egalitarian traditions, but in the 1960s there were renewed and more determined attempts to implement them.

While setting the chronological boundaries of this study, and especially focusing it on the 1930s and 1960s, was fairly easy to resolve, selecting particular works as source material was more problematic. It required deciding who the important and influential Western intellectuals are. By what criteria should one choose among the many who qualify? Obviously the choices were to be made among those who were at some stage in their life strongly critical of their own society and favorably disposed toward one of those mentioned before and, moreover, expressed such sentiments in published writing. I was not concerned with the durability of such attitudes, or with the proportion of the authors who subsequently changed their political sympathies. The process of political disillusionment is a subject of inquiry in its own right and deserves extended analysis as much as the issues being grappled with here. I was interested in the growth of political faith and its particular manifestations and not in the process of disillusionment, however often it followed.

As far as the nationalities of "Western" intellectuals were concerned,

---

* By the end of the 1970s it had become fashionable to talk about declining expectations in the United States and the West in general, tied to economic difficulties.

they ended up being primarily American,[31] British, and French. There were more of them, more distinguished figures among them, and they wrote more about their political tours. This, however, did not exclude interesting and relevant materials produced by other Western nationalities.

It may be suggested that I "loaded" the sample by picking authors whose attitudes and writings illustrated the points I wanted to make. While to some degree this is true, the crucial fact is that such a group could be selected without any difficulty: there were more than enough intellectuals of importance who went on these trips and wrote the kind of travelogues which support the propositions I entertained about Western intellectuals. I seriously doubt that a counter sample of a similar size could easily be assembled consisting of prominent Western intellectuals who had visited the same countries and wrote indignant exposés on their return. It is a historical fact that large numbers of prominent (and less prominent) Western intellectuals have been (or were) sympathetic, with varying degrees of intensity and duration, toward regimes they perceived as socialist and intent on implementing the most idealistic teachings of Marxism.

Not *all* the travelers chosen for this study were seekers of utopia. Rather, they represent a range of attitudes which includes the quest for utopia as well as milder degrees of favorable predisposition and susceptibility toward the appealing facets of the new societies. Not every traveler set out to find a close approximation of his ideals and longings, but many did. Others went on their tours out of curiosity or because they felt that it was important that they themselves evaluate societies often seen as misrepresented in the mass media of their own countries. Numerous visitors embarked on these trips because of specific concerns and interests: wanting to know how particular problems unresolved in their countries were handled, from race relations to public health, from industrialization to day-care centers, prison reform, or the state support of the performing arts. Thus, while many intellectuals projected extravagant hopes on the countries concerned, envisioning a totally new way of life and a radical break with all the familiar imperfections of the past and of organized social existence, others focused on the more tangible and specific accomplishments, on new forms of economic organization or administrative techniques, on various more rational (or seemingly more rational) solutions to age-old problems. It stands to reason that the perceived attractions of these countries depended—in addition to the particular historical circumstances and spirit of the times—on the personal and social background of the visitors. Different individuals had different susceptibilities. Occupational backgrounds doubtless played an important part in the selective appreciation of the various features of the countries inspected.

Could the political pilgrims be regarded as fellow travelers? Certainly there is a similarity between the concept of the political pilgrim and that of the "fellow traveler." Both share a critical stance toward Western societies and sympathy toward "socialism." Many fellow travelers even traveled to the USSR. However, "fellow traveler" had a more limited meaning: it referred to Soviet and Communist sympathizers of the 1930s and 40s who made no formal political commitment and remained outside the Communist party for various reasons. Their services were eagerly sought by the party and the Soviet Union, since their symbolic neutrality seemed to enhance their credibility and propaganda value. They had no organizational commitment and therefore a greater freedom of action and expression. On the whole, the views of the fellow travelers represented slight modifications or variations of the official line, or its softened version.* The term lost much of its applicability in the post–World War II period when the original species, the devoted helper of the Soviet cause, loosely affiliated with the Communist party (through front organizations), gradually disappeared. The term implies, despite some appearances, a more enduring, stable, and structured political commitment, which the Western intellectual of the 1960s and 70s seldom had. It would seem that the cycle of commitment and disenchantment accelerated in our times. Intellectuals may visit Cuba or China in a sympathetic frame of mind, write a book or some articles reflecting such sentiments, and a few months or couple of years later their enthusiasm fades. They may be getting ready to find a new object of veneration. After all, Mao shook hands with Nixon, and the Chinese regime reintroduced competitive examinations at universities, while Castro has been persecuting homosexuals. Things may be different in Albania or Mozambique. Thus, the locale of enthusiastic interests may shift once more, though not the core of estrangement which underlies these shifting susceptibilities.

---

* Fellow travelers usually purveyed what Gabriel Almond designated as the "exoteric" view of the party line which would appeal to the greatest number of people and offend the fewest sensibilities—the most diluted and palatable version of the party line, that is.[32]

Unlike David Caute, the English writer and academic, I find it difficult
to reduce the phenomenon of the utopian susceptibility of contemporary
Western intellectuals to a "postscript to the enlightenment," the subtitle
and main theme of Caute's book.[33] He locates the basis of pro-Soviet
fellow-traveling in values and attitudes deriving from the Enlightenment,
which include rationality, belief in progress, the benefits of science and
technology, planning, or, more generally speaking, benevolent intervention in social affairs. If fellow-traveling (and political utopia-seeking)
was a postscript to anything, it was more to nineteenth-century romanticism than eighteenth-century rationalism, though admittedly there was
an overlay of rationalism. I also share Lewis Feuer's criticism of Caute's
thesis:

> Men of the Enlightenment . . . were ready to denounce the suppres-
> sion of freedom from whatever quarter it issued; they were enemies of
> every despotism. They liked to imagine themselves as influencing
> monarchs, but they never wrote apologies for Prussian or Russian
> serfdom. They also retained a scepticism concerning grandiose politi-
> cal claims. . . . The fellow-travelers, on the other hand, were less
> children of the Enlightenment than the heirs to the platonic aspiration
> toward the status of philosopher-kings.[34]

The appeals of the social systems considered here (including the Soviet Union in the 1930s) transcend the rationalistic themes and boundaries Caute proposed. It is one of the main contentions of this study
that the major attractions of the new societies have not been political,
not at least in the relatively narrow and conventional sense of the word,
despite all appearances to the contrary. Instead, I found that these appeals have coalesced around two main themes. One of them is certainly
social justice and its many tangible components—material, economic, political, cultural, and organizational. The second theme is more elusive
but probably the more important. It comprises the achievement of or
the striving for "wholeness," the sense of identity and community, meaning and purpose in life. Such appeals mirror a malaise which goes beyond and beneath dissatisfaction with specific political arrangements,
the defects of capitalism and the particular forms of social injustice
found in Western societies. They derive their force from "civilization
and its discontents," some of which are endemic, while others intensify
in an increasingly secular society that can no longer either legitimate
the curbing of individualistic impulses and fantasies, or offer fulfilling
social myths and values which could divert attention from the growing
preoccupation with the self. Behind the metaphors of wholeness, iden-

tity, and community lies a craving for a universe that has meaning, purpose, and direction. Apparently such a craving is, contrary to what some might expect, more pronounced among intellectuals than among "ordinary" people. Of late it appears that the former find it less tolerable and more troublesome to live in a world of "disenchantment" from which "the ultimate and sublime values have retreated"—as Max Weber characterized the corrosive process of secularization. It is one of the paradoxes of our times that intellectuals, once the vanguard of secularization, seem to have become its struggling victims, unwilling or unable to come to terms with an existence, personal and social, that offers so few authentic versions of "enchantment."

Western Traditions of Utopia-Seeking

The utopian susceptibilities of contemporary Western intellectuals are part of a long-standing tradition of seeking heaven on earth which took more specific form when the belief in a heavenly heaven, as it were, began to lose its hold on the imagination of Western man. This is not to say that utopian and religious designs are antithetical, but that the utopian ones often feed on and derive from religious impulses. While the underlying desires for heaven on earth and for supernatural gratifications may be presumed to be similar, there are empirical, observable differences between orientation toward gratification here and now, or at an other-worldly plane of existence.

While utopias differ in respect to their specific objectives and the methods proposed for their attainment, the hoped-for benefits of utopias have much in common.[35] They all are blueprints or proposals for some radical, sweeping alteration and improvement of the human condition, for the rectification of widely shared human frustrations and discontents. Utopias differ from other plans of such improvement by their universality—they are in principle applicable to all mankind—and also by the comprehensiveness of their objectives. As Adam Ulam noted, they "must promise not more of the same but an entirely different and marvelous world. . . ."[36] It is on account of their bold designs and ambitiousness that utopias are often thought of as unrealistic.

Utopias incorporate both themes peculiar to the strains and discontents of a particular historical period and elements, secular as well as religious, which are common to many cultures and eras. Isaiah Berlin has firmly grasped the latter, more universal core of all utopian beliefs and aspirations:

. . . the belief that somewhere, in the past or in the future, in divine
revelation or the mind of an individual thinker, in the pronouncements
of history or science, or in the simple heart of an uncorrupted good
man, there is a final solution. This ancient faith rests on the conviction
that all the positive values in which men have believed must, in the
end, be compatible, and perhaps even entail one another.[37]

Berlin's point goes to the heart of the notion of utopia, namely, harmony: harmony between different values and goals, between individuals,
between groups, between society and the individual, human society and
nature, between public and private interest, aspiration and achievement, desire and opportunity. That is to say, utopia is a form of social
organization which has banished scarcity, frustration, and conflict, which
maximizes happiness, freedom, and self-realization through the combination of communal bonds and the creation of material and institutional
opportunities for self-development. Utopia is obviously not compatible
with poverty, scarcity, inequality, coercion, or repression. It is a state in
which individual and group satisfactions converge rather than conflict.

Another core component of the utopian idea is that society (or the
community) must assume full responsibility for the individual. Utopians
do not believe that "The attainment of happiness should be left to our
private endeavours."[38] They lean to the belief that most people do not
know what is good for them, that the individual pursuit of happiness is
inefficient and often leads to the collision of the desires of different individuals (which could be averted in the utopian framework proposed).
It follows from the compelling character of many utopian schemes that
those intent on their realization cannot, in good conscience, exclude the
use of force to bring it about and to maintain it.[39]

The fact that most utopias involve plans and call for implementation
helps to distinguish them from myth or collective fantasy. Furthermore,
the somewhat contradictory blend of rational and religious elements, including the orientation toward change, reminds us that utopian thinking
is a relatively modern phenomenon dating back no further than the Renaissance and receiving new impetus from the French Enlightenment
and the advances of science in the nineteenth century.[40] ("To seek salvation on this earth, to achieve human perfectibility in this life would have
been inconceivable before the onset of rationalism.")[41]

Utopian thinkers (and doers) are inclined to consider human nature
and needs more or less fixed, allowing for the ultimate reconciliation of
divergent human values and wishes. This perspective creates tension
between human nature (and behavior) as it is, here and now, and

"true" or "real" human nature, which is supposedly realizable in every-body when this positive, universal essence is unearthed and allowed expression thanks to the efforts of the utopian educator, revolutionary, or philosopher king. Utopians often view their task as removing obsta-cles from the path of self-realization, or creating conditions for it. In practice this tends to lead to programs and policies aimed at modifying and changing human nature, or at least observable behavior, in conjunc-tion with the long-term objectives of the utopian plan. Lewis Mumford identified a major pattern in regard to conceptions of human nature and utopian proclivities:

> If the medieval thinkers were convinced that, on the whole, nothing could be done to rectify men's institutions, their successors in the 19th century committed the opposite error and absurdity: they believed that human nature was asocial and obstreperous only because the church, the state, or the institutions of property perverted every human impulse. Men like Rousseau, Bentham, Godwin, Fourier and Owen might be miles apart from one another in their criticism of so-ciety, but there was underlying consensus in their belief in human nature. They looked upon human institutions as altogether external to men; these were so many straitjackets that cunning rulers had thrown over the community to make sane and kindly people behave like madmen.[42]

Marx and his followers also entertained similar beliefs about the rela-tionship between human nature and social institutions. Marx's utopia—communism—entailed not only changes in the system of production and other institutional arrangements but also the unfolding of human poten-tial and the appearance of human characteristics which do not over-whelm us with their presence through recorded history (e.g. unselfishness, kindness, lack of aggression, rationality). The successors and disciples of Marx accepted his premises but projected the rejuvenation and total renovation of human nature to the more distant future and made these transformations dependent on not only structural changes in society but also patient didactic efforts through education and propaganda.[43]

It is hard to conceive of utopian schemes which exclude the belief in virtually unlimited human potential. All existing political systems dis-playing utopian pretensions take this position, for understandable rea-sons. Professing faith in a virtually unlimited and universal perfectibil-ity of human nature is compatible, in the short run, with treating actual human beings like raw material whose present nature leaves much to be desired, but can be radically improved by relentless molding.

From the contemporary perspective the most important distinction among utopian designs appears to be between what may be called traditional-rational and less rational or non-rational conceptions of utopia. This is a difference between the emphasis on making social organization more rational and perfecting control over the physical environment, as opposed to the more recent interest in creating liberating, non-repressive, unregulated, or quasi-anarchistic social arrangements. Eugene Goodheart refers to these two currents of thought and attitude as the "utopianism of reason" versus the "new utopianism of the passional imagination."[44] The new utopians include preeminently Herbert Marcuse, Norman O. Brown, R. D. Laing, and Theodore Roszak. The difference between the two utopian currents is of some relevance for our study as it underlies certain differences between the "pilgrimages" of the 1930s and those of the more recent period. It may be suggested, at the cost of somewhat oversimplifying the issue, that the first wave of utopia-seeking approximated more closely the "utopia of reason," while the more recent one approximated that of "passional imagination," with its focus on freedom from societal and sexual repression and liberation from all "unnecessary" restraints. The new utopianism also incorporated elements of anti-intellectualism, including hostility to science, industry, and technology. Correspondingly in the 1930s Soviet society was appealing on account of its rationality, planning, and benevolent application of science and technology, while such themes were less prominent in the 1960s when much of the emphasis shifted to a yearning for simplicity, authenticity, and community, discerned in the newly discovered societies.

If the outlines of utopias have much in common, so do the various forms of utopia-seeking. The least arduous is what may be called armchair utopia-seeking, that is, theorizing and speculation without attempting to implement the schemes proposed. A more serious pursuit of utopia has been the setting up of small-scale utopian communities cut off from the rest of society, such as the nineteenth-century utopian communities in the U.S., the American communes in the 1960s, and the kibbutz in Israel (the third example differs from the first two in that it emerged not in opposition to but in support of society as a whole, although it remained limited in scale). Setting up small-scale utopian communities may also be combined with the geographic move from one country or even continent to another. Indeed this has been the origin of many American utopian communities, most recently of the Peoples' Temple in Guyana.

The pursuit of utopia can also take explicitly political forms when through a revolution or uprising an attempt is made to create a social order so different from other known or existing systems that the utopian appellation becomes justified.

Lastly, there is the pilgrimage to distant lands in the hope of finding utopian social arrangements at places unknown or poorly known. The hopes of such a discovery may be intense or tentative, the motives may range from mild curiosity (about the prospect of finding something better than the familiar social arrangements) to the more intense expectation and even certitude that social systems far superior to those known must exist and can be found. This is the form of utopia-seeking most central to this study. The motives underlying such political pilgrimages have certain things in common with some of the impulses which prompt people to travel in less purposeful ways. The essential motive behind much travel is the desire for new experience, for escaping the familiar. The pursuit of the unusual, exotic, or exciting has for centuries been a part of the tradition of traveling, especially as practiced by members of the upper classes, adventurers, artists, and intellectuals—categories which often overlap. Expectations of adventure, enrichment, and above all, new experience of a transforming character have always been part of the lure of travel. In this regard travel and revolution have something in common. Both are routine-shattering, seen as open-ended and leading to some, not fully definable, transformation of personal lives. There is also the hope, often associated with travel, of finding instructive lessons about how to lead a fuller, richer life, of learning from the "natives." Such impulses have been viewed by some authors as part of an age-old quest for some lost paradise, or innocence. Manes Sperber has written that "a yearning for paradise includes both wanderlust *and* homesickness, a longing for vanished childhood, lost youth, the fire of burnt out passions. Anything lost in time, or undiscoverable, we tend to seek in a remote place, in Utopia."[45]

The compensatory functions of utopia-seeking through travel is also a major theme of Baudet's study of European images of non-European man. In his introduction Franklin L. Baumer wrote: "The European's images of non-European man are not primarily if at all descriptions of real people, but rather projections of his own nostalgia and feeling of inadequacy. . . . The outsider, whether primitive or civilised, is held up as a model of what he (the European) has been in happier days, or of what he would like to be and perhaps could be once again."[46]

The view expressed by British historian V. G. Kiernan of the part played by the Orient in nineteenth-century Western imagination could be generalized to other times and parts of the world: "To its own denizen a realm of necessity or destiny, to Western fantasy this Orient was one of freedom, where man could expand beyond all common limits, with the unlimited power that Napoleon dreamed of there . . . all those inordinate things that orderly modern man had to renounce and live as if born, . . . with a bit in his mouth. If, as we are now told, our dreams are necessary to our mental equilibrium, Europe's collective day dream of the Orient may have helped to preserve it . . ."[47]

In our times there has been a new spurt of self-consciousness about the personal and social problem-solving potentials of travel, an increasingly stereotyped linking of "discovery" and "self-discovery." Much of this has only limited political significance and may instead be considered one among the many by-products of the upsurge of individualism in Western countries and especially in the United States. Thus travel for many has become increasingly an ego-enhancing activity, a rejuvenating device which provides new settings against which to display and re-examine the same old ego. Travelers often look for a stage where they can place themselves, in the hope of rediscovering youth, strength, forgotten interests or talents, a more harmonious relationship between the self and nature, or the self and the social world. The expectations which can be attached to travel are virtually endless and contradictory. We may travel to be alone or to find company; to solidify existing ties or to forget about them; in pursuit of knowledge or escape; with the burden of social responsibility or of total irresponsibility. Travel is especially irresistible to those—and their numbers may be increasing—who seek instant solutions to personal or social problems. Moreover, movement—*going somewhere*—suggests a clear purpose. (This may also help to explain why Americans move so much within their own country and why they like to attend meetings and conferences in different places.) "This promise of a change of scene," Sperber wrote, "is virtually an announcement of imminent solution or salvation."[48]

It might be expected that there would be a high representation of intellectuals among different types of contemporary travelers and especially among those whose movements are propelled by more ambitious motives and imaginings. While undoubtedly more intellectuals in our times travel in search of some form of political fulfillment or enlightenment, the phenomenon of intellectuals traveling with more in mind than diversion or recreation is far from new. Men of letters in the past, though smaller in number and usually more privileged in their social origins, often responded to the same impulse when embarking on visits to distant and poorly known lands. Those tired of or uneasy with their own culture and civilization have frequently cast wistful glances at far-away places where the uncorrupted natives dwelt in innocence, harmony, and authenticity. European, and more recently American, culture has for many centuries been permeated by ambivalence toward itself, toward the complexities, restraints, and pretenses that go with civilization, with high levels of social organization and differentiation. A better human condition was assumed to exist either in the past, or in distant, little known regions or—more recently—in a future utopian state that combined some characteristics of this idealized past and idealized spatial remoteness. As Baudet has observed:

> . . . the old, never entirely forgotten idea of an ideal age has, through constantly changing interpretations, continued to offer opportunities for culture to make contact with that unfaded prehistory; all idealism, all morality, all unattainable dreams of happiness from humanity's obscure beginnings, which form a vivid contrast with present day shortcomings, will then shine forth. . . . So the "noble savage" or a tenuous prefiguration of him, has been present in our culture from earliest times. . . .
>
> The glorification of all things primitive, the culture-less as a characteristic of the true, the complete, the only and original bliss: that is one of the fundamentals of our Western civilization.[49]

Many times in European history such longings intensified at times of crisis when dissatisfaction with existing conditions prompted a quest for alternatives. Thus the more recent twentieth-century travels to new societies may fit into a broader, long-standing historical pattern. This is suggested by one recurring theme of the accounts of both sets of travelers: the theme of simplicity, community, and authenticity allegedly found among the peoples of the new societies ("The natural goodness that developed so harmoniously in others formed a striking contrast to our errors and corruption . . ." again, as Baudet put it).[50]

The repository of all this "natural goodness," harmony and authenticity, was the Noble Savage, whose image continued to exert a powerful influence on the fantasies and wishes of Westerners and who keeps reemerging in forever new incarnations but incorporating the core elements—whether he is projected on the preliterate "native," robust proletarian, earthy peasant, or tenacious Third World guerilla. The Noble Savage was everything the traveling aristocrat, artist, patrician, or intellectual was not. Judged by his remarkably stable configurations, some of the major discontents and frustrations of Western civilizations have changed little over the centuries, at least as experienced by these travelers and explorers. V. G. Kiernan sees the Noble Savage as a "compound of . . . open-mindedness and self-deception" characteristic of the age in which it originated (at least in its most elaborate version in eighteenth-century France), and ". . . it suited the mood of the middle class pining for 'freedom' [and] a Europe burdened with its own complexities. Commonly the ordinary man, in or out of Europe, was regarded as a born Caliban, only redeemable by paternal control. But perhaps on the contrary, what he was suffering from was too much control, too much artificiality and class division. If so, man in his primitive condition might be expected to exhibit naturally the virtues that civilized men had to toil painfully for. The idea went through many metamorphoses, and Noble Savages turned up in all sorts of places. . . ."[51]

Ignacy Sachs, another recent student of Western attitudes toward the non-Western world, emphasizes the more novel elements of ambivalence in such perceptions:

> Average Europeans continue to see the inhabitants of the Third World . . . through two contradictory stereotypes which are, however frequently linked together in very different combinations. This "other" appears now as the cannibal, the Anti-Christ, the destructive demon preparing to overwhelm the developed countries in his demographic tidal wave, and now as the being on the right side of the angels, the child of nature, the creator of exquisite cultures, worthy of our greatest respect . . .[52]

The pursuit of uncorrupted simplicity was not the only source of the tradition of wistful curiosity about distant lands on the part of the literati. On closer inspection one finds yet another appeal, in many ways diametrically opposed to that of the simple, spontaneous, unregulated life associated with the Noble Savage. In this view, order and rational design are imposed by enlightened authority and contrasted with the familiar scenes of disorder, pettiness, and pursuit of conflicting group interest which obstructed the realization of higher purpose in their own society. Eighteenth-century French intellectuals were notable precursors of contemporary intellectuals impressed by the enlightened, orderly designs of socialist systems such as the Soviet or Chinese. As is so often the case, Tocqueville had some pertinent observations about a phenomenon which has persisted from his lifetime to the present:

> Not finding anything about them which seemed to conform to their ideals they went to search for it in the heart of Asia. It is no exaggeration to say that everyone of them in some part of his writings passes an emphatic eulogy on China. . . . That imbecile and barbarous gov-

ernment . . . appeared to them the most perfect model for all nations of the world to copy.[53]

L'Abbé Baudeau, an eighteenth-century admirer of China, wrote:

> More than 320 million people live there as wisely, happily and freely as men can ever be. They live under a most absolute but most just government, under the richest, the most powerful, the most humane and the most welfare-conscious monarch.[54]

Another eighteenth-century writer, Poivre, claimed that "China offers an enchanting picture of what the world might become, if the laws of that empire were to become the laws of all nations." Voltaire too believed that the Chinese empire "is in truth the best that the world has ever seen, and moreover the only one founded on paternal authority."[55] Russia was held in a similar esteem by the French men of letters of the period. Their admiration also foreshadowed the twentieth-century veneration of the Soviet Union and especially its capacity to overcome backwardness and modernize itself with such apparent dispatch and speed. They believed, as Lewis Coser put it, that

> Everything . . . is possible, if in a country that had been until recently wholly barbaric, one man aided by right reason could transform a whole people. Russia had made enormous progress within the short span of a few decades. . . . It moved ahead so fast that, in many respects, it was already a model of other countries of much older civilization. And what, if not enlightened despotism, had allowed the Russians to make such giant steps forward? . . . Russia's advance revived the spirits of those discouraged by the anarchy and apparent hopelessness of the political scene at home. . . . In enlightened Russia, in contrast to Western Europe, the sovereign was not hindered by all sorts of obsolete and obsolescent resistance to his beneficient actions. There one could paint with broad strokes upon the canvas of the future.[56]

Kiernan has explained the appeals of enlightened despotism for the eighteenth-century intellectuals rather persuasively: "What these intellectuals of an aristocratic society were predisposed to look for and to admire was something resembling themselves, a class of men of enlarged minds and sympathies benevolently guiding ordinary mankind."[57]

Just as the eighteenth-century French intellectuals were impressed by the powerful central authority found in both Russia and China, capable of bringing about desirable social change, their twentieth-century counterparts found much to admire in the methods of government and determination displayed by the rulers of China and Russia in their times. The attitudes being sketched here reflect a dislike of political pluralism shared by many intellectuals of the eighteenth as well as the twentieth century. Again, as Coser put it:

> Suffering from a multiplicity of laws and authorities, fragmentation of political will, lack of concerted planning in governmental affairs and all the privileges accruing to favored estates and orders, the philosophers yearned for a body politic that would be efficiently run by a central administration. . . . Reason could not be expected to prevail in a society split into autonomous, warring powers. . . .[58]

Finally, certain patterns in the eighteenth-century veneration of China and Russia foreshadowed yet another source of the more recent approval of these countries on the part of Western intellectuals—an appreciation of the treatment extended to their fellow intellectuals by the rulers: "China and Russia to the *philosophes,* were unlike in many respects, but they had one thing in common and a most important thing at that: in both these great empires, the men of letters served in places of eminence, at the very center of things. . . . There the powerful knew how to give due honor to the men of letters."[59]

The attitudes toward distant lands, past or present, may also be probed with the help of the metaphors of romantic lover and religious pilgrim. Parallels with the latter are the more obvious. The political pilgrim, like the religious one, is propelled by faith and hope on his visits to the holy places of his secular religion. They may be Lenin's or Mao's tomb (a rather literal parallel), the walls of the Kremlin, the symbolic heart of socialism (as Moscow used to be considered),[60] a commune in China, the setting of sugar-cane harvest in Cuba, a school for reformed prostitutes, a model prison, a new factory, a folk dance festival, a political rally—or any other setting, event, or institution in the countries concerned that symbolizes the realization of the dreams and values of the pilgrim. He returns to his homeland, after the pilgrimage, spiritually refreshed and rejuvenated. The pilgrimage functions either to confirm and authenticate the beliefs already well established, or if they are faint, to produce a conversion experience (which may or may not endure).

The political pilgrim also resembles the romantic lover in that his passions are fueled by the unattainability of the love-object, by the carefully retained obstacles to the fulfillment of his longings. He knows that he will not live in the society he admires but will return to the boredom and comforts of the one he despises. G. B. Shaw spoke for many such travelers when he said, embarking on his return trip from the Soviet Union in 1931, "Tomorrow I leave this land of hope and return to our

Western countries of despair."[61] Although the traveling intellectual seeks to immerse himself in the setting of his ideals, he will not become a part of it. Distance remains, and it helps to conserve the dreams. Usually he knows neither the language nor the unappealing features of the country visited, and he is shielded by his hosts from a close embrace with the object of his affections. Mysteries will persist, although he may succeed in convincing himself that he knows all that is to be known. Both the institutions and individuals representing the longed-for social order will remain partially and poorly known. He can continue idealizing and projecting his desires.

It is in part by a process of elimination that the search for utopia comes to be focused on specific historical societies which become the objects of what Peter Berger called "redemptive expectations."

In our times traditional religious beliefs do not, as a rule, provide psychic sustenance for intellectuals. Likewise, religious innovations, though widely pursued by various churches and denominations, especially in the United States, had only a limited and transient impact. The more traditional secular values—for example the American belief in success, hard work, social mobility, and material acquisition—were also found wanting in the 1930s as later in the 60s. Political ideologies offer alternatives, but their implementation in the domestic context has proved difficult. By contrast, distant countries provide examples of the apparent implementation of the political beliefs attractive to many Western intellectuals.

2

Intellectuals, Politics, and Morality

In every society . . . there are some persons with an unusual sensitivity to the sacred, an uncommon reflectiveness about the nature of their universe and the rules which govern their society. There is in every society a minority of persons who . . . are inquiring and desirous of being in frequent communion with symbols which are more general than the immediate concrete situations of everyday life. . . . In this minority there is a need to externalize this quest in oral and written discourse, in poetic or plastic expression, in historical reminiscence or writing, in ritual performance and acts of worship. This interior need to penetrate beyond the screen of immediate concrete experience marks the existence of the intellectuals in every society.

EDWARD SHILS[1]

. . . unable to hurt a fly [they] are capable of becoming ferocious in the name of an idea. JULIEN BENDA[2]

Essential Attributes and Conflicting Images

Since this is a book about a large segment of contemporary Western intellectuals, we should pause for a more general discussion of what is meant here by intellectuals, how they have been defined by others, and what roles they were allotted in modern society. Reminding ourselves of the ways in which the term is generally used and understood is also necessary for its reevaluation. Although it has not been its prime objective, the findings of this study will suggest certain revisions of the prevailing conceptions of the intellectual.

For Karl Mannheim, perhaps the first major social scientist to be preoccupied with intellectuals, they were "social groups whose special task is to provide an interpretation of the world . . ." for their society. He contrasted the intelligentsia (used instead of "intellectuals") in more static societies with those of more recent times:

The more static a society is, the more likely is it that this stratum will acquire a well-defined status or the position of a caste in that society. Thus the magicians, the Brahmins, the medieval clergy are to be re-

garded as intellectual strata, each of which in its society enjoyed monopolistic control over the moulding of that society's worldview. . . .
   . . . the decisive fact of modern times, in contrast with the situation
during the Middle Ages, is that this monopoly of the ecclesiastical interpretation of the world which was held by the priestly caste is
broken, and in place of a closed and thoroughly organized stratum of
intellectuals, a free intelligentsia has arisen. Its chief characteristic is
that it is increasingly recruited from constantly varying social strata
and life-situations, and that its mode of thought is no longer subject to
regulation by a caste-like organization. . . . the fundamental questioning of thought in modern times does not begin until the collapse
of the intellectual monopoly of the clergy.[3]

Mannheim's observations are suggestive of both the enduring and
changing attributes of the intellectual. Indeed the "special task to provide an interpretation of the world" is crucial, whether it is merely an
unfulfilled aspiration (on the part of intellectuals) or a fact of their social existence in actual societies. Intellectuals would certainly like to
provide such interpretations, and they often do. The extent to which
these are accepted, ignored, ridiculed, or defined as authoritative depends on concrete historical situations and the type of society they live
in. It is useful, in the context of this study, to remember that the intelligentsia (or intellectuals) have a much longer history as the upholders of traditional worldviews and supporters of authority than as
performers of their (more recent) social role which prescribes the questioning of authority, marginality, and highly developed critical faculties.° Not everybody would agree with Mannheim's inclusion of priests,
Brahmins, and magicians of the pre-modern world in the definition of
intellectuals, as will be seen below. Yet if it is accepted that intellectuals
are the group which specializes in the interpretation of the world, then
the priestly groups cannot be excluded, and if so, doubt is cast on the
generally presumed, universal disposition of intellectuals to function as
critics of society.

Mannheim's discussion can serve as a reminder that this older tradition is by no means extinct and has in fact revived vigorously since he
wrote *Ideology and Utopia* in the early 1930s. Today and in the last few
decades, in many countries of the world a new type of intellectual has

° "To view them as something other than iconoclasts or heretics, to dwell on their
importance as 'the creators and carriers of tradition' is to present them in an unaccustomed role." More infrequently it has also been noted that ". . . all debunkers
have a bashfully hidden pedagogic vein." Koestler is one of the few intellectuals
who commented on this duality of "the iconoclastic and the pedagogic, the destructive and constructive. . . ."[4]

arisen whose functions and roles are comparable to those of the medieval priestly groups who had a "monopolistic control over the moulding of that society's world view." I am referring here to what might be
called the party-intellectuals in totalitarian countries who may occupy
important positions in the party apparatus and especially in the so-called
agitation and propaganda departments, or ministries of culture and similar agencies. While such intellectuals may have little autonomy, they do
provide authoritative interpretations of the world backed up by the
power holders of their society. At times even the supreme political
power may be held by an intellectual of sorts (or quasi-intellectual) as
in the case of Lenin, Mao, or Castro. Needless to say it is not the task
or inclination of such intellectuals to engage in a "fundamental questioning of thought." Intellectual revolutionaries, or revolutionary intellectuals
(such as Lenin or Castro) just as readily shed their critical-subversive
roles and impulses in the realm of ideas as in that of political action, and
become the secular priests of the new social order, the upholders of official dogma, and the suppressors of critical tendencies. There is of course
nothing unusual in the perennial change of roles associated with the
move from powerlessness to power. What is more unusual—in the case
of the revolutionary intellectual—is the apparent ease and completeness
with which one outlook on life, style of thought, and set of values are
discarded and replaced by others more suited to the exercise than the
quest for or criticism of power. This transformation has been especially
striking when those involved were Marxists, and its quality may be related to the peculiar suitability of Marxism to be an ideology both for
revolution and status quo—as perceptively noted by Adam Ulam:

> Marxism in power is the exact opposite of Marxism in revolution.
> . . . One may think of Marxism as a two stage ideology. The revolu-
> tionary stage drops off after the revolution. The democratic undertones
> of Marxism are disposed of, revolutionary anarchism is extirpated, and
> the task of construction, in spirit and by means antithetical to the
> revolutionary stage, is begun. The process is neither smooth nor auto-
> matic. It comes in a series of realizations . . . that a faithful applica-
> tion of the principles under which the Party had been carried to power
> would, in the post-revolutionary era, hamper and make impossible the
> construction of socialism.[5]

Another historical perspective on the contemporary usage of the term
is provided by the evolution of the concept of "intelligentsia" in the second half of the nineteenth century in Russia, where groups of educated
middle- and upper-class individuals provided the purest examples of

what we generally mean today by intellectuals. Indeed I see no reason for not using the two terms, "intellectuals" and "intelligentsia," as inter-changeable except for a slight difference in emphasis due to historical factors: "intelligentsia" implies (because of the specific Russian conditions which gave rise to the concept) deeper ideological commitments and concerns with the state of the world.[6] Thus it may be argued that the current value-laden connotations of what constitutes an intellectual (or "true" intellectual) developed largely out of the nineteenth-century Russian historical context which provided unusually fertile ground for the rise of attitudes which combined negation and affirmation.

James Billington, the Russian historian, described the period and the attitudes it generated as follows:

> . . . these alienated urban intellectuals of late imperial Russia created something that can only be described as a new religion. . . .

Preceding and predisposing to these attitudes

> . . . was the almost physiological spasm of negation that swept through the young student generation in the five years between 1858 and 1863. Even though this half decade saw the tide of reform reach its highest point, the basic reaction was not gratitude, but increased discontent.

As to the concept itself,

> . . . the word [intelligentsia] acquired by the last sixties [1860s, that is] the sense both of a group separated from ordinary humanity and of a suprapersonal force active in history, with . . . "critically thinking individuals" as its special agents.[7]

In those decades "intelligentsia" came to be linked with a sense of historical mission which still lurks beneath even the more modest designs of what it means to be an intellectual.

Julien Benda's famous treatise provides another classical point of departure for defining intellectuals:

> I mean that class of men whom I shall designate "the clerks" by which term I mean all those whose activity essentially is *not* the pursuit of practical aims, all those who seek their joy in the practice of an art or a science or metaphysical speculation, in short in the possession of non-material advantages, and hence in a certain manner say: "My kingdom is not of this world." Indeed, throughout history, for more than two thousand years until modern times, I see an uninterrupted series of philosophers, men of religion, men of literature, artists, men of learning . . . whose influence, whose life, were in direct opposition to the realism of the multitudes.[8]

For Benda (and many others after him) intellectuals constituted a disinterested, idealistic elite unconcerned with practical matters and material advantage, immersed in the realm of ideas, in art, science, literature, and reflection.

Lewis Coser, a contemporary sociologist and specialist on the subject, echoes the notions of both Mannheim and Benda:

> Intellectuals live for, rather than off ideas . . . [they] exhibit in their activities a pronounced concern with the core values of society. They . . . seek to provide moral standards and to maintain meaningful general symbols . . . modern intellectuals are descendants of the priestly upholders of sacred tradition, but they are also and at the same time descendants of the biblical prophets, of those inspired madmen who preached in the wilderness far removed from the institutionalized pieties of court and synagogue, castigating the men of power for the wickedness of their ways. Intellectuals are men who never seem satisfied with things as they are, with appeals to custom and usage. They question the truth of the moment in terms of higher and wider truth; they counter appeals to factuality by invoking "impractical ought." They consider themselves special custodians of abstract ideas like reason and justice and truth, jealous guardians of moral standards. . . .

At the same time and in addition to such weighty concerns,

> The modern intellectual is akin to the jester[9] not only because he claims for himself the freedom of unfettered criticism but also because he exhibits what . . . we may call "playfulness.". . . Ideas for him have far more than mere instrumental value: they have terminal value. Intellectuals may not be more curious than other men but theirs is what Veblen has aptly called *idle* curiosity.[10]

This is what might be called "the best case" definition of intellectuals, as it stresses moral uprightness, social conscience, unfettered critical impulses, as well as playfulness and creative curiosity.

Similar, if somewhat more abstract, definitions are offered by other contemporary sociologists. According to Edward Shils:

> Intellectuals are the aggregate of persons in any society who employ in their communication and expression, with relatively higher frequency than most members of their society, symbols of general scope and abstract reference, concerning man, society, nature and the cosmos. . . . Intellectual interests arise from the need to perceive, experience and express—in words, colors, shapes or sounds—a general significance in particular, concrete events.[11]

More simply Robert Nisbet uses the term to refer ". . . to those individuals who quite literally live by their wits or by the resources of their knowledge about some aspect, small or large, of the world, society, or man. Added to this is a certain adversary status with respect to culture and the social order, a built-in polemical, critical, even combative stance with respect to the norms and dogmas by which most of us live."[12]

It has also been proposed that "the contemporary image of the intellectual is . . . essentially a literary one." While this conception is weakened by excluding those belonging to non-literary occupations, there is a very close fit between the literary occupations and the qualities and attributes most commonly associated with intellectuals. Bennet Berger justifies his claim as follows: "In our time literary men have pre-empted the intellectual's role because of their maximal freedom (within their status as literary men) to make large and uncompromising judgements about values and their maximal freedom from institutional restraints."[13]

Berger would probably agree that today many academic settings provide comparable if not identical freedoms for intellectuals for making "large and uncompromising value judgements" and that the restrictions on free expression or on the use of time created by affiliation with academic institutions are far from severe. Likewise the recent vogue for interdisciplinary studies substantially reduced "the parochial demands for specialization." In support of these observations it should also be pointed out that a very substantial number of literary intellectuals make their living from their associations with academic institutions, either as resident writers or, more frequently, members of the faculty. In short, affiliation with academic institutions is highly compatible with the range of attitudes and activities typically associated with being an intellectual at least in Western societies.

Richard Hofstadter, the social historian, emphasizes the distinctive qualities of the mental processes of the intellectual: "we do not think of him as an intellectual if certain qualities are missing from his work—disinterested intelligence, generalizing power, free speculation, fresh observation, creative novelty, radical criticism . . . a playfulness and piety."

Hofstadter also included the guardianship of moral values among the tasks of the intellectuals: ". . . in a very important way the role of the intellectual is inherited from the office of the cleric . . . intellectuals have often tried to serve as the moral antennae of the race, anticipating and if possible clarifying fundamental moral issues. . . . The thinker feels that he ought to be the special custodian of values like reason and justice which are related to his own search for truth. . . ."[14]

In contrast with such emphasis on creativity and guardianship of moral values, a more cynical observer, Tom Wolfe, singles out the status-seeking aspects of the intellectual role, at any rate in contemporary American society where the numbers of those claiming intellectual status has multiplied:

> The intellectual had become not so much an occupational type as a status type. . . . by the 1960s it was no longer necessary to produce literature, scholarship or art—or even be involved in such matters, except as a consumer—in order to qualify as an intellectual. It was only necessary to live *la vie intellectuelle*. A little brown bread in the bread box, a lapsed pledge card to CORE, a stereo and a record rack full of Coltrane and all the Beatles albums from *Revolver* on, white walls, a huge *Dracaena marginata* plant . . . a stack of unread *New York Review of Books* . . . the conviction that America is materialistic and deadened by its Silent Majority . . . three grocery boxes full of pop bottles . . . destined . . . for the Recycling Center, a small uncomfortable European car—that pretty well got the job done.[15]

While one may question the specifics of the life style or consumption patterns used above to define this type of "intellectual," it is hard to deny that characteristic uniformities exist and that certain values are increasingly projected and signified by patterns of consumption among intellectuals (as well as other status groups), thanks to the instant availability of a wide range of goods and services. Certainly clothing, hair styles, eyeglasses, cars owned, vacation spots frequented, furnishings of living rooms, and other components of life style have come to bear increasingly heavy messages of ideology or belief, or have become self-conscious "statements" about the self. We may also view this phenomenon as a variety of a domesticated and popular bohemianism (a cousin of the counter-culture) which used to be a preserve of the struggling artist but has recently become available to large numbers of people in forms modified to be compatible with greater creature comforts. By contrast for Raymond Aron, the French sociologist, creativity represents the core in the definition of the intellectuals, while marginal cases may include "popularizers . . . bent only on success or money, slaves of the supposed tastes of their public. . . ."

Aron, like Mannheim and a few others, is somewhat skeptical of the attribute of alienation as a perennial defining characteristic.

> It is not true that intellectuals as such are hostile to all societies. The writers and scholars of old China "defended and illustrated" the doctrine . . . which put them in the front rank of their society and consecrated the hierarchy. Kings and princes, crowned heroes and wealthy

merchants, have always found poets (not necessarily bad ones) to sing their praises. Neither in Athens nor in Paris, neither in the fifth century before Christ, nor in the nineteenth century of our era, did the writer or the philosopher incline spontaneously towards the party of the people, of liberty or of progress. Admirers of Sparta were to be met with in no small quantity within the walls of Athens, just as in our day, admirers of the Third Reich or the Soviet Union could be met with in the cafes of the Left Bank.[16]

According to Lewis Feuer, the American social philosopher, alienation when present is not so much a result of hostility to those in power, but rather arises out of the sense of exclusion from power. He wrote that "The frustration of their will to rule has been the deepest unconscious source of the intellectual's alienation. With it have been allied . . . their longing to merge themselves . . . with the physical power of the people—peasantry, proletariat, primitive peoples, colored races or backward nations."[17]

Once political orientations and criteria are introduced into definitions of the intellectual, ambiguities arise. Seymour Martin Lipset, among others, raised the question: "The problem of definition is sharpened by the existence of intellectuals in Nazi Germany and the Soviet Union who used, or still use, the tools and training associated with the *intelligentsia* in the service of anti-intellectual values. Are they really intellectuals?"[18]

As we have seen, there are those who stress the disinterested qualities and concerns of the intellectual and those who consider his guardianship of core values important. There is clearly a gap between those who view him as a detached, often marginal and alienated critic of prevailing social values and institutions, and those who see him as a guardian and articulator of major social and moral values.

Peter Viereck, a conservative author, defines intellectuals

> as all who are full-time servants of the Word or the word. This means educators in the broadest sense: philosophers, clergymen, artists, professors, poets, and also . . . editors and the more serious interpreters of news. When they fulfill their civilizing function, intellectuals are the ethical Geiger counters of their society, the warning-signals of conscience. . . . Indirectly and in the long run their influence can be decisive. . . . Even more so today, there being no universal established church as guardian of values.[19]

Not surprisingly, what for some observers satisfies the criteria of being "ethical Geiger counters" or "moral antennae" for others is a sell-out and "treason of clerks." Indeed, a major focus of controversy in the definition

of intellectuals and of their social role has to do with the universality or
essential quality of the adversary role.

Is guarding the core values of society compatible with the critical
function? To what extent does it entail reminding the public of the discrepancy between traditional values and existing realities, of the gap between ideal and actual? *How much* of such a discrepancy justifies the
adversary role? What, if any, balance between social criticism and
affirmation is possible for the intellectual in fidelity to his critical role?

Whatever the ideals and aspirations of intellectuals, and whatever
roles social scientists and the wider public may assign to them, their
activities and attitudes are greatly dependent on certain "objective realities," on the social-political setting of their lives which they may be
powerless to alter. This is particularly true in regard to their ability to
become or remain the critics of society. Historians such as Martin Malia
are more keenly aware of this fact than those not accustomed to comparative-historical perspectives. He has written: "The existence of critical intellectuals . . . presupposes a predominantly secular, pluralistic,
and liberal culture which makes a positive value of free expression and
of intellectual competition in the 'market place of ideas.' "[20]

It may now be possible to summarize the main thrust of the definitions reviewed.

Intellectuals are generally defined on the basis of shared attitudes, interests, and predispositions, rather than on the basis of either occupational specialization, or the substantive content of the ideas they adhere
to. The emphasis is on a "mindset" more than anything else. They are
usually seen as generalists, rather than specialists, having a special concern with ideas which ultimately springs from disinterested sources (although this involvement with ideas may be part of their profession), as
being—to varying degrees—creative, playful, sensitive, inquisitive, and
somewhat impractical.

As far as the moral-ethical aspects are concerned, they are depicted
as idealistic, critical, irreverent, iconoclastic, imbued with altruistic-
ameliorative impulses, deep moral concerns, and commitments.

In regard to their social roles and position they are usually regarded
as outsiders, yet the conscience of society, the upholders of its true
values and ideals. There is obviously a tension between the role of upholding the traditional, or core, values of society and several of the attributes reviewed above. The intellectual cannot be at once an alienated
social critic, the angry conscience of society, and the potential revolu-

tionary on the one hand and on the other, the guardian of prevailing values and traditional (or established) authorities.* Thus the question keeps coming up: Can an intellectual approve of or legitimate a given, social order without ceasing to be a "true intellectual"? In the eyes of some, he cannot; in the eyes of others it depends on the social order. As will be seen later, the intellectuals, whose political attitudes and values are scrutinized in this study, found no difficulty in endorsing and legitimating certain societies—but not their own.

Nevertheless it is safe to say that there is a tradition that looks with suspicion on the intellectual who is too well integrated into his own society, has more than a fair share of status, influence, and access to material goods, and is close to the holders of power. In times of Vietnam they are "New Mandarins" in the eyes of Noam Chomsky and his followers.[21] In times of the New Deal (or the Kennedy administration) proximity to the centers of power is more acceptable. Some Western intellectuals may applaud those of their colleagues in distant revolutionary societies who seize the gun and subsequently head departments of education, propaganda or planning. There are those who insist that the true intellectual must remain pure and untainted by power under any and all circumstances, and there are those who find consorting with the power holders occasionally acceptable and even laudable. The two positions cannot be reconciled.[22]

Idealism and power-hunger, disinterestedness and commitment, the legitimation of the social order and its subversion, autonomy and the readiness to be coopted, the display of critical impulses and their subordination to ideological objectives, reflectiveness and action-orientation—all these are parts of the conflicting images of intellectuals.

Among these contrasts and contradictions this study will pursue primarily those which accompany the tension and fluctuation between the critical and uncritical attitudes of Western intellectuals, the shifts from disbelief to belief.

---

* The tension between these two positions may be somewhat reduced if we substitute for traditional values, ideal or authentic ones. Since most societies deviate most of the time from their own basic, core values, intellectuals have little trouble pointing to the gaps between theory and practice, ideal and actual—one of their favorite activities. Pointing to such discrepancies is an activity that may be congenial for both the embittered critics of the social order and those who wish to bolster it. The former are motivated by the desire to discredit the system (exposing its hypocrisy), the latter by wanting to make it more authentic and stable by reducing the gap between "ought" and "is."

Intellectuals and Power

A number of references have already been made to the political roles and attitudes of intellectuals. It will be recalled that this book evolved out of the interest in (and doubts about) the political judgments of contemporary Western intellectuals. Several among the authors trying to define the essential attributes of intellectuals alluded to their ambiguous attitudes toward power. While most of the authors surveyed stressed the marginal position and the critical roles of intellectuals there were some (e.g. Feuer) who suggested that intellectuals secretly lust for power and that the frustration of this lust explains a great deal about their attitudes and behavior, including the recurring errors in their political judgments.

In the following pages I will examine some major criticisms of intellectuals relating to their political roles. Although in a sense this whole book is an examination of the political judgments of intellectuals and of their attitudes toward politics (defined rather broadly), it will be useful to look at some of the characteristic criticisms which had been made of intellectuals in regard to their attitudes toward power. Needless to say, much of the critical analysis of intellectuals has been the work of intellectuals.

We may start by observing that the very activity or disposition which in more recent times has been a major source of self-esteem of intellectuals, namely the critical, probing, or unmasking disposition, has not always been perceived in unambiguously positive terms. Nietzsche, for instance, wrote that ". . . theoretical man, whom I take to be the intellectual, takes delight in the cast garments and finds his highest satisfaction in the unveiling process itself which proves to him his own power."[23]

Tocqueville saw a clear connection between the generalized "unveiling disposition" and more specific social criticism:

> As a result of this incessant probing into the bases of society in which they lived, they were led both to examine its structure in detail and to criticize its general plan.

There is a fundamental sociological proposition (revived and expanded by Durkheim) buried in this observation. It is that once the nature of the social order ceases to be taken for granted, once its basic premises are closely examined *and* questioned (two processes invariably implying one another), the social fabric begins to unravel and social cohesion erodes. In other words, the raising of fundamental questions about any social order has inherently subversive implications because neither social order nor solidarity can rest on purely or predominantly rational grounds. Thus ratiocination, a key activity of intellectuals, even unwittingly undermines social order. Tocqueville further points out (talking about the pre-revolutionary French intellectuals, the carriers of the values of the Enlightenment) that "their starting point was the same in all cases; and this was the belief that what was wanted was to replace the complex of traditional customs governing the social order of the day by simple, elementary rules deriving from the exercise of the human reason and natural law."[24]*

Tocqueville's criticism of the political attitudes of intellectuals has become paradigmatic of many contemporary critiques. In his view the excessive belief in reason and rationality almost inexorably leads to its opposite: lack of realism and irrationality. He wrote:

> Their very way of living led these writers to indulge in abstract theories and generalizations regarding the nature of the government, and to place blind confidence in these. For living as they did, quite out of touch with practical politics, they lacked the experience which might have tempered their enthusiasm. Thus they completely failed to perceive the very real obstacles in the way of even the most praiseworthy reforms, and to gauge the perils involved in even the most salutary revolutions. . . . As a result, our literary men became much bolder in their speculations, more addicted to general ideas and systems. . . .

Almost identical observations have been made about the Russian intelligentsia, its exclusion from politics, inexperience, and resulting propensity to grand illusions and beliefs divorced from social and political realities. This is worth stressing, since these two groups, the French Enlightenment intellectuals and nineteenth-century Russian intelligentsia, represent the core of the historical tradition and the principal models to which contemporary Western intellectual sensibilities reach back, consciously or not. It follows, according to Tocqueville, that intellectuals are tempted to compensate for the disorder of their social world by constructing imaginary ones:

> Thus alongside the traditional and confused, not to say, chaotic, social system of the day there was gradually built up in men's mind an

---

* Even Lenin, not exactly a child of the Enlightenment and champion of reason, was susceptible to the irresistible appeal of such "simple elementary rules" as was indicated in his *State and Revolution*. In it he suggested that after the masses learned how to administer production and exercise informal social control over the remnants of the former ruling classes ". . . the *necessity* of observing the simple, fundamental rules of human intercourse will very soon become a *habit*."[25]

imaginary ideal society in which all was simple, uniform, coherent, equitable and rational in the full sense of the term.

The men of letters, complained Tocqueville, "imported literary propensities into the political arena."[26]* In a similar spirit some contemporary intellectuals thought to discern and applauded the blurring of the lines between politics and the arts in the countries they visited in the course of their political pilgrimages.

A further example of the lack of realism of "the men of letters" that Tocqueville cited was their belief (still with us in modified forms) that "The only safeguard against State oppression they could think was of universal education."[28]

Tocqueville was only one of many who considered the central problem of intellectuals to be their ambiguous relationship to political power. Intellectuals who entertain great liberating ideas and propose alternatives to existing social and political arrangements find idling on the sidelines unsatisfactory. To nurture great schemes without the hope of translating them into reality is ultimately frustrating. At the same time the occasional and limited involvement with the exercise of power also tends to prove frustrating and often taints the intellectual. He may be accused of assisting a less-than-perfect government, of shoring up a questionable status quo. To become a full-time helper or employee of the government is even more difficult for most Western intellectuals than to serve in some part-time, partial advisory capacity. Therefore power remains a nagging temptation—it can neither be totally renounced nor fully embraced, at least not in Western societies. In Western societies, which have historically provided the maximum freedom of expression and room to work for the intellectual, what comes most naturally is to assume the function of the social critic, "unveiler," "faultfinder," or "discrediter." The inability to resolve the proper relationship to the powers-that-be usually leads to an undifferentiated stance of alienation. In the words of Richard Hofstadter, "it appears then, to be the fate of

---

* The contemporary social philosopher Isaiah Berlin also noted the dangers of the encounter between the literary-artistic temperament and politics, and of the application of artistic sensibilities to matters social and political: ". . . I may conceive myself as an inspired artist, who moulds men into patterns in the light of his unique vision, as painters combine colors or composers sounds; humanity is the raw material upon which I impose my creative will; even though men suffer and die in the process, they are lifted by it to a height to which they could never have risen without my coercive—but creative—violation of their lives. This is the argument used by every dictator, inquisitor, and bully who seeks some moral, or even aesthetic, justification for his conduct."[27]

intellectuals either to berate their exclusion from wealth, success, and reputation, or to be seized by guilt when they overcome exclusion. They are troubled, for example, when power disregards the counsels of intellect, but because they fear corruption they are even more troubled when power comes to intellect for counsel." Thus alienation becomes something of an obligation—moral, social, and political. Again, as Hofstadter points out, this is a tradition which springs not only from political sources but also bohemian-artistic ones. ("Their conviction that alienation is a kind of value in itself has a double historical root in romantic individualism and in Marxism. For more than a century and a half the position of creative talent everywhere in the bourgeois world has been such as to make us aware of the persistent tension between the creative individual and the demands of society.")[29]

This "forced morality of alienation" may be the most obvious source of the political misjudgments and misperceptions of Western intellectuals, or at any rate of large numbers among them. Lewis Feuer, one of the most outspoken contemporary critics of intellectuals, believes that

> The Intellectual Elite in both the United States and Europe has a record of recurrent misjudgement and misperception of social reality. Its members have yielded to wish fulfillment, emotional indulgence and even insincerity while claiming to the public at large that they were inspired by scientific reasoning. They have too often also turned out to be authoritarians rather than democrats.[*]

Feuer also believes that the alienation of such intellectuals stems ". . . basically from an obstructed will to rule."[31] By contrast, it has also been argued that the adversary roles and attitudes of Western intellectuals stem less from exclusion from power, social marginality, or the type of education received but rather from the nature of the societies they belong to, that is, capitalist society, which has created an ethos conducive to critical thinking and aversion to illusions. Thus Joseph Schumpeter believes that "capitalism creates a critical frame of mind, which, after having destroyed the moral authority of so many other institutions, in the end turns against its own; the bourgeois finds to his

---

[*] A similar view has been held by Robert Conquest: "It has long been the misfortune of the intelligentsia that its most vocal section has been taken as its representative and plenipotentiary. For this has the worst record of any part of the community when it comes to judging foreign affairs. Current lists of signatories contain stratum after stratum of names recognisable to political geologists as what a ruder commentator might call Guilty Men—apologists for the Moscow Trials, supporters of the 1940 movement for peace with Hitler, signers of Stalin's 'peace' appeal, excusers of North Korean Aggression, sponsors of the Germ Warfare hoax, and so on . . ."[30]

amazement that the rationalist attitude does not stop at the credentials of kings and popes but goes on to attack private property and the whole scheme of bourgeois values."[32]

There is more than a faint parallel between Schumpeter's view of capitalism (as its own gravedigger, which subjects everything to the merciless scrutiny of rationalistic critical inquiry) and Marx's perception of capitalism as a ruthless demystifying force that "strips away" all that is hallowed in social institutions and relations, a system that in the final analysis delegitimates itself by its own inexorable drive toward secularization, by eroding all sacred tradition.* To be sure Marx did not go so far as to suggest that a social system may collapse as a result of "delegitimation," the loss of ideological-spiritual justification rather than that of economic malfunctioning and contradictions.

George Orwell was among those who believed that the political attitudes (and errors) of intellectuals were rooted in their exclusion from power: "The whole left-wing ideology, scientific and Utopian, was evolved by people who had no immediate prospects of attaining power."[34] In other words, exclusion from power led to ignorance, illusions, and misplaced political sympathies, the most prominent being sympathy toward the Soviet Union and associated left-wing causes in recent times. Orwell was a connoisseur of the political naiveté (or worse) of Western intellectuals and a relentless critic of their double standards in judging Western societies and the Soviet Union. He bitterly concluded that Western intellectuals cared less about free expression than ordinary people, the common man.

Another prominent contemporary and critic of the political obtuseness of Western intellectuals was Arthur Koestler. Both Orwell and Koestler arrived at their critical views of their fellow intellectuals from an earlier

---

* Marx has written: "The bourgeoisie . . . has put an end to all feudal, patriarchal, idyllic relations. It has pitilessly torn asunder the motley feudal ties that bound man to his 'natural superiors,' and has left remaining no other nexus between man and man than naked self-interest, than callous 'cash payment.' It has drowned the most heavenly ecstasies of religious fervour, of chivalrous enthusiasm, of philistine sentimentalism, in the icy water of egotistical calculation. It has resolved personal worth into exchange value. . . .

"The bourgeoisie has stripped of its halo every occupation hitherto honoured and looked up to with reverent awe. . . .

"The bourgeoisie has torn away from the family its sentimental veil. . . .

". . . All fixed, fast-frozen relations, with their train of ancient and venerable prejudices and opinions, are swept away, all new-formed ones become antiquated before they can ossify. All that is solid melts into air, all that is holy is profaned . . ."[33]

involvement with left-wing causes, including participation in the Spanish Civil War on the side of the anti-Franco forces. They differed in that Orwell never belonged to the Communist party whereas Koestler did. Likewise Orwell did not visit the Soviet Union, while Koestler had.

Koestler (like Orwell) was outraged by the willingness of left-wing intellectuals to support political systems and movements—that is, the Soviet Union and Communist parties over which it had control—devoted to the destruction of free speech and other intellectual freedoms. He too had found disturbing the spectacle of Western intellectuals, who, while enjoying a wide range of civil liberties and free expression, admired from their comfortable niche of estrangement societies and movements where these rights were non-existent.[35]

Koestler offered a summary of what he considered the "deadly fallacies" of the politics of Western intellectuals. It included the belief that the Soviet system is a socialist one (a fallacy no longer widespread); the attitude of "soul-searching" which makes it difficult for Western intellectuals to be critical of the Soviet system as long as imperfections remain in Western democracies; the equation of the flaws of Western societies with those of the Soviet Union (e.g., Hollywood "purges" versus Moscow Purges); the "anti-anti attitude" (more recently known as anti-anti-communism),[36] that is, the fear of being labeled anti-communist and the resulting identification of the liberal Western intellectual with politically unsavory elements in his society (an attitude very much alive).[37]

It would be a serious omission to neglect pointing out that the Vietnam War and American participation in it have substantially changed the terms of the discourse on these topics. Throughout the 1960s many alienated Western intellectuals no longer accepted the contrast between totalitarianism and Western democracy as presented by Koestler and others sharing his outlook. The United States itself was, in these years, likened to a totalitarian, fascist, or Nazi system. The inclination to make what the social critics regarded as fine distinctions has become increasingly attenuated. Thus in the eyes of many it was no longer the question of choosing between bad and worse, or tolerable and intolerable, but between either two equally (if somewhat differently) unappealing systems, or between two of which the non-Western one was actually more appealing at least in the long run. Thus for example while by no means pro-Soviet, Marcuse found the Soviet system superior in its *potentials*.[38]

In the 1960s, in the United States at any rate, a more clear-cut split emerged between intellectuals working for the government (usually in some advisory-consultative capacity) and the social critics "uncontaminated" by such connections. The segment of intellectuals associated with the government was subsequently disowned by the spokesmen of the estranged intellectual subculture, as almost every form of work for, or with, the government came to be defined as odious. A minor witch-hunt emerged at many universities, focused on the financial sources of research grants. In this period there was also an upsurge of criticism of one intellectual by another on grounds of selling out to the powers-that-be by assisting the government in devising or implementing its foreign policy, in Vietnam and elsewhere. Cooperation with the military or the CIA by academics was particularly severely censured. In short, a part of the intellectual community was chastised by the other for not remaining properly alienated from the system.

Noam Chomsky was probably the most prominent exponent of these views, expressed in his influential essay on the responsibility of intellectuals.[39] Rather than offering general propositions as to these responsibilities, the essay is almost exclusively an attack on the relatively small number of American intellectuals who supported the U.S. government policies on Vietnam and provided advice or legitimation for these policies. Chomsky was also (almost equally) angry at those who, while not working for the government, stood aside in comparative indifference and failed to protest.* Underlying the essay is a deeper hostility toward the intellectual who ceases to be "free floating" and instead "sells out" by becoming an adviser, a "scholar-expert," or "academic apologist" or "welfare state technician" in the service of the government. There are also undertones of a relentless hostility toward technology, behavioristic social science, and more importantly, American intellectuals who are not, or are only insufficiently, estranged from their government and society, and who "achieved power and affluence." Although Chomsky proposes unarguably that the responsibility of intellectuals is "to speak the truth and expose lies," nothing in his essay suggests that these activities should ever be directed at targets other than the government of the

---

* Like Sartre (whose views will be discussed below) Chomsky too evinces a peculiar compulsion to obliterate the distinction between actual misdeeds and passivity. Thus if you don't fight some injustices you are just as guilty as if you committed them. This passionate refusal to take more differentiated political views is a hallmark of many contemporary intellectuals and it often appears in combination with the fervent embrace of collective guilt. Chomsky seems to overlook that when all are equally responsible for the specific misdeed of some, or when you fail to establish the distinction between doing and not doing, the whole idea of responsibility washes away. When all are guilty nobody is guilty in any meaningful sense. Eldridge Cleaver, in his radical phase, popularized this idea by proposing that "if you are not a part of the solution, you are part of the problem."

United States. His single-minded preoccupation with the United States as the fountainhead of all evil in this world—shared by many Western (and non-Western) intellectuals—reflected the spirit of the times (the 1960s and the Vietnam War protest) but also a genuine inability to conceive of any country other than the U.S. as being capable of committing significant historical outrages or conducting aggressive policies.

Chomsky's discourse suggests three archetypal positions intellectuals may take toward political power. The first, to which the most lip-service has been paid in recent times, is never to get involved; any association with power corrupts and subverts the integrity and critical impulses of the intellectual. To perform his true functions and duties the authentic intellectual must stand apart; he must remain detached from the exercise of power (and the temptations of the marketplace). He must observe, expose, and analyze from the sidelines.

The second position, while it recognizes the essential merits of detachment and non-involvement, allows for a restrained, carefully limited involvement with the powers-that-be (unless they are totally and self-evidently evil and beyond redemption). The intellectual in such a limited advisory association would help to purify, tame, and enlighten the exercise of power from the inside while retaining mental reservations. This is a circumscribed involvement which precludes identification with the power-holders.

Adherents to the third position simply propose that intellectuals should under no circumstances get mixed up with bad political systems, while nothing should restrain them from plunging into total commitment to a good political cause or system to which their skills and talents should be made fully available. In our times this advice comes, as a rule, from those who define bad systems as Western, pluralistic, capitalistic industrial societies and the good ones as the adherents of some type of left-wing revolutionary doctrine of Leninist derivation.

While a fair amount has been written here (and elsewhere) about the political attitudes and errors of Western intellectuals connected with their sympathy for Marxist movements and regimes (especially of the earlier, pro-Soviet variety) much less is known and has been said about political misjudgments of the opposite character. There is, for example, a very limited awareness today in the Western countries, and especially among the younger generations, of the popularity Nazism enjoyed among university students in Germany in the 1920s and 30s and of the substantial moral and political support German intellectuals gave to the Nazi movement and regime. Wilhelm Röpke, for instance, claims that "There is scarcely another class in Germany that failed so fatally as that of the intellectuals in general . . ." in resisting Nazism, and that ". . . the faculties of social science provided a special opportunity for practicing intellectual treachery and preparing the way for Nazism."[40] Likewise few among our contemporaries know, or care to remember that

> As many adhering to the Left journeyed to the USSR, there to offer thanks and admire all that they were shown, so did their corresponding type of the Right make Hitler their hero and the Third Reich their paradise. If the Rev. Hewlett Johnson detected in the Soviet regime the highest extant realization of Christian principles, Major Yeats-Brown . . . made the more guarded statement that it was his "honest conviction that there is more real Christianity in Germany today than there ever was under the Weimar Republic." . . . Corresponding to the ladies who had met Russians whose eyes glowed proudly when Stalin's name was mentioned, were other ladies who had met Germans whose eyes similarly glowed when Hitler's name was mentioned. . . . Against Lord Passfield [Sidney Webb] reverent in Moscow, might be set Lord Rothermere reverent in Munich.[41]

Certainly the appeals of Nazism and fascism were more short-lived, yet not altogether different from the appeals of communism. Stephen Spender, among others, noted that "Fascism offered political answers to criticisms of modern technological society . . . ," an attribute which it shares more with what used to be known as the New Left (in the 1960s) than with the more traditional Left. Likewise New Left sympathies toward assorted left-wing regimes and movements in more recent times resembled the attitudes of intellectuals decades earlier ". . . who supported Fascism . . . more because they were against other politics than because they were for it."[42]

Alastair Hamilton, one of the few students of the appeal of fascism to intellectuals, thought that "the barrier between those who chose Communism and those who preferred Fascism seems to me, in many cases, so slim that we are less than entitled to say that a certain type of man, a certain type of psychology tended towards Fascism." He believed that what united many intellectuals who ultimately ended up as fascist or communist sympathizers respectively, was their anti-democratic or authoritarian dispositions. "These were rebels whose main enemy was the status quo, the quiet, peaceful, complacent and somewhat hypocritical liberal State." Another attribute of fascism that intellectuals found appealing (and which in turn resembles an appeal of communism) "was the prospect of the 'new man,' the elite of heroic supermen, 'artist-tyrants' of whom Nietzsche had dreamt° . . . The myth of the 'new man' was connected, in its turn, with the desire for renewal, for revival, for invigoration . . ." Lastly, fascism also appealed to intellectuals because it offered a solution to the problem of anonymity which began to haunt intellectuals in this century. It promised to solve the problem of the frustrated need for self-assertion and individual distinctiveness *and* that of belonging and community at one stroke.[43]

It was not my intention to discuss or document here the similarities between the appeals of fascism and communism to certain Western intellectuals. I merely wished to remind the reader that the attraction of a sizeable number of famous Western intellectuals† to fascism was neither totally insignificant nor is it irrelevant for a better understanding of the political attitudes this study is concerned with. The sympathy with fascism, however short-lived, was an aspect of the politics of contemporary Western intellectuals which cannot go unmentioned in a study which claims at least in part to be an exploration of their political misjudgments.

Among the factors which help to explain the intellectuals' attitudes toward political power is the unresolved tension between their elitism and egalitarianism (or individualism and collectivism). Although rarely confronted, many contemporary Western intellectuals suffer from the clash between their declared commitment to equality and a sense of belonging to a select group. Because of the latter, intellectuals often believe that they deserve power, although this conviction is not readily admitted or expressed. The intellectual's desire for, or sense of, entitlement to power derives from the belief in his superior, elite status. This claim to superiority follows in part from the value placed on knowledge in contemporary societies but even more from the functions intellectuals have increasingly assumed in the articulation of social values. As Andrew Greeley puts it, "The most basic value [of intellectuals] is the conviction that the articulation of ideas is the most dignified form of human activ-

---

° As will be shown later, images of heroic super-men were also attractive for left-wing Western intellectuals in the 1960s, among them especially for Sartre who had discovered their most recent personifications among the Cuban leaders of Castro's Cuba.

† Such distinguished intellectuals include W. B. Yeats, Ezra Pound, T. S. Eliot, G. B. Shaw (subsequently he turned to the Soviet Union), Henry Williamson, James Burnham, Lincoln Steffens (who like Shaw also abandoned fascism for communism), Oswald Spengler, Ernst Junger, Martin Heidegger, Charles Maurras, Louis Céline, Jean Cocteau, Filippo Marinetti, Benedetto Croce, Luigi Pirandello, Gabriel d'Annunzio, and Giovanni Gentile.

ity; and closely related is the notion that those whose role it is in society to articulate ideas are not only the most superior members of that society, but also the ones really qualified to run it."[44]

The intellectual, whether in his role as a morally involved social critic, creative artist-thinker, or—occasionally—expert-adviser, has *some* reason to believe that he knows more about certain things than most of his fellow citizens. Such a sense of superiority, or elite consciousness, is especially strong when the intellectual's self-image is fortified by either some form of certification, or social recognition, or both. Paradoxically even the most embittered and critical Western intellectuals have been the recipients of such recognition and rewards. Most Western intellectuals dealt with in this study enjoyed high social status, received substantial financial compensation for their work, and rose to high positions in various hierarchies (academic, literary, artistic, publishing, and so on). Such rewards and recognition obviously enhance the sense of self-importance of the contemporary Western intellectual and in turn sharpen the conflict between his egalitarian values and sense of superiority over the masses, and over their undistinguished political representatives. (The contempt for the democratic politician is particularly pronounced among American intellectuals.) As will be more fully discussed later, the commitment to equality is the cornerstone of the value system of intellectuals; it is reflected in their criticism of inequality in their own societies and in their praise of others which have attained a greater measure of equality or seek to do so. Yet, concurrently the intellectuals on their political tours were much impressed by the important political roles of intellectuals in these countries, by their proximity to the supreme power-holders, by the apparent commitment of these regimes to intellectual values and sometimes also by the privileges granted to intellectuals.

The tension between the professed egalitarianism and the benevolent, paternalistic elitism of self-selected leaders (frequently of an intellectual background) is especially noteworthy in revolutionary situations and regimes. The revolutionary must at once believe in his mission and his superior skills but also in the limitless perfectibility of the masses. Since he cannot help thinking of himself as their saviour, uplifter, and selfless mobilizer, he cannot also think of himself as being one of them, and no better than they. To be in a position of leadership *and* to feel equal to the led is a difficult psychological feat.

In its early phases the Soviet system satisfied such contradictory yearnings shared by many Western intellectuals:

Everyone [that is, who visited the USSR] found what he wanted most, and a sense of superiority into the bargain. It was easy to feel superior to the rabble who stood on lines, who were shooed off trains to make way for the cash customers, who regarded a tweed skirt or a fountain pen as a miracle, who were rationed and liquidated and mobilized for parades. *The only place in the world where you could stand at the apex with dictators and merge ecstatically with the masses simultaneously: a synthesis of absolute power and absolute humility* heretofore vouchsafed only to rare mystics and martyrs.[45]

To be sure, it proved impossible to sustain this synthesis at any rate in the Soviet context. Nonetheless many Western intellectuals caught in the dilemma of being both elitists and egalitarians persevered in their efforts to resolve the conflict by humbling themselves in front of the mythical masses* and fantasizing about their authenticity. In an interview in 1971 Sartre said:

Today it is sheer bad faith, hence counter-revolutionary, for the intellectual to dwell on his own problems instead of realizing that he is an intellectual because of the masses and through them; [he did not elaborate on this mysterious proposition] that he owes his knowledge to them . . . he must be dedicated to work for their problems not his own.

. . . I was only the mouthpiece of the miners . . .

In the same interview he also expressed the hope that "names be altogether eliminated" from the revolutionary press he was helping to publish. Yet there was an irrepressible and unselfconscious paternalism: "Each time there is a seizure of a plant by workers, for example, our job is to make sure that it is the workers themselves who explain why they did it, what they felt and learned from it. Our job is to help them, etc., but never interpreting them, never telling them what they should say." Trying further to clarify his relationship with the masses or the workers he added: "It is that I am with workers in actions that counts, not the

---

* It should be noted that the sociological components of the mythical concept "The Masses" are rather unstable. While for almost a century, alienated Western intellectuals identified the masses with the proletariat, or the industrial workers, since the 1960s the emphasis has shifted to other conceptions of the masses. The newly idealized version of the masses often includes, especially in the United States, non-white slum residents, convicts, and students. Special place is reserved in the current conceptions of the progressive masses (such as entertained by Sartre) for the young, including adolescents and occasionally even children as yet uncorrupted by their elders. As far as non-Western societies are concerned, the poor peasants (perhaps even tribesmen?) have also gained admission to the category.

fact that I may live differently and better in Paris. No, language is a much more serious problem. . . . You know it's much easier for a philosopher to explain a new concept to another philosopher than to a child. Because the child, with all its naiveté, asks the real questions. So do the workers." The basis of Sartre's faith in the masses and of his conviction that intellectuals are in their debt remains obscure. The masses for Sartre, as for many other intellectuals, are an abstraction apparently made up of equal imaginary parts of authenticity, innocence, strength, and simplicity, qualities intellectuals either rarely experience or do not have in sufficient supply.

Throughout the discussion Sartre exhibited considerable hostility toward his fellow intellectuals. His position seemed to be that intellectuals are guilty and despicable as long as they behave like intellectuals; they can only redeem themselves by "commitment," by political action and association with the mythical workers. He said, for example, "the intellectual who does all his fighting from an office is counterrevolutionary today, no matter what he writes." Sartre also entertained a grotesquely exaggerated and undifferentiated view of the responsibility of intellectuals that makes sense only as a mirror image of a correspondingly inflated notion of their political and social importance:

> A leftist intellectual . . . forsakes his privileges, or tries to, in action. . . . A white leftist intellectual in America, I presume, understands that because he is white he has certain privileges which he must smash through direct action [a euphemism for the violence Sartre approved of]. Not to do so is to be guilty of murder of the blacks—just as much as if he actually pulled triggers that killed . . . the Black Panthers murdered by the police, by the system. . . . the intellectual who does not put his body as well as his mind on the line against the system is fundamentally supporting the system—and should be judged accordingly.
> . . . when the youth confronts the police our job is not only to show that it is the police who are the violent ones but to join the youth in counterviolence.
> . . . the intellectual, more than anyone else . . . must understand and act accordingly, that there are only two types of people: the innocent and the guilty. . . .[46]

Sartre's refusal to entertain distinctions finer than between guilty and innocent and his compensatory concern with action and commitment reflected a certain immoderation that is often characteristic of the intellectual's attitude to politics and power. He (like Chomsky) is contemptuous of intellectuals who do not share his political beliefs and are disinclined to participate in the symbolic political actions he favors (such as distributing "revolutionary" newspapers or participating in demonstrations).

The spurts of veneration for manual labor in political systems run by intellectuals (or erstwhile intellectuals) is also related to the issues raised here. It is unlikely to be an accident that in Cuba, ruled by a semi-intellectual like Castro (earlier in association with Che Guevara), there has been an unusually great emphasis on the redeeming qualities of manual labor—a policy almost compensatory in style. The same was true in China, especially during the Cultural Revolution. Again, Mao's quasi-intellectual background and aspirations may provide some clues for the veneration of manual labor and the belief in its purifying qualities.* By contrast, in a country like the Soviet Union, which has been run for some time by former peasants and workers, the stress on the redeeming qualities of manual labor has been noticeably more muted and the attempts to escape it more willingly tolerated. Perhaps the attitudes to manual labor provide clues to the conflicts that rend the intellectual psyche. The more ambivalence toward the life of the mind, and the more guilt over the privileges it can secure, the greater the outward emphasis on the superior virtues of physical exertions and manual labor. Thus it may be possible to conjecture about the relative political weight of intellectuals (or former intellectuals) in revolutionary systems on the basis of the official emphasis placed on manual labor.

The changing balance between elitism and egalitarianism in the post-revolutionary period is illustrated by Che Guevara's observation about leadership. He said: "Revolutionary institutions . . . permit the *natural selection* of those who are *destined to march in the vanguard,* and who dispense rewards and punishments to those who fulfill their duty or act against the society under construction."[47] Such undisguised elitism—and a revealing terminology (natural selection, destiny, marching vanguard) more congenial with the spirit and hero worship of fascist movements and ideologies than with Marxism—is another reminder of the apparently insurmountable problems revolutionary (and many non-revolutionary) intellectuals face in their relationship to the masses and in their attempts to resolve the conflict between their own elitism and egalitarianism. In recent history this conflict was all too often settled by the elitist impulses gaining the upper hand. Eric Hansen, a political scientist, writes:

---

* The obsession of the highly educated, formerly Francophile rulers of Cambodia with transforming the entire population into agricultural laborers is a more recent example of the same phenomenon. (I was referring to the Pol Pot regime since ousted by the Vietnamese.)

> As all intellectual-led social movements from Martin Luther to Mao Tse-tung indicate, the intellectual's sympathies with the plight of the masses cools considerably with access to power. The very introverted nature of intellectuality, the relative inability to move out into the other fellow's place . . . tends to substitute dogma, polemics, and fiat for dialogue and democracy. The intellectual because he is deficient in the quality of empathy, except in the poetic sense, tends to love all mankind in general while being intolerant toward the short-comings and imperfections of men in particular.[48]

Hansen's observations pinpoint another characteristic form the elitism of intellectuals may take, namely their tendency to dismiss the needs of ordinary people for certain freedoms on the assumption that such requirements are the luxury of the few while the masses should rightfully concern themselves with satisfying their more immediate material needs. From Lincoln Steffens to George Bernard Shaw, Scott Nearing (the long-lived American radical), and all the way to Susan Sontag the line stretches in unbroken continuity as far as such attitudes are concerned. All of them, and many others, made it clear that they could not live in the restrictive societies they had visited and admired. Nonetheless they highly recommended them to others, and especially to the native residents. Lincoln Steffens said it for all his fellow-pilgrims and successors:

> . . . I am a patriot for Russia; the Future is there; Russia will win out and it will save the world. That is my belief. But I don't want to live there.

Scott Nearing explained his decision to stay in the United States, notwithstanding his profound revulsion from American society:

> . . . I decided that, committed to the socialization of the planet earth, my post of duty was in the United States, difficult as it was to live in. . . . I had made visits to socialist countries and would continue to do so but my base of operations must remain in the West because my roots were there and also a possibility that I could still make a contribution to the thinking and attitudes of at least a few of my fellow Americans.[49]

The avowed avoidance of ethnocentrism, that is, the imposition of one's own cultural values and standards on other societies, often served to justify such paradoxical attitudes and bolstered the belief that non-Western masses cheerfully accept deprivations Western intellectuals would find painful. Needless to say, such beliefs have little empirical basis and, as Peter Berger has shown, those who entertain them are unaware that many basic values of non-Western societies also support important personal and group freedoms and rights.[50]

While the unresolved conflict between elitism and egalitarianism underlies the attitudes of many intellectuals toward political power, it is even more difficult for them to arrive at a satisfactory position toward the possession of power per se. While I do not doubt that there are many intellectuals who lust for power and relish it when attained, a far greater number of them, I believe, remain torn between the desire for it and the awareness of the moral dilemmas its possession creates.

Moral Impulses and Political Preferences

As was shown earlier, a key component in the conception of the intellectual is a highly developed moral sensibility, a concern with moral values and their social-political implications. Correspondingly, authentic intellectuals are characterized by strong value commitments and their vigorous expression. The moral impulses and political stands of intellectuals are supposed to be joined together, not by self-interest but by higher purpose.

In our times there appears to be a new outpouring and proliferation of moral passion connected with a great variety of political commitments and the fragmentation of values in contemporary Western societies. Intellectuals have been in the forefront of articulating moral sentiments and applying them to matters political. It often seems that in the contemporary world moral passion and indignation have become more potent political forces than they used to be, or at least there is a greater propensity to advance moralistic arguments in the political arena than ever before. Likewise, intense commitments and partisanship have resulted in new ways of suppressing moral indignation, in rationalizing and legitimating moral outrages. In short, double standards in moral-political judgment have achieved unusual prominence.

A possible explanation of this development might be that intensified political commitments exert a greater pressure toward prejudgment and the biased weighing of evidence. Gwynn Nettler, a Canadian sociologist, proposed that "it is in the ethico-political arena that we are most prone to use our heads to justify our interest and to rationalize our personal discontent . . ." and that there is the "possibility that ethico-political commitment produces inaccurate use of information."[51]

Much of this book suggests that this may indeed very often be the case. Both when a social system is rejected and when it is admired, information and evidence turn out to be secondary to predisposition. Intellectuals more than most people are highly skilled in finding factual "bases" to support their values.

It is not clear why moral concerns and rationalizations have increasingly invaded politics without political practices themselves becoming more infused with moral principles and considerations. Probably such developments are connected with the displacement of meaning-seeking impulses from the religious to the secular-political sphere. Perhaps as long as most people sought and found some meaning in life with the help of religion—and concurrently managed to separate the religious from the political compartment—it was easier to be brutally candid about the pursuit of political power and interest, and to resist camouflaging personal and group interest in lofty moralizing justifications. Correspondingly, as politics has become more ideological, the temptation to moralize about its ends and practices has become irresistible. This may in part explain the phenomenon being discussed here, namely the proliferation of moral standards and judgments on the part of intellectuals and the wide variety of moral legitimations of unappealing political practices.

Indeed the "rediscovery" that the intensity (or degree) of moral passion could not be adequately explained by the quality of the acts which provoked it may be added to the motives which prompted me to undertake this study. In other words, I noted that the magnitude of a moral outrage (as defined for example by the number of human beings killed on the basis of some a priori, abstract scheme or criteria) had, strangely enough, little to do with the way people, and especially intellectuals, reacted to it. Given the fact that moral sentiments, indignation and compassion alike, play a large part in social and political affairs, the issue seemed worth investigating and pondering.

International affairs, and particularly the relationship between outrages commited in various parts of the world and the varied public responses to them, provide striking examples of the peculiar patterns of moral indignation and indifference and the multiplicity of double standards. Outrages and atrocities of gigantic proportion are often all but ignored, meekly lamented or barely protested, while other acts or events, morally objectionable but of more modest dimensions, provoke vocal and prolonged protest. If one were to assume that the number of people and especially civilians mistreated in any particular conflict should lead one to anticipate or predict the intensity of moral indignation, many events of the recent past and the response to them deflate such expectations.

The "selective genocide" in Burundi in the early 1970s was among the outrages of recent times which provoked little protest from intellectuals, governments, or churches, African or Western.[52] A few years later the more publicized massacres in Uganda failed to get the attention (let alone action) of either the United Nations or the organization of African states.[53] A less colorful but more durable dictator in the African state of Guinea proudly observed that "A denunciation can bring about the arrest of anyone anywhere in this country in five minutes," and there was much else to indicate that this was indeed an exceptionally brutal police state lavishly meting out death sentences.[54] Little public criticism greeted such events as was also the case with Equatorial Guinea, where, according to Jack Anderson, an even more unrestrained dictator ". . . Francisco Macie . . . has been executing everyone he fancies may be against him. He celebrated one Christmas Eve by hanging and shooting 150 of his countrymen in a soccer stadium. . . ."[55] Neither Western or Third World intellectuals nor public opinion was interested in or moved by the fate of the Kurds napalmed, bombed, and otherwise denied self-determination by Iraq and Iran respectively.[56] Tribesmen in Laos could count on massive international unconcern as they were abandoned to the tender mercies of their Vietnamese neighbors and their Soviet patron willing to try out new weapons (chemical in this case) on these enemies of progress.[57] As we move back in time, the forgotten victims of history and power politics multiply. Few tears were shed by Western intellectuals for the subjects of "Operation Keelhaul," the "forcible repatriation of Displaced Soviet citizens" numbering in the hundreds of thousands after World War II.[58] While vigorous protest greeted the misdeeds of American troops in Vietnam, little was said about the atrocities committed by the other side. Mary McCarthy, the American writer, could not, for example, believe that the North Vietnamese were capable of mistreating American prisoners; according to her they were making a careful distinction between the person and his crime. In regard to the Hue massacres she could not accept that the other side could have done it: "There is no way of knowing what really happened. . . . I should prefer to think that it was the Americans. . . ."[59]

Currently another chapter is being written in the long history of selective moral indignation and compassion by many former champions of political morality in connection with the hundreds of thousands of refugees pouring out of Indochina, once more "voting with their feet" as ordinary people have done so many times during the past half century. William Kunstler, the radical lawyer, said "he sympathizes with the plight of the boat people but added that the problem is inevitable following the massive upheaval created by the U.S. . . ."[60] Even the Pol Pot regime of Cambodia, credited with the killing of millions of people, found its defenders among Western intellectuals, as Noam Chomsky emerged to offer a most striking personification of selective moral outrage. His attempts to minimize the atrocities in Cambodia were reminiscent of the pleadings of the last-ditch defenders of Stalin's Russia for whom there was never enough solid evidence of the Purges and Soviet concentration camps. With vehement scorn and certainty Chomsky dismissed "the tales of Communist atrocities" (still "tales" for him in 1977) as he cited, accepted, or rejected with the required selectivity the available evidence. Alluding to the findings of unnamed but "highly qualified specialists"* (whom he does not quote for "limitations of space" in an article well over 6000 words and otherwise teeming with quotations) "who have studied the full range of evidence"—an activity he reserved for those whose views he found congenial—Chomsky claimed that these experts concluded, in his words, that "executions numbered at most in the thousands; that these were localized in areas of limited Khmer Rouge influence and unusual peasant discontent where brutal revenge killings were aggravated by the threat of starvation resulting from American destruction and killing." Elsewhere in this article, in a startling reversal of his skepticism about refugee accounts ("extremely unreliable"), he prefers to accept the explanation given by the revolutionary government for the evacuation of Phnom Penh (shortage of food) and criticizes François Ponchaud for arguing that it was due to political-ideological reasons.[62]

Chomsky exemplifies the morally selective intellectual who cannot revise or modify his political commitments—in this case a very deep and emotional rejection of the United States and all it stands for. Everything seems to follow from this commitment, from this basic hostility. The social critic of this type will defend the enemies of his enemies (Cambodia in this case) who are by definition his friends and allies. He cannot acknowledge evil in the world—or rise to genuine indignation about it—

---

* It was said of Chomsky that he "drew on his training in the field of linguistics to create an impression of scrupulous reasoning and meticulous scholarship; on the surface his political articles bore all the marks of responsible scholarly discourse, including—always including—a large number of footnotes."[61]

if there is no way to implicate the prime object of hate, in this case the United States. Correspondingly he will display great industry and ingenuity to show that the United States is culpable in all significant moral outrages in the world in our times.* Chomsky, like many others, has in his mind a rigidly fixed scenario as to the representatives and embodiments of good and evil in our times. The case of Cambodia does not quite fit into his moral universe, but he tries his best to squeeze it in. The juices of his moral indignation will not flow unless and until his candidates of evil can be made to bear the responsibility.

Among the factors which inhibit a more impartial expression of moral impulses among Western intellectuals is the largely unverifiable and unexamined article of faith of our times, that left-wing authoritarian regimes are singularly adept at improving the material conditions of life for the masses. While sympathizers may concede that such improvements are attained at the expense of certain civil liberties, there is widespread belief that poor people have no interest in personal freedom. According to a study published by the American Friends Service Committee (the Quakers), "Those in misery cry 'Bread' and as long as they do not have bread they do not, and will not, respond to our slogan of 'Liberty.'"[64] The point of view quoted is deeply entrenched and persists despite the tens of millions of people who left left-wing dictatorships as much for economic as for political reasons, indicating that the alternatives do not reduce to "bread" or "liberty" but that in such political systems both tend to be in short supply. (The 1980 exodus from Cuba provides the most recent example of this.)

Many Western intellectuals are also reluctant to make moral judgments about the behavior of Third World governments or political movements, because they feel disqualified to deplore wrongs done by the erstwhile victims of colonialism and racism. They seem to believe that

---

* In a similar frame of mind Michael Parenti, an American political scientist, could not let the suggestion pass that the U.S. was *not* guilty of the psychiatric repression of prisoners Soviet style; Cora Weiss, social critic and activist, was convinced that it was the fault of the U.S. that China attacked Vietnam in 1979; the Rev. Sloan Coffin felt uneasy about the American criticism of Iranian hostage-taking unaccompanied by some reference to the misdeeds of his country, and the P.E.N. Club of the U.S. demonstrated even-handedness by including among the "repressed" of the world American pornographers and Soviet political prisoners alike. More recently, on his pilgrimage to Teheran, Ramsey Clark used the occasion to flagellate the U.S. and virtually absolve the Iranians of responsibility for the hostage-taking. Apparently he could not help feeling sympathetic toward a regime hostile to the U.S. and perceived as its erstwhile victim.[63]

an earlier status of victimization automatically confers moral superiority on the former victim. In an interview, Dr. Philip Potter, secretary general of the World Council of Churches, was asked:

> Why does the World Council of Churches confine itself to seeking the mote in the eye of white racialists and find it barely worth mentioning such massive beams as the brutal expulsion and despoliation of Asians in Uganda or the interracial massacres in Burundi?
>
> Dr. Potter: We have taken careful note of these things—in fact . . . we did condemn the events in Uganda. However, the worst racial discrimination is that of the whites in South Africa *because* [my emphasis] of the forces underlying it; colonialism, imperialism, and economic exploitation. The most shocking aspect of it is that it is perpetrated by nations with a Christian background. Where Uganda is concerned, you should examine the role played by Indians with British Government support. You may then derive *some understanding of this brutal conduct* [my emphasis] on the part of a nation which has only just gained its independence.
>
> Q: Does your magnanimous forgiveness also extend to another country where persecution directly concerns the World Council of Churches . . . because it is religious, not political . . . I refer to the muzzling of the Russian Orthodox Church . . . the Baptists, who even today share the lot of intellectual opposition in forced labor camps and insane asylums? Isn't this religious persecution of Soviet Russian Christians of more urgent concern to the churches than political and social discrimination in Africa?
>
> Dr. Potter: We make no distinction between religious, political and social persecution. We certainly concern ourselves with the lack of religious freedom in Communist countries *insofar as it is proven.* [My emphasis] On the other hand, it makes a great difference whether one is dealing with regimes which profess themselves to be Christian or with those which openly profess atheism. . . .
>
> Q: In other words, because Christians are subject to a higher responsibility you beat the Western breast . . . whereas the Communists, from whom no decency can be expected in view of their depravity or perhaps original sin, get off virtually scot-free.[65]

Jonas Savimbi, the leader of the guerillas fighting the Cuban-backed regime in Angola, noted that "the World Council of Churches, instead of denouncing the ill-treatment of the many members of the Christian Church in Angola, has sent a delegation that has engaged in a fundraising campaign for Angola, thus contributing to the consolidation of another Russian satellite in Africa."[66]

Another example of a similar political morality was reflected in the attitude of Julius Lester, the American black writer,° toward the Soviet invasion of Czechoslovakia in 1968 and those among the radicals who disapproved of it. Lester wrote:

> Many radicals were disturbed and confused by the Russian invasion. . . . Almost all felt that they had to choose who was right and wrong in this context and the Czechs won . . . everybody wept a few sentimental tears for occupied Prague.
>
> This kind of reaction to the recent events in Eastern Europe is more a reflection of our youth and untested idealism than it is a reflection of whatever might have occurred there. What would have been our reaction if Fidel had had to send troops onto the campus of the University of Havana to put down a student uprising there? What would have been our reaction to Ho Chi Minh's unhesitating elimination of thousands of political foes in the mid 50's . . . ? And our reaction is decidedly negative to the purges under Stalin, even though we know nothing about them.
>
> This will undoubtedly be interpreted by some as a covert approval of Russian action against Czechoslovakia. It is not. Nor is it disapproval. Perhaps the correct position on the matter was that taken by China and Cuba—condemnation of both Russia and Czechoslovakia. Neither country is a model of socialism . . . and serious questions can be raised as to whether either country is totally worthy to be called socialist. But all of that is irrelevant to our infant movement taking sides because we see pictures of tanks entering a city, and, like well-conditioned animals, we scream that he at whom the tank is aimed has been wronged. This kind of reaction reveals an all too typical American syndrome—apolitical morality.[67]

A group of Quaker intellectuals were similarly restrained in their condemnation of the Soviet invasion, noting that ". . . it is still too early for adequate analysis of the continuing event." Not unlike Chomsky and the World Council of Churches, they found the available information insufficient for deploring matters they were disinclined to deplore to begin with. Elsewhere in the same volume they referred to the entire range of Soviet (and Communist Chinese) political violence from the 1920s to the 1960s as "repressive episodes."[68] Here as in other instances, the choice of words reveals the moral sentiments behind them. Since the Quakers

---

° It should be noted here that in subsequent years Lester's political morality has undergone significant, and in my opinion, admirable, change. One decade after he wrote the above he was willing to judge severely those he would not have criticized in his New Left-radical period, including American black leaders who had shown an all too reverential attitude toward the Palestine Liberation Organization. Such and similar stands earned him considerable unpopularity among his colleagues in the Afro-American Studies Department of the University of Massachusetts, who wanted to prevent him from teaching a course on blacks and Jews.

were far more disturbed by anti-communism than by communism (as was indicated by the entire volume from which I quoted) it is hardly surprising that they played down, by the selection of words and otherwise, the moral outrages associated with communist systems and the specific events reflecting them such as the invasion of Czechoslovakia.

The intellectual's capacity for the uneven display of moral concerns was also illustrated, at another level, by the reactions of the late Pablo Neruda, Nobel prize-winning Chilean poet, to the difficulties of his fellow writer Alexander Solzhenitsyn:

> Interviewed on the last day of his week long visit here [in the U.S.] the 68-year-old Chilean poet spoke reluctantly about the problems Mr. Solzhenitsyn has faced in trying to have a suitable ceremony for the presentation of the Nobel prize medallion . . .

> "I don't want to become part in a dispute involving highly personal passions," Mr. Neruda said . . . "And I have no intention of becoming an instrument for anti-Soviet propaganda."

> "After all," he went on, "there are more novelists in the capitalist countries who have conflicts with their governments than in the socialist countries."

He also said in the same interview:

> "One no longer knows who is saying what . . . The whole thing has become a big bore and everybody should allow time to pass so that the issues can be seen in a cooler perspective."[69]

Evidently Neruda's long-standing commitment to the support of the Soviet regime precluded sympathy with Solzhenitsyn's fate; it also prompted him to try to trivialize the persecution of Solzhenitsyn by calling it a "big bore." Even more irrelevantly he suggested that as long as writers in capitalist societies were persecuted (an assertion belied by his own position, among many other things) Solzhenitsyn's problems deserved little attention.

Another, less prominent, apologist of Soviet policies, Arnold Kettle, the English literary critic, took a similar position in regard to the Soviet treatment of Pasternak after he was offered the Nobel prize. First he suggested that the awarding of the prize was a political act—as if that justified the Soviet official abuse of Pasternak. Second, he proposed that in any case most Russians regarded Pasternak as a traitor just as the British and American people had regarded P. G. Wodehouse and Ezra Pound as traitors during World War II. He also asserted that all such matters are worse in capitalist societies:

Can anyone really imagine that the present appalling state of culture in this country any more than its economic state, is going to be solved by laissez-faire? One of the essential differences between a socialist and a capitalist society is that in the former the burden of full responsibility is accepted by its leaders. . . . Responsibility involves error and abuse; but it is none the less a higher, more humane attitude than irresponsibility. Most Western intellectuals in practice wash their hands of 90% of the culture in their own countries. . . .[70]

In defending the Soviet treatment of Pasternak, Kettle in effect appealed to higher values and the Soviet leaders' sense of responsibility concerning cultural affairs. He also argued that the whole matter was culturally relative, so to speak, and subject to criticism only by the application of bourgeois standards and values. None of this really explained why Pasternak was prevented from receiving the Nobel prize, had his books banned in the USSR, and was vilified. Both Kettle and Neruda were among the numerous Western intellectuals who considered free expression their inalienable right while they readily rationalized its absence for others in societies they endorsed.

It may be concluded from this brief, preliminary review of the moral impulses and political preferences of many Western intellectuals that the intensity of their moral passion is far more significantly determined by the identity of the actors engaged in the morally questionable conduct than by the conduct itself.[71]

3

The First Wave of Estrangement: The 1930s

Above all, calamities caused by unseen or unknown agencies—plague or famine, gross inflation or mass unemployment . . . —may then produce an emotional disturbance so widespread and acute, such an overwhelming sense of being exposed, cast out and helpless, that the only way in which it can find effective relief is through . . . a sudden, collective and fanatical pursuit of the Millennium.   NORMAN COHN[1]

Could an outcast from a dying social order exist frugally and decently and at the same time have sufficient leisure and energy to assist in the speedy liquidation of the old social order and its replacement by a more workable social system?   SCOTT NEARING[2]

There is always something wrong with society for the sensitive and critical intellectual who takes seriously the task of pointing to the gaps between social ideals and their limited actualization. But to observe such propensities is not to deny that at certain times in history there are far better reasons for finding fault with society than in others. If estrangement is the combined product of inner pressures and response to external conditions, the balance between these two forces varies. There are also different ways in which the external conditions impinge on the sensibilities of the intellectual. He may be disenchanted with the social order because it fails to provide him with a sense of purpose and meaning in life, or because there are too many hungry people around. The two motives for estrangement may converge at times, although more typically they tend to exclude one another. The quest for meaning usually declines when more tangible deprivations abound and must be dealt with.

It was in the early 1930s that the first major twentieth-century wave of estrangement swept through Western societies and intellectuals. To unearth the source of these attitudes requires less a digging in the psyche of intellectuals than the taking note of the economic, social, and political problems of the period. Becoming a critic of Western societies at the time required no unusual or overdeveloped critical faculties, eso-

74

teric sensibilities, colorful neuroses. As Daniel Aaron has written, "The Great Depression, with its hunger marches, its Hoovervilles, its demoralized farmers, its joyless youth and bankrupt entrepreneurs, was not the projections of sick personalities."[3]

The material-economic dimensions of the crisis merged into a deeper, more pervasive sense of insecurity (which later on readily gave way to the type of security found in firm political commitments): ". . . by 1931 many people in England certainly had begun to see the crisis in which they lived as more than a temporary economic reverse—to see it rather as the collapse of an inherited system of values, and the end of a secure life."[4]

No attempt will be made here to retell the history of the 1930s in the United States and Western Europe, which has been told many times competently.* My concern with the 1930s will be limited to those of its features which seemingly predisposed or contributed to the estrangement of intellectuals and which were also echoed in their travel writings, as they contrasted the defects of their society with the accomplishments of the Soviet Union.

It is interesting to reflect why the estrangement of American intellectuals (and its corollary, the sympathetic interest in the USSR) was not more strongly developed before the 1930s and why World War I did not leave more of a residue of bitterness and cynicism; why Prohibition and its failure, the trial of Sacco and Vanzetti, and other domestic social problems failed to raise significantly the level of social criticism of intellectuals. Why was there not a sense of letdown as the Wilsonian ideal of democracy around the world—justifying American involvement in World War I—failed to materialize?

In attempting an answer to these questions it might first be noted that the awareness and concern of American intellectuals with what was go-

---

* There has been, in recent years, a revival of interest in and something of a celebration of the 1930s. Many nostalgic glances have been cast back at the period, when political issues seemed easier to grasp, alliances were more clear cut, and the commitments of intellectuals to good causes more readily forthcoming—or so it might seem in retrospect. Moreover, the hardships of the period, while greater and more tangible, were also easier to overcome. There was little ambivalence about material well-being or "affluence" such as developed since the 1960s, when it acquired associations with emptiness, spiritual torpor, boredom, status seeking, and wasteful consumption. The 1930s were also impressive in retrospect because of the artistic-intellectual ferment and creativity we tend to associate with that decade. At last the recent revival of interest in the period has presumably also been inspired by the easily discernible parallels between the political passions and turmoil of the 1960s and the 1930s.

ing on in different parts of the world was at the time limited, especially since distant events did not impinge on their lives. The socially and politically mixed results of World War I did not make much difference to them. Even more important was that the 1920s was a period of material prosperity and loosening of moral restraints. Many intellectuals during that period clustered in apolitical bohemian subcultures, or became temporary expatriates in Western Europe. They seemed to be more concerned with what came to be called "self-expression," in the 1960s, or the quest for identity and cultural radicalism, than with social and political issues. The attitudes germinating in these years, although manifestly apolitical, were not unrelated to the subsequent resurgence of political commitments and the more active and politicized rejection of the system. As Dos Passos recalled them: "American Bohemia was in revolt against Main Street, against the power of money, against Victorian morals. Freedom was the theme. Freedom from hard collars, from the decalogue, from parental admonitions. . . . The businessman could never understand. . . . When artists and writers found it hard to make themselves a niche in industrial society they repudiated the whole business."[5] (It may be noted here that the tendency to "repudiate the whole business" survived well after the artists and writers and other intellectuals found more than a "niche" in industrial society, as became apparent in the 1960s and 70s). In any event in the 1920s the confidence in the status quo of other elite groups, such as businessmen and politicians, had yet to be shaken. Nor did major domestic traumas motivate the intellectuals to turn their attention to other societies. Relatively little was known about the Soviet Union during the 1920s; the October Revolution did not provoke great curiosity on the part of many intellectuals. It is also possible that for those among the intellectuals who were more radically inclined, much of the 1920s in the Soviet Union was not particularly inspiring or heroic, given the retreat from revolutionary policies embodied in the NEP (New Economic Policy) period, which lasted from 1921 to 1928. It is one of the paradoxes of the attitudes of American as well as other Western intellectuals (which will be explored more fully) that they found Soviet society less interesting and less appealing both at the time of the relatively bloodless, but nonetheless dramatic, October Revolution and during the 1920s when more rational and humane attempts were made to reconstruct society, than during the 1930s when Stalinist terror reached its climax, famine raged, and immense hardships resulted from the collectivization campaign.[6]

Frank A. Warren had written: "Most liberals had been vaguely sympathetic to Russia during the twenties, but they had not felt its impact directly. Significantly the Five-Year-Plan did not generate intense excitement until 1930—two years after it had begun. What happened to cause this excitement was 1929 and the depression, the real impetus in turning the liberals eastward toward Russia."[7] Similar comments were made by Peter Filene, the historian: ". . . the preponderant American feeling toward Soviet Russia in 1933 was decidedly more benign than at any time during the twenties, and, of course 1918–1919." The diplomatic recognition of the Soviet Union by Roosevelt in 1933 was made possible because ". . . by the early thirties, open-mindedness had finally surpassed hostility toward the USSR."[8] Eugene Lyons had a different explanation for the shifting American attitudes:

> Where had all these enthusiasts been in the thirteen years of the Bolshevik Revolution before 1930? Certainly there was a larger element of honest idealism, a smaller admixture of horror, in those years. No less certainly the Soviet regime had more need of their enthusiasm in its earlier stages. These Americans became pseudo-communists . . . when Russia became less communistic . . . more brutally totalitarian. . . . They were drawn to the Great Experiment by its magnitude and seeming strength. Under the guise of a nobly selfless dedication they were, in fact, identifying themselves with Power.

He also observed: "In the early years of the Russian experiment American eulogists were relatively few. Their books showed a romantic, almost lyrical acceptance of the revolution. The facts, no matter how harsh, were usually admitted and assimilated as part of the agony of birth. . . . But in the years now under discussion [the 1930s] the attitude is quite different. There is for the most part a literature of apologetics, ranging from panicky rationalization and self-deception to deliberate concealment."[9]

Throughout the 1920s many American intellectuals were disenchanted with their society—its business ethic, crassness, obsession with material values—but responded more by withdrawal and aesthetic criticism than by becoming politicized. Indirectly however, the apolitical estrangement of American intellectuals in the 1920s paved the way for the passionate commitment of the 1930s and to receptivity to the appeals of Soviet society. As one social historian saw it: "The decade of the twenties . . . robbed them [the intellectuals] of old and outworn values without providing them with new values. It made them cynical about capitalism without making them cynical about all power."[10]

The Depression beginning in 1929 suddenly dramatized all the ills and evils of capitalism and politicized the estrangement of intellectuals and artists. The defects of the capitalist system ceased to be abstract or primarily aesthetic when people lost their jobs, savings, or investments, as the case may be. The sight of the unemployed silenced the apologists of the status quo. The "contradictions of capitalism" became palpable and undeniable when one could contrast the spectacle of American farmers destroying food with the Hunger Marchers or those lined up at the charities. Not only did many become impoverished, but poverty also became all too visible.

As is often the case, some intellectuals derived a sense of satisfaction and exhilaration from the disaster. For many it confirmed their views of the rottenness of the society they lived in, while for others the disruption of normal routines and expectations was in itself an exciting novelty. "One could not help being exhilarated," wrote Edmund Wilson, "at the sudden unexpected collapse of that stupid gigantic fraud. It gave us a new sense of freedom; and it gave us a new sense of power. . . ."[11] In a somewhat similar spirit Scott Nearing was convinced that ". . . the Great Depression was not an accident but . . . the logical outcome of a private enterprise economy. . . ."[12]*

Unemployment in particular provided a potent source for the moral indictment of capitalism, since few would dispute that the right to work is a most basic and elementary human right. Moreover, by failing to provide work for all who wished to work American capitalism was also vulnerable to the criticism that the equality of opportunity was a myth. There was no way to justify or legitimate inequality when work was unavailable to millions who wished to work. The unemployed were hardly in a position to compete in the free enterprise economy, and the poor could thus not be blamed for their condition because of their allegedly deficient industry, ambition, or diligence. And if this was no longer pos-

---

* The denial of accidents is a favorite activity of intellectuals, propagandists, and demagogues, but their respective motives are somewhat different. Propagandists and demagogues deny accidents in order to maximize the culpability of particular groups or individuals and thereby to provoke and intensify indignation and incite to hostility. It is also easier to interpret the social world governed by ill-will and goodwill respectively than one determined by impersonal social forces and imprinted by the unanticipated consequences of human intentions and interactions. Alienated social critics including intellectuals may fall prey to the same impulses when they seek to make moral sense out of the social-political universe. Intellectuals are also prone to take an overintegrated view of society—it is an expression of analytical thinking and of the desire to impose meaning and order on social phenomena. Passionate social critics have always been dedicated to the proposition that the defects of society flow from a constellation of inter-related evils and identifiable wrongdoers.

sible then clearly the broader social system was to take the blame. There was no plausible way left for rationalizing the contrasts of poverty and wealth, and the implications of economic malfunctioning became increasingly moral and ethical. The entire social order came to be seen as bankrupt because of its economic irrationality, inefficiency, and wastefulness. All the worst suspicions of intellectuals about capitalism and the American business civilization were confirmed. Not only was the system objectionable on aesthetic and moral grounds, now its economic defects too became glaring.

In 1932 Granville Hicks described the conversion of an apolitical estrangement into highly politicized alienation: "How easy it was to drift in 1927, 1928, and 1929! Though the social order still seemed viciously inefficient and indecently corrupt, there was, I consoled myself, nothing that I could do about it. I was very much occupied with personal problems and tasks of literary criticism, and I managed to forget about the world in which I lived. . . . Then came the crash! . . . the depression wiped out the illusion of security, as I saw my friends and even relatives losing their jobs and witnessed every time I went on the street the spectacle of the unemployed. I no longer tried to conceal from myself the fact that the system was rotten. . . ."[13]

A similar process of politicization and radicalization among the intellectuals was taking place in Britain, also largely under the impact of the economic crisis.

> . . . between 1928 and 1933 a change occurred in their [the intellectuals'] outlook. . . . Their pursuit of pleasure ceased to be satisfying. A new seriousness came to the fore in the place of the former *joie de vivre*. Increasing attention was given to politics. Whereas sex and aesthetics had been the major topics of conversation, now everybody began to talk politics. As time passed the politics of the intellectual moved leftward to socialism and communism. What began as a political awakening became a great radicalization. Radical politics flourishes in a seed-bed of catastrophe. Great Britain during the thirties experienced a series of shattering domestic and international crises. Of most immediate impact was the severity of the Great Depression.[14]

While the economic crisis created moral indignation, social criticism, and an increasingly politicized estrangement among intellectuals, the social injustices of capitalism were not the only factors sustaining the spirit of alienation and the subsequent susceptibility toward the Soviet Union and the political organizations which represented its interests abroad. The spectre of Nazism and fascism, which began to cast its shadow over Europe, also predisposed to alienation and sympathy to the Soviet Union. While the British and French governments did little to prevent the spread of Nazism, the Soviet Union and the communists in general succeeded in projecting the image of being the only staunch and determined opponents of Nazism and fascism. This impression was enhanced by the Spanish Civil War, in which the communists supported by the USSR appeared to be the best organized force rallying to the support of the Loyalists, whereas Western European governments stood aside and did nothing to hinder the triumph of Franco. Pablo Neruda, who was a resident in Western Europe at the time, spoke for many when he said: "The Communists were the only organized group [in Spain, that is] and had put together an army to confront Italians, Germans, Moors and Falangists. They were also the moral force that kept the resistance and the anti-Fascist struggle going."[15]

The impotence of the British and French governments in arresting or discouraging fascism may have been a more important factor in the estrangement of Western European intellectuals than the corresponding inaction of the American government, in view of the distance and the traditions of isolationism in American foreign policy.

The European democracies also failed to discourage the attack of Mussolini on Abyssinia in 1935 and the Japanese conquest of Manchuria earlier. Thus not only the economic chaos but also impotence in international affairs contributed to an enfeebled, decadent image of Western democracies. Whereas intellectuals may come to terms, in one way or another, with a social system that is authoritarian but promotes social justice, or with one that is unconcerned with justice but projects strength, the combination of feebleness and social injustice is the most potent encouragement to moral indignation and hostile estrangement.

The Nazi menace in particular contributed to a more indulgent attitude toward the communists and the Soviet Union; whatever was unappealing about them was dwarfed by the monstrosity of the Nazi movement and ideology. Alfred Kazin's views were typical:

> The danger was Hitler, Mussolini, Franco . . . I found myself more sympathetic to the Communists. They had . . . they still seemed to have, Silone, Malraux, Hemingway, Gide, Rolland, Gorky, Aragon, Picasso, Eluard, Auden, Spender, Barbusse, Dreiser, Farrell, while the Socialists seemed to have only their own virtue. I was tired of virtue, and now wanted to see some action. . . . Fascism was the main enemy and I feared any division on the left. . . .

Malcolm Muggeridge, who chronicled the period in England, further described these attitudes:

> Looking round the field anxiously, they saw, as they thought, one reso-
> lute enemy at least. Against outstretched arms, clenched fists were
> raised defiantly. Let them, then, raise a clenched fist in defense of
> freedom and culture, peace and happiness. . . . Stalin became their
> antidote to Hitler; Marxist hate should abolish Nazi hate, and Marxist
> falsifications correct Nazi ones. . . . Even the Duchess of Atholl had
> come to treat sympathetically what once had been anathema to her;
> even Mr. Garvin, faithful admirer of Mussolini, had reached the con-
> clusion that 'there is in fact, no firmer ally than Russia in the defense
> of freedom.'[16]

In some instances these attitudes were carried to their ultimate conclusion by a few intellectuals (especially in Britain) who volunteered
their services to Soviet espionage organizations. Anthony Blunt, the
English art historian lately exposed as a spy of long standing (and part
of the Burgess-Maclean-Philby team), stated, "In the mid 1930s it
seemed to me and to many of my contemporaries that the Communist Party and Russia constitued the only firm bulwark against fascism,
since the Western democracies were taking an uncertain and compromising attitude toward Germany. I was persuaded by Guy Burgess that
I could best serve the cause of antifascism by joining him in his work
for the Russians."[17] Blunt's recruitment to the Soviet espionage apparatus
is among the contemporary parables of good intentions and idealism.
His and his friends' services were certainly not bought by money or
through blackmail. Nor was their becoming Soviet spies a reflection of
personal or class interest. They became spies in order to assist the Soviet
Union, "the bulwark against fascism" and the counterpoint to everything
they rejected in their own society. The case of Blunt in particular indicates that the intellectual role and the immersion into the world of
ideas, art, and aesthetics provide no immunity or protection against
serious political misjudgments and misconduct.

The encounter between Western intellectuals and Marxism during this
period was also significant in deepening and articulating their estrangement and social criticism. The Marxist view of the world provided an
impressively coherent explanation of all the disturbing phenomena of
the times: the Depression, unemployment, poverty, and the rise of Nazism. For many intellectuals their limited exposure to Marxism was a
revelation; suddenly everything fell into place. ("Here at last were the

answers . . . to most of the questions raised by the depression . . .")[18]
The chaos of empirical social reality coalesced into understandable patterns, laws, and regularities. Disorder gave way to contradictions, the
problems of human nature to those of economic and social organization.
Most importantly, everything appeared to be interrelated and thus made
sense. Marxism came to satisfy the need for wholeness and meaning
which was intensified by the times:

> The depression had done more than disturb their lives; it had ripped
> apart the fabric of their values and beliefs, leaving them cold and shiv-
> ering in the winds of uncertainty. Intellectuals may deal professionally
> with ideas, that is, with problems, but like the rest of humanity they
> find it hard to refrain from the narcotic of certainty; not many are able
> to suffer a prolonged acceptance of a mode of life that is inherently
> problematic. The new converts . . . came rushing in quest of a sys-
> tem . . . they wanted to feel that, at the very moment the world was
> being shattered, they found the key to its meaning.[19]

The impact of Marxism was all the more powerful since many of the
new devotees had earlier been totally apolitical and quite naive in political matters; they leapt, as it were, from a state of complete non-
involvement with politics to intense commitment aided by Marxism.[20]
Granville Hicks wrote: "As I read a little in the works of Marx and his
followers, I found the answer to one question after another that had
been bothering me."[21] Marxism helped to convert apolitical aestheticism
and individualism, and a rejection of society based upon them, into
more systematic social criticism. It also helped to overcome pessimism
and a largely passive political attitude:

> Intellectuals believed that the Marxist diagnosis of dying capitalism
> was accurate, that history was on their side. There was a sense of pur-
> pose, of excitement, of exhilaration in their commitment to politics.
> They felt they were on the offensive—against war, fascism, and eco-
> nomic exploitation.

Interestingly enough, the Marxism cherished by the British intellectuals of the 1930s resembles the versions resurrected by their New Left
successors in the 1960s. Marxism or communism came to mean a philosophy of personal action, a moral force for good: "The thirties model of
Marxism in England was not the traditionally conceived deterministic
doctrine . . . but rather the idea that there was an interaction between
man and his environment, to which man contributes an active, striving
force."[22] Nor, for that matter, was the appeal of Marxism for American

intellectuals that different, as described by John P. Diggins, the intellectual historian:

> . . . Marxism seemed the resolution of the eternal dualism of facts and values, science and aesthetics, reality and desire. Marxism also appeared to have resolved . . . how to attain a perfect society with imperfect human beings.

> . . . Marxism did restore meaning and purpose to life by offering a sense of historical direction . . . and an organic version that dared to be monistic. In an age when all truths seemed relative and fragmentary, Marxism could provide a rare glimpse of the totality of existence, an exciting synthesis that broke down the classical dualisms between self and society, idealism and realism, contemplation and action, art and life.[23]

For quite a few of these intellectuals it was not only the theory of Marxism but also its professional executors, the communists (and not only in Russia), who were attractive. Claud Cockburn, the fellow-traveling English journalist, revered them not only for being the most militant anti-fascists, but more generally because "they were a lot nearer being a creative force in British politics than any other I could see. Also, they were a force that was small, poor and adventurous, and the distance between their thoughts and their actions appeared to be a lot shorter than it was when you came to the Labor people, the 'progressive intellectuals.' "[24]

Many American intellectuals who became fellow travelers or party members entertained similar perceptions of the American communists. Granville Hicks was one of them: "A socialism of deeds, not of words, was what we were looking for, and it was true that the Communists were active in every strike and every unemployment demonstration and that they were being beaten and jailed and sometimes killed. By comparison the Socialists seemed tame and ineffectual . . . 'Nobody in the world' [Lincoln] Steffens wrote 'proposes anything basic and real except the Communists.' " More generally speaking, intellectuals were attracted to the party

> For Communism [Malcolm Cowley wrote] not only furnished a clear answer to the problems raised by the depression . . . and not only promised to draw writers from their isolation by creating a vital new audience . . . but it also seemed capable of supplying the moral qualities that writers had missed in bourgeois society: the comradeship in struggle, the self-imposed discipline, the ultimate purpose . . . the opportunity for heroism and the human dignity.[25]

Even in retrospect Pablo Neruda had no second thoughts and felt that supporting the Communist party was the right choice under the prevailing historical circumstances:

> We poets of this age have had to make a choice. The choice has not been a bed of roses. . . .
>
> In my party, Chile's Communist Party, I found a large group of simple people who had left far behind them personal vanity, despotism and material interests, I felt happy knowing honest people who were fighting for common decency, for justice.[26]

The self-evidently irrational nature of the Western economic problems also narrowed the alternatives for Louis Fischer, the American political writer-journalist: "Outside Russia, the years beginning in 1929 found governments confounded by deep crisis, with able workingmen in bread lines, farmers seeing their precious crops plowed under or destroyed by dust and intellectuals in a quandary. An endless stream of thirsty minds flowed into Russia from the capitalist West. How did Russia do it? Was it because of planned economy? . . . What was the secret of Bolshevik success and capitalist failure? Books on the Five Year Plan headed the bestseller list."[27]

Some of the contemporaries recalled yet another form of alienation of the period, which manifested itself in excessive sympathy for the defeated in World War I, the underdogs of the period. Claud Cockburn wrote:

> For obvious psychological reasons . . . a lot of young men of my generation had a compulsive urge to love and cherish the peoples defeated by our fathers. On countless journeys between Oxford and Budapest I had taken time off in Germany, in the Rhineland, in Heidelberg, in Bavaria, seeing very few people but intoxicated by the loveliness of those lands, and when I did see people, seeing them through the haze of that kind of political mysticism which I had built up around them.[28]

Sentiments of this nature bring to mind the 1960s when among the youth of the West another, somewhat similar political mysticism arose in regard to "Third World Peoples" largely unknown to them. In the 1960s (as in the 1920s and 30s) many young Western intellectuals felt a somewhat similar, reflexive sympathy with, what could be considered, the enemies of their parents' generation: Cuban, Vietnamese, or Chinese communists, Palestinian Arabs, and other groups. To understand this phenomenon one need not invoke hostility toward one's parents as the explanation. More simply, once a state of estrangement from the prevailing social-political order develops (for the many reasons noted above, which need not include generational conflict) attitudes on specific issues often become reflexive. Thus if the dominant social-political system designates the Germans (or Vietnamese or Chinese or Cubans) as the enemies, then the enemies of my enemy become my friends. In the 1930s this applied with a particular intensity to the attitudes toward the Soviet Union: "We were bound to look with sympathy on Soviet Russia, if only because the defenders of the status quo were so frightened by it and told such outrageous lies about it."[29] This attitude has persisted among left-wing intellectuals in the West to the present and it helps to explain why so many of them cannot bring themselves to criticize outrages committed by putatively socialist regimes when these are *also* criticized by the political groups and powers which such intellectuals despise.* And if they succeed in taking, however reluctantly, a stand against such systems (say, after the evidence of the existence of Soviet concentration camps can no longer be rejected as unreliable), they do so at the price of great anguish, as illustrated by, among others, Lillian Hellman's retrospective reexamination of her pro-Soviet attitudes in her *Scoundrel Time*. Such Western intellectuals obviously paid no heed to Trotsky's advice: ". . . the stupidity and dishonesty of one's enemies is no justification for one's blindness."[31]

The Western attitudes toward the Nazi totalitarian threat of the times are also reminiscent of the more recent Western attitudes toward the Soviet Union. With all due acknowledgment of the considerable differences between the Soviet and Nazi leaders, regimes, policies, tactics, and values, certain resemblances between the two situations remain: in both periods Western countries faced unfriendly and militant powers (Germany and Italy in the 1930s, the Soviet Union and its allies and client states in the 1960s and 70s) and at both times many Western politicians, opinion-makers, intellectuals, and segments of the public opinion tried to persuade themselves and their constituents that behind the appearance of unfriendliness and menacing gestures, reasonableness and accommodation could be found. Then as now the threatening voices were often dismissed as mere rhetoric, and understanding was earnestly solicited for the potential aggressors and their grievances. Then, as more recently, lack of information and the failure of imagination played a considerable part in the misperception of the countries hostile to the

---

* Thus Garcia Marquez, the Colombian writer, recently revealed that he had written a book critical of Cuba but decided against publishing it, since "it could be used against Cuba."[30]

West. According to the British historian A. L. Rowse, the British in the 1930s were "too decent to imagine that there were such people in the world" (as the Nazis) and the tendency to give them the benefit of doubt was matched by the unwillingness to learn about their ideas and beliefs[32]—observations which would apply just as well to the attitudes of many Americans of the 1960s and 70s toward the Soviet Union and many Soviet-supported governments and movements.

Then as now the temptation was irresistible for many Westerners to assimilate the personalities and attitudes of totalitarian leaders to those of Western politicians, at bottom reasonable fellows, capable of give-and-take even if given occasionally to fiery rhetoric. In particular it was difficult for pragmatic Western liberals to conceive of people who took ideas seriously and who attempted to make ideologies relevant to their policies. Then, as in more recent times, there was much store put on face-to-face meetings between world leaders; Chamberlain seemed to believe, Muggeridge wrote, that "A chat with Mussolini or Hitler, even a friendly nod to Stalin, would make all the difference."

The attempts to compromise with Hitler and Mussolini were played out against a background of ardent if occasionally inconsistent pacifism, largely a response to the bloodletting in World War I. 150,000 American students participated in 1935 in a "Student Strike Against War."[33] The famous pledge of the Oxford Union (of students) not to fight for king and country reminds one, again, of the more recent avowals of American students ("Hell no, we won't go") refusing to fight in Vietnam or to register for the draft in 1980. To be sure, although the moods in these two periods appear similar, the outcomes were not. The British and American students did fight when they were called upon in World War II—most American students in the 1960s did not, either because they were not called upon or, if they were, because they evaded the draft, one way or another.

Such were some of the major events and characteristics of the times which spawned the first great wave of estrangement among Western intellectuals.

The social criticism produced by intellectuals during these years was not confined to the all too obvious economic hardships, material deprivations, and the malfunctioning of identifiable social institutions. Soon enough other targets and broader issues emerged; the perception of particular flaws led to the sighting of others, more elusive and encompassing. It appeared, for instance that beyond the concern with poverty and the inherent deprivations, intellectuals were especially disturbed by poverty suffered for no good reason or higher purpose. As will be shown later, intellectuals are capable of regarding poverty as a wholesome condition when it is associated with purity, egalitarianism, and the subordination of material needs to higher, spiritual purpose. The travel reports indicate that in the societies admired by the visiting intellectuals, poverty was viewed either as a transient residue of the past or as a meaningful sacrifice, or redefined as a simple, uncorrupted way of life. In short the intellectuals' attitude toward poverty depended very much on its context. Certainly "poverty amidst plenty" was more unjust than poverty as a general condition.[34] Yet the implicit distinction between meaningful (socialist) and meaningless (capitalist) poverty has been problematic insofar as the meaning of socialist poverty is predicated on the future, which is hard to predict. The second problem is that the "meaning" may not be sensed by those undergoing the deprivations but only by those—the planners, leaders, ideologues—who impose it upon them.[35] Such a contextual evaluation of poverty also enables intellectuals to reevaluate other matters associated with it, for example, child labor. Under capitalism child labor is degrading and incompatible with a happy and healthy childhood. In revolutionary societies however it may symbolize social unity, common effort for the good of society, reflect early socialization to respect work, possibly even the removal of barriers between the generations.[36] Likewise manual labor under capitalism is usually seen as demeaning, especially when dirty and fatiguing; under socialism the joyless routine on the assembly line or in the fields acquires new meaning; coolies carrying baskets of dirt on their heads become transformed from wretched slaves into valiant builders of a new society; even garbage and nightsoil collectors (as in China) become ennobled in their otherwise unattractive calling when such toils are performed on the altar of collective well-being. In short there is more (and less) to the intellectuals' concern with poverty and deprivation than often meets the eye.

The contextual evaluation of various social phenomena prevailed both with respect to the Soviet Union and the United States. It may be stressed again that although it was the Depression and the associated material hardships which opened the floodgates of social criticism, behind the critiques of economic malfunctioning there emerged other, more fundamental objections to the social system the intellectuals experienced. Poverty, as revealed by the Depression, was doubtless an intolerable condition, particularly as it was joined with inequality. But both poverty and inequality were part of a broader, deeper, more general malaise. It should be noted that most of the intellectuals whose views are being discussed here were, despite the Depression, not lacking in employment or income and were materially comfortable to varying degrees. Hence their concern with povery was vicarious, unlike the sense of deprivation they experienced far more directly due to the lack of meaning and purpose in their society.

In the social criticism of the period there was a link between the concern with poverty and inequality on the one hand and the obstacles to self-realization on the other. Self-realization was a broad enough concept to accommodate both the most obvious forms of deprivation—lack of adequate food, shelter, clothing, medical care, and so on—and the more elusive, mental-spiritual needs and gratifications. The concern with self-realization was among the preoccupations the alienated intellectuals of the 1930s shared with their successors of the 1960s. Their moral indignation was further inflamed by knowing that the deprivations witnessed were not uniformly distributed and barely, if at all, justified.[37]

As we probe further the social criticism of the 1930s we also encounter the rejection of the prevalence of material values. Deploring the scramble for money, the crass commercialism, and the related impoverishment of the aesthetic-spiritual sides of life was not an entirely new development, of course. The critique of the pervasiveness of the "cash nexus" has been, at least since the publication of the *Communist Manifesto,* a staple of the social criticism mounted by Western intellectuals. It was among the appeals of the new societies, such as the Soviet, that they seemed free of the preoccupation with money ("for the first time in my life I was sharing the breath of a great city with a folk which has not fouled the air by perpetual forced incense to the cult of money,"[38] observed Waldo Frank joyously upon his arrival to Leningrad in 1932).

Hewlett Johnson, the Dean of Canterbury, stressed appropriately enough the moral-spiritual consequences of poverty, inequality, and the cash nexus:

> . . . our own competitive system of every man for himself and the devil take the hindermost, with the profit-making motive as the chief incentive; men being used as means and not ends. . . . Folly culminates in wastage of human material. Stunted and narrow lives are the result.

> . . . Slumps and booms, unemployment, and mis-employment the dole and the multimillionaire, the scales weighted for financiers and against the workers. . . .[39]

Scott Nearing, the versatile American radical author and organizer, wrote off Western civilization as a whole for similar reasons: "I said adieu to Western civilization first because I was disgusted with its professions of belief in Christian doctrine of 'love God and serve your neighbour' coupled with its hypocritical practice of 'every man for himself and the devil take the dropout.' "[40]

Inequality, waste, and poverty are the attributes which for many intellectuals define capitalism as an uncaring, irresponsible social system. (By the same token, as will be seen later, societies like the Soviet exercise their attraction in part because of an image of caring and responsibility. It is often difficult to separate, in the accounts of our authors, expressions of indignation and criticism in regard to one social system from the praise and approval of the other.) Scott Nearing became "a pacifist, a vegetarian, and a socialist" because of the ". . . woeful discrepancy between riches and poverty, the inequity of exploitation and the wickedness of deliberate, wholesale destruction and killing."[41]

Anna Louise Strong longed for a world "where society organized assignment of work . . . and looked after all workers . . ." and "where 'chaos and waste' were abolished." Yet at the same time she also confessed that ". . . I came to condemn capitalism not through any oppression endured by me personally, but through that very deification of efficiency which capitalism had taught me. . . ." Strong, like many other Western intellectuals, remained unaware of the cult of efficiency present in socialist industrial societies which are just as capable of treating human beings as interchangeable parts as the capitalist industrial machine. She was convinced that as soon as such ills of capitalistic exploitation and profit hunger were abolished abundance would immediately be ushered in and thus betrayed some surprise when she first arrived in Russia in the early 1920s: "My Utopia . . . was in ruins; famine and pestilence swept the land. We in Seattle had reasoned, when we observed the graft and exploitation of capitalism, that as soon as these were abolished, widespread comfort would begin."[42]

While Strong's criticisms of American society were less extensive—she spent much of her adult life in the Soviet Union and later in China—she expressed an attitude and experience that were widely shared among estranged intellectuals and especially Americans. I am referring to idealism, high expectations, and hopes which had been routinely frustrated. She had written: "I grew up expecting justice and kindness as natural rights of man: if anyone treated me with unkindness, I assumed it must be through my fault."[43] While not all intellectuals surveyed here would admit to such attitudes or would express them in the same manner, most of them seemed to entertain similar hopes and ideals. It may well be asked here how capitalist society, despite its ethos of the cash nexus, cult of efficiency, impersonality, profit hunger, and greed allowed the development of values and attitudes so clearly anti-thetical to its spirit, so subversive of business civilization? If the ruling ideas and values of any historical era are those of the rulers (the capi-talists, in this case) they clearly failed to impose them successfully on society or else they allowed very substantial pockets of autonomy for people who upheld ideas opposed to those of their rulers—a state of af-fairs at odds with what Marx and Engels envisaged. They had written:

> The ideas of the ruling class are in every epoch the ruling ideas: i.e., the class which is the ruling material force of society, is at the same time its ruling intellectual force. The class which has the means of material production at its disposal, has control at the same time over the means of mental production. . . . The ruling ideas are nothing more than the ideal expression of the dominant material relationships.[44]

Few statements became less applicable to contemporary pluralistic-capitalistic societies. More generally speaking, the proposition is hard to apply to any society, since it provides no specification or approxima-tion as to when ideas are "ruling"—how much dissent or criticism of the ruling classes is compatible with the claim that their ideas are ruling? Are, for example, the ideas of corporate capitalism "ruling" American so-ciety today, when in fact such ideas are rejected or derided by a large portion, if not the great majority, of influential intellectuals and opinion-makers and satirized in the arts, literature, and even popular entertain-ment?

The explanation of idealism and the rejection of the supposedly ruling ideas of society may be found, in the United States at any rate, in cer-tain historical factors rather than in the prevailing modes of production and ownership. What became the United States was settled by people of high expectations and some of their expectations could at least in part be realized. Many immigrants sought and found not only economic but also religious, political, and cultural opportunities. This history of the United States is one of many earnest new beginnings. Even many Amer-ican capitalists managed to conjure up a peculiarly American combina-tion of hard-nosed business attitudes with a degree of social conscience and sentimentality.[45] Well before the crisis years of the early 1930s it was fairly clear that the ethic of capitalism had not proved as pervasive or dominant as was thought to be the case by Marx and his followers. Unlike what Marx had envisaged, the social setting of ideas is fragmented—at any rate in large-scale, complex societies—and subject to influences other than economic ones. Modern society has made possible far more variation in its cultural products than was allowed for by all those who overestimated the extent of its integration, whether on economic or political grounds.

While it is difficult to ascertain what the precise character of the "ruling ideas" was in the period under consideration, socially conscious intellectuals were troubled less by the substance of such ideas than by the discrepancy between social ideals and practices. Again, this was a particularly American concern, perhaps a form of historical innocence enabling American intellectuals to observe time and again with pained surprise that "In almost every branch of American life there is a sharp dichotomy between preaching and practice"[46]—as if such disjunctions between ideals and implementation were a unique failure of American society.

Malcolm Cowley's diagnosis in 1934 of the ills of American society has retained a startling freshness and closely resembles the social criticism of the 1960s and early 70s. In this archetypical critique of American society and culture the focus shifts from poverty and inequality to inauthenticity, to the gaps between ideal and actual, theory and practice, professed value and observable behavior. He wrote:

> . . . almost the whole of American culture was becoming false or flimsy. The stage dealt with problems that had no meaning in terms of daily life; the movies offered dreams of impossible luxury . . . the popular magazines were merely vehicles for advertising and the popular newspapers effectively disfranchised their readers by failing to give them the information they needed as voters. . . . Worst of all . . . was the hypocrisy that had come to pervade the whole system, with businessmen talking about service when they meant profits, with statesmen proclaiming their love for the common man while taking orders from Wall Street (and sometimes money from oil operators . . .)
>
> In those days hardly anyone seemed to believe in what he was doing—not the workman on the production line, or the dealer forced to sell more units . . . to more and more unwilling customers . . . or the salesman with a foot stuck in the door while he repeated an argument learned by rote, or the underpaid newspaperman . . . despising his readers—not even the people at the head of the system, the bankers and stock promoters and politicians . . . everybody was in it for the money. . . . The advertising men who served as priests and poets of American prosperity were the biggest cynics of all.

> Like the advertising men . . . they [the writers] suffered from a
> feeling of real discomfort. Something oppressed them. . . . They did
> not understand its nature, but they tried to exorcise it by giving it
> names—it was the stupidity of the crowd . . . it was Mass Production,
> Babbittry, Our Business Civilization; or perhaps it was the Machine,
> which had been developed to satisfy men's needs but which was now
> controlling those needs and forcing its standardized products upon
> us. . . . The same social mechanism that fed and clothed the body
> was starving the emotions, was closing every path toward creativeness
> and self-expression.[47]

A strikingly similar summary of the defects of American life was to
appear in the 1960s in one of Mailer's shorter pieces, pointing to the
continuity in certain themes of the rejection of American society. The rejection of the machine in the 1920s and 1930s was hardly different in
spirit from the loathing of computers and all they stood for in the 1960s.
In turn, the relatively apolitical condemnation of the Machine Age in
the 1920s prepared the ground for the more politicized, wholesale rejection of capitalism of the 1930s.

The reminiscences of Joseph Freeman (a prominent communist intellectual in the 20s and 30s) of life in Greenwich Village in the early 20s
conjure up the images of the more recent quests for authenticity and
"alternative life styles":

> It was in the Village—with its enthusiasm for Varnum Poor's handmade
> pottery—that the revolt against the machine was the purest. Sur-
> rounded by the most mechanized and industrialized country in the
> world, the little island burned candles not only symbolically—at both
> ends—but literally. The inhabitants wore handmade batik blouses in-
> stead of factory-made dresses, sandals instead of shoes. They were,
> spiritually at least, machine wreckers. For many of them art was not
> an attempt to express contemporary civilization, but to escape from
> it into dreams of a nonindustrial world assumed to be full of peace,
> beauty and love.

Alfred Kazin's recollections of the 1930s suggest further similarities
between the phenomenon of "dropping out" then and in the 1960s:

> I would find myself evenings in Communist social halls, surrounded
> by classmates who had gone "proletarian," who had taken jobs as
> countermen in cafeterias, and who . . . boasted an aggressive "class"
> hardness that shamed me. They had broken with the studious patterns
> we had all been raised in; they had given up solemnly trying to inch
> their way up the ladder. They had broken with the bourgeois world
> and its false ambitions.[48]

Such sentiments foreshadowed many attitudes and criticisms of American society which emerged in the 1960s, including the concern with the corruption spread by capitalist industrial society drowning its members in useless consumer goods.

While apprehension about the machine and the various ravages of industrialization is a familiar enough theme in the writings of Western intellectuals for well over a century, there was a new outpouring of such sentiments in the period being discussed here. (Waldo Frank for instance referred to Americans as "barbarians of the machine.")[49] There was a preoccupation with depersonalization, standardization, lack of proper levels of spirituality and humane warmth, in the social critiques of the 1930s which was to reach full fruition in the 1960s. Many intellectuals already in the 1930s were convinced that the problems of American and other Western societies were not merely or predominantly economic, material, or organizational, but rather spiritual. Malcolm Cowley for example emphasized that "we are dealing here with what was essentially a religious experience. The problems of the time were not only political but also moral and personal. . . . Many of [the writers] were also unconsciously seeking a religious solution, a faith that would supply certain elements heretofore lacking in their private and professional lives as middle-class Americans." (He also included the "casting out of old identities" among these "religious elements.") Even earlier, in the 1920s, a group of thirty New York intellectuals concluded that "Life in this country is joyless and colorless, universally standardized, tawdry, uncreative, given over to the worship of wealth and machinery."[50] And again, Waldo Frank spoke with contempt "of that flabby relativism that goes by the name of liberalism in the West and which is so often nothing but a want of conviction. . . ."[51]

Thus the wave of alienation and social criticism which was triggered by the Depression and had manifestly economic causes broadened into a questioning of the entire value basis of capitalist society: "Our system lacks moral basis. . . . It gives rise . . . to that fatal divergence between principles and practice of Christian people, which is so damning to religion. . . . The gap between Sunday, with its sermons on brotherhood . . . and Monday with its competitive rivalries . . . becomes so wide that many of the better men and women of today remain outside the Churches altogether."[52]

None of the foregoing is to suggest that all criticisms of Western society and capitalism were focused on spiritual malaise, defective values, lack of purpose. Rather my argument is that even the criticisms of narrowly defined shortcomings and of specific institutions were permeated and informed by a sense of a rejection of the entire system and a profound lack of faith in it. This is, after all, what we mean by alienation. Intellectuals who could envisage significant improvements within the existing or modified institutional framework—for example through the government providing jobs, better educational opportunities, health care, etc.—were not really alienated even if they were critical of the problems and injustices present in their society.

There were, in any event, many clearly focused criticisms of Western societies which often complemented the praise of corresponding Soviet policies, practices, or institutions. Thus, for example, if Waldo Frank castigated the American legal system because of "the damaging barrier of legal technique between the human issue and the official judgement,"[53] this was to contrast it to the superior humanness and informality of the Soviet one. Julian Huxley, the British scientist, was all the more critical of British society for its niggardly support of scientific research, lack of planning, contrasts of unemployment and overproduction, the stranglehold of vested interest groups, since all such deficiencies have been thoroughly remedied in the Soviet Union. He too felt it necessary to link such specific ailments to the broader problem of values, such as the preponderance of undue individualism in English society.[54]

The feeling that something was fundamentally wrong with Western societies and that their failings transcended the more specific and easily identifiable ills (such as poverty, unemployment, lack of planning) was certainly widely shared, though probably not as intensely held as similar attitudes in the 1960s. There was also a difference in the favored terminology of social criticism and a lesser readiness, in the 1930s, to relate the personal problems of the social critic to those of larger society. There was, nonetheless, in many instances, a similar sense of irremediable flaws, of decadence and aimlessness prevailing in the societies which bred the critics who became the pilgrims. Thus Lion Feuchtwanger, the German novelist, wrote:

> I came to the Soviet Union from countries where complaints are the general rule and whose inhabitants, discontented with both their physical and spiritual conditions, crave change. . . . The air which one breathes in the West is stale and foul. In the Western civilization there is no longer clarity and resolution. . . . One breathes again when one comes from this oppressive atmosphere of a counterfeit democracy and hypocritical humanism into the invigorating atmosphere of the Soviet Union. Here there is no hiding behind mystical, meaningless slogans, but a sober ethic prevails.

G. B. Shaw felt the same way:

> The bourgeoisie is rotten. The army is rotten. The monarchies are rotten. Above all parliamentary institutions are rotten.

Corliss and Margaret Lamont perceived the contrast in these terms:

> The direction in the Soviet, from both the material and cultural standpoints, seems steadily and on the whole upward, and the problems those of growth. Elsewhere in the world the direction seems downward and the problems those of decay.

J. D. Bernal, the British scientist, recalled:

> I went round the Soviet Union in those rather rough, primitive and casual days when one saw very much of the difficulties . . . [in 1931, that is] And yet there was no mistaking the sense of purpose and achievement . . . in those days of trial. It was grim but great. Our hardships in England were less; theirs were deliberate and undergone in an assurance of building a better future.

At last, according to John Strachey, "Even today . . . before a classless society has fully emerged, there is perceptible an exhilaration of living which finds no parallel in the world. To travel from the capitalist world into Soviet territory is to pass from death to birth."[55]*

The images and metaphors of staleness and freshness, growth and decay, topdogs and underdogs were recurring elements in the social criticism of Western societies and in the susceptibility to the Soviet system. Louis Fischer accounted for the state of mind which led to his pro-Soviet attitudes as follows:

> I preferred fresh sweeping winds to stale stagnant air, and well-intentioned pioneers to proved failures. I liked the Soviets because they were an experiment in the interests of the downtrodden majority, because they destroyed the privileges of the powerful few, because they were weak, and because the world's conservatives and reactionaries opposed them.[57]

---

* Decades later the same feelings were still voiced by some of the intellectuals who in the end succeeded in tearing themselves away from the invigorating atmosphere of the superior societies they visited. Thus wrote Scott Nearing, referring to his numerous visits to various socialist countries since World War II: "Each time I returned to our subsistence farm in Maine I was increasingly convinced that the socialist countries were moving ahead to their goals, that the western capitalist countries were drifting, rudderless, and leaderless, on a sea of troubles. . . ."

In a similar spirit Garcia Marquez, "Despite his frequent trips to Havana . . . says he could not settle there. 'I could not live in Cuba because I haven't been through the process,' he said. 'It would be very difficult to . . . adapt myself to the conditions. I'd miss too many things.' "[56]

Even when some of the intellectuals recognized certain flaws or liabilities of Soviet society, they were usually dwarfed or reduced to insignificance by comparing them to the apparently far more serious defects of their own societies. And there was always the feeling (in the early and mid-1930s at any rate) that the defects of capitalist societies were inherent and irremediable while those of the Soviet were ephemeral, transient pains of growth rather than the diseases of decline and disintegration. Thus for example, while acknowledging that Russia was not exactly free politically, Stephen Spender nevertheless concluded that ". . . whereas Russia advances toward greater freedoms, the British Empire finds itself compelled to choose between disintegration and repression."[58] Discussing the appropriate and inappropriate views of the Soviet system, Joseph Freeman wrote:

> You could travel to Russia . . . and write volumes of backwardness and hardship you saw. . . . Even though every instance you recorded were by itself true, your picture of the Soviet Union as a whole would be false. . . . When people saw only the negative side of the October Revolution . . . and at the same time ignored the great changes, the construction, the immense movement forward—they lied monstrously.[59]

Freeman and others sharing his faith attempted to remedy the situation by taking the diametrically opposed attitude. Instead of ignoring or slighting the positive features of the regime, they ignored or played down whatever was negative. More than that: they fervently denied, dismissed, disbelieved, and rationalized those "details" that would detract from the shining whole; they went to the other extreme by refusing to admit or discuss *any* imperfection. On the infrequent occasions when they would perfunctorily acknowledge some deficiency, they refused to see any connection between the defect in some detail of the great design and the quality of the whole system.[60] This kind of contextual reasoning (already referred to) was a major determinant of the way in which the intellectuals in question thought of both their own societies and the counter-model. Insofar as they considered their own social systems historically doomed, even their more appealing aspects (for example, freedom of expression) came to be devalued, or redefined as trivial, meaningless, and unimportant. And by the same token the (rarely acknowledged) shortcomings of Soviet society could also be dismissed on contextual grounds: in the light of the fundamentally progressive and desirable nature of the Soviet system, such shortcomings mattered little and, in any event, were bound to wither away and become extinct. This attitude saved time and anguish to many critics-admirers of the two types of societies respectively. Once their minds were made up as to the *essential corruption* of one and the *essential goodness* of the other, details were no longer important and worth careful scrutiny. If they did not fit into the whole (of either type) they could be dismissed or ignored. Or, as E. J. Hobsbawm, the contemporary social critic, put it: "modern political choice is not a constant process of selecting men or measures, but a single or infrequent choice between packages in which we buy the disagreeable part of the contents because there is no other way of getting the rest, and in any case because there is no other way to be politically effective . . . the communist intellectual, in opting for the USSR . . . did so because on balance the good on his side seemed to outweigh the bad."[61] This is little more than saying that ends justify the means or you cannot make an omelet without breaking the eggs. By contrast, the eventual breakdown of faith in the Soviet Union on the part of many intellectuals occurred precisely because of their inability to assimilate more and more increasingly incongruous details into the whole, as it were, or because of their growing belief that the unattractive parts did not add up to a desirable "package." Disillusioned intellectuals testifying to the breakdown of their faith in *The God That Failed*[62] and similar volumes vividly describe this painful process.

Most social criticism entails a belief that there is a connection between personal happiness and fulfillment (or their absence) and the nature of the social world; that personal lives are, to a large extent, socially determined, and that society should help people to live better and make their lives more meaningful and well spent. Most critiques of society also entail the conviction that the ills of society can be remedied and that some people or groups can be held responsible for them. Without such beliefs social criticism would be psychologically difficult and make no more sense than a criticism of nature.

There is no "natural criticism," even though nature has always imposed hardships and scarcities on human beings, confronting them with an uncaring, often harsh physical environment. Much of the earth is infertile and difficult to wrest a living from. The weather in many parts of the world (and many times of the year) is either too hot or too cold, too wet or too dry. The seas are stormy, the mountains rocky, the uplands hard of access. Floods, earthquakes, and drought often menace life more directly and dramatically. Many plants and animals are unfriendly. It is easy to catch disease. We must all die. "The struggle with nature" is not an idle phrase, in spite of what seem to be increasingly costly human victories in our times.

Yet few would think of pointing an accusing finger at nature—neither the religious nor the irreligious among us, though for different reasons. By contrast we blame and hold society responsible for all the reasons we do not blame and criticize nature: because we cannot praise or blame without some, whether boldly or half-heartedly articulated, conceptions of good and evil that are entertained even by the most seemingly dispassionate, social scientific, and deterministic observer. We criticize and hold society responsible because we assume that alternatives to existing (or past) social arrangements and institutions can be found that reduce hardships, scarcity, and deprivation, because we believe that such alternatives would yield more human satisfaction. Social criticism can flourish because it is deeply felt that human will plays a crucial part in social arrangements despite all talk about blind, impersonal, or inexorable social forces and historical processes.[63] The flaws of social arrangements and systems are criticized in a spirit quite different from the regretful comments of travelers traversing a bleak landscape which allows the inhabitants bare survival. Social criticism tends to be passionate because of the underlying conviction that things could be better and different; that suffering and deprivations are needless and could be removed or reduced if only human beings, some human beings, would cease to be greedy, power-hungry, selfish, irrational, wasteful, perverse, cruel, imprudent, or indolent. Such reflections help to explain the tone and character of social criticism that has been reviewed in this chapter, and will be summarized below.

Approximately five or six principal themes constitute the critique of Western capitalist-pluralist society. They have been present as long as capitalism, commerce, and industry; certainly as long as there have been writers, artists, and thinkers who stood apart from their societies, their dominant values, and social-political forces. The main components of this criticism were contributed by Marx and other nineteenth-century socialists and have survived with remarkable tenacity to the present day in partial disregard of substantial social changes.

The five or six main themes represent two types of criticism. One is directed at social institutions and organizations (at institutional malfunctioning), the other more at values and beliefs, or at their failure to move, motivate, or inspire people.

Thus in the 1930s (as in other periods) a prime focus of criticism, besides the economic crisis and its consequences, was the value system (or ethos) of society which was supposed to sustain its members and properly guide its institutions. Capitalism failed to provide worthwhile spiritual values and a sense of purpose (other than excessively individualist preoccupation with material-financial achievement). At the same time, the critics believed that the concern with material values, or the cash nexus, undermined the sense of community and personal relationships, objectifying people. This theme merges into the critique of competitiveness and excessive individualism. No sense of community can develop when people are engaged in merciless competition with one another for money, jobs, material possessions, status, and other questionable attainments. Excessive individualism both reflects and further deepens the inherent conflict between private and public interest which dominates life in capitalist societies. Cultural life too becomes impoverished and oriented to cheap entertainment and unadulterated escapism. The pursuit of profit taints everything.

Inequality unredeemed by any higher purpose or future compensation—the contrasts between widespread want and narrow privilege—was another crucial failing of the capitalist systems.

Capitalist societies were further criticized on political grounds. Few if any critical intellectuals were willing to grant that despite economic failings, rampant inequalities, multitudes of social problems and injustices, there was at least some agreeable political and cultural freedom under capitalism. Most critics took the position that whatever political freedoms existed were rendered meaningless by the enormous discrepancies between the rich and poor; there was refusal to allow any independence or autonomy to the political or cultural realm. Money was power and the lack of money total political powerlessness. The rich could buy power, education, justice, and publicity.

The theoretical rights of the poor were of little use. Everybody had equal rights to sleep under the bridge or run for president or parliament.* In short, economic inequality was viewed as the single determi-

---

* Estranged intellectuals failed to recognize, in the 1930s as well as at other times, that there was, and always is, a link between political rights and economic well-being, and that the so-called bourgeois freedoms or formal rights are not as meaningless or secondary as many Marxists proclaimed. Rosa Luxemburg, for one, recognized the importance of this issue long ago: "the remedy which Trotsky and Lenin have found, the elimination of democracy . . . is worse than the disease it is supposed to cure; for it stops up the living source from which alone can come the correction of all the innate shortcomings of social institutions. . . . Socialist democracy

nant of political power. Under such conditions nominally existing political rights were nothing but sham. The government was no more than an executive committee of the most influential capitalists.

The political defects of capitalism also included racism and colonialism (sexism was added in the 1960s as another product of capitalism). Sometimes it was conceded that capitalist political arrangements were less repressive in the heart of the colonial empires (that is, England and France), but this was achieved at the expense of the more downtrodden and exploited colonial masses. By the same token, in the absence of colonies the formal rights or bourgeois freedoms available in the U.S. were accompanied by the specially savage exploitation of the Negro population at the expense of which all segments of the white population could enjoy some rights and some status.

Finally, as we have seen, there was the critique of irrationality, inefficiency, and wastefulness, directed at both the institutions and organizational practices of capitalism and the values which allowed such a state of affairs to exist. Again, it was the economic crisis which highlighted all other deficiencies of the social system.

The social criticism of the times, especially of the American intellectuals, was also characterized by a self-critical temper which was to surface again in the 1960s and which obstructed the transfer and application of the social-critical impulses to other societies. For example, Henry T. Hodgkin, a Quaker author and sympathizer with the Soviet Union, believed—as did many of his contemporaries—that not only capitalism but also Christianity failed "to create a world where human relations are happily adjusted and where men and women have a chance for full development." His views of Soviet society were conditioned by the critical perception of his own: "Is all well with us? Is voting free? Is the Negro really enfranchised?" The answer was bound to be a resounding "no." In the same spirit he lamented: "Our communist friends can indeed come back to us with some very awkward questions and these we dare not evade."[65]

As noted earlier, in the 1930s as at other times the Quakers were frequently in the forefront of such critical self-examinations of the United States, which invariably resulted in the devaluation of American society and in giving all benefit of the doubt to societies which called

---

is not something which begins only in the promised land after the foundations of socialist economy are created; it does not come as some sort of Christmas present for the worthy people who, in the interim, have loyally supported a handful of socialist dictators."[64]

themselves socialist. Doubtless historical circumstances, and in particular a long tradition of "unremitting preoccupation . . . with the purity of their own souls . . ." help to account for these attitudes. More generally it has also been observed that many social critics of the period "retained enough Calvinist background to have a sense of personal guilt for the sorrows of the unemployed."[66]

While such a blending of religious and political attitudes made a contribution to the larger reservoirs of alienation and utopia-seeking, Americans probably more than any other people have shown a tendency to be outraged by every departure of the social arrangements and realities from the social ideals which had inspired them and by every indication of the failure to implement the ceremonial values and public beliefs of the founders of their country.[67] The awareness that their society has failed to live up to its core values has remained for many intellectuals an endless, nagging source of guilt or at least ambivalence toward their country. Such self-critical propensities are bound to intensify in times of crisis such as the 1930s.

4

The Appeals of Soviet Society:
The First Pilgrimage

Of course, it is no worse than Hollywood (though the penalties—death and deportation—are greater).　　　　　　　EDMUND WILSON[1]

Is it assumed that a visit of this kind affords an ideal opportunity to snoop on one's hosts?　　　　　　　OWEN LATTIMORE[2]

They are unquestionably one of the wonders of the age, and I shall treasure . . . the spectacle of them travelling with radiant optimism through a famished countryside, wandering in happy bands about squalid, over-crowded towns, listening with unshakeable faith to the fatuous patter of carefully trained and indoctrinated guides, repeating like school-children a multiplication table, the bogus statistics and mindless slogans endlessly intoned to them.

Their delight in all they saw and were told, and the expression they gave to this delight, constitute unquestionably one of the wonders of our age. There were earnest advocates of the humane killing of cattle who looked up at the massive headquarters of the Ogpu with tears of gratitude in their eyes, earnest advocates of proportional representation who eagerly assented when the necessity for a Dictatorship of the Proletariat was explained to them, earnest clergymen who walked reverently through anti-God museums and reverently turned the pages of atheistic literature, earnest pacifists who watched delightedly tanks rattle across the Red Square and bombing planes darken the sky, earnest town-planning specialists who stood outside overcrowded ramshackle tenements and muttered: 'If only we had something like this in England!' The almost unbelievable credulity of these mostly university-educated tourists astonished even Soviet officials used to handling foreign visitors. . . .　　　　　　　MALCOLM MUGGERIDGE[3]

Predispositions and Perceptions

The process by which certain societies, slowly or abruptly, become the focus of interest and hopeful expectations is not simply a matter of more information becoming available about their achievements. Indeed, reliable information may hinder this process.

The case of the Soviet Union is among the best illustrations of this phenomenon. Learning more about it had little to do with the upsurge in its popularity in the late 1920s and early 1930s in the United States and Western Europe. It was rather the changed attitudes toward Western societies which pre-dated and determined the emergent appeal of the Soviet. This makes it easier to understand why the October Revolution itself had a relatively limited impact on Western intellectuals despite its historic and symbolic significance as a step toward ending injustice, inequality, and traditional autocracy. At the time, and through much of the 1920s, the United States and the countries of Western Europe were more self-confident, economically secure, and politically stable than in the years which were to follow. Consequently there was less interest in finding a model country which would exemplify the solution to various social and economic problems. Thus the estrangement of intellectuals from Western societies and their admiration for the Soviet were almost totally fused. Most of those who became estranged sooner or later discovered the attractions of Soviet society; and those enchanted by the latter were invariably alienated and highly critical of their own society. The two attitudes rarely existed independent of one another, although in theory this could have been possible: alienation need not have led to the admiration of the Soviet Union, and it might have been possible for people comfortable with their own society to find the Soviet Union appealing. This however was not the case. Evidently people do not simultaneously become interested in other societies or cultures, at any rate not in large numbers unless something becomes problematic in their own, which makes them anxious to learn about social arrangements elsewhere.

It is difficult to realize today, at a time when the Soviet Union stands largely discredited (or ignored) by most Western intellectuals, how widespread its appeals were in the late 1920s, the 1930s,* and the World War II period. This is not to deny or overlook that for many intellectuals these appeals proved short-lived, that many of them changed their mind following some dramatic historical event or disclosure about the Soviet

---

* For example, a collection of writings about the Soviet Union by Western intellectuals published in 1932 contained tributes from well over one hundred prominent authors (the largest contingents were German, American, French, and English) including such figures as Heinrich and Thomas Mann, Johannes Becher, Egon Ervin Kisch, Gerhart Hauptmann, Ernst Toller, Anatole France, Henri Barbusse, Romain Rolland, André Maurois, G. B. Shaw, H. G. Wells, Theodore Dreiser, Stuart Chase, Sherwood Eddy, Anna Louise Strong, Michael Gold, Albert Rhys Williams, John Dos Passos, Upton Sinclair, Floyd Dell, Martin Andersen Nexo, and George Lukacs.[4]

system. The significant fact remains that many Western intellectuals did go through an intensely pro-Soviet phase and exhibited highly patterned, virtually uniform attitudes of admiration and enthusiasm toward the Soviet Union, if only for a limited period (usually a few years).

Julian Huxley's recommendation as to how one should view Soviet society was widely adopted by sympathetic visitors, as it enabled them to discard the ballast of their critical faculties with a clear conscience. He wrote: "It is no good viewing everything Russian through your own imported atmosphere, for that merely acts as a distorted lens to the facts . . . the visitor to Russia must attempt to discard some of his bourgeois ideas about democracy, religion and traditional morality, his romantic individualism, his class feelings, his judgements of what constitutes success, and pick up what he can of the atmosphere in which the Russians live immersed."[5]

As already noted, predisposition played the major part in the favorable perceptions of the Soviet Union. These perceptions rested primarily on the feelings of disenchantment with one's own society, a disenchantment feeding on many sources. The social criticism reviewed earlier provides the most accessible explanation. More elusive but also important might have been the particular life experiences and personality dispositions of the visitors, which cannot be explored here. Suffice it to say that most of them were idealistic, hopeful, and ready to believe that radically new departures were possible in remodeling the organization of society and that social policies and personal needs could be fully harmonized.

It is difficult to conjure up today the spirit of joyous anticipation in which so many travelers in the early 1930s set forth on their trips to the Soviet Union. Malcolm Muggeridge observed some of them aboard a ship he shared with them:

> On their way to the Soviet Union they were in a festive mood; like a cup-tie party on their way to a match, equipped with rattles, colored scarves and favours. Each of them harboring in his mind some special hope; of meeting Stalin, or alternatively, of falling in with a Komsomolka, sparkling eyed, red scarf and jet black hair dancing the *carmagnole;* above all, with very enlightened views on sex, and free and easy ways. In any case equipping themselves with special, authoritative knowledge which would enable them to embellish their articles and lectures . . .
>
> In their dealings with the crew and the stewards they were punctilious in cultivating an egalitarian attitude; the word 'comrade' was often on their lips. . . . These fellow-passengers provided my first experience of the progressive elite from all over the world who at-

tached themselves to the Soviet regime, resolved to believe anything they were told by its spokesmen. For the most part they were academics and writers—the clerks of Julien Benda's *La Trahison des clercs;* all upholders of progressive causes and members of progressive organizations, constituting a sort of Brechtian ribald chorus in the drama of the twentieth century. Ready at any moment to rush on to stage, cheering and gesticulating . . . a western version of the devotees of Krishna who throw themselves under the wheels of the great Juggernaut.[6]

The enthusiasm of the visitors persisted after their arrival. William C. White, an American residing in Moscow at the time, wrote of them:

> They are wildly enthusiastic over all they see but not always logical; they were enthusiastic before they came and their visit only doubly convinces them. A schoolteacher from Brooklyn was on a tour of one of the newspaper plants. She saw a machine which did wonders with the paper that was fed to it. 'Really, that is remarkable,' she commented. 'Such an amazing invention could be produced only in a country like yours, where labor is free, unexploited, and working for one end. I shall write a book about what I have seen.' She was a trifle embarrassed when she walked to the rear and saw the sign: 'Made in Brooklyn, N.Y.'[7]

Those who regarded the USSR as the true land of opportunity and fulfillment were confident that their particular (and occasionally peculiar) causes would there be taken up. Sometimes disappointment followed: "There was an American who felt that universal salvation lay in Communism plus the adoption of Esperanto and a diet of only nuts for all people; he departed disillusioned when his suggestions about more pecans for the proletariat and no meat were turned down."[8]

There were many other, less frivolous, motives for visiting the Soviet Union. According to Lewis Feuer, a generation of Americans went to the Soviet Union in search of inspiration and to find specific remedies for problems which loomed large and seemed well-nigh insoluble in their own society at the time:

> The social worker was ready to see the Soviet Union as a kind of Hull House on a national scale, as the land of public health and mental hygiene; the progressive educator was ready to see the Soviet experiment as a nation-wide Laboratory School, happily freed from the surveillance of university presidents and boards of trustees; the religious leader who saw the Social Gospel ignored and disused in Coolidge's America recognized witnesses to his creed in the party of dedicated political missionaries, who despite their atheism were evidently moved by a selfless emotion . . . ; the crusader for birth control and liberal

divorce laws who found himself trammeled and sometimes jailed in his
own Puritan-bound and Catholic contained America saw a land where
sexual love was more nearly unfettered; radical labor leaders, who bore
the memory of judge's injunctions, militiamen's bayonets and policemen's clubs, found themselves welcome in a land whose political chief
talked with them for several hours and called them: "Comrades"; the
social scientists found themselves singularly at home in a society which
was guided by fellow social scientists who aimed to build a rational,
planned world.[9]

Eugene Lyons, who surveyed the visitors from inside the Soviet Union
at the time, also commented on the multiplicity of its appeals:

> Hard-boiled capitalists found the spectacle to their taste: no strikes, no
> lip, hard work on a bread-and-water diet; and one good look at a
> Soviet factory cured them of the fear of Russian competition. Soft-
> boiled idealists found familiar slogans, day nurseries, model prisons,
> bigger and better uplift. Pale advocates of juiceless causes—birth con-
> trol, Esperanto, new calendars, sex equality, prison reform, big families,
> futurist dancing, modern education—found surcease from contempt.
> Everyone . . . who accounted himself enlightened and advanced
> veered toward Intourist under the pleasant illusion that Bolshevism was
> a new, more gloriously intransigent bohemianism.[10]

Such visitors failed to grasp that the Soviet system was puritanical,
stressed discipline and self-denial, and was thoroughly averse to any
form of bohemianism, or liberated self-realization as understood by
Westerners. Occasionally this created problems:

> Finally there are those who come feeling that the Soviet Union is a
> paradise for rebels; such people, weary of bourgeois hypocrisy or unsat-
> isfied under capitalism, have read of Soviet Russia and dreamed
> dreams. A young couple from New York sold everything they owned
> and came to Moscow to "express their real selves!"* . . . They learned
> that cabbage soup and black bread constitute a monotous diet . . .
> worse, the wife fell sick and after two weeks managed to get into a
> free hospital. She fled the food and the crowded wards in three days.
>   In the meantime the husband was discovering that the Soviet Union
> was not as he dreamed it; lauding its social aims he, a pacifist . . . dis-
> approved of the drastic and direct measures that are often employed
> to achieve these aims. "We want no such sentimentalists," said one
> Communist to him. . . . The couple returned to New York. . . .[11]

Richard H. Pells, the American social historian, divided the American
sympathizers into three major groups. There were what he called "the

_____

* Their spiritual heirs in the 1960s were content to engage either in purely domestic experiments—on their road to self-expression—or limit their forays into the promised lands of their times to a few weeks.

natural rebels against all types of tyranny" (exemplified by writers such as Dos Passos and Edmund Wilson); there were those who misidentified the Soviet regime as "a modern version of Christian brotherhood" (a group which included Waldo Frank and Granville Hicks); and at last there were those who were attracted to the Soviet system largely as a reaction against the economic chaos and inefficiency in their own society.[12]

On the whole there was a notable convergence between the varied needs and shared predispositions of the travelers (and potential travelers) and the objectives of the Soviet government: "The positive image which the Soviet authorities wished to disseminate was multifaceted," Sylvia Margulies wrote. "There was something in it to appeal to everyone. To the worker, the Soviet Union was to appear as a revolutionary fortress, a land of opportunity, the only home for the world proletariat. For the intellectuals, the society became a humanitarian one . . . devoted to the advancement of mankind. And to the businessman, it was a thriving society, desirous of co-operating economically with the capitalist world in mutually beneficial arrangements."[13]

While the Soviet regime tried, for pragmatic reasons, to maximize its appeals among diverse strata of the Western public, its efforts were the most successful among intellectuals. For them, the Soviet system exercised a contradictory yet irresistible attraction: "Admiration for Russia could . . . satisfy at the same time two apparently contradictory sentiments: rage for order and support for revolution,"[14] in Lewis Coser's words. Nevertheless it is to be noted that this upsurge of interest in and endorsement of the Soviet system on the part of intellectuals in the early 1930s took place against a broader background of a generally improving image of the Soviet Union. The increasingly favorable perceptions of the Soviet Union rested largely on Soviet economic achievements or what a contemporary observer called "a respectful and attentive regard for planned economic effort."[15]

Before a closer examination of the diverse appeals of Soviet society I would like to comment further on the exceptionally close relationship between predispositions and perceptions. It is no exaggeration to suggest that a large number of visitors entering the Soviet Union with feverishly positive anticipations succeeded in discovering exactly what they expected and wished to discover.* We may never know which was the

* Surprisingly few visitors strove to erect defenses against the techniques of hospitality or had shown awareness of the problem of contrasting and oscillating perceptions pondered by Gyula Illyés, the Hungarian writer, in his little-known travelogue dating from the early 1930s: "The traveler to Russia, whatever his point of de-

greater force shaping their highly selective perceptions: their inner drives and desires or the assistance rendered by their obliging hosts in selecting what they could perceive. These two factors obviously interacted but, as noted earlier, without predisposition the official efforts to manage their impression would not have been successful. The connection between predisposition and perception was so close that even sights or experiences unappealing or indifferent in other contexts were transvalued and redefined in the Soviet. Eugene Lyons wrote of his arrival in the Soviet Union in 1928: "Neither a forlorn looking station, nor cold, nor darkness could douse our mood of expectation. . . . Elsewhere dinginess might be depressing. Here it seemed to us romantically proletarian. . . ."[17] In the same spirit Anna Strong exulted as she approached the Soviet border in 1921: "Exhaustion, vermin, dysentery, were birth pangs to joy, the initiation to chaos where a new world was being born beyond the border."[18]

While sometimes the sordid or bleak were redefined as exciting and exhilarating, at other times the perfectly ordinary sent the observer into raptures over something he would have paid little if any attention to in his own country. Thus Julian Huxley found extraordinary pleasure in contemplating the crowds during a summer weekend at the Moscow River and even managed to endow them with physiques superior to those of his countrymen: "It [the scene] all seemed simple, natural and pleasant but perhaps it would not be pleasant in England until the physique of the average man and woman is up to that of the Russians."[19] Such perceptions and sentiments document and support the notion that what makes travel an adventure and a source of exhilaration is not only the possibility that it may lead to the discovery of the unusual, but also that it may transform the ordinary into the extraordinary. Many of the intellectuals who traveled to the Soviet Union in the 1930s succeeded in effecting such transformations. Waldo Frank discovered virtues in a Russian train he would not have been able to find in similar pieces of

---

parture, sets out in a suspicious frame of mind and by the time he reaches the border, he duly contracts the Potemkin-complex . . . its prime symptom is that at times the eye becomes a magnifying lense making an elephant out of a flea, while at other times it turns a cow into a mole. . . .

". . . In the beginning one stares with dilated pupils at the most unremarkable shack and keeps looking until two of them emerge simultaneously: one is tidy and neat, the other dilapidated and about to collapse. The miracle may be transferred into reality and the photograph of the shack may be one kind or the other depending on whether or not it is published in the Sunday supplement of an anti-communist or communist newspaper."[16]

machinery traversing capitalist rails: "There is something about a Russian train standing at a station that thrills. . . . The little locomotive is human.° . . . The dingy cars are human. . . ." The insides of this magic little train provoked similar ecstasy: "The compartment was dirty with scraps of food, spilled water, moist soot: clothing and bags lay indiscriminate on the floor . . . the air was thick with cigarettes." Monotonous factory work too became an occasion for jubilation for the enthusiastic observer, if not the workers: "Here are happy workers, because they are whole men and women. . . . Dream, thought, love collaborate in the tedious business of making electric parts, since these toilers are not working for a boss—not even for a living."[21] Eugene Lyons observed the ". . . Voks [agency dealing with tourists] sell the glories of mass production to a couple of California back-to-nature, hand-loom faddists. Vegetarians . . . swooned in ecstasy of admiration for Soviet slaughter-houses."[22]

Selective perception, combined with projection, allows for the almost total neglect of what objective reality is like. What occurs is not so much an outright denial of reality—after all, Waldo Frank did not claim that the railroad compartments were clean or that making electric parts was not tedious—but rather the redefinition of situations or events by means of the context in which they are found and which is supposed to impart new meaning to them. Such contextual redefinitions in turn facilitate selective perception. Thus Corliss and Margaret Lamont could reconcile themselves to manifestations of militarism in Soviet kindergarten by asking, "in a setting of a socialist state may not all this have a different aspect?"[23] Feuchtwanger attributed good-natured patience to the Soviet people in the same spirit: "The citizens of Moscow joke about minor inconveniences, usually if not always, with complete good humor, but they never think of allowing these shortcomings to blind them to the big things which life in the Soviet Union alone can offer. . . ."[24]

The favorable predisposition and the associated selective perceptions were not the only explanations of the overwhelmingly favorable accounts produced by the visitors. There was also the powerful pressure of apprehension that should they report something unfavorable they would be automatically (and "objectively") aligned with the forces of

---

° Perhaps the fascination with steam engines has to do not only with the ideological transvaluation of objects and sights but also with the sense of deprivation Americans experienced as such machines were replaced by more unromantic Diesel engines. Sympathetic visitors to China in the early 1970s were also impressed by the trains, and in revolutionary Cuba LeRoi Jones noted that "Everyone in the train seemed to be talking excitedly and having a wild time."[20]

reaction and evil in their own societies, an apprehension that continues to haunt and color the public assessments of supposedly socialist regimes on the part of liberal intellectuals even in our day. Recalling the intellectual climate of the times, Dos Passos wrote: "The other inhibition [to truthful reporting from the Soviet Union in the late 1920s, that is] was the fear of writing something that would be seized on by anti-Soviet propaganda in the West. That was a period in which American capitalism seemed a much greater danger to the Russian experiment than the other way around." (Several decades later similar motives restrained Hans Magnus Enzensberger, a German admirer of Cuba, from publishing his critical account of his visit[25] as they had Garcia Marquez.)

Louis Fischer offered another familiar explanation of similar attitudes: "Why, instead of holding my tongue, did I not come out in 1937 or 1938 as a critic of the Soviet regime? It is not so easy to throw away the vision to which one has been attached for fifteen years. Moreover, in 1938, the Soviet government's foreign policy was effectively anti-appeasement and anti-Fascist, much more so than England's or France's or America's. It helped China. . . . It helped Spain with arms to fight the Nazis and Mussolini. It encouraged Czechoslovakia to stand firm . . . I hesitated to throw stones in public. . . ."[26]

The expression of critical attitudes toward the Soviet Union was inhibited not only by such tactical considerations—that is, that it would play into the hands of the enemies of progress and the most biased critics of the Soviet system—but, as noted earlier, also by a more diffuse attitude of humility, most discernible among Americans, especially restrained by their pervasive misgivings about their own society. Henry T. Hodgkin exemplified these attitudes as he exhorted: "Merely to repudiate the violent and terrible measures used in establishing and maintaining the Bolshevik regime does not seem enough. There are enough evils here without looking across the Atlantic or Pacific to find them."[27]*

It should also be recalled that another attraction of travel to the Soviet Union (as was also the case later with China and Cuba) could be found in the combination of the more usual motives (e.g. change of scenery, excitement, adventure, etc.) with the more serious purpose, that is, learning about a new system of government and forms of social organization. The latter was especially attractive for educated and serious-minded Americans as it appealed to the dutiful streak in them. The

---

* It may be noted here that no such restraint, or self-critical humility, is recommended by authors like Hodgkin when they do feel genuine moral outrage about "violent and terrible measures" in other parts of the world.

possibility of joining serious purpose with pleasure mitigated the self-indulgent or frivolous associations of travel, as if one combined dining out with a lecture on lung disease among coalminers, or á day on the beach with a lecture-tour of a nearby fish processing plant (in fact such combinations abounded on the visits of the Soviet Union and the other countries).[28] The attitude perhaps also reflected the time honored American proclivity to combine business with pleasure, the joy of vacationing with the collection of sociological information, sightseeing with statistics. This approach remains well and alive.

Social Justice and Equality

Although the various appeals of Soviet society tended to coalesce in the eyes of the visitors, some were singled out for special praise and attention. Probably social justice and equality (seen as either already attained or about to be) were the most highly regarded achievements of the regime. There was widespread consensus that whatever residual inequalities could still be found, the sharp distinctions between the rich and the poor, which troubled and deeply offended intellectuals in Western societies, disappeared in the Soviet Union. Edmund Wilson reported:

> One gradually comes to realize that, though the people's clothes are dreary, there is little, if any, destitution; though there are no swell parts of the city, there are no degraded parts either. There are no shocking sights on the streets: no down-and-outers, no horrible diseases, no old people picking in garbage pails.
> I was never able to find anything like a slum or any quarter that even seemed dirty.[29]

Theodore Dreiser wrote, "There is no show, no luxury. [In the Soviet Union] . . . you will see thousands who are comparatively poorly dressed to ten—at most a hundred—who are well dressed. And yet generally speaking, a sense of well-being—none of that haunting sense of poverty or complete defeat that so distressed one in western Europe and America. It is not to be found. Yet in Moscow there is poverty. There are beggars in the streets. . . . But Lord, how picturesque! The multi-colored and voluminous rags of them!"[30]

The apparent absence of deference in social intercourse was equally heartening, especially for those coming from highly stratified societies like England, where manners of speaking and ways of dressing reflected social status. The Americans, more accustomed to informality and little deference in their own society (however unmatched by the underlying

reality of vast discrepancies of wealth and concomitant social position),
were particularly appreciative of the absence of conspicuous consumption and display associated with the striving for higher social status.
Whatever aspect of the perceived equalization of status, opportunity,
and reward was noted, the visitors were deeply moved by the thought
that they were encountering a historically new and unique attempt to
do away with inequality in a deliberate and purposeful way. Even when
what were regarded as residual, lingering inequalities were observed,
there was a profound conviction that—like any other surviving weakness
or blemish in Soviet society—these too were doomed to extinction.

Underlying the concern with equality and social justice, many visitors
discerned a conception of human nature they found highly congenial
and assumed to animate the Soviet leadership. An English Quaker, D. F.
Buxton, wrote:

> the really fundamental thing in a change of attitude towards human
> nature in general. The Communist view of human nature seems to me
> far more inspired by Faith, Hope and Charity than our own. To them
> the prime cause of evil . . . is the poison of wealth which stultifies
> men's natural instincts of fellowship. Once a State is delivered from
> this perversive influence acting on any of its citizens, and granted also
> a certain degree of education, all can be trusted to receive equal rights.
> Their confidence in unspoilt human nature forbids the Communists to
> believe in self-interest as the indispensable motive by which alone the
> economic machine can be kept going.[31]

More specifically Buxton (like many others) felt that "Of all flunkeys
and flunkeyism there was a complete and (to my mind) blessed absence.
There was in fact, *one* standard of manners, not several. . . . In Russia,
with the disappearance of the upper class, the foibles of fashion have
disappeared too. The only class that remains is the one great class of
'The People.'" He had much praise for the egalitarianism of the rulers:

> As an example of the new order of incentives, the self-denying ordi-
> nance of the Communist Party in the matter of salaries is significant.
> . . . The simple unostentatious life of Russia's rulers represents a
> notable advance in *real* civilization—real because based on a more en-
> lightened interpretation of human nature, both of its needs and capac-
> ities; an interpretation which incidentally is also a more Christian
> one.[32]

Theodore Dreiser, during the same period, also praised the modesty
and pecuniary restraint of the Soviet leaders:

The rooms of Lenin in the Kremlin . . . offer perhaps a classical example of the simplicity and frugality of the present-day rulers of Russia. Lenin, however was not alone in this. Most of the leaders live in
simple hotel rooms or in single rooms in the Kremlin.
Monsieur Stalin . . . receives for himself 225 rubles per month (about
$112) plus three rooms in the Kremlin. . . . And . . . Tchicherin,
the Minister of Foreign Affairs, no more. Lunacharsky, the Minister of
Education . . . receives no more! In fact, I could find no one in any
high position who received a penny more. . . . Yet among the Communist workers I could not find any who were earning less than 50
rubles and thousands upon thousands who were receiving 150, 175,
200, 225 or more![33]

Egalitarianism was not confined to the modest salaries of the leaders;
it was also detected in the lack of officiousness and in the warmth of
Soviet officials. Joseph Freeman, the American communist writer, upon
arrival aboard a freighter in Baku (in 1926) was astonished by the behavior of the Soviet official who inquired:

"Did you have a good trip?" We exchanged glances. This had not happened in Constantinople. It did not happen in any other port. Control
officials never came to the fo'c'sle to chat with the seaman. This one,
to our surprise, asked us about our health, our voyage, our wages,
hours, working conditions, food, about the general situation in our
country, the American labor movement.[34]

It should be noted here that such comments on the part of the earlier
generation of visitors to the Soviet Union were based not merely on their
misperception and misinterpretation of Soviet social realities and official
policies but also on the surviving remnants of revolutionary egalitarianism which could still be detected in the second half of the 1920s. The
new and well-defined system of stratification which took final shape in
the early 1930s was not yet fully discernible. In the meantime, that is,
through much of the 1920s, Western visitors were able to project egalitarian dreams and wishes on to Soviet society more easily and with less
self-deception than became possible in subsequent years. By contrast,
from the beginning of the 1930s the denial of inequality required more
ingenuity; the new inequalities had to be redefined and explained away
with more determination than was necessary earlier. Thus for example
Hewlett Johnson, a lifelong admirer of the Soviet Union, admitted (in
1940) that income inequalities existed but was not disturbed by them
since they were based on "a carefully thought-out plan" and acted as incentives. He felt assured that such differentials would not lead to "class
differentiation."[35] Feuchtwanger too recognized the presence of inequali-

ties but found them "utterly reasonable," being based on the principle "to each according to his achievement."[36] Harry F. Ward, professor of Christian Ethics at the Union Theological Seminary in New York, and another durable friend of the Soviet regime, also found much to justify Soviet income differentials. First of all, they were transitional. Secondly, they were linked to the good of society. After all, work in the Soviet Union benefited (by definition) the entire society. Hence the more work and better quality work, the greater the social benefits. The latter in turn justified higher rewards. Reassuringly, Stalin's attack on petty bourgeois egalitarianism "was amply supported by quotations from Marx and Lenin." Moreover, ". . . the stimulus of increased monetary rewards . . . operates differently in a socialist society where social disapproval falls more heavily upon the 'snatcher' than it does in the capitalist world." Ward even managed to justify the introduction of tuition fees and the limitation of stipends which some people considered, mistakenly, "a narrowing down of opportunity." This too was "a temporary device" designed "to raise the scholastic average and weed out the incompetent." The crux of it all was that no matter how hard anyone would try, the system was so designed that work would benefit society whereas asocial impulses could find virtually no outlet: "In general the situation in the Soviet Union offers satisfaction to ambition only in terms of social service. It offers creative adventure: the chance to pioneer in the improvement of human organization . . . youth is offered the satisfaction of its socially justifiable ambitions without having to climb up the ladder trampling upon the less able. *The ladder is abolished. All go up together or none go.*"[37] The apologists of the new inequalities rarely if at all confronted the fact that if income differentials had to be introduced as incentives to attain greater productivity, or as a reward for acquiring higher skills, then the moral-spiritual or service-oriented incentives were obviously not providing sufficient motivation for hard work or, more generally speaking, socially beneficial exertions. The justifications of Soviet inequality on the part of the sympathetic intellectuals followed the official Soviet line, which amounted to the Soviet version of true meritocracy. That so many of the visitors were capable of retaining their enthusiasm for the Soviet regime even after the restratification of Soviet society indicated once more that what outraged the conscience of many Western intellectuals was not inequality as such. Rather, it was inequality poorly justified and without sound purpose, such as they confronted in their own society.

For a large contingent among these visitors, the public ownership of the means of production (or what was taken for public ownership, i.e., state control) was a sufficient guarantee of social justice and a firm foundation for building an egalitarian society. In 1932 Julian Huxley still felt that social justice was being realized in "a system in which the results of work go primarily to raising the general level of well being instead of seeping away into private channels. . . ."[38] Unhesitatingly the sympathizers equated these new forms of control over the economy with a sense of mastery and participation in decision-making on the part of the masses. Joseph Freeman wrote:

> Here, where the individual was supposed to subordinate himself to the general interests of society as a whole, he actually expanded by virtue of being part of something greater than himself. Except for the remnants of the former privileged classes, everyone acted as though the general good was his personal good, as though his personal difficulties could be solved by conquering the common difficulties. At home, in America, the "average" man—the worker, the farmer, the office employee . . . —was despised and rejected; he had no real voice in the management of the national economy or public affairs. . . . Here the "average" man felt himself master of everything. . . .[39]

Edmund Wilson also felt that "Here the people in the park do really own it and they are careful of what is theirs. A new kind of public conscience has come to lodge in these crowds. . . ." Furthermore, "the crowds move like slow floods of water—not straining, not anxious like our people, not pitted against an alien environment, but as if the whole city belonged to them. . . ."[40]

Alexander Wicksteed, an English visitor of the same period, had an identical point of view: "for the first time in history the common man feels that the country belongs to him and not to the privileged class that are his masters." He too was impressed by the lack of deference:

> Next I would mention the complete equality that one finds in Russia . . . on the economic plane the Marxian ideal of a classless society may still be a thing of the future, but on the social side it has been realized to an extent that is wonderfully refreshing to any Englishman of democratic aspirations.[41]

Thus there were various ways to get around the problem of inequalities, depending on the exact period of time and the ingenuity of the observer. In the 1920s inequality was residual, a vestige of the past; in the 30s (and later) a temporary measure introduced for pragmatic purposes. In any event the inequalities permitted were compatible with the lack of deference, social justice, good fellowship, sense of community, the absence of class distinctions and class antagonism. Inequalities were also mitigated by a sense of national unity and the steady decline of the divergence between public and private interest. Legends of the public-spirited Soviet citizen were legion, as were tales of self-sacrifice either on the altar of peaceful construction or later when confronting the German invaders. (We learn for instance about the "voluntary" donations of peasants to the Red Army, a campaign that was intiated, among others, by "the beekeeper Feropant Golovaty, who donated out of his life savings 100,000 rubles for a fighter plane."[42])

Another important component of social justice was the security of employment. It was hardly surprising that the absence of unemployment should impress the visitors who had witnessed its ravages in the United States or Western Europe. Corliss and Margaret Lamont discerned a relationship between full employment and the disinclination of Soviet workers to save some of their income: "Indeed why should Russians save when they have no fear of unemployment and when society as a whole is pledged to take care of them and their families in sickness and old age."[43] (They did not entertain other possible interpretations of this phenomenon, such as that Soviet workers' earnings were too modest to allow for savings.) Feuchtwanger commented on the "comfortable certainty [of the citizen] that the state is really there for him and not he for the state."[44]

The beneficial effects of such profound security were not lost on the visitors. Ward spoke for many of them as he concluded that "Those who have grown up in the Soviet land have never known the fears that shadow the paths of a predatory society . . . the record shows that people who grow up without the tormenting fear of economic insecurity work with a freedom, a joy, and a power that cannot exist when the natural desire of man to create is limited by fear and want."[45]

Dyson Carter, a Canadian scientist, pondered the good fortune of those who grow old in the Soviet Union:

> Perhaps we should have called Soviet old folks the second privileged class. [Children were the first.] Every possible care and comfort is given those who have retired from active life. The fear of poverty in old age has been completely banished by pensions for all. For the sick and infirm there are rest homes and sanatoriums in beautiful surroundings. For those who still feel young in body and mind there is leisure to enjoy the infinite variety of experiences that abound in the vigorous new land of the Soviets.

He thus summed up the triumph of social justice and material security:

No color lines, no "dirty foreigners," no filthy overcrowded slums, no unattended sickness, no criminal vice and prostitution, no lifelong toil shadowed forever by insecurity. . . . The Soviets abolished all these evils. . . .[46]

The popularity of the Soviet system among clergymen and Quakers was one of the paradoxes of the times, not only because one would expect servants of God and those devoutly religious to be sensitive to political repression but also because they admired a political system which was dedicated, in word and deed, to the eradication of religion. Here again the belief in the Soviet success in achieving social justice was helpful to overcome whatever problems the anti-religious stand of the regime created. Hewlett Johnson personified many such servants of God who were irresistibly drawn toward the Soviet Union on account of its material accomplishments and who succeeded in viewing it as a social system, which, despite its overtly irreligious nature, came closer to the ideals of Christianity than Western societies which merely paid lip service to religious values:

> The experiment which is being worked out in a sixth of the earth's surface is founded on a new organization of economic life based on clearly defined principles which are thoroughly understood and gladly accepted. . . . Our system lacks moral basis. . . . It gives rise . . . to that fatal divergence between principles and practice of Christian people, which is so damning to religion. . . . Such is the moral aspect of contemporary economic society. Its scientific aspect is the wholly irrational wastage of wealth, the artificially induced shortage, the poverty amidst plenty. . . . In opposition to this view of the organization of economic life is that of the Soviet Union where co-operation replaces competitive chaos and a Plan succeeds the riot of disorder. . . . The community rather than the self-seeking individual stands in the centre of the picture. The welfare of the whole and of each individual within it replaces . . . the welfare of a select class or classes. The elimination of the profit-motive makes room for the higher motive of service. . . . A new attitude towards human life is the natural counterpart of the new economic morality. Individuals, all individuals, become ends as well as means. The development of the human potentialities of each individual receives fullest opportunity and encouragement. . . .[47]

Johnson's statement is also typical of the sentiments voiced by many sympathetic Western visitors, clergymen or not,* which characteristically

* In refusing to accept at face value the Soviet professions of anti-religious purpose, Johnson and others anticipated a trend especially pronounced in our times among the advocates of detente, namely the designation and dismissal as "rhetoric" of the Soviet expressions of hostility directed at the U.S. and other Western societies.

combine the glorification of Soviet achievements with a strong sense of shame over the defects of Western societies. (The same basic attitudes survived intact into the 1960s, although at that time exaltation was evoked by other societies.)

For those who looked upon the Soviet Union as the most outstanding contemporary embodiment of social justice, the question of material scarcities and especially food shortages was an important one. It is hard to institute social justice in a society in which crippling scarcities prevail and in which the satisfaction of basic material needs is problematic. Many visitors went to the Soviet Union to dispel "misinformation" about such scarcities, which were mentioned in the Western press in the 1920s and 30s, although their magnitude was not known even among the detractors of the Soviet Union at the time.[48] Not surprisingly, the visitors were not given many opportunities to experience shortages. Their predispositions were exemplified by a gesture of G. B. Shaw, who ". . . before crossing the Soviet border . . . had flung a supply of provisions out of the train because he was convinced that there were no shortages in Russia."[49]* Julian Huxley "got the impression of a population not at all undernourished, and at a level of physique and general health rather above that to be seen in England."[51] Feuchtwanger found a great variety of food available at low prices and "People with modest incomes entertaining an unexpected guest with surprising lavishness."[52]

Louis Fischer, who as a journalist was better informed, though no less sympathetic to the Soviet system, observed more cautiously that "Lest a false impression be conveyed, it must be stated that nobody starves. The population of the entire country, however, suffers from the poor quality of food and from lack of variety." Yet, he also noted, "Despite the universal shortage, Russians are complaining less about living con-

---

* Eugene Lyons at the time in the Soviet Union also remembered this famous episode and some of the Soviet reactions to it: "The vision of good English food thrown away in Poland [he did so before crossing the Soviet border] was mockery of the underfed audience. Shaw's listeners gasped. . . . Even before he reached Russia, Shaw assured them, he knew that this talk of food difficulties was poppycock. Why, he had been overstuffed ever since he reached Moscow. . . . At a luncheon in the Metropole next day Mrs. William Henry Chamberlain [wife of another American resident correspondent] remarked to Shaw that Russians were sorry he did not wait to throw away his food on Soviet soil. Shaw looked around the restaurant and asked cutely: 'Where do you see any food shortage?' Mrs. Chamberlain tried to tell him. 'I have a four-year old daughter,' she said. 'As a foreigner I can buy all the milk she needs but if I were dependent on the Russian milk rations my little girl would suffer terribly.' 'Why don't you nurse her yourself?' Shaw retorted. 'But she is four, she is too old . . .' 'Nonsense! Certain Eskimos nurse their children till the age of twenty.' "[50]

ditions than they did before."[53] He refrained from speculating about any other possible reason why Russians were complaining less about living conditions or any other matters in the early 1930s.

This issue of famine—and more generally the regime's inability to meet the basic material needs of the population in the early 1930s—exemplifies the magnitude of misperceptions on the part of the visitors and the regime's capacity to conceal. Malcolm Muggeridge was one of what must have been a handful of outsiders who found out and reported the acute food shortages *at the time.* (He was also one of the few sympathizers of the period whose favorable predispositions were undermined by what he had experienced while living in the Soviet Union. To be sure, he spent more time there than most visitors, being correspondent of the *Manchester Guardian*, but for others like Walter Duranty, Louis Fischer, or Anna Louise Strong prolonged residence made little difference.) Muggeridge wrote:

> . . . I did break my journey several times, and can never forget what I saw. It was not just a famine. . . . This particular famine was planned and deliberate; not due to any natural catastrophe like failure of rain, or cyclone, or flooding. An administrative famine brought about by the forced collectivization of agriculture; an assault on the countryside by party apparatchiks—the very men I'd been chatting so amiably with in the train—supported by strong-arm squads from the military and the police. . . .
>
> As it happened, no other foreign journalist had been into the famine areas in the USSR except under official auspices and supervision, so my account was by way of being exclusive.* This brought me no kudos, and many accusation of being a liar . . . I had to wait for Khrushchev . . . for official confirmation. Indeed, according to him, my account was considerably under-stated. If the matter is a subject of controversy thereafter, a powerful voice on the other side will be Duranty's, highlighted in the NY *Times,* insisting on those granaries overflowing with grain, those apple-cheeked dairymaids and plump contented cows, not to mention Shaw and other distinguished visitors who testified that there was not, and could not be, a food storage in the USSR.[55]

At another extreme there were those who would entertain the possibility of famine as yet another temporary necessity or setback. Maurice

---

* Eugene Lyons discussed at some length how "The Press Corps Conceals a Famine," ch. XV in *Assignment to Utopia.*

Another rare glimpse of the famine by a foreigner was had by Homer Smith, an American Negro who was at the time a temporary expatriate in the USSR. He reported on his firsthand observations in the book he published after his return to the U.S.[54]

Hindus, an American author and early specialist on the Soviet Union, wrote:

> "And supposing there is a famine in Russia," continued my interlocutor, an American businessman, . . . "what will happen?"
> "People will die of course," I answered.
> "And supposing three or four million people die."
> "The Revolution will go on."[56]

Anna Louise Strong, despite being a full-time propagandist of the Soviet government (writing and editing for both foreign and domestic consumption), was at the time assailed by doubt about suppressing the news of the famine: "I protested to Borodin. 'Why does everybody keep this deadly silence? Every communist to whom you mention the hunger glares as if you talked of treason. . . . Why aren't we allowed to tell the facts?' "[57] She was evidently persuaded that her "journalist passion to tell things" was not to take precedence over the interests of the party.

For sympathizers it has remained an article of faith up to the present that the Soviet Union has, in a historically unparalleled way, raised the living standards of the entire population, and even if it is not exactly egalitarian, created social justice by providing adequate minimum standards and equality of opportunity for all. Although Western intellectuals attracted to the Soviet system are neither numerous nor vocal these days, those retaining their earlier commitment have persisted in such beliefs. Thus for example Ruth Epperson Kennell, who acted as a guide for Theodore Dreiser in the 1920s, wrote in 1969 that "Their [Soviet] socialist society provides a standard of living for all the people approaching the level of an average American middle class family—with no extremes of wealth and poverty."[58]

Sense of Purpose and Cohesive Values

Among the main appeals of Soviet society the sense of purpose and the invigorating social values seem almost equal in importance to social justice and egalitarianism. The attractions of purposefulness and integrative values were to a great extent apolitical and spiritual. It need not be unduly perplexing that the Soviet system had certain crucial appeals which were of a spiritual nature and that these (and other) appeals of Soviet society climaxed at the time when Western societies were shaken by economic rather than spiritual crisis, when the contrasting model of Soviet economic rationality exerted its greatest attraction.

Here again we must be reminded that the visitors responded selectively to the appeals of Soviet society, depending both on personal susceptibilities and particular occupational backgrounds. Scientists, economists, and engineers were certainly less touched by spiritual appeals and more impressed by planning, by the apparently rational use of resources and the practical problem-solving capacity of the regime. Yet even as we acknowledge such diversity in attitudes the fact remains that for most visitors the material-economic accomplishments, important as they were, signified something deeper and pointed to the paramount achievement of the "Soviet experiment," namely the creation of a society permeated by cohesive and sustaining values and a sense of purpose without which, they felt, the great material strides would have been impossible. Just as the economic crisis of the West could not be isolated—in the eyes of the intellectuals—from a crisis of values and beliefs, so the Soviet economic accomplishments seemed to have been inseparable from a sturdy system of values. As Lewis Coser put it:

> It was perhaps not the economic Depression itself that caused the intellectuals disaffection but the accompanying social disorder. The times were hopelessly out of joint, and nobody seemed able to put them together again. It seemed to many intellectuals that the Western world was drifting without plan, guidance or goal. The Depression revealed the apparent shipwreck of Western assumptions and values. The whole house of liberal civilization . . . seemed suddenly to collapse. What use was the whole framework of safeguards for the individual, of concern with the reign of law and freedom and democratic process . . . when people were hungry and lived without hope and purpose. . . . What use all the niceties of civil liberties and political freedom when young talented writers could not publish, when it seemed impossible to find a job even with the highest professional degree, when nobody seemed able to answer the insistent question, What of tomorrow?[59]

For Beatrice and Sidney Webb (as for many other intellectuals) what mattered was not so much the specific institutional accomplishments but the underlying higher purpose: "The marvel was not that there should be parks, hospitals, factories; after all, these could be found in England as well. The marvel was that they should all, as the Webbs thought, be inspired by a collective ideal, a single moral purpose."[60]

John Maynard Keynes argued strongly and prophetically that the appeals of communism and the Soviet system were, for intellectuals in particular, not primarily economic. His observations are even more relevant for understanding the 1960s and 70s than they were for the 1930s: "Communism is not a reaction against the failure of the 19th century to organize optimal economic output. It is a reaction against its comparative success. It is a protest against the emptiness of economic welfare, an appeal to the ascetic in us all. . . . It is the curate in Wells, far from extinguished by the scientist, which draws him to take a peep at Moscow. . . . The idealistic youth play with Communism because it is the only spiritual appeal which feels to them contemporary. . . ."[61]

John Dewey was convinced that "the most significant aspect of the change in Russia is psychological and moral rather than political. . . ." He went on to say:

> I had the notion that socialistic communism was essentially a purely economic scheme. . . .
> That the movement in Russia is intrinsically religious was something I had often heard and that I supposed I understood and believed. But when face to face with actual conditions, I was forced to see that I had not understood it at all . . . for this failure there were two causes. . . . One was that, never having previously witnessed a widespread and moving religious reality, I had no way of knowing what it actually would be like. The other was that I associated the idea of Soviet Communism, as a religion, too much with intellectual theology, the body of Marxian dogmas, with its professed economic materialism, and too little with a moving human aspiration and devotion. As it is, I feel as if for the first time I might have some inkling of what may have been the moving spirit and force of primitive Christianity.[62]

Sherwood Eddy, the American churchman, author of several books on the USSR, and YMCA leader, wrote:

> Russia has achieved what has hitherto been known only at rare periods of history, the experience of almost a whole people living under a unified philosophy of life. All life is focused in a central purpose. It is directed to a single high end and energized by such powerful and glowing motivation that life seems to have supreme significance. It releases a flood of joyous and strenuous activity.[63]

Edmund Wilson was of the opinion that despite the defects of the Soviet system (some of which he noted even in his enthusiastic phase), "you feel in the Soviet Union that you are at the moral top of the world where the light never really goes out. . . ."[64] Thus the spiritual gains attributed to the system were widely commented upon. Even such a relatively pragmatic admirer of the Soviet Union as Beatrice Webb, who was primarily interested in and approving of the efficiency of various social and economic institutions, was compelled to emphasize the sense of purpose and higher values which animated the Soviet leaders: "The new rulers of Russia professing a crude scientific materialism, have done more for the soul than the body!" She also spoke of their "impassioned insistence on the spiritual no less than on the material side of life."[65] Beatrice Webb was one of many visiting intellectuals who relished what they perceived to be the apparent paradox between an allegedly godless, materialistic political system and its idealistic, puritanical leaders who acted with determination on the many moral precepts and principles Western religions avowed but failed to implement. Not unlike the capitalist who could heartily endorse selected aspects of the Soviet system, such as the absence of strikes and the unchallenged authority of the management, sympathetic clergymen were able to filter out parts of the system which could have disturbed them. As noted before, there was something for everybody. "Many clergymen found the Soviet's strict social morality reassuring—the opposition to excessive use of alcohol; the emphasis on 'clean' motion pictures, made neither for money nor entertainment but for education; the new sex standards . . ." Already in the 1930s (and late 1920s) many members of the American clergy were fearful of losing touch with their flock, of not being sufficiently up to date, or, in recent vernacular, "with it": "Many clergymen abhorred the popular stereotype of the pious, other-worldly minister, and their eagerness to associate with radicals . . . stemmed in part from a rebellion against this stereotype."[66] Association with the cause of the Soviet Union or communism in general offered a posture of this-worldly spirituality, display of social conscience, a new way of revitalizing old values. Such attitudes intensified during the 1960s when the anti-war movement provided a similar rallying ground for activist ministers.

The praise for the new Soviet combination of the secular and spiritual appeared alike in the writings of those imbued with religious impulses and obligations and those without them. Thus Dreiser quoted with apparent approval a Russian friend of his who insisted that "these Communists, while calling themselves materialists, are the greatest Utopians and fanatics of the modern epoch; they are the children, though hating their parents, of the old Russian idealists. . . ."[67]

D. F. Buxton devoted many earnest passages to this welcome paradox:

> I came to the conclusion that what impressed me most in Russia was a sense of the moral advance represented in the new order of society which the Communists are trying to establish. . . .
>
> In the emphasis they place on the spirit of service, the Communists have taken to heart some of the most important maxims of the New Testament. . . .

In their social ideal there is no doubt that the Communists have introduced ethics where we have been content with snobbery. . . .

The communists repudiate, of course, the language of religion, but their actions are so much more important than their words that I do not feel we need take the latter very seriously. . . .

The Communists have, in fact revived and applied what are, historically, essentially Christian ideas, and applied them where they always ought to have been applied, i.e., to society and our social duties . . . in spite of all their irreligious jargon their society is a more Christian one than ours.[68]

The American Quaker Henry Hodgkin sounded the same theme: "As we look at Russia's great experiment in brotherhood, it may seem to us that some dim perception of Jesus' way, all unbeknown, is inspiring it. . . ."[69]

Sherwood Eddy, also described as an influential molder of "informed Protestant opinion on the USSR" (he organized annual seminar-tours of the Soviet Union for educators, religious leaders, and businessmen), was also fascinated with the new, Soviet forms of brotherhood: "The communist philosophy seeks a new order, a classless society of unbroken brotherhood, what the Hebrew prophets would have called a reign of righteousness on earth."[70]

A key attraction of Soviet society, implicit in several of the admiring comments quoted, was its seeming authenticity. It was in the process of closing, at long last, the gap between social ideals and their realization, implementing the age-old ideal of Western civilization and religions. This was irresistible for Western intellectuals frustrated by their powerlessness to actualize their ideals and irritated by the sham and hypocrisy found in their own societies. In the Soviet Union, it seemed, these incongruities were being wiped out. The Soviet regime succeeded in combining the highest level of idealism and aspiration with hard-headed practical measures. The very problem of authenticity in a modern society—which preoccupied Western European as well as nineteenth-century Russian intellectuals—was being solved. Here was the long-sought-for unity of theory and practice, the antidote to the chronic anxiety of intellectuals about their propensity to do little else but talk, write, theorize, and criticize. In the Soviet Union (as in other more recent revolutionary societies) the distasteful gulf between ideal and actual, thought and deed was being bridged, even obliterated—or so it seemed. A sense of purpose and high moral aspiration permeated every corner of Soviet society as it refused to compromise with the imperfections of social existence ("It does one good after all the compromising of the West to see an achievement such as this, to which a man can say Yes, yes, yes, with all his heart . . .").[71]

Authenticity permeated politics too. Edmund Wilson thought that, notwithstanding occasional misrepresentations of truth, "The Communists . . . in the long run . . . must always give way to any serious pressure from the people: they have to deliver the goods. When you have made a clean slate of the past, when you have got rid of all the systems of private profit which have come between the people and the fulfillment of their needs, you make it difficult to satisfy them with words. Think of the reservoirs of delusion and false values which flood our minds at home. . . ."[72] Soviet children also benefited from this atmosphere totally free of hypocrisy and contradiction, according to Frankwood Williams ("one of the leading psychiatrists in the United States" and former medical director of the National Committee for Mental Hygiene):[73] "The principles he has absorbed in nursery, kindergarten, and school are precisely the same principles that are observed by the adults in his environment. As he grows older he has nothing to unlearn. There never comes a time when he has to 'get wise.' Never a time when he has to choose between what he believes to be right and what is expedient."[74]

While, generally speaking, the visitors lauded the Soviet system for its success in uniting ideals with reality, on the rare occasions when some discrepancy between theory and practice was allowed, the sympathetic Western intellectual found ways to squelch his doubts by reminding himself that much greater discrepancies of this kind abounded in his own society.[75] The admiration of Soviet society, whatever aspects were concerned, was hardly ever detached from lamenting the wrongs of the Western world. Thus Hewlett Johnson exclaimed:

> From this capitalist world of storm and stress, where ancient pillars of society collapse, where morals are outraged, where science is balked, production impeded, and poverty unchecked, we turn at last to the Soviet world.

Again, paradoxically it was in large measure because of his own Christian, spiritual values that this world was so entrancing for him:

> Here was something wholly new. Here was something laid down as a programme by men at the head of affairs in a great nation, which we as Christians had been told by our own men of affairs, was pleasant as

an idealistic dream and might even happen in a far-distant future, but was wholly impracticable in the world as it is today. . . . this Soviet programme regards men as persons and plans for them as brothers. There is something singularly Christian and civilized in this attitude and intention. . . .

Hewlett Johnson also encountered Soviet moral purpose in other forms:

> . . . Russia is the most moral land I know. During many months in Russia, in great towns and small, in country places and seaside resort, in back streets and front streets, at all hours of the day and night, in bookshops and railway stalls, in theater and picture house, I never saw a sight I would screen from the eyes of a young girl.[76]

Moral purpose was found by Maurice Hindus in the new Soviet literature too: "The significant feature of all these new books is that they are dedicated to a positive purpose. Nowhere is there a subject or title suggestive of doubt, scepticism, regret or contrition."[77] Bernard Pares, the English historian, found a "more purposeful look" even on the faces of ordinary citizens.[78] Lion Feuchtwanger discovered purposefulness in the life of Soviet youth:

> How sturdily and with what calm confidence do they face life, feeling that they are organic parts of a purposeful whole. The future lies before them like a well defined and carefully tended path through a beautiful landscape.

He also discerned in the future city plans for Moscow "more purposeful cohesion than anywhere else in the world."[79]

W. E. B. Du Bois upon visiting the Soviet Union in 1936 observed that "This was no longer a people struggling for survival, it was a nation sure of itself."[80]

The sense of purpose pervading Soviet society was often contrasted not only with the chaos of the Western world (economic or spiritual) but sometimes with the state of affairs which prevailed in Russia in the years following the October Revolution. Anna Louise Strong was drawn to the Soviet system because of this process of imposing order. She confessed that "It was the chaos that drew me, and the sight of creators in chaos . . . I saw in Russia and its communists mystically, as that group of creators in chaos . . . I was ready to take a Russian communist as oracle, not only on revolution, but on personal plans and details of personal life."[81]

Others established a deeply satisfying connection between the sense of purpose and the future. It was the former that made the latter unthreatening, secure and to be looked forward to. According to Corliss and Margaret Lamont:

> the many stresses and strains still existent in Russia are justified in the light of the great goal ahead. The masses of people are making what may be called *constructive* sacrifices, with a splendid purpose held consciously and continuously in mind. This makes all the difference in the world. For purposeful giving of all that is in you may lead to happiness not only in the future but also in the present. And consequently we believe that there is a great deal of happiness in Russia today. People here are giving their complete allegiance to a great object of devotion which drives their personal worries and Freudian complexes into the background.[82]

The viewpoint expressed by Mr. and Mrs. Lamont certainly supports the argument that in the Soviet Union Western intellectuals sought—and for a while, found—not merely new manifestations of social justice, but a social order in which the individual was free from aimlessness, confusion, and uncertainty such as the intellectuals experienced in their own societies and which are endemic to contemporary secular, pluralistic societies. Naturally these feelings of unease and confusion intensify at times of crisis such as the Depression of the early 1930s. In the latter period not only were Western intellectuals outraged and disturbed by the irrationality of the social-economic order under which they lived, they also felt more profoundly estranged from their society because it provided few if any long-term goals and ultimate values worthy of pursuit and possible of attainment. The sense of purpose perceived in the Soviet Union, as well as its seemingly benevolent social policies, made it what Feuer called "a conscience model," attracting their idealistic impulses. The Western intellectuals' sense of meaninglessness was intensified by feelings of isolation, by the lack of widely shared remedies for personal problems, and by considering their societies indifferent and irresponsible.

The Lamont quote highlights these issues. It suggests, as did other visitors' comments, that deprivations and scarcities *by themselves* do not represent a serious problem *if* they are viewed as "constructive sacrifice," that is, if they are embedded in a context of meaning and values and are predicated on the hopes and fulfillments of the future. We must also take note of another important point rarely made so explicit, i.e., that personal lives become meaningful and "personal worries and Freudian complexes" recede when the individuals concerned give "their complete allegiance to a great object of devotion." It is interesting that neither the Lamont couple nor others who found such benefits accruing to the individual in the Soviet system discerned a similarity between the object of their admiration and what Erich Fromm called "the escape from freedom" in another political (though not historical) context, namely Nazi Germany. It is doubtless true that intense political allegiances—such as the sympathizers admired and found so wholesome in Soviet society—can provide diversion, escape, and relief from personal problems and frustrations. Such devotion, however, may be rather costly to both society and the individual.

People and Community

Although it was the novelty of the social system and the apparent superiority of its institutions which first attracted Western intellectuals to the Soviet Union, in the course of their visits their attention was also drawn to "The People," both beneficiaries and creators of this new society. At times the qualities of the people were praised without reference to the social system under which they lived, at other times the two were considered inseparable: the wonders of the system derived, to a large extent, from the admirable qualities of the population while the system got credit for capitalizing on these excellent qualities and bringing out the best in the people. John Dewey considered "the essence of the Revolution . . . its release of courage, energy and confidence in life." He also wrote: "The people go about as if some mighty, oppressive load had been removed, as if they were newly awakened to the consciousness of released energies." And he spoke of "this achieved revolution as a determining power in the shaping of their ultimate fate."[83] It would have been difficult to remain unimpressed by people whose attitudes reflected the goodness of their advanced social institutions and norms. And yet at times one could detect a veneration for the people which had no clear or necessary connection with the admiration of the political system. It seemed as if many of the visitors would have been just as impressed by the Russian people (and especially the peasants) in the pre-revolutionary era as in the post-revolutionary one. There was often an element of wonderment at the timeless quality of their virtues. It is hard to avoid the impression that people perceived in this way would have been admired any time and anywhere, regardless of the political system prevailing in their country.*

While in most cases the appreciation of the People was largely due to perceiving them as being very different and exotic (even in their simplicity and authenticity), not a few among the American visitors rejoiced over the discovery of familiar traits among them. There have always been many Americans whose attitudes toward things foreign were conditioned by the degree of familiarity they could assign to foreign countries and their inhabitants. If successful in finding such familiar traits, they felt reassured. This was particularly the case when the visitors started out with bizarre preconceptions as to how different Soviet people must be, to be followed by a diametrically opposed conclusion upon encountering *any* similarity between them and Americans. Soviet foreign propaganda seeks to exploit this propensity by stressing the common human element in people regardless of the political system they live under. (By contrast, domestic audiences are lectured on the pitfalls of universalistic moral positions devoid of class or political content.) The American mass media, in turn, have unwittingly fostered these contradictory images of Soviet people and society, alternatingly presenting them as totally and almost incomprehensibly different, and hardly different at all.

An American advertisement of a television program about the Soviet Union (and the program itself) illustrates this phenomenon: "Can the Russians keep up with the Joneses? Do you picture the typical Russian citizen as a servant of the state, toiling in a drab collective vineyard? Look again. He lives in a comfortable apartment. His wife enjoys a day at the stadium or an afternoon of boating. Tonight you get a candid view of 'Ivan Ivanovich' as ABC News takes you on a visit with a typical Russian family."[84] In the same spirit, the Citizens Exchange Corps, an organization devoted to promoting face to face meetings between Russians and Americans (in the hope of thereby alleviating political tension between the two countries), ran an advertisement in the New York *Times* which asked: "Do the Russians have horns?" implying, perhaps

---

* It has indeed turned out that many widely perceived and praised attributes of ordinary Russians had much in common with the corresponding attributes of ordinary Chinese, Cuban, or North Vietnamese people. This is one of the findings of the study which suggests that such perceptions might have depended as much on the projection of desires and preconceptions as on empirical observations. On the other hand, it may also be true that what is good in people, and accessible to superficial observation, is the same everywhere.

humorously, that such drastic preconceptions prevail and must be combatted. It is not surprising that those who initially assume that "Russians" are totally different (they rarely grasp the fact that the Soviet Union is not exclusively populated by Russians) are shocked to discover that this is not the case, and this startling discovery often leads to instant conversion to the opposite point of view, namely that there are no differences worth mentioning.

The above may help to explain why in many instances encountering the familiar in the Soviet Union was as exhilarating as the discovery of the different and exotic. Ambassador Joseph Davies joyfully seized on this morsel of similarity: "The people at the railroad station seemed warmly clad and not much different, insofar as being dressed warmly is concerned [!], from country people to be seen in rural frontier districts in the United States."[85] (Davies was among the relatively few Westerners who succeeded in combining an extended stay in the Soviet Union with the preservation of total innocence about the nature of the Soviet system.) Henry Wallace too was reminded in the Russian countryside of American farmers.[86] Ella Winter found broader basis for the similarities: "The people were like Americans; they discussed and argued and gossiped and grumbled, they criticized and appreciated. . . ."[87]

For the most part however the visitors were captivated by the unfamiliar and the exotic, the primeval authenticity of the people and the seeming harmony between people and nature. Sometimes the attractiveness of the people, of the physical setting and the social system all merged in the eyes of the beholder. The late Pablo Neruda, Stalin prize winner and lifelong supporter of the Soviet Union, wrote:

> What first impressed me in the USSR was the feeling of immensity it gives, of unity within the vast country's population, the movements of the birches on the plains, the huge forests so miraculously unspoiled, the great rivers, the horses running like waves across wheat fields.
>
> I loved the Soviet land at first sight and I realized that not only does it offer a moral lesson for every corner of the globe where human life exists, a way of comparing possibilities, an ever increasing progress in working together and sharing, but I sensed that an extraordinary flight would begin from this land. . . . The entire human race knows what a colossal truth is being worked out there . . . I was in the middle of a forest where thousands of peasants in traditional festive costumes were listening to Pushkin's poems. Everything hummed with life: men, leaves, vast stretches of new wheat. . . . Nature seemed to form a triumphant union with man. . . . A heavy rain came down while the

peasants were at the celebration. A lightning bolt struck close. . . . It all seemed a part of the torrential nature scene.[88]

Neruda made these observations during his first visit in 1949 at a time when there were fewer reasons to misperceive Soviet society than in the early 1930s when Waldo Frank succeeded in fusing the characteristics of the physical setting, the people, and society. Upon his arrival on the Soviet border he already assessed some major qualities of the Russians met at the railway station: "What struck me about these men, and the girls too, was their good will. The good will of persons sure of themselves, sure of their place in a world that, being theirs, held no terrors for them." Later in the course of his travels the appeal of the people (and of their "organic" relationship to both nature and the man-made environment) intensified. In the Russian village he found

> a homogeneous world: man and animal and fruit, air and wood and earth, were a single substance whose parts slowly vibrated round its core—the sun.
>
> . . . I stood in the village mud and sensed the organic rhythm of this telluric world—the pulse of earth and beast and man together. The peasant, the unsophisticated toiler, has a self knowledge, humble but authentic. This our Western culture has merely covered and destroyed with a patina of lies. And that is why there is more hope in the uncultured workers of all races. . . .

Such impressions further deepened aboard a ship on the Volga where he was a passenger:

> That night a great peace fell upon the boat. We were lifted out of time . . . I tasted the substance of a people. Men and women sat motionless on deck, children slumbered, couples moved close together . . . songs drifted down the river. . . . Slowly, sweetly, fertilely we swung in the equipoise of life . . . together.* And I knew in that moment the essential health of what was happening in Russia. A fresh spirit was born, and was whole.

Like so many other intellectuals before and after him, Frank was held in thrall by the vision of wholeness: "the immediate human, the want of stereotype, that makes Russia so exciting. There are no separate things in Russia, no separate persons . . . every person is in full flowing

---

* A mood not unlike that which overwhelmed Father Berrigan several decades later in Hanoi: "a dreamlike trance seemed to lie gently upon people and trees and animals."[89]

action with the folk about him. Therefore he is vital—with the whole vitality of Russia."

The contemplation of the expressive exuberance of the singing and dancing masses led Frank to conclude that "Here was the deepest proof—music and folk dance do not lie—that the Communist Revolution is Russian,"[90] that is to say that there is an organic, authentic link between the present and the past, revolution and tradition, the character of the people and their new institutions. Corliss and Margaret Lamont were also receptive to the charm of such displays: "As we finish supper . . . . the Comsomols of the Commune gather outside and sing to us." The songs were "strong, vigorous and unsentimental."[91]* Even Julian Huxley, the scientist, and an unlikely candidate for being swept up in some collective ecstasy, joined a group in street dancing and relished this "brief immersion" in the joyous, communal spirit of ordinary people: "all of us, from medical students to Harley Street specialists and scientific professors, experienced a real exhilaration from our brief immersion in this organized mass activity shared with four or five hundred other human beings."[92]

Joseph Freeman captured some of the broader implications of this sense of release and gratification: "The sense of isolation which haunted the declassed intellectual [and evidently even the non-declassed], the exploitation which darkened the worker's day, the persecution which hounded the militant proletarian and the revolutionary were like a frightful chimera rapidly dissolving in the dawn . . . for the first time I saw the greatest of human dreams assuming the shape of reality. Men, women and children were uniting their efforts into a gigantic stream of energy directed toward destroying the evils of life, toward creating what was healthy and good for all."[93] A more understated vision of unity was entertained by Bernard Pares, who observed that "Certainly there was, in all I saw, no suggestions whatever of a sullen and disgruntled people . . ." and that "government and people were of the same stock." He found this unity extended so far that even peasants were "now really converted to the collectivised system." Pares found Stalin a faithful chronicler of the spirit of the times as he quoted approvingly his words:

---

* It may be noted here that there is a remarkable uniformity among modern nations of varied political ideologies and systems of government in respect to the political uses of folk art, especially dancing and singing, as a legitimating device. Revolutionary and conservative regimes are at one in wishing to convey, particularly to visitors, a sense of the organic past and a high regard for the genius of ordinary people. They are saying in effect that governments which preserve and respect such enduring and widely appealing traditions cannot be bad.

" 'Now Comrades, life is better, life is brighter' and this corresponds to the mood of the time."[94] Sense of community and harmony, between people and the government were also duly noted by Feuchtwanger:

> I was at first surprised and dubious when I found that all the people with whom I came into contact . . . were at one with the general scheme of things, even if they were sometimes critical of minor points. Indeed everywhere in that great city of Moscow there was an atmosphere of harmony and contentment, even of happiness.[95]

While in general the wholesome attitudes and sense of community prevailing among the Soviet people were linked both to the soundness of the Russian character and to the beneficial social transformations permeating the masses, sometimes more specific explanations were offered. Frankwood E. Williams focused on the new ways of upbringing. He found the key for the virtual extinction of mental illness and for the proliferation of well-adjusted people in the combination of parental happiness and the most enlightened forms of communal childcare: "The child's parents are likely to be robustly healthy adults in the early or middle twenties. . . . They are well informed in regard to all matters pertaining to sex, including birth control . . . the child lives and grows in association with others of his own age. He sees much of his parents—but not too much—and the parents he sees are likely to be happy people with a fund of affection for him and not people weighed down by anxiety, worry, frustration and broken illusions. . . ." Williams also believed that the other source of the success of Soviet child-rearing practices, of happy family life, low incidence of juvenile deliquency, and alcoholism* was the absence of exploitation from all spheres of life. He thus summarized his findings:

> A wanted child, in a home of purposeful, secure, unanxious, unfrustrated adults, a child with a purpose conscious of being wanted and needed . . . his security firmly anchored in the group, his personal ambition attainable within a frame of larger purpose—that is his mental hygiene! A mental hygiene inherent in a social organization . . .[96]

Another explanation for the sterling character of the new Soviet generation was offered by Beatrice Webb: "If I had to pick out any one institution of Soviet Russia as the most striking in its hopefulness, it would be the Comsomols with their attendant Pioneers. The combination in this organization of Communist youth . . . of the passion for

---

* "Alcoholism . . . was a very serious problem some ten years ago. It is still a problem but a rapidly diminishing one."

self-improvement and self-discipline, with the passion for social service, and the consequent growth in the younger generation of personal initiative and personal responsibility, is one of the finest disciplines the world has ever seen. . . ."[97]

Not infrequently the visitors were struck not only by the appealing personal qualities and emotional health of the population but also by the physical well-being and attractiveness of the citizens of this new society. Julian Huxley wondered: "Is it in Russia that there is destined to grow up a new attitude toward the human body, more like the Greek ideal, than anything possible in a country tinged with the Christian attitude?" Observing the people along the Moscow River, he found that "Almost all were deeply bronzed with the sun, and the great majority were of fine physique. . . . None of our willowy, boyish figures [as far as the women were concerned]—solid, robust, healthy, they swam and sunbathed and enjoyed themselves. . . ."[98] Such scenes along the Moscow River also fascinated Maurice Hindus: "Their bodies are dusty with sunburn and sweat rolls off them in shiny streaks . . . their hunger for sun is insatiable. . . . As you watch these multitudes of young people you are impressed with their superb appearance."[99]* Frankwood Williams too found in the public behavior of Soviet people proof of their inner serenity: "One sees this same lack of neurotic tension in the thousands of young adults who on an evening crowd the streets of a city like Rostov or Yalta . . . or the parks of recreation and rest in Leningrad, Moscow, Stalingrad, Tiflies, Odessa, Kiev. These young men and women . . . are alert and quick moving. There is nothing phlegmatic about them. . . . They are out for a good time and they are obviously having it as they promenade up and down, but there is none of the rushing about, pushing and shoving, raucous laughter, shrill screams of our young people at Coney Island or in a public park."[101]

Such simple, healthy, authentic, open people had wholesome personal relationships and emotional lives. As Waldo Frank saw it, "There is intense emotion in Russia's personal life. Women here are women indeed. . . . In their sexual relations they [the women] meet men freely—spirit to spirit, unaided, untrammelled by conventions." Russian men and women were "childlike and wise." Sex and socialism met and merged

---

* It was, doubtless, the spirit of enhancing the physical beauty of the population that enabled Edmund Wilson to report on the prevalence of beauty parlors on collective farms: "Among the collective services, there was a homely, rustic Beauty Parlor [at the collective farm he had visited]. It seems that all the farms have them now that the women are being encouraged to look attractive."[100]

in the most satisfactory manner: "All their mind, all their will, all their emotion, was given to the single cause whose intricate parts their separate deeds embodied—the cause of socialism. But their acts moved mellow in a glow of sex that worked like a lubricant within them."[102]

Ella Winter summed up her favorable impressions of Russians as follows: "Russia! The frank, gay, hospitable, childlike people; their pride, enthusiasm, whole-heartedness. . . . I had seen little pettiness or meanness. Their faith and their energy. . . . In an age of anxiety they [the Russians] know what they wanted."[103]

Finally, a contrasting vision of depth and mystery captivated Edmund Wilson:

> I can understand how people get fascinated with Russia: the old ambiguous borderland between the West and the East, uncharted, unsurveyed, undelimited, unplowed, unmastered, unaccountable till now to civilization. The people seem to have deep resources like the minerals of Kuznetsk and the Urals. . . . What is there beneath the murmur of this immense and amorphous life which lies all around me here?[104]

The variations in the way Soviet people were perceived and their characteristics identified must not obscure the fact that they had several predominant traits such as good mental and physical health, strong communal feeling, commitment to public affairs, kindness, generosity, wisdom, and simple authenticity. It was an image that combined the time-honored elements of the Noble Savage, the Earthy Peasant, the Happy Poor, the Powerful Proletarian, and a glimmer of the Renaissance Man of Utopia.

Triumph Over the Past

One of the most obvious and least questionable accomplishments of the Soviet system was the reduction of economic backwardness and various related liabilities of the past. The efforts to overcome backwardness were among the most appealing features of the regime, and the visitors responded eagerly and with enthusiasm. They lauded social change, especially the application of scientific principles and techniques to social and economic affairs, and the regime's determination to tackle problems which had been unresolved for centuries. These were indeed aspects of Soviet society which could be related to the values and principles of the Enlightenment,[105] to nineteenth-century rationality and belief in progress, to the sympathy toward the new, the experimental and path-breaking.

Economic and physical transformations were certainly among the most conspicuous and impressive aspects of change in the Soviet Union. Invariably the visitors were shown great construction projects, factories, dams, canals, hydroelectric plants, new farms, schools, housing, and the like. The visible transformation of the landscape, the sight of new cities, industrial plants, flood control projects, roads, bridges, newly cultivated lands—all these offered tangible and indisputable proof of the great changes taking place.

Julian Huxley noted that in Siberia "cities spring up almost overnight, called into being out of barren steppes at the behest of central authority, all in due relation with the natural resources of the region and the planned lines of communication and electrification." For Huxley as for many others, the Soviet Union of the 1930s was "an enormous experiment" which differed "in two fundamentals from any other type of civilized society. It is organized as much as possible on a communal or collective as against an individualist basis, primarily for the benefit of the working class, and with the incentive of private profit reduced to the smallest proportions; and its economy is planned throughout." Huxley also found "science . . . an essential part of the Russian plan. Marxist philosophy is largely based on natural science."[106] Feuchtwanger summarized the feelings of many visitors when he wrote: "I sympathized inevitably with the experiment of basing the construction of a gigantic state on reason alone."[107]

In the 1930s Western intellectuals still believed in the successful application of reason to human affairs.* To the extent that the Soviet Union could be perceived as a society in the process of waging war on the past, on its traditional values, inequities, and material backwardness, she was deserving of warm support. Characteristically, a group of prominent American intellectuals defending the Soviet system against charges of being dictatorial included in their list of its superior attributes the claim that "It has replaced the myth and superstitions of old Russia with the truths and techniques of experimental science, extending scientific procedures to every field, from economics to public health."[108]

While the appreciation of the material achievements of the Soviet regime was understandable (especially as long as their social and human

---

* As will be shown later, this was no longer the case in the 1960s or 70s when rationality, if not outright rejected, was played down among the appeals of the then glorified societies. Correspondingly domestic social criticism incorporated the rejection of what was conceived to be excessively rational and hence impersonal aspects of modern industrial society.

costs were not known or were ignored), sometimes it verged on ecstatic veneration which went beyond a hearty endorsement of progressive industrialization. These attitudes apparently were a part of the worship of power and mastery; mastery over nature, the past, tradition, inertia, resistance to change. In the eyes of many visitors Soviet construction projects symbolized a transcendence of the human condition with all its limitations. Pablo Neruda wrote in his memoirs: "I shall never forget my visit to that hydroelectric plant overlooking the lake, whose pure waters mirror Armenia's unforgettable blue sky. When the journalists asked me for my impressions of Armenia's ancient churches and monasteries, I answered them, stretching things a little: 'The church I like best is the hydroelectric plant, the temple beside the lake.' "[109] Many similar comments were made about the miracles of Soviet industrialization. Many Western visitors seemed to forget that they were describing inherently ordinary objects—factories, hydroelectric plants, bridges, schoolhouses, or movie theaters (if some of them rather large, like the dam on the Dnieper River or the steel works of Magnitogorsk)—which under capitalism would provoke little excitement. All such inherently ordinary or prosaic projects and constructs were transformed, in the eyes of the beholders, by their new purpose and context. Bigness helped but it was not the main thing. Louis Fischer wrote:

> The entire Soviet Union felt inspired in the presence of this spectacle of creation and self-sacrifice. I too was swept away. . . . A whole nation marched behind a vision. . . . in Russia the factory was conquering . . . I had lived in Ukranian villages. I had stood at train windows during night hours . . . crossing the flat face of Russia. No light. Hunderds of miles of darkness. People lived in that all their lives. . . . Now the electric bulb was invading the bleak black village; steel and iron were vanquishing Russia's wood civilization. I translated Five Year Plan statistics into human values.[110]

These were obviously still times when Western visitors could unabashedly praise industrialization and urbanization without ambivalence, without thinking of their own environmentalist crusades and laments about cities and factories encroaching on nature. Smokestacks dotting the countryside and dams rising over the rivers were still symbols of benevolence and purposefulness, not of pollution, waste, and folly. Visitors in the second period sometimes found it difficult to reconcile their praise of industrialization in Cuba or China with the criticism of industrial life in their own countries.

Some visitors even managed to find similarities (and thereby a reassuring familiarity) between the Soviet planned construction and the New Deal in the United States. H. G. Wells said in his conversation with Stalin: "It seems to me that what is taking place in the U. S. is a profound reorganization, the creation of planned, that is, socialist economy. You [Stalin] and Roosevelt begin from two different starting points. But is there not a relation in ideas, a kinship of ideas and needs, between Washington and Moscow?"[111]*

In any event, the material transformations of Soviet society and the dynamism symbolized by the huge construction projects were especially attractive in the early 1930s because they contrasted with the economic stagnation in the West. Even the later work projects inspired or funded by the federal government of the United States (and associated with the New Deal) did not match in grandeur, scale, and scope those undertaken in the Soviet Union between the late 1920s and during the 1930s. It must also be remembered that industrialization in the Soviet Union entailed the settlement of sparsely populated or totally unpopulated areas of the country, changing the ways of life of primitive tribal people in some instances, introducing modern technology and communications into some of the most remote parts of the world—in short, efforts which were genuinely dramatic and pioneering and had few Western counterparts in the twentieth century.

The great social-economic transformations observed and praised were inseparable from a rational and energetic application and organization of work. Western visitors expressed amazement at both the scale and intensity of work being accomplished and the new meaning it held for those performing it. Waldo Frank described a Soviet engineer at work:

> The engineer . . . is a pure proletarian Russian. His pockmarked face is gentle, the eyes cast warmth over its pallor. . . . The men work intensely, yet with a quiet reserve. They have no mechanical ease like the operators in an American plant . . . when the engineer stops a group of them, in order that we may ask them questions, they seem to emerge from a distant realm like poets suddenly recalled into the surface of a prosaic world.

Another worker was glimpsed as "a sensitive man . . . he was closer to the artist than to the Western factory worker. His eyes burned with

* Such was an early rudimentary version of the convergence theory. During its more formal launching sometime in the 1960s it was rarely if ever noted that it was a far from original idea but has been around ever since Soviet-American differences and tensions were to be reduced through wishful thinking. The Soviet attitude toward these ideas was the same in the 1930s as in the 1960s and 70s: Stalin was totally unreceptive just as his successors have been.

an ascetic flame . . . he might have been a saintly artisan in some medieval convent. . . ." The factory manager was "utterly different from the American magnate risen, like himself, from the ranks. There is in this Russian an essential *innocence*. He is ruthless but he is *clean*."[112]

Corliss and Margaret Lamont also found Soviet workers vastly superior and actively engaged in the transformation of their society: "Those workers up there [at a Leningrad district committee on housing], carelessly dressed, coatless and collarless—lacking most of the superficial qualities found in capitalist society—those workers, and men like them are running the new Russia. . . . They are intelligent, they are resolute, they are direct, they are forceful. And the recognition of the common task to be performed for the common good unites the comrades in the audience with the comrades on the platform."[113] Important British members of Parliament were impressed by "the keenness and intensity of labour" and the "genuine enthusiasm of the workers."[114] Commenting on the Soviet shockworkers (that is, those who regularly exceeded their production norms), G. B. Shaw suggested that "In England such privileged workers are not loved by the working masses. Here in Soviet Russia they are the most popular and are showered with honors by their fellow workers. Comrades, I am very glad to see such great enthusiasm here."[115]*

Dyson Carter assessed the level of motivation of the agricultural labor force with a similar acuity: "the Soviet farmer is constantly striving to increase the crop yield . . . and the milk output of his dairy herds, without the slightest regard for market prices or surpluses of wheat and milk. His concern is to step up farm production so that there will be ever more food available." Like many other scientists Carter was overwhelmed by the support and attention the Soviet system gave to science and by what he considered its centrality in Soviet life:

> There is no phase of life in the Soviet Union that is not guided by this new kind of science—Soviet science.
>
> . . . Science has shown the 180 million people of the Soviet Union how to banish starvation and sickness, how to improve farming and industry so that universal civilized living becomes a reality for all, how

---

* Such observations of this famous writer, noted cynic and iconoclast, provide impressive illustrations of the extraordinary combination of unmitigated gullibility in one setting and the vigorous exercise of critical faculties in another. Bertrand Russell said of Shaw that "he fell victim to adulation of the Soviet government and suddenly lost the power of criticism and of seeing through humbug if it came from Moscow."[116]

to lift the burden of oppressive toil from the shoulders of millions, how to give the whole population leisure and health enough to live a more joyous life.

J. D. Bernal, the famous British scientist, was also persuaded that "the cornerstone of the [Soviet] Marxist state is the utilization of human knowledge, science and technique, directly for human welfare."[117]

Such jubilation was not the singular attitude of a handful of scientists—though more common among the scientific than literary intellectuals—but was shared by other sympathizers who believed that the ever-widening application of science to every conceivable human problem provides the key solution to human happiness.

Humane Prisons and Other Reconstructed Institutions

Although the appeals of Soviet society were diffuse and the fascination it exerted due to certain generalized beliefs about its character, the visitors were also keenly interested in the specific institutions implementing the grand design. Almost invariably they generalized from the particular to the general. Indeed, as John Dewey said, there tended to be "a marked disproportion between the breadth of . . . conclusion and the narrowness of the experience upon which it rests."[118] The process was dual. On the one hand people came to the Soviet Union with an image, a sweeping preconception, and they filled in the details by means of what they could experience, no matter how narrow this sampling of reality had been. On the other hand those who came with more of an open mind and fewer preconceptions succeeded in conjuring up a grand design from the particular experiences they were able to have. Most of these experiences involved the observation, however cursory or superficial, of certain institutions connected with work, health, education, or the administration of justice.

Not surprisingly, in view of their backgrounds, the intellectuals were keenly interested in educational institutions and the spread of knowledge and culture to the masses. Improvements observed in this sphere held a strong appeal both on account of their close association with equality (it has become axiomatic in our times that education is the major stepping stone to equalizing opportunities) and also because of the vision of unearthing the hidden potentialities of human beings, making them better, kinder, more sensitive and spiritually enriched. Comments such as the following were typical: "In whatever museum we enter in Leningrad we run across workers' tour groups thirstily drinking in the knowledge which is offered to them by guides especially trained for the purpose . . . if you glance at their faces you find that they are all alike in having an eager, awakened look."[119]

Dyson Carter wrote: "In the Soviet Union every child, regardless of nationality, color, religion or income of its parents, is educated up to the limits of his or her capabilities. Every young person is sure of a job when school days are over. College students are paid wages, and may even marry while still taking courses. To us this seems like a fairy tale, a story out of a dream world."[120]

The regime also succeeded in claiming and receiving credit for promoting cultural activities which pre-dated the October Revolution and had no inherent connection with its policies. Eugene Lyons recalled, "I took in the Russian theater, ballet and opera in great draughts. Ardently, if illogically, I gave the revolution credit for everything cultural that it had inherited from the tsarist era."[121] This attitude was widespread. The Soviet regime was lavishly praised for the encouragement of all kinds of cultural and educational activities—drama groups, folk dancing, instruction in painting and handicrafts, the expansion of book publishing, evening and correspondence schools, and even the enlightenment spread by the mass media. Ella Winter was impressed by the educational role of the Soviet press: "What they print is directed towards making an active, conscientious, responsible human being. Journalism in Russia, like all other means of communication, is dedicated, in the fullest sense of the word, to the education of all people."[122]

Improvements in public health and childcare too made a deep impression on the visitors. The caring, humane attitude of the regime was most symbolically expressed in the development of various childcare institutions: nurseries, kindergarten, pre-natal clinics, and the like. Undoubtedly great strides were made in improving public health, and reducing infant mortality in particular. (More unkindly, one might note that while infant mortality declined, adult mortality had sharply increased, at any rate during the 1930s.) The visitors were invariably acquainted with some childcare institutions and usually commented on the healthy, cheerful and happy demeanor of the children seen.[123]*

Schools and kindergarten were not the only Soviet institutions which

---

* There is a parallel between the use of children and folk art as legitimating devices. Again, as with folk art, and even more effectively, the message the regime intends to convey is that a political system that is good to children must be generally humane. For most people it is hard to entertain the idea that a social system can create *both* well-run children's camps and totally degrading concentration camps for adults.

impressed the visitors favorably. Readers of these pages may be startled to learn that among the Soviet institutions which were found appealing by the guests from abroad prisons also ranked high. Aware of the iniquities of the system under Stalin which were denounced by Khrushchev and passionately exposed by Solzhenitsyn and other former inmates of Soviet labor camps, it may be hard to believe today that many Western visitors, and especially intellectuals, found Soviet penal institutions and policies among the outstanding accomplishments of the regime. Harder still is to believe that they contrasted Soviet prisons with Western ones most favorably and found the Soviet penal system exemplary in its concern with humane values.

The Western intellectuals' perception of the Soviet prisons and their judgment of the Soviet penal system is one of the most fascinating aspects of the pilgrimages. It is also the most thought-provoking and disturbing. The positive evaluation of Soviet penal institutions exemplifies both the outer limits of gullibility (rooted in favorable predisposition) and of the great impact the skillful, selective presentation of reality can have on reasoned judgment. Whichever played the greater part, predisposition to believe or selective display, the outcome was disquieting as it cast the most serious doubt both on the value of the on-the-spot fact-finding experience and the capacity for critical thinking of many intellectuals.

It must be stressed that the admiration of the prison system was part of the more general enthusiasm for all Soviet institutions ostensibly dedicated to the reshaping or reeducation of the individual, especially the liquidation of undesirable attitudes left over from the past.* The institutions involved with the creation of new human beings encompassed all those concerned with education, from nurseries to universities, houses of culture at factories and farms, clubs devoted to the cultivation of particular talents. Prisons were especially impressive, in this regard, since they provided a most unlikely setting for the upgrading of human nature. It was precisely the association of prisons with evil, degradation, and deprivation on the one hand and their apparent novel utilization for such high purpose as the remolding of human beings that was so dramatic and remarkable in the eyes of the visitors. This dialectic of making something good out of something bad was hard to resist. If even prisons could be perfected and made more humane, how much more plausible it became to accept the claims of the regime about its other accomplish-

---

* Anna Louise Strong observed that "This remaking of criminals is only one specialized form of the process of remaking human beings which goes on consciously today in the Soviet Union."[124]

ments and institutions! How much easier to believe in the constructive design and purpose of other inherently less odious institutions!

Here then was an example of both the new humanism displayed by Soviet society and its rational, ingenious problem-solving capacity. The spirit of punishment (repugnant to so many Western intellectuals) and the associated demeaning living conditions were replaced by prisons oriented toward the rehabilitation of the wrongdoer who was to reemerge as a reformed and a useful member of society. The new terminology introduced signaled these lofty aspirations, as was reported by Dr. J. L. Gillin, a former president of the American Sociological Society and "one of the leading authorities on penology in the United States":

> In accordance with the spirit of the Revolution the terms current in capitalistic penology are discarded. There are no "crimes"; there are "wrongs." . . . There is no "punishment" only "measures of social defense." . . .
>
> It is clear that the system is devised to correct the offender and return him to society.[125]

Ella Winter explained the basic principles of Soviet criminology as follows:

> Crime, according to Soviet law, is the outcome of antagonisms existing in a society divided into classes; it is always the result of faulty social organization and bad environment. The word "punishment" is not approved of: it has been replaced by the phrase: "measures of social defense." . . . Sentences are short and once the sentence has been served the miscreant is readmitted into everyday life with no . . . scar of shame, no brand of having been a "convict" . . . Soviet criminology seems to assume that the "criminal" is not a criminal. He is not to be treated an an outcast. . . . He is an "unfortunate," sick, weak or maladjusted and must be trained to become . . . a functioning member of society. This theory is carried out in practice in the communes run by the OGPU.[126]

D. N. Pritt, the British Barrister and King's Counsellor, wrote:

> Terms of imprisonment are on the average shorter than in England and the treatment of prisoners is one of the most remarkable features of the whole system. The Russians apply fully and logically the theory that imprisonment must be reformatory, and not in the smallest degree punitive; and they regard society as sharing with the criminal the responsibility for his crime. They speak of "social correction," not of "punishment" and they succeed in creating in their penal establishments a very striking atmosphere of co-operative endeavour to effect

a real cure of bad habits and a full restoration to the normal life of society and to the rights of citizenship.[127]

Harold Laski, the famous British political scientist, contrasted favorably the environmentalist, social-determinist approach prevailing in the USSR with the state of affairs in Britain:

> The principle that since society is to be regarded as partially responsible for crime, the object of punishment must be reform, has consequences in Russia wholly unknown in Great Britain. The first is the direct interest of the judiciary in the penal system. The second is the insistence that the prisoner must live, so far as conditions make it possible, a full and self-respecting life. . . . The view is taken that the severe discipline characteristic of older systems destroys morale and makes the return of the prisoner to normal life difficult. . . . The final principle . . . is the effort, through the creative organization of leisure, to prevent that deterioration of character which seems so frequent in our normal prison population through deprivation of the habits and opportunities associated with normal social relations.[128]

Anna Louise Strong wrote:

> Soviet justice . . . aims to give the criminal a new environment in which he will begin to act in a normal way as a responsible Soviet citizen. The less confinement the better; the less he feels himself in prison the better.[129]

Mary Stevenson Callcott, an American criminologist, concurred:

> There has been a steady effort to remove what they term the "prison spirit." There is, they tell you, no such thing as a "captive" or "prisoner." The idea is to keep the person deprived of his liberty from feeling in any measure isolated. He is given work to do such as he would have outside and he is always conscious of its useful nature.
>
> . . . In doing away with handcuffs, with solitary confinement, with any type of corporal punishment, and with any prison garb the enunciation of policy does its part, but in the approach of the immediate staff to the inmates there is seen a wholesomeness that no [penal] code could account for.[130]

Wicksteed, the English author (held in high esteem by Beatrice Webb), was also fully convinced that "The whole idea of punishment has been frankly dropped and the aim of reformation alone pursued."[131]

Sidney and Beatrice Webb, relentlessly trying to sound matter of fact even about their objects of admiration, reported that "the [prison] administration is well spoken of* and is now apparently as free from physical cruelty as any prison in any country is ever likely to be." Some of their beliefs must have undoubtedly been based on their visit to Bolshevo (the model prison also favorably described by Bernard Pares and Gillin and many other visitors who were taken there). They found Bolshevo "a remarkable reformatory settlement, which seems to go further, alike in promise and achievement, towards an ideal treatment of offenders against society than anything else in the world." They felt that at Bolshevo the inmates were shown "that a life of regulated industry and recreation, with the utmost practicable freedom, is more pleasant than a life of crime and beggary."[132]

Maurice Hindus, the veteran reporter on Soviet affairs, put it more strongly:

> Vindictiveness, punishment, torture, severity, humiliation, have no place in this system. The Soviets are acting on the assumption that it is not the criminal who is under obligation to society but that society is under obligation to the criminal. Implacable environmentalists, they believe that under normal conditions of living the human animal . . . would not commit antisocial acts.
>
> . . . On good behavior which is easy in Soviet jails, as easy as in Soviet schools, the sentence is pared down. Constant amnesties on the occasion of revolutionary holidays bring further reductions. During the period of confinement criminals experience no other hardships than the enforced separation from home. Unless they violate the light discipline that they must observe they never are made to feel the yoke of the stigma of prison life. There are no chain gangs. There are no severe compulsions. There is no lockstep. There is no striped or any kind of uniforms. There are no limitations to the amount of literature or correspondence they may receive. Indeed the prison exists not for punishment but for ministration.[133]

Corrective labor was seen as central to the ambitious program of rehabilitation. In the words of Anna Louise Strong: "The labor camp is the prevalent method for handling serious offenders of all kinds, whether criminal or political. . . . The labor camps have won high reputation throughout the Soviet Union as places where tens of thousands of men have been reclaimed."[134] And according to Mary Stevenson Callcott,

---

* We are not told of the source of the appreciative comments. It may however be presumed that the Webbs did not glean them from random encounters with inmates or with ordinary Soviet citizens passing on to them the nice things they heard from friends or relatives with prison experience. It may be safe to assume that the prisons were "well spoken of" by the guides, interpreters, and the prison official who kept the Webbs informed of such matters.

"The authorities seek to use labor that is constructive as to character and useful economically, and not the kind that brings indignity and resentment when resorted to as punishment or disciplinary measures."[135]

George Bernard Shaw's vision of the successful Soviet rehabilitation procedures was even more vivid:

> In England a delinquent enters [the jail, that is] as an ordinary man and comes out as a 'criminal type,' whereas in Russia he enters . . . as a criminal type and would come out an ordinary man but for the difficulty of inducing him to come out at all. As far as I could make out they could stay as long as they liked.[136]

Shaw was not the only one who believed that Soviet prisoners found conditions so pleasing that they were reluctant to leave after they served their sentence. "So well known and effective is the Soviet method of remaking human beings," wrote Anna Louise Strong, "that criminals occasionally now apply to be admitted."[137]

D. N. Pritt reported that "The prisons are of several types, most of which should not be and are not in practice, called prisons at all, being in the nature either of open or semi-open camp or fully open communes or colonies. The closed prison . . . will, it is expected, be a thing of the past in a few years." Like most of his visiting countrymen, Pritt found that "There is none of the restriction and futility created by the over-regimented life of so many English prisoners. . . ." Under such circumstances recidivism sank to "negligible proportions" and no stigma whatsoever attached to the released prisoner. The most advanced penal establishments could hardly be distinguished from a regular village, and many prisoners were reluctant to depart: "Small wonder that in such a 'prison' a substantial part of the population . . . nevertheless prefer to continue living in the 'prison' bringing up their children in the surroundings which helped themselves back to normal life. . . . Small wonder, even, that a high official of the Ministry of Justice spent three months in one of the 'prisons' as an ordinary inmate, to see how he liked it."[138]

Mary Callcott observed at the labor camp established on the site of the Moscow-Volga Canal that "I could never see what kept men in this camp unless they wanted to stay there. No convicts I have known would have any difficulty if they wanted to break away."[139]

Thus not only was there an extraordinary amount of freedom inside Soviet prisons but also it was easy to escape. Hardly any guards were seen, and those occasionally spotted did not bother to carry weapons. Many of the institutions visited had no walls, fences, or watchtowers.

The prison system overflowed with trust. Being in the Soviet penal institutions was good for the character, the life of the mind, healthful for the body, and a joyful experience for those temporarily detained. G. B. Shaw, upon inspecting a prison for women, opined that "none of these women would have been better off as innocent persons earning their living in an English factory," and found being in a Soviet jail a "privilege" compared to those in capitalist countries.[140] Mr. and Mrs. Lamont met prisoners who informed them that they did not feel at all as if they were in a prison.[141]

Did the prisoners ever complain under such delightful conditions? Given the peculiarities of human nature and the capacity of some people to find fault with everything, the possibility could not be ruled out. Lenka von Koerber, a German student of Soviet prisons, asked one of the prison official she met: "Is there any dissatisfaction among the prisoners?" She was told that "Naturally there is a little sometimes but very seldom. Our prisoners have unlimited right of complaint."[142]

The actual experience of visiting the Soviet prisons, labor colonies, or corrective labor camps was nothing short of idyllic. The visitors often felt, without any irony intended, that there was little difference between conditions inside and outside the penal institutions.[143]

Mary Callcott saw inmates in the Sokolniki prison who were "talking and laughing as they worked, evidently enjoying themselves. This was the first glimpse of the informal atmosphere that prevailed throughout, and which caused us to look in some amazement at occasional scenes such as encountered as we entered the auditorium where a good pianist was playing and other men stood beside him or leaned on the piano, at ease and absorbed in the music." In the course of her visit she commented on the interaction between "attendants" (guards) and prisoners: "There seemed to be no feeling of restraint in their presence, but on the contrary an existence of comradeship showed."* "As we were leaving the yard an incident happened that impressed us greatly. From the flower garden, one of the men [a prisoner] came with an armful of flowers that he wished to present to a member of the party. . . . He did it with the air of one who brings a bouquet from a prized garden of his own." Upon the suggestion of the prosecutor accompanying her party she proceeded to the auditorium where, once more, "an informal atmo-

---

* Laski was likewise "struck by the excellent relations between the prisoners and the warders, and the sense of men who were living a useful life untainted by that torture of separation from the power to fulfill personality which is the dominant feature of our own system."[144]

sphere prevailed that it would be hard to give an impression of. The men talked in low excited tones, the music continued, the prosecutor and the prison director leaned against the piano. . . . It was difficult to believe that this was indeed a prison of a more serious type. It had all the earmarks . . . of a community affair of local talent about to start. The program was given with zest and enjoyment." Out in the yard "some of the prisoners demonstrated their athletic ability and performed gymnastic feats on bars. We noted their carefree attitude."

The same scenes and impressions repeated themselves in the Moscow Novinsky Prison for Women. The girls chatted and laughed gaily and were also "unrestrained by the presence of attendants or directress. . . . The parting word from our hostess was: 'I wish I might visit a prison in America with the same freedom with which I have shown you this.'" At the Bolshevo Labor Commune Dr. Callcott was at a loss "what to call this place. To say that it is a penal institution is misleading. . . ." Here, even more than in other institutions that she visited, "the principle of 'trust' [was] held like a shining torch before the eyes of incredulous youngsters."[145]

Lenka von Koerber came away with impressions similar to those of Dr. Callcott. She too noted the continuities between prison life and the world outside. For instance: "All Russian prisoners are caught up in the general drive, and the majority of them work extremely hard and make the most of every minute." On one of her visits at the prison for women in Perm she witnessed the presentation of awards to outstanding workers:

> Troopers stepped forward to a flourish from the orchestra. One prisoner solemnly presented another with the "Red Flag." Then the fourth group was given a wooden shield on which was painted a tortoise, because they had been last in the competition. But the representative of the fourth group, a young gipsy . . . with flaming eyes she declared that her group would not keep the tortoise long, but would soon win the "Red Flag."

Even at the prison of Tjumen, near Sverdlovsk, Koerber found "Most of the prisoners . . . quite cheerful, which puzzled me because it is a closed institution and also a clearing house for prisoners . . . to be sent to far off colonies in Siberia. In spite of educational work and self-administration one inevitably finds some men in closed prisons who look depressed and who appear to suffer under their captivity. Perhaps the freedom from depression of the prisoners of Tjumen had something to do with the wonderfully clear, invigorating air."[146]

Harold Laski too applauded not only the underlying principles of pe-

nal policy but also their reflections in the living conditions of the prisoners he himself observed during his visit:

> The prisoner . . . must live a full and self-respecting life. All prisoners
> do normal industrial work, and they all receive wages. They have the
> right to a vacation; they receive a generous allowance of visits; their
> privilege of writing and receiving letters is practically unlimited and
> uncensored. . . . No one who has seen over a Russian prison, and
> compared that experience with a visit to one in England, can doubt
> that the advantage is all on the Russian side. The prisoners with whom
> I talked were . . . men who were conquering themselves. . . . They
> had not been disciplined into machines. They had learned the value
> of regular labor. They had not been made to feel that they were cut
> off from the outside world. They had no sense of being under the con-
> tinuous supervision of an unfriendly eye. There was neither furtiveness
> nor fear about them. I think, on any showing, that these are great
> gains which say much for the theory which underlies their treatment.

He also noted that

> The degree to which prisoners are put on their honor has also an ex-
> cellent effect. The unaccompanied holiday at home, the uncensored
> correspondence, the right to receive visitors without supervision, all
> remove that constant sense of being humiliated which I believe to be
> one of the most destructive features of our own system.[147]

There was virtually no aspect of the prison conditions and penal policies that failed to provoke the enthusiasm of such visitors. Cultural, educational, and recreational facilities were among the most highly praised.
For example:

> Prisoners have absolute quiet in the reading rooms where they have a
> good supply of newspapers, periodicals and books.
>
> In Taganka prison an official pointed with great pride to a large field
> of wild flowers which adorned the exercise ground.
>
> . . . the prison audience is very critical, and if a play is boring the
> organizers are called to account. . . . The complaint is then brought
> before the dramatic circle which has chosen a dull piece and they are
> asked to make a more careful selection in the future.[148]
>
> Wireless, classes in cultural and vocational subjects, gymnastics, books,
> dramatic performances, concerts both for, and by, the prisoners, a
> prison newspaper, in which the right to make complaints is an essen-
> tial feature, all these are universal.[149]

Involving the prisoners in public activities was also much praised:

> Prison administrators as well as other authorities on penal policy in the
> Soviet Union are of the opinion that the development of public activ-

ities among the prisoners has yielded splendid results of a social nature. They point to the success of a "book subbotnik" (one day's salary
given for books) which netted 100.000 rubles. . . . Another incident
showing a desirable spirit was the collection among the convicts of
31.818 rubles for an aeroplane which was presented to the fleet.[150]*

Since the visitors considered the Soviet attempts to rehabilitate the
prisoners successful it is not surprising that many identified with the
official Soviet viewpoint, still confidently expounded in the 1930s:

> An eventual disappearance of crime is expected by Soviet authorities
> as the mental habits produced by a socialist system become established
> in Soviet life. For crime, in the Marxian view, arises from the conflicts
> of a class-exploiting society and will follow classes and exploitation
> into oblivion. . . . The labor camps which supplanted prisons are
> themselves diminishing, partly because they have "cured" their in-
> mates, and still more because the normal free life of Soviet society is
> becoming strong and prosperous enough to have a direct regenerative
> influence on those social misfits that remain.[151]

It will not be necessary, I hope, to argue and document further that the
Soviet authorities were successful in creating an impression among many
visitors almost totally at odds with what we have known about Soviet
penal establishments from their former inmates. This achievement was
not solely due to elaborately organized deception (of which more will
be said below), the naiveté of the visitors and their predisposition to see
only the good things in Soviet society—although certainly these factors
explain most of their impressions. There are some other factors also to
be considered, although their precise impact is not easy to determine.
First it must be noted that some of the site visits reported took place in
the early 1930s when the more enlightened penal policies of the 1920s
had not yet been completely wiped out, as far as *non-political offenders*
were concerned.[152] (There was never any serious attempt to rehabilitate,
or treat with minimum decency, the politicals.) Secondly, the visitors
were as a rule exposed only to non-political offenders (though they usually believed their circumstances were not different from those of the
politicals)[153] whose treatment was always better than that of political
prisoners.

One important exception must be mentioned. This was the construc-

---

* Had Dr. Callcott been more familiar with the various meanings and manifestations
of "voluntarism" in the Soviet Union—whether in the realm of "voluntary" donations
of money or labor—she might have drawn different conclusions from the "book
subbotnik."

tion site of the Belomor Canal where political prisoners labored and which was shown to foreign visitors. It was a project the Soviet authorities took pains to publicize and present as an outstanding example of rehabilitation through work. Not only was a Soviet play written on this theme,[154] but no fewer than thirty-four Soviet writers (including such notables as Gorki, Vera Inber, Kataev, Alexei Tolstoi, Zoschenko, and others) produced collectively what might be called today a documentary novel. In the preface of its English translation, the editor, Amabel Williams-Ellis, wrote that "For the first time we are here told the story of what goes on in a Russian labor camp. . . ." Further, "This tale of accomplishment of a ticklish engineering job, in the middle of primeval forests, by tens of thousands of enemies of the State helped—or should it be guarded—by only thirty-seven GPU officers, is one of the most exciting stories that has ever appeared in print."[155]

The Webbs too felt called upon to comment on Belomor and draw some general conclusions from it:

> The latest example of the constructive work of the OGPU will strike the British or American student of public institutions as even more remarkable than its prison reform or child rescue work. . . .
>
> These convicts serving their sentences rose to the height of the occasion. Realizing that they were engaged on a work of great public utility, they were induced to enter into "socialist competition" . . . as to which could shift the greatest amount of earth, erect the greatest length of concrete wall . . . within a given number of hours or days. . . .
>
> It is pleasant to think that the warmest appreciation was officially expressed of the success of the OGPU, not merely in performing a great engineering feat, but in achieving a triumph in human regeneration.[156]

There has been an inimitable surrealistic quality to the thoughtful observations of the Webbs which lent distinction to their massive misapprehension of Soviet society, even as compared to other misapprehensions of similar magnitude. Their perceptions of the OGPU (the Soviet political police, today called KGB), a unique blend of innocence and unintended understatement, provide further illustrations of this quality. Thrilled by its "strong and professionally qualified legal department" they averred that "When they do strike [the OGPU] they strike sure and hard. Their case is practically watertight."* Nor did they hesitate to

---

* This was approximately the same time when Muggeridge reported the following conversation between Ralph Barnes, an American reporter, and a Soviet GPU official: "Another coup Barnes pulled off . . . was to procure an interview with some-

attribute their own assessments of this unique police force to the Soviet population at large: "there is now, we think, little or no sign of general disapproval among the four fifths of people who are manual workers in industry or agriculture, either of its continued existence or of its vigorous activities. . . ." They cheerfully concluded their review of this versatile organization by noting that among "the other functions of this extensive government department, is the considerable social services rendered by its uniformed staff, and its achievements of a reformatory character, now constitute a larger proportion of its work than its criminal prosecutions or the imposition of death sentences."[158] And yet the Webbs were taken seriously not only at the time of the writing of the above, but for decades to come, and their influence was not limited to their fellow Fabians. Vladimir Dedijer, a Yugoslav author and former associate of Tito, has recalled the impact of their writing on his political thinking at the time of the Purge Trials when he was first assailed by doubt about the Soviet system: "[I] clung to hope that all would be well in the end. Sometime in 1938 Sydney and Beatrice Webb published a new edition of their great study of the Soviet Union. The subtitle to the first edition had been 'A New Civilization?' whereas the second edition was printed without the question mark. I castigated myself thinking: 'Look what a suspicious intellectual you are. You are being taught a lesson—and by social democrats at that . . . —that there should be no doubt about the prospects of development in the Soviet Union.' "[159]

Needless to say, the influence of the Webbs was the greatest in their own country where, despite their quasi-radicalism, they enjoyed establishment status, and their remains were enshrined in Westminster Abbey along with the other great sons and daughters of the British nation.*

Admiration for the good works of the OGPU (or its predecessors and successors) was not peculiar to the Webbs. Their friend G. B. Shaw heartily endorsed even its non-reformatory activities: "we cannot afford

---

one who purported to be fairly high up in the GPU. In the course of their conversation Barnes put to him the naive but fundamental question: Why is it that in the USSR innocent people get arrested? The GPU man, it seems, fairly shook with laughter at this, to the point that it was quite a while before he could get his answer out. Of course we arrest innocent people, he said at last in effect; otherwise no one would be frightened. If people are only arrested for specific misdemeanours, all the others feel safe, and so ripe for treason."[157]

* The importance and influence of the Webbs was also reflected in the collection of admiring pieces published shortly after their death. See Margaret Cole, ed., *The Webbs and Their Work*, London, 1949. More irreverent were the recollections of Malcolm Muggeridge and Bertrand Russell.[160]

to give ourselves moral airs when our most enterprising neighbor [the USSR], . . . humanely and judiciously liquidates a handful of exploiters and speculators to make the world safe for honest man."[161] Jerome Davis, sociologist, professor at Yale Divinity School, and lifelong friend of the Soviet Union, had this to say about the head of this remarkable organization:

> Lavrenti P. Beria has, until recently, been Commissar for Internal Affairs, handling security police work similar to our FBI. Balding, bespectacled, he looks like the former achitect he is. Somewhat inaccessible and seldom interviewed, one must depend on knowledge of how very little war-time sabotage and espionage took place in the Soviet Union to realize that he is a successful administrator.[162]

The misjudgment of the character of the Soviet penal institutions and policies was not merely a product of favorable predisposition, crucial as it was. The visitors were in fact shown some attractive correctional institutions and thus their favorable expectations were given tangible substance; their beliefs and their experiences were gratifyingly united. Should they have suspected that what they were shown was the exception rather than the rule and hardly typical of the prison system as a whole? They were not inclined to be suspicious of their hosts, or to "snoop on them" as Owen Lattimore put it. They were favorably disposed toward the regime and therefore could not easily entertain the possibility of being the victims of an elaborate scheme of deception. Applied on such a scale, the techniques of hospitality, which included visits to the model prisons, were historically new. The highly organized efforts of the Soviet regime to impress foreigners were genuine innovations, produced by the enormous propaganda apparatus and its meticulous attention to detail—an enterprise both unfamiliar and unfathomable for most Westerners.[163] Although students of Russian history knew of Potemkin's villages (arranged for the benefit not of foreigners but of the monarch), the idea of such elaborate manipulations was at the time foreign to both Western intellectuals and public opinion at large. It was especially hard to imagine that model prisons or labor colonies might be established as mere prototypes, not for general use but as special exhibits to impress public opinion both abroad and at home. Possibly such exhibit-institutions were in part created to satisfy the more idealistic aspirations of the Soviet leaders themselves, to prove that humane institutional innovation was after all taking place. Similar factors may account for various Western interpretations of the Moscow Trials; no matter how implausible, indeed absurd the plots and confessions had been, many

Western intellectuals were unprepared to conceive of elaborate, stage-managed didactic show trials.

At last, nobody, and least of all intellectuals (who take pride in their ability to see through sham) like to admit to being vulnerable to deception. It would have been intolerable for most visitors to face the possibility that their judicious assessments arrived at during these fact-finding tours were the product of the cynical manipulation of what they had seen and experienced. Thus to believe or not to believe was also a matter of retaining self-respect.

Further light is shed on this process by the unusual and revealing case of a Polish socialist who was exposed to both the staged view of the Soviet penal institutions provided for the benefit of foreigners and the inside view accorded to the inmates. Jerzy Gliksman visited the Soviet Union in 1935, member of a tour group organized by Intourist. A few years later, after the German-Soviet treaty and the joint Nazi-Soviet occupation of Poland, he was one of tens of thousands of Poles sent to Soviet labor camps. Much of his book narrates his camp experiences, but there is one flashback to his 1935 visit which included an excursion to the model prison at Bolshevo, near Moscow. His recollections of this visit deserve to be quoted at some length as they are unique on two counts. Gliksman may well be the only person who had a double exposure to Soviet prisons, first as a visitor being taken to a showcase and then as an inmate of the "real thing." Secondly, his account of the visit is probably the only one which is a retroactively critical and analytical description of such a conducted tour. It is also one of the most detailed of such accounts and thus helps us understand the techniques of hospitality more generally and not only as applied to penal establishments.

> I awaited the trip to the prison-camp at Bolshevo with great impatience. Neither the Intourist nor the VOKS customarily included such visits in their excursion schedules. I was assured that I had been granted a special privilege.

> And indeed, I traveled to the camp with a distinguished group of people, which included correspondents of great foreign newspapers, several writers, artists, labor leaders etc. . . . My immediate neighbor in the luxurious Intourist bus . . . was a noted Mexican painter. Most of the conversation during the ride concerned the good will shown by Soviet authorities in consenting to show to foreigners even the detention place of criminals. What other government in the world would as easily agree to such a visit? . . .

> After a short ride we arrived at Bolshevo . . . our bus entered a lovely park containing numerous trees and flower beds. . . .

We started our inspection in one of the buildings containing the inmates' dormitories. We saw nice white beds and bedding, fine washing rooms.

Everything was spotlessly clean. . . .

Then we visited various workshops. . . . Everyone worked at a special occupation chosen by him of his own free will. . . .

The young men were working eagerly, with interest. Our entrance did not impress them in the least—apparently they were used to such visits. . . .

Finally we were taken to a large dining hall. At dinner we partook of the same food as prepared for the inmates; it was tasty and nourishing. . . .

It sounded incredible, but the camp was not guarded and the gate stood open.

After listening to a speech by the tour guide who stressed the two basic principles permeating the institution, namely self-government and voluntary activities, the author

saw tears in the eyes of an elderly English lady. They were tears of appreciation and joy. "Wonderful! Wonderful!" she kept repeating.

"How beautiful the world could be!" a French movie director who happened to be sitting at my side whispered into my ear.

Our guide had something more to offer. "I should like to convince you of the truth of my statements" he told us. "I should like to call a group of young people in the room and leave them here with you, all by themselves!" . . .

The inmates repeated almost everything we had been told by our guide. They were happy in the camp, they said. Everything was ideal, nothing could be better. . . .

Our visit to Bolshevo took up almost the entire day. During the return trip the participants exchanged lively comments about the wonderful institution. Our guide's face glowed with joy.

"If you are not tired," he told us, "we could visit still another institution today, one that should complete in your minds the picture of our educational homes. I propose that we visit the home for former prostitutes."

We were of course enthusiastic about the proposal. . . .

The directress of the home, an elderly, stoutish, intelligent-looking woman, received us with utmost friendliness. And what good fortune! She spoke English, French and German.

Politely she explained to us the working of the home.

> "This is the way the Soviet Union fights this plague and shame of mankind, prostitution." The VOKS representative proudly emphasized, "Not by means of harsh police methods like in your capitalist countries, but through proper education!"

Gliksman and some other visitors wondered whether or not the fallen women thought it humiliating to be visited and stared at: "One of the girl attendants reassured us. 'It does not matter,' she said; 'they are used to these visits. Foreign tourists are brought on a visit here almost every evening.' "[164]

We are fortunate to have other published accounts of Soviet labor camps which highlight the difference between the view from the outside and inside. In this instance it was not the same person who reported from both perspectives but rather accounts of the same penal institution are provided by two visitors and one inmate recalling their visit. The year was 1944 and the place Magadan (in the Kolyma region in the Soviet Far East), one of the most notorious places of detention and forced labor.[165] Unlike Bolshevo it was not designed as a model prison camp, therefore it had to be converted into one, or at least be made presentable enough for the benefit of important visitors. They were Henry Wallace, vice-president of the United States, and Owen Lattimore, professor at Johns Hopkins University, a member of his party. Their experience was more unusual than that of many other visitors (who inspected and commented favorably on carefully selected penal institutions) in that Wallace and Lattimore throughout their visit remained unaware of being in the middle of a vast complex of labor camps. (They shared this distinction with G. B. Shaw, who had earlier been taken to timber producing areas near Archangel to prove that no slave labor was used. "The method of refutation was the dismantling of the barbed wire and sentries' towers, and the marching of the prisoners into the depths of the forest for a few days. . . . This proved effective.")[166]

Wallace wrote:

> At Magadan I met Ivan Feodorovich Nikishov, a Russian, director of *Dalstroi* (the Far Northern Construction Trust), which is a combination of TVA and Hudson's Bay Company. On display in his office were samples of ore-bearing rocks in this region. . . . Nikishov waxed enthusiastic and Goglidze [an aide] commented jestingly: "He runs everything around here. With *Dalstroi's* resources at his command, he is a millionaire." "We had to dig hard to get this place going," said Nikishov. "Twelve years ago the first settlers arrived and put up eight

prefabricated houses. Today Magadan has 40,000 inhabitants and all are well housed."

Subsequently Wallace's party was "flown north along the Kolyma Road to Bereliakh, where we saw two placer gold mines. The enterprise displayed here was impressive. Development was far more energetic than at Fairbanks [in Alaska], although conditions were more difficult. . . ." He continued:

> We went for a walk in the taiga. . . . The larch were just putting out their first leaves and Nikishov gamboled about, enjoying the wonderful air immensely. . . . The Kolyma gold miners are big, husky young men, who came out to the Far East from European Russia. I spoke with some of them.

Wallace also recalled having been taken in Magadan to "an extraordinary exhibit of paintings in embroidery . . . made by a group of local women who gathered regularly during the severe winter to study needlework. . . ." He could not have guessed, given his level of information about the area and its inhabitants, that they too were prisoners. As to the NKVD troops (another incarnation of the political police) assigned to his party: "In traveling through Siberia we were accompanied by 'old soldiers' with blue tops on their caps. Everybody treated them with great respect. They are members of the NKVD . . . I became very fond of their leader, Major Mikhail Cheremisenov, who had also been with the Wilkie party."[167]

Owen Lattimore's vision of Magadan was very similar to that of Wallace:

> Magadan is also part of the domain of a remarkable concern, the Dalstroi (Far Northern Construction Company), which can be roughly compared to a combination of Hudson's Bay Company and TVA. It constructs and operates ports, roads and railroads, and operates gold mines and municipalities, including, at Magadan, a first-class orchestra and a good light-opera company.

> At the time we were there, Magadan was also host to a fine ballet group from Poltava. . . . As one American remarked, high grade entertainment just naturally seems to go with gold, and so does high-powered executive ability.

> Mr. Nikshisov, the head of *Dalstroi*, had just been decorated with the Order of Hero of the Soviet Union for his extraordinary achievements. Both he and his wife have a trained and sensitive interest in art and music and also a deep sense of civic responsibility.[168]

It is hardly surprising that things looked rather different to the more permanent residents of these parts. Elinor Lipper, a former inmate, devotes several pages in her book to her recollections of the visit of Wallace and Lattimore, whose accounts she subsequently read.

> He [Wallace] does not mention, or does not know, that this city was built solely by prisoners working under inhuman conditions. . . . He does not say—or does not know—that this highway [which Wallace made admiring references to] was built entirely by prisoners and that tens of thousands gave their lives in building it. . . .

As to his remarks about "Nikishov gamboling about" she says

> It is too bad that Wallace never saw him "gamboling about" on one of his drunken rages around the prison camps, raining filthy, savage language upon the heads of exhausted, starving prisoners, having them locked up in solitary confinement for no offense whatsoever and sending them into the gold mines to work 14 and 16 hours per day. . . .

As to the exhibit of embroidery done by local women on long winter evenings she notes that

> "The group of local women" were female prisoners, most of them former nuns, who were employed to do needlework for such highly placed ladies as Nikishov's wife.

In regard to Lattimore's comparison of *Dalstroi* with TVA and Hudson Bay Company she remarks that, among other differences, neither of these two use forced labor or shot their workers if they refused to work.[169]

Wallace and Lattimore cannot be fully blamed for failing to notice the surrounding realities.° Not only did they have no preconception of the Soviet penal system but their hosts made a determined and successful effort to remove the reminders of the true facts of life in Magadan and

---

° Subsequently Owen Lattimore was indignant about criticisms of his and Wallace's account of their visit to Kolyma. In his letter written in 1968 to the *New Statesman* he was in no mood to be self-critical ("Is it assumed that a visit of this kind affords an ideal opportunity to snoop on one's hosts? Should one return fully briefed to write an intelligence report 'exposing' what one has not seen?"). He went so far as to imply scornfully that after all Nikishov, the camp commander, could not have been such a tyrant ("the 'unspeakable Nikishov' . . . must have slipped up in his control"), since Elinor Lipper survived to write her book. He seemed to suggest that being on a goodwill mission and allied to the Soviet Union were good enough explanations of the euphoric accounts he and Wallace produced. Finally, as if to forestall further criticism of those who had written such accounts, he invoked the spectre of "possibly [a] second wave of Joe McCarthyism"—a singularly inaccurate foreboding in the late 1960s.[170]

Kolyma. They went about this task with characteristic thoroughness, and their activities provide one of the best examples of the techniques of hospitality on record. Lipper writes:

> Wallace traveled through the Asiatic portions of the Soviet Union in order to observe the capacity of Soviet industry. I do not know what he saw in the rest of Soviet Asia, but in Kolyma the NKVD carried off its job with flying colors. Wallace saw nothing at all of this frozen hell with its hundreds of thousands of the damned.
>
> The access roads to Magadan were lined with wooden watch towers. In honor of Wallace these towers were razed in a single night.
>
> At the edge of the city there were several prison camps, among them the large women's camp with its several thousand inmates. . . . Every prisoner who was there at the time owes Mr. Wallace a debt of gratitude. For it was owing to his visit that for the first and last time the prisoners had three successive holidays. On the day of his arrival, the day of his visit and the day of his departure, not a single prisoner was allowed to leave the camp. This was not enough. Although the route for Mr. Wallace and his suite was carefully prepared in advance, there was still the possibility that by mischance the visitor would catch sight of the prisoners in the camp yard—which would not have been an edifying spectacle. Therefore, on orders from above, movies were shown to the prisoners from morning till night for three days. No prisoners went walking in the yard.
>
> To some extent the prisoners of Magadan did repay him, but probably Mr. Wallace did not know it. How could it occur to him that the actors whose performance he enjoyed one evening in the Gorky Theater of Magadan were mostly prisoners? He never met any of these actors, because immediately after the curtain fell they were loaded aboard a truck and returned to the camp. After all, it would have been embarrassing if one of the actors had happened to know English and had mentioned to Mr. Wallace that he was one of hundreds of thousands of innocent prisoners serving a ten-year sentence in Kolyma.
>
> And how could Mr. Wallace know that the city of Magadan, which had risen so swiftly out of the wilderness, had been built exclusively by prison labor; that women prisoners had carried the beams and bricks to the building sites? He probably did not realize that he had sowed confusion among the prettily dressed swineherd girls at the model farm on the twenty-third kilometer from Magadan by asking them a harmless question about the pigs. For these girls were not swineherds at all; they were a group of good-looking office girls who had been ordered to play a part especially for Mr. Wallace's visit. They took the place of prisoners who actually did take care of the swine. However, the interpreter saved the situation and the visit went off smoothly.
>
> Mr. Wallace was also gratified to note the rich assortment of Russian merchandise in the shop windows of Magadan. He made a point

of going into a store to examine the Russian products and to buy some
trivial item. The citizenry of Magadan were even more amazed than
Mr. Wallace at the Russian goods that appeared overnight in the shop
windows, because for the past two years all the strictly rationed goods
which could be bought had been of American origin. But the NKVD
had gone to the trouble of digging stuff up from the remotest stores
and precious private hoards in order to impress Mr. Wallace. . . .
Then Mr. Wallace went home and published his enthusiastic report on
Soviet Asia. The watch towers were put again, the prisoners sent out
to work again, and in the empty shop windows were to be seen nothing but a few dusty and mournful boxes of matches.[171]

The surrealistic misperception of Soviet society reached its apex in the
prison reports sampled above. Evidently there are few defenses against
well-planned deception no matter how extraordinary its scope and aspiration, if there is no predisposition to be on guard.

The Purge Trials

The misjudgments of the Purge Trials on the part of many Western intellectuals are comparable in their enormity to the misapprehensions displayed with respect to the Soviet penal institutions and policies. Similar
processes were at work in both cases, predisposing to a genuine incomprehension of what transpired. The trials, not unlike the prisons, were
viewed against a background of generally sympathetic perceptions of
the Soviet system, including its judicial institutions. Waldo Frank's comments about (non-political) court proceedings he witnessed in Leningrad capture this spirit: "this crowd is different. Here, no recognizable
lawyers; no heavy jowled judges sweeping with black robes into their
chambers, followed by bald clerks with servile mouths; no sleek litigants
of civil suits marshalling their witnesses, nursing their dollars, groomed
by professional manipulators of human weakness . . . it came to me
that this was the first court of human justice I had known."[172]

Even when the Moscow Trials produced at least mild consternation or
a measure of unease, the sympathizers tried to assimilate such a less appealing occurrence (as the trial) to the generally benign vision of Soviet
society and to reduce dissonance between the particular and the general. This was done in several ways. Jerome Davis, among others, argued that the whole issue of the purges and trials was blown up out of
all proportion, and they had little impact on the tranquil and contended
life of law-abiding Soviet citizens:

To the rest of the world it seemed at the time that Russia was enveloped in a smothering atmosphere of plots, murders and purges. Actually this was a superficial view since, although the rest of the world was morbidly interested in the trials to the exclusion of anything else about Russia, only a tiny percentage of the population was involved and the same years which saw treason trials saw some of the greatest triumphs of Soviet planning. While the screws tightened on a tiny minority the majority of Soviet people were enjoying greater prosperity and greater freedom.[173]

The trials were reasonable proceedings, so the argument often ran, but even if they were not, they should not detract from the great accomplishments of the regime. Davis evidently believed that those upon whom "the screws tightened" fully deserved such discomfort, but even if their fate was perhaps a tiny bit harsh, that was a small price to pay for the rising tide of contentment all around. (Did not Stalin himself say at the time that life was becoming happier and more cheerful?) In a similar spirit "on the occasion of a dinner given in his honor by the newspaper *The Nation*, André Malraux declared that 'just as the Inquisition did not affect the fundamental dignity of Christianity, so the Moscow trials have not diminished the fundamental dignity of communism.' "[174]

Others judiciously argued that there was insufficient solid evidence to cast aspersions on the soundness of the judicial proceedings, and while admitting that certain aspects of the trials were not quite to their liking they deferred jumping to conclusions unwarranted by incontrovertible evidence. Supporters of the regime would also argue that the apparent ruthlessness and possible irregularities were due to the circumstances and the times: the serious external threats and the unprecedented exertions required for rapid modernization, necessitating drastic measures against the opponents of the government. Defenders of the trials did not, as a rule, entertain doubts about the guilt of the accused, who had, after all, made full confessions.[175] Upton Sinclair's reasoning as to the authenticity of the confessions was fairly typical, as seen in his criticism of the views of Eugene Lyons:

> You speak in your letter of "obviously phoney trials." That is, of course, begging the question. That the trials were "phoney" seems obvious to you, but the exact opposite seems obvious to me. Over and over I ask myself: Is there any torture, any kind of terror, physical, mental or moral, which would induce them to do such a thing?
>
> These men had withstood the worst that the Czar's police could do . . . my belief is that the Bolsheviks would have let the GPU agents

tear them to pieces shred by shred before they would have confessed
to actions which they had not committed.[176]

Sinclair also succeeded in persuading himself that the famine and violence associated with the collectivization of agriculture in the early 30s
was necessary to avert far greater evils in the future: "They drove rich
peasants off the land and sent them wholesale to work in lumber camps
and on railroads. Maybe it cost a million lives—maybe it cost five million—but you cannot think intelligently about it unless you ask yourself
how many millions it might have cost if the changes had not been
made." He added: "Some people will say that this looks like condoning
wholesale murder. That is not true; it is merely trying to evaluate a revolution. There has never been in human history a great social change
without killing. The French Revolution cost millions [sic] lives. . . ."[177]

It was not merely the ardent desire to give the Soviet system every
benefit of doubt that led to such reasoning. Upton Sinclair and most
other American and Western European intellectuals had no frame of
reference for evaluating the Purge Trials and insufficient imagination for
divining the way in which they were designed and implemented.

Jerome Davis concurred with Upton Sinclair in defending the veracity
of the confessions, drawing on his experience and expertise as chairman
of the Legislative Commission on Jails in Connecticut:

> The accused were tried in open court with representatives of the whole
> world listening in. There was not then and is not now a scintilla of
> evidence that any of them had been tortured. They knew they were
> facing death, and yet did not protest innocence although the world
> would have been prone to believe them. The defendants were ex-
> revolutionists who had never confessed under the Tsar's regime to
> save their lives or their families. Further, both Mr. Pritt . . . and
> Ambassador Davies . . . say that it would have been absolutely im-
> possible for the defendants to prepare fake confessions which would
> square with the rest of the evidence and all other testimony. They
> claim that fourteen defendants could not rehearse their parts in ad-
> vance and stick to their roles . . . even if they decided, for some un-
> known reason, to take part in such a farce.
>
> Again, it is said, why should guilt make people confess? It so hap-
> pens that I was chairman of the Legislative Commission on Jails in the
> State of Connecticut for many years. I have seen hundreds of crimi-
> nals who confessed when confronted with overwhelming proof of their
> guilt.[178]

Clearly, it did not occur to Davis that it was not the defendants who
prepared their confessions but the prosecuting authorities, who had lit-

tle trouble, for the most part, "squaring" the confessions with "the rest of the evidence."

Henri Barbusse, the famous French writer, was genuinely shocked by what the trials revealed: "What subterranean maneuvers, what scheming and plotting! . . . The same people who blew up bridges and whatever public works during the Civil War still remained in liberated Russia, gasping for breath, who threw emory into the machines and put the few remaining railway engines out of action—these same people put powdered glass into cooperative food supplies in 1933."[179] Jerome Davis reported that Yagoda had arranged that the office of his successor Yezhov be sprayed, no less than seven times, with a mixture of mercury and acid.[180] (Both were heads of the political police.)

Bertolt Brecht, the popular German writer and selective cynic, somewhat in the manner of G. B. Shaw, explained the trials as follows:

> Even in the opinion of the bitterest enemies of the Soviet Union and of her government, the trials have clearly demonstrated the existence of active conspiracies against the regime. . . . We must try to discern behind the actions of the accused what was to them a conceivable political conception—a conception which led them into a quagmire of infamous crimes. . . . This false political conception led them into the depths of isolation and deep into infamous crime. All the scum, domestic and foreign, all the vermin, the professional criminals and informers, found lodging there. The goals of this rabble were identical to the goals of the accused. I am convinced that this is the truth, and I am convinced that it will carry the ring of truth even in Western Europe, even for hostile readers.[181]

A remarkable tribute to the Soviet system of justice was offered by Feuchtwanger, who personally observed the trials of Pyatakov and Radek:

> as long as I was in Western Europe the indictment of the Zinoviev trial seemed utterly incredible. . . . But when I attended the second trial in Moscow . . . I was forced to accept the evidence of my senses, and my doubts melted away as naturally as the salt dissolves in water.
>
> It cannot be denied that the most impressive feature of the confessions is their precision and coherence. . . .
>
> There was no justifications of any sort for imagining that there was anything manufactured, artificial or even awe-inspiring or emotional about these proceedings. If a producer had had to arrange this court scene, years of rehearsal and careful coaching would have been necessary to get the prisoners to correct one another eagerly on small points and to express their emotion with such restraint.

In wishing to further clarify aspects of the proceedings that might puzzle the Western observer he found an illuminating parallel:

> It is this common feeling which enables judges and accused to work together with such unanimity of purpose—a feeling somewhat akin to that which in England links the government with the opposition so closely that the leader of the opposition receives a salary of 2000 pounds from the state.[182]

Walter Duranty (reporter for the New York *Times*) was similarly persuaded:

> No one who heard Piatakof or Muralov could doubt for a moment that what they said was true, and that they were saying it from no outer drag of force. . . . Their words rang true, and it is absurd to suggest or imagine that men like this could yield to any influence against their own strong hearts. . . . it is unthinkable that Stalin and Voroshilov and Budenny and the Court Martial could have sentenced their friends to death unless the proofs of guilt were overwhelming.[183]

Joseph Davies, ambassador of the United States at the time, also attended the trials and was more than satisfied with their authenticity:

> To assume that this proceeding [the Pyatakov-Radek Trial] was invented and staged . . . would be to presuppose the creative genius of Shakespeare and the genius of Belasco in stage production.

As to the Bukharin trial (which he attended without an interpreter) he thought that guilt was established "beyond reasonable doubt." These proceedings also led him to reflect that "There can be no doubt . . . that the Kremlin authorities were greatly alarmed by these disclosures and the confessions of the defendants." Davies believed that the Purges truly "cleansed the country" and "rid it of treason," which explained why there were no fifth columnists when the Germans invaded. (He evidently did not know that the Germans had no difficulty in recruiting a whole army under General Vlasov.) His comments on the prosecutor are reminiscent of Harold Laski's, who considered him far superior to his British counterparts and believed that law reform was his passion. "The attorney general is a man of about sixty and is much like Homer Cummings; calm, dispassionate, intellectual, able and wise. He conducted the treason trial in a manner that won my respect and admiration as a lawyer," Davies wrote. Moreover his attitude "was entirely free of browbeating. Apparently it was not necessary. . . . [he] conducted the case calmly and generally with admirable moderation."[184]*

Jerome Davis defended the trials even while admitting that not all confessions were genuine. He wrote: "in the main these trials are genuine and the men guilty," adding "Of course . . . there is a lot of false testimony in a trial of this kind. Nothing less should be expected." At last, according to Owen Lattimore "the purge of top officials showed the ordinary citizen his power to denounce even them, and [Lattimore] concluded, 'this sounds like democracy to me.' "[186]

While the sample of reactions to the Purges and Moscow Trials may seem improbable in retrospect it becomes less so as we remind ourselves that belief in the authenticity of the Moscow Trials was an integral part of deeply held beliefs about the superiority of the Soviet system as a whole. As long as the latter remained an article of faith, it was possible to ignore, justify, rationalize, or explain away the Purge Trials. There were also some specific beliefs which provided more direct support for digesting the Purges. These included faith in the integrity of the Soviet leaders and Stalin in particular and in the soundness of the political and law enforcement institutions of Soviet society. If and as long as it was believed that "the USSR is the most inclusive and equalized democracy in the world,"[187] monstrous abuses of power associated with the trials were hard to conceive of. Likewise if you felt that the NKVD was a superb organization it was difficult to credit it with masterminding the trials and subjecting their victims to a wide range of deprivations. Sympathetic intellectuals like Jerome Davis had nothing but praise for the vigilance of the Soviet security police ("In traveling about Russia during World War II, I was often taken into custody by the NKVD. I always made it a point to compliment them on their alertness in spotting a foreigner who might be a spy. In every case I found that the NKVD had exceptional men in charge, picked leaders with training and intelligence. They always released me promptly after I had shown my American passport and my credentials from the Foreign Office").[188]

---

* He was referring to the same Vishinsky who routinely called the defendants dogs, snakes, rats, brigands, degenerates, vermin, etc. Pablo Neruda recalled his funeral in his *Memoirs* as follows: "I look out the window. There is an honor guard in the streets. What is happening? Even the snow is motionless where it has fallen. It is the great Vishinsky's funeral. The streets clear solemnly to let the procession pass. A profound silence settles down, a peacefulness in the heart of winter, for the great soldier. Vishinsky's fire returns to the roots of the Soviet mother country."[185]

Yet even as one adds up everything—the predisposition of the sympathizers, the thoroughness of the staged proceedings, the confessions of the accused, the threat of Nazism during this period, an appreciation of the rapid economic progress the regime made—the credulousness of Western intellectuals still remains somewhat daunting *if* one clings to the view that intellectuals are by definition critical and skeptical.

As already suggested, explanations of credulousness must not focus on isolated misperceptions, however spectacular, such as those of the prisons and the Purge Trials. For the most credulous visitors the attractive features of Soviet society formed a "package" which was hard to pull apart. They could not bring themselves to think or say, for instance, that the decline of illiteracy and infant mortality was admirable but clearly the Purges and police terror were not. Those who admired the decline of infant mortality persuaded themselves (with some notable exceptions) that the judicial proceedings too were admirable. In some extreme cases, like that of Jerome Davis (and others like Shaw, Hewlett Johnson, the Webbs, Corliss Lamont, Harry F. Ward, Ambassador Davies), the believers could not bring themselves to stop believing.* They became political addicts; like the alcoholic who cannot remain a social drinker, the most credulous among the sympathizers were incapable of drawing the line. If he believed X why not also believe Y? If Jerome Davis could believe that those who confessed in the Moscow Trials were guilty why not also that the Baltic people welcomed annexation by the Soviet Union? Why not the Soviet professions of innocence in the Katyn massacre in Poland? Why not the Soviet version of why the

---

* Even in 1957 and in 1959—his faith surviving the Soviet domination of Eastern Europe, the Berlin Uprising in 1953, Poznan and Hungary in 1956, the "Secret Speech" of Khrushchev in 1956—Jerome Davis was still taking visitors on group tours of the Soviet Union and organizing seminars for the proper appreciation of the Soviet system.[189] Such tenaciousness of faith, however, was rare. Many others similarly inclined found new countries to venerate. Waldo Frank discovered Cuba, others China; Hewlett Johnson ecumenically worshipped both the Soviet Union and China as well as other Communist-dominated regimes in Eastern Europe. Likewise W. E. B. Du Bois paid friendly visits to the Soviet Union, East Germany, Czechoslovakia, Poland, Rumania and China.

There have been other indications that youthful political commitments, like bad habits, are difficult to break and bury unceremoniously. The latest trends in preserving or wistfully dignifying past political attachments include the sentimental obliteration of facts, confusing good intentions with good results, the making of good clean fun of serious moral blunders, disclaiming information and other techniques.

These new trends in prettifying the political past have been displayed to various degrees and in different combinations in books by Vivian Gornick, Jessica Mitford, Peggy Dennis, and others.[190]

Soviet Army halted at the gates of Warsaw in 1944 and let the Nazis slaughter the non-communist Polish resistance fighters?

As long as the generally favorable attitudes toward the regime persisted, the Soviet version was always the more credible and the blemishes found in Soviet society and Soviet policies could be "put into context,"* compared with (allegedly) greater historical outrages elsewhere, and ultimately digested. Of course for many people the accumulation of "blemishes" finally led to a collapse of faith, or the demise of favorable predisposition; when this happened no part of the system was any longer appreciated, none of the impressive statistics on infant mortality or hydroelectric plants mattered any more. But that is another story. What concerns us here are the appeals of Soviet society, what they were, how they related to one another, and how they survived as long as they did.

The misperception and misjudgment of particular institutions or events, however colossal, cannot be understood in isolation from the enthusiasm for the system as a whole. For those looking for alternatives to their decrepit and uninspiring society it was not possible to admit to flaws in the counter-model. Either the Soviet Union was wholly or overwhelmingly admirable and exhilarating, or else it ceased to be of interest altogether.

Wise and Caring Leaders

It should not be surprising that admirers of the Soviet system were also enthusiastic about its leaders. Even those who considered equalization the prime achievement of the Soviet regime felt that in an egalitarian system too there must be leaders who inspire the multitudes. It appears that the appeal of the leaders was as powerful as that of specific institutions.

Again this is particularly understandable in view of the historical circumstances. The chaotic, "rudderless" state of Western societies in the 1930s engendered craving not only for a sense of purpose but also for leaders who could provide and personify the latter. There was no agreement among the visitors as to how indispensable the leader was for the system but there was widespread appreciation for his role and personality.

---

* Even *Life* magazine had no difficulty in voicing the familiar argument: "When we take account of what the USSR has accomplished in the 20 years of its existence we can make allowances for certain shortcomings, however deplorable." And they certainly were made. In the same editorial article *Life* assured its readers that "If the Soviet leaders tell us that the control of information was necessary to get this job done, we can afford to take their word for it for the time being."[191]

While in the context of the 1930s Stalin was the key leader, some visitors also commented on Lenin, usually in connection with the obligatory visit to his mausoleum. Corliss and Margaret Lamont "[paid] homage to Russia's greatest leader and [took] strength from his impersonally beautiful and resolute face. . . ."[192] Edmund Wilson was similarly impressed on inspecting the mausoleum and found that Lenin's was "a beautiful face, of exquisite fineness; and,—what proves sufficiently its authenticity—it is profoundly aristocratic. . . . Yet it is an aristocrat who is not specialized as an aristocrat, a poet who is not specialized as a poet, a scientist who is not specialized as a scientist."[193]

Lenin's aristocratic traits also impressed Shaw. On his trip to the mausoleum he declared: "A pure intellectual type . . . that is the true aristocracy. . . ."[194] Doubtless the appeals of Lenin were both enhanced and circumscribed by the circumstance that he was dead because death created a distance between the man and his errors (or less appealing features), making his achievements more visible than his mistakes. Moreover he was the unquestioned founding father, whose personality and organizational contributions enriched the foundations of the new society and became an enduring source of its legitimation. By displaying his bodily remains the regime literally enshrined and canonized him. The official materialism notwithstanding, his successors tried their best to suggest that his preserved body was symbolic of the eternal survival of his spirit. Mayakovsky, the poet, was not the only one to entertain this idea. Among Western intellectuals Pablo Neruda more recently reflected on Lenin's continued "presence": "On the morning of November 7, I watched the people's parade. . . . They marched with sure and firm step through Red Square. They were being observed by the sharp eyes of a man dead many years, the founder of this security, this joy, this strength: Vladimir Ilyich Ulyanov, immortal Lenin."[195]

Almost inevitably the appeals of the living leader, in direct charge of all the thrilling social transformations, were bound to overshadow those of the deceased father. Thus more comments were made of Stalin than of Lenin, especially since some of the more important visitors were given an opportunity to meet with him. Others could at least behold him at receptions or on the reviewing stand as he was dispensing benediction to the masses below.

It was the combination of great power and apparent modesty and simplicity which fascinated many intellectuals about Stalin (perhaps because they had little of either). Stalin seemed to tower above the masses, possessed virtually superhuman qualities, and yet somehow managed to be at one with them and dedicate his life to them. He personified the resolution of the conflict between elitism and egalitarianism discussed earlier. As Stalin himself put it: "The art of leadership is a serious matter. One must not struggle behind the movement, nor run in front of it lest one become in both cases separated from the masses. Whoever wants to lead and at the same time maintain his contact with the masses must fight on two fronts; against those loitering in the rear, and those speeding on ahead,"[196] a formulation which impressed many sympathizers by its judiciousness if not precision.

In any event the sympathetic intellectuals were not too concerned with the dangers of concentrated power as long as it was in the right hands and used for lofty purposes. Above all they were yearning for a political system in which "things got done." They certainly did in the Soviet Union. G. B. Shaw wrote: "Mussolini, Kemal, Pilsudski, Hitler and the rest can all depend on me to judge them by their ability to deliver the goods and not by Swinburne's comfortable notions of freedom. Stalin has delivered the goods to an extent that seemed impossible ten years ago; and I take off my hat to him accordingly."[197]*

While the intellectuals were impressed by Stalin's power (though not all of them quite so unabashedly as Shaw), they often took pains to insist that he was no autocrat or despot. The Webbs were the most ardent on this subject:

> He [Stalin] has not even the extensive power which the Congress of the United States has temporarily conferred upon President Roosevelt, or that which the American Constitution entrusts for four years every successive president.

They further argued that ". . . Stalin is not a dictator . . . he is the duly elected representative of one of the Moscow constituencies to the Supreme Soviet of the USSR. By this assembly he has been selected as one of the thirty members of the Presidium of the Supreme Soviet of the USSR, accountable to the representative assembly for all activities . . . [Stalin] has persistently asserted in his writings and speeches that as a member of the Presidium of the Supreme Soviet of the USSR he is merely a colleague of thirty other members, and that so far as the Com-

---

* Here as elsewhere Shaw revealed not only his admiration for Stalin but a more general fondness for dictators, regardless their ideological complexion, who get things done. Shaw displayed most nakedly a vicarious gratification in identifying with the "strong men" who exercised power with gusto and few inhibitions. Lincoln Steffens and John Reed were also among those who switched from the admiration of Mussolini to Stalin (or perhaps indulged in them concurrently for a while).[198]

munist Party is concerned he acts as general secretary under the orders of the executive."[199]

Hewlett Johnson was similarly persuaded: "Stalin is no oriental despot. His new Constitution shows it. His readiness to relinquish power shows it. His refusal to add to the power he already possesses shows it. His willingness to lead his people down new and unfamiliar paths of democracy shows it. The easier course would have been to add to his own power and develop autocratic rule."[200] Feuchtwanger believed that "the realization of the socialist democracy" was Stalin's "ultimate goal."[201] Ambassador Davies considered Stalin a stubborn democrat, unwilling to make any concession to autocratic ways of governing: "Stalin, it was reported,* insisted upon liberalism of the constitution even though it hazarded his power and party control. . . . It is stated that Stalin himself decided the issue of projecting actual secret and universal suffrage which the new constitution calls for."[202] Doubtless, the Ambassador would have agreed with I. F. Stone's assessment of the significance of universal suffrage: "There is only one party, but the introduction of the secret ballot offers the workers and peasants a weapon against bureaucratic and inefficient officials and their policies."[203] According to Albert Rhys Williams, the American writer, Stalin took no initiative to gain power: "By no coup d'etat did Stalin seize the reins of government. Nor did he arbitrarily arrogate to himself the vast powers he exercises. They were bestowed upon him as Secretary of the Communist Party."[204] Evidently Stalin was temperamentally incapable of exercising autocratic rule: "It would be an error to consider the Soviet leader a willful man who believes in forcing his ideas upon others," wrote Jerome Davis. "Everything he does reflects the desires and hopes of the masses to a large degree." W. E. B. Du Bois thought "He [Stalin] asked for neither adulation nor vengeance. He was reasonable and conciliatory."[205]

The unique combination of being powerful without being autocratic was not Stalin's only trait that elicited the admiration of the visitors. He was also a good man to have power: kindly, simple, good-natured, unpretentious and self-denying. "His demeanour is kindly, his manner almost deprecatingly simple, his personality and expression of reserve, strength and poise very marked."[206]

Emil Ludwig, the German writer, upon visiting Stalin "found a lonely man who is not influenced by money or pleasure or even ambition. Though he holds enormous power he takes no pride in its possession,

---

* We never learn by whom this was reported, not unlike the identity of those who assured the Webbs of the popular satisfaction with the prison system.

but it must give him a certain amount of satisfaction to feel that he triumphed over his opponents."[207] Feuchtwanger considered Stalin "the most unpretentious" of all the men known to him who held power, the Soviet leaders in general "as good as their word," ready to receive criticism and "exchange frankness for frankness."[208]

Ambassador Davies stressed the reassuring aspects of Stalin's personality: "His brown eye is exceedingly wise and gentle. A child would like to sit on his lap and a dog would sidle up to him."[209] He was not the only one who found Stalin's parental-paternal qualities attractive. Emil Ludwig confessed that "I had expected to meet a Grand Duke of the old regime, stern, abrupt, and unfriendly. But instead . . . I found myself for the first time face to face with a dictator to whose care I would readily confide the education of my children."[210] The Webbs, in the same spirit, were also deeply impressed by what we would call today Stalin's caring attitudes. They quoted him approvingly and without the slightest touch of irony: "As Stalin said, 'man must be grown as carefully and attentively as a gardener grows a favorite fruit tree.' "[211]

Stalin was not only gentle and kind, but also farsighted and correct in his policies: "Riding over every obstacle and opposition and driving the First Plan through to completion, he launched the country on a Second and a Third Plan—each a more comprehensive and colossal undertaking. There were many who protested against the terrific speed and tempo; who resented the hardships imposed upon them; who questioned the wisdom of the whole undertaking. But they do so no longer."[212] Those familiar with the history of the period will readily agree that the last sentence was more true than its author realized. Williams was content not to elaborate on the precise reasons why the questioning of Stalin's policies had ceased.

Stalin's powers of concentration were another source of amazement among the visitors. Louis Fischer, for example, recalled how during a meeting which lasted over six hours (Stalin received an American group which included Jerome Davis) he never once left the room or received any messages, devoting his full attention to his guests. But there was more to his genius than powers of concentration. As J. D. Bernal saw it, Stalin " 'combined as no man had before his time, a deep theoretical understanding with unfailing mastery of practice . . . [and] a deeply scientific approach to all problems with his capacity for feeling. . . .' "[213]

Of all his impressive qualities perhaps his simplicity and unpretentiousness elicited the most heartfelt praise. Hewlett Johnson discoursed on these (and related) attributes at some length, since he was a beneficiary of a private audience. He reported that "Stalin is calm, composed, simple, not lacking in humor, direct in speech. . . . There was nothing cruel or dramatic . . . just steady purpose and a kindly geniality. . . . Here then was a man who had helped to plan a new order and a square deal for the masses . . . the man who would see that justice was done on the broad scale . . . whom no assault could terrify . . . the man who through fifty years' tenacity of purpose has earned and won the name . . . Stalin or steel." The Dean of Canterbury humbly and effusively told Stalin of his pilgrimage to certain shrines in Georgia:

> "I went to Gori . . . and visited the cottage where your Excellency was born. The new setting of marble which protects your old home in no way clashes with the little house it shelters.* The gardens were full of bloom. I was presented with an armful of roses. Next I visited the seminary in Tbilisi where you were taught and the small suburban house in whose deep and hidden cellar you operated your illegal press. . . . Finally . . . I stood bareheaded before the tomb of your mother in the church up the steep hillside above Tbilisi."
>
> "My mother was a simple woman" [responded Stalin].
>
> "A good woman," I added.
>
> "A simple woman," he repeated, with a friendly smile, which broadened as I added: "One often sees the portrait of the mother in the disposition of the child."

Such tones of reverence were not peculiar to Johnson,† though he excelled among his fellow pilgrims perhaps because of the occupational requirement of humility toward the divine here transferred to his dialogue with the new, secular deity. In the course of the same audience he at last summoned up his courage to ask Stalin about some thirty Russian girls who married Englishmen during the war and were not allowed to join their husbands. He broached the delicate topic as follows:

> "I speak with diffidence and hesitation, for I would avoid all appearance of meddling with your internal affairs; but one matter, small in

---

* A most astonishing assurance, since a veritable Greek temple was superimposed on the peasant cottage.

† Jerome Davis also extended reverence from the son to the mother. He actually met her (in 1927) and had a long talk with her about Stalin's boyhood. Of her he said: "Her face was remarkable for its strength, its will power and its serenity. She was obviously very proud of her son. . . ." Among his early accomplishments she recounted that "Once he demonstrated his superiority by going around a complete circle of trees hanging from the branches by his hands without once touching the ground, a feat that none of the other boys succeeded in doing. He was very sensitive to the injustice all about us."[214]

comparison with greater affairs, but apt to cause ill-feeling out of all proportion to its magnitude, troubles us and we are anxious to remove any and every unnecessary cause of friction between our peoples. . . ."

Stalin exchanged meaningful glances with Molotov (who was present during the meeting) and intimated that the problem might be cleared up, though, as he said, "it is a matter for decision by the Supreme Soviet."[215] The Dean of Canterbury left in something of a daze (as his recollections suggest), reflecting on the encounter with the wise, steely, yet genial man.

In his *Memoirs* Pablo Neruda attempted a retrospective historical summation of Stalin's significance: "This has been my stand: above the darkness, unknown to men of the Stalin era, Stalin rose before my eyes, a good-natured man of principles, as sober as a hermit, a titanic defender of the Russian Revolution. Moreover this small man with his huge moustache had become a giant in wartime."[216]

There was a consensus among the sympathetic visitors both in the 1930s and early 40s about the cardinal virtues of Stalin. His appeals were as highly patterned as those of the system he fashioned. Nor was every ingredient in his image a product of misperception or deception. Stalin had indeed possessed great powers of concentration, his manners were simple, and he was knowledgeable about the subjects he discussed with his interlocutors from abroad. As to kindness, modesty, tolerance, and gentleness, the impressions of the visitors were less than accurate as both the record of history and the recollections of closer associates and contemporaries suggest.[217]

The Treatment of Intellectuals

The appeals of Soviet society examined above did not have much to do with personal (or group) interests as they are conventionally defined. Thus I have argued in effect that Western intellectuals were attracted to the Soviet Union, largely for disinterested, idealistic reasons. There remains one feature of Soviet society the appeals of which cannot be explained primarily with reference to idealism and the altruistic impulses of the visiting intellectuals. This is the treatment of intellectuals within the Soviet Union as it appeared to the visitors.

Several circumstances commended the approval of these tourists as far as the position and treatment of intellectuals was concerned. Most importantly they were taken seriously. John Strachey wrote: "Communism offers no one of this generation a ticket to Utopia. But it does offer to intellectual workers of every kind the one road to escape out of a paralysing atmosphere of capitalist decay, into a social environment which will give a limitless stimulus to the achievement of the mind of man."[218] In a society where ideas were regarded and used as weapons intellectuals were closer to the seats of power, their advice was sought, they even seemed to share power. They were well integrated into society, not living on its margins as sulking, often ignored eccentrics, as they sometimes conceived of themselves in Western societies where their position was more ambiguous. Waldo Frank felt that Soviet artists and intellectuals were not "cut off from the core of national life" as they were in many countries in the West. The proletarian writers he met at a writers' conference differed even in their physical appearance: "Unlike the intellectual writers these boys and girls had supple bodies; and on their eyes and mouth there was the mark of *will.*"[219]

The integration and importance of intellectuals was also recognized by Edmund Wilson:

> There has been in our times no parallel . . . to the position of Gorky in the Soviet Union. In the past a close friend of Lenin, he is at present a kind of Commissar of Literature; and is perhaps closer to sharing the glory of Stalin than any one public man.
>
> The effect on a writer of a visit to Russia is therefore both flattering and sobering. Nowhere else in the world does the writer receive so much honor; nowhere else to the same degree is he made conscious of responsibility.[220]

Not all recognition was symbolic. Many visitors observed wistfully that the material circumstances of artists and intellectuals were commensurate with their social importance. Feuchtwanger wrote, "They are appreciated, encouraged and even pampered by the state both with prestige and large incomes. . . . The books of favorite authors . . . are printed in editions of a size which makes the foreign publisher gasp."[221] Large editions and royalties were not the only indicators of the favorable material circumstances of writers and other intellectuals. Writers and artists supportive of the regime were also provided with good apartments in the city and houses in the country; with special rest homes, sanatoria, clubs, access to scarce goods, and traveling privileges. They were clearly members of the elite and given due recognition, symbolic as well as material, for their services.

The moral and material recognition and rewards given to the loyal intellectuals were not merely due to their functional importance, their contribution to the building of the new society, or their willingness to become "engineers of the soul." There was also a genuine affinity between political leaders and intellectuals in this society, or so it seemed to many visiting intellectuals. After all, many of the leaders were intellectuals or had intellectual leanings. Stalin himself was a voracious and wide-ranging reader, had an extraordinary mind, was deeply concerned with and impressively knowledgeable about the arts and literature, a major theoretician of political economy and philosophy who enriched and further developed Marxism-Leninism in our times. He was also conversant with the sciences, especially biology, and even mastered (later on) intricate questions of linguistics. He was intimate with many writers and artists, often read their manuscripts before publication, previewed their films, talked to them over the phone or in person.[222] The more ominous significance of these attentions, and what it portended to the autonomy of the arts and intellectual activities, usually escaped the visitors. It was more gratifying to think of Stalin as philosopher king, the thinker and doer, great theoretician and practitioner of the social and political revolution taking place. He was bound to have a deep spiritual kinship with intellectuals.

Sometimes more direct ways of softening up visiting intellectuals were used. Not only were they exposed to the good life of their fellow Soviet intellectuals, but they themselves became beneficiaries of the generosity of the regime as recipients of lavish hospitality, and also as a result of the attention given to their work. Arthur Koestler's description of his literary good fortunes in the USSR when he was still a pro-Soviet writer from Germany is revealing. For instance, upon arriving in a provincial capital:

> The editor of the magazine declared that it had been for many years his dearest wish to publish a story by me. . . . The director of the State Publishing Trust asked for the privilege of publishing a Georgian translation of the book I was going to write. I thus sold the same short story to eight or ten different magazines from Leningrad to Tashkent and sold the Russian, German, Ukranian, Georgian, and Armenian rights of my unwritten book against advance payments which amounted to a small fortune. And as I did all this with official encouragement, and as other writers did the same, I could wholeheartedly confirm that Soviet Russia was the writer's paradise and that nowhere else in the world was the creative artist better paid or held in higher esteem. Human nature being what it is, it never occurred to me that my contracts and cash advances had been granted not on the strength of my literary reputation but for reasons of a different nature.[223]

Waldo Frank recalled in his *Memoirs* another instance of Soviet generosity toward the Western intellectuals:

> Were these royalties or a retainer of my good will—in fact a bribe?
> The year before I had written to Michael Koltsov, editor of *Pravda*
> . . . asking if I had enough rubles in the Soviet bank to take my son
> Thomas for a visit to Russia. He had answered: "You have enough
> rubles to come to Russia with your son. You have enough rubles to
> put him into school and to rent a villa in the Crimea. You have enough
> rubles to place a mistress in your villa. And if you need more rubles
> we can always order a few articles for *Pravda*."[224]

Thus the Soviet rulers, like their predecessors in eighteenth-century Russia, "knew how to give due honor to the men of letters" or so it seemed.[225] Unhappily, the visitors were not in a good position to learn about the more characteristic fate of Soviet intellectuals, many of whom perished or were imprisoned during the purges. They were enthusiastic about the position of Soviet intellectuals largely because they knew little about it and especially about those among them unwilling to serve the regime. Least of all did they realize that in the words of Vladimir Nabokov, "had [they] and other foreign idealists been Russians in Russia . . . they would have been destroyed . . . as naturally as rabbits are by ferrets and farmers."[226]

Even if some visitors caught some glimpses of the limitations on free expression (an undeniable blemish on the position of intellectuals), they felt that such restrictions were of temporary necessity and did not constitute a major interference with intellectual work. Or else they were considered to be a small price to pay for effective participation in a new social order, for escaping social isolation, being taken seriously by the political leadership and finding life pulsating with new purpose and meaning.

5

The Rejection of Western Society
in the 1960s and 70s

We human beings developed as part of the earth, which holds all we need to satisfy all our material requirements, and which gives us the senses to appreciate the beauty of water, air, land, life and each other. This planet, literally rolling in the heavens, is potentially the paradise imagined in most of our religions. We now confront the last class of men who claim to hold this planet as their own private property and who force the majority of us to toil. . . . We live in the early dawn of human history, when we can see the possibility of communism—a world of peace, abundance, creativity, and freedom.   BRUCE FRANKLIN[1]

It is technologically possible to build subways that are virtually noiseless, and relatively pleasing inside, as well as to provide good live entertainment on some cars and total quiet for reading or contemplation on others. . . .

As a beginning, of course, we want every neighborhood to be equipped with adequate musical supplies, sports supplies, painting supplies, sculpture supplies, knitting, embroidery, macrame, etc. Each neighborhood should have facilities for the development of film, and facilities for the presentation of concerts and plays, as well as printing press for leaflets, poetry, books and community newspapers. . . .

We ought to develop new needs. One of the new needs we must develop in the course of the revolution is the need for universal self-fulfillment.   MICHAEL P. LERNER[2]

It was an easy life. The weather was warm and the seasons hardly changed. . . . You could always get by selling dope. Or you could hawk the *Barb* on the weekend and make enough money for the rest of the week. There were always guilty professors to panhandle . . . some people started handicraft industries . . . right on the Avenue. Nobody starved in the streets of Berkeley.   JERRY RUBIN[3]

177

The recurring references to the 1960s require qualification. Insofar as this chronological designation refers to a cohesive constellation of events, attitudes, and beliefs, it does not correspond to the actual decade. Many of the major themes of social criticism formulated during the 60s were discernible in the 1950s,[4] although these critiques had a very limited impact until a decade later. The 1960s, as they live in popular imagination and social history, did not begin in 1960 and did not end in 1970. Viewed as a period of social unrest, political turmoil, cultural change, and activism, it began around 1964. The Berkeley Free Speech Movement and the associated demonstrations in that year may be taken as the first major events that set the tone of the decade and were duplicated and replicated across American college campuses for the next six to eight years. Certainly, the more dramatic and visible manifestations of the spirit which permeated the period—the demonstrations, riots, civil disobedience, bombings—had subsided by the middle 1970s. On the other hand, many of the values and beliefs we associate with those years, and which seemed daring or deviant at the time, have become the conventional wisdom of the 70s, as Tom Hayden suggested with no small satisfaction.[5]

In retrospect it is not difficult to find explanations of the political conflicts and intensified social criticism which characterized this period in both the United States and Western Europe. From our present vantage point at the beginning of the 80s we are hardly at a loss to account for the spirit of the 60s. Yet in the 1950s and early 60s much of what came to transpire had not been anticipated.

An examination of the social conditions, currents, and concerns of the 1960s will make clear the connection between the discontents of the period and the renewed propensity to idealize a new set of societies—a propensity which found tangible expression in the pilgrimages to Cuba, Vietnam, and China.

Affluence, Security, and Individualism

The character of the 60s in the United States may be grasped at two levels. On the one hand, one may follow the route of pointing to observable historical events and cultural developments as explanations of what transpired during the period. There was the Vietnam War, the civil rights movement, the ghetto riots, the spread of drug taking, the growing influence of the mass media. In other words, there were tangible social problems and situations which elicited certain responses from various groups of the population. At the same time, the 60s may also be seen and understood as the reflection of more elusive trends and developments. It is my belief that the attitudes, beliefs, and negations which flourished during these years would have arisen without the Vietnam War and without race riots. They might have taken somewhat different forms and perhaps the timetable of their emergence might have been different, but the rejection of society on the part of substantial segments of the middle classes, and especially the middle-class young, was in the cards, so to speak. The Vietnam War helped to channel and bring to the surface these impulses and dispositions, but it did not create them.

A variety of circumstances of different degrees of "tangibility" or observability created the *Zeitgeist* (the spirit of the times) that I am trying to capture here. If I were to rank them according to their relative importance, I would start with what came to be called "affluence," and the associated sense of security. It certainly was not the first occasion in modern history that a combination of the unproblematic satisfaction of material needs and a related sense of security made a major contribution to restlessness, unease, diffuse rebelliousness, and finally political activism or (non-political) thrill-seeking. Writing about the origins of the romantic movement in Europe, Bertrand Russell observed that "By the time of Rousseau, many people had grown tired of safety, and had begun to desire excitement. . . . The romantics did not aim at peace and quiet, but at vigorous and passionate individual life. . . ."[6]

Sometime in the late 1950s, affluence began increasingly to not merely denote high standards of living, but also acquire a stigma, a taint, a suspicion. The "Affluent Society"[7] of private wealth and public squalor was nothing to be proud of, as John Galbraith argued in a book that was among the first to cast doubt on the still untroubled satisfaction that millions of middle-class and lower middle-class Americans derived from private consumption. While he did not seek to discredit consumption or the material values associated with it, in the manner that became customary in the decade to follow, Galbraith helped to subvert the innocent and taken-for-granted nature of the pleasures private consumption entailed. The social critics who followed shifted the emphasis from the imbalance between private and public expenditures (and the attendant social injustices) to the undesirable spiritual consequences of being materially comfortable, associating the latter with self-centeredness, emotional torpor, and stagnation. Gradually "affluence" became something of a dirty word, often prefixed by "empty." The influence of the concept can hardly be overestimated as the background against which much of the rebelliousness and protest of the 60s was played out.

Perhaps most crucial for the 60s, and especially their beginning, was the realization on the part of a large number of young people that contrary to all previous conviction, expectation, and (implied or explicit) parental assurance, money and financial security did not automatically and predictably make one happy or guarantee the discovery of the true ends of life. As E. J. Hobsbawm put it, "What lies behind the revival of revolutionism in the 1960s is . . . the discovery that the solution by capitalism of the problem of material scarcity reveals, perhaps even creates, new problems (in Marxist terms 'contradictions') which are central to the system and possibly all industrial society."[8] According to Kenneth Keniston, the young demanded no less than answers to the questions: "What lies beyond affluence?" and "Beyond freedom and affluence, what?" They were young people "brought up in family environments where abundance, relative economic security, political freedom and affluence are simply facts of life, not goals to be striven for."[9]

The phenomenon was not limited to American society, although it is likely that this scenario was played out in the United States more often and has been given more attention—journalistic, literary, and social scientific—than elsewhere in the West. Jan Myrdal, Swedish radical (son of Gunnar Myrdal, the famous sociologist), admirer of the Third World, and pilgrim to China and Albania, wrote: "I saw the family life of the suburbanites and their loveless love-life. . . . Told myself in my life, love won't be their love. I will never live in a dead asceticism, neither will I let myself be swindled into accepting a dull habitual married life. . . . Promised myself not to conform, not even if I were to be given a two-car garage, a model railroad and a pat on the back."[10]

These were the times when middle-class parents were routinely reproached for their lack of idealism and emotional intensity, for their small-mindedness and material concerns. Indeed, in the post–World War II period, more families acquired the proverbial suburban house with the two-car garage, more households were outfitted with dishwashers and washing machines and television sets. There was undeniable evidence of "materialism," of affluence—much to react against, including the Cold War, McCarthyism, the parents' tales of the Depression, and World War II, the routine expectation of college attendance, the overprotectiveness of the middle-class upbringing.

While affluence did not confer widespread contentment and make life fulfilled and meaningful, it did create a sense of security which permeated and informed the behavior of hundreds of thousands of young middle-class Americans in various ways. Most importantly, it encouraged and for a while helped to sustain dissent and defiance of authority because it was hard to imagine that serious repercussions would follow. Few of the protesters and dissenters felt *truly and seriously threatened* by the system they called "repressive" day in and out.* Even those in the front ranks of the public protests, the full-time activists such as Jerry Rubin, often treated the "System" and its halting attempts to bring disorder under control as a big joke. He wrote:

> Those who got subpoenas became heroes. Those who didn't had *subpoenas envy.* It was almost sexual. "Whose is bigger?" "I want one, too." "Let me see yours."

> I went to a pay phone . . . to ask the Red Squad if I got a subpoena too. Just as I put the dime in, I felt a tap on my shoulder. It was Chick Harrison of the Berkeley Red Squad. "Jerry Rubin," he said. "This is for you. A subpoena from the House Committee on Un-American Activities."

> I snatched it out of his hands and ran through the Student Union, jumping up and down, clicking my heels together. It was the biggest, most beautiful subpoena in the world!

> Within two hours I was on the steps of San Francisco City Hall in front of four television cameras, five photographers, four newspaper reporters, and seven radio stations, denouncing HUAC as a "witchhunter."[11]

Susan Stern, a former "Weatherman" ("Weatherperson"), member of the "Seattle Seven" and participant in "The Days of Rage" in Chicago, wrote:

> I was more curious than frightened, this being my first arrest. I couldn't really relate to being arrested; to me, it was still a wild adventure. Jail was just another part of that adventure. . . .

> I was charged with three counts of aggravated assault and battery, and one count of assault with a deadly weapon. Each charge was a felony, punishable by up to ten years' imprisonment. Still enthralled by the adventure and excitement of my first bust, I was not very staggered by the thought of forty years in prison. I didn't believe that it could happen to me . . . [as it turned out, she was largely correct]. I looked at my mother, all made up and expensively dressed and thought

---

* I suspect that what they meant by "repression" was not the type of activities we associate with police states, but rather any form of constraint. This interpretation helps to explain the wide range of situations and institutions to which the term came to be applied by the radicals: the nuclear family, schools, colleges, places of work, examinations, correct spelling—almost any situation in which behavior was regulated to any degree.

"How nice that I can fight one day in the streets of Chicago, and then fly to New York the next and have my mother pamper me." Then I thought of the black women I had left behind in prison. . . . There was no way I could explain it to my mother . . . how much I hated my white skin. . . .

An account of courtroom behavior is equally revealing:

Boredom threatened to overwhelm us. . . . The next day we brought wine and put it in the water pitcher. . . . We got stoned in our defense room. We didn't even worry about the smell, surrounded as we were by judges, federal marshals, and other pigs.[12]

If Jerry Rubin and Susan Stern and other members of their generation treated the upholders of law and order, from street policemen to congressional committees and judges, with disrespect and lack of fear, this was not only because of the self-conscious, programmatic rejection of authority, but because they were genuinely incapable of believing that any serious retribution would follow. Courtroom proceedings were envisioned (by and large correctly) more as opportunities for denouncing and mocking the System than as preludes to lengthy jail sentences.

"Dropping out" was another manifestation of this underlying sense of security which, according to Susan Sontag, had revolutionary implications:

America is a cancerous society with a runaway rate of productivity which inundates the country with increasingly unnecessary commodities. . . . This country has a surplus energy, whose predatory overflow . . . must be contained. Hence the revolutionary implications of dropping out—of taking drugs (thereby reducing efficiency, clarity, productivity), of disrupting the school system (which furnishes the economy with docile personnel), of concentrating on unproductive hedonistic activities like sex and listening to music.[13]

Whether or not it had revolutionary implications, the young people dropping out of college or graduate school, or giving up regular jobs, instinctively (and correctly) believed that they would not lack what they considered essentials of life, that there would be food, shelter, "joints," clothing, stereo sets, guitars, and access to cars. They felt assured that somehow somebody would take care of them.[14] Nobody (or very few) starved on the streets of Berkeley or Cambridge. There were part-time jobs, welfare agencies, fellow students or non-students with "crash pads," communes, and also parents, in the last resort.

The sense of security also had much to do with the protest against American participation in the war in Vietnam. Although for most college students the possibility of being drafted was remote, it enraged the sense of security enjoyed heretofore. Brought up during and impressed by the tranquility of the 50s, tired of the "Cold War rhetoric" of their elders, seeing the Cold War (that is, anti-communism) discredited by its most vocal American representatives on the Right (McCarthy and co., and his spiritual heirs), and familiar with the power of American technology, this generation saw no reality or credibility in foreign threats. For them World War II was ancient history, one of the stories fathers told and just as boring as other nostalgic parental recollections of hardship (such as those of the Depression). Thus this sense of security and the ignorance of history had a bearing on the war protest. Evidently the absence of corresponding historical experiences had exerted a similar influence on an earlier generation too, the alienated English intellectuals of the 1930s. Orwell wrote:

> If you have grown up in that sort of atmosphere it is not at all easy to imagine what a despotic regime is like. Nearly all the dominant writers of the thirties belonged to the soft-boiled emancipated middle class and were too young to have effective memories of the Great War. To people of that kind such things as purges, secret police, summary executions, imprisonment without trial, etc. etc., are too remote to be terrifying.[15]

If American power and security in the world seemed unchallenged and unshakeable how could such a war be justified? Only the wildest conspiratorial theories could explain it. ("Vietnam and the school system are the two main fronts in America's campaign against the youth. Jails and mental hospitals follow closely.")[16]

The 50s and early 60s left many yearnings and impulses unfulfilled among young middle-class Americans. The connection between security and boredom on the one hand and political activism on the other deserves more attention than it has been given. Roland Stromberg, an English author, observed: "the young radicals . . . represented . . . the first generation to have absolutely nothing to believe in and an abundance of leisure in which to do it."[17] A combination of material security, leisure, few (if any) responsibilities, encouragement to self-expression (from parents and the educational systems), the daily routines of life in the suburbs and on the college campuses added up to a constellation of circumstances out of which rebellious activism could easily arise. John W. Aldridge speculated:

> perhaps the crucial factor . . . is simply the boredom of the vast majority of students. . . . Without strongly internalized ambitions and

interests that are satisfiable within the university system, average students, like average people everywhere, are entirely dependent upon outside stimuli to provide them with the distractions needed to make life bearable. The greater the intellectual vacuum, the greater need for distraction, a vacuum in people presumably even more abhorrent than it is in nature. . . .

. . . all the great occasions for challenge and adventure seem to have passed them by. They were born twenty years too late to have a part in that knightly crusade which World War II now seems sentimentally to symbolize for their fathers. They did not even have the small but appealing satisfaction of going hungry in the Depression. And to make matters worse, the only available war is one they cannot morally accept. . . .[18]

Jerry Rubin wrote: "We want to be heroes, like those we read about in history books. We missed the first Amerikan [sic] Revolution. We missed World War II. We missed the Chinese and Cuban Revolutions. Are we supposed to spend our futures grinning and watching TV all the time?"[19]

Not only the young on the campuses but their academic elders too often searched for new paths to a more fulfilling existence. The following advertisement in the personal column of the *New York Review of Books* was among many which reflected the spirit of the times:

Twenty years in the academic jungle is enough. College teacher, published scholar, combination of 19th-century's Burton and Thoreau invites serious correspondence from anyone with hope and guts enough to change, pool funds, abilities, respect for natural and human qualities, start a new life style, simple and unmanipulative, in Hawaii or elsewhere in near future. Age, race, and sex irrelevant. Receptivity, vigor, patience essential.[20]

By any comparative-historical standards, life in the United States was no more unfulfilled in the 1960s and 70s than in most other societies. However, material and political security created or contributed to new needs for stimulation and adventure. Routines became increasingly intolerable and oppressive—more than anything else the 60s was a decade of escalating expectations far more in evidence in the Western world than in the underdeveloped countries to which the concept (the revolution of rising expectations) was first applied. Political activism provided an arena for excitement, adventure, the pursuit of high expectations, and service to various causes of social justice. It is not easy to determine what mixture of idealistic, altruistic, and thrill-seeking motives lay beneath the political protests directed against both the war and domestic injustice.[21] According to an English observer of the American scene, Henry Fairlie, "When they [the activists] wished to regard themselves as a class that was oppressed, they had to reach outside their own experience . . . as 'white niggers,' claiming that their long hair was their black skin and that they 'felt like' Indians and blacks and Vietnamese."[22]* The inauthenticity of the political identification of young, white, middle-class radicals was a characteristic by-product of their efforts to break out of the secure middle-class existence and experience.[23]

A more elaborate explanation of this phenomenon was offered by David M. Potter, the historian:

> In the impulses of the present day to identify with the wretched of the earth, there may be altruistic compassion, but one is justified in suspecting also a component of negative identification. . . . Negative identification is itself a highly motivated, compensation-seeking form of societal estrangement. Sometimes when identification with a person fails, a great psychological void remains, and to fill this void people incapable of genuine interpersonal relationships will identify with an abstraction. An important historical instance of identification with abstract power has been the zealous support of totalitarian regimes.[24]

The political activism of the period attained its most characteristic expression in what came to be known as "confrontation politics," which combined idealism with the desire for adventure, the defiance of authority as well as elements of pragmatic political purpose. Escalated civil disobedience, verbal or physical attacks on authority figures, and the presentation of "non-negotiable demands" were among the major techniques used to compel the system to reveal its true colors.[25] Confronting the authorities entailed physical action, togetherness, spontaneity, and risk-taking. A "Weatherwoman" activist recalled:

> With a great eagerness the women waited for the coming riot to begin. . . . We wanted to fight. . . . the mood of a great portion of the crowd was hilarious, not serious. . . . The riots were a real ex-

---

* It was an interesting expression of the spirit of the times that various groups engaged in arduous verbal competition for the status of the most victimized. College students, middle-class women, the young in general, prisoners, mental patients, welfare clients, homosexuals, minority groups variously defined, all vied with each other—with considerably varied justification—for the status of the most victimized, most oppressed. Such claims not only helped to authenticate the critiques of the "System" but insofar as they found official acceptance they also qualified the claimant for compensatory action on the part of the authorities.

It is probably generally true that groups or individuals will not claim or publicize a victimized status unless psychic, political, or economic rewards can be anticipated from doing so.

pression of frustration . . . although it had little to do with over-throwing the government. . . . The pigs represented an authority that was restrictive and one-sided. . . . We had a women's meeting after the riot, and it was full of electric energy. It was so high. . . . Nothing but action, running in the streets, actually fighting with the pigs could have released such a pent-up force. . . . Eyes glowing we looked at each other warmly.[26]

Confrontation politics also helped to "demystify" authority by showing disrespect toward it. Jerry Rubin, a major theoretician and practitioner of confrontation tactics, wrote:

Satisfy our demands and we got twelve more. . . . All we want from these meetings are demands that the Establishment can never sat-isfy. . . . Demonstrators are never "reasonable." We always put our demands forward in such obnoxious manner that the power structure can never satisfy us. . . . Then we scream, righteously angry, when our demands are not met. . . . Goals are irrelevant. The tactics, the actions are critical.[27]

Although we tend to associate with the 1960s dissent, non-conformity, and unusual forms of self-expression, social historians of the period will also take note of the new forms of conformity and regimentation which sprang up. An advertisement in the New York *Times* (for Macy's department store) captured these aspects of the spirit of the times. It showed a smiling man in military-style clothing, and it read: "It is fun to wear olive drab, especially when you know you don't have to. . . . It's a kick to go regimented. . . ."[28] Macy's message was not lost; sartorial regimentation flourished.* Blue jeans, farmer outfits, boots, and the like appealed to the impulse to identify with the poor, who were mistakenly assumed to favor such styles of clothing. In turn the untamed look was intended to shock and convey contempt for convention and middle-class norms of respectability. Again, Jerry Rubin grasped the gist of the matter:

We were dirty, smelly, grimy, foul, loud, dope-crazed, hell-bent and leather-jacketed. We were a public display of filth and shabbiness, living-in-the-flesh rejects of middle-class standards.

* Competing for its share of the radical chic market, Bloomingdale's offered Chinese worker's suits: "All the people . . . are waiting. To live together in peace and joy. Someday soon. Is this a symbol? The people's suit. Once in a great while, something exciting happens. Something everyone wants. It's happening now. The worker's suit has arrived from Mainland China."
    In the 1930s Malcolm Cowley observed a similar phenomenon when ". . . the Communists one met were mostly intellectuals and politicians disguised in working-men's clothes (cap, blue-or checked shirt, army shoes, leather jacket)."[29]

We pissed and shit and fucked in public; we crossed streets on red lights; and we opened Coke bottles with our teeth.

We were constantly stoned and tripping on every drug known to man.

We were outlaw forces of America displaying ourselves flagrantly on a world stage.[30]

At the same time, the knowledge that wearing ragged clothing was a matter of choice and not necessity must have been reassuring. For most members of the counter-culture and for the middle-class political activists, involuntary scarcity was not easy to visualize. The inability to conceive of scarcity was a pillar of the social criticism of the period, especially as it combined with a relatively sudden awareness of the deprivations of blacks and some other minority groups. If there was so much to go around only the most vicious irrationality and human ill will could account for the material inequalities which were now brought to the attention of this generation by the mass media and social science teachers in the colleges.

The outraged disbelief in scarcity rooted in daily experience was given theoretical confirmation and elaboration in the works of Marcuse, Roszak, Reich, and others. The denial of scarcity, as an immutable condition of human existence, had its material as well as non-material aspects. Disbelief in material scarcity was predicated on the technological development attained in the United States and Western Europe which, combined with a less wasteful and more rational use of resources and further automation, would make it possible to banish material want. The denial of non-material scarcity was based on the belief that the emotional resources of human beings too are unlimited, not unlike their celebrated potential for "growth." Disbelief in scarcity and the exuberant growth of individualism went hand in hand. The growth of individualism has of course been a long historical process which appeared to accelerate after World War II due to a combination of three circumstances: the spectacular rise in living standards (allowing the concern for material necessities to recede), the spread of higher education (which provided new ideas to more people about various forms of self-fulfillment and higher aspirations), and the political freedoms and pluralism which allowed a stable institutional framework in which the new needs for choices and options could be expressed and realized.[31] Tom Wolfe notwithstanding, the "Me Decade," a term he coined and applied to the 70s, began in the 1960s with its programmatic hedonism, cult of drugs, sexual experimentation, rock music, rejection of routinized work, exultation of leisure, and belief in limitless self-expression through art, political participation, and communal ties. To be sure, the emphasis on both community and individuality obscured the primacy of individualism over the communitarian pursuits and gestures. Although hundreds and possibly thousands of communes were formed during the period, few endured—a fact suggestive of the strength of individualism and the inability to submit to the type of discipline, authority, and routinization that can make communities endure. Much of the counter-culture was, by and large, a replay (on a mass scale) of romantic individualism to which dashes of Marxist social criticism have been added.[32] Age-old forms of romanticism were revived and absorbed into the counter-culture, attitudes innocently celebrated as if they were brand new cultural inventions. Bertrand Russell's observations about eighteenth- and nineteenth-century romantics and romanticism still held:

> They admire strong passions, of no matter what kind, and whatever may be their social consequences. . . . the habit of foregoing present satisfactions for the sake of future advantages is irksome, and when passions are roused the prudent restraints of social behavior become difficult to endure. Those who, at such times throw them off, acquire a new energy and sense of power . . . and though they may come to disaster in the end, enjoy meanwhile a sense of godlike exaltation . . . the romantic outlook prefers passion to calculation. . . . The romantic movement, in its essence, aimed at liberating human personality from the fetters of social convention and social morality.[33]

It was also the resurgence of individualism which led to the new definitions of repression, to the equation of almost any situation of scarcity with repression. Edward Shils observed at the time that "Whatever hampers the fulfillment of whatever happens to be desired at the moment—whether it is a student housing arrangement which stipulates the hours of visiting in halls of residence, or an examination, or a convention regarding dress, or sexual behavior in public places—is repressive." Such expansion of sensitivity to "repression," or such a redefinition of what was "repressive," could not have taken place without a new and vastly enlarged sense of what constituted individual rights and needs and prerequisites for self-development and self-expression. Correspondingly there was a tendency to regard almost any demand imposed from the outside as unspontaneous, inauthentic, and repressive.[34]

Andrew Hacker stressed the spreading of such sensibilities, at any rate in the American context:

In the past ordinary people thought of themselves in unpretentious terms, acknowledging their limitations and accepting stations relatively consonant with their capacities. But the emergence of individuality has changed self-conceptions, creating discontents . . . that were unlikely to occur . . . [in] earlier years. Once persuaded that he is an "individual" entitled to realize his assumed potentialities, a citizen will diagnose himself as suffering quite impressive afflictions. . . . Alienation, powerlessness, and crises of identity come into being only if citizens decide to invest their personalities with potentialities ripe for liberation. . . .[35]

Heightened individualistic expectations help to explain not only the general tone of the times but also some more specific social movements such as women's liberation, largely white middle class and college-based. At the core of the feminism of the 6os and 70s was the surging demand for self-realization, self-expression, liberation, autonomy, the rejection of (profoundly anti-individualistic) social roles and role relations. Even institutions of public higher education ran courses, or workshops (such as "Project Self" at the University of Massachusetts at Amherst) in which participants were exhorted and instructed in ways to expand their range of personal expectations and fulfillment. A favorite activity in feminist groups was the painstaking dissection of personal problems, frustrations, and impediments to gratification. Support and consciousness-level raising groups thrived on catering to and cultivating these expanding egos. The popular schools of psychotherapy and new religious cults as well as some of the established churches stressed growth, gratification, and liberation. Self-help literature advertised the glories and justifications of being, or becoming, egocentric.[36] Tom Wolfe summed it all up:

The old alchemical dream was changing base metals into gold. The new alchemical dream is: changing one's personality—remaking, remodeling, elevating and polishing one's very *self* . . . and observing, studying, and doting on it. (Me!) This has always been an aristocratic luxury . . . since only the wealthiest classes had the free time and the surplus income to dwell upon this sweetest and vainest of pastimes. . . . By the mid-1960s this service, this luxury had become a standard approach. . . . Outsiders hearing of these sessions wondered what on earth their appeal was. Yet the appeal was simple enough. It is summed up in the notion: "Let's talk about *Me*." No matter whether you managed to renovate your personality through encounter sessions or not, you had finally focused your attention and your energies on the most fascinating subject on earth: *Me*. Not only that, you also put *Me* onstage before a live audience. . . . Just imag-

ine . . . *my* life becoming a drama with universal significance . . .
analyzed, like Hamlet's, for what it signifies for the rest of mankind. . . .[37]

It was among the paradoxes of the times that the growth of individualism and heightened personal expectations were accompanied by a
spreading popular belief in the socio-cultural determination of personal
lives as the "system" was held responsible for an increasing number of
personal problems and frustrations.[38]

Affluence, expanded educational opportunities, and a permissive po-
litical-institutional environment were not the only sources of the new
flowering of individualism which marked the 60s. The characteristic
ways of middle-class upbringing and the attendant intensified youth
cult were additional contributing factors. The more youth is venerated,
the more adult authority and competence is devalued by implication.
The youth cult reflected the loss of confidence of the older generations.
It was hardly surprising that so many among the young rejected adult
authority (or what was left of it) when "authority figures" joined the
young in their criticism of authority[39] and tried to signal with words,
beards, or blue jeans that their hearts were in the right place, despite
their age, social position, or educational qualifications. There were many
adults on the college campuses who, after some soul-searching, concluded that they had to take their cues from the young and who were
unable to resist youthful demands once they were sanctified by the
mystique of change that always strikes a responsive chord with Americans. Thus according to Robert Hutchins, former chancellor of the University of Chicago,

> students in the Spring of 1968 not only should be granted full amnesty
> for taking over five college buildings for six days [at Columbia Univer-
> sity] but should be honored at special graduation ceremonies for
> forcing open the door to university reform. . . . "Instead of worrying
> about how to suppress the youth revolution, we of the older genera-
> tion should be worrying about how to sustain it," advises John D.
> Rockefeller, 3rd. "The student activists . . . perform a service in
> shaking us out of our complacency. We badly need their ability and
> fervor in these troubled and difficult times."[40]

The concern with identity was part of the self-conscious individualism
Tom Wolfe poked fun at, and it reflected the unwillingness of a growing
number of people to define themselves with reference to such impersonal and standardized criteria as social roles, age, sex, ethnicity, or
class. Forms of middle-class upbringing contributed to such develop-

ments as much as what Peter Berger called "The pluralization of social experience."[41] More specifically, the transmission of parental values also supported youthful estrangement and social criticism. The generational conflict was exaggerated, even mythical as far as the most radical students were concerned.[42] Diana Trilling pointed out that

> a decent proportion of the decent American middle-class mothers and fathers of these young people, as well as other energetic spokesmen for progress, supported their offspring. Mr. (Lt. Col.) Rudd, father of Mark, strode the campus boasting his paternity; Mrs. Rudd, mother of Mark, gave the proudest and tenderest of interviews to the *Times* about how her son-the-rebel plants tulips in their suburban garden. Some two hundred or so mothers and fathers of students at Columbia banded into a Committee of Concerned Columbia Parents to back their children and further harry the administration. Dwight Macdonald, who is supposed to loathe all violence, wrote his friends a letter of appeal for funds for the SDS. . . . And the Columbia clergy . . . threw themselves with hearts bleeding and souls aflame into this newest movement of youthful idealism. . . .[43]

The influence of the family on the young radicals was naturally easier to trace in such well-known instances as those of the proud parents of Mark Rudd, or Herbert and Bettina Aptheker (father old line pro-Soviet Communist party functionary, daughter leading Berkeley rebel, Du Bois club leader), Leonard Boudin the radical lawyer and his even more radical Weather-underground activist daughter Kathy (of the Greenwich Village bomb factory fame). "As one close friend of the Boudins said: 'His kids were immersed in this far left world and it would be abnormal if all the people, the talk, the cases wouldn't in some way shape their lives.' "[44] The political encouragement parents provided to their children was often related to the parents' concern about their own "selling out"; that is, accepting the social system as it was, giving up their youthful political commitments, settling into soft middle-class life, and living well materially in the society they still despised and considered unjust. To such parents the activism of their children was a form of surrogate rejuvenation and redemption: *they* tried to realize their parents' dreams, *they* would not compromise with the imperfections of the world and be bought off with degrees, good jobs, vacation homes, European trips. This was particularly the case with academic parents and professors sympathetic to their radical students, who were often similar to their own children.[45]

Not all influences emanating from the older generations—parents or college teachers—were heavily political in their implications. More intangible processes were also at work, especially during childhood: "the modern child . . . comes to feel very early that he is a person of considerable importance," observed Peter Berger. "He learns that he has a dignity and rights that belong to him as a unique individual. He also learns that society (that is, the elders who serve as 'administrators' of the world of childhood) is pliant and responsive to all his needs. Typically, he acquires a low frustration threshold." These attitudes are not only building blocks of the type of individualism discussed earlier, but also explain the peculiar abhorrence of bureaucracy which was such a key part of the social criticism mounted by the younger generations:

> Modern childhood is marked by values and by a consciousness that are emphatically personalistic. Modern bureaucracy, by contrast, has an ethos of emphatic impersonality. Put simply, an individual shaped by modern childhood is most likely to feel oppressed by modern bureaucracy. . . . Thus people today feel oppressed, "alienated" or even "exploited" simply being subjected to bureaucratic processes . . . that a generation ago would simply have been accepted as pragmatic necessities. Any process in which the individual is "treated as a number," even if the process is set in motion for indisputably benign purposes, is experienced as an offense to human dignity.[46]

In brief the characteristic middle-class ways of upbringing contributed to the ethos of the 1960s by creating high and diffuse expectations of personal fulfillment, intense dislike of impersonality and standardization, hostility toward authority and a sense of security. Egalitarianism in the home also led to a paradoxical combination of expecting egalitarianism in society at large *and* expecting to be treated as unique.*

The Mass Media and Mass Culture

It was the mass media which gave rise to the pervasive awareness of the social problems, tensions, and political protest of the period. The "Revolution" could not have become a "theater"[47] without television, and the participants and creators of this revolutionary theater were keenly aware of the importance of publicity, and especially visual publicity, and the opportunity it provided for dramatizing political discontents. Jerry Rubin was basically right in his analysis of uses of the media:

> TV is raising generations of kids who want to grow up and become demonstrators. Have you ever seen a boring demonstration on TV?

* These forms of upbringing may also have contributed to the conflict between individualism and collectivism which the radical counter-culture could not reconcile.

> Just being on TV makes it exciting. . . . Television creates myth bigger than reality. . . . The mere idea of a "story" is revolutionary because a "story" implies disruption of normal life. Every reporter is a dramatist, creating theater out of life. Crime in the streets is news; law and order is not. A revolution is news; the status quo ain't.
>
> The media does not *report* "news," it *creates* it. An event *happens* when it goes on TV and becomes myth.
>
> The media is not "neutral." The presence of the camera transforms a demonstration, turning us into heroes. We take more chances when the press is there. . . .[48]

Renata Adler, the critic, also detected the affinity between the media and revolutionary rhetoric and posturing: "the cry of alienation made good fellows and good copy. The gesture and rhetoric of revolution were well suited to that natural creator of discontinuous, lunatic constituencies, the media."[49]

This is how Susan Stern experienced the attentions of the mass media and the blessings of publicity:

> Suddenly I was someone. I knew I was someone because there were so many people hanging around me asking me questions, looking to me for answers . . . offering to do things for me, to get some of the glow from the limelight. Half a dozen lawyers came to visit me in jail, asking if they could take the case. Newspapers across the country carried my pictures along with those of the other defendants. Reporters came to the jail to interview me. A priest came to comfort me; law students attempted to get credentials to visit me. My cellmates gave me their commissary, telling other inmates: "I'm in the cell with Susan Stern. You know, from that conspiracy thing, the Seattle 7."[50]

Certainly what Rubin called "the living commercials for the revolution" multiplied during these years, not only for the reasons possibly inherent in the nature of the media but also because the people working for the media were not unsympathetic to the protesters and generally gave them favorable rather than critical coverage. It was hard to be critical of the idealistic, educated young, or the oppressed minorities.[51] Thus dissent was made to appear at once pervasive and more respectable as it became a part of daily life through the evening news and a powerful reminder for the public at large of the ills of society.

The presentation of the Vietnam War by television also helped to set the tone of the period. The daily images of personalized and vivid suffering lent great moral authority to the war protest and indirectly helped to legitimate *all* critiques of American society.

It has also been suggested that the mass media, and television in particular, contributed to the desire for instant gratification among the young, to their low thresholds of boredom, and the attendant pursuit of quick and easy stimulation and excitement.[52] Renata Adler wrote: "The new enemy was boredom, in the sense of lack of drama. The new currency was fame."[53] Moreover, compared with other times, it was relatively easy to become "famous"; this was the era of instant if ephemeral celebrities risen from the world of street politics, low-grade mass entertainment, political protest, crime, or almost any form of bizarre act. Murderers, kidnappers, bombers—political and non-political—derived considerable satisfaction from the knowledge that their acts were not to be relegated to oblivion and anonymity. They could (and did) count on the media to reward sensational or outrageous forms of behavior with generous coverage, regardless of race, religion, sex, age, national origin, or moral substance. The craving for publicity permeated public life. Artists, entertainers, academic pundits, literary intellectuals, politicians, members of street gangs, all participated in the scramble for publicity. The aspiration to attain celebrity status was compatible with a variety of political persuasions. In the era of the radical chic, political radicals and counter-culture heroes embraced the media as zestfully as pop singers and TV starlets. As Robert Brustein commented, "the new political radicals demonstrated how it was possible to be avant garde, popular and rich all at the same time." Even artists and intellectuals of substance succeeded in persuading themselves that it was no longer in their best interest to remain impecunious, unrecognized, and wanting in acclaim and exposure. They too wanted "simultaneously to be serious and respected, and to be rich, famous and popular." The spirit of the times and particularly its trendy anti-elitism made it possible to convert popularity and easy access to the media (earlier thought to be unbecoming for a serious artist or intellectual) into an asset, a proof of authenticity:

> Thus it was that the Beatles, the Rolling Stones, Woodstock, "Easy Rider" and "The Graduate," The Living Theater, "Hair," "Lenny" and "Jesus Christ Superstar," psychedelic adventures and the antics of Abbie Hoffman could be validated as authentic cultural achievements precisely because they *were* popular, and anything private, singular or idiosyncratic could be condemned as square, establishment-oriented or counterrevolutionary.[54]

Those in pursuit of publicity excelled in devising new ways to obtain it by various special effects, contortions of the personality and revelations of private lives for public inspection. "Instant recognition" was the highest aspiration of entertainers and politicians alike* as both groups sought the blessings of publicity. But the mass media, and television in particular, probably had other, more momentous and widespread effects as well. In all likelihood they contributed to the growing intolerance of routines, to the desire for the spectacular, and heightened expectations of rising from obscurity to fame. They also stimulated a hunger for novelty. The craving for the new was by itself among the most powerful sources of social criticism and the rejection of existing society, its institutions and values. Daniel Bell (as Tocqueville before him) considered the quest for novelty a central, defining characteristic of contemporary American culture: "society has done more than passively accept innovation; it has provided a market which eagerly gobbles up the new because it believes it to be superior in value to all older forms. Thus our culture has an unprecedented mission: it is an official, ceaseless search for a new sensibility. . . . A society given over entirely to innovation, in the joyful acceptance of change, has in fact institutionalized the avant-garde. . . ."[56]

While the "generation gap" was a complex and contradictory phenomenon, one of its dimensions was tied to the mass media and culture, and to the rapid succession of fads and fashions:

> The much-discussed "generation gap" was . . . largely the result of neophilia, the restless neuroticism of modern life. Fashions in everything change so often that only people of very nearly the same age can share those intimacies of culture, such as songs, jokes, books, vocabulary, that are the instruments of personal understanding. Youth and age, inevitably different in their views of life, could once at least share the same classics of literature and art and music, the same dances, and stories and blandishments. The frenzied replacement of all styles every few years imposes a further obstacle to social intercourse and augments the isolation of modern souls.[57]

Television was also criticized for weakening the cultural foundations of society, for contributing, however indirectly, to the decline of educa-

---

* The desire for publicity, and its attendant financial rewards were such that distinguished artists such as the late Arthur Fiedler of the Boston Symphony would appear in television commercials endorsing orange juice, while Lillian Hellman, author and social critic, posed for an advertisement of "the world's finest natural dark ranch mink" in the *New York Times Magazine*.[55] The late Eugene Burdick, the author of *Failsafe*, posed for beer commercials in magazines and on television. Bella Abzug would wear a special hat for instant recognition (her "trademark"), while William Kunstler would often pose with his sunglasses pushed up in the middle of his head, rain or shine. Senators would perform an impromptu jig at senate hearings or play their fiddle for the benefit of commuters at an air terminal. The pursuit of publicity shrank the distance between entertainment, art, and politics.

tional standards and to illiteracy. William V. Shannon observed that "television's most subtle debilitating influence is that it makes audiences passive and accustoms them to expect instant gratifications."[58] There seemed to be a connection between the cries for "relevance" in the colleges and high schools and this television-fed impatience with the unfamiliar and the non-contemporary. Indeed, ignorance of and disinterest in history were among the major characteristics of the 1960s, more precisely of the groups which set its tone. Many criticisms of formal education were also stimulated by and implicitly based on the model of the relationship between television and its audience. The attention span of students shortened, and teachers became increasingly apprehensive about boring their audience.

Although still predominantly escapist, the mass media and mass culture during these years became influenced by cultural radicalism and certain forms of social consciousness. There emerged what might be called a Western socialist realism (complementing the original Soviet one) designed to convey political messages. Political demonstrations often included "guerilla theater," the most simplified of all such devices. Many writers and literary critics debated the new ways in which literature and the arts must respond to the new social and political concerns. The centerpiece of these Western forms of socialist realism was the demand for "role-models," which was another way of saying that literature (and the mass media) ought to show things not the way they are but the way they ought to be.[59] Thus a play ("That Certain Summer" by Richard Levinson and William Link) was criticized by a representative of the Gay Activist Alliance for presenting a homosexual who was not entirely fulfilled by being a homosexual and could not make up his mind whether or not homosexuality was a pathology. The critic suggested that the playwright *should have* picked from the "countless healthy and [happy] gay men and women" instead of portraying an unhappy one and thereby discouraging "a great number of young viewers who are gay but still hesitant to come out." Another correspondent chastised the play for "making homosexuality as pertinent and interesting as a dead bromo fizz" and also for not helping "the young and [those] searching for answers" to make up their mind about the choice between heterosexuality and homosexuality.[60] William Styron, the author, was criticized in the same spirit for allowing the portrait of Nat Turner to incorporate certain characteristics detracting from an unreservedly heroic image and for presenting him as having had an unbecoming sexual interest in a white girl.[61] Not surprisingly, at a gathering of black artists it was proposed that "Our art must be seen as part of the struggle, part of the worldwide societal revolution . . . ," that "All art is propaganda," and "We must go to the masses, learn from them and be nurtured by them."[62] In turn feminists complained of the insufficient number of inspiring role models in the mass media, of the insufficient representation of the new woman of raised consciousness, unusual occupational attainments, and a reduced interest in men and family affairs. A report on the proportional representation of "minorities" (including women) on television went so far as to suggest that in this realm, too, quotas might be useful.[63] Museums too were to become "relevant," that is, serve political purposes, and the methods used in the pursuit of such goals were similar to those popular on the campuses. Such was the case when, for instance, the "New York Artists Strike Against Racism, Sexism, Repression and War" invaded and disrupted a meeting of the American Association of Museums.[64] Louis Kampf, professor of literature at M.I.T. and president of the Modern Language Association, forcefully expressed truly radical attitudes toward matters cultural:

> The movement should have harassed Lincoln Center from the beginning. Not a performance should go by without disruption. The fountains should be dried with calcium chloride, the statuary pissed on, the walls smeared with shit.[65]

The theater too came under the influence of these trends; indeed, it proved to be an especially vulnerable target. According to Robert Brustein, "The theatre is attractive [to the young activists in quest of meaning and relevance] because it is a communal activity and thus offers promise of the same kind of togetherness held out by T-groups, communes, encounter sessions, sensitivity exploration, and all the other current forms of quasi-tribal expression."[66]

Perhaps it was a willful lack of discrimination, a self-consciously impaired ability to differentiate—between art and politics, religion and therapy, learning and entertainment, political freedom and repression, mental health and mental illness, and so on—which was a hallmark of the period and of many of its most visible and publicized cultural activities and preoccupations.

Vietnam

It is virtually impossible to think about the 1960s without recalling the impassioned protests against the American involvement in Vietnam, the teach-ins, the daily news items on television, the draft-card burnings and the prolonged acrimonious debates the war provoked. Much of the political activism of the period was anti-war activism; much of the social criticism generated during those years was a part of, or closely related to, the criticism of an unjust war waged by an unjust society. For almost a decade Vietnam was in the forefront of the attention of public opinion, and it especially preoccupied students, academics, and other intellectuals. Its coverage in the mass media was probably more extended and thorough than that of any war in history. It generated a vast number of books, articles, studies, documentaries, and even some plays. °

Protests against the war were rarely confined to the American participation and ways of waging it; they almost invariably became the basis of a broader critique of American society and system of government. As Susan Sontag put it: ". . . Vietnam offered the key to a systematic criticism of America." And as Jerry Rubin said: "If there had been no Vietnam war, we would have invented one. If the Vietnam war ends, we'll find another war."[69] As such statements suggest, indignation about American intervention in Vietnam had sources other than the aggrieved concern with the consequences of war per se. Vietnam mobilized the rejection, criticism, or hatred, as the case may be, of American society that had been dormant or partially articulated earlier. The war gave new vehemence and assurance to the social critics who languished during the placid 50s without major issues or causes that could have "offered the key to a systematic criticism of America." Vietnam was more a catalyst than a root cause of the rejection of American society in the 1960s. It confirmed all lurking apprehensions about the United States among the critically disposed and the estranged.

Indignation over American involvement in Vietnam was also connected with the decline of the conviction that the Soviet Union and other communist states represented an unfriendly force in the world and thus resisting their expansion was justifiable. (Subsequently this view of the Soviet Union and its allies was assigned to the "myths" generated by the Cold War.) Such earlier assessments of the Soviet Union and its global intentions also explain the lack of protest over American involvement in the Korean War, although in certain ways it resembled

° Peter Weiss entitled his play, "A Discourse on the Early History and the Course of the Long Lasting War of Liberation in Vietnam as an Example of the Necessity for the Armed Struggle of the Oppressed Against Their Oppressors as Also on the Attempts of the United States of America To Destroy the Foundations of the Revolution."[67] The high school in Scarsdale (N.Y.) offered a course on guerilla war tactics modeled after Vietnam,[68] justified on the grounds of relevance.

that in Vietnam and especially its objectionable features. Thus in Korea too the U.S. supported an undemocratic regime, the war was fought in a distant place not vital for American interests, napalm was used, and civilians suffered. Despite such similarities there was no protest because it did not yet seem abhorrent that the United States should assert itself militarily against a communist regime. The illusions and expectations of the post-Stalin period were yet to be born; memories of the Berlin Blockade, the Soviet take-overs in Eastern Europe were fresh; the Sino-Soviet conflict was yet to emerge, and belief in American power was still at high levels. The Cold War was then a reality, not a fantasy based on mutual misunderstanding or American ill will (as many subsequent revisionist historians and their followers came to believe), and it made sense that Soviet-supported expansion had to be stopped, even in distant places (like Korea). Memories of World War II and of the appeasement that preceded it were also fresher. The idea that there might be external threats to the United States was not yet seen as bizarre and incomprehensible as it has become in subsequent years for the younger generation. Moreover the Korean conflict differed from the Vietnamese in being more clear-cut. It was not a guerilla war. North Korean troops in uniform crossed the border and attacked. There were no pro–North Korean guerillas in the South. At last, and most importantly, it was not a televised war, and thus the suffering it exacted remained easier to ignore or forget.

By the latter part of the 1960s the Cold War was seen in a new light in the United States and Western Europe and much of it retroactively reinterpreted. There was widespread impatience with the costs and tensions associated with it, and the absence of any major and spectacular act of Soviet aggression helped to discredit concern with Soviet global intentions. There was a parallel rise of domestic preoccupations, with poverty, racial equality, feminism and the "quality of life," some of them connected with the ethos of affluence and security discussed earlier. The number of people who believed that the United States had any mission or moral mandate in the world was declining; the threat of communism, especially in distant places, was not persuasive and had been largely discredited by the late Senator McCarthy.[70] Under these circumstances it was hardly surprising that there was so much outrage, especially among the middle classes, about risking lives in Vietnam.

The view that Vietnam was both a catalyst and independent source of social criticism is also supported by the experience of other contemporary Western societies. In Britain too similar, underlying attitudes of estrangement attached themselves to more specific causes and targets of criticism. Thus, for instance, in a careful study of the beliefs and values of adherents of the British Campaign for Nuclear Disarmament (CND), Frank Parkin, an English sociologist, found that the ". . . CND is not to be understood wholly as an expression of protest against the Bomb, but as a somewhat more complex affair. It will be claimed that much of the movement's attraction derived from the fact that *it also served as a rallying point* for groups and individuals opposed to certain features of British society which were independent of the issue of the Bomb, but which the latter served dramatically to symbolize." And what Parkin said about the major predictor of British attitudes toward the CND is readily applicable to Vietnam and the American "normative order" as well: "men's relationship to the normative order provides a far surer guide to their support for, or opposition to, CND than any 'rational' considerations of defence or deterrence."[71]

The quality and quantity of social criticism unleashed by the Vietnam War in the United States (and to a lesser extent in several Western European countries) further support this argument. Statements such as Daniel Berrigan's claim that "the American ghetto and the Hanoi 'operation' were a single enterprise—a total war in both cases,"[72] cannot be explained merely by the nature of the war and the American policies associated with it. The routine attribution of genocidal intent or the recurring equation of the United States and Nazi Germany did not, and could not, spring from the evidence and events of the war itself. Such sweeping, totalistic hyperboles and denunciations fed from deeper reservoirs of hatred and estrangement. They were not created but intensified by the war.

Racial Problems

If the protest against the Vietnam War and the varieties of student activism were an essential part of the social history of both the United States and Western Europe in the 1960s, the race riots and associated problems were more peculiarly American. Their impact was twofold. On the one hand the new awareness of the deprivations of blacks and other minorities (Puerto Ricans, Mexican-Americans, American Indians) did much to discredit the United States in the eyes of the nations of the world, especially in Africa and Asia. At the same time the intensification of racial-ethnic conflict was also a major source of domestic instability and loss of collective self-esteem among Americans. The Civil

Rights movement, which began in the South where discrimination and segregation were most entrenched, spread during the 1960s throughout the whole country. It inspired both legislative measures, voter registration drives, and, indirectly, urban riots. In the course of the decade great gains were made by the black population, but there was also growing dissatisfaction with the progress achieved. Ghetto riots, arson, black extremism (and separatism), on the one hand, affirmative action and white self-recrimination on the other contributed to the tone of the decade. Since the riots were not concentrated in cities where the black population experienced the greatest material hardships, it is likely that heightened expectations as much as objective deprivation played a part in these activities.[73]

The feelings of guilt on the part of large segments of the white middle-class population were occasionally reflected in the actions and policies of the federal government. Thus, for instance, the destruction wrought by a group of American Indians in a federal building (the Bureau of Indian Affairs) was passively tolerated by the government; there was no attempt made to prevent the ransacking of the building or to punish the wrongdoers. Although the damage was extensive in the course of the six-day occupation, the occupiers were promised that no one would be prosecuted, and the U.S. government gave the protesters $60,000 for return travel expenses.[74]

The facts of black (or American-Indian) deprivation were not mythical and provided a compelling basis for social criticism in the 1960s. It is noteworthy that the injustices visited upon the minorities barely touched the social critiques of the 1930s when discrimination was unalleviated by the federal government and unquestioned by the general public. Such historic wrongs became a matter of concern at the time when they were in the process of elimination (or no longer perpetrated), that is, in the 1960s, suggesting that the massive sense of guilt among many white liberals toward the black population was combined with, and perhaps intensified by, other sources of unease.[75] Certainly out of this unease came positive accomplishments: legislative, judicial, political, educational. More controversial were the policies of reverse discrimination, designated as affirmative action.[76]

The popularity of black militants and prisoners among white intellectuals and college students was also characteristic of the times and represented a form of social criticism. Eldridge Cleaver in particular became something of a cult figure, perhaps because he was not only black but also tough, imprisoned, radical, and a self-made writer.[77] His book

Soul on Ice became a widely used text in sociology courses all over the country during the 1960s. (Cleaver's popularity went into sharp decline after he ended his exile and returned to the United States in the mid-70s with a newfound appreciation of American society following his prolonged sampling of life in various communist and Third World countries.) Huey Newton was another cult figure of the times, a self-styled "minister of defense" (of the Black Panthers). His poster showing him holding a rifle in one hand and spear in the other decorated countless rooms in college dormitories together with those of Che Guevara.[78]

The fact that a high proportion of prison inmates belonged to minority groups with a long history of mistreatment transformed them in the eyes of many social critics from convicted criminals into political prisoners and a new revolutionary vanguard. While there is a long-standing Western tradition of viewing the outlaw as romantic hero and socially conscious defier of oppressive authority* (viz., Robin Hood among others), at times of social unrest and rejection of dominant social values it becomes especially tempting to regard the breakers of law (and even the more violent ones among them) as representatives of authentic alienation and victims of social injustice.[79] They are, after all, people who rejected the norms of society not only by word but also by deed. The well-publicized prison riots in the same period also drew attention to this segment of the population and contributed to regarding them as victimized and abused. Coretta King, widow of Martin Luther King, referred to the "nobility" of those kept in the jail on Rikers Island in an address to the inmates of the same institution and compared their plight with the jailings of her husband.[80]

The radical social critics' attitudes toward race relations, black and white guilt, and the law were epitomized in the comments of William Kunstler, the radical lawyer, as he discussed the death of a white policeman in Oakland, California:

> In my opinion he deserved that death . . . the crowd justifiably, without the necessity of a trial and in the most dramatic way possible, stomped him to death. The reason was one that comes from 400 years, from the pillaging and marauding of black communities throughout the United States and the world by white power structures that have preyed upon the ghetto the way vultures prey upon meat. . . .[81]

* The American mass media and entertainment industry of recent times also provide many examples of this tradition with their portrayal of the criminal as tragic hero, victimized by a variety of social forces or circumstances. (See, for example, *Bonnie and Clyde, The Godfather, Mean Streets*, etc.)

Radical intellectuals and political activists were not alone in equating imprisonment with political persecution and the criminal with the political rebel. There were also some social scientists who concluded that people defined as criminals by the existing laws were not merely victims of social forces which forced them into lawbreaking behavior but that the laws themselves defining such behavior were arbitrary and unfair. Such laws served the interests of the elite groups and provided no basis for assessing the guilt or innocence, or the moral quality, of allegedly lawbreaking behavior.[82]

This phenomenon was not limited to American society either. Academic students of crime in Western Europe too often preferred to identify or align themselves with those violating the law rather than those upholding it. A Scandinavian criminologist, Nils Christie, wrote: "We have now made it clear that our role as criminologists is not first and foremost to be received as useful problem-solvers *but as problem-raisers. . . .*" (Social workers in Scandinavia helped to organize prison inmates into unions.) In Britain three criminologists, Ian Taylor, Paul Walton, and Jack Young, proposed that

> the politicisation of crime and criminology [is] imminent . . . a criminology which is not normatively committed to the abolition of inequalities of wealth and power . . . is inevitably bound to fall into correctionalism. . . . For us, as for Marx and other new criminologists, *deviance* is normal—in the sense that men are now consciously involved (in the prisons that are contemporary society and in the real prisons) in asserting their human diversity.[83]

It was a basic impulse inherent in the estrangement of the period to extend sympathy to all the groups outside the dominant cultural values and institutions, be they black, Puerto Rican, homosexual, prison inmates, or those in mental institutions. While blacks were the most prominent among the underdog groups and the most obvious victims of social injustice, the sympathy toward them was part of a broader pattern of identifying with *any* group that could be considered a victim of the System.

The Themes of Social Criticism

Characteristically the social critics viewed the ills of society (in the United States and Western Europe) as parts of a totally interdependent and predetermined pattern. Susan Sontag wrote: "To us, it is self-evident that the *Reader's Digest* and Lawrence Welk and Hilton Hotels are organically connected with the Special Forces' napalming villages in Guatemala . . .".[84] Everything that was bad—from sexual repression to air pollution, advertising, or racial discrimination—was caused by some identifiable social forces and their human agents. American society was controlled by the Power Elite, the Military-Industrial Complex, the Giant Corporations, or the Corporate (sometimes liberal) Fascists.[85] Such critiques of the political system, despite the new terminology, were anchored in the Marxist conception of the relationship between the polity and the economy, though enriched with the notion of "repressive tolerance"—that is, repression disguised as tolerance designed to confuse and deceive those thus repressed.[86]

While in the 1930s the main theme and target of social criticism was poverty, in the 1960s a striking shift came about in the perception of the ills of American and other Western societies. Poverty per se ceased to be the major thrust of social criticism, although there were occasional outcries about certain of its manifestations. These tended to be focused on the poverty of blacks and other minority groups. Certainly in the United States, poverty in general, and the poverty of white people in particular, was not a prime concern of the social critics. Moreover, there emerged a new idealization of poverty and the poor, almost invariably associated with the idealization of certain minority groups: blacks and Puerto Ricans in particular. Stereotypes about the spiritual benefits of poverty revived. The poor were "real people"; they were tough but possessed of an underlying humanity; they had a sense of community; they were capable of strong feelings; they had guts; they defied authority. They knew how to sing and dance and express joy uninhibitedly despite the bleakness of their lives.[87] Sometimes the radical social critics confused poverty with the voluntary renunciation of the world of material pleasures and vanities. The poor seemed free of the original sin of consumption, crass materialism, and hollow status-seeking that infected the rest of society. And the poorer, the better. The unemployed, those on welfare, juveniles, the "lumpen-poor" (or the "underclass") were seen as possessed of a higher level of consciousness than the working poor who internalized the values of the system and hankered after its rewards. It was the shift from the critique of poverty to the criticism of affluence that explains this phenomenon.

In the 1960s it was no longer possible to mount the type of broad, frontal attack on capitalism which in the 1930s had focused on poverty and unemployment. Insofar as and in part because it was less feasible to attack capitalism on such predominantly economic grounds, in a striking switch its economic successes became the new basis for its rejection. Now it was the baleful results of the high standards of living and the associated empty material values and competitive individualism that became the grounds for social criticism.[88] The rejection of society could no longer be based predominantly on the decline of material conditions which were so evident in the 1930s.

A similar trend could be observed with respect to work. While in the 1930s unemployment was a major focus of social criticism, in the 1960s the emphasis shifted to the quality of work since unemployment was no longer a major problem. Now critics directed their fire at the routinized, meaningless, demeaning, or dead-end jobs. While undoubtedly there were many such forms of work, this was neither a new development nor peculiar to the United States or Western Europe. Again such criticisms reflected the rising expectations of an increasing number of people.

The American literary critic Morris Dickstein credited the 60s with a form of religious thinking which "encourages us to make exorbitant, apocalyptic demands upon life and tells us that we can break through the joyless forms of everyday existence toward a radiant communality and wholeness."[89] A well-known sociologist, Philip Slater, concluded his book with the following ringing paragraph:

> Past efforts to build utopian communities failed because they were founded on scarcity assumptions. But scarcity is now shown to be an unnecessary condition. . . . We need not raise the youth of new utopias to feel that life's primary gratifications are in such short supply. Hence the only obstacle to utopia is the persistence of the competitive motivational patterns that past scarcity assumptions have spawned. Nothing stands in our way except our invidious dreams of personal glory. . . .[90]

Shulamith Firestone's vision of the future included "the abolition of the labor force itself under a cybernetic socialism, the radical restructuring of the economy to make 'work,' i.e. wage labor, no longer necessary . . . [and] the freedom of all women and children to do whatever they wish to do sexually."[91]

A statement by Carl Oglesby, an early leader of the SDS (Students for Democratic Society), also reflects the high aspirations and hopes of the period: "Our best concern . . . is to make love more possible. We work to remove from society what threatens and prevents it—the inequity that coordinates with injustice to create plain suffering and to make custom of distrust. Poverty. Racism. The assembly line universities. . . . The ulcerating drive for affluence."[92]

In the 1930s there was no revolution of rising expectations; rather, people wanted to hold their own; they wanted to keep their jobs, savings, social standing already attained. They wanted to be able to feed their families, pay their rent or mortgage, fend off disruption and cataclysmic change in their way of life. Any job was better than no job. The house in the suburbs was a dream not a nightmare. There was no doubt about the reality of scarcities. This is not to say that there were no forerunners of the criticisms of affluence and consumption we learned to associate with Herbert Marcuse in particular. As early as the 30s Scott Nearing had pioneered the type of rejection of American society which stressed the evils of technology, materialism, and elaborate consumption. He despised "Capitalist society . . . founded on habit-forming generations of gadgetry" and "[parted] company with Western civilization,"[93] retiring to his farm in Vermont and later to Maine.* Nearing's critique of American society also encompassed some of the countercultural values which focused on the virtues of simple life, self-sufficiency, nature, and the soil.

While it has been long believed (by those to whom it was available) that wealth and material comforts are sources of spiritual corruption,[95] these beliefs surfaced and spread with a renewed vigor in the 60s as they were also linked to the new fears about the evils of technology. Marcuse was the main spokesman and theorist of the spiritual horrors of the combined effects of mass production, mass culture, high technology, capitalism, and Western-style political institutions. In his writings the critique of capitalism often merges into a more general critique of modern industrial society. Yet whenever Marcuse spoke about modern industrial society in its most evil and stultifying incarnation, his

---

* Nearing was one of the few social critics whose alienation spans the decades of both the 30s and 60s, and whose social criticism was congenial to both periods. So were his enthusiasms as he managed to visit and admire ecumenically both the Soviet Union and China, Cuba and the Eastern European "socialist" countries including Albania. He averred that he was converted "into a citizen of the world, carrying in my pocket, when I travel, a United States passport, but ashamed to show the document or admit the association to intelligent, sensitive, aware people abroad. I am able to justify myself by saying: the alienation is complete. I live in the United States only because my post of duty is there. I carry this humiliating document only because it enables me to go abroad and get a breath of fresh unpolluted air. I am ashamed of any connection with the oligarchy which presently misgoverns, exploits, plunders and corrupts the United States and the World."[94]

model was the United States. He and other critics in the 60s were especially angered and concerned over two aspects of American (and to a lesser extent Western European) society. One was its productive capacity, which allowed the satisfaction of the material needs of the majority and thereby undermined their desire for more basic transformations of the social world and their personal lives. It was a new version of Lenin's "trade union consciousness" that Marcuse castigated, perceiving the novel inducements capitalism offered to disarm the masses. Secondly, there was "repressive tolerance." Tolerance, not unlike affluence, was repressive because it allowed people the illusion of freedom, while the satisfaction of material needs allowed people the illusion of general well-being.

Marcuse's social criticisms were classically elitist. If his notions of good life and fulfillment were not embraced by the masses, he diagnosed them as suffering from false consciousness:

> If the individuals are satisfied to the point of happiness with the goods and services handed down to them by the administration, why should they insist on different institutions for a different production of different goods and services? And if the individuals are pre-conditioned so that the satisfying goods also include thoughts, feelings, aspirations, why should they wish to think, feel and imagine for themselves? True, the material and mental commodities offered may be bad, wasteful rubbish—but *Geist* and knowledge are no telling arguments against satisfaction of needs.[96]

In effect, Marcuse was indignant about some basic facts of cultural socialization and appeared to overlook that historically such socialization always succeeded to the extent of making most people at least resigned to the social system they lived under. The idea that American society was uniquely or exceptionally successful in legitimating itself was plainly wrong by all standards of historical comparison, and as the 60s proceeded this became increasingly obvious. To be sure, in *One-Dimensional Man* Marcuse was still reacting to the relative stability and tranquility of the 1950s, yet he continued to be preoccupied and distressed with what he perceived as the enormous capacity of American society to lull and seduce, and buy off dissent and social criticism.

Although Marcuse acknowledged the existence of scarcity outside the Western world, his emphasis on its conquest in the West and his association of abundance with waste, corruption, and inauthenticity became the most influential theme of social criticism of the period. This was perhaps the gist of the argument:

In the contemporary era, the conquest of scarcity is still confined to small areas of advanced industrial society. Their prosperity covers up the Inferno inside and outside their borders; it also spreads repressive productivity and "false needs." It is repressive precisely to the degree to which it promotes the satisfaction of needs which require continuing the rat race. . . .[97]

Social-political stability was maintained by what Marcuse called "the technology of pacification." For instance: "The little man who works eight hours a day in the factory, who does an inhuman and stultifying work, on the weekend sits behind a huge machine much more powerful than himself, and there he can utilize all his antisocial aggressiveness. . . . If this aggressiveness were not sublimated in the speed and power of the automobile, it might be directed against the dominant powers."[98] Correspondingly Marcuse also believed that the second pillar of stability in a repressive society is television and the mass media: "The mere absence of all advertising and of all indoctrinating media of information and entertainment would plunge the individual into a traumatic void . . . such a situation would be an unbearable nightmare. . . . The non-functioning of television and the allied media might thus begin to achieve what the inherent contradictions of capitalism did not achieve— the disintegration of the system."[99]

Generally speaking the social criticism of the 60s was far more unabashedly elitist and paternalistic than the criticism of the 1930s. Marcuse was not only perturbed because there was no true freedom in modern industrial society (i.e., the United States), but also irritated by undue permissiveness in certain areas of life. Thus he remarked that "To the denial of freedom . . . corresponds the granting of liberties where they strengthen repression. *The degree to which the population is allowed to break the peace . . . and silence, to be ugly and to uglify things, to ooze familiarity, to offend against good form is frightening.*"[100] Despite such hauteur and elitism, Marcuse's social criticism became widely diffused and very much a part of the conventional wisdom of the 1960s and 70s. Thus the hostility toward technology was adopted not only by the anti-war movement—whose spokesmen often suggested that it was the use of advanced technology which made American war-making particularly repugnant—but also by the back-to-nature, back-to-the-land people and much of the counter-culture at large. One of the aims of the back-to-the-land movement (stretching well into the 70s) was "less machinery, less technology, less everything that comes from and depends on big business. . . . Thousands of the new rural families heat and cook with wood. 'Labor-saving' devices like tractors are examined skeptically and used sparingly. Mule-drawn equipment is reappearing."[101]

The back-to-nature movements were truly characteristic of the estrangement of the 1960s: although ostensibly part of the rejection of affluence, urban amenities, and material comforts, they could not have arisen without affluence. Leaving the cities and setting up communes, or small studios, workshops, businesses, required money to buy land, homes, equipment, tools. Besides the rejection of technology and routinized, bureaucratized work situations, those moving to the rural areas were also motivated by the concern with the physical environment. Here was also a reflection of the greater aesthetic preoccupations of the more recent social critics. The countryside was more appealing than most cities and suburbs, and natural beauty was important for those who did not have to worry unduly about the basic necessities of life.*

The aversion to technology and urban ways of life were not the only novel features of the social criticism in the 1960s and early 70s. Impurities in personal relationships were also under scrutiny, and American society stood accused of having a peculiarly debilitating effect on human beings and their relationships. The charge somewhat resembled the venerable Marxian critique of the cash nexus, of calculation at the expense of spontaneity and human fellowship, but there were new anti-rational twists added to the notion of authenticity. D. H. Lawrence had brilliantly anticipated and summed up the related, underlying counter-cultural beliefs and attitudes of our times half a century ago in a letter written to Bertrand Russell:

> Why don't you drop overboard? Why don't you clear out of the whole show? One must be an outlaw these days, not a teacher or preacher. . . . Do for your pride's sake become a mere nothing, a mole, a creature that feels its way and doesn't think. Do for heaven's

---

* In earlier times, including the 1920s and 1930s, it was the urban bohemia (the Village, parts of London, Paris, and other Western capitals) which functioned as subcultural islands, though far less insulated from society at large than the communal (or individual) farms of more recent times in Vermont or Maine. Joseph Freeman wrote of the bohemians of Greenwich Village in the 1920s: "The radical bohemian . . . suffered from the infantile expectation that the Golden Realm of 'art and revolution' should have, while capitalism still dominated the world, some of the characteristics of the classless society. There must be no money, no debtors and no creditors; we were to live in a little utopian South Sea isle of 'communism' surrounded by the raging sea of capitalism; and on this happy island we were to fulfill Marx's dictum, from each according to his abilities, to each according to his needs."[102]

sake be a baby and not a savant anymore. Don't *do* anything more—
but for heaven's sake begin to *be*.[103]

Similar sentiments were at the root of the attacks on social roles and
role relations. According to Jerry Rubin, "Amerika puts her people into
prisons by carefully defining their roles."[104] Members of the Venceremos
Brigade (American radicals who journeyed to Cuba to cut sugarcane
and show their solidarity with Castro's regime) wrote: "We had all been
taught to relate to people in their social roles. . . . In Cuba this was not
the case. . . . Amerika does a lot of ugly things to people. It puts walls
between them. . . . Amerika tries to make pieces of everything. . . .
Not long ago I was in pieces. All the experiences of my life had con-
spired to fragment my understanding. . . . I suffered from the prime
Amerikan problem: middle class consciousness, the inability to feel."[105]
A similar vision of the deadening qualities of American life (or perhaps
an early version of "repressive tolerance"?) permeated Norman Mailer's
lament:

> In Cuba hatred runs over into the love of blood; in America all too
> few blows are struck into flesh. We kill the spirit here. . . . We use
> psychic bullets and kill each other cell by cell. We live in a country
> very different from Cuba. We have had a tyranny here, but it did not
> have the features of Batista; it was a tyranny one breathed but could
> not define; it was felt as no more than a slow deadening of the best of
> our possibilities, a tension we could not name which was the sum of
> our frustrations. . . . By law we had a free press; almost no one
> spoke his thoughts. By custom we had a free ballot; was there ever a
> choice? We were a league of silent defeated men. . . . In silence we
> gave you our support. [To Castro] You were aiding us, you were
> giving us psychic ammunition . . . in that desperate silent struggle
> we have been fighting with sick dead hearts against the cold insidious
> cancer of the power that governs us, you were giving us new blood to
> fight our mass communications, our police, our secret police, our cor-
> porations, our empty politicians, our clergymen, our editors, our cold
> frightened bewildered bullies who govern a machine made out of peo-
> ple they no longer understand, you were giving us hope they would
> not always win.[106]

These critiques were more than a rehash of the cash nexus argument.
The depersonalization envisaged was broader, deeper, and more diffuse,
and it could not be attributed to greed, acquisitiveness, or monetary
calculation alone. What the critics were rejecting was their perception of
an excessive and pathological rationality, a far-reaching "cultural warp-
ing of human emotionality" (as Philip Slater called it) which, they felt,
was peculiarly American. Slater believed that American culture "deeply

and uniquely frustrated" major human needs and desires. He offered a revealing image of the inauthenticity and emotional barrenness of American life: "There is an uneasy, anesthetized feeling about this kind of life—like being trapped forever inside an air-conditioned car with power steering and power brakes and only a telephone to talk to. Our world is only a mirror, and our efforts mere shadowboxing. . . ."[107] Slater too voiced the widespread counter-cultural criticism of American society: that it was sickly puritanical, overcontrolled, and that people were not "in touch with their feelings"—a proposition that became one of the key cultural and therapeutic clichés of the period (still with us). Here many different strands of social criticism came together. Repression was the magic word, the glue holding them together. People were repressed not only sexually and emotionally, but also politically and economically. Internal and external repression met and fortified one another.

It was among the paradoxes of the times that although individualism flourished (in the senses discussed earlier; that is, especially in respect to the refusal to accept restraints on personal gratifications), the counter-cultural and radical critiques of American society also deplored individualistic achievement orientation. This again was something new that had no parallels in the 30s. In the 1960s many culture critics felt that the old work ethic (or Protestant Ethic) was obsolete and the source of all repression and inextricably interwoven with equally dated notions of scarcity.[108] The vehemence with which achievement orientation was criticized was also related to the belief that self-esteem should not unduly depend on work, or work-connected achievements, as this would allow the perpetuation of inequality and invidious distinctions. (It was this outlook that also inspired the assault on grades and examinations as they too led to differentiation and inequality.)

The critiques of achievement orientation were closely associated with the rejection of competition and competitiveness, which were considered destructive of the sense of community, trust, and mutual respect. Such criticisms were not limited to the ethos of commerce and capitalism but extended even to competitive sports and games. Achievement orientation and the associated competitiveness were also regarded as inimical to wholeness, leading to fragmented attitudes and experiences, to specialization and role relations. Social roles and role relations in turn were antithetical to openness, flexibility, sincerity, spontaneity, informality, free self-expression. Not for nothing was "uptight" a major term of opprobrium in the counter-culture.

Another main theme and motif of social criticism in the 60s was the hatred of bureaucracy. Its relationship to the growth of individualism is obvious: bureaucracy represents the negation of the individual and of his unique needs or capabilities. Bureaucracy is, or is supposed to be, impersonal and standardized, neutral, objective and detached. It is profoundly unemotional, un- and anti-romantic; it is prosaic, calculating, and tedious. It strives for "the administration of things," not the nurturing of ego. It will be recalled that the Berkeley student movement in 1964 elevated the rejection of bureaucracy to one of its central themes. Its early leader, Mario Savio, spoke impassionately and scornfully about "The Machine" and about people being reduced to computer cards. (Subsequently computer centers became targets of hostility in many campus protests.)

The abhorrence of bureaucracy and depersonalization did not, by implication, lead to the defense of the family, which may be seen as antithetical to large-scale impersonal organizations. The family and marriage also became a focus of criticism in this period, albeit from a narrower portion of the ideological spectrum, namely the radical feminists. Shulamith Firestone wrote: ". . . Marriage in its very definition will never be able to fulfill the needs of its participants, for it was organized around and reinforces a fundamentally oppressive biological condition. . . ." For feminists, motherhood and procreation too were suspect. ("Pregnancy is barbaric . . . the temporary deformation of the body for the sake of the species. Moreover childbirth *hurts*. . . . It is not fun. . . .")[109] While most feminists did not go as far as Shulamith Firestone, they blamed the nuclear family for the status of women and the defects of monogamy. Hostility toward the nuclear family also rested on its association with patterns of elaborate and privatized consumption and a routinized existence deplored by radical social critics.

Not surprisingly the attack on inequality was a major theme of the social criticism of the 1960s, although it differed in emphasis from its antecedents in the 1930s. Inequality had different dimensions and consequences in an affluent society than in one which suffered from unemployment and economic depression. In the 1960s as noted before, poverty per se was no longer the issue; rather it was the deprivation of racial-ethnic minorities and, to a lesser extent, of women. The concern with inequality was at once narrower and broader; narrower because of the focus on minorities, but broader because the material aspects were not all-important. Inequality often came to refer to *any* barrier to self-fulfillment and the realization of human potential. At the same time inequality has remained a particularly painful condition in American society, given the widespread belief in equal opportunity. Apparently in Western Europe, where the facts of social stratification were more readily accepted, inequality was easier to bear—few people expected, even under conditions of various welfare states, to attain a full equality of opportunity, let alone equality of condition or result. The latter, expressed in demands for the proportional representation of certain minority groups and women in various occupations, educational institutions, or public offices, was a new conception of equality which was absent in the 1930s.

There was also a difference between the old and new criticisms of inequality as to who or what was blamed for it. In the 30s these matters, in the light of a more orthodox Marxist explanation, were clearer. Inequality was inherent in the capitalist mode of production, in the private possession of the means of production. It was economically determined and, when necessary, politically supported and upheld. The experience of the Soviet Union and similar regimes—to the extent that they were known to the alienated students and intellectuals in the 60s—made this analysis somewhat problematic. Evidently it was possible to have inequalities of all kinds and of considerable magnitude in societies where the means of production were not privately owned, in societies calling themselves socialist and which, whatever else they could be called, were not capitalist.

Non-economic explanations of inequality were now also proposed, such as the pleasure derived from keeping others down, or that of the invidious distinction. Philip Slater argued that the desire for status or for "fame, power or wealth . . . are inherently invidious needs; they are satisfied only in relation to the deprivation of others."[110] Michael Lewis, another American sociologist, further elaborated the status and self-esteem building functions of inequality:

> Invoking the individual-as-central-sensibility° . . . many Americans make of their commonplace successes praiseworthy achievements by viewing disadvantage as the just desert for insufficient effort born of moral infirmity or incompetence . . . the culture of inequality mandates the existence of visible failure and therefore the persistence of major social problems in our midst . . . it necessitates the continuing victimization of the disinherited. . . .[111]

In other words, inequality is not solely or predominantly a product of scarce resources and their unjust and/or irrational distribution; inequality survives so tenaciously because it gives comfort to large numbers of

° That is to say, individualism or excessive individualism.

people, as it enables them to look down on others. Self-esteem is invidious and all the more so since most of us never live up to our aspirations,
which are inflamed by American culture. As a statement of the human
condition the argument is persuasive. On the other hand, the suggestion
that we have large numbers of poor and otherwise disadvantaged groups
in our midst mainly because their contemplation pleasurably bolsters
self-esteem and this pleasure subverts any serious attempt to alter their
condition—such a proposition carries less conviction. (The author also
suggested elsewhere in the book that the same considerations explain
the persistence of crime: "Our response to crime has in fact been more
consistent with the need to sustain it as a highly visible component of
the American experience than with the ostensible desire to reduce its
impact upon our lives . . . for many Americans, criminals serve as a
negative reference group whose violations of common decency render
such decency uncommon and praiseworthy.")[112]

Among the novel streams of social criticism in the 60s and 70s the
feminist critique of American society was preeminent and had no counterpart in the 1930s. Here again, the crucial difference may be found in
the different material circumstances of the eras. In the earlier one, social
criticism was directly inspired by economic crisis and material deprivation. Among the issues and grievances of the 30s there was little room
for feminism and especially the kind which became prominent in the
late 60s. As has been observed before, the women's liberation movement
of the 60s was a predominantly white middle-class, college-based (or
educated) movement. Its main concerns were not material but psychic-
emotional or spiritual deprivation. Obviously, feminists demanded equal
pay for the same work for women, but the issues most strongly agitating
them were not the "bread and butter" ones. Rather, the main thrust of
the feminist movement was directed at a complex of obstacles which appeared to interfere with self-realization. Women were encouraged to
break free of whatever felt restrictive: childcare, housework, uninter-
esting or menial jobs, residence in a particular place, mundane routines,
the yoke of monogamy, heterosexual relations, as the case may be. The
feminist movement shared many of the counter-cultural sensibilities.
Members of support groups encouraged one another to follow their impulses, to do what "felt right" or "good," to be spontaneous, to seek new
challenges. The urge to realize submerged potentials was central to the
women's movement. As to other matters, the new feminists shared the
basics of the New Left–radical critique of American (or Western) society
and inclined to link sexism and capitalism. The women's movement also

shared with the New Left a preoccupation with matters expressive and symbolic, including the ideologically proper ways of dressing, use of language, and address (viz., Ms., chairperson, personhood, herstory, and other linguistic innovations).

The part played by Marxism in the social criticisms of the 1960s was not quite as important as its corresponding role in the 1930s, when for American intellectuals it was more of a novelty, a delicious, and until then somewhat forbidden, fruit. In that period the Soviet Union was still untarnished in the eyes of Western intellectuals and the only society claiming to implement Marxism and using it as a legitimating device. The Soviet example had enhanced rather than detracted from the prestige of Marxism. By the 1960s the situation was different as the Soviet Union became morally discredited* and Western Marxists were hard put to cite the Soviet experience as vindicating Marxism—they remained (or became) Marxists in spite of the Soviet experience. Nor did the proliferation of societies each claiming to be Marxist help. In turn, Communist parties and movements around the world splintered and reflected the schisms and conflicts among various socialist countries, especially the Soviet Union and China. In the West a wide variety of Marxist schools flourished as revisionists of different stripes were at work salvaging, reinterpreting, highlighting, or deemphasizing different aspects of Marxism. Far more than in the 30s Marxism became many things for many people. None of this means that it did not enter into or color the social criticism of the times. There was, after all, a strong if romantic anti-capitalist strain in the criticisms mounted by the New Left and the counter-culture. Even more importantly, the concept of alienation and its many varieties remained useful and stimulating. The language of Marxism—its passionate ethos of protest, polemics, and denunciation— was also appealing. Moreover, certain basic propositions of Marxism still made good sense and were easy to grasp, such as the condemnation of the profit hunger, of acquisitive urges and the attendant indifference to our fellow human beings. "People Before Profit" was the type of slogan in the 60s that was easy to applaud (not unlike "Make love not war"). It was also tempting to link the war protest to the critique of capitalism: the corporations profited by the war; some critics asserted that the United States got involved in Indochina because of the raw materials

* There were some exceptions. For example, in the words of Carl Oglesby, many in the SDS believed that "Stalinism was 'Right on.'" And an American political scientist noted that "the Marxism that the Movement incorporated was a harsh and dogmatic variant."[113]

and minerals the corporations were after.[114] Thus many of the estranged
intellectuals in the 60s discovered and rediscovered aspects of Marxism.
Susan Sontag rejoiced: "That I've begun to use some elements of Marxist
or Neo-Marxist language again seems almost a miracle, an unexpected
remission of historical muteness, a new chance to address problems that
I'd renounced ever understanding."[115] Angela Davis embraced Marxism
more in the spirit of the 30s:

> When I learned about socialism in my history classes, a whole new
> world opened up before my eyes. For the first time, I became ac-
> quainted with the notion that there could be an ideal socioeconomic
> arrangement. . . .
> The Communist Manifesto hit me like a bolt of lightning. I read it
> avidly, finding in it answers to many seemingly unanswerable dilem-
> mas which had plagued me. . . . Like an expert surgeon this docu-
> ment cut away cataracts from my eyes . . . it all fell into place. . . .
> The final words of the Manifesto moved me to an overwhelming
> desire to throw myself into the communist movement. . . .[116]

Admittedly Angela Davis was somewhat atypical, not only in regard
to the fervor displayed in embracing Marxism but also in becoming a
staunch supporter-functionary in the pro-Soviet American Communist
party and an old-style admirer of the Soviet Union.[117]

The lesser importance of Marxism as a source and inspiration of social
criticism also had to do with the fact that the critics of the 60s were generally less interested in theorizing—a circumstance that was one of several differences between the Old and New Left. The radicals of the 60s
were more action-oriented, more interested in immediate gratification,
as it were, accessible through some form of political activism. Similar
trends were also noted in Britain. For example, the great majority of the
supporters for the Campaign for Nuclear Disarmament (a fairly characteristic English New Left organization) "declared themselves in favour
of a style of politics in which the achievement of concrete goals is not
the prime consideration. From this point of view, politics is concerned
with the strict adherence to principles, and the making of gestures felt
to be morally right, even though ineffective in practical terms."[118] "Gestures felt to be morally right" were at the heart of the politics of the new
radicals. Action-orientation often bordered on anti-intellectualism. Jack
Newfield, a sometime admirer and charter member of the New Left,
was pained as he observed that

> There is an appalling anti-intellectualism among the newer SDS mem-
> bers. [This was written in 1967.] Not only do they read few novels

and almost no scientific or philosophical literature, they have read little within the radical tradition. Of twenty-five activists interviewed, none had ever read Rosa Luxemburg, Max Weber, Eduard Bernstein, John Dewey, Peter Kropotkin, or John Stuart Mill. Less than five had actually read Lenin or Trotsky, and only a few more had ever read Marx. Almost all of them had read C. Wright Mills and Camus, and about half had read Goodman, Franz Fanon and Herbert Marcuse. . . . Most of those questioned justified their sparse reading by saying either that they had little to learn from the past or that the demands of activism took up most of their time.[119]

The main theoretical inspiration for the social criticism of the period was not so much Marxism but rather secondhand versions, interpretations, modifications, and adaptations of Marxism and of Leninism. Certainly Marcuse, Mills, and Goodman were popular, as were Fanon, Che Guevara, and Mao. But such authors were used more as a source of slogans and "role models" than for theoretical enlightenment. Social criticism in the 1960s was less cerebral, sometimes self-consciously garbled, inchoate, and atheoretical.[120] At a time when deep feeling and spontaneity were prized, articulate theoretical elaborations and expositions commanded less respect and interest.

Some of the differences between the quality and tone of social criticism in the 1930s and 1960s may be due to the fact that in the latter period social criticism became a mass movement, a vast subcultural phenomenon, whereas in the 1930s it was more of an elite activity of "certified intellectuals," writers, and journalists.

Not only were many themes of social criticism peculiar to the 60s, the underlying quality of estrangement was also different.[121] Unlike in the 30s, in more recent times political involvements acquired a more personalized aspect, especially in the United States. Perhaps it was merely a resurgence of "a persisting American habit of appropriating political ideas as narcissistic supplies for a self which demanded nothing less than imaginative possession of the world. . . ."[122] If so, there were far more Americans in the 60s than in the 30s who indulged this habit.

In the 60s it seemed as if many among the critics believed that it was simply impossible to lead decent personal lives in American society, such was the corrosive effect of corrupt social institutions and values. Philip Slater claimed "that although we live in the most affluent society ever known, the sense of deprivation and discomfort that pervades it is also unparalleled."[123] There was a new insistence on the close interdependence of the social and personal spheres. In the writings of American social critics of the 1960s there was far more personal anguish, frustration, and resentment than in those of their counterparts of the 1930s.[124] Those of the earlier generation rarely complained, for example, of society paralyzing their capacity for genuine feeling (a complaint belied, incidentally, by the emotional outbursts and cries of despair of many of those voicing it in the 1960s).* The critics of the 1930s did not berate their social environment for whatever personal or spiritual malaise and discomfort they experienced, nor did they find in society the source of feelings of personal inadequacy. The earlier generation rarely lamented "fragmentation" and infrequently expressed longings for a more intense capacity for emotion. Their writings seem less agonized, less suffused with a generalized quest for a meaning in life supposedly denied to them by their society. In the 1960s (and 1970s) there were more social critics and estranged intellectuals who might be suspected of using politics as personal problem-solving devices.† Not that this was a novel situation: in all ages one may find connections between personal injuries and certain forms of political protest, between intimate personal motives and socially derived grievances. At the same time it has never been easy to establish the precise nature of such connections or the direction of causality. Certainly, no easy inferences can be made from the motives of adherents of a political movement to the content of their social criticism or the objectives of the movement. A society may be oppressive and particular social institutions corrupt even if people are led to recognize this (or are sensitized to this) through childhood traumas, parental neglect, sibling rivalry, physical unattractiveness, or any other personal misfortune or misadventure. What may be argued is that the quality of social criticism and estrangement may undergo a noticeable change when people arrive at it via the route of personal grievance rather than a more detached and impersonal assessment of social-political injustice

---

* This paradox is somewhat similar to another one that alienated critics of American society often proposed, namely, that we have all been "brainwashed" by the mass media. It is of no avail to ask, how, if this is so, the complainer has managed to remain highly critical of American society. Nor will these critics be swayed by the observation that those brainwashed are rarely aware of it, or willing to confess with such joyous vehemence to such a debilitating experience.

† It is however worth pointing out that the recent linking up of the personal and political spheres had its precedent in the attitudes of many of those attracted earlier to the Communist parties of Western Europe and the United States. Gabriel Almond found that "More than half of the respondents (58%) saw the party at the time of joining as a way of solving personal problems or attaining personal ends. . . . Substantially more of the American respondents (73%) perceived the party as a means of satisfying non-political ends."[125]

and institutional malfunctioning. Alienation when closely tied to personal problems assumes a more troubled, tortured character, as has been the case with many of the, often younger, "second generation" travelers in my study. When alienation is more personal in its origins, the need to prove that the prevailing social institutions are bad becomes more urgent and compelling. As if nagging doubts were to be fought off about the validity of the social criticism which emanates from a self-doubting individual who often feels guilt on various grounds (e.g., a privileged social background, middle- or upper middle-class membership, being white, male, American, European, well educated, etc.). By contrast the social criticism expressed by blacks and members of other genuinely deprived groups was less personal, less suffused with a generalized quest for meaning in life, and far more focused on specific and corrigible ills of society.

Radical social critics of privileged backgrounds also exhibited what appeared to be a compensatory reverence and submissiveness toward the authentic underdog groups: blacks, American Indians, Third World guerillas, prison inmates, and others. Many of these attitudes and especially the qualities of estrangement in more recent times are illuminated in the self-revelations of members of the Venceremos Brigade:

> White people . . . came to Cuba with only the most fragile sense of themselves as people . . . they were often paralyzed with shame and despair over the values which a competitive, individualistic and racist middle class culture had instilled in them.
>
> After her disillusionment with the anti-poverty program, she started travelling through Europe for a year. . . . She got to Berkeley. . . . She could not relate to Berkeley politics. . . . She hopes the Brigade will get her off her individual trip.
>
> This morning there was a meeting of all the women. Most of the vocal whites emphasize guilt, "we are all guilty"; most of the blacks attack. People tiptoe around blacks because you don't argue with a black—everything you say will be attacked as racist. The other white move is to attack other "liberal" whites and ally themselves with the blacks. . . . The whole thing was about what slobs we were. The Cubans were disgusted about . . . the way we made a mess, leaving clothes around; and the amount of water we used taking long showers. . . . And as the Cubans cleaned out the bathroom we continue to bicker about who was guilty.
>
> I am all fucked up. Too many problems that I have to deal with. I am amazingly selfish. . . . That's certainly how we are taught in capitalist society. . . . Right now I have the very real problem of getting out to the field every day [to cut sugarcane]. Is Communism simply an act of will?

People at the meeting were so untogether it was pathetic. Some questioned the Third World leadership itself. . . . All in all there is a lot of hostility and confusion developing among brigadistas. Blacks and whites are not relating too well. Women's Liberation people are regarded by almost all others with biting sarcasm. . . . Everyone is just so untogether. Someone has been writing "Off the People!" and "Off Chicks!" on the tents. The Cubans must be tearing their hair out trying to deal with us.

The white caucus meeting was the most diseased, frightening meeting I have ever seen. The central force in it was fear—everyone was scared shitless of himself and the next person. . . . One girl finally stood up in tears and pleaded with everyone to please stop hating each other. . . . She was almost hysterical. . . . For the first time in my life I felt deep in my gut a real powerful shame of my whiteness. It is a paralyzing feeling.

[Upon arrival in Cuba] I felt kind of shameful that I could fuck around with drugs and sort of take advantage of all the leisure and abstraction—what everyone [sic] is into in the U.S.

The questions we asked [of a visiting Vietnamese delegation] were in hushed, respectful tones and every word of the confident answers was anxiously waited for. One American asked whether the guerrilla soldiers ate white rice or brown rice.

I am beginning to understand how very thin is the line between neurosis and oppression, and consequently how in the most profound way the solution to what formerly seemed our most personal problems is deeply political.

I can fight the system because I truly hate it. I hate how it has warped the people of our country. How it tries to warp me and everyone it can. . . . Amerika we will rip you up—tear your guts apart from the inside.[126]

What is one to make of this type of estrangement? What makes it so intense and personal? These were not, by and large, people who had firsthand experience of racial discrimination, police brutality, or the humiliations and deprivations of poverty, unemployment, bad housing, insufficient medical care, lack of educational opportunity.

The negative self-images such as displayed by members of the Venceremos Brigade (and some other middle-class radicals) had no counterpart in the 30s when evidently estrangement and social criticism could coexist with a more balanced conception of the impact of society on the individual, and when in fact social criticism was more selective. In the 60s all major social institutions and values were discredited in the eyes of these critics: it was not only or predominantly the political and economic system; schools, colleges, mental institutions, prisons were all equally hellish (even "childhood [was] hell");[127] the mass media brainwashed; mass culture was junk; the police a new Gestapo; the place of work a place of slavery; the family the oppressor in the home—there were just no places to go, figuratively speaking, so pervasive was corruption, injustice, and oppression.[128] Given such a view of society, both the tone and psychological correlates of criticism were bound to be different, as shown above. At the same time the very broad, sweeping, and increasingly ritualistic character of social criticism had a certain hollowness to it. John W. Aldridge had drawn attention to "the oddly obscure vocabulary they use to describe the evils they wish to overthrow. They talk compulsively and ritualistically about 'power structures,' 'systems,' 'establishments,' 'bureaucracy,' 'technology,' and the vagueness of these words, their failure . . . to describe specific conditions in a real world, is symptomatic of their function as empty pejorative metaphors for problems not personally engaged by those who use them."[129]

Perhaps the standardization of the language of social criticism also reflected the virtual institutionalization of the adversary posture itself, especially in academic settings, as the initially iconoclastic and irreverent attitudes of social criticisms turned into the new forms of conventional wisdom.

At last we must briefly consider the possibility that the quality of alienation was also affected by the unsuccessful waging and subsequent losing of the war in Vietnam—as distinct from the criticisms directed at the objectives and methods of the war. While this possibility has not been widely recognized, it seems to me that not doing well in the war and finally being defeated is likely to have made a significant contribution to the general delegitimation of American society. Not only was the System bad, it also proved impotent in the final analysis. Edward Shils was one of the few observers of these processes who realized that losing the war by itself was of crucial importance, regardless of whether it was a just or unjust one, a good or bad cause. He wrote:

> A war is an undertaking which involves national identity and, as such, it touches on the deepest roots of the acknowledgement of legitimacy. The loss of a war endangers the real and symbolic existence of the entire national community and it thereby weakens the readiness to acknowledge the right to rule of those who have taken to themselves the care of the name and safety of that national community.[130]

I reviewed in this chapter some of the major social and political developments, cultural trends, and group beliefs which characterized the late 1960s and early 1970s in the United States and Western Europe. In doing so I attempted to capture the spirit of the times and the themes of social criticism which flourished and eventually gave rise to a new set of favorable predispositions toward countries which became the new, if again transient, symbols of social justice and political rectitude.

6

New Horizons: Revolutionary Cuba
and the Discovery of the Third World

There's direction. Here you have all these things happening and disagreement. There you get this singleness of purpose, from the university to the cane fields.   HUEY NEWTON[1]

Cuba is the first purposeful society that we have had in the Western
Hemisphere for many years—it's the first society where human beings
are treated as human beings, where men have a certain dignity, and
where this is guaranteed to them.   SAUL LANDAU[2]

. . . every man was a brother; there was never any place, except perhaps Paris on liberation day, so full of hope and glory as Cuba then.
For us, there was the tremendous excitement of just being there, the
thrill of standing in the center of History.   WARREN MILLER[3]

. . . it seems sometimes as if the whole country is high on some benef-
icent kind of speed, and has been for years.   SUSAN SONTAG[4]

Each of my two visits to Cuba was a pilgrimage and an adventure.
                                                         JONATHAN KOZOL[5]

The alienation of the 60s and the discovery of Cuba as a new source of
political inspiration, or counter-model to American (and other Western)
societies, did not precisely coincide. In the beginning enthusiasm about
Cuba was less a product of a social crisis—such as was the case in the
early 1930s when the admiration of the Soviet Union surged against the
background of the Depression—than a form of escape from what the social critics considered the stifling atmosphere and stagnation of the
1950s. Cuba was the welcome relief, the outlet for the accumulated frustrations, the counterpoint to a rather unrevolutionary period in American (and Western European) history. It was an alternative not so much
to a crisis-torn, tottering capitalism, but to a smug, undynamic, inau-

thentic social order (especially in the United States). Many intellectuals turned to Cuba, at any rate during the first revolutionary years, more out of despair with the durability of their own society, showing few signs of imminent collapse, rather than because it offered a feasible alternative for replacing their own social system. ("The young intellectual living in the United States inhabits an ugly void," wrote LeRoi Jones. "He cannot use what is around him, neither can he revolt against it.")[6] Just as important was Cuba's role in proving that the socialist transformations dreamt of in the philosophy of Marx were not preempted by the Soviet case, which by the time of Castro's revolution was thoroughly discredited even among left-wing intellectuals. It was of crucial theoretical and personal importance, for some Marxist intellectuals, to find a new, unsullied incarnation of their hopes. Paul Baran, the economist, was one of them.

"The Cuban Revolution," Baran declared, "was born with a silver spoon in its mouth." Having come to power with tremendous popular support and comparatively minor internal opposition, the Cuban revolutionaries, he believed, could bypass an extended period of collective sacrifices. In this "paradisiac garden," the agricultural problems would melt away as the potential economic surplus, which "assumes . . . gigantic proportions," was rapidly actualized. "Enabled . . . to organize an immediate improvement of the wretched living conditions of the masses, the Cuban Revolution is spared the excruciating but ineluctable compulsion that has beset all preceding socialist revolutions: the necessity to force a tightening of people's belts today in order to lay the foundations for a better tomorrow."[7]*

In turn, Paul Sweezy, a political economist, succeeded not only in rekindling his hopes in a better realization of socialism but in restoring his faith in mankind:

> To be with these people, to see with your own eyes how they are rehabilitating and transforming a whole nation, to share their dreams of the great tasks and achievements that lie ahead—these are purifying

---

* In fact such belt tightening has not been avoided. Neither food nor consumer goods have been abundant, and at the time of this writing a system of comprehensive rationing persists. There have been recent (1980) reports of graffiti in Havana protesting food shortages. Moreover, besides the scarcities which characterize the Cuban economy, inequalities have also surfaced: between the elites and the masses, between foreign tourists and the natives as well as the citizens of Soviet bloc nations stationed in Cuba and the Cubans. Both categories of strangers benefit from special shops, prices, accommodations, and goods and services not available for ordinary people.[8]

and liberating experiences. You come away with your faith in the human race restored.[9]

Thus Cuba was "discovered" before estrangement intensified and the rejection of society became a mass phenomenon in Western societies. There were obvious historical reasons for this: the Cuban Revolution triumphed at the end of 1958, and its romantic heyday lasted through approximately 1960–61. Dennis Wrong noted that "Castro's triumph coincided with the closing years of the Eisenhower administration . . ." which many liberal and potentially radical intellectuals found dull, insidiously conformist, and lacking in idealism and social conscience.[10] Cuba offered a welcome contrast for those who longed for drama, heroism, and new departures in politics:

> Cuba represents several "firsts": the first successful popular social revolution with a worldwide impact in many years; the first political event in Latin America for decades to have had great repercussions in the United States; the first under-developed country to produce a leader capable of moving Western intellectuals to entranced identification with him; the first country geographically remote from the Communist bloc nations to pattern itself internally on them and to give them its full allegiance; the first country to become a victim of an American act of aggression since the beginning of the cold war.[11]

In short, the Cuban Revolution was "a fresh new cause" which appeared quite different from the state socialist bureaucracies of Eastern Europe and the Soviet Union, further discredited by Khrushchev's revelations in 1956. Yet if the old leftists among the intellectuals approached Cuba with a sense of relief for appearing so different from Soviet-type societies, their predisposition to believe in the genuineness and durability of these differences was not so dissimilar from that of the new generation of youthful radicals.[12]

On the whole, the patterns in the attitudes and attitude changes toward Cuba were less clear-cut than corresponding patterns regarding the Soviet Union. While the interest in and enthusiasm toward the Soviet system peaked during the early 1930s, that is, almost a decade and a half after the revolution of 1917, it was the revolutionary beginnings of the Cuban regime which instantly and widely attracted Western intellectuals in the United States as well as Western Europe. Such affections toward the new regime were intense during the first few years, and much of it lingered on throughout the entire decade of the 1960s. Even when disillusionment set in (at different times for different people) it was neither as massive nor as dramatic as it had been in the Soviet case earlier. There was more quiet disenchantment than angry denunciation or pained rejection. Many of the previously enthusiastic intellectuals preferred to keep their change of heart or soul-searching to themselves and tried to salvage some of their initial admiration.

A number of developments and events accounted for the declining appeal of Cuba during the late 1960s and through the 1970s. Che Guevara, identified with the most idealistic aspects of the revolution and the most admired leader next to Castro, died in 1967. There was a steady growth of Soviet ties and influences, reflected among other things in Castro's support of the Soviet invasion of Czechoslovakia in 1968 and more recently of Afghanistan. There was the arrest and confession of the poet Padilla in 1971, and the persecution of homosexuals. The 10-millon-ton sugar harvest did not materialize in 1970, while the attempt to achieve it did much harm to the economy, increasingly regimented as the 60s came to a close. Rationing and scarcities stubbornly persisted. Throughout the 1970s there was a gradual but perceptible abandonment of the more idealistic and revolutionary features of the regime: material incentives came to prevail, after all the heated arguments and avowals, over moral ones at the place of work; the militia was phased out, new ranks and uniforms introduced in the army; restrictions were imposed on the mobility of labor; it became apparent that the Committee for the Defense of the Revolution was as much an auxiliary of the police as an incarnation of the new communal spirit.

Nevertheless, some of the appeal of Cuba persisted despite such set-backs, although the composition of the admirers has changed. Certainly some of the most famous dropped by the wayside* but new enthusiasts

---

* Simone de Beauvoir wrote (evidently also on Sartre's behalf): "There is one country we looked upon, for a while, as the very embodiment of socialist hopes—Cuba. It very soon stopped being a land of freedom—homosexuals were persecuted and the least trace of nonconformity in dress made the wearer suspect. And yet on the whole the air was easier to breathe in Cuba than in the USSR. . . . The discussion at the congress [the January 1968 Cultural Congress] was perfectly free and open. . . . All our friends who had attended . . . spoke of it with enthusiastic approval on their return.

"Very soon they were obliged to eat their words. In that same year Castro adopted a more cautious attitude. . . . In July he uttered no word in favour of the Mexican students murdered by the police, and Cuba took part in the Mexican Olympic Games. His speech after the entry of Soviet troops into Czechoslovakia showed that he was now unreservedly following the policy of the USSR. He has never diverged from this attitude since then. . . . Since they are condemned to near-famine, the people are unsatisfied, and their discontent leads to repressive measures. In an atmosphere of this kind intellectuals are allowed no freedom of any sort. As early as 1969 the museum of modern art was closed and the cultural budget

came forward, especially after American policy-makers decided in 1976–77 to move closer to the reestablishment of diplomatic and trade relations. This new group of sympathizers included politicians, journalists, businessmen eager for new trade, a few intellectuals who tenaciously clung to their early commitments,[15] and some who belatedly discovered the accomplishments of the regime.[16] The Venceremos Brigade maintained continuity in the veneration of Cuba and, in effect, institutionalized a type of annual pilgrimage which combined sightseeing with work and systematic pro-Cuban propaganda upon return. (". . . the trip itself is only half of the Brigade experience. Throughout the year across the United States, brigadiers are active—hosting discussions and rallies, sponsoring films, showing slides, appearing on talk shows and panels—in an effort to break through the blockade of misinformation about Cuba.")[17]

The attitudes among members of the Venceremos Brigade represented both the extremes of social criticism directed at American society and the extremes of reverence toward Cuba. A journalist not unsympathetic toward Cuba commented in 1977 on these attitudes:

> the brigade's tendency to chant slogans at every opportunity, and to give standing ovations to every stirring phrase in every speech, left me standing aside. . . .
> Nor was the brigade's atmosphere conducive to a critical approach. All too often the *brigadista's* response to Cuba did not go beyond "Oh, wow!"

Evidently there was continuity not only in the brigade members' attitude toward the U.S. and Cuba (the expressions of estrangement and admiration quoted earlier were published in 1968) but also toward one another:

> if the *brigadistas* tended to gaze upon Cuba with adoring eyes, they did not feel the same about one another. Even with Maoists and

---

cut to a minimum. Five hundred youths were arrested for having long hair. In January 1971 Castro promulgated his own version of the Soviet law against the 'idle.' . . . The charge of 'parasitism' allows the most arbitrary forms of persecution and imprisonment. In April the poet Padilla was denounced as counter-revolutionary and gaoled; he was released after having signed a 'self-criticism,' a document filled with utter nonsense from beginning to end—it accuses René Dumont and Karol of being agents of the CIA! . . . Castro has also threatened other counter-revolutionary intellectuals. The 'honeymoon of the revolution' that had so enchanted us is over and done with."[13] It should be noted that the disenchantment was mutual. Castro had no patience with intellectuals criticizing his regime "no matter how moderate or qualified" their criticisms were.[14]

Trotskyists absent, the faction-ridden state of the movement was obvious. Politics was discussed from dawn to past midnight. . . . But the mood often strayed from comradely exchange toward uglier emotions. Charges of sexism, racism, liberalism, revisionism and ultra-leftism left scars. . . . All this suggested one reason for the *brigadista's* passionate and indiscriminate embrace of Cuba: it helped to maintain a group spirit that might have otherwise turned surly.[18]

The institutionalization and growing respectability of visiting Cuba in the second half of the 1970s had other manifestations besides the annual journeys of the Venceremos* group and senatorial tours. At Hunter College in New York the "Center for Cuban Studies" in conjunction with the "Center for Lifelong Learning" offered a course on Cuba followed by a trip. Unmistakably this was an exercise in political propaganda, signified both by the fact that the instructor for this course was none other than Sandra Levinson (also director of the Center for Cuban Studies) who was the co-editor of the volume-length celebration of Cuba published in 1971[20] and by the circumstance that the course had explicitly excluded former Cuban citizens whose perspectives presumably would have conflicted with those of the instructor.[21]

Thus, while many of the early admirers of the Cuban Revolution became disenchanted and fell silent by the second half of the 1970s, the persistent supporters (such as the Venceremos Brigade) were joined by newly interested politicians and businessmen. (In the Soviet case all three strands merged more or less simultaneously: intellectuals were most enthusiastic at the time when diplomatic relations were resumed, while businessmen were keen and eager since the late 1920s.) Irving Louis Horowitz, the well-known sociologist, who had been more sympathetic to Cuba earlier, commented on such recent developments:

> The Cuba lobby is comprised essentially of two elements—liberal senators and conservative businessmen. . . .
>
> The vanity of Congress-and-business people is such that it takes little more than a casual wining and dining, and a midnight visitation, to turn the heads of the American guests of the Cuban leadership. Senator George McGovern, kingpin figure in the Cuba lobby . . . rarely misses the opportunity of noting that "Castro is something of a Ho Chi Minh of Cuba"† . . .

* For over a decade they had no difficulty recruiting, after careful screening, approximately 200 enthusiasts annually among "people who are involved in sectors of the progresive movement . . . [or] some sectors of the movement for social change"[19] as the pamphlet put it.

† As if such a comparison would by itself confer instant legitimation on Castro and vindicate his policies.

There is a strong whiff of Vietnam that hangs over everything that McGovern says, and it leads to some facile formulas: tiny Vietnam, tiny Cuba.

McGovern's attitude toward Cuba and Vietnam illustrates the durability of the underdog image as a source of political sympathy well beyond any historical justification. Thus Vietnam which defeated the United States and has occupied Laos and Cambodia and threatens Thailand is no better candidate for the underdog status than is Cuba with the largest military establishment in all Latin America and an expeditionary force of approximately 50,000 soldiers in Africa. Presumably for McGovern and others of similar political disposition, the single major factor conferring underdog status on a country is its involvement in some conflict with the United States, since the latter retains the overpowering topdog image despite all recent evidence to the contrary.

As far as American (and most other) businessmen were concerned, it seems true as Horowitz argued that "the business community knows no politics other than those of doing business. . . ." Yet even businessmen and especially American businessmen feel sometimes uncomfortable about doing business with dictatorships. It is for that reason that the search for business contacts with Cuba had been accompanied by journalistic and public-relations efforts aimed at redefining and prettifying the Cuban regime. Kirby Jones and Frank Mankiewicz, producers of a very favorable book on Cuba and of an exclusive television interview with Castro, have been in the forefront of such efforts.* Perhaps it is such squeamishness which impels American businessmen to convince themselves—or seek out those who would convince them—that the repressive regime they are about to trade with has some merit. Mr. Kendall, head of the Pepsi company and a leading proponent of trade with the Soviet Union, exemplifies these attitudes against greater odds, since these days the American public is less receptive to favorable reassessments of the Soviet Union than to those of Cuba. It is also harder to find journalists or intellectuals willing to redefine the Soviet Union in a more favorable and less critical manner.

* Horowitz had this to say of their activities: "The interface between the business and political sides of the Cuba lobby is the offices of Kirby Jones and the organization he runs, called Alamar Associates. Jones himself is a veteran of the presidential campaigns of Kennedy and McGovern, having served as press secretary in the 1972 election campaign. . . . A further linkage is through the offices of Frank Mankiewicz, formerly McGovern's campaign director, who along with Jones formed the National Executive Committee. This organization brought politicians and business leaders together in seminars, which led to the trips to Cuba. . . ."[22]

On a smaller scale and less conspicuously, a similar scenario has been played out in the academic world. As scholars sought to establish or re-establish ties with Cuba, the retention (or development) of a critical perspective has become an impediment.[23]

All in all the appeals of the Cuban system did not fluctuate as sharply as those of the Soviet, which ripened gradually in the 1920s, reached great intensity during the early 1930s, declined after the Purges, and revived once more during World War II to fall off completely in the post–World War II period and decline even further after Khrushchev's 1956 speech. The years of peak appeal—from the victory of the Cuban Revolution in 1958 through 1961—were not followed by a sudden or abrupt decline. As late as in 1968 in connection with the Cultural Congress, it was clear that Cuba still had many prominent friends among intellectuals in many Western and non-Western countries. Those attending the Congress included David Dellinger, David Cooper (the English author and psychiatrist), Jules Feiffer, Eric Hobsbawm, Magnus Enzensberger, Susan Sontag, Sir Herbert Read, Arnold Wesker, and many others of similar prominence.[24]

The revival and persistence of a measure of sympathy toward the Castro regime, in the United States in particular, was probably also related to the growing difficulty of maintaining an emotional and ideological investment in China in the post-Mao period. The retreat from revolutionary idealism in China appeared sharper than corresponding developments in Cuba. In Cuba there seemed to be a greater continuity with the heroic revolutionary days symbolized by the presence of Castro, whereas China might have appeared to be taken over after Mao by a group of aged "faceless [party] bureaucrats." Moreover, the new Chinese leaders openly reversed and covertly denounced the inspiring revolutionary policies of their great predecessor. The shifts which have taken place in Cuba were less conspicuous and not widely noted abroad. Those who wished to persist in embracing a highly idealized image of the Cuban regime could fall back on techniques and attitudes familiar from the 1930s in regard to the Soviet Union. Ronald Radosh, a friendly critic of Cuba, wrote:

> To many North American radicals, the contradictions of Cuban policy are to be ignored or wished away. Their response to Cuba is reminiscent of that shown by many Western travelers to the Soviet Union during the 1920s and 1930s. It was during that period when an institutionalized model for travel to socialist nations was developed. Radicals, wary of life and politics in America, turned their own alienation

from and despair about the United States outward. Identification with the great Soviet experiment became a substitute for their own impotence at home. Any criticism of Russia, any candid discussion of Soviet problems . . . was considered grist for the mill of pro-Axis and reactionary forces. . . . Like those of the Old Left, many members of the New Left have come to idealize one or another socialist country. The process was explained by Todd Gitlin back in 1968: "For generations the American Left has externalized good: we needed to tie our fates to someone, somewhere in the world who was seizing the chances for a humane society." Cuba became that place for many of the New Left.

Once Cuba was chosen for that purpose it became difficult to look upon the process of the Revolution dispassionately. Like the Russians, the Cubans arranged carefully guided tours. . . . But it was not the tours that produced a distorted judgement. The visitor saw only what he or she wanted. . . .

Like travellers to Russia in the 1920s,* members of the group that traveled to Cuba with me revealed a familiar psychological attitude. To criticize Cuba, they argued, was to aid the Revolution's enemies. . . . The job of North American radicals is to "offer political support," not to indulge in the bourgeois luxury of independent criticism. . . .

The argument is an old one: refrain from criticism, lest you fall into the waiting hands of reactionary forces.[25]

These reflections recall the argument proposed earlier in this book, that the rejection of one's own society and the admiration for another one are indissolubly linked, and that rejection precedes the projection of hopes. The point may be obvious, yet we need to remind ourselves of this relationship to fully comprehend the characteristic reluctance to come to grips with the emerging realities of the new societies when they conflict with the original hopes and expectations. (Few would divorce their spouses in the knowledge that they will not be able to find a better partner. Belief in alternatives is vital for almost any form of rejection. By the same token the propaganda campaigns and vigorous censorship in so many "socialist" countries need to be interpreted less as an effort to persuade the population of the merits of the system under which they live than an effort to deprive them of the contemplation of alternatives.)

Frances Fitzgerald, another sympathizer with the Cuban Revolution (better known as a writer critical of American involvement in Vietnam), also observed that "many North American radicals who visit Cuba or live there have performed a kind of surgery on their critical faculties

* The attitudes referred to became much more obvious and widespread in the 1930s.

and reduced their conversation to a form of baby talk, in which everything is wonderful, including the elevator that does not work and the rows of Soviet tanks on military parade that are 'in the hands of the people.' "[26] Jorge Edwards, a Chilean writer and former diplomat under Allende, representing his country in Cuba, also pondered the suppression of critical impulses among intellectuals:

> we showed a perhaps more serious and ominous intellectual submissiveness toward Havana's dictates. The reasons for keeping silent were familiar; the fragility of the revolutionary island and the terrible power of the blockade could be compared with the solitary socialism of Stalin's years, but history had changed and we new Latin American writers, blinded by pig-headedness of youth, had not assimilated its lessons.[27]

For others who suspended their critical faculties it was perhaps a question of priorities. Theodore Draper wrote: "In this conception [of socialism] all that essentially matters is that the economy should be nationalized. The nationalizing state may be murderous, mendacious, guilty of duplicity, brutal and arbitrary, but it is still 'socialist.' "[28] It must be added that the fetish of nationalization, on the part of those who give it such a high priority, is linked to the desire for social equality and the rejection of capitalism. Therefore allowances are made once this basic evil is believed to have been done way with. Regimes seen as being "on the right track" (by eliminating the private control over the means of production) are then given every benefit of doubt.

In other instances the suspension of critical sentiment and uncritical endorsement resulted from putting form ahead of content, or certain institutional change ahead of a careful scrutiny of its substance. Horowitz commented on this attitude: "True, schools *are* widespread, education *is* universal; but curiously, what is taught therein remains unreported. Children do indeed work 15 hours weekly in farm labor; but to celebrate child labor in Cuba hardly represents necessary or sufficient grounds for full diplomatic relationships."[29]

As in the Soviet case, contextual redefinition, resting on such favorable predispositions, profoundly altered the visitors' perception of the social-political landscape. Thus Angela Davis could observe that "The job of cutting cane had become qualitatively different since the revolution" not because the job itself became less arduous but because "during the cane season everyone pitched in" (neglecting to note that some did much less "pitching in" than others) and because the workers were no longer exploited. Likewise giant billboard posters, held in contempt when filled with the sloganized praise of capitalist products, were instantly transformed into devices of dignity and beauty when they advertised the blessings of the political system ("Many of these billboards had been used in the past to advertise U.S. products. . . . I felt great satisfaction knowing that the Cubans had ripped down these trademarks of global exploitation and had replaced them with warm and stirring symbols that had real meaning for the people. The sense of human dignity was palpable").[30] She was also capable of complaining of "the incredible bureaucracy in which one must become embroiled merely as a prerequisite for living an ordinary life" in Western countries, without noting the far more demanding and encompassing routines and regulations which are the "prerequisites of ordinary life"[31] in countries such as Cuba (or the Soviet Union) which she admired. Presumably if pressed she would have admitted to bureaucracy in socialist countries but would have dismissed its significance on the grounds either that these bureaucracies were fundamentally benevolent or that they were transient aberrations rather than systemic features of the social system in question.

Since the above was written, approximately 120,000 Cubans poured out of Cuba within a short period of time (in the spring of 1980) adding a new element to the recent perceptions and assessments of the Cuban regime. The bulk of them consisted of people who grew up under the Castro regime and were difficult to classify as remnants of the old ruling or middle classes contaminated by the values of capitalism and unable to adapt to the new system. Those who could be described in such terms were among the approximately one million Cubans who had left since 1958 but prior to the recent wave. The new refugees like the previous ones sought to escape both material hardships and political repression.[32]

Notwithstanding such self-evident expressions of popular discontent with the system, there are already some indications that some supporters of the regime will find ways to retain their beliefs. Thus for example Philip Brenner of the Institute of Policy Studies in Washington dismissed the recent refugees as materialistic malcontents whose dissatisfaction was no reason to pass judgment on the Cuban regime; moreover (despite their age) "they were animated by nostalgia for the Batista regime." By contrast, a more innovative sympathizer, Andrew Zimbalist, an economist at Smith College, resourcefully suggested that far from being contaminated by the past, the new refugees ("in their twenties") left because they did not know how bad things used to be before Castro and thus had no basis for comparison.[33] Such explanations of the exodus left few age groups properly qualified to appreciate the benefits of the regime. Attempts to reconcile the phenomenon of refugees with the preservation of the image of superiority of the system they leave behind were not limited to the Cuban case, as similar responses to the Indochinese boat people will also show. The attitudes involved in these rationalizations suggest once more that the appeals of these soceties have far less to do with their ascertainable achievements, and their reflections in popular satisfaction, than with the estrangement from one's own society.

A Charismatic Leader

Of all the political systems considered in this book which provoked widespread (if transient) enthusiasm among Western intellectuals, it was in Cuba that the personality of the leader was the most important. Despite the enormous weight of similarly positioned leaders—such as Stalin, Mao, Ho Chi Minh, Enver Hoxha, or Kim Il Sung—it was in Cuba that the entire social-political system was the most clearly and convincingly legitimated (and authenticated) by its unique leader. In short, a major appeal of the Cuban system was Fidel Castro. There were a variety of explanations of this; some had to do with the personality and style of Castro, others with the spirit of the times. Let us start with the latter.

By the late 1950s many people in the West, and especially intellectuals, were ready to be receptive to the appeals of a charismatic leader—within or outside their own societies. In the previous decades most political leaders with a heroic bent either proved to be evil or lost their charisma to the corruptions of political office and secure power. They included Hitler, Mussolini, and Stalin. (Curiously, Tito, despite excellent heroic qualifications, never—not even in his early phases—quite managed to capture the imagination of Western intellectuals.) De Gaulle might have been charismatic but hardly revolutionary. Others had some of the required attributes but lacked the dynamism and vivid interaction with the masses.

Throughout the late 1940s and the 50s the lack of the heroic element in Western societies has created a predisposition to find it in the most unlikely places: among entertainers, sportsmen, gangsters. The retreat of the heroic from the life of Western societies did not mean that the thirst for it has also disappeared. The new forms of the heroic and their personifications have been of a diluted, synthetic quality without the moral underpinnings more in evidence in the past. The "hero" of our era has often been the transient celebrity catering more to the desire for novelty, excitement, and vicarious gratification than to moral impulses and inspiration.[34] This development may in part be explained by the vested interest of the mass media in manufacturing new heroes and celebrities to capture the interest of their audience. In the process the distinction between hero and celebrity has become increasingly blurred. These developments may also be understood, as Daniel Boorstin emphasized, with reference to moral uncertainties and confused intellectual values which provide few guidelines as to what human accomplishments and attributes are worthy of attention and admiration.

The sources of the hero worship in our times, proposed by Hans Speier decades ago, are still with us:

> There is a sharp contrast between heroic society and modern social organization. Power now is centralized and largely anonymous; law has restrained self-reliance. . . . A truly bewildering specialization of work . . . has created a web of interdependence which all of us help to spin and in which each of us seems caught. . . . We are divorced from the naive and full assertion of life. . . .
>
> Modern hero worship is a devastating inarticulate criticism of the shortcomings of a civilization in which the goals of socially approved aspirations are difficult to attain, in which the rewards of conformity bring only scant and clandestine release from the self-restraint expected of conformists. . . . Modern man, brought up with the expectation that happiness is a right, finds at best that life offers diversions —"fun" but not "joy." While he may not be aware of the difference, it is in hero worship that he betrays a deep need for release from the yoke of civilization.[35]

More recently Robert Nisbet observed: "It is almost universally conceded that ours is an age of singular mediocrity in its leadership—a word I use to include spheres beyond politics alone." Having surveyed various areas of contemporary life—including politics, arts, science, scholarship and others—Nisbet concludes that "in area after area we have been stripped of heroes. . . . Between heroism and modernity there has been a fateful conflict. The acids of modernity, which include egalitarianism, scepticism and institutionalized ridicule in the popular arts, have eaten away much of the base on which heroism flourished."[36]

The retreat of the heroic element in Western life fed of many sources. We have been losing even evil heroes. There has been a growing tendency since World War II to see as sick, maladjusted, or socially undesirable what was earlier viewed as evil. Eichman exemplified "the banality of evil,"[37] and the moral implications of his actions shrank. The tremendous interest and morbid fascination created by Stanley Milgram's experiments on obedience to authority[38] mirrored the predisposition to the view that no distinction need be attached to even the most repugnant forms of behavior, since anybody is capable of engaging in them under appropriate external pressures. Also, with declining belief in individual responsibility, conceptions of good and evil became harder to maintain. If it was no longer possible to attach any sort of distinction to even the Eichman-like behavior; if even the most monstrous forms of cruelty and inhumanity could be derived from obedience to authority; if, as was increasingly believed, anybody could commit misdeeds of murderous proportions under certain conditions; if, in short, evil was perceived as banal, commonplace, and impersonal—then clearly it could not retain any diabolic-heroic dimension.

Thus the decline of the heroic element in modern life is inseparable from the growing moral-ethical relativism which, in turn, is an obvious by-product of the advanced secularization of Western societies. Insofar as the religious roots of morality dried up, and religious definitions of good and evil ceased to carry conviction, the only alternative source of such definitions could be found in intensely held political ideologies and beliefs, such as were upheld in distant, revolutionary societies. Among the appeals of these societies were their invigoratingly heroic aspects to which many intellectuals turned their attention.

Norman Mailer's confession was characteristic of the impulses and needs which entered into the initial veneration of Castro. He wrote: "So Fidel Castro, I announce to the City of New York that you gave all of us who are alone in this country . . . some sense that there were heroes in the world. One felt life in one's overargued blood as one picked up in our newspapers the details of your voyage. . . . It was as if the ghost of Cortez had appeared in our century riding Zapata's white horse. You were the first and greatest hero to appear in the world since the Second War." Mailer also hoped that Castro's historical mission would prove durable: "you give a bit of life to the best and most passionate men and women all over the earth, you are the answer to the argument of Commissars and Statesmen that revolutions cannot last, that they turn corrupt or total or eat their own."[39]

Sartre's account of his meetings with Castro and other leaders offers an even more remarkable illustration of the susceptibility of Western intellectuals to the appeals of strong, routine-shattering, charismatic leaders. While his observations may reveal more of Sartre than of those he writes about, they provide an unintended summary of some of the characteristic longings of many contemporary Western intellectuals. Not surprisingly, Sartre was most impressed by Castro's authenticity, the unity between word and action, theory and practice that he personified. Thus Sartre reports Castro's explanation of what he meant by being a professional revolutionary:

> "I can't stand injustice."

> What pleased me in this anwer was that this man—who fought, who is still fighting for a whole people and who has no other interest than theirs—first recalled for me his personal passions, his private life.

> . . . He learned the inanity of words.

There is more to Sartre's admiration than respect for devotion to social justice and the selflessness Castro embodied. Castro and his cohorts exerted a magnetic, almost hypnotic influence on him and rekindled hopes of transcending the human condition; they conjured up a new version of the age-old dream of the triumph of mind over the body, spirit over the flesh. They ignited his imagination with a promise of immortality and sense of rejuvenation. This is how Sartre describes a visit to Che Guevara's office at midnight:

> I heard the door close behind my back and I lost both the memory of my old fatigue and any notion of the hour. Among these fully awake men, at the height of their powers, sleeping doesn't seem like a natural need, just a routine of which they had more or less freed themselves. [Sartre too, electrified, as it were, sleeps less during these days, he reports] . . . they have all excluded the routine alternation of lunch and dinner from their daily program.

> . . . Of all these night watchmen, Castro is the most wide awake. Of all these fasting people, Castro can eat the most and fast the longest. [They] . . . exercise a veritable dictatorship over their own needs . . . they roll back the limits of the possible.[40]

Powerful, dynamic, and heroic renaissance men exercising iron-willed command over their body and mind, tirelessly reshaping their society— this was the exciting vision many Western intellectuals, such as Sartre, were ready to embrace. Theirs was a full-blown hero worship (though not always as extreme as that of Sartre) suggestive of a variety of social and personal conditions from which such cults spring.° Thus beyond the

° Hans Speier's further observations on modern hero worship seem applicable here: "Modern hero worship is a safe and underhanded way of obtaining vicariously what life refuses to give freely. Hero worship is a worship of active unbridled life . . . modern hero worship comprises three main components: first the primeval veneration of strength and freely chosen risks in defiance of Christian and middle class ethic; second, the specific misery created by the clash of socially approved other attractions of the new societies, the appeal of the heroic looms large and is embodied both in the styles of the leaders and the newly meaningful and dramatic aspects of everyday life no longer humdrum or prosaic.

For Abbie Hoffman, as for Mailer and Sartre, Castro's appeal had much to do with the macho image, the condottiere on the white horse—or tank: "Fidel sits on the side of a tank rumbling into Havana on New Year's day. . . . Girls throw flowers at the tank and rush to tug playfully at his black beard. He laughs joyously and pinches a few rumps. . . . The tank stops in the city square. Fidel lets the gun drop to the ground, slaps his thigh and stands erect. He is like a mighty penis coming to life, and when he is tall and straight, the crowd immediately is transformed."[42]

On his visit to the United States, it was reported, ". . . Fidel, to the stupefaction of everyone, suddenly jumped over the barrier [in the Bronx Zoo] into the lion's den. The diplomats and the FBI didn't dare to shout to him to get out of there for fear of startling the lions. Fidel stood there for some minutes without the lions paying any heed to him and then left calmly."[43] (A story to gladden the heart of Norman Mailer.)

Castro, like the true charismatic leader, inspired his followers and was totally devoted to them. Elizabeth Sutherland (journalist, critic, book and arts editor of *The Nation*) wrote:

> He [Castro] seems, first of all, utterly devoted to the welfare of his people—and his people are the poor, not the rich. When he speaks, it is as if his own dedication and energy were being directly transfused into his listeners with an almost physical force.* Possessed of an extraordinary instinct for rhythm and voice pitch, he builds his speeches . . . like long poems.[45]

Frank Mankiewicz and Kirby Jones found him

> one of the most charming and entertaining men either of us had ever met. . . . Castro is personally overpowering. U.S. political writers would call it a simple [sic] case of charisma, but it is more than that. Political leaders often can be and are charismatic in a public sense, but rather normal in more private moments. Such is not the case with

---

values of work, humility and self sought happiness as a right with a life experience in which aspirations are curbed, desires censored and in which risks are ubiquitous but imposed; third, the passivity which modern civilization promotes. . . ."[41]

* Theodore Draper offered a more somber assessment of such performances: "The individuals in the outdoor spectacles have a direct relationship only to Castro personally, not to each other. The demonstrations are as 'democratic' as Hitler's Nuremberg rallies and Mussolini's balcony speeches once were."[44]

Fidel Castro. He remains one of the few truly electric personalities in a world in which his peers seem dull and pedestrian.[46]

Characteristically, different observers responded to different aspects of Castro's personality and appeals, or projected different attributes on him. If Sartre, Mailer, or Abbie Hoffman were most receptive to strength and masculinity, others of a more anarchistic or anti-elitist disposition succeeded in discovering new forms of leadership associated with Castro. Julius Lester, the black writer, noted:

> To become a public personality in Western society is to become a prisoner of a media-created image. To become a public personality in a revolutionary society is to become so at one with the people that quite unconsciously they see you in them and you see yourself in them. The West says a "cult of personality" exists in the figures of Mao and Fidel. That is not true. Revolutionary consciousness and revolutionary commitment have destroyed the ego in Mao and Fidel, and in that destruction, they as men became free. Mao is China. Fidel is Cuba. China is Mao. Cuba is Fidel.[47]

For Saul Landau, Castro was "a man who has been steeped in democracy . . . a humble man. . . ."[48]

While visitors might have differed in their emphasis on the heroic versus the humble, they all seemed to agree on the warmth, compassion, and humanitarianism of the Cuban leader. Leo Huberman and Paul Sweezy wrote: "First and foremost, Fidel is a passionate humanitarian . . . in the meaningful sense that he feels compassion for human suffering, hates injustice because it causes unnecessary suffering, and is totally committed to building in Cuba a society in which the poor and the underprivileged shall be able to hold up their heads. . . . He treats people within this framework—kindly, sternly, implacably, according to their actual or potential role in creating or hindering the creation of the good society."[49] Angela Davis reported that "Talking to almost any Cuban about Fidel, it soon became clear that they did not see him as being anything more than extraordinarily intelligent, exceptionally committed and an extremely warm human being endowed with great leadership talents. He made mistakes, human errors, and people loved him in large part because of his honesty with them. Fidel was their leader, but most important he was also their brother in the largest sense of the word."[50]*

---

* This completely brotherly, humble, egalitarian image of Castro was not universally shared even among the sympathetic visitors. According to David Caute, "Castro is like a loving, intelligent and autocratic father who, when he has decided what is best for his children, sits them on his lap and asks them gently to express their own wishes . . . when they are finished he 'persuades' them precisely why they

Senator McGovern found him, "In private conversation at least, soft-spoken, shy, sensitive," whereas Castro's views made Julian Bond think of the "connection between socialism and Christianity."[52]

More than any other leader in recent times Castro (and Che Guevara) impressed the visiting intellectuals by conveying to them the image of a fellow-intellectual, but with a difference: an intellectual in power, a doer, a maker of history, not a critic or dreamer. Nobody quite fitted this image so well since Lenin. Castro's qualifications for the part were unique. First, he was a true revolutionary, a guerilla fighter in the mountains, young, strong, tall, well built, spontaneous, and unpretentious. Here was the man who at last bridged the gap between word and deed and promised to redeem the good name of socialism after the discredit that was brought upon it by Stalinism and bureaucratic state socialism. Second, not only was he a doer; he was a talker too (often nonstop for hours), willing to discuss any idea. With great skill he cultivated important Western intellectuals, at any rate during the beginning stages of the new regime. Who among them could have resisted attentions such as were lavished on C. Wright Mills:

> One day, Fidel Castro had looked him up in his hotel, telling him straight out that his *Power Elite* had been a bedside book of most of the *guerrilleros* in the Sierra Maestra. Castro invited him to come on a tour—una vuelta—of the country. They spent three and a half days together, devoting an average of eighteen hours in every twenty-four to discussions.[53]

He also read Karol's book and "wanted to discuss it."[54] Waldo Frank, Sartre, Senator McGovern, Ernesto Cardenal, and many others were taken on whirlwind tours conducted by Castro using helicopters or jeeps often driven by himself. According to Senator McGovern, "The reality of the man matches the image. He was, as always, dressed in freshly pressed military fatigues. Youthful in appearance at the age of forty-eight, hair and beard still black, cigar constantly in hand, he was

---

really want to do what he wants them to do." K. S. Karol commented on Castro's "aristocratic conception of political power and leadership: the men who 'know best,' 'deserve trust' . . . ." Elsewhere he expressed misgivings about Castro's tendency to be "an infallible expert in all fields of technical endeavor. . . ." He also noted that "All his [Castro's] arguments betray an aristocratic spirit, a faith in the role of the elite, rather than trust in the converse of equals, in fruitful exchange of ideas between the rank and file and its leaders." In turn, René Dumont recalled that "Traveling with Castro I sometimes had the impression that I was visiting Cuba with its owner, who was showing off its fields and pastures, its cows if not its men."[51]

poised, confident and questioning. . . . He responds knowledgeably on almost any subject from agricultural methods to Marxist dialectics to American politics."[55]

He had everything going for him, everything a Western intellectual (or a type of Western intellectual) would admire and long for; he was an aristocrat of sorts, son of a landowner, graduate of law school, authentic underdog guerilla fighter, subsequently the holder of great power unhindered by parties, parliaments, sordid interest groups, petty politicians—a man with dreams and the power to implement them. He was also well read. (While Castro was in jail, David Caute tells us, he "used the time to read voraciously and eclectically—St. Thomas Aquinas, John of Salisbury, Luther, Knox, Milton, Rousseau, and Tom Paine—any notable authority he could lay his hands on.")[56] As seen by an American admirer, he was "above all an educator of his people and constant self-educator. When he spoke in public, the scene often resembled a huge and very relaxed classroom. . . . A concern with morality, especially honesty, often dominated his teachings."[57]

He was personally checking everything in his country, responding to letters of ordinary people, dropping in at factories, stopping by on beaches, testing the quality of ice cream on the street, finding out directly without intermediaries how his subjects lived and how his underlings carried out his orders and plans. Like the kings and princes of folktales, he would suddenly and unexpectedly materialize in different parts of his realm and minister to the needs of the poor.

> Let's follow him on one of his inspection tours. He finds a bridge in bad shape and gives orders for it to be repaired immediately. Fifty miles further along, his jeep bogs down . . . on a muddy road. . . . "See to it that a good asphalt road is built here." On another occasion (this time during the dry season) an entire agricultural zone is visibly suffering from the drought. "See to it that the area gets a little dam." At another place the crops appear neglected. "I want an agricultural school here."[58]

Castro's attention to detail was a trait he shared with other supreme leaders (such as Stalin, Mao, and Hitler), but Castro was also informal and had a sense of humor. His knowledge seemed awesome and wide-ranging:

> He does know for example . . . the annual construction rate of schools, housing, factories, and hospitals. He knows the number built and being built, their scheduled dates for conclusion, and the building plans projected for the next five to ten years. He knows the number of

students at each level of the educational process, is familiar with the curriculum, knows how many . . . will graduate this year and in 1980 and 1985. He knows the standards for the promotion from one school to the next. . . . He knows the monthly water temperatures at the fishing ports and when they are most favorable for catching various fish. He knows how many feet can be spanned by concrete—and at what stress. And he knows sugar—probably better than anyone in the world. . . . He knows, almost hourly, sugar's price on the world market and is familiar with its fluctuations. . . .

Castro's encyclopedic knowledge does not extend only to things Cuban.[59]*

Vigorous, handsome, passionate, informal, undogmatic, open, humane, superbly accessible and yet immensely powerful, equally interested in problems small and big, knowledgeable of animal husbandry, international affairs, armaments, and the quality of lemonade sold at popular vacation spots—he was a leader easy to warm to even without the strong predisposition the visitors had. Nor was it beneath him to pick up the machete (on selected occasions) and join the masses in cutting sugarcane.[61]

Castro, and his image, had many affinities with the spirit of the times and the unmet needs of many Western intellectuals of the period. As Dennis Wrong put it,

Fidel Castro was a natural hero for the New Left from the first . . . a genuine hero in an age of characterless bureaucratic leaders. Moreover, he and all his men were young and wore unruly beards, the newly publicized symbol of rebellious youth. His air of informality and creative improvisation . . . stood in delightful contrast to the managed appearances of other politicians in this age of TV . . . [he was] determined to carry out without delay genuinely egalitarian reforms . . . Sartre and Mills came back from Cuba reporting that there was something new under the sun. . . .[62]

* The other side of the coin of course was that, as K. S. Karol observed, "A single person cannot be an infallible expert in all fields of technical endeavour, cannot be competent on questions of cattle breeding and irrigation, on the best method of cutting sugar cane and on the advantages of coffee plantations in the *Cordon de la Habana*, not to mention a thousand other spheres calling for special knowledge of the soil and of the political realities." Even more serious were the reproaches of René Dumont (a French agricultural expert invited by Castro and subsequently denounced by him): "Castro is no longer content with his claims to military and political fame and his undeniable value as a human being. He has to feel himself recognized as the leader in both scientific research and agricultural practice. He's the man who knows everything . . . the prolonged exercise of power has convinced him that he understands every problem better than anybody else. . . ."[60]

Just as the Cuban Revolution and the regime it had ushered in differed from other regimes claiming to be socialist (in particular the Soviet Union and its East European satellites), so Castro differed from what had since the death of Stalin been learned about the "real" Stalin (as opposed to his idealized image) and from other socialist leaders who had modeled themselves after Stalin.

Not only Castro but also Che Guevara occupied a special place in the affections of those sympathetic to Cuba. While alive he was reputed to be the most idealistic, self-denying, and puritanical of the Cuban leaders. Sir Herbert Read, the British art historian, compared him with Tolstoi.[63] On top of such attributes he was martyred in the prime of life trying to liberate the poor of Bolivia. Richard Lowenthal observed that "the asceticism and heroic self-sacrifice of Che Guevara have permitted the growth of a legend around him that combines Christ-like features with those of a militant secular leader."[64]

Such human attributes immensely enhanced the credibility and appeal of the policies and institutional transformations the visitors could observe in revolutionary Cuba.

Sense of Community and Purpose

In Cuba the appeals of the sense of community and purpose are so closely intertwined that it seems contrived to discuss them separately. The affinity of these two appeals for one another grows out of the ethos of the 1960s and of the outlook and predisposition of the new generation of pilgrims. Their virtual interchangeability reflected the quality of estrangement in the 1960s characterized by declining levels of theoretical discourse and a somewhat impoverished ideological elaboration of the prevailing discontents. If it was true to say that Marxism in the 60s (and 70s too, one might add) was used more as a myth than a theory, more as a slogan (or collection of slogans) than ideology, and if it was true that political actions were more often based on emotional impulses than on theoretical blueprints, if indeed action-orientation and spontaneity increasingly replaced carefully thought-out political programs, if all that is true, then it should not come as a surprise that the *sense* of purpose overshadowed the specific components of purpose, and the latter, in turn, merged with the sense of community just as ardently sought after.

Cuba, at least in the beginning, made it easy for these susceptibilities to merge. The Cuban Revolution and its leaders were young, appeared flexible, experimental, independent, free of the dead hand of the past; they were not part of the Old Left and its errors, no inheritors of its dogmatism. (David Dellinger wrote of "the restless idealism of the Cuban revolutionaries" and beheld "the possibility of a genuine libertarian communism.")[65] For members of the Venceremos Brigade, "Cuba [was] real, the way a day of childhood is real—all fresh and vibrant and immediate. It is a magnet for visitors from the heart of prehistory. . . . It is a pattern that reveals the whole. . . ."[66] A pragmatic idealism was among the most notable virtues of this new revolution, all the more enticing as it had not fully or narrowly spelled out its objectives and thus seemed replete with limitless possibilities. But certain things were clear from the beginning. This was not going to be a society stamped by the cash nexus which deformed human relationships in the capitalist world. Michael Parenti wrote:

> what struck me and other members of the group about the people in Havana was the absence of the kind of "struggle" one experiences in North American cities. . . . Cubans are not preoccupied with money anxieties of the kind that plague most Americans, and the absence of money problems and all related competitiveness, personal fears and aggression has a palpable effect on social relations.[67]

In the same spirit Ernesto Cardenal, the Nicaraguan priest-poet, commented:

> the streets [of Havana] were filled with people but nobody was buying or selling anything. People were *strolling* through the streets . . . nobody was chasing after money. No face was strained by poverty. There were no . . . prostitutes, no bootblacks, no beggars.[68]

From the very beginnings, visitors perceived a radiant sense of community which characterized the relationship of leaders and the led as well as that of ordinary citizens with one another. Even more than in the Soviet case, community was a central appeal of Cuban socialism. If the Soviet Union in the 1930s was seen as the antidote or polar opposite of the chaos and "rudderlessness" of Western societies, Cuba in the early 60s was the counterpoint to alienation, social isolation, depersonalization, and other ills of mass society. Huey Newton (often referred to as the "chief theoretician" of the Black Panther party and, if so, an intellectual as well as political activist) regarded the major difference between American and Cuban society as being that in the latter "truly everybody is an extended family and [has] concern for everybody else's welfare. . . . They are interested in each other's life in a brotherly way."[69] Likewise members of the Venceremos Brigade "found out that people . . . could love one another. That really blew my mind."[70]

Several factors combined to make the communal-communitarian aspects and appeals so prominent. There were the circumstances of the victory of the Revolution: the small, heroic, and romantic band of guerilla fighters, intellectuals of sorts (many of them) joining forces with the peasants and liberating them from their wretched state. There was also the size of Cuba: a relatively small country, more compact, more capable of creating a sense of community. Perhaps even more importantly, there were also the Latin-Hispanic aspects and the nostalgic stereotypes they evoked especially in North Americans and Northern Europeans. The sense of community perceived in Cuba not only was nurtured by the political designs and ideology of the system, but had its subterranean reservoirs and supports also in the stereotype of the joyful, life-affirming attitude attributed to the musically gifted, song-and-dance-loving natives, their natural and politically engendered vitality. Susan Sontag wrote: "The Cubans know a lot about spontaneity, gaiety, sensuality, and freaking out. They are not linear, desiccated creatures of print-culture. . . . The increase of energy comes because they have found a new focus for it: the community." She also believed that "Perhaps the first thing a visitor to Cuba notices is the enormous energy level. It is still common, as it has been throughout the ten years of the revolution, for people to go without sleep—talking and working several nights a week."[71] Todd Gitlin, radical writer-journalist, related a conversation with a seventeen-year-old tractor driver who informed him that he worked sometimes twenty-four hours a day (" 'You don't sleep?' 'No, don't sleep' ").[72]

As will be recalled, the lack or reduced amount of sleep also made a deep impression on Sartre as he observed the way of life of the young leaders. More generally, it is the apparent combination of high energy levels with the disruption of routinized life styles that is so appealing and is often taken to be the most authentic hallmark of revolutionary situations and periods. Members of the Venceremos Brigade wondered, "Do the Cubans ever get tired? On four, five, six hours of sleep all they do is cut cane and dance. Singing while they cut, while they sweep the floor, and then dancing with the broom. . . . The Cubans are like superthyroid freaks; the men will make music and dance and screw around at the drop of a hat."[73] Such a vision of the New Society entailed the removal of repressive routines and artificial barriers between people and the ecstatic submersion of the individual in the group. The follow-

ing account is a spectacular counterpoint to the social isolation and estrangement so many visitors to Cuba (and the other new societies)
complained of; it reaffirms the proposition that the appeals of the sense
of community (and of the attendant self-transcendence and loss of individuality) arise out of essentially apolitical urges and impulses:

> At the end of their performance, the entire crowd of us—performers,
> the directors of the camp, all the companeros—surged out in a happy,
> dancing, hugging, silly, singing herd [sic] with this tremendous, over-
> whelming group energy. We stamped and yelled and improvised our
> way around the entire camp, people banging on all kinds of things:
> empty wooden boxes, drums, spoons, bottles, anything.
>   . . . Here people are high on their lives all the time. A group called
> Los Bravos charged in from back, parting the crowd, sounds of deep
> drum, a bell, a guitar, and sticks, charging deep rhythm. Everyone
> went wild. . . . An actual physical force seemed to surge through the
> room, men dancing with men, women with women, everyone's hands
> on everyone else's shoulders, a huge snake line forming and chugging
> around the hall: lawyers, translators, drivers, cane cutters, students,
> waiters, an absolute frenzy of brotherhood and excitement. . . .
>   . . . At lunchtime . . . the whole crowd spilling out onto the
> lawn, falling down sweaty, screaming at the top of their lungs, rolling
> down the hill . . . that much unadulterated emotional give is almost
> unbearable. I begin to really conceive of being part of a current, that
> in the process of a revolution you are both very important and very
> small; we're talking about something bigger than all of us, and that is
> the transformation of an entire people, the liberation of that kind of
> energy we saw this evening, the beginning of building the new
> man. . . . High on the people! Woooiiieeeeeeeee!![74]

In a somewhat similar spirit, Waldo Frank (who had transferred his
admiration from the Soviet Union to Cuba) observed, on another occasion, "young men and women sparkling with animal spirits."[75] Although
not every visitor was similarly seized by such an "absolute frenzy of
brotherhood and excitement," the spectacle of large gatherings and apparently enthusiastic crowds was hard to resist. Even a cool and somewhat detached (though not unsympathetic) English writer like David
Caute was compelled to muse at a big rally: "But what for me is so odd,
so dreamlike, so elusive about this gigantic demonstration of solidarity? . . . this is the first demonstration I have attended where the
Government (damn it) is the sponsor!" Yet he was ultimately impressed:
"As we walk home . . . the demonstrators are climbing into their trucks
and buses, euphorically happy and proud as any festival's children
could be. For us, Cuba has suddenly fulfilled her promise and we too

are happy."[76] LeRoi Jones too relished the Cuban crowds: "At each town, the chanting crowds. The unbelievable joy and excitement. The same idea, and people made beautiful because of it. People moving, being moved. I was ecstatic and frightened. Something I had never seen before exploding all around me."[77]

What accounts for the intellectuals' propensity to be so fascinated with the crowds, the rallies, marches, assemblies?° The response to the Cuban crowds was by no means unique. The massed multitudes of Soviet citizens had evoked similar responses in earlier periods as did the Chinese ones later on. The reactions to crowds in the unfamiliar, idealized society and to those at home are noticeably different. Intellectuals in their usual habitat are noted for being individualistic, cherishing their privacy, requiring much "space," literally and figuratively, to be comfortable; they tend to avoid crowds at places of entertainment or recreation, and are hardly moved by them when encountered in routine aggregations, for example at rush hour in a city.

The favorable reaction to crowds in Cuba (and other similar societies) has its sources both in the process of contextual redefinition and in a misinterpretation of what the intellectuals had actually seen. As will be recalled, the objects of contextual redefinition may include material scarcities, hard manual labor, physical discomforts, and other depriving situations endured for higher purpose, and endowed with dignity because of the elevating context or meaning attached.† While the specta-

---

° I am not suggesting that all intellectuals responded to crowds in the same way, but that a very large portion of them did. There were occasional exceptions. Ronald Radosh, for instance, "did not detect [at a gathering in a Havana neighborhood] any sense of joy or dedication but, rather saw hundreds of people sitting around idly with bored expressions, perhaps annoyed that they had to endure this event after a full day's work. Here was another example of how the Revolution demands mass participation—but it could hardly be called an example of socialist democracy."[78]

† For example: ". . . Havana is dilapidated but not sad, and its shabbiness has charm."[79] Concerning the Cuban dismissal of affirmative action to correct past racism: " 'It would be unfair,' said a Cuban Union official of black skin, 'to hire a black over a white regardless of skill and experience: the solution was time for the Revolution's commitment to equal education to work itself out.' What would be a liberal platitude in the United States was for him a secure faith. . . ."[80] Evidently also for Todd Gitlin making the comment. For Andrew Salkey a Las Vegas–type floor show at the Havana Tropicana night club complete with chorus girls "was more than merely ersatz North American dance-collage . . . it was done with . . . electric thrust, professional gusto and the kind of charm that would . . . disarm the most severe critic."[81] Maybe so. The same spectacle also became a subject of ideological contention (and illustrated even more clearly the process of contextual redefinition) among members of the group Ronald Radosh belonged to: "When two of us term the contents [of the show, that is] sexist and backward we are

cle of a sweaty and boisterous crowd at a football game may hardly move a Western intellectual, a similar crowd at a political rally in a country of higher purpose brings about profoundly different reactions as the onlooker finds the latter assemblage admirable, heartwarming, and inspiring.

In addition to such a contextual redefinition, there is also a frequent and basic misapprehension of the circumstances under which crowds in highly regimented societies assemble: seeming spontaneity is confused with genuine spontaneity; enthusiasm over getting a day or a few hours off from work (on account of the rally or parade) may be confused with enthusiasm over the political meaning of the event; the highly organized carnival atmosphere (often complete with appointed cheer or chant leaders) with impulsive, spontaneous outbursts of good cheers. Furthermore, the enthusiastic crowds come to symbolize genuine, popular democracy, the unity of the leaders and the led, the ultimate and most tangible bestowal of legitimacy on the system, more lively and authentic than casting votes in little privatized polling booths; more personal and more filled with vitality than the covert lobbying, backroom bickering, and influence peddling associated with pluralistic politics, where large numbers of the citizens rarely meet and merge in joyous crowds and listen to lengthy perorations of their leaders. It may very well be that it was the spectacle of the politically assembled Cuban crowds in general and their attitude toward Castro in particular that convinced people like C. Wright Mills that the regime was legitimated by the "enthusiastic support of an overwhelming majority of the people of Cuba"[85] and like Waldo Frank that "A revolution such as Castro's is nourished by the direct, almost physical embrace of leaders and people."[86]

The fascination of intellectuals with such political crowds is a remarkable phenomenon, even if we assume that the political gatherings

---

pounced upon. 'Sexist?' says one woman in our group. 'What's wrong with a woman showing her body and moving it on stage?' " In a visit to Havana's "impressive psychiatric hospital" (another standard item on many itineraries) "the administrator who takes us around mentions that the hospital uses large doses of tranquilizers on patients and practices shock therapy. . . . Despite great surprise expressed by some of us, other members of our visiting group are again uncritical."[82] Cardenal called the same institution the "place where the tenderness of the Revolution may be seen."[83]

Perhaps David Dellinger had the best formula for capturing the attitude beneath contextual redefinition: the capacity for "relating even the simplest daily events to the purposes for which the Revolution exists."[84]

witnessed were truly enthusiastic and more spontaneous than critical observers would judge them to be. After all, there were many historical instances when intellectuals remained unimpressed by political regimes and their leaders despite the most authentically frenzied endorsement of the crowds—Nazi Germany and fascist Italy being good examples. In such instances, it was understood that mass enthusiasm may be ephemeral, volatile, irrational, and subject to manipulation. It is only when the intellectuals assume that the social-political system organizing these spectacles is basically sound and well intentioned that they will abstain from a critical analysis of crowd behavior. Such abstention from asking more hard-nosed questions about the meanings of crowd behavior and its relevance to the assessment of the political system could also be explained by the desire to seek and find community. Hence the frequent confusion of community with the excited, enthusiastic behavior of crowds. LeRoi Jones's remarks are suggestive of this state of mind: "What was it, a circus? That wild, mad crowd. Social ideas? Could there be that much excitement generated through all the people? Damn, that people still *can* move. Not us, but people. It's gone out of us forever."[87] "Us," North Americans, intellectuals, are dead, incapable of such communal ecstasy and group enthusiasm. They, the fresh, new young people, are capable of generating it. Forms of behavior extinct or inauthentic in the U.S. flourish in Cuba. LeRoi Jones shared with Norman Mailer the concern with vitality and the belief that American society was decadent, lifeless, without passion and intensity.

> The rebels among us have become merely people like myself [wrote LeRoi Jones in his report on his Cuban visit] who grow beards and will not participate in politics. Drugs, juvenile delinquency, complete isolation from the vapid mores of the country, a few current ways out. Something not inextricably bound up in a lie. Something not part of liberal stupidity or the actual filth of vested interest. There is none. It's much too late. We are an old people already. Even the vitality of our art is like bright flowers growing up through a rotting carcass.[88]

The cheering, marching, boisterous crowds of Cuba radiating purpose and solidarity provided a striking counterpoint to such feelings. The sense of the contrast between what was lacking in their own society and what was present in the Cuban (or Soviet, or Chinese) society was almost ever present in the minds of the visitors. Joseph A. Kahl, a social scientist, wrote in his essay, "The Moral Economy of a Revolutionary Society": "the young militants are convinced that they are building a superior society. . . . To talk with them was profoundly moving, especially in contrast to the disillusion and cynicism of many of the best of young Americans. Cuban youth are not alienated, bitter, or 'turned off.' "[89]

If in the United States work was drudgery or at best a routinized way of making a living bereft of any higher purpose, in this new society the people "young and old, proudly dressed in work clothes, [were] singing as they made their way to the country. . . . On these faces reigned the serenity of meaningful work—the passion of commitment."[90] Small wonder that upon returning to the United States the first sensation that hit some of the visitors was that "society gave . . . no spiritual sustenance" and that "life was meaningless."[91] It was a culture Susan Sontag judged to be "inorganic, dead, coercive, authoritarian," full of "dehumanized individuals," and "living dead," especially if they worked for "IBM, and General Motors, and the Pentagon and United Fruit"; a "culture which produces the heartless bureaucrats of death and empty affluence." In such a society it was imperative to "retreat from the rough, dehumanizing embrace of the corporate life-killers (family, school, jobs, the Army). . . ."[92]

Todd Gitlin spoke for most visiting intellectuals who admired Cuba when he said that "We look to Cuba not only because of what we sense Cuba to be but because of what the United States is not."[93] Perhaps it should not be startling that the yearning for community made so many Western intellectuals unaware of or insensitive to the oppressive qualities of totalitarian societies, whether they were of the Soviet, Cuban, or Chinese variety. Just as the alienated, urban intellectuals generally forgot or ignored the constraints inherent in small traditional communities in their moments of nostalgia for a simple life, they were equally oblivious to the implications of the community restored and reimposed under totalitarian political auspices. They rarely grasped that totalitarian systems multiply all the restrictive potentials inherent in small communities as they strive to make life more visible and observable, as they seek to reduce privacy and enlarge the public domain. Among others, Jose Yglesias, the American writer of Hispanic origins, rejoiced in precisely such developments: "The workers and campesinos in the CDR's [Committee for the Defense of the Revolution, a vast neighborhood organization] had taken the first step toward a new cultural attitude. . . . They brought a wonderful sanity and healthiness to their organization's pushiness about people's lives: an insistence that the open life—open to the view of one's neighbors—is the natural life of man. I decided that this might well be what would make Mayari a valley of paradise."[94]

It is far from accidental that certain appeals of totalitarian countries resemble those of traditional societies and that there is in fact a vital connection—however frequently overlooked—between traditional and totalitarian societies. Totalitarian regimes often build on the residues of a traditional society which include the generalized respect for authority, disrespect for privacy, the prevalence of informal social controls (in neighborhoods and villages), the belief that ordinary people's freedom and autonomy must be inherently and severely circumscribed, and that the decisive forces in this world—religious or secular-political—are both inaccessible and unaccountable to ordinary people.

Social Justice and Popular Support

There was little difference between the attractions of Cuba and the Soviet Union with respect to the appeals of social justice. The Cuban regime got things done too: abject poverty was rapidly being liquidated, especially among the poorest peasants. Sweeping public health measures were taken: new hospitals and clinics built, doctors assigned to rural areas, medications made available to everybody; children were given special attention. A campaign against illiteracy was waged with great success; the property of the rich was expropriated: mansions which had earlier belonged to wealthy families were turned into children's homes or workers' resorts.

The emphasis on the liquidation of rural backwardness and poverty was especially appealing, since this was clearly an area where urgent and radical changes were warranted and appeared most dramatic when implemented. The severity of rural poverty in Cuba was indisputable,[95] even if living standards in the country as a whole were not as low before the Revolution as many visitors thought to be the case.[96] Furthermore, the emphasis on rural development and the concern with the welfare of peasants contrasted attractively with the Soviet policy toward the countryside, which represented one of the worst features of the Soviet system.* Here then was an important example of the Cuban avoidance of the errors of the Soviet regime. Finally, the Cuban interest in rural development struck a responsive chord in the visiting intellectuals who by the early 1960s shared, and were often in the vanguard of, the

---

* I am referring to the forced collectivization of agriculture in the early 1930s and the general Soviet policy of squeezing the peasantry for the sake of rapid heavy industrialization, as well as the persisting neglect and backwardness of the countryside.

growing disenchantment with life in modern industrial societies. For this reason they were increasingly susceptible to the appeals of nature, the countryside, the simple rural life, and authentic peasants. To be sure, the Cuban regime was modernizing the countryside. Nevertheless, such policies seemed more decentralized and humane than the construction of gigantic industrial plants Soviet-style and preferable to the Soviet emphasis on upgrading urban amenities at the expense of the rural areas.

The attention the Cuban regime paid to agriculture was also symbolized by Castro's preoccupation with milk production and cattle breeding, and his turning into an amateur geneticist to improve the herds of Cuba. Repeatedly he himself would show the model-experimental farms and cattle breeding stations to important visitors. Of all the major sights representing the accomplishments of the regime none were shown more often and regularly than such model farms. (The other three types of projects most frequently displayed were schools, hospitals, and new housing.)

The new egalitarian social relationships were most strikingly symbolized in the Cuban concern with manual labor and the policies aimed at assuring its universal practice. These policies focused on sugarcane cutting for obvious economic as well as ideological reasons. The participation in cane cutting was hailed by many sympathizers as the highest expression of social solidarity, egalitarianism, and part of the assault on what might be called the original sin of the division of labor. Such popular participation reflected both the determination of the government to spread around the most backbreaking forms of manual labor and the dedication of the people to share in the building of the new society by contributing to its economic objectives. The apparently voluntary nature of it all was the most essential and impressive. As Angela Davis put it, "It seemed as if every able-bodied resident of Havana was rushing to the fields as though to a joyous carnival."[97] Barry Reckord, a Jamaican writer, discussed with a Cuban friend why he cut cane:

> Because there is moral pressure on him to go. But it is *moral* pressure. If he has no morality he needn't go. He can stay in the office and still draw his salary. There is a legal necessity to go to the fields only one day a week. . . . But most people go not only once a week, but one of two Sundays a month and a month or two each year.[98]

Andrew Salkey, another West Indian writer-poet (expatriate living in London and more recently in the U.S.), visited with volunteer workers on the outskirts of Havana:

Talked also with a young psychiatrist, as she sat flat in a shallow trench between two long rows of ploughed dark red earth. Her face was streaked with perspiration and dirt. "We all do it," she said. "You'll find students, professional people, people in the Government, housewives, youngsters at school, everybody. It's got to be done and we volunteer to do it. As simple as that."[99]*

Thus the mobilization of the entire population for bouts of manual labor—regardless of age, sex, marital or social status, training, or expertise—was an important proof of the commitment to equality. Not unlike the cultural revolution in China, which was aimed at the destabilization of privileged social positions and hierarchies, the "volunteering" for manual labor in Cuba was also supposed to reduce or undermine, if not abolish, the distinction between manual and mental labor, soft and backbreaking work, the privileged and less privileged, the leaders and the masses. Occasionally even Castro participated and mixed freely with ordinary people. ("There is so little condescension here. That is the most beautiful thing. Every man, no matter what he is doing, is contributing. Every man and woman, and Fidel brings this out constantly, is just as important as he, Fidel is.")[101]

Even the strict and pervasive rationing was acceptable and even praiseworthy, since the visitors viewed it as yet another thoughtful measure designed to assure that all will receive a decent minimum to satisfy basic needs. Some of them succeeded in associating it with spiritual gain. Cardenal said to a Cuban friend of his: "This system that delights you because you're a communist delights me because I find it evangelic. I also am fond of scarcity: I am a monk. I hope you will never have too much abundance."[102] Often the shortages and rationing were blamed

---

* Another interpretation of volunteering was offered by John Clytus, a black American who lived in Cuba for three years and left in the end because, among other things, of disillusionment over the regime's racial policies: "Some vegetable or fruit acreage or factory needed them [office workers] on Sunday to do 'voluntary work.' Frequently I participated in this work. No one was forced to do so, but everyone in each office was asked if he was going to participate in this 'patriotic' venture. He could refuse but thenceforth he would be looked upon as being unfriendly to the revolution. He could not expect to be promoted . . . and as soon as some other calling himself a revolutionary was found who could perform the same duties, he would be replaced." An even darker explanation was offered by a Cuban factory worked quoted by a French journalist: ". . . anyone who refuses to put in the extra hours or asks payment for them is accused of counterrevolutionary plotting. Then G-2 [the political police] takes a hand, raids his home, questions his neighbors, rakes through his past and makes all kinds of difficulties. If the obstinate worker persists . . . the union delegate convokes the workers to 'vote' for his expulsion."[100]

on the American blockade[103] (with some justification in the early 60s and much less later on) as if it could be anticipated that its lifting would induce the Cuban government to start importing consumer goods in substantial quantities. More recently, Castro made it clear that this will not be the case: "In a major speech last September (1977), President Castro warned that if trade resumes, Cuba would not spend its scarce resources on 'junk and trinkets,' meaning imported consumer goods."[104]

There was, among sympathetic visitors, less of a denial of the scarcities (depending also on the time of the visit) than a positive interpretation of them, and of the rationing system as an instrument of socioeconomic equality. Still, the latter had to be balanced against "the inadequacies of a supply system that forces the people to stand in line for every item of food or clothing. In Havana, where the shops open at six in the morning, housewives have to spend their nights waiting outside."[105] Jonathan Kozol, the American author on education, was under the impression that "The long lines . . . the ration cards, and other forms of deprivation do not seem to dampen the high spirits of most people. . . ."[106] Other visitors conjured up an approaching state of affairs in which scarcity will be banished:

> Each year more and more workplaces eliminate time clocks and other forms of attendance records; more and more places grant workers unlimited paid sick leaves; more and more new towns and farms and factories and schools provide free meals, free clothes, free housing. Already there are experimental areas such as the Isle of Youth where money is almost unseen.[107]

It did not come to pass: "Free telephone calls, free water and other free social services also ended last year"; that is, in 1976. In turn, saving electricity became so pressing that "so-called 'click patrols' . . . [were] empowered to enter any home or establishment and switch off lights they consider unnecessary." The labor laws of the 70s reenforced rather than eliminated time clocks, and apparently the Isle of Youth experiment folded or has been phased out.[108]

On the whole the discovery of material and social inequalities on the part of the sympathizers has been a slow and incomplete process; most sympathizers have never confronted it, although by the early 1970s a fair amount of information began to accumulate. John Clytus, for instance, wrote in 1970 about the special shops for privileged foreigners. K. S. Karol regarded wage differentials "as enormous" in 1970, with engineers earning up to 1700 pesos per month as against 100 earned by "the average worker."[109] René Dumont reported salaries ranging from

85 to 900 pesos per month. There were also the non-income privileges for the political elite groups characteristic of one-party socialist systems:

> Castro, *le grand seigneur*, lives very comfortably; he understands that his aides have extensive needs, and he sometimes recompenses them in a lordly fashion. His faithful were recently given free Alfa Romeos: a modern conception of the feudal grant. . . . In July 1969 it was said that there were six hundred of these cars in Cuba and that the man who drew up the lists of recipients could be in a position to know who *really* held the reins of power that year. If the rector of the University of Havana still goes to work in a Soviet jeep it's only because he is not eager to have the students see his handsome Alfa Romeo. . . .
> But it is not just a matter of cars. There are also the beautiful villas and the magnificent Varadero beach where officers and their families vacation free of charge.[110]

There was also a general decline of egalitarian concerns on the part of the regime over time. These developments had an unmistakable resemblance to the Soviet change of policies under Stalin in the late 1920s and early 1930s when inequality as an incentive was officially reestablished. Jorge Dominguez, an American specialist on the Cuban system, commented:

> By the early 1970s egalitarianism was losing out. It was denounced by Prime Minister Castro at the thirteenth labor congress in the fall of 1973; both wages and the wage share of gross product have declined. There was other evidence of increasing income inequality as well. Preferential access in the rationing system in the 1970s was used as a new individual material incentive to produce. In 1973, one hundred thousand television sets were given to vanguard workers through labor assemblies, and party and union recommendations. Refrigerators and electrical appliances were also distributed in this fashion. Technicians, physicians, and labor-union leaders had preferential access to new cars. . . . The rationing system, which had once been an instrument for equality, now became a method to benefit the elite. . . .[111]

If by the 1970s some observers could raise critical questions about the distribution of material privilege, it was harder to dispute the achievements of the regime in public education.

Jonathan Kozol wrote:

> There are these words in the Bible: "Where there is no vision, the people will perish." In Cuban schools . . . the vision is strong, the dream is vivid and the goal is clear. There is a sense, within the Cuban schools, that one is working for a purpose and that that purpose is a great deal more profound and more important than the selfish pleasure

of individual reward. The goal is to become an active member in a common campaign to win an ethical objective.[112]

The early campaigns against illiteracy were particularly impressive: "When Sartre was interviewed on TV, he said that what moved him above everything else in the Cuban revolution was the idea of every literate Cuban teaching five illiterates to read and write and the absence of any preconceived ideology which made the Cuban experience free of dogma and so different from traditional communist revolutions."[113] Jose Yglesias was also touched by the educational policies of the regime. In an evening class for adults, "The classroom had the air of a moralistic, 19th century print: Abe Lincoln reading law by the light of a log fire." And at the reform school for juvenile delinquents, he wrote: "I was unprepared for the classroom where I sat with a sixth grade class: models of deportment and participation. . . . The boys crowded around me after classes . . . there was nothing to suggest that they had ever been a problem to anyone. . . ." The commitment to education was part of the concern for the young: "the revolution is committed to the young . . . the tone of its ideology and the success of its economic development . . . relies on the enthusiastic participation of the young."[114] Other visitors too were most favorably impressed by the social-political role of the young, their prominence in positions of power and decision-making. The youthfulness of the Cuban Revolution, of its leaders and most ardent followers, was by itself one of its major appeals. It symbolized the rejuvenation of socialism, of the myth of the revolution, and the ideas of Marxism.[115]

Amid the widespread praise of extending the reach of education, few questions were asked about its content, or about what an English writer called "the uses of literacy."[116] In this regard the premises of the Enlightenment retained their original force: education per se was considered to be an undifferentiated good, not something that could also be misused or abused, employed to narrow people's outlook and understanding of the world rather than broaden them.

More generally speaking, even when mild apprehensions about certain aspects of the system surfaced—when, for example, occasionally some visitors perceived, however dimly, the limits placed on civil liberties or free expression—the achievements of the regime easily outweighed its liabilities:

> I couldn't help thinking about how life would be for that Indian woman [the author quoted here, Joe Nicholson, an American journalist, had seen begging on a sidewalk in Mexico City]—or the rest of the

poor majority in Latin America—in Communist Cuba. She wouldn't be assured all of the civil liberties of a Jeffersonian democracy, but she would be guaranteed a decent job. Her children would be enrolled in free day-care centers or schools. They wouldn't be wearing rags and they wouldn't have to worry about getting enough to eat. . . .

For the poor of Latin America, Cuba offers dignity that is even beyond the grasp of large segments of America's citizens, the penniless elderly and migrants, the impoverished whites of Appalachia and poor blacks of inner cities.

This dignity is composed of rights Cubans have gained under their Communist Revolution: the right to a decent job . . . to wages sufficient to cover basic needs . . . to an equal—and adequate although not yet generous—share of rationed food and clothing, the right to inexpensive housing . . . free health care and free education. . . .[117]

This then was the familiar argument for social justice, or positive freedom as against the niceties of free expression or the intangibles of negative freedoms. By contrast, at the time and soon after the Revolution many visitors hoped that the Cuban regime would avoid the fateful choice between "bread and liberty"; that is, the path traversed by the Soviet Union and several Eastern European countries under its control.

Barry Reckord, while pondering the intractability of human nature and the slow emergence of the "New Cuban Man," nevertheless felt that

The individual who is unjust works in a society that shares its food fairly evenly, doesn't discriminate against blacks, gives priority to hospitals and schools over Cadillacs and mansions, wipes out unemployment with the money it borrows. The society is moral even if the individual is not. Men are more just, more humane in a collective sense.[118]*

On an even more positive note other visitors concluded that

. . . Castro's Cuba is prosperous and its people are enthusiastic, reasonably content and optimistic about the future. Perhaps the overriding impression of three trips to Cuba is the enthusiasm and unity of the Cuban people. They are proud of their accomplishments and sing songs about themselves and their country that reflect this self-pride. . . . The people work together and work hard—for what they believe to be the good of their neighbors and therefore their country.[120]

Whatever the actual levels of pride were among the population, the regime ceaselessly urged them to contrast the achievements of the pres-

* At the same time Reckord also quoted the views of a Cuban who pointed out that "the more equal men get, the more watchful they are about a trace of privilege. . . . And of course there is bound to be privilege so the greater the equality the more the misery."[119]

ent with the liabilities of the past and encouraged visitors to take full measure of such differences.[121]

It is not being suggested here that the gains made by the Cuban system under Castro in reducing rural poverty or improving public health were spurious. One-party systems such as Cuba's, inspired and legitimated by some version or variety of Marxism-Leninism, have been successful in eliminating certain forms of backwardness and deprivation (e.g., illiteracy, high rates of infant mortality, the worst forms of malnutrition, and so on). At the same time many of their claims are not subject to verification and sometimes turn out to be fabrications years or decades later (as did, for instance, the Soviet claims concerning material improvements in the life of the population in the early 1930s, when in fact famine conditions prevailed, or the Chinese claims concerning the benefits of the Cultural Revolution).

There is also the question of the *costs* at which such gains in the redistribution of wealth, in education or public welfare have been attained and of the measures taken against those segments of the population which resisted the programs and policies of the regime. The Cuban government, unlike the Soviet in its earlier period, rarely if ever included visits to model prisons in the typical itinerary of the visitors.* Some were shown former prisons converted into less forbidding structures; some were taken to reform schools for juvenile delinquents or prostitutes. Members of the staff of Senator Edward Kennedy were shown "other-than-maximum-security-areas" and observed that "conditions appear adequate."[123] Other visitors learned secondhand about the system of forced labor that "parasites" and political unreliables were subjected to.[124] Regular, bona fide penal institutions, especially those housing political prisoners, were not displayed to the visiting intellectuals, or to others. This absence of "humane prisons" from the itinerary is not easy to explain. It was certainly within the power and resources of the regime to develop and exhibit at least a small number of such institutions. Its failure to do so may be due to the reluctance to expose the visitors to a prisoner, and particularly to political prisoner population, insufficiently docile—there have been reports of prisoners refusing to undergo political reeduca-

---

* I cannot be certain that such accounts do not exist. However in my immersion in the travel literature I did not come across reports of visits to model prisons, Soviet style. There were references to "prison transfers . . . made for cosmetic reasons: to show foreign visitors that the prisons dating from Batista's rule were being shut down, with no mention that the prisoners had simply been moved elsewhere. When presented in public, prisoners were seen in civilian clothes and without handcuffs—to give the impression of a happy, well-treated lot."[122]

tion. It is also possible that prison conditions in general were too poor, and the regime simply did not bother to improve them. Cuba has never allowed the Red Cross, Amnesty International, or U.N. groups to inspect prisons; as recently as in 1977 Castro insisted that these were purely internal matters.[125] At last there is also the possibility that both political and non-political crimes were considered such a sensitive issue—perhaps because of the very idealism and moral claims of the regime—that any reminder of its failure to eradicate or reform its political enemies, or reeducate its non-political misfits, was to be repressed and removed from the agenda of public discourse. Certainly what has been learned about the conditions of Cuban prisons and political prisoners encourages such speculation. Although not nearly as well known as corresponding practices in Soviet penal institutions, the treatment of those regarded as the political enemies of the regime appears quite similar to the tradition established by the Soviet Union. There is, to begin with, the secret or security or political police, the G-2. As was noted of the Soviet state security organ, the KGB, its Cuban relative (or descendant?), the G-2, was also an atypically efficient part of the system. Jorge Edwards observed:

> How could room service be so inefficient, with breakfast frequently arriving an hour late, with coffee instead of tea, one cup for two people and three cups for one, the milk jug without milk, with the bread forgotten and the eggs stone cold; while the service of the machine [of the secret police, that is], on the other hand, was immaculate and precise, as if in this field the improvisation and lethargy of the tropics and absenteeism did not count?[126]

Not unlike in the Soviet system under Stalin and the Chinese under Mao, in Cuba too "the defendant is expected to establish his own guilt: he is questioned and prodded by the prosecution until he produces an acceptable self-critique, detailing his crimes against the revolution."[127] Reports of physical and psychological mistreatment in Cuban prisons have been numerous since the early 1960s, but such accounts, including eye-witness reports and recollections, have not received wide publicity either in the United States or Western Europe. They included reports of overcrowding, exceptionally unsanitary conditions, starvation diets, physical mistreatment by guards and interrogators, sleep deprivation, special punishment cells, lack of medical care, and extra punitive measures against those refusing to participate in ideological retraining.[128] Huber Matos, an early leader of the revolution imprisoned by Castro for twenty years, described his treatment as ranging "from brutal to subhuman"; it included years spent in solitary confinement in underground cells or concrete boxes (the latter "two-and-a-half meters wide and three feet long," another one three feet wide), many beatings, and a year during which "he was given no clothes and subsisted in his underwear."[129] Such treatment of political prisoners could hardly be viewed as manifestations of revolutionary violence or overreactions to the sabotage conducted by anti-Castro exiles, though the latter certainly played a part, up to a point. By the 1970s neither domestic revolutionary, self-defensive violence, nor defensiveness over the exiles offered reasonable excuses or explanations of the political repression. By 1976 "Relatively few figures of the old Batista regime [were] still in jail . . . prisoners today range from Fidel's former comrades in the 26th of July Movement to young peasants who were infants when Castro took over."[130] According to Jorge Dominguez, "Cuba's rate of political imprisonment is well above that of other authoritarian Latin American governments."[131]

Like the Soviet regime, the Cuban authorities too eventually ran into peasant hostility, although initially their policies were far more generous toward peasants than the Soviet ones:

> Although initially the revolution had the support of the rural population, in the early '6os, when the government reneged on its word "to give the land to the toilers," the regime began to have difficulty in enforcing its collectivization policies. In 1967 Lee Lockwood, in his very favorable account of the Revolution, pointed out that ". . . the majority of the internees are not, as one might assume, men of urban backgrounds, but 'campesinos,' peasants. . . . Most are serving terms ranging from two to twenty years. . . ." Since then, the revolutionary leadership has tightened its controls, prohibiting the peasants from slaughtering their animals and requiring that their crops be sold to the government.

The regime's efforts to tighten labor discipline became another source of repression:

> The application of government labor decrees has also contributed to the number of politically oriented "crimes" in Cuba. Since 1970 the regime has enacted a series of decrees punishing "absenteeism" and "loafing." The government has also introduced the "worker's biography," a type of labor passport that records a worker's behavior, attitudes and production quotas.[132]

The unusually intense persecution of homosexuals has been another manifestation of repression and a peculiarity of the Cuban regime. According to a generally sympathetic visitor,

the Revolution has created a new class of outcasts, the homosexuals.
. . . They are officially classified as "anti-social" . . . they are barred
from mass political organizations, and relegated to second-class citizenship—perhaps outlaw status is more accurate—that makes U.S. blacks
seem emancipated. In Cuba, everybody's life depends on his support
for—or at least cooperation with—the Revolution; it is a prerequisite
for a good job, a chance to enter the university, and even the opportunity to buy rationed consumer goods—a refrigerator, a radio, a wrist-
watch. For homosexuals, many of these things are impossible, all of
them difficult.[133]

Castro himself said that "homosexuals should not be allowed in positions where they are able to exert influence upon young people." Other
high party functionaries described homosexuals as people of "weak
character" who carry on "immoral acts." Homosexuals were excluded as
new tenants from housing projects;[134] and they were highly represented
among those placed in forced labor units (UMAP, or Military Units for
Aid to Production).[135] Evidently the persecution of homosexuals can be
explained not only by cultural traditions or machismo—plausible as it
might seem to be—but also by the totalitarian puritanism of the new regime and its zealous pursuit of conformity in all walks of life. Apparently
prior to the revolution no comparably massive and systematic repressive measures were taken against them.[136]

Another innovation in repressive techniques and grass-roots surveillance has been the Committees for the Defense of the Revolution, variously assessed as benevolent neighborhood groups devoted to taking
medicine to old widows and tending flowerbeds in local parks, or sinis-
ter organizations entrusted by the police to watch the day-to-day activities of fellow citizens, making sure that no islands of privacy remain.
K. S. Karol believes that they "have a purely repressive function" and
are "mere appendages" of the police.[137] According to Jose Yglesias,

vigilance was the first task of the CDR's, and members were set to
watch the activities of people on their block, particularly of people
known not to sympathize with the Revolution. The information was
passed up to the municipal level and they turned it over to the security police. If the police . . . had reason to worry about reports that
some unsympathetic person had come home at an unusual hour carrying a strange package then they investigated.[138]

Although the above state of affairs existed predominantly at the time
when invasion and counter-revolutionary sabotage were real possibilities, other reports suggest that the CDRs remain committed to the struggle against privacy and to the enforcement of conformity. A critic of the

regime confided to Barry Reckord: "They know who visits me and who I visit. . . . Under Mr. Castro it's suddenly my neighbor's duty to know how I live. . . . Here in Cuba every jackass is knocking on your door to give you advice about who you should see and who is dangerous."[139]

The state of civil liberties and free expression in present-day Cuba as compared with the state of affairs under Batista was summed up by Hugh Thomas, the historian of Cuba:

> The chief difference between Batista and Castro was not that the first was ruthless and the second just; on the contrary, Batista's tyranny seems, from the angle of the present, a mild and indolent undertaking,* an insult to responsible citizens no doubt, but far removed from the iron certainties imposed by Castro.[141]

For most visitors, however, the facts of repression were either not known, or seen as temporary necessities (or evils), outweighed by other benefits brought by the regime.

The Position of Intellectuals

As in the Soviet case, the position of intellectuals in Cuba was by itself among the major attractions of the regime in the eyes of the visiting intellectuals—at any rate until the late 1960s and early 1970s when disillusionment set in among many sympathizers, as was noted earlier. (The treatment of the poet Padilla and of the homosexuals was among the major catalysts of such sentiments.)

The belief that the Cuban regime was congenial to intellectuals rested in part on the perception of the leaders as fellow intellectuals, or former intellectuals who had much affinity with other intellectuals—or so it seemed. Castro was not only trained as a lawyer, he was also a voracious reader, amateur geneticist-biologist, agricultural expert, military genius, eloquent statesman, a renaissance man (not unlike Stalin, but seemingly more modest), and in the words of one of his admirers, "not a leader but a teacher . . . above all an educator. His speeches are long because they are lessons he gives to the Cuban people."[142] Waldo Frank reported that he planned to set up "a community for writers" on the

---

* Symbolic of such differences is the manner in which Castro was punished for organizing the armed revolt against Batista; he was released by an amnesty after less than two years and given ample opportunity while in jail to read and write under comfortable conditions. By contrast, Castro treated even his former allies (like Huber Matos) with whom he had policy disagreements with extraordinary cruelty.[140]

Similar differences could be found between the treatment of political prisoners by the authorities in Tsarist Russia and under the Soviet system.

Isle of Pines and this project was "as urgent to his intimate needs as the solution of the problem of sugar monoculture."[143] (Evidently neither of these objectives has been accomplished at the time of this writing; there is no writers' community on the Isle of Pines and sugar has remained the backbone of the Cuban economy.) Che Guevara too qualified as an intellectual, indeed a most unusual one: trained as a medical doctor, becoming a full-time revolutionary, reading Goethe in the lulls of the battle,[144] and becoming also a great theoretician of the revolutionary struggle.

Lesser functionaries—such as the executive director of INRA (the National Agrarian Reform Institute), Dr. Nunez—conveyed a similar image in that they combined the attributes of the articulate intellectual and the tough revolutionary: "he was beautiful. A tall, scholarly looking man with black hair and full black beard, he talked deliberately but brightly about everything, now and then emphasizing a point by bringing his hands together and wringing them in slow motion, something like college English professors. He wore the uniform of the rebel army with the black and red shoulder insignia of a captain. A black beret was tucked neatly in one of his epaulets. He also carried a big square-handled .45." LeRoi Jones was led to "the wild impression . . . that it [the country] is being run by a group of young radical intellectuals. . . ."[145] A woman directing secondary level adult education was, according to Jonathan Kozol, "one of the most explosive, non-statistical, unconventional human dynamos of any government or nation . . ." while the minister of education "lifted his glass, held it to me—then drank it in one gulp. The atmosphere in the room was gentle and relaxed. I wondered if any other country in the world had ever had an adult education minister quite like Ferrer."[146] These were people who could inspire confidence in the visitors and convey the feeling of being fellow intellectuals, speaking the same language, sharing the same concerns.

As to the position of intellectuals in Cuban society, it appeared that they had almost everything estranged Western intellectuals desired. There was, to start with, ample official recognition. They were taken seriously and, if loyal to the regime, given generous opportunities to share in power and the management of the new society. They were given responsibilities such as the visitors rarely enjoyed in their own societies. For the most part these were, in the words of Susan Sontag, "pedagogical functions," and "a major role in the raising of the level of consciousness."[147] The jubilation on the part of the visitors, as they witnessed Cuban intellectuals moving into positions of power and responsibility, signaled their relief that at long last intellectuals could abandon their traditional roles as social critics and outsiders and could now joyously affirm, endorse, and assist an ongoing social system. At last the painful dichotomy between thought and action was dissolved; Cuban intellectuals were men of action, some actually fought as guerillas; others became revolutionary deans of universities, revolutionary officials in ministries of education, culture, or propaganda, revolutionary writers, film-makers, academics. Most of them shared, from time to time, the manly burden of manual labor with the masses. Most importantly, they were fully integrated into society, there was nothing marginal about them.

Under these circumstances, it was also possible to accept with a clear conscience the material benefits and privileges the regime bestowed on them, unlike in Western societies, where the material privileges and status advantages of estranged intellectuals often become a major source of their bitterness, inner conflict, or self-contempt. Wishing to be severe social critics of the societies they lived in and half expecting some measure of retribution or mild martyrdom for their criticism, instead they often found themselves either ignored by the holders of power or, worse, in positions of influence and high social status despite their relentless castigation of the social system which continued, almost absent-mindedly, to feed generously the mouths that so regularly bit it. Having been so benignly treated, many social critics in the West felt ineffectual: not being denied material rewards and social status (let alone political freedom) was proof that they failed to become a threat to the system. Dark suspicions would arise: did they unwittingly sell out? By contrast in Cuba (as in the Soviet Union and China) it was possible to enjoy the blessings of good life, that is, to consume without guilt and without twinges of doubt because this was taking place in a rational, benevolent, and egalitarian system. To each according to his ability and contribution to the good of society—so for some generations has socialism been defined. The regime did consider the contribution of intellectuals important and treated them accordingly. The Cuban writers' and artists' club (UNEAC) was among the symbols of such official recognition:

> housed in once fashionable Vedado in a large elegant family residence: spacious reception hall, lounge with well-stocked bar, esplanada-veranda with colonial style garden furniture, meeting rooms, exhibition areas and offices; in the buildings off the house, very impressive club library, bookshop, studios, workshops. We saw many writers' books on show, and tasteful displays of lithographic and lino-cut work, posters

and book illustrations. All-round excellent atmosphere for encouraging young unestablished writers and artists. Union altogether enviable (no P.E.N. Club gloom here) . . .[148]

Cardenal was told by a young Cuban poet (fundamentally committed to the regime) that "there are writers who take advantage of the Revolution to obtain favors: 'There is Guillen, who's been a communist all his life, and now he has a car with a chauffeur at his door and he's always running off to Paris. . . . Or Retamar, who is also always traveling, he has a fine house and a splendid table.' "[149]

More important than the material privileges, many visitors felt, was the historically unique opportunity for intellectuals to attain a new degree of wholeness and integration not only with society and the masses, but within themselves. No longer was it necessary for intellectuals to be splintered into various, often conflicting roles. Politics and art, among other things, could now harmoniously mesh:

> I asked her about the possible clash of interests between her political work and her artistic career. Weren't the demands dissimilar? Weren't the energies conflicting and hardly mutually supporting?
> "I can choose" she said. "We're free to decide what we want to do in the society. I have to be an artist and I want to be a Party worker. I like it that way. This is good for me. I use my imagination both ways."

By the same token film-makers were also allowed "maximum room for exploration, comparative criticism and development." Andrew Salkey (as others before and after him) was also assured of other varieties of free expression, including that enjoyed by the academic publication *Pensamiento Critico* (banned since the early 1970s). One of the editors told him: "Our editorial freedom is absolutely strictly within the terms of the Revolution, so to speak, and we're within the Revolution."[150]

"Working within the Revolution" was precisely the state of affairs that visiting Western intellectuals envied, as it seemed to hold the promise of neither "selling out" to the powers-that-be, nor being impotent bystanders. By definition, "working within" or for the revolution could not be a sell-out; at the same time it was a way to be effectual.

Was there any recognition of the price to be paid for such bliss? Susan Sontag put matters into proper perspective:

> Americans are, perhaps, over-zealous when they visit Cuba about the fate of oppositional forces within the society. . . . This is understandable, since Americans who visit Cuba tend to be "intellectuals"—probably a majority of them write, if they are not actually professional

writers, journalists, teachers or students—and most of the rest are exceptionally well-educated and atypical professional people. An American radical visiting Cuba is therefore more likely to be interested in the fate of his opposite number, a student, or writer or teacher or artist, than he is of a dairy farmer or of a fisherman and he is likely to leave relatively unquestioned the traditional role which intellectuals play in our society: being a critic of the system. . . . American radicals can barely envisage a new role for intellectuals which goes beyond the traditional oppositional one . . . [Whereas] . . . intellectuals in a revolutionary society must have a pedagogical function. . . . Still, it is natural to feel concern about those who refuse this task . . . when there is a public attack on one of the younger apolitical writers, the poet Herberto Padilla, there might be reason to worry. But again there might not.

Sontag was confident that no Cuban writer "has been or is in jail or is failing to get his works published."[151] Since her lines were written it has been learned that

Armando Valladares, a poet and painter, has been imprisoned for the last 19 years . . .

Ernesto Diaz Rodriguez smuggled out of prison a number of poems that were published in the United States in 1977 . . .

The young poet Miguel Sales was given a 25-year sentence in 1974 after he was found preparing to flee Cuba with his wife and infant daughter . . .

Another poet, Angel Cuadra . . . served two-thirds of a 15-year sentence . . .

Another parolee, Tomas Fernandez Travieso, lost his freedom after his play . . . was produced in Miami in 1976 . . .

Amaro Gomez, a member of the Cuban Institute of Cinematographic Arts and Industry, was fired from his job after being accused of "ideological deviation" and was thereafter unable to work except as a bricklayer and waiter. When a police search of his home turned up some of Mr. Gomez's own writings and a copy of . . . Gulag Archepelago, he was tried and sentenced to an eight-year term in prison. Similarly Rene Ariza, winner in 1967 of a Cuban Writers' Union Award, was given an eight-year term for defaming the revolution after manuscripts of poetry, a play and a novel were seized in his house . . .

Raul Arteaga Martinez, a founder of the Association of Free Poets and Writers of Cuba, a clandestine organization that circulates samizdat . . . was to be released after completing his 15-year sentence. But when guards found unorthodox poetry in his cell he . . . received an additional sentence . . . in February 1979 . . .

Roberto Ponciano . . . fled the island in a homemade raft, taking his manuscripts with him. Apprehended on the high seas, he was sentenced to seven years' imprisonment—three for his unsuccessful escape; four for his confiscated literary work . . .

Also despairing of Government permission to emigrate the young black writers Esteban Luis Cardena Junquera and Renaldo Colas Pineda sought asylum in the Argentine Embassy in Havana on March 21, 1978 . . .

Cuban penal legislation prescribes sentences of up to eight years for those who "create, distribute or possess" written or oral "propaganda" "against the socialist state" . . .

. . . artists in Cuba committed to the revolution—are easily accessible. Dissidents on the island are not.[152]

Many Western intellectuals unaware or uninterested in such facts and generally gratified by the social role of intellectuals in Cuba seem to have taken the position that while there might have been some infringements on intellectual freedom (the perception of which varied with the emotional support given to the regime), "The independent intellectual, the critic of all societies and all beliefs, is a luxury they [the Cuban regime] cannot afford."[153]

It is indicative of the ambivalence toward themselves and their social functions (in Western societies) that many intellectuals regard their most characteristic and significant activities as "luxuries" a truly purposeful society can do without.

Vietnam, Albania, Mozambique

Of the Third World countries that became the focus of attention and affection of Western intellectuals during the latter part of the 60s, none was more prominent than North Vietnam. The trips to North Vietnam followed, for obvious historical reasons, the journeys to Cuba. As will be recalled, Cuba attracted attention because of the 1958 revolution. North Vietnam had its revolution in the late 40s and has had a "revolutionary system" ever since. Western intellectuals began to take notice of North Vietnam only after it became the David confronting the Goliath of the United States in the early and mid-1960s. As Susan Sontag put it: "During the last years Vietnam has been stationed inside my consciousness as a quintessential image of the suffering and heroism of the 'weak.' But it was really America 'the strong' that obsessed me—the contours of American power, of American cruelty, of American self-righteousness."[154] It was a remark that once more underlined the intimate connection between the rejection of one's society and the irresistible rise of sympathy toward those which were locked in conflict with one's society. It is doubtful that without this confrontation there would have been many pilgrimages to North Vietnam—a suggestion supported by the fact that since the end of the war (1975) the number of visiting Western delegations has drastically dropped.

The attractions of North Vietnam, even more than of the Soviet Union, Cuba, and China, were the most obviously proportional to the aversion felt toward the United States, both by Americans and Western Europeans. More than any among the countries which had been idealized, North Vietnam could be regarded as a victim, in the most direct sense of the word, of the United States and of naked and brutal military force.

The war provided inspiration for sympathy and visiting in other ways too. Mary McCarthy wrote: "As a common purpose, repelling the invader is a more enlivening goal, it would appear, than building socialism, a sometimes zestless affair; here building socialism is not just an end, which may seem perpetually receding, like a mirage, but a *means;* the reason for making sacrifices is clear and present to everyone."[155] And the Reverend William Sloan Coffin, in a somewhat similar spirit, admitted to the expectation to have his "passion rekindled by the bomb damage"[156] as he embarked on his trip to North Vietnam. The more unjust and irrational the American intervention appeared, the more warmth there was for North Vietnam (and its Southern allies, the Vietcong). At the same time, the clearer it became that the United States would not be able to subdue North Vietnam, the more the sympathizers were ready to confer the type of "moral" superiority on the system that accrues to the winner. Thus paradoxically they succeeded in deriving vindication from regarding North Vietnam both as underdog and as winner.

It is important to bear in mind that most visits to North Vietnam took place during the war—unlike the visits to the USSR, Cuba, and China. For that reason there was an additional sense of elation among many visitors, as they exposed themselves to a measure of personal danger. Among the Americans there was a further cause for elation mixed with apprehension, since they defied their government, which discouraged trips to North Vietnam. (As it turned out, the apprehension and elation were groundless, but they added drama and "zest" to the visits.) There was also the thrill of "arrival in a combat zone" which induced what one visitor called "a kind of sober, middle aged nostalgia." Mary Mc-

Carthy "half wish[ed] for some *real* excitement, for the bombs to come a bit nearer and make a louder bang."[157]

The end of the war and the absence of feelings it had generated are probably not the only explanations for the decline of the political tours of Vietnam. From the official Vietnamese point of view, visiting foreign groups served a very clear political purpose: they were to return to their countries with impressions and beliefs calculated to influence both public opinion and policy-makers in a manner helpful for the successful conclusion of the war.[158] Once the war was over, the pressure diminished in this regard. From the Western and especially American viewpoint too, there were fewer reasons to visit: the war was over and with it the gratification of identifying with the victim and denouncing the aggressor. There was yet another development which damaged in some measure the earlier enthusiasm about the North Vietnamese regime and the type of society they were building in the South. It was the flood of refugees pouring out of Vietnam that was difficult to reconcile with the earlier images of the Vietnamese communists and their putative popularity among the people. There were two ways of stifling the rise of critical sentiments toward the victors: either the United States had to be blamed for the plight of the refugees or the refugees were to be blamed by assigning them some variety of false consciousness or guilt.

An advertisement signed by many prominent critics of the war (including Richard Barnett, David Dellinger, Richard Falk [who had also professed admiration for the Ayatollah Khomeini on another occasion],[159] Corliss Lamont, Paul Sweezy, and Cora Weiss) assured the American public in 1977 that "The present suffering of the Vietnamese people is largely a consequence of the war itself for which the United States bears the continuing responsibility." As to the charges of repression by the new regime:

> We have examined these charges [of human rights abuses] and find them to be based on distortion and exaggeration. True, some Saigon collaborationists have been detained in re-education centers, perhaps 40,000 at present. But such number is surprisingly small. . . . Many of those detained engaged in crimes against their own people. . . . On balance consider the terrible difficulties left behind by the war and made worse by America's continued hostility. The present government in Vietnam should be hailed for its moderation and for its extraordinary effort to achieve reconciliation among all its people. . . . In fact almost all the Vietnamese who worked for the Saigon regime, and who remained have by now returned to their families and are pursuing normal lives.[160]

Two years later a much diminished but still self-assured group of former war critics (which still included Corliss Lamont) attacked Joan Baez for her public criticism of the new regime in Vietnam and insisted that "Vietnam now enjoys human rights as it has never known in history" and approvingly quoted a resolution of the National Lawyers Guild on the subject:

> the reeducation program for former Saigon personnel carried out by the Socialist Republic of Vietnam was absolutely necessary and [the National Lawyers Guild] does further recognize and acknowledge the remarkable spirit of moderation, restraint and clemency with which the reeducation program was conducted.[161]

Despite such assessments of the situation, several hundred thousand people left Vietnam under difficult and dangerous circumstances and have given many indications of escaping the conditions created by the new regime rather than by the war. Far from blaming the United States for their plight, it was their fervent hope to gain admittance to it. Those remaining sympathetic toward the communist regime, including some groups of Quakers and Mennonites, preferred not to pry into matters which might have thrown further light on the much disputed motivation of the refugees:

> Neither Mr. Ediger [a Mennonite social worker], nor the Quaker team which toured in February, asked to see the re-education centers where, it has been alleged, the authorities have interned tens of thousands. . . .
>   Wallace Collett, a Cincinnati businessman who headed the six-member Quaker group, said its members did not go on an inquisitorial mission to check on allegations of repression. . . .
>   He said the Quakers were told that if the accusations of widespread repression had been true, the religious leaders and others [Vietnamese, that is] would have protested rather than waiting for outsiders to speak out.[162]

It may be recalled that Mr. Lattimore, in rebutting charges of ignorance and naiveté in connection with overlooking repression in the Soviet Union, suggested that it would have been distasteful "to snoop" on his hosts (see pages 102, 158).

As far as the visits during the war were concerned, the attractions of North Vietnam proved to be almost identical to those found in the other countries considered in this book. Indeed, the atmosphere of military conflict enhanced many of the same attractions; it also made it easier to overlook, or make allowances for, almost any unappealing aspect of North Vietnamese society. Thus it did not take long for the visitors to be deeply moved by the sense of purpose, unity, and social cohesion they found in that beleaguered nation. Ramsey Clark, former U.S. attorney general, observed in 1972:

> My experience tells me that, as has been told by Aristotle, the chief and universal cause of the revolutionary impulse is the desire for equality. You see no internal conflict in this country. I've seen none.* You feel a unity in spirit. I doubt very seriously that I could walk in safety in Saigon or the cities and villages of South Vietnam, as I have here, because of the division and the confusion and the lack of faith and belief there.[163]

Susan Sontag observed with apparent surprise that "The phenomenon of existential agony, of alienation just don't appear among the Vietnamese. . . ." and that "The Vietnamese are 'whole' human beings, not 'split' as we are."[164] The concern for wholeness was, of course, a hallmark of the 1960s when the experience of affluence without spiritual content became more and more burdensome. The visitors to Vietnam, like those to Cuba (and like Sontag, many visited both places), were eager and predisposed to come upon social systems which solved the problems of wholeness and identity:

> Even before arriving in Hanoi we were struck by the grace, variety and established identity of the Vietnamese. . . . Our impression of an effectively organized society, with its own genuine character, was deepened as we flew over the Chinese border into Vietnam. Below rolled miles of delicately manicured fields.[165]

If Staughton Lynd and Tom Hayden succeeded in associating neatly cultivated fields with a sense of identity, Daniel Berrigan experienced in Hanoi (as was noted earlier) a "dreamlike trance [which] seemed to lie gently upon people and trees and animals." This dreamlike state might have been among the explanations for his association of Ho Chi Minh with the saints and martyrs of his church, and for his finding that a "naive faith in human goodness [was] powerfully operative in North Vietnamese society."[166]

Perhaps in part because the Vietnamese were so foreign, so different, so exotic—especially to Americans—and because of the concern over the

---

* A remark reminiscent of Shaw's comment in 1931 (in the Soviet Union) that he had seen nobody starving in the Soviet Union (see page 118).

human consequences of American bombing,* much attention was paid to the personal characteristics and behavior of the Vietnamese people. Susan Sontag made these observations:

> I am overcome by how exotic the Vietnamese are—impossible for us to understand them . . . we see charming, dignified people living amid bleak material scarcity and the most rigorous demands on their energies and patience.

> . . . in Vietnam one is confronted by a whole people possessed by a belief in what Lawrence called "the subtle, lifelong validity of the heroic impulse" . . .[168]

An explanation of such (and some other) impressions and beliefs may lie in the psychological tension and its cathartic relief due to the great (if unjustified) initial burden of guilt these visitors carried, and its joyous dissipation as they, literally and figuratively, embraced those whom their country injured. The Reverend William Sloane Coffin, Jr., wrote: "Already I began to experience a very special feeling for the North Vietnamese, a feeling I attributed to the fact that we were friends because we had deliberately refused to become enemies."[169] There were embraces between the Reverend, his companions Cora Weiss and David Dellinger, and Premier Pham Van Dong, a most impressive leader. "The very special feeling" toward the Vietnamese† is also reflected in the ways in which various Vietnamese and Patet Lao officials and citizens were described: there was "astonishing passion" in a Patet Lao leader encountered by Father Berrigan, completely lacking "in the dead looks of the leaders who confront us at home"; the chairman of a farming commune had "a good, weathered, intelligent face"; other peasants were described as "leather faced, smiling, older folk[s]." Father Berrigan also beheld "healthy, skittish children ranged along the wall, ready to sing for us."[171] Both the people and the landscape were often characterized as "gentle" (sometimes "the gentlest people we had ever known").[172] Susan Sontag (along with Mary McCarthy) was convinced that these

---

* It was symptomatic of this guilt and the naiveté of the visitors that many of them expressed surprise at the absence of hostile behavior on the part of the population,[167] as if the natives did not know that any foreigners could only have been there as important guests of the government and as such protected by it quite literally too, by the ever present official guides.

† Even when encountered abroad, Vietnamese people inspired awe and a special reverence: "To sit in the same room, to cut cane with the people who symbolize the strength and the consciousness we are striving for, and then to be able to talk to them, ask them questions, answer their questions, *to be considered comrades in struggle by the Vietnamese people*—that was the thing."[170]

gentle and kind people "genuinely cared about the welfare of . . . captured American pilots."[173] Dr. Coffin found the North Vietnamese official first encountered "serene and dignified," a North Vietnamese judge full of vitality, and the chairman of the "solidarity committee," "a middle aged man with a quick mind and a lively sense of humor." The prime minister was not only "unusually energetic," "his laugh was infectious."[174] Father Berrigan saw him as a person with "a face of great intelligence" and "great reserves of compassion," "A humanist in an inhuman time."[175] Mary McCarthy said that he was "a man of magnetic allure, thin, with deep-set brilliant eyes, crisp, short electric grey hair, full rueful lips. . . . The passion and directness of his delivery matched something fiery but also melancholy, in those coaly eyes. An emotional, impressionable man, I thought, and at the same time highly intellectual."[176] Tom Hayden and Staughton Lynd (who "constantly heard poetry and music of all kinds" in the streets of Hanoi) connected the appealing qualities of the people to the system:

> We knew too what the Vietnamese contribution to a humane socialism would be; it was evident in the unembarrassed handclasps among men, the poetry and song at the center of man-woman relationships, the freedom to weep practised by everyone . . . as the Vietnamese speak of their country. . . . Here we began to understand the possibilities for a socialism of the heart.[177]

Even the one-party system was transformed: "when love enters into the substance of social relations, the connection of people to a single party need not be dehumanizing," wrote Susan Sontag,[178] and Daniel Berrigan thought that "The mystery of the resources of this people" could be explained by "its political leadership . . . exercising power in so new a way."[179]

Such comments and others suggest that the visitors, and especially the Americans among them, projected upon Vietnam their ideals and desires with a remarkable abandon and deeply misunderstood the nature of that society in a manner comparable to the misapprehension of Soviet society at earlier times. There was also the predictable process of contextual redefinition. For instance, while healthy and happy-looking children in an American kindergarten would not have been regarded as proof of the superiority of capitalism over socialism, in North Vietnam "the presence of beautiful children . . . is evidence of the regime's benevolence."[180]

It is perhaps also significant that in the case of Vietnam there seems even more emphasis, in the accounts of the visitors, on the spiritual qualities of the people and the system than with respect to Cuba and the Soviet Union. This was not just a progressive, just, and advanced society; it was also quite extraodinary, totally different from everything experienced before, dignified and uplifted in a distinctive way, its people and government alike in a virtual state of grace. Again, such perceptions and descriptions undoubtedly had to do with the exotic character of the place and people, the (misplaced) guilt of many visitors and the state of war and the hardships and dangers it imposed, which heightened every impression and deepened every appeal. Father Berrigan captured this frame of mind eloquently:

> Evidently something extraordinary is happening to me, which I am not in a position to analyze very thoroughly now. But a great gift, granted to few Americans, is in my hands. I am so strangely and so immediately at home in this new world, where myths are being shattered by the immediate experience of suffering and survival. . . . For the man of faith such an experience induces reflection on what God may mean by granting this trip. . . .[181]

While the circumstances of war added unusual elements to the pilgrimage to Vietnam and heightened certain appeals of the North Vietnamese regime (such as those of shared purpose, sense of community, and social cohesion), they also enhanced the egalitarian aspects of the society and brought its distributive justice into sharper focus. The social-economic transformations were rendered particularly impressive because of the war: every effort to better the life of the population was made in spite of the war and the diversion of resources it required. Thus Daniel Berrigan admired "a people, who in the midst of a rain of death conceive and push to fruition a museum of art. . . ."[182] Somewhat predictably the visitors commented most favorably on the achievements of the system in the spheres of education, including adult education, and the overcoming of illiteracy,[183] on public health,[184] housing in the villages,[185] and also on the cleanliness and orderliness experienced[186] which was tempting to associate with the puritanical elements of the social system. Several visitors were also impressed by the frugality, simplicity, and limited use of technology. As Susan Sontag succinctly put it, "To observe . . . a society based on the principle of total use is particularly impressive to someone who comes from a society based on maximal waste."[187]

Finally, in North Vietnam (as in Cuba and China) the achievements of the regime were enhanced by contrasting them with the deprivations and backwardness of the past—in addition to viewing them against the background of the war.[188]

Vietnam and Cuba were not the only Third World countries idealized by Western intellectuals, although they were the most important and attracted the largest numbers of visitors. While the end of the war and the boat people diminished the attractions of North Vietnam, the popularity of Cuba declined for the reasons noted earlier. Inevitably, there was also a loss of novelty and revolutionary freshness as the twentieth anniversary of the Cuban Revolution approached and passed. Thus, at least some Western intellectuals had reason to turn their attentions to other countries in the Third World. Besides China there were fleeting flirtations with Algeria, Albania, North Korea, Tanzania, Mozambique, and even Cambodia.[189] Albania and Mozambique in particular enjoyed some measure of popularity among radical Western European intellectuals. According to Jan Myrdal:

> Due to its principled struggle, the small Albanian people have become the focus of interest for militant trade union activists in the Swedish mining districts, Polish dockers fighting for socialism against their new bosses, students from Africa, leaders of the underground resistance against the fascist generals in Chile, and many others. And Tirana, which once was a secluded Balkan city, is becoming a meeting place for discussing and exchanging experiences.[190]

If Jan Myrdal perhaps overestimated the impact of Albania on the world outside, he himself was unquestionably its best-known admirer (he had earlier also visited and praised China). His account suggests that the appeals of Albania were strikingly similar to all the other countries considered in this study, and especially those of Cuba. As Jan Myrdal saw it, Albania was a tiny, super-underdog country bullied not only by the Western imperialists, but also by the new pseudo-socialist topdogs such as Yugoslavia and the Soviet Union.[191] Myrdal, while trying to rehabilitate Albania, so to speak, and defend her against both Soviet and Western slander, also seemed to uphold the indulgent Albanian view of Stalin and Stalinism.[192] Myrdal liked Albania for being small, defiant, and independent of the great powers and for exactly the same reason others were attracted to Cuba, namely, for rescuing the good name of socialism tarnished by the Soviet-type bureaucratic, inegalitarian system of government.[193] In Albania true collectivism reigned, genuine egalitarianism flourished, bureaucracy was dealt one blow after another: officers in the army "wore no indication of rank," manual and mental labor were being merged, income differentials were shrinking, and party democracy prevailed. ("The party does not stand above the people. The working class is in power; the party serves the working masses.") There was also, need it be said, an impressive and authentic sense of community in this beleaguered nation. Even the individualistic, household-based bread-baking methods were overcome, though evidently not without some resistance. Albanian centralized planning produced harmony with nature. Vast improvements in education and public health took place.[194] Albania too, like the other countries admired, came complete with a wise, inspiring, powerful, popular, and durable leader: Enver Hoxha, "one of the great working-class leaders and Marxist-Leninists of our time," "one of the great figures in Albanian history and one of the outstanding Communists in the world today. For this he is respected and beloved. But he is not the subject of a cult of personality; he does not stand above or outside the people. . . . he is applauded not as a personality but as a founder and servant of the party."[195] Myrdal himself realized that his portrait of Albania had an all too familiar ring: "So far the description sounds like one from the Soviet Union in the 1930s. A USSR in construction, but on a much smaller scale on the shores of the Adriatic."[196]

Besides Jan Myrdal and the Scandinavian students (to whom reference was made in the first chapter) Albania had at least one well-known American admirer, Scott Nearing, who found its people "'rested, secure, hopeful, cheerful' in a land without poverty, where 'they are building solidly and fundamentally for a better future.' "[197]

Albania was not the only country in recent times whose attractions recalled those discovered in other lands by other generations of seekers. According to a French author, Serge Thion, "Quite a few people in Europe and Africa consider Mozambique a revolutionary success story. President Samora Machel's speeches receive slowly rising quotations on the revolutionary theoreticians' stock exchange. We have known enough other examples of these infatuations in which the political intelligentsia is prone to see what it searches for. . . ."[198]

Evidently Tom Wicker of the New York *Times* was one of those who found "Hope and Discipline" in Mozambique during his "brief but intense visit." After noting that housing projects in Mozambique were superior to many in the United States, and finding the communal villages, to which the "rural population is drawn—not forced," impressive, he concluded: "something seems to be going on here that has resulted in hope and discipline, and people of all races working toward a new society from the wreckage of colonialism and war." Mozambique, too, like Cuba and Albania, was, in the eyes of this beholder, a new departure, not a "carbon copy."[199]

Evidently Tom Wicker was not alone. It was reported in the New York *Times* that

> The idealistic left, in Africa, Europe and America is now looking to this country [Mozambique] as it once looked to Ghana, Algeria and more recently Tanzania as fertile ground for the nurturing of socialism's "new man" . . .
>   . . . it is largely the influx of Westerners that serves to underscore Mozambique's particular role in testing the idea that the seeds of scientific socialism can flower in Africa without repression, or economic chaos.

In Mozambique the *Times* reporter found "social innovations through which [the] . . . Government is seeking to transform this country . . . into a nonracist, nontribal, nonexploitative and self-reliant society." The reporter also noted, during his two-week visit, grass roots organization, social cohesion, pragmatism, concern with the personal problems of members of various collectives, and "an appearance of movement and orderliness." It was "clear" to him "that President Machel's Government enjoys popularity and support." At last it may be noted that a publication of the American Friends Service Committee ("Letters from Mozambique") also "paint[ed] a picture of Mozambican society that is as pretty as Bragg's [another Quaker official] vision of the new Vietnam."[200]

Even the new Iranian system under Ayatollah Khomeini was capable of arousing high hopes. In the words of Richard Falk, "Having created a new model of popular revolution based, for the most part, on nonviolent tactics, Iran may yet provide us with a desperately needed model of humane governance for a third-world country."[201]

It is unlikely that the appeals of Albania or Mozambique will become widespread or enduring. Nevertheless, even if confined to smaller numbers of devotees, the accounts of visits to these countries suggest that the ingredients of what make countries appealing for Western intellectuals are remarkably constant and changed very little from the 1930s to the 1960s and from the 1960s to the 1970s.

7

The Pilgrimage to China:
Old Dreams in a New Setting

To me China seemed a kind of benign monarchy ruled by an emperor priest who had won the complete devotion of his subjects. In short, a religious and highly moralistic society.   URIE BRONFENBRENNER[1]

. . . a people is marching with a light step and with fervor toward the future. This people may be the incarnation of the new civilization of the world. China has made an unprecedented leap into history.
MARIA ANTONIETTA MACCIOCCHI[2]

. . . life in China today is exceptionally pleasant. . . . Plenty of fond dreams are authorized by the idea of a country where the government pays the people's way through school, where generals and statesmen are scholars and poets.   SIMONE DE BEAUVOIR[3]

The people seem healthy, well fed and articulate about their role as citizens of Chairman Mao's new China . . . the change in the countryside is miraculous. . . . The Maoist revolution is on the whole the best thing that happened to the Chinese people in centuries . . . Maoism . . . has got results . . .   JOHN K. FAIRBANK[4]

. . . a country which has become almost as painstakingly careful about human lives as New Zealand.   HANS KONIGSBERGER[5]

The pilgrimage to China is the final example of the apparently endless search for superior social systems on the part of Western intellectuals.

In regard to the visits to China, somewhat sharper differences may be noted between the attitudes of Americans and Western Europeans than in the case of the journeys to the Soviet Union and Cuba. Western Europeans have been going to Communist China for a longer period than Americans—since the early 1950s, that is, while few Americans went to China before 1972, owing to the ruptured diplomatic and political relations. By the same token, following 1972, American visitors probably outnumbered the Western European ones as the trip to China suddenly became possible and highly desirable among elite and up-to-date intellectuals and many politicians.* For Western Europeans, whose countries extended diplomatic recognition to China long before the U.S., visiting China did not have the same associations of daring adventure or delicious novelty which it has acquired for many Americans. Unlike Americans, European intellectuals traveled to China without feeling the need to expiate the sins of their country and with less of an expectation of an impending crisis in their own society. Their visits spanned decades; those of the Americans clustered in the years of the earlier 1970s. While the ethos of the 1960s provides a backdrop to many visits, European as well as American, the 60s were more turbulent in the U.S. and more devastating for the collective self-confidence of Americans than Western Europeans. Unlike Western Europe, the U.S. was deeply involved in the Indochina War and torn by racial conflict. The rejection of society in the U.S. was probably more widespread, if not more intense, than in Western Europe, not only for the reasons noted above but also because of a far greater proportion of college students in the population.

In many ways the social-political, if not economic, conditions in the U.S. in the late 1960s and early 70s were reminiscent of those which prevailed in the late 1920s and early 30s: both sets of conditions were conducive to a search for political and spiritual alternatives. As in the 30s, the waves of disillusionment with American society carried the intellectuals (and many non-intellectuals) to the shores of a new society, this time China, even more mysterious, distant, and poorly known than the Soviet Union used to be. The sense of crisis and malaise was similar in both periods even if the specific sources and expressions of discontent were not.

China, even more than the Soviet Union in the 1930s, was seen by many Western intellectuals as a country shrouded in ignorance, maligned in the mass media, and mistreated by the politicians. A very high proportion of the visitors to China, and especially the Americans among them, went in a spirit of rectifying this state of affairs. They wanted to

---

* Lucian Pye, an academic "Old China Hand," observed that "A current status symbol among American opinion-makers is to have traveled to China. . . . One delegation after the other comes back to report that they too have . . . toured the Great Wall, the Ming Tombs, the Forbidden City . . . visited the same communes, factories, neighborhood committees, nursery schools and industrial exhibitions; attended identical briefings about economic planning, educational policy, and the contrast between before and after 'liberation' in the peoples' livelihood."[6]

dispel misinformation, lay to rest hostile stereotypes, clear up misunder-
standings, "break through the walls of ignorance,"[7] and correct misconceptions.[8] It was also significant that most of the trips (at least on the
part of the Americans) were undertaken in the aftermath or toward the
end of the Vietnam War, when disenchantment with "Establishment"
views and attitudes, especially toward communism, was at a high level,
particularly among intellectuals. If American policy-makers and those
supportive of them had hitherto been critical of China, this *ipso facto*
called for a rebuttal. If views of China were until now colored by the
spirit of the Cold War and anti-communism, both discredited by American involvement in Vietnam, this called for vigorous reaction, for demystification. If Communist China was presented in the American mass
media and in some books as unfree, regimented, or totalitarian, it was
incumbent on the generation of new visitors to refute or modify such
views. The new truth about China was bound to be different from the
old one.

Another circumstance related to but not reducible to the after-effects
of Vietnam played a part in the new American perceptions of China.
The pervasive disenchantment with American society among intellectuals in the late 60s and early 70s made it generally difficult for many
of them to be critical of other societies.* The who-are-we-to-lecture-
others attitude gained a new momentum in these years comparable to
the negative, self-reproachful disposition prevalent among intellectuals
in the early 1930s. For example Hans Konigsberger, the American
writer, asked:

> what right do we Westerners have, freshly back from plundering the
> world for four centuries, fat and rich and worried about calories, what
> nerve do we really have, to poke around here and see if there's dust
> on the political piano, and worry so nobly whether these people [the
> Chinese], whose former drowning or starving by the millions didn't
> make our front pages, have enough democratic rights?[9]

Unlike the 1930s, in the late 1960s and the early 1970s it was not an
economic depression that shattered the self-confidence of the general
public and deepened the estrangement of intellectuals. As noted in

---

* Except those seen as in some way affiliated with or dependent upon the United
States: for example, Taiwan, South Korea, Greece (under the military dictatorship),
or South Africa. In all these, and other similar instances, the criticism directed at
these societies derived its fervor from the possibility of linking whatever deplorable
conditions existed in the countries concerned, in some manner, to American policies.

Chapter 5, this was more a spiritual crisis, one of value, belief, and cultural standards.

The background of the visits to China also differed from that of the tours of Cuba. It will be recalled that interest in Cuba was at its peak at the time and immediately after the Cuban Revolution, and it reflected conditions in the United States—associated with the 1950s—quite different from those of the early 70s. Moreover, the visits to Cuba never equaled in volume and media attention those to China. The admiration of Cuba remained the domain of a smaller number of intellectuals; the reverential interest in China became a deluge; it ranged from the pronouncements of elite intellectuals to the enthusiasm of mass circulation magazines. After many years of isolation, China was more of a novelty, and a country much bigger and more important than Cuba. The varied manifestations of interest in China included growing enrollment in Chinese courses at colleges, interest in Chinese theater, music, dancing, medicine, history, and even fashions. The New York *Times* noted that

> The Chinese impact has been most noticeable in fashions and decorating. Veronika Yhap . . . in charge of sales and marketing for Dragon Lady, a company that imports apparel from China, said: "The interest is fantastic. The buyers will take anything. . . . It's incredible." Even Mrs. Richard M. Nixon has been affected by the Chinese craze. The *Ladies' Home Journal* has on the cover of its February issue a picture of the First Lady in a Chinese style gown. . . . Describing this situation Mrs. Yhap said: "We try to introduce Americans to the real China of today—the people's suits worn by the workers and peasants." She said the suits, which sell for approximately $130, are popular in colleges. . . . Professor Alexander Eckstein . . . a specialist on the Chinese economy commented: "There is a fantastic mystique. I have been amazed. . . . I never expected Ping-Pong would evoke the kind of reaction that it did. There is an incredible amount of curiosity, goodwill and sympathy."[10]

While the focus of this study is upon the intellectuals, it should be noted that the pilgrimage to China was not confined to them, nor to those who had a prior, ascertainable sympathy toward China. Joseph Alsop, the well-known American newspaper columnist who had earlier been hostile, was invited, and "his columns, which are distributed to 250 newspapers, were full of a sense of amazement and admiration at what he called 'the new China.' " His reports of his one-month journey "reflected much of the new warmth of the revised American image of China."[11] Harrison Salisbury, another well-known journalist who had earlier reported on the Soviet Union, was also caught up in the mood: "it seemed to me," he wrote, "that there could be no more vital task than to apprehend in some measure the density, the velocity, the viscosity, the sheer magnitude of the Chinese spirit."[12] Even some of the disabled went, as testified to in the "Observations of a Wheelchair Traveler in China."[13] A British social scientist, Peter Worsley, commented on the new wave of interest and its broad basis:

> People want to find out because they feel that China represents two things: the revival of hope in the possibility of change, including very radical and revolutionary change, and a fascinated interest in the detailed lineaments of the Chinese model itself . . .

> What is striking . . . in the new wave of enthusiasm for China is that it is not . . . a response mainly among the young; older people are equally interested. Nor is it an interest confined to the Left.[14]

Thus, for many intellectuals, American and Western European alike, China was important (as Cuba had been earlier) as the exemplar of a new type of socialism untainted by the bitter experiences and flaws associated with the Soviet model. David Kolodney wrote in *Ramparts*:

> At the same time that we adopted the Chinese model of revolutionary purity as a political touchstone . . . we drew upon it as a source of energy and hope. China served as proof that the revolutionary process can make a difference, that it can realize a vision of fundamental social change. . . . China's intransigence gave us hope. . . . The real importance of the Chinese revolution to the American Left was . . . in the widely held conviction that . . . this revolution was really revolutionary.[15]

Maria Macciocchi, an Italian writer-journalist, advised that "we should [not] cling to the Chinese experience as blindly as we did to that of the USSR . . . or transfer to China the hopes placed earlier in the Soviet Union. One historical error cannot be redeemed with another."[16] These warnings notwithstanding, she proceeded to render a largely uncritical account of what she had seen.

K. S. Karol "had seen [as a former resident in the Soviet Union] the deceptions practised on foreign visitors: the ragged people sent out of sight, the shops filled for the occasion. . . . He also knew that being unable to speak Chinese or to contact people except through official interpreters, he would find it difficult to penetrate deeply into Chinese life." In spite of all this "he concluded that in China things were very much as they seemed . . . that Chinese society is fundamentally more decent and less hypocritical than the society he knew in the USSR."[17]

Such and similar assessments of China have undergone considerable change after the demise of the "Gang of Four" which followed the death of Mao. Yet it is safe to say that throughout the 1960s and early 70s the appeals of China, like those of Cuba, derived to a great extent from the belief that China successfully avoided the errors of the Soviet Union, including the undue emphasis on industrialization at the expense of agricultural development, and the attendant food shortages and mistreatment of peasants, the bloody purges and, more generally, the terror and coercion associated with the rule of Stalin.° By the late 1970s many people were not so sure. Bernard Frolic, a Canadian student of both China and the Soviet Union, concluded that "the Stalinist thirties and the China of the Great Leap and of the Cultural Revolution are quite similar" and that "the Chinese experience is rather akin to that of the Soviet Union of the twenties and thirties (and today)"[18] in regard to elite and mass relationships, bureaucratization, and egalitarianism. Another visitor to China Peter Kenez (a historian of the Soviet Union) also found much too much similarity:

> I was unprepared for the narrowness of the limits of possible subjects for discussions, facts and events to be publicly mentioned.
> China in this respect is a caricature of the Soviet Union of the 1930s and 1940s. There, too, facts became facts only if they received official recognition. . . . Even there [in the USSR, that is] it never happened that the meeting of the Party Congress was announced only two days after it adjourned. Even Stalin never disdained the people to such an extent as to keep in secret the place of meeting.[19]

Such comments and parallels were, however, unusual not only because few people visiting China were well informed about Soviet society, but because of the prevalence of a predisposition to find virtue in China that could no longer be found in the Soviet Union. Frolic provided a retrospective summary of the attitudes involved:

> From the events of 1966–71 there evolved a Chinese concept of development that captured our imagination with its simplicity and promise. The Chinese were going to develop without the chaos and disruption that had previously accompanied modernization throughout the rest of the world, capitalist or socialist. The Soviet Union had succumbed to the evils of industrialization and Westernization, but need it be so for the Chinese?
>
> . . . In the "developed" West, the idea of an emerging Chinese model appealed to many of us for a variety of reasons. The occupation of

---

° It was a belief that in turn reduced sensitivity to those unappealing features of the Chinese regime which were not of Soviet derivation.

Czechoslovakia had just taken place. . . . We were, therefore, more willing to listen to the Chinese and to be more sympathetic to their cause if only because they were so aggressively anti-Soviet. (We knew too much about the Russians and, as it turned out, perhaps too little about the Chinese.) Second, China was exotic to most of us, a repository of the wonderful secrets of the mysterious East. So why not accept the proposition that this strange culture may actually have found a superior way to modernize? . . . Third, commitment to the new China was a form of expiation for some Westerners who felt that China had been wronged and exploited in its encounters with the West. . . . Fourth, for many intellectuals struggling to cope with the moral crisis of the sixties, the Chinese model was a beacon of salvation showing that there still was hope for mankind. . . . Finally, for radicals throughout the world, the Chinese example was one last try for utopia, a more plausible socialist synthesis than anything tried in the past.[20]

Whatever the similarities and differences between the appeals of China in the 70s and the Soviet Union in the 30s, the general frame of mind of the intellectuals embarking on their trips was similar in both instances.

Now, as before, the visitors were anxious to avoid the imposition of standards or values which could lead to the making of critical judgments. According to Macciocchi, "The traveler who judges China by Western standards will understand nothing and be at a complete loss."[21] This attitude was paradoxical on two counts. First, Western standards were the only ones Western visitors could apply, hard as they might have tried not to. Secondly, it was precisely in the light of Western standards—of social justice, equality and radical social change—that societies such as Communist China could be admired, to the extent that they appeared to live up to these standards.

A delegation of Quakers pondered the same issue:

How shall the Westerner look at China and its people? . . .

The American social experience of pluralism and diversity and the relatively ungoverned U.S. economy do not constitute the lens through which Americans can successfully examine the basis of Chinese society. . . . We had a concern for world peace and friendship. . . . We were determined to see with friendly eyes, but also with as much objective discernment . . . as our own national and cultural conditioning would allow.[22]

David Selbourne, an English playwright, proposed what might be called the socialist-realist travel perspective:

in spite of the richness of detail which is there to be seen, the structures and processes which have brought the Chinese masses to their
"present," and which are bearing them to a future different in every
respect from that which now confronts Western civilization, are not—
cannot be—visible to the "naked eye." . . . To get behind the im-
mediacy of those appearances, to discover the inner structure of this
great historic movement, we need a change of focus, a switch of lens,
a mode of writing which does not "stick to appearances," which is not
transfixed by the naturalistic illusion.[23]

In short, as Zhdanov, the Soviet authority on the arts, explained,
reality had to be captured not as it is, visible to the naked eye, but as it
unfolds, in its emergent essence—a suggestion designed to obliterate the
distinction between the way things are and the way they ought to be,
according to ideological requirements.

Some visitors in attempting to "understand" what the new Chinese
regime had done came close to endorsing the very policies which limited
their own access to the people and the country. Professor John K. Fairbank, the Harvard sinologist, wrote: "Today China's strict limitation of
access is a refreshing contrast in Chinese eyes to the subservience of
treaty times. The revolutionary generation deem it only appropriate that
foreign contact like all other developments should be under rational and
purposeful control."[24] E. H. Johnson, secretary for research and planning of the Board of World Mission of the Presbyterian Church of Canada, wrote about his preparation for the visit:

> In planning our visit . . . we purposely excluded contact with the
> Church as one of our objectives. Positively we wanted the focus of
> our visit to be on development in contemporary China so that we
> could give full attention to understanding the China experiment as the
> Chinese themselves would present it. Negatively, we felt it better not
> to seek Church contact lest it might be embarrassing to Chinese Chris-
> tians trying to carry on church activities quietly.[25]

Such attitudes were not uncommon among visitors who were determined to avoid situations that might detract from the spirit of goodwill
and approbation they brought with themselves. Happily, Mr. Johnson's
intentions and those of his hosts converged: he was ready to absorb
favorable impressions and they strove to impart them.

In the case of journalists, professional as well as sentimental factors
combined to create self-censorship and a readiness to be cooperative
with the hosts. Stanley Karnow wrote:

> most American newsmen visiting China these days are reluctant to
> pose tough questions. . . . For example we hesitated to ask about

China's defense establishment . . . and we made no attempts to seek out dissenters. . . . Nor did we complain when the Chinese refused to show us such innocuous places as a newspaper office or a television station . . . I think that our mildness was partly motivated by the opportunistic concern that we might be blacklisted from getting back to China. . . . But more significantly we were probably sentimental enough to believe that we could not be discourteous. Subliminally perhaps we still viewed the Chinese as underdogs to whom we owed our sympathy, and thus we bent over backwards to be polite.[26]

Like the sympathetic visitors to the Soviet Union and Cuba, many travelers to China were also ready to see things in a more favorable light because of the context. Felix Greene wrote: "No experience in my life shook me so deeply as this first visit to China. I was not blind to the mistakes that were being made or the extent of poverty that still existed. I knew something, too, of the suffering and bloodshed that had accompanied the birth of this new China. But all this took on a new meaning in the light of the accomplishments that I could see around me. . . ."[27]

Sometimes grotesquely unrealistic and improbably negative anticipations led to the equally unrealistic reversal of the expectations. Ruth Sidel, an American social work specialist, confessed that "We expected to see a poor country with some of the usual signs of poverty—teeming cities with beggars in the streets . . . a country with a strong military presence, marching men, and a highly visible army. . . ."[28] Having found none of these, she produced a most enthusiastic and largely uncritical account.

Generally speaking, the generation of American political tourists of the early 1970s embarked on the journey to China with reverence, solicitousness, and guilt, a blend of attitudes that rarely stimulates the exercise of critical faculties. These attitudes were also discernible in regard to cultural exchanges:

> For American citizens, cultural exchanges offer the exciting possibility of learning more about a long-forbidden land. For many Americans, there also seems to be an added dimension of feeling that it is necessary somehow to make amends for the years of enmity between the two countries. For a few Americans enthusiasm for almost any aspect of exchange becomes a form of *mea culpa,* for what they thought went wrong during the McCarthy period. Consequently, there is a widespread American taboo about making any kind of criticism not only of what is learned about China, but also about the manner in which the Chinese conduct their side of exchanges.[29]

China was unusually well suited to become a candidate for the part of the virtuous underdog-nation in American eyes. First, the U.S. sinned against the Communist regime by aiding Chiang Kai-shek in the civil war; later, by refusing to grant diplomatic recognition and blocking U.N. membership. Moreover, such actions contrasted sharply with earlier more benign if paternalistic policies toward China: a special ward of the United States teeming with American missionaries, educators, advisers.

Not unlike the Soviet Union in the 1930s, China had something for everybody: for the puritan, a hard-working, simple, efficiently modernizing country; for the cultural connoisseur, thousands of years of Chinese culture; for the frustrated leftist, a Marxist-Leninist regime restoring the good name of Marxism; above all, and for most visitors, there was a land of mystery, beauty, purpose, and order, a former victim acquiring power and dignity, a nation seemingly possessing all the virtues Americans sorely missed in their own society during and after the war in Vietnam.

Yet, when all is said and done, the extent to which such predispositions altered perceptions and judgments was quite remarkable, especially since it had happened before (in the Soviet case) and also because there existed by the 1970s a body of informative and judicious literature on China. The latter included both the work of American specialists such as Doak Barnett, Jerome Cohen, Martin Whyte, and Ezra Vogel and also numerous books produced by Western European authors. It was not until the climate of opinion changed after the death of Mao that, for the first time in over a decade, a book sharply critical of China, *Chinese Shadows* by Belgian sinologist Simon Leys, was given widespread attention and a respectable hearing. Leys's remarks about Solzhenitsyn (made elsewhere) could have been applied to the impact of his own writings: "the most amazing thing about Solzhenitsyn's impact is that the West reacted to it as if it was *news*. Actually Solzhenitsyn's unique contribution lies in the volume and precision of his catalogue of atrocities—but basically *he revealed nothing new*."[30] Although the volume of critical writing (before Leys was published) on China was smaller than the corresponding literature on the Soviet Union which had accumulated prior to Solzhenitsyn (between the 1930s and 1960s), there was such information but it did not get attention and found no resonance. Let us take the basic issue of how much the visitor could learn about Chinese society in the course of a few weeks' visit.

Herbert Passin, an American sociologist, wrote as early as 1963 about the aim of the Chinese cultural exchanges:

> the Chinese have a much clearer conception of their goals and a greater sense of urgency about them. Nothing is left to chance. . . .
>
> The ultimate advantage . . . is the ability of the Chinese Communists to control and focus the entire experience, both because of their great organizational skill and their control of the environment. . . . Most of the visitors come on whirlwind tours in delegations. . . . For the period of his stay, which may vary from a week to two months—the average is probably three weeks—the visitor is treated as an honored guest. He is shown every courtesy, surrounded by luxury, and given every attention. . . . one of the·key operational principles of Chinese cultural diplomacy [is] *to make contact with the susceptibilities, preoccupations and dispositions of the visitors.* . . .
>
> The itineraries are very carefully planned. . . . Normally the visitor is taken to model institutions—schools, factories, kindergartens, collective farms, people's communes. But since many visitors are prepared for the Potemkin village technique, the Chinese very skillfully have alternatives available. . . . in virtually all cases, the alternatives too have been pre-selected.
>
> . . . non-official Chinese will be very careful not to involve themselves in unauthorized contacts with foreigners. . . . Moreover the visitor cannot have private, unscrutinized contacts. If he visits "an ordinary worker" in his home there will be guides, interpreters, or hosts. . . .
>
> The visitor's insulation from real contact with the people is therefore heightened by the careful control of the environment as well as by his own lack of language ability, unfamiliarity with people and with the country, and by the normal, initial reserve of the Chinese people. And when this is a matter of state policy as well, his chances of real contact are almost non-existent.[31]

Robert Guillain, a French writer, observed in 1957:

> There is no Bamboo Curtain, and yet a more subtle veil was always kept skillfully and firmly drawn between China and myself . . . there are six hundred million Chinese, but in two months I was never left alone to speak with one of them without a witness . . . I was never able . . . to visit with my guides at random a house in some district of my choice. I could never stop and make enquiries in a factory, a farm, an institution . . . unless the visit had been planned in advance. . . . I went nowhere without an interpreter by my side. . . . Nothing is left to chance. . . .
>
> Finally—an unbreakable rule—the attentive guides never show the visitor anything that is not excellent or even exceptional but they refrain from telling him so. . . .[32]

Lorenz Stucki, Swiss political commentator and correspondent for the *Neue Züricher Zeitung,* wrote in 1965:

> Even more forbidding than the walls within walls is the official Chinese travel agency . . . the foreign visitor is made utterly dependent on it; he cannot escape its ministrations, and soon he realizes that the attention lavished on him is a device meant to isolate him from everyday China.
>
> Whether visiting a nursery school or a university, a factory, hospital or people's commune, the routine is invariably the same; the visitor is shown to a reception room where the chief administrator or his deputy, in the presence of at least two other men or women, delivers a standard talk. . . .
>
> The visits to schools, factories, hospitals, handicraft shops, etc., do not open up anything. On the contrary, by erecting glittering props, they isolate. . . . It is impossible to find out or even sense what is in the minds of the people. . . . There is no personal contact, hardly even a glance, a smile or a gesture. One experiences nothing, discovers nothing, learns nothing that is spontaneous, unrehearsed, natural and open. . . .[33]

Jacques Marcuse, a French journalist, wrote in 1967:

> The special correspondent is given the VIPP (Very Important Potential Propagandist) treatment. . . . He is taken straight to the marketplace, so to speak, there to make his choice and do his professional shopping. He does not always realize that it is a *special* market and a sham market. . . . by and large, the shorter the stay, the more favorable the report.
>
> In Shanghai the beautiful simplicity of the system struck me with even greater force: you do not allow visitors to see anything but that which you want them to see.[34]

Jules Roy, a French writer, noted in 1967 after his trip:

> I had labored for six months and had accumulated twenty pounds of notes before leaving for China, yet I had known nothing and I know very little more today. . . . I had only gone from hotel to hotel, from city to city, always escorted by my little group of mandarins . . . the bulk of our conversations converned nothing but commonplaces. . . .[35]

Another French author and regular contributor to *Le Monde,* Alfred Fabre-Luce, wrote in 1959:

> Everything fell into place around me as though by a miracle . . . surrounded with attention but deprived of all initiative, a silent traveler, both prince and prisoner. . . .

> Like conjurors able to produce rabbits from a hat, they are prepared
> to offer you a factory, a circus, a curiosity shop, a doctor, a workers'
> club, and even a capitalist.[36]

As early as in 1959, a former Chinese guide, Robert Loh, who had de-
fected, provided a wealth of information on the elaborate techniques,
as seen from the inside, that the Chinese regime used to make favorable
impressions on the visitors. For example:

> The Party selected certain cities where the travelers could "freely
> choose" to go. . . . In these cities, the best hotels were chosen for of-
> ficial guesthouses. . . . Top quality consumer goods such as tea, silk,
> brocade and the works of art unavailable in the open market were sold
> to visitors at ridiculously low prices. . . . in every city the authorities
> made careful arrangements to give the illusion that nothing was pre-
> arranged and staged.[37]

There were other books published in the 1960s which were critical of
various aspects of the system and had little impact on public opinion
(especially American) or on that of intellectuals, and which certainly
failed to dampen their enthusiasm a few years or a decade later when
they went on their tours. They included Sven Lindquist's *China in Crisis*
(1963), based on his experiences as a student, and Alberto Moravia's
Red Book and the Great Wall (1968), which expressed distaste at the
extinction of free expression in the arts and literature, among other
things. Hugo Portisch, a German journalist, had his *Red China Today*
published in English in 1966, as did Harry Hamm, another German
correspondent, his *China*. There was Susan Labin's *The Anthill*, based
on interviews with refugees in Hong Kong, published in 1960. This and
other information provided by refugees was often shunned by sympathizers (though not by China scholars) on the grounds that since refugees were hostile to the system their reports could not be trusted. Manes
Sperber's essay "Pilgrims to Utopia"[38] was also ignored. There was even
an account by a disillusioned African student, Emmanuel John Hevi
(published in 1963), which likewise had little impact. The eager "delegations" of American visitors which sprang upon China in the early 70s
acted as if there had been little worth knowing about China until they
stepped on its soil. (This attitude, needless to say, did not characterize
most China scholars.) That virtually all available unfavorable information on China was ignored or brushed aside by the most recent generation of political tourists is another indication of the weight that predispositions carry in the making of political judgments. Ironically this
occurred in part because of the value attached to "being-on-the-spot" and

"seeing-things-for-oneself."[39] The mystique of personal experience as the only authentic one was especially strong in the early 70s when the values of the 60s stressing the importance of feeling and direct experience were still much alive.

"The truth" or the many truths about China will not for some years be established or widely agreed upon. Still, it is worthwhile to remember in the late 70s (when this study was written) that much that came to light in the wake of the fall of the "Gang of Four" was already known and noted by many in the 1960s. It may yet become possible to apply to the study of Chinese politics and society under Mao what Adam Ulam said about the study of the Soviet Union under Stalin:

> We who study Soviet affairs have . . . a skeleton in our filing cabinets. To describe this skeleton let me invoke a fictitious case of two fictitious characters, X and Y. In his attempt to learn as much as possible about the Soviet Union, X, between roughly 1930 and 1950, read nothing but the works of reputable, non-communist authors. He grounded himself on the writings of the Webbs and Sir John Maynard. Turning to American academicians, he followed the studies of Soviet government . . . which might have come from the pens of a professor at Chicago, Harvard, Columbia, or Williams. . . . His friend Y had an equal ambition to learn but his taste ran to the non-scholarly and melodramatic . . . he would seek the key to Soviet politics in the writings of the avowed enemies of the regime, like ex-Mensheviks; he would delight in the fictional accounts à la Koestler or Victor Serge. Sinking lower Y would pursue trashy or sensational stories of the "I Was a Prisoner of the Red Terror" variety. He would infuriate X by insisting that there were aspects of Soviet politics which are more easily understood by studying the struggle between Al Capone and Dan Torrio than the one between Lenin and Martov, or the dispute about "socialism in one country." Which of the fictitious characters would have been in a better position to understand the nature of Soviet politics under Stalin?[40]

Sense of Purpose in a Moral Society

To find the source of happiness and contentment in the non-material realms of life has been an ancient dream of Western man, increasingly implicated in and dependent on the material world for its comfort, sense of security and mastery. Freedom from the temptations of the material world has also been the centerpiece of major religious beliefs. *To be poor and happy* has been a desire that intensified in proportion with the decline of poverty and the increase of self-conscious dissatisfaction with the materially secure but spiritually unfulfilled life. A wide variety of groups and individuals—monks, mendicants, hermits, bohemian artists, political activists, hippies and communards of more recent times—have in common the overpowering desire to be poor and happy, unencumbered by possessions, material aspirations, possessiveness, greed.

China had much to offer to gratify such longings. It was undeniably a poor nation, but its poverty was of an elevating, not debilitating, nature. Felix Greene, the English writer, ably captured the sentiments felt by many Western visitors upon encountering this type of poverty:

> In the streets, I walked into the throbbing life of a Chinese city. The poverty hit me almost like a physical blow! I had forgotten how poor the Chinese are. But it's not a sullen or apathetic poverty. . . . Here, in spite of squalid surroundings, a general atmosphere of vitality. Children playing lustily everywhere. . . .[41]

Maria Macciocchi liked that "Everyone's hair is washed with soap and water. Makeup doesn't exist. . . . Everything is poor, clean, honest, basic." Or, as members of the American Committee of Concerned Asian Scholars put it: "The people live simply but their spirit is impressive."[42]

In the 1960s, even more than in the 1930s—a time when Western intellectuals had also yearned for a life guided by sound spiritual values—the sense of a spiritual vacuum was overwhelming for many of those who eventually found their way to China. This time, what may be called a crisis of values did not arise from the malfunctioning of the capitalist economic system. On the contrary, it was the material gains and the proverbial emptiness of affluence (for those who enjoyed it too long) which had swollen the quest for sustaining values and a moral society harboring them. Since the new generation of travelers of the 1960s and 70s could argue with less conviction that in their societies the masses were poverty-ridden, the emphasis has shifted to the spiritually debilitating nature of Western, capitalist societies. These societies were contrasted with the moral fiber and strength of poor countries (such as China or Cuba) inhabited by dignified and simple people free of the afflictions of the more affluent Western countries the visitors came from.

As in the case of past pilgrimages, the new travelers were immediately struck by the contrast between the corruptions of their own society and the rectitude of the new. Carol Tavris, an American psychologist, wrote:

> When you enter China you walk through the looking glass into a world that reflects a reality antithetical to ours. You leave Watergate, the energy crisis, crime, privacy, dirty movies, cynicism and sex at the

border, and step across into safety, stability, enthusiasm, clean streets, clean talk and positive thinking.

Most of all, you leave diversity and controversy, the hallmarks of America, to be wrapped in a uniformity of belief and singlemindedness of purpose.[43]

Staughton Lynd and Tom Hayden were equally impressed by the differences between the two worlds, much of which reduced to the difference between a purposeful and purposeless society:

We landed in Peking early in the afternoon. . . . The sense of a different world was immediate. . . . We could feel the West was behind us. . . . The Communist "Internationale" boomed with conviction from outdoor loudspeakers at the large modern airport.
. . . Walking before breakfast . . . we passed a group of women energetically singing before starting a day's work. Everywhere is the pulse of purposeful activity.[44]

The corruptions of Hong Kong (from which most travelers entered China) were often contrasted with the purity of the new, non-commercial world, untainted by the cash nexus: "Behind me, the aggressive vendors, the gaudy clothes, the Coca-Cola," noted Ross Terrill, the Australian China specialist, "Ahead, a world which is sterner in its political imperatives, but which in human terms may be a simpler and more relaxed world."[45] While "relaxed" may be a questionable word in this context, life was certainly simpler in a society permeated by singleness of purpose. Thus were the appeals of a sense of purpose and of a simpler life intertwined. As Barbara Wooton, the British social scientist, put it: "to anyone coming from a world which threatens to strangle itself in its own complications, it is the apparent simplicity of Chinese life which makes an irresistible appeal."[46] Entering China, Shirley MacLaine, the actress,° rejoiced: "There were no hawkers selling goods, no frenzied bargaining. Nobody was buying and nobody was selling. . . . There were no billboards screaming out their false promises, no slums. . . . Serene, I said to myself. That is the word. Serene."[47]

° Admittedly Shirley MacLaine is a questionable choice as an "intellectual." However, actors or actresses (and other artists) may qualify as intellectuals if they are not totally absorbed by their occupational roles and have some demonstrated ability to reflect on and articulate larger issues and ideas, if they engage in social criticism. On these grounds Shirley MacLaine as well as Jane Fonda may be considered intellectuals if one abstains from judging the quality of their reflections and concerns. In any event both were fierce and popular social critics with ample access to the mass media to express their ideas. Shirley MacLaine also wrote two books.

The reactions of David Rockefeller, the capitalist, were indistinguishable from those of radical intellectuals, estranged social critics:

> One is impressed immediately by the sense of national harmony. From the loud patriotic music at the border onward, there is very real and pervasive dedication to Chairman Mao and Maoist principles. Whatever the price of the Chinese Revolution, it has obviously succeeded not only in producing more efficient and dedicated administration, but also in fostering high morale and community of purpose.
>
> General economic and social progress is no less impressive. . . . Today, almost everyone seems to enjoy adequate if Spartan food, clothing and housing. Streets and homes are spotlessly clean and medical care greatly improved. Crime, drug addiction, prostitution and venereal diseases have been virtually eliminated. Doors are routinely left unlocked.[48]

For a student, her stay in China was "an exhilarating change from her days as an aimless undergraduate at Yale" which "gave [her] life much more direction." For a physicist from Johns Hopkins, "moral regeneration" was the key to the achievements of the regime.[49] Churchmen discovered the moral lessons the new China could teach:

> If the reports [presented at a theological conference in Belgium] had a common theme, it was that Christianity had much to learn from the social transformation in China. . . .

Many theologians saw the hand of God at work in China. "China has come to exert some particular impact on our understanding and experience of God's saving love,"[50] one report asserted.

It will be recalled that the Soviet Union in the 1930s had also been perceived as realizing the best values of Christianity, notwithstanding its anti-religious façade and slogans. Indeed, Hewlett Johnson, one of those making these claims in the Soviet case, had no difficulty in extending them to China a few decades later. "China, I feel," he wrote, "is performing an essentially religious act, entirely parallel with this Christian abhorrence of covetousness . . . freeing men from the bondage of the acquisitive instinct and paving the way for a new organization of life on a higher level of existence."[51] He was persuaded that "no persecution of missionaries or Christians has been countenanced by the Government. . . ."* and found (an example of) the Chinese criticism and

---

* He "returned to England with highly important documents presented with great formality entirely on their own initiative by the Christians in China to the Christians in England, challenging them to join the Chinese Christian Churches in denouncing an act of wickedness never equalled before" namely, the "scatter[ing] of exterminat-

self-criticism practice "reminiscent of the primitive Christian professions of a humble and contrite heart, and also . . . of the communal foregiveness of the early Christian communities . . . an outlook [which] gives promise of unimaginable moral strength."[53] James Reston thought that Chinese communist doctrines and the Protestant ethic had much in common and was generally impressed by "the atmosphere of intelligent and purposeful work."[54] The atmosphere was so full of virtue, Hans Konigsberger wrote, that it was no longer "strange or unbelievable . . . that government tax collectors became incorruptible, that waiters *really* don't want tips, that a lost wallet is always brought back, that doors do not have to be locked† and that some intellectuals want to prove that they no longer feel contempt for peasants by lugging buckets of manure in their free time."[56] As early as in 1952, Hewlett Johnson noted the operation of "new codes of honour," for instance, in the fact that at bookstalls there were no attendants and people left the price of their purchases in boxes. Likewise, Arthur Galston, an American scientist, believed that "Law and order . . . are maintained more by the prevailing high moral code than by threat of police action."[57]

Another expression of high moral standards was found in sexual relations, which were reportedly almost exclusively confined to the marital union. Felix Greene reported that "China is today an intensely, almost compulsively 'moral' society. Of the many communes I visited, all except one denied any knowledge of any children born out of wedlock."[58] Looks played hardly any part in interpersonal attraction as "in certain major ways, the Chinese have succeeded in fundamentally altering the notion of attractiveness by simply substituting some of these revolutionary attributes for the physical ones . . ."[59] wrote Orville Schell, an American writer. The preoccupation with work also reduced the preoccupation with sexuality and hedonism in general. "The advantage of prolonged celibacy as it [was] practised in China" was that it helped to "avoid the privatization of love,"[60] noted Claudie Broyelle, a French sympathizer. On the whole, sexuality was de-emphasized and the people were appealingly, if quaintly, modest.[61] According to Shirley Mac-

---

ing disease on the masses of Chinese." This was in reference to the "bacteria warfare" fabrication of the Korean War period, which the Dean of Canterbury also believed. The hoax was subsequently exposed, among others, by Tibor Meray, a former Hungarian communist correspondent in Korea.[52]

† Simon Leys observed: "As for foreigners who say there is no more theft in the People's Republic, I am afraid it shows that they have never been to a bicycle parking lot: most of these . . . have watchmen; bicycles have chains and the watchmen always remind you about locking them up."[55]

Laine, "women had little need or even desire for such superficial things as frilly clothes and makeup, children loved work and were self-reliant. Relationships seemed free of jealousy and infidelity." Macciocchi saw the Chinese "emanating purity . . . men without sin. . . ."[62]*

Comments such as those cited suggest once more that what was most impressive for the visitors frequently transcended the issues of material improvement or political change. Nothing short of changing human nature was discerned, as Jan Myrdal, among others, made clear.[64] In turn Peter Worsley was most pleased, it seems, by "the Chinese attempt to transform human values and personal relationships at the level of everyday life, to challenge assumptions that certain modes of behavior are naturally 'entailed' under conditions of industrial or city life . . . that some form of class system . . . is inevitable . . . that the attractiveness of material gratifications must, in the end, reassert itself. . . ."[65] In short, he and others were delighted that the Chinese were providing new ammunition against the skeptics who disbelieved that radical transformations in the human conditions were possible. In effect the Chinese re-opened the avenues of utopian hope and thinking. As in the case of Cuba, the new hope of socialism was based on the belief that what was attempted in China went beyond the alteration of social institutions, fundamental as they were, and was going to lead to the "resocialization of people in new, positive, humanistic social values. . . ." Worsley, like many other Western intellectuals, was looking for a type of "Socialism that is not just about forms of ownership: it is about participation, democracy and altruism: a human texture of life."[66]

An earlier English visitor, Basil Davidson, a political writer, thought that the Chinese believed "in the good and peaceful destiny of mankind" and this belief was the "mainspring" of their revolution, creating "a sense of unity and a unity of enthusiasm . . . which other peoples have sometimes known in their great moments of history."[67]

For James Reston,

> China's most visible characteristics are the characteristics of youth . . . a kind of lean, muscular grace, relentless hard work, and an

---

* Moreover, sin was punished. "After the revolution many male opera singers were persecuted because they impersonated women. Sodomy and rape can be punished by death. Females get five years for extra- or pre-marital fornication. A married man who seduces a married woman gets ten years. A married man seducing an unmarried woman will receive an indeterminate but heavy sentence and his partner a light one . . . the once widespread homosexuality is no longer tolerated . . ."[63] according to Bao Ruo-Wang, who spent many years in Chinese penal institutions.

optimistic and even amiable outlook on the future. . . . The people seem not only young but enthusiastic about their changing lives.

He also believed that young people from the city who worked as manual laborers in the rural areas "were treating it like an escape from the city and an outing in the countryside."[68] The American Friends Service Committee observed that the young "all seemed imbued with an immense youthful revolutionary fervor. They expressed complete dedication to the goals and objectives of the revolution. . . ."[69] Even relatively skeptical Canadian observers like Pierre Elliot Trudeau and Jacques Hebert were moved to comment on the "Chinese people[s] confidence in the future and an active faith in their own destiny."[70] In a similar vein, Ruth Sidel wrote that "People go about their daily work with a purpose and even a sense of mission. . . . The feeling which comes through most clearly and which we found most moving was this sense of mission, this sense of participation and commitment to an ideal greater than one's self."[71] An American political scientist of Chinese descent concurred: "When I asked a child whom he loved most, the answer was inevitably 'Chairman Mao.' The parent came next. When I asked a girl what was the most important qualification of the man whom she would like to marry, she would always say: 'a man with correct political thinking'. . . ."[72] Members of the Committee of Concerned Asian Scholars elicited answers to the effect that the Chinese did not mind being separated for long periods from their family and unhesitatingly put work, or the interest of society (as defined by their leaders) ahead of personal or familial concerns.[73] Simone de Beauvoir had a simple explanation for these attitudes: "Far and away from being in contradiction, personal aspirations and duty to the country jibe. . . ."[74]*

Under these circumstances, Basil Davidson believed, there was "no more need for workers to strike,"[76] indeed such action would have been inconceivable under the conditions of harmony, unity of purpose, and dedication to the interests of the society which he and other visitors perceived.

Thus morality and politics were joined together: "under Mao the Chinese Revolution has become not only an advance in the industrial arts . . . but also a far-reaching moral crusade to change the very human

---

* In her more recent reflections on China she expressed some skepticism concerning such issues: "When I am told that the workers have a right to three weeks of holiday but that they give them up because of their socialist enthusiasm, what stays in my mind is that they do not take holidays; enthusiasm *cannot be* institutionalized."[75]

Chinese personality in the direction of self-sacrifice and serving others.
. . . Politics and morality are . . . intertwined . . . political conduct is
a manifestation of moral character. . . ." wrote Professor Fairbank. This
welcome union of politics and morality was also reflected in China being governed "by exemplary moral men, not laws." He felt that "Americans may find in China's collective life today an ingredient of personal
moral concern for one's neighbor that has a lesson for us all."[77] For
Macciochi, China was "the most astounding political laboratory in the
world" where morality permeated politics and thus "politics means sacrifice, courage, altruism, modesty and thrift."[78]

As in Cuba, the sympathetic visitors found purposefulness associated
with vitality. "No one can be in China for more than a few hours without sensing an almost tangible vitality and an enormous optimism,"
wrote Felix Greene. "I saw in the people a buoyancy and a confidence
which was utterly unlike my expectations."[79] A decade later the young
American Asia scholars reported that "the overwhelming impression of
China is vitality—the enthusiasm, the humor, and the tremendous commitment of her people to this new China." They were also impressed by
such expressions of political commitment and purposefulness as that of
the bus conductors in Canton who led "their riders in reciting quotations by Mao, singing revolutionary songs and calling out slogans . . .
as they walk[ed] up and down the aisles, selling tickets. . . ."[80]

For many sympathetic foreigners the Cultural Revolution. was the
most dramatic and elevating manifestation of the sense of purpose, a
climax of idealism and a society-wide spiritual renewal. This is how
Joshua Horn, a British physician who had settled in China, described it:

> It is difficult to write about the Cultural Revolution without running
> into a plethora of superlatives. . . . It sets itself no less a task than
> discovering how Man can make the leap from the past millennia of
> class society to the Communist society of the future. . . .
>
> It is an unprecedented movement to disinfect society, to clear away all
> pests, to expose political degenerates . . . to prise out the spies, rene-
> gades, traitors, all those whom the Chinese so graphically describe as
> "Demons and Monsters." It is a vast demolition operation to bring
> down the age-encrusted edifice of institutions, customs, values and
> morals of the man-eating past, to clear away the rubble and to drive
> the foundation piles for the society of the future. . . . It is an ex-
> ploration to discover forms of organization and of government which
> will be proof against corrosion by bureaucracy and nepotism. . . .

History may see it as the harbinger of the emergence of Communist Man; as the fanfare proclaiming the entry of the future on the stage of the present.[81]*

The intellectuals (and non-intellectuals) visiting China in the 1960s and early 70s shared, to a varying degree, a disenchantment with excesses of individualism, the moral relativism and ethical uncertainties of their own societies. The sharply defined and binding values of Chinese society appeared as refreshingly firm guideposts to life which freed people of the burden of agonizing choices, of living with ambiguity and uncertainty. The moral vacuum painfully felt in the West did not exist here. The sense of purpose so much in evidence was all the more impressive because of the vast number of people whose life it had seemingly permeated.

The Chinese puritanism had its own appeal too. It was a welcome experience to be in a highly moral society for those who came from countries where pornography was rife, where all forms of sexual obsessions and pathologies abounded (and were often catered to), where the mass media and entertainment industry appeared to thrive on the lowest common denominator, where hedonism ran rampant, where "not making value judgments" and not being "judgmental" have increasingly become prevailing cultural norms. The high moral tone of China was for many visitors a virtual spiritual rebirth, for most, a purifying experience, a moving moral uplift.† Once more a distant and poorly known society appeared to possess and provide Western intellectuals with something essential they were deprived of in their own.

---

* Subsequently it had been revealed that the "disinfection and cleansing" of society entailed in the Cultural Revolution included making the "Demons and Monsters" eat "night soil or insects, being subjected to electrical shocks, forced to kneel on broken glass, being hanged by the arms and legs." It was also reported that "By Peking's own admission, the losses were heavy. . . . There are some partial figures: Han Suyin . . . acknowledges 90,000 victims in Szechuan province *alone* (this figure is probably a fraction of the real one). Li Yi-che in his manifesto states that Lin Piao's repression of 1968, in Kwantung province *alone*, had 40,000 victims. . . ."[82]

In general the more recent reassessments of the Cultural Revolution, both Chinese and foreign, stressed the great damage it had done to the Chinese economy, educational system, the development of science and technology and cultural life—in addition to unleashing a period of fanaticism, quasi-puritanical violence, and repression.

† Shirley MacLaine stopped smoking on the second day of her visit and also stopped picking her fingers and biting her nails. She "began enjoying sunsets and trees and food instead of rushing through each day because time meant money." She also slept less because she "felt so much more alive when [she] was awake."[83]

Equality

One major reason why the recent generation of political tourists gravitated toward China lay in the hope that China might have been (or was) successful where the Soviet Union failed, that is, in the attainment of equality and social justice. The awareness of the Soviet failure magnified the attractions of China, rather than creating a reservoir of skepticism about the prospects of large-scale social engineering and experimentation. Instead of the growth of doubts or immunization against utopian hopes, the longings frustrated by the outcome of the Soviet "experiment" were readily transferred to China by many Western intellectuals. To be sure, that "transference" was carried out largely by a new generation barely familiar with the developments which marked the end of revolutionary idealism and egalitarianism in the Soviet Union. Thus the hope of finding a society dedicated to the achievement of social equality has remained irrepressible among Western intellectuals, and Chinese policies lent plausibility to the belief that the Soviet failure to achieve it—or to pursue it with prolonged determination—has not prejudiced similar attempts in other parts of the world. Peter Worsley perceptively characterized this longing: "At an almost invisible level, there is, I suspect, a deeper, residual, unextinguished, sneaking but very repressed and virtually lost hankering human feeling that the cardinal communist virtues—equality and fraternity—*are* virtues after all and virtues we lack."[84]

The Chinese experiment not only revived such hopes, but also made the visitors more conscious of the connection between the persistence of inequality and certain social values bolstering it. Arthur Galston, an American scientist, along with Worsley and many others reflected: "Visiting China . . . made me wonder whether 'human nature' as we know it in the competitive West is the only course of development model possible for mankind. It reawakened some of my youthful idealism and made me question some of the deep-rooted cynicism prevalent in our society."[85]

The Chinese attack on inequality seemed to take two forms, as reported by the visitors. One was the attempt to transform competitive, individualistic, acquisitive values and attitudes through education and propaganda. The other, perhaps more dramatic, pertained to the conditions of work, as the Chinese regime engaged in redefining not only the values (and monetary rewards) associated with work but also the actual work situation. This made a profound impression on Western visitors well aware of the fact that social inequalities were linked to and reflected in the evaluation of different types of work. Western intellectuals knew full well, and felt considerable unease over the fact, that not only were different jobs regarded differently in most societies but, contrary to all elementary notions of justice, the more onerous, demeaning, and boring jobs were usually also the most poorly paid, in part because they required the least training and hence could be performed by anyone. No society offered the same pay to engineers and ditch diggers, nuclear scientists and street cleaners, generals and privates, jet pilots and pedicab drivers—but in China at least, the wage differentials appeared smaller. Moreover, the Chinese redefined the meaning and prestige attached to different jobs, in particular the manual ones, far beyond the lip service paid to the glories of manual labor in the Soviet Union. It appeared to many visitors that the Chinese system made significant progress in endowing many types of work, neither inherently pleasant nor gratifying, with a new meaning. Galston, for example, observed that "Service workers in the cities—elevator operators, clerks at hotels, drivers of limousines, street cleaners—all perform their task with a cheerful acceptance of what life has brought them. Every worker seems fortified by the implicit knowledge that all tasks contribute to the well-being of his country, and that knowledge accords dignity and satisfaction to even the most ordinary duty."[86]

In the same spirit, Simone de Beauvoir found nothing disturbing about the survival of pedicabs under socialism, assuming that since the task performed was useful for society it ceased to be degrading.[87] Many Western intellectuals came to believe (even more than in the Soviet and Cuban cases) that great strides had been made by providing a contextual alleviation of disagreeable forms of labor. The Concerned Asian Scholars reported the remarks of an old woman whose job was to remove and collect slivers of metal from oily rags and whose hands were "covered with cuts from the slivers." Upon asking her if it was not painful to do this, she answered, "When you are working for the revolution, it doesn't hurt."[88] In this way even painful activities were transformed by their context and purpose, that is, by the perceived or imputed contribution to the good of society. Such transvaluation of tasks regarded as arduous or demeaning (in other settings or contexts) was even more striking in relation to garbage disposal and the collection of human excrement,[89] widely used in China as an agricultural fertilizer. Nothing could be more symbolic of the attempt to redefine the meaning of work than the policy of allocating such unattractive tasks in a more equitable way adopted during the Cultural Revolution. This meant the involvement of former city dwellers, white collar workers, or bureaucrats in the performance of such chores. Maria Macciocchi called it the "conquest of loathing" and was greatly impressed by self-improvement via garbage and excrement collection in the May 7 cadre school she had visited.[90] It is very likely that the specialists and administrators the regime regarded as truly indispensable (for instance those engaged in weapons research and development) were permitted to forego this form of character development. The sending of highly qualified people to the May 7 schools was a practice of questionable economic rationality to Joseph Kraft, the columnist, but a young woman scientist in one of these schools assured him of the benefits of working with peasants and of the necessity to rotate jobs in this manner.[91] Clearly, such efforts were inspired by ideological rather than economic considerations, since it could hardly be argued that there was a shortage of labor in rural areas or that urban people were going to make agricultural production more efficient.[92] Jan Myrdal viewed the sending of intellectuals to the villages in itself as a form of reeducation: "Today intellectuals and city dwellers of various sorts are out in the villages of China to be transformed by work and to be reeducated by poor peasants . . . to overcome the notion that intellectual work is more respectable than manual work. . . ."

The resettlement of intellectuals in the countryside signified the far-reaching alteration of the entire social structure. According to Myrdal, "What is happening in China just now is that the cultural barriers which used to separate 'intellectuals' from ordinary people are being broken down, like the barriers which used to separate town from country."[93] The Concerned Asian Scholars also approved of the resettlement of "educated young people" and believed that those among them they had met were typical in rejoicing about their new assignments. These Americans asserted confidently that "by far the majority [of those resettled] expect to live their lives in the countryside, becoming peasants and making their contribution to China there." They believed not only that the majority of uprooted intellectuals found happiness in the country but also that their departure from the cities was voluntary.[94] While at no time had this been plausible, since Mao's death it became widely known that these rural assignments were both unpopular and coercive. For instance, Claudie and Jacques Broyelle, two disillusioned French supporters of the regime, reported: "One frequently hears of local Party cadres . . . who, on the receipt of bribes from educated youths . . .

allow them to return to . . . the city. A friend told us: 'The boys can buy the local cadre by paying him with money or cereal coupons but more often . . . by volunteering labor. For instance, the cadre lets everyone know that he wishes to build himself a new house. The boys . . . volunteer to build it. . . . As for the girls, they most often pay with their bodies.' "[95]

The visual manifestations of social equality have also been remarked upon by the visitors. Macciocchi wrote, "my first 'images' of China are of these sumptuous restaurants crowded with ordinary people instead of wealthy customers." Beauvoir discerned equality in the appearance of street crowds: "What is most striking about the tranquil and gay crowd at one's side is its homogeneity. Men are not all of the same station in China but Peking offers a perfect image of a classless society. Impossible to tell an intellectual from a worker . . . this crowd's unity stems from a deeper source: nobody is arrogant here, nobody is grabby, nobody feels himself above or below anybody else. . . ."[96]

Orville Schell discerned diversity in homogeneity: "Everyone is dressed in the practical unisex clothes. . . . These baggy uniformlike tunics—consisting of pants, jacket and cap—far from blurring people like sameness, seem to accentuate their faces."[97]

For the most part, the visitors took it for granted that the uniformity of clothing was an indicator of equality. They generally failed to discern the finer distinctions concealed behind the identical style of clothing. According to Simon Leys,

> The Cultural Revolution has hypocritically masked some of the most obvious forms of class divisions, without changing their substance. In trains, for instance, first, second, and third classes have disappeared *in name*, but you have now 'sitting hard' . . . , 'sleeping hard' . . . , and 'sleeping soft,' which are exactly the same classes as before* and with the fares, as before, ranging from single to triple prizes. External insignia have nearly completely disappeared in the army; they have been replaced by a loose jacket with four pockets for officers, two pockets for privates. . . . In cities one can still distinguish between four-pocket men in jeeps, four-pocket men in black limousines with

* This was exactly the same remedy as the Soviet Union and Soviet-controlled East European regimes have found against "class distinctions" on trains. This type of magic thinking (if we rename something it will go away) was also apparent in the United States in the 1960s when educators, intent on doing away with elitism and competitiveness, decided that grades symbolized and perpetuated such evils and replaced them with verbal evaluations which, in more cumbersome ways, continued to convey that their pupils' performance and ability differed.

curtains, and four-pocket men who have black limousines with curtains and a jeep in front.[98]

Among the American visitors, Edward Luttwak was probably the first to note that "Perhaps the most transparent of all the simulations of social equality . . . is the mock-equality of dress. Almost everybody wears the . . . Mao uniform. But some are made of rough cotton and others of delicate gabardine, and still others of good-quality wool. Senior partymen would wear their equality in carefully tailored worsted wool . . ." standing apart from "the blue cotton outfits of ordinary people."[99]

It should be noted that these iconoclastic discoveries were made and widely publicized mostly in the post-Mao period when China began to invite such hardnosed guests as Luttwak, provided their anti-Soviet credentials were well established. Lucian Pye, another of the more critical visitors, pointed out that "The leveling of incomes has, to my observations, tended, oddly enough, to accentuate status and power differences. In any group we never had much difficulty in spotting officials from non-officials. Power seems to allow for more visible gradations than income differences. . . ."[100]

In connection with the egalitarian appeals of China, the apparent absence of bureaucratization must also be noted, since it was often favorably contrasted with the advanced and oppressive bureaucratization of the Soviet Union. It may be recalled here that in the 1960s Western intellectuals, and preeminently among them the younger Americans, developed an intense loathing for bureaucracy and all it had symbolized in their eyes: hierarchy, inequality, routinization, depersonalization, and lack of feeling. A major reason behind the unpopularity of the Soviet Union among this generation was due to the realization that it too was a highly bureaucratized society. China was thought to be different, and the Cultural Revolution in particular suggested that this regime was not going to tolerate the growth of bureaucracy. Macciocchi, among other visitors, was fully convinced that "any hierarchical or bureaucratic mentality has disappeared."[101] The absence of deference was another aspect of egalitarian social relations as "comrade" became the universal form of address.[102] Status distinctions* were also to be eradicated at the work-

---

* We have since also learned more about bureaucratic and other status distinctions in China. For instance, Simon Leys brought to the attention of Western readers that "the Maoist bureaucracy today has thirty hierarchical classes, each with specific privileges and prerogatives." Moreover, "Various gastronomical privileges distinguish officials of a certain level from mere mortals. . . . if a new phrase must be found

place: "the Chinese have set out to break down some of the distinctions which make working in an American factory so unrewarding. The traditional and clear differences between 'management' and 'labor,' for example, are being attacked. . . ." According to the Concerned Asian Scholars, the "breaking down of elitism" (especially since the Cultural Revolution) also had a beneficial impact "in the field of culture itself where, for the first time, everyone can participate, sing, dance, act . . . and does with enthusiasm!" Elsewhere they noted that "the idea is that everyone is an artist. . . ." Such participation was a "part of being a while person."[104] Felix Greene perceived an "intellectual renaissance" and "cultural explosion" taking place.[105]

The democratization of artistic creativity had much in common with a somewhat similar attempt to democratize and collectivize scientific activities—also heartily endorsed by the Concerned Scholars. On their visit to the Nanking Observatory they were told that "Now the people of the Observatory work together. . . . No individual research is done."[106] The struggle against individualism was an integral part of the new egalitarianism. Young Americans coming from a competitive, individualistic society and embracing some version of the counter-cultural or political collectivism of the 60s were particularly receptive to this.° (At that time

---

to qualify modern mandarins, 'Those-who-ride-in-cars' would probably be the most appropriate. . . . Since all cars are official cars the simple fact of sitting in the back seat of a limousine is equivalent to a *laissez-passer*. . . . If you come by car . . . the various watchdogs will swing the iron grille of the gate wide open . . . without even having to slow down . . ."

The post-Mao revelations about the privileges of high officials included the information that " 'Senior officials can buy commodities at cheap prices and . . . also . . . commodities that are in short supply,' according to a wallposter that was torn down shortly after it appeared . . . at Peking University. . . . Officials even have their own brand of filter cigarettes . . . not sold in Chinese stores. . . ." The existence of special stores serving foreigners and Chinese officials has also been reported. Revealing glimpses into the lifestyle of the Chinese rulers was also provided by Roxane Witke in the course of her interviews with Mao's wife, Chiang Ch'ing, who had shown every indication of relishing luxurious living conditions, clothing, food, and entertainment which was not only materially inaccessible to the Chinese people but also ideologically frowned upon (such as Western movies and skirts).

Prior to Mao's death the only accounts detailing material privileges and luxuries concerned the life style of reformed capitalists exhibited to some visitors. Thus Colette Modiano's group was taken to such a specimen (the former owner of a large cotton mill, now its manager) who displayed a "gleaming black Jaguar and a very recent model at that" and who had tea and little cakes served to the guests in his spacious drawing room by "two maids in white aprons."[103]

° An example of this receptivity to collectivism was the preference for collective authorship of the book produced by the Committee of Concerned Asian Scholars unwilling to elevate to the status of author or editor any member of the group.

communitarian impulses had stronger political underpinnings; in the 70s, the same impulses found more a religious-therapeutic expression.)

To the Westerners who, as children of the 60s, abhorred "elitism" (or any form of differentiation), the egalitarian policies which erupted in China with the Cultural Revolution were especially congenial. Even the profession of science was to be purified and demystified, and another group of young Americans (calling themselves "Science for the People") devoted their visit to finding out how the Chinese accomplished this. Their collective product (similar in inspiration to that by the Concerned Asian Scholars) informed the reader in the introduction that "We saw China as the Chinese presented it to us and readily admit that we believed what we saw and heard. The reader may feel that our presentation lacks an element of objectivity or skepticism. If so, it is probably because we were deeply impressed by New China, and our impressions are no doubt in part based on a clear political bias."[107] In spite of its designation the group included few trained scientists and, not surprisingly, its major concern was the de-professionalization of science, that is, the elimination of its "elitist," hierarchical aspects. The group also wished "to redirect the priorities of American science away from 'following the logic of profit.'" In view of such predispositions, members of this group found much to be enthusiastic about on their visit to China:

> Science in China . . . is becoming the property of the entire people and is integrating all problems into a scientific methodology. . . . In Chinese theory science is not the exclusive domain of those with special training . . .

> Science in short is being demystified in China. . . . a vast exercise in sharing knowledge is being carried out through the length and breadth of China to make science a part of mass culture.[108]

It remains to consider the more tangible economic manifestations of the egalitarian policies pursued by the regime. On these matters there was virtual unanimity among most visitors, who found that the range of income differentials was gratifyingly narrow. Moreover, according to some, even "those with a larger income do not seem to express interest in living at a higher standard."[109] It is probably safe to say that Galbraith spoke for the majority of Western visitors when he declared:

> Somewhere in the recesses of the Chinese polity there may be a privileged Party and official hierarchy. Certainly it is the least ostentatious ruling class in history. So far as the visitor can see or is told, there is—for worker, technician, engineer, scientist, plant manager, local official, even, one suspects, table tennis player—a truly astonishing approach to

equality of income. . . . Clearly, there is very little difference between rich and poor.[110]

Although such impressions were widespread, there was a minority, and especially the China scholars among them, who discerned greater inequalities even in Mao's lifetime. Martin Whyte, for example, noted that "Officials and employees in the state bureaucracy were ranked from level 1 (top national leaders) to level 30 . . . and the differential between the highest and lowest levels was about 28 : 1. . . . Technical personnel . . . were ranked on a separate 18-grade scale with a differential of roughly 10 : 1. . . . In regard to income differentials, then, one can say that the existing situation is quite different from the impression that the egalitarian rhetoric of the Cultural Revolution or the uniformity of dress of the population may convey."[111] According to Donald Zagoria, "There are greater inequities in China than are generally imagined . . . there are inequities between the rural communes close to the cities and communes in more remote areas . . . between rich and poor brigades, between different work teams in the same commune. . . . There are also substantial differences between urban and rural incomes. . . . In Chinese industry . . . the ratio of the highest to the lowest wage is about three to one, from about 40 yuan a month . . . to 110 yuan at the top. Engineers can earn . . . 150 yuan. University teachers earn about 70 to 350 yuan. . . . Top government officials can earn as much as 450 yuan. . . ."[112] Edgar Snow reported that military pay differentials ranged from the equivalent of $2.50 per month for a private to $24 for captains, $62–64 for colonels, $192–236 for full generals, $360–400 for marshals.[113]

Despite such information, most visitors seemed to believe in far greater degrees of equality than actually prevailed. This was due to a combination of the predisposition to believe, limited access to conflicting information and the need to balance—for those who took note of such matters—the loss of political freedoms against compensating gains in other spheres.

The appeals of social justice and equality were similar in the Soviet and Chinese cases, although the preoccupation with their specific components varied and changed over time. In the 1930s the relevant Soviet policies were seen as historically novel and pathbreaking, and were viewed against the background of economic chaos, dislocation, and crisis in the West. Western visitors to the USSR during these years were particularly impressed by a system that could provide full employment. By contrast, visitors to China in the 1960s or early 70s were less concerned with issues of employment and unemployment in their own societies and, hence, did not consider full employment per se an especially noteworthy achievement of the Chinese regime; at any rate, they commented on it less frequently. At the same time the Chinese egalitarianism acquired greater significance against the background of the corresponding Soviet failure. As noted before, by the 1960s many of the Western intellectuals who went to China were aware of the flaws of Soviet society and its bureaucratic, hierarchical, and stratified nature and, therefore, all the more appreciative of a society which allowed them to renew the hopes of an earlier generation, or those of their own youth.

The recent generation of travelers has taken a broader view of equality than their predecessors, as the emphasis shifted from its material underpinnings to concerns with competitiveness, wholeness, and more general issues of social differentiation.

Western intellectuals in the 1960s and 70s remained preoccupied with social equality because they found the progress toward its attainment unsatisfactory in their own societies. Few of them were prepared to say about their own country what one of them, Ross Terrill, said about China: "In a magnificent way, it has healed the sick, fed the hungry and given security to the ordinary man. . . ."[114]

The People and the Setting

Entering China, Shirley MacLaine wrote, "I stepped into the mystery that had haunted me for most of my adult life," into a country she had "dreamed of . . . since childhood."[115] Audrey Topping, the American journalist-photographer, after crossing the railroad bridge from Hong Kong to China for the third time, "felt it happening again. I could feel the enchantment of China seeping into my whole being. The whole world seemed new and more colorful." For her it was a homecoming of sorts that intensified the sentimental impact and emotional appeal of the visit. She was revisiting a country, or, as she put it "a world that has attracted my family since the late 1800's and intrigued me since I was old enough to remember."[116] The appeal of China for those who had been there before the Communist regime was established represents a distinct chapter in the history of Western, and particularly American attitudes toward China. They were primarily missionaries or diplomats (and their children) and their recollections and impressions (such as being quoted above) reflect experiences and attitudes far removed from politics. The appeal of China for this group was part of the nostalgia for their youth, for old friends; in their fond memories hardship and enjoyment blended. In the case of Audrey Topping, the childhood memories were a result of her father, Chester Ronning, spending extended periods of time in China as a Canadian diplomat before World War II.

Many visitors registered their favorable impressions immediately upon arrival. "As we emerged from the train in Canton . . . the atmosphere was almost a physical shock," recalled members of the Committee of Concerned Asian Scholars. "After Hong Kong—noisy, pushy and crowded —the busy streets of Canton seemed gentle by comparison. People almost sauntered, their pace purposeful but relaxed. Everyone looked healthy, no one wore rags, or begged, or jammed an elbow into you. . . . We heard people chattering and laughing, bicycles ringing, occasional buses, and a few whispered comments and giggles at the sight of us. But no raucous horns or street vendors shouting. . . ."[117] Norma Lundholm Djerassi, an American poet, found the people in Canton, where she "perspired freely all the time . . . fresh and clean. . . ."; in Peking "voices and laughter are muffled. They seem gentle, soft-spoken, kind people. They smile readily. . . ." Most importantly she saw "none of the role-playing and power-pushing I find so unpleasant in my own society. . . . To feel none of that here is most refreshing. People are who they are and are happy in their usefulness to society."[118] Joshua Horn and his family "from the moment of landing . . . felt enveloped equally by the warmth of the autumn sunshine and by the friendship of the people. No stiletto-heeled, charm-trained air hostesses here! Just pigtailed girls with rosy cheeks who smiled because they were happy. . . ." Arthur Galston and his family were "knit into a friendly group by virtue of singing together" with the Chinese passengers on the domestic flight.[119]

Despite vast cultural and characterological differences between the Chinese and the Russians, the qualities Western visitors found appealing in the Chinese did not much differ from what their predecessors admired in the Russians. They were mainly authenticity, simplicity, courage, endurance, friendliness, hospitality, helpfulness, and wholeness. Yet the Chinese were obviously different, more exotic, more mysterious, and more unfamiliar even in their physical appearance. Unfamiliarity made the projection of appealing attributes easier. The Chinese, even more than the Russians (or Cubans), acquired their aura of admirability in a peculiar perceptual process in which affective tension was created by the blending of the familiar and the exotic, the ordinary and the ex-

traordinary.[120] Basil Davidson's description of Chinese soldiers and rail-
waymen provide an example of this process:

> Possibly they were no different from any other group of Chinese sol-
> diers in China now. And yet they were exceedingly differe⁻t from any
> other peasant army I have seen; . . . they looked like men who had
> elected to serve. And this impression, it will be said, was highly sub-
> jective—caused in me, no doubt, by the accident of a sunny morning,
> the pleasure of striding along a station platform after many hours in
> the carriage, the fact that half a dozen soldiers grinned their willing-
> ness to make way for me to buy *yang-to.* . . .
>
> Perhaps it was subjective. The railwaymen, I confess, produced the
> same kind of effect in me; they looked so sure that they owned their
> own railways, so determined to make their railways run well. . . .[121]

The remarks of Peter Townsend, a British student of China, about his
preference for travel in third class (in China) also reflect the glamor
ordinary objects and settings can acquire under certain conditions: "I
went along to the third class. Third meant hard seats, but it was alive.
Children cluttered the corridors and slept on luggage racks. Groups of
soldiers played cards, and there was a hubbub of talk and song. . . ."[122]

The fascination with trains was especially noticeable among American
travelers who responded to them with an almost pre-industrial nostalgia.[123]* The Concerned Asian Scholars were deeply impressed by the first
Chinese train they beheld, presumably on account of the quaint fact that
it was pulled by a steam engine: "The train had a steam engine; it was
modern and gleamed from constant washing. The cars were not air-
conditioned, and the windows were wide open. . . ." Shirley MacLaine's
first Chinese train was "a thing of beauty," and for Arthur Galston, "The
train itself was a wonderful surprise and worthy of emulating by American railroads."[124]

The appeals of the Chinese people and of the places they inhabited

---

* It may also be noted here that our travelers were divided in regard to the appeals
of picturesque squalor versus ideologically commendable cleanliness. Waldo Frank
was among those, probably the minority, who had a certain affection for dirt and
disorder, as they associated the latter with spontaneity, the untroubled acceptance of
hardship, human warmth, simplicity and communal togetherness. For Frank and
some others, especially among the Americans—forerunners of or adherents to the
counter-culture—a certain amount of dirt and disorder was more appealing and authentic than the antiseptic, dehumanized cleanliness they associated with middle-
class life. Many of them did not succeed in resolving their conflicting sentiments on
these matters. (For example, the members of the Venceremos Brigade felt guilty
about using up too much water for their showers.) On the whole, it is probably safe
to say that more visitors were impressed by the historically progressive cleanliness,
especially in China and North Vietnam, than by picturesque and authentic squalor.

were often difficult to separate. The poetic qualities of the Chinese countryside were especially hard to resist. For many visitors it was inconceivable that there could be disharmony between mellow landscapes, gentle people, and the political system superimposed on them. Simone de Beauvoir wrote:

> Of the memories I preserve of China the most ineffaceable is of that countryside I crossed during the 40 hours by rail from Hanchow to Canton. . . . Before the light fails, it is an unaltering scene that slips by: distant mountains are the landscape's backdrop. . . . The villages nestle under clumps of trees . . . to each village there is a pond; their houses are tile-roofed, walls are of whitewashed brick. . . . These mountains over the horizon, this sparse foliage over rooftops, the water, the flat light compose a China—at last—similar to the one prints show: many Sung era painters treated these landscapes.[125]

The view from the train had a similar impact on Felix Greene:

> The view from the train window was like a scene from a Sung painting. . . . Old clustered villages with their curved roofs among the terraced rice fields. Tiny silver waterfalls sparkled from terrace to terrace, an irrigation system two thousand years old and still working. Peasants in the fields in their wide cone hats. . . . And water buffalo. And brakes of bamboo and banana trees; everything green and lush.[126]

For Basil Davidson, "With the sunset there came a sense of calm and peace upon this endless land; and the last thing I remember before going to sleep was a glimpse of junks floating downstream with their slack sails raised. . . ." Even Galbraith waxed lyrical over the Chinese landscape: "To see things from a train is divine. The rice fields are golden; other crops are green . . . cotton fields with the first white bolls . . . lots of towering multitargeted sunflowers."[127]

It is not difficult to understand why the serenity of the Chinese countryside made such an impression on the highly urbanized visitors from the West. For many of them the social order of China symbolized less a new mode of industrialization than an excursion into a pastoral past where sturdy rural values merged with and prefigured the humane essence of Marxism. Sometimes the roots of such a predisposition were revealed by the visitors themselves. Thus Jan Myrdal explained why he was so strongly attracted to the Chinese peasants and rural life in China: "With this book on China I unburdened myself of my debt to my ancestors. Only afterwards did I become fully conscious of this emotional drive behind my work. So, in a way, I did write a book about our village, even though I wrote of a village in China."[128]

Harrison Salisbury's observations of the Chinese countryside and its people also recall those made by Waldo Frank in Russia four decades earlier, and suggest once more that the perceptions being discussed here derive from a common and deep source:

> As we drove deeper into the countryside, the feeling grew in me that I was experiencing not a prevision of the world's future but a retrospective glimpse into our own American or European past,—the world in which men and women labored with their own hands, with a few animals, a few primitive implements—experiencing a life so simple, so integrated with the land, the weather and the plants that its symmetry seemed almost magical.[129]

The temptation to discover in China's present the good old days of the (American) past also proved irresistible for James Reston, who remarked that "One is constantly reminded here of what American life must have been like on the frontier a century ago. The emphasis is on self-reliance and hard work, innovation and the spirit of cooperation in building something better and larger than anything they have known before."[130] For Paul Dudley White (a prominent medical professor and cardiologist), "To be in Peking was like going back to the Puritan days of my youth . . . when it was safe to walk the streets of Boston even in the dark, and when thefts were relatively rare."[131]

The harmony of the landscape and the social system detected by some of the visitors was further paralleled by the harmony between the character of the people and the social-political order being built. It was a system without any appearance of conflict at any level, including the interpersonal. Shirley MacLaine "had not seen any examples of hostility in China . . . not even a simple quarrel between bus driver and passengers." (Visiting China for a period of six months during approximately the same time when Shirley MacLaine was there, Simon Leys "saw more quarrels, even brawls, than in five years in Hong Kong—which is not a markedly relaxed or gracious city.") Arthur Galston observed (on the commune where he and his family spent some time) that "No one seems ever to have to tell anyone else what to do in this harmonious world."[132]

The harmony of the Chinese character and personal relationships was also mirrored in (and supported by) the upbringing and the behavior of children. The visitors reported without fail that the children seen were happy, healthy, and well cared for, that kindergartens were excellent, the staff thoughtful and dedicated, the parents kind and attentive. Ruth Sidel (among others) argued that there was a direct connection between the happiness of the people and the progress made in child-care. She admitted that "Much of this book may sound unduly optimistic; people may seem unbelievably happy; there may seem to be a striking lack of conflict."[133]

According to Joshua Horn, the children were "full of fun, overbrimming with joy. It is rare to see children fight or cry in Peking and even rarer to see them scolded or hit." He believed that the decline of juvenile delinquency was due to "the ending of exploitation [which] has greatly reduced social tensions and insecurity."[134] Urie Bronfenbrenner, the American specialist in child development, declared: "Any thought that these were exploited automatons lacking in childhood spontaneity or warmth was quickly dispelled as the little ones ran forward to take us by the hand. . . ." Not all visitors were totally persuaded by the same expressions of warmth and spontaneity. Hebert and Trudeau (the present prime minister of Canada) recalled their visit to the Children's Palace in Shanghai: "About a hundred of them were awaiting us, commissioned to overwhelm us with their importunate friendliness. They are used to it since every foreigner comes to see this place . . . it leaps to the eye that one boy and girl have been told to attach themselves to each of us. With exquisite graciousness, the little couples take our hands and lead us from room to room."[135]

At last harmony, happiness, joy, and other appealing personal qualities could also be observed in aggregate form, so to speak, when a segment of the vast population assembled on some special occasion. The propensities of Western intellectuals with respect to crowds were discussed in the previous chapter, and much of that discussion applies here. In the Chinese, as in the Soviet and Cuban cases, ambivalence toward crowds was replaced by admiration, since the crowds in question assembled for a higher purpose in a praiseworthy context. In China (as in Cuba) such crowds were usually viewed as exuding the communal spirit and symbolizing the sense of purpose permeating the whole society. The Chinese authorities in turn capitalized on these susceptibilities and strove to expose their visitors, and especially the more important ones among them, to such spectacles. Herbert Passin noted that "Since the overwhelming majority of the visits are political and ceremonial in character, we find a heavy clustering at the time of national celebrations, principally May Day and National Day (October 1). This is the time the Chinese can make their greatest impression of dynamism, national unity, and power. . . ."[136]

In most instances, the visitors' reactions fulfilled the expectations of the authorities. Joshua Horn, watching the National Day Parade, "had never before experienced such a mass demonstration of unity, joy and confidence." As to the marchers, "Rosy cheeked, red scarved, cheering lustily, full of vigor and happiness, they surged forward like a tidal wave. . . ."[137] For David and Nancy Milton, young Americans who taught English in China, the National Day parade: "was a marvel of enormous numbers and perfect order . . . long rows impeccably straight, their animation and seriousness contagious . . . their purposefulness stamped upon the celebration the authority of a people cognizant of their destiny."[138] Simone de Beauvoir reflected an initial ambivalence (of the individualistic Western intellectual) toward the mass spectacle that soon dissipated:

> The parade continues . . . we cast sidelong glances at each other: Poles, Frenchmen, Italians, we were all bred in irony, to keep our emotions on a leash . . . each of us wonders to himself whether he is alone in feeling moved by the earnest joyousness of this crowd on the march. It is a relief to hear Infeld murmur: "When you see that, you don't much want to be a cynic anymore . . ." Now it is Nenni who expresses our common remorse as shaking his head he murmurs: "Impossible to imagine anything like this happening in Rome or Paris. . . . One has to have a certain freshness in the soul; and we have gone stale somehow."[139]

Despite their inability to communicate with the people without the mediation of interpreters (or without their presence), the visitors often drew sweeping conclusions about the qualities and personal attributes of the Chinese people and felt free to generalize their impressions. Irene Dawson, a Canadian consultant for a library and art museum, wrote: "Our brief visit left me with deep feelings of admiration and affection for these dedicated and intellectually disciplined people. Their modest and loving attitude toward each other and ourselves was a lesson in itself and one I hope not to forget in my future Continuing Education work."[140] Shirley MacLaine observed "the glorification of selflessness [in a nursery school, that is], the gentle education of one who does not conform, the refusal to ostracize her. . . ." She felt every day, during her visit, "powerful vibrations because of the massive, anonymous, healthy group of human beings called the Chinese people."[141] Professor Fairbank made similar assessments of the prevailing modes of personal relationships: "The great ingredient of Chinese life . . . is the human warmth of personal contact. Chinese live very much together. . . .

The personal quality of China's government is evident if one compares the very human aura of Chairman Mao's thought as a final arbiter with the rather impersonal legal concepts of the American Constitution."[142] It is no wonder that visiting intellectuals were persuaded about the extinction of alienation. As Macciocchi put it, "There is not a trace of alienation in China, nor of those neuroses or that inner disintegration of the individual found in the parts of the world dominated by consumerism. The Chinese world is compact, integrated, an absolute whole."[143] Her compatriot, Alberto Jacoviello, foreign affairs editor of *Unita*, reached a similar conclusion: "the most striking observation is the absolute absence of what in our society is called alienation, and in others de-politicization. There is no alienation in China. And there not only is no de-politicization but, on the contrary, there is mass political passion such as I have not found in any other part of the world."[144]

The absence of alienation, sense of participation and wholeness were the key characteristics of the setting in which Chinese people could "grow and develop into a well-rounded complete person."[145] Ultimately, the virtues of the social system came to be revealed at the individual level.

Material Progress and Humane Modernization

Until the recent upsurge of environmental awareness, and the associated ambivalence toward industry, science, technology, and mastery over nature, it was easy to impress Western man with material progress. At least as far back as the French Enlightenment, there was a confident expectation that material progress entailed spiritual gains as well, and that the great, visible works of man transform not only nature but also human beings, and for the better.

In each country visited by Western intellectuals and discussed in this volume, material progress commanded widespread approval, unifying the attitudes of many visitors who might have disagreed on other matters. It would have been difficult not to endorse more schools, new housing, better public health, flood control projects, the harnessing of natural resources for human needs, the progressive elimination of material hardship. Moreover, accomplishments of this kind were the most visible, the most indisputable. Chester Ronning, who had been born in China, wrote: "The naked mountains of China have been reforested. The wheat and rice fields produce yields surpassing anything China has ever known. Industry is gaining momentum. The Chinese people are fed, clothed and sheltered. They are solving their own problems by co-operation and self-reliance."[146]

Andrew March, an American professor of geography, also conveyed a vivid image of the material progress accomplished: "in the valleys of the Yellow and Yangtze rivers live a people healthy, well-fed and reasonably housed, mostly literate, articulate and happy with socialism." And Seymour Topping, a New York *Times* correspondent, reported that "the evidence of construction, the lush, well-tended fields, the markets full of food and consumer necessities and the energy exhibited everywhere add up to the impression that the basic needs of the people are being met and the foundation is being laid for a modern industrial country."[147]

Thus the visitors saw "with their own eyes" the new housing, the schools, canals, industrial plants, and other construction projects, while they had to rely more on conjecture and intuition in regard to other matters, such as the sense of purpose, love of the government, and various human qualities of Chinese citizens.

The great material transformations were all the more impressive because they were being carried out without modern technology, predominantly by the manual labor of the huge masses. Literally, mountains were moved by hand, and it was generally assumed by the visitors that popular enthusiasm was the mainspring of these impressive undertakings: "none of us will ever forget the image of sun and wind-burned peasants pitted optimistically against this massive and forbidding landscape,"[148] wrote members of the People for Science group. The famous Red Flag Canal, for example, was hewed out of solid rock "with rather elementary tools."[149] Leys believed that "The function of the Red Canal is only accidentally economic, agricultural or hydraulic; its real significance is religious. . . . Monuments like the Great Wall or the Pyramids capture the imagination of millions . . ." In the same spirit Maria Macciocchi considered "The Nanking bridge . . . a shrine."[150] Thus were relatively ordinary objects again transformed by their higher purpose, a phenomenon noted in the Soviet context earlier. For Urie Bronfenbrenner, the scene of a dam construction was "an unforgettable experience" as he beheld "a landscape dotted with people of all ages, pushing wheelbarrows, shoveling, grading, helping each other." Staughton Lynd and Tom Hayden saw "progress . . . everywhere. Millions of Chinese are involved in its creation. In Peking we saw thousands of people digging a canal while music blared from outdoor loudspeakers. . . ."[151]

While the appeal of material progress has retained its Enlightenment roots and continued to exercise an attraction to all who were capable of compassion toward the poor, at least since the 1960s new currents of ideas have entered the attitudes of Western intellectuals toward modernization. The desirability of material progress, of modernization, became qualified by two considerations. One has been the growing realization that it is a painful and disruptive process under whatever political auspices it takes place, and that it certainly had been one in the Soviet Union. The second reservation has been more recent and follows from the new concern with the physical-environmental consequences and by-products of material "progress." As will be seen below, most visitors to China considered it a distinctive accomplishment of the Chinese regime that it avoided both of these pitfalls.

Western intellectuals, anxious and pained about the decline of community in their own society, were hopeful that the same corrosive processes would spare the Third World. They thought that China managed to combine material improvements (modernization) with the sense of renewed community—a perception which offers the key to the attraction of socialist ideologies and regimes for Western intellectuals. Peter Berger observed that "Socialism is the secular prototype *par excellence* of projecting the redemptive community into the future . . . its secularized eschatology incorporates in addition to the central aspirations of modernity—a new rational order, the abolition of want and social inequality, and the complete liberation of the individual. Socialism, in other words, promises all the blessings of modernity *and* the liquidation of its costs . . . including . . . the cost of alienation."[152]

Under socialism, such as was found in China, even a harmonious relationship between man and machine could be created. According to Kurt Mendelsohn, a British physicist,

> For the workers in the West . . . industrialization always savours of enslavement and exploitation. The industrial revolution has left a bitter taste. Things are different for the Chinese. There, the Communists are not, as with us, a force which tries to destroy a well-established pattern of society. On the contrary, they have brought order and peace.· . . . Technology is a great and joyful experience, an adventure into which they have thrown themselves with enormous enthusiasm.[153]

In the same spirit Hewlett Johnson concluded that "Chinese communism has illustrated the way in which the cold technicality of the machine can be inspired with the warmth of vital relationships. So that a man enters a laboratory, a field, or a factory with an absolutely new conception of his role in life and society. He and his fellows are parts of a great throbbing whole of life. Their little selves are gone. The thing we had dreamed of as an essential element of true religion has come." Professor Fairbank was confident that "China will not copy the American automobile civilization but will create a new balance of man and machine in her own way."[154]

The material (and non-material) accomplishments of the Chinese system were magnified in the light of the contrast between the present and the past on the one hand and between China and the West on the other. There was also the staggering demographic background to these accomplishments. The Quakers pointed out that "In terms of the numbers of people affected, the Chinese experiment is without precedent . . . the great mass of this immense population has been affected almost uniformly."[155] As to the past and present, Scott Nearing (who in his long life admired and visited virtually all countries calling themselves socialist) "found China completely transformed [in the winter of 1957–58] since my first trip in 1927. The Communists have eliminated the scourges that were rife thirty years earlier. . . . Industrialization was being enthusiastically promoted. . . . A flood of energy, idealism and high striving marked the mood of China at that period."[156] Joshua Horn recalled "The swarms of beggars* of all ages. . . . All having in common their poverty, their degradation. . . . The prostitutes. . . . The hunger-swollen bellies. . . . The rummaging in garbage bins . . ." and contrasted such sights with "a complete absence of beggars, vagrants, teddy-boys and prostitutes. In the shops, fixed prices, no persuasion, scrupulous honesty and no bartering" in post-revolutionary Shanghai.[157]

Material progress and the elimination of various social problems went hand in hand. A delegation of the American Association of State Colleges and Universities reported that "Our group discerned no evidence of hunger, vagrancy or alcoholism. The people are industrious. Everyone seems to have a task and is conscientiously engaged in that task."[158]

---

* The elimination of public begging may be one of the most distinctive psychological accomplishments of left-wing dictatorships which can be fully appreciated as one contrasts the visual image of a city teeming with beggars with one without them. For Western visitors, and especially intellectuals, few spectacles can be more abhorrent than beggars—symbols of degradation, deprivation and extreme inequality. At the same time no far-reaching conclusions can be drawn from the presence or absence of beggars by itself as to the standard of living in general; being allowed to beg is a matter of administrative controls and of cultural values and not merely an indicator of the distribution, or depth of poverty.

Frequently the achievements of the Chinese were assessed and appreciated in the light of the Western failures:

> It is the certainty of success that most dominates the Chinese mood today [wrote Carol Tavris]. Their accomplishments assume dreamlike proportions in the cold light of an American day. They virtually have eliminated many of the social problems that nations are heir to: prostitution, drugs, theft, rape, murder and litter. They have eradicated many of the diseases that flesh is heir to: . . . No one starves, no one begs. The old do not feel useless, the young do not feel helpless.[159]

On occasion the Chinese successes were contrasted with the shortcomings of other Asian countries: "It is difficult to convey our growing amazement as we explored Shanghai. China has overcome almost all the tragic problems of Asia's cities," which included slums, lack of electricity, sewage, urban transportation.[160] Paul Dudley White had similar impressions: "On good authority we were told that their problems of alcoholism and drug addiction had been conquered, that venereal disease . . . was no longer encountered and that other endemic and epidemic infections were under control. . . . Their problems of pollution were minimal compared with ours. . . ."[161] (Celebrating the absence of pollution and traffic problems in China was, in the words of Leys, somewhat like "praise[ing] an amputee because his feet aren't dirty.")[162] Corliss Lamont, who admired both the Soviet Union and China, was convinced that "the [Chinese] Communists are determined that they will not permit the bad by-products of modern technology that have brought pollution and other evils to the United States and other capitalist nations."[163] There were those among the visitors who distinguished between legitimate material improvements and the evils of consumerism, and expressed pleasure over China's policies of steering clear of the latter. Peter Worsley was one of them: "The Chinese . . . do not wish to create a consumer society. They have not *tried* to produce cars, television or phones on a mass scale, since they do not wish to. Hopefully the boulevards of Peking will never be choked with thousands of private cars. . . . Instead, the two million bicycles, the modern, cheap buses and the new Underground will keep the traffic moving."[164]

Thus by the 1970s Western visitors were less inclined to gape in wonder at every sign of industrialization and the associated technological accomplishments than in the 1930s when smokestacks in the Russian wilderness inspired lyrical outpourings, not cries of horror. Growth per se was no longer admired; instead, frugality, simplicity, and the avoidance of waste (recycling) struck a responsive chord, especially in Americans coming from a rather wasteful society. An injunction of the Cultural Revolution, reported the Concerned Asian Scholars, was "waste nothing, use all."[165] Edward P. Morgan, the journalist, described in the *Sierra Club Bulletin* how the Chinese utilized human waste:

> Where Shanghai shines—if that's the word—is in the conversion of human waste . . . into precious fertilizer. . . . A fertilizer company collects 9,000 tons a day of "night soil" and sends it to the countryside. Each district is responsible for the retaining tanks at its respective sewer head. Where there is no plumbing, residents use chamber pots . . . and the company collects their contents too.[166]

This generation of visitors was probably more interested in the improvements in the countryside than in those of the urban areas, as they came with considerable ambivalence toward urban life in modern industrial societies. They also hopefully assumed that material improvements in the rural areas would prove compatible with their special charm and authenticity. Harrison Salisbury, among others, was thrilled by the rural images he recorded on a visit (in Honan Province) which was "like driving straight into the early 19th or late 18th century." He saw "in the fields men and women bowed to the waist stride swiftly through the high golden grain, cutting it with their scythes and quickly binding the sheaves with a strand of fiber, just as Americans did before the days of the McCormick reaper."[167] After his tour of China, Dr. Norman E. Borlaug, the Nobel Peace Prize-winning plant breeder, said, "You had to look hard to find a bad field. . . . Everything was green and nice everywhere we traveled."[168] Simone de Beauvoir recalled: "I made a tour of the village. Not one speck of garbage, not a pool of stagnant water left; the air smelled clean—I had not thought that a village could be so neat." Not only the villages were neat. Arthur Galston observed that the "most striking characteristic of these cities are orderliness and cleanliness, the sense of well-being and hope, and freedom from crime and strife." Cleanliness was greatly enhanced by the various campaigns against dogs, sparrows, flies, and any and all other insects.[169] It was a well-managed society. "There can be no doubt," wrote Galbraith, "that China is devising a highly effective economic system. . . . there is massive evidence of great continued movement—new housing, new industrial plants, new building at old plants, the impressive figures on the increase in local industrial and agricultural production." The system for distributing consumer goods was also, in his opinion, "remarkably efficient."[170]

What of the costs of such progress? Was there a price to be paid for the achievements the Chinese regime was given credit for? On this issue there was little difference between the attitudes of the recent and earlier generation of intellectuals, those who were inspired by the Soviet Union on the one hand and by Cuba and China on the other. If and insofar as some losses were detected, the conclusion was easily reached: the gains outweighed the losses. Ross Terrill, among others, provided a plausible summation of such attitudes:

> Easy for pluralist America, which has 6% of world population and about 35% of its wealth, to attack the regimentation of China, which has about 25% of world population and 4% of its wealth.[171]

Only after the death of Mao did a new set of questions begin to emerge, however cautiously, and a new set of moral dilemmas arise. The new issue Western intellectuals had to confront was not whether or not the loss of personal freedoms was adequately compensated for by improvements in distributive justice (conquest of hunger, public health care, etc.) but rather *how many* of the material gains of the regime were real and how many fictitious. How much material progress had actually been accomplished at the expense of civil liberties?

As in the Soviet case (until the death of Stalin), doubts about the performance of the Chinese regime were largely rejected until confirmation came from the new rulers who replaced Mao and his entourage. Interestingly enough, it was not so much that suddenly a wealth of new information was discovered. Rather, much of the already available information was seen in a new light and was paid more attention to. As in the Soviet Union, the self-delegitimation of the regime—its admission that many of its earlier policies were incorrect, and many of its earlier leaders (notably the Gang of Four) were vicious and incompetent—changed the climate of opinion in the West. As Adam Ulam noted with reference to the Soviet Union, once the facade of total self-assurance and uncritical self-adulation began to crumble, the receptivity of Western intellectuals diminished. Since the regime itself sanctioned a more critical assessment of its policies, or rather, of those who had been in power before, it became more acceptable to criticize China. The *New York Review of Books* published lengthy excerpts from Simon Leys's iconoclastic and bitter denunciation of China under Mao and of the Western travelers who came back with stories of a fairy tale land after the carefully conducted tours. The New York *Times* began to publish more and more articles and reports casting doubt on the economic "miracles" performed by the regime.[172] Increasingly, the Cultural Revolution came to be seen as a destructive and bloody rampage and not an elevating upsurge of radical idealism designed to restore the revolutionary purity of the system. ("Attempting to be radical, the 'Cultural Revolution' did indeed succeed in bringing about a radical decline in production, and with it, of the people's standard of living.")[173] One after the other, the exorbitant claims made by both the Chinese authorities and Western pilgrims came to be called into question if not totally exploded. The new eagerness of China to buy from the West all it could—food, machinery, technology, weapons—suggested that self-sufficiency was far off. A few examples will illustrate the change of tone and climate of opinion in regard to the hitherto undoubted material (and moral) progress China had achieved in the eyes of so many Western intellectuals:

> China's agricultural technology is so backward that roughly 75% of its 900 million people still must till the land. . . .

> Given its poor management and often shoddy standards of work China may not be able to absorb all the new technology which it has already begun to import. The Communist Party paper, *Jemnin Jih Pao*, recently reported that of the $4 billion worth of farm machinery stored in China, one-third was unsaleable because of low quality. . . . Will Peking be able to rekindle the traditionally strong Chinese work ethic among an urban work force disenchanted by years without material incentives? American businessmen . . . are often surprised to find that Chinese bureaucrats go to lunch promptly at 11:45 A.M. and do not come back until 2 P.M. . . . How will China pay for the $70 billion or more in foreign commitments Peking is currently discussing?[174]

The flaws of Chinese collectivized agriculture turned out to be startlingly similar to those of the Soviet: Chinese peasants too seemed unmotivated to till the collective land and zealous to toil on the private:

> This lack of productivity of collective agriculture [the Broyelles wrote] is quite astounding and is probably equalled only by the Soviet Union; the most telling illustration of this failure of "socialist" agriculture is provided by the *People's Daily* itself which stated recently that 25% of non-cereal agricultural production sold to the state came from family plots which themselves constitute only 5% of all cultivated lands. . . . this figure does not include family produce sold legally on the free market . . . nor the produce sold on the black market, nor that which is of course directly consumed by the producers themselves.[175]

In a series of articles in the *New York Review of Books* designed to reassess the performance of the Chinese system, Nick Eberstadt, a researcher at the Harvard School of Public Health, reached similar conclusions: "Visitors are almost always moved by the dedication and self-lessness of the commune workers they meet, but the fact remains that the 5% of China's cropland allowed to remain in private hands produces about a fifth of China's food output." (Soviet figures illustrating the contribution of the private plots to the national food production are strikingly similar.)

Now it was also discovered that "it would be unreasonable to claim that China is the best-fed poor country"—in fact, countries such as Taiwan, South Korea, and Sri Lanka provided their population not only with more civil rights (without, of course, being Western-style democracies) but also with more food and higher life expectancies. In matters of birth control—another area where China was supposed to have accomplished miracles—it was now found that "China's population growth rate really has not been dramatically different from that in many other parts of the poor world," such as Bangladesh, Indonesia, Pakistan, and the African Continent. In regard to literacy and the status of women, Eberstadt concluded that "China's . . . achievements had been exaggerated." Likewise, the extent of hunger was underestimated and improvements in public health exaggerated.[176] Of the latter Claudie and Jacques Broyelle had this to say:

> Contrary to widespread Western delusion, health services are not free in China even for workers. For every medical consultation there is a tax of one mao (1/10 of a yuan). The wife and children of the insured person are covered for only half of their medical expenses. Dentist and eye care must be paid entirely or nearly entirely by the patient himself. Tonics, vitamins, etc. must be paid for. . . .

> A Latin-American friend was hospitalized at four A.M. When his car arrived near the hospital, he saw a huge, tightly massed crowd of people . . . queueing before the hospital gates. . . . At 8 A.M. they could receive a ticket marked with a serial number, which would entitle them to return later in the day. . . .

> Not everyone, however, must endure this. Follow Chang-an Avenue to the west; there in the outskirts of the city . . . you will encounter in a quiet suburban setting a certain very large, modern and somewhat forbidding building, guarded by a soldier whose fixed bayonet glistens. . . . This too is a hospital—but no queue here! A discreet but vigilant inspection of official passes is all that is required for admission. Inside, all is luxurious, calm and clean; private rooms, silent corridors, nurses in spotless and elegant uniforms. . . . Access to the hospital is strictly controlled; with the exception of a few privileged "foreign friends," only high Party and Army officials may enter here. In Peking most foreigners go to a large hospital . . . a special wing is

reserved for them. . . . Once or twice we succeeded in losing our way and finding ourselves in the "ordinary Chinese" section: there we were confronted with chaos and misery beyond description. The common wards teemed with people, the very corridors were packed with beds. . . . Hygiene was appalling. . . . The hospital itself provides only medical care, while everything else, such as bedding, washing and meals, had to be seen to by the relatives.[177]

As the weight of official censorship lightened in the post-Mao period, all sorts of unexpected trouble-spots came to light. Who, for example, would have thought that "China's meager forest resources have been badly depleted in recent years by indiscriminate and illegal logging," according to the Chinese press itself, and that "The damage has been so great that some areas have had changes in climate, the Yellow River has become more silted than ever and agricultural output has suffered."[178] Surely this was exactly the sort of thing, one would have believed, the Chinese were good at: patient toil on the hillsides, planting seedlings along the railroad tracks or city streets, great social discipline as well as official rigor that would stand in the way of "indiscriminate and illegal logging."

The assessment of the performance of the Chinese economy on the part of the visitors has not been a simple matter either, contrary to the belief of Galbraith. He wrote: "Without question we were taken to see and were told about the best. But in all travel one sees much that one is not shown, and Potemkin . . . would have had more difficulty dealing with decently experienced economists." More realistically, Padmai Desai, an Indian economist, declared: "I refuse to believe that if one has seen one commune or factory, one has . . . seen them all."[179] It was also pointed out by more critical observers—and subsequently acknowledged by the Chinese authorities themselves—that highly centralized economic systems tend to make more consequential mistakes which are more difficult to correct.[180]

Thus in the post-Mao period we are witnessing a reassessment of material progress in China. There is little doubt today that it had been overestimated—by how much we will not know for a long time. Successive governments of China are unlikely to delegitimate their predecessors (and themselves) by revealing *the full extent* of the gap between theory and practice, since doing so would disrupt political continuity and might create more unrest.

Part of the explanation of the Western overenthusiasm about material progress in China must be sought in the association of higher purpose with the material improvements taking place. Although, as was noted above, several underdeveloped countries attained and surpassed China's material progress, this failed to elicit jubilation; indeed it was barely noted—in countries like Taiwan or South Korea—because their achievements occurred under political-ideological auspices many Western intellectuals found uncongenial. There was no higher purpose attached to South Korean highways, Taiwanese hydroelectric dams, or public health projects in Pakistan. Furthermore, Westerners knew little about the limits of material progress in China: the defects of Chinese public health system, the modest gains in food production, the inefficiency in industry, and various areas of backwardness and underdevelopment. Peter Berger might have been right in suggesting that "Perhaps Third World dictatorships only appear to solve the problems of development because they control our information about these problems."[181]

The Leaders

The leaders of the Chinese society constituted an important part of its appeal for the visitors who, as a rule, found their own "leaders" unimpressive at best, corrupt and malevolent at worst. Although Mao, the supreme leader personifying the best qualities of the new Chinese society, was the focus of their admiration, Chou En-lai, the second-ranking leader, also commanded the respect of the visitors, partly because he spent far more time with them than Mao. He had made a more deliberate effort—an obvious part of the techniques of hospitality—to befriend and impress them, at any rate the more important ones.[182] Chou was more accessible; it was possible to have conversations with him; he was also more cosmopolitan and knowledgeable of the ways of the world outside China. With Mao it was more a matter of listening reverentially to a somewhat remote oracle, a mysterious and inscrutable presence.[183]

In comparing the attractions of the various leaders discussed in this study, the most noteworthy similarities are to be found between the demeanor and perception of Stalin and Mao. (By contrast Castro stands apart: indisputably charismatic, relatively young, informal, and romantic in the Western tradition.) Mao (like Stalin) was old, formal, full of dignity, and somewhat inaccessible (even when one was in his presence). Neither Mao nor Stalin knew or cared much about the outside world. Neither spent much time with people or addressed crowds—an obvious limitation of their charisma. It is debatable to what extent Mao was a charismatic leader;[184] he was too much a godlike figure, remote from the masses, to inspire or move them in a more direct way. The "Little Red Book" (or any other book) is no substitute for the live interaction between a charismatic leader and the masses, though in the Chinese case a good try was made to turn his writings into an ever-ready, sacred inspiration.° The "Science for the People" group reported that his works were used "in daily application to very concrete problems," and even the blind and deaf-mute read and benefited from his thought. According to Dick Wilson, a British specialist on China, Mao "wanted to be remembered, above all, as a teacher." Jan Myrdal went as far as to suggest that "What is holding China together is the discussion of Mao Tsetung's thought."[186]

Mao, like other leaders admired by Western intellectuals, was also an embodiment of the renaissance man and the philosopher-king. "Both a philosopher and politician . . . he combined qualities which rarely coexist in one being with such intensity. He was an inquisitive thinker, who savored power, a visionary who remained an activist . . . mercurial yet disciplined, benevolent yet ruthless, solicitous yet tyrannical," wrote Michel Oksenberg, an American political scientist. In addition, reported Edgar Snow, "Mao probably had a better knowledge of Western classics read in translation than any Western ruler had of Chinese literature. . . . Recently he surprised a French visitor with an apt allusion to the character of Marguerite Gautier, La Dame aux Camélias."[187]

Although resembling Stalin's in certain ways, the image of Mao also entailed features that set him apart and added to his appeal. Being a poet was one such attribute, which not even the most sycophantic admirers of Stalin had ever claimed on his behalf. Mao's life and struggles before gaining power were also more dramatic than Stalin's: the Long March and the Yenan Period were more exciting chapters in Mao's life than Stalin could boast of in his before taking power. Moreover, Mao was, so to speak, both the Lenin and the Stalin of the Chinese revolution; there was never any question as to who was to take power, never a separation between the theoretician–founding father and the man who seized and held power. Despite such divergencies, many of the actual personality traits attributed to Mao were very much like those projected upon

° Reportedly between 1966 and 1968, 740 million copies of the "Little Red Book" were distributed; there were also 150 million copies of his 4-volume *Selected Works*, 140 million *Selected Readings*, and 96 million copies of his poems. It should be noted here that Mao's cult was not one of the "excesses" of the Cultural Revolution—although it had intensified during the latter—but went back to the earliest years of the regime.[185]

(or, perhaps, correctly ascribed to) Stalin, as will be seen below. By the same token, Mao was unlike the demystified and discredited image of Stalin which gained acceptance after Khrushchev's revelations in 1956: "Stalin was a man in a hurry, who believed in physical liquidation. Mao is a man who moves fast but is extremely patient, and believes in debate and re-education." Moreover, also unlike Stalin, Mao had "an ever-present concern with the practical application of democracy."[188]* This was Han Suyin's view. (She was a half-Chinese writer who regularly visited China and wrote much about it.) In a similar spirit Edward Friedman, an American scholar of Chinese politics, stated that "Mao was almost invariably responding in a uniquely creative and profoundly ethical way to deep political crises."[190]

Despite his enormous and largely unchallenged power, many Western intellectuals could not bring themselves to conceive of Mao as an autocrat. Again, as in the Soviet and Cuban instances, it was claimed that in China the leaders exercised power in a new way. Felix Greene wrote: "China is not being led by a group of men hungry for personal power who have fastened themselves on a resentful population. It is, rather, a leadership that has shown itself genuinely concerned with the welfare of the people. Though changes in the leadership take place from time to time, there is no evidence of that jockeying for power or of the personal rivalry that we have so often seen in the Kremlin."[191] (This, of course was a post-Stalin view of Soviet politics.) Mao—like the other leaders discussed in this volume—was seen as combining in his character self-denying puritanism, idealism, and incorruptibility[192]—qualities rarely detected in Western politicians. The attribution of these characteristics is probably a major explanation for the singular indifference Western intellectuals had shown to the issues of political intolerance and the concentration of political power. To put it simply, as they saw it, good men were in power who could be trusted and were not going to abuse their power; their political system was not going to degenerate into a scramble for power for its own sake (or for the sake of material privilege).

* It may be recalled here that many similar assessments were made of Stalin's commitment to democratic and tolerant ways of government in the 1930s; for example, Anna Louise Strong noted that Stalin's "method of running a committee reminded me somewhat of Jane Addams . . . or Lillian D. Wald. . . . They had the same kind of democratically efficient technique, but they used more high pressure than Stalin did."[189] Similar observations were made by the Webbs, Ambassador Davies, and others. A. L. Strong ended up in China performing almost identical services for the Chinese government (e.g. publishing "Letters from China" for Westerners) as she had in the Soviet Union where she had also worked on an English language publication produced for Westerners.

There was no need to worry about safeguards and controls over power as long as it was in the right hands, as long as the holders of power were (seen as) decent, benevolent, idealistic and puritanical men. In effect, most of the visiting intellectuals tacitly believed that defenses against corruption and the abuse of power are only needed when bad people run the government. Political institutions were unimportant when good people had the power.

Shortly after Mao's death Orville Schell assessed Mao's significance for China:

> I was struck in a very forceful way by the fact that even prior to his death, Mao had transcended his own personality. . . . For Mao had transformed his being, even his personality, into a series of carefully thought out and organized ideas. Mao was a thinker as well as a doer. He conceived of the Chinese revolution, and then helped cause it to happen. And, in the process, the thought of Chairman Mao became inculcated in almost every Chinese. The word almost literally became flesh. And it seemed clear, even before Mao died, that his death could not erase the way in which he had almost become transubstantiated in his people.[193]

Placing his remains on display, like those of Lenin, was doubtless designed to provide the Chinese people with a somewhat less abstract and more tangible reminder of his "transubstantiation," or perhaps to preserve the legend of the founding father as a permanent and visible source of legitimation—no matter how much his successors would depart from his policies.

Jan Myrdal was confident that "as the third in line with Marx and Lenin . . . [Mao] solved the problem how, after the revolution the people can secure the revolution. . . . How the revolution can be prevented from degenerating. . . ." John K. Fairbank also believed that China was governed by "exemplary moral men."[194] As there was so little doubt about the rectitude of Mao (and his fellow leaders), it was inconceivable that they would abuse their power. Moreover, Mao ruled by popular mandate. Hewlett Johnson described the popular attitudes toward Mao:

> It was not hard as you talked with Chairman Mao to understand the deep affection men feel for this man. . . . All men—intellectuals, peasants, merchants—regard Mao as the symbol of their deliverance, the man who shared their troubles and has raised their burdens. The peasant looks at the land he tills: Mao's gift. The factory worker thinks of a wage of 100 lb. rice instead of 10: Mao's gift. The intellectuals re-

joicing in freedom from the menace of armed censorship regard that too as Mao's gift.[195]

The question must also be raised: how could Western intellectuals come to terms with the full-scale religious veneration of Mao that even exceeded the discredited "cult of personality" which surrounded Stalin? How could they reconcile their conception of China as a rational, "truly democratic" and profoundly egalitarian society with the deification of Mao and the total self-abasement before him, which became a social norm in China?[196] In the eyes of some Western visitors, the perceived popularity of Mao neutralized their potentially negative reactions toward his cult.[197] For the most part the cult of Mao (as Stalin's and Castro's) was viewed as a reflection of the popularity of a beloved leader and not much different from the publicity that surrounds the powerful politician in the West. If, on the other hand, it was admitted that the cult of Mao was a qualitatively different phenomenon from the publicity Western politicians seek and often get, then it was presumed that Mao himself found it distasteful and would do all he could to restrain such extreme expressions of respect and popularity. Lord Boyd Orr, a high official of the World Health Organization, and Peter Townsend, for example, believed that Mao "won't have streets or places named after him either, or any of the usual honours" and that he even objected to celebrations of his birthday.[198]* According to Dick Wilson, he "often exhibited a refreshing personal humility." The Concerned Asian Scholars reported that "Mao himself has said that he did not like the 'personality cult' aspects of this veneration. . . ."[200] It is likely that some Western intellectuals had no difficulty in grasping the paternalistic element involved in the cult: after all, ordinary people craved father figures.

The drama of actually meeting either Mao or Chou was heightened by the Chinese custom of making those selected for this honor wait for a mysterious phone call in their hotels at unusual hours and then "whisking" them to the prearranged meeting place.[201] Hewlett Johnson was among the relatively few Westerners who had a face-to-face meeting with Mao (as he had with Stalin too). What struck him most "was something no picture had ever caught, an inexpressible look of kindness and sympathy, an obvious preoccupation with the needs of others: other

---

* By contrast, Robert Jay Lifton felt that, at any rate in the course of the Cultural Revolution, "Mao's active participation in the creation of his own cult has become increasingly clear."[199] It may be recalled that an integral part of the cult of personality in virtually all cases had been the attribution of modesty to the leaders basking in the cults.

people's difficulties, other people's troubles, other people's struggles—these formed the deep content of his thoughts and needed but a touch or a word to bring this unique look of sympathy to his face." To David and Nancy Milton, who also had a chance to meet him personally, "Mao was surprisingly warm, almost grandfatherly in manner," whereas Chou was described by them as "legendary statesman and diplomat of exquisite sensibilities . . . but what many people looked to him for was his understanding of their personal difficulties."[202] Simone de Beauvoir too captured in her narrative both Mao and Chou:

> We sit about little tables on which there are teacups, cigarettes, fruit, candles. . . . Chou En-lai moves amid the guests exchanging words, shaking hands; then similarly at ease Mao Tse-tung, by himself, with quiet unostentation makes the rounds of the tables. What is so winning about the Chinese leaders is that not one of them plays a part; they are dressed like anybody else . . . and their faces are not deformed either by class mannerism or by . . . the need to maintain a front . . . these are just faces, plainly and wholly human.[203]

As noted before, Chou's personal diplomacy had made him a highly visible figure among the Chinese leaders as he sought (and succeeded) to make a most favorable impression on the more important visitors. Audrey Topping was among those who received the full treatment:

> Dinner with the Premier of China is not only a gourmet's delight, it is mixed with words of wisdom and wit. Every visitor leaves with his own impressions of Chou, but everyone seems to agree that he radiates intelligence and worldly charm. I found him to be a virtual prism, shooting off flashes of light in all directions, yet he possesses a calm dignity and projects an inner strength that to me reflects the face of New China itself.

Moreover, "Premier Chou looked relaxed, extremely handsome and much younger than his seventy-three years."[204] He had also fired Harrison Salisbury's imagination: "He walked with an easy gait, slightly thrusting his feet ahead of his body. I imagined it was a gait that had become customary on the Long March, and I fancied that even now, he could start out on the trail in the morning and end up at nightfall fresh and unwearied."[205] Hewlett Johnson described him as "Handsome, courteous and gently spoken," hiding "under a modest urbane presence a courage of steel with reasoning power swift and trenchant as a rapier. . . . Mr. Chou's face once seen is never forgotten. An alert and kindly face, youthful, almost boyish. . . . A very warmly kind face too, and with eyes that look straight at you. I cannot imagine a less aggres-

sive face, or a gentler one. . . . Chou is an intellectual. He is cultivated
. . . has all the elements of literary genius." Norma Lundholm Djerassi
noted his "beautiful hands" and "kind and gentle face."[206]

Linking the personality and even the looks and physique of the leaders to the attributes of the regime was part of the process of fusing the
characteristics of individual leaders with the appeals of the social system they had created or inspired. It would have been simply inconceivable to behold a glorious social order which could not boast of outstanding leaders. These linkages were part of the harmony sought after
and perceived—between society and the individual, leader and the
masses, theory and practice.

The Regime and the Intellectuals

It is one of the ironies of our times that the position of intellectuals in
Communist China was among the sources of attraction Chinese society
exercised for numerous Western intellectuals. In few societies in our
times—including the Soviet Union—have intellectuals (and artists) been
more harshly treated, humiliated, and deprived of autonomy than in
China under Mao, especially during and after the Cultural Revolution.
As was belatedly discovered, intellectuals and artists of various kinds
were silenced, imprisoned, tortured and made to perform menial labor.° Writers allowed to publish were forced into the straitjacket of the
most primitive forms of socialist realism;† books were literally destroyed
(and not only banned) as were many monuments and works of art.
Bookshops stood empty but for the works of Mao, Stalin, Kim Il Sung,
and Enver Hoxha; in the National Library at Peking *"all traces of the
twentieth-century literary and historical works that do not conform to*

° Harrison Salisbury reported how "The riddle of the non-presence of writers and
artists in 1972 was solved. Almost every person I met in 1977 has been in prison in
1972, or confined to his home, exiled to a farm in the countryside, or put to some
other form of disgrace." Academics in turn fell victim to what Edward Friedman, an
American political scientist, called "Marxist McCarthyism," many of them "forced
into endless, tortuous, vacuous confessions" and suicides.[207]

† Chiang Ch'ing decreed, for example, that only positive characters could be emphasized in films (none of which produced before 1966 could be shown) and no
heroes were allowed to die.[208] Manuscripts had to meet the following conditions:
"All novels, essays, articles, works of art . . . must 1) exalt with deep and warm
proletarian feelings the great Chairman Mao; exalt the great, glorious and infallible
Chinese Communist Party; exalt the great victory of the proletarian revolutionary
line of Chairman Mao; 2) following the examples of Revolutionary Model operas,
strive with zeal to create peasant and worker heroes. . . ."[209]

Maoist orthodoxy have simply vanished." As to the monuments, "if a
tourist perversely escapes from his guides and beyond the circuit of Potemkin monuments he sees only desolation and ruin where famous buildings used to stand." Although perhaps the bulk of such depredations
(directed at both books and works of art) were linked to the Cultural
Revolution, what Simon Leys called "the death warrant of Chinese intellectual life" goes back as far as 1942, to a talk given by Mao in Yenan
on "arts and letters" and to policies which resulted in "the near-total extinction of Chinese intellectuals *as such*. There only survive specialized
technicians in propaganda, science and technology; others have been
'recycled' in the fields and factories; an irreducible minority of them
have committed suicide or been liquidated."[210] In a similar vein Robert
Guillain observed in 1956 that "The intelligentsia of the old days, with
its liberalism and general culture, has no place in a society where repetition and imitation are the order of the day, where free thought and free
information are forbidden."[211] If, as has increasingly been confirmed
since the fall of the Gang of Four, these were among the characteristics
of intellectual life in China under Mao, how can we account for the favorable impressions of the sympathetic Western intellectuals?

The same triad of factors accounts for the misperceptions of Western
visitors in these matters as in others examined before. There was the
strong predisposition to find virtue in China, including virtue in its
treatment of intellectuals; there was a bitter dissatisfaction with Western societies, including the condition of their intellectuals; and there was
ignorance, probably even greater than in the Soviet and Cuban cases,
and fortified by the techniques of superb hospitality, about conditions
of intellectual life in China and about the life of intellectuals. In certain
instances the respect accorded by the Chinese authorities to the work
of the visitors also helped to confirm the belief that nothing could be
wrong with intellectual life in China. Thus, for example, Scott Nearing
recalled that "on my latest trip to China I was told by Rewi Alley, a
New Zealander who has made Peking his home for the last twenty years,
that the book [Nearing wrote about China in 1927] still has a recognized place in the history and development of the Chinese revolution."
As to Rewi Alley, he has lived in China since 1927 and has been a
prominent propagandist of the regime (similar in stature to Anna Louise
Strong), playing an active part in the reception and guidance of important foreigners.[212]

In discussing the treatment of intellectuals it must also be noted that
their treatment during the decades Western visitors observed China had

not always been as harsh as during the Cultural Revolution, though it was always worse than what the visitors judged it to be.

The position of intellectuals in China won hearty endorsement for exactly the same reasons it was applauded in the Soviet Union in the 1930s and in Cuba in the 1960s. Chinese intellectuals appeared to be well-integrated, useful members of society, trusted by the highest power-holders, and often sharing power with them, taken seriously and well treated materially. Felix Greene's account affords a few glimpses of such privileges:

> the Writers' Association in Shanghai . . . was a palatial building with paneled rooms, wide staircases, spacious gardens. It has been, I learned, the private home of a Shanghai capitalist. . . .

> As for Mr. Hu [a Chinese writer he had met], he is clearly one of the rising stars among writers. . . . He wears silk shirts, new shoes, speaks humbly in an assured sort of way . . . a veritable Jack London story of success.

> I asked him if it were not true that writers were enormously better off than steelworkers. He agreed that they were. "There is a move on to reduce the royalty given to writers," he said. "One author recently earned 140,000 yuan for a single novel; it is now thought that writers ought to lower their scale somewhat. The purpose of writing," he stated, "is not to make money, but to help the people understand what they are working for."[213]

Simone de Beauvoir reported approvingly on other dimensions of the condition of intellectuals in one of the earliest Chinese travel reports:

> The Communist Party's policy toward the former society's intellectuals is to leave none of them adrift. They have all been given suitable employment. . . . By and large Chinese writers have never enjoyed such material prosperity . . . authors' royalties being 10 to 15%, earnings may be very high. . . . If moreover a writer wishes to travel, to undertake research, if he needs spare time for study or creative work, if he needs medical care or rest, all sorts of facilities are at his disposal. This preferential service is paid for: in China whoever receives must give; the writer is expected to render *service*. . . .

She found it preferable to be given "advice" by fellow professionals (i.e., the functionaries of the Chinese Writers Association) than to be subjected to the commercial pressures of "the merchants in the book game." Simone de Beauvoir also believed that writers in China were not subject to political pressures ("each writer decided for himself what his next book is to be about").[214] As Hewlett Johnson saw it, "Under Mao's inspiration, Chinese artists and writers left their dens of 'escapism.'

They went into field, factory and army, went and lived, and wrote as they lived . . . their writings reflect the deep emotions which they share with the people." Basil Davidson was persuaded by Chinese officials that the "remoulding" of intellectuals was a humane and benevolent exercise and that there was no censorship. Jan Myrdal, as has already been noted, was enthusiastic about the dispatching of intellectuals into the villages and what amounted to their loss of intellectual status and sphere of activity. The Concerned Asian Scholars did not doubt that the exodus of "intellectual youth" to the countryside was voluntary and desirable.[215] The authors of *China—Science Walks on Two Legs* were also greatly pleased by the fact that intellectuals ceased to be intellectuals, at least as we usually understand this concept.° As they and other estranged Western visitors saw it, the merging of intellectuals with the masses was a part of the attainment of social equality, of the struggle against social differentiation and essential for becoming truly integrated into society. Obviously, for those who were disenchanted with the qualities and activities which historically defined intellectuals— such as detachment, skepticism, critical thinking, sense of autonomy, etc.—the loss of these qualities was hardly a matter of concern. On the contrary, these Western "intellectuals" welcomed a society in which their occupational identities could in effect be dissolved, where they no longer stood apart from the rest of society by virtue of their intellectual status. (They were not in a position to assess the costs of such enforced integration as against the discomfort of whatever social isolation they experienced in the West.) In any event, there was a higher purpose in China that redeemed and redefined everything including the changing life style or loss of autonomy of intellectuals. Alberto Jacoviello, an editor of *Unita*, wrote: "there has been talk [in the West] of 'oppression' of intellectuals. The truth is that all intellectuals whom we met told us that contact with the people and work with the people made them different and better. It made them, in other words, men among men, all aiming at building a new Chinese socialist society." In his view China was "a country of philosophers."[217]

Two further speculations may be added to the reflections about the attitudes of Western intellectuals who were favorably impressed by the

° Their preferences coincided with the policies of the Chinese government which predated the Cultural Revolution. Robert Guillain observed on his visit in the early 1960s "That an intellectual should be an intellectual and nothing more is something that the authorities are not going to allow much longer in China."[216]

position of intellectuals in China. It is possible that whatever overt admiration Western intellectuals expressed on account of the integration (and subordination) of Chinese intellectuals, it was interwoven with the unexpressed feeling that it cannot and will not happen to them. Hence they could dismiss the chilling implications of what they had seen, and admire the "integration" of their Chinese colleagues from the safe distance which separated the visiting from the resident intellectuals.

We may also dust off here the old aspersion about the self-destructive impulses of Western intellectuals who found the condition of their Chinese counterparts enviable. Certainly the admiration and support for a political system (on the part of one set of intellectuals) which brings about the destruction of intellectuals as a group suggests a rather weak will to survive and a questionable dedication to function as voices of reason and critical conscience of society.

Reeducation, Not Imprisonment

Sympathetic visitors to China—like their predecessors to the Soviet Union in the 1930s—were favorably impressed by the penal system and its underlying philosophy. Their views were conditioned not only by their limited and selective exposure to penal institutions but also by their relative unconcern with civil liberties. Lord Boyd Orr and Peter Townsend, for instance, informed their readers at the outset that "In writing this book we avoided the question of civil liberties which has preoccupied some writers on China." They stated bluntly, "The important thing for the West is not so much the political system as the industrial and economic development."[218] Their position rested on the customary dual assumption that, since the vast majority of the population never had such liberties, they will not miss them now, and that the material gains outweighed whatever losses there might have been in respect to political rights.° Almost twenty years later the same attitude was echoed by Robert W. Barnett, former State Department official and

° Simon Leys proposed a typology of those engaged in such and similar arguments: "On the question of human rights in China an odd coalition has formed between 'Old China hands' (left over from the colonial-imperialist era), starry-eyed Maoist adolescents, bright, ambitious technocrats, timid sinologists ever wary of being denied their visas for China, and even some overseas Chinese who like to partake from afar in the People's Republic's prestige without having to share any of their compatriots' sacrifices or sufferings. The basic position of this strange lobby can be summarised in two propositions: 1. Whether or not there is a human rights problem in China, remains uncertain: 'we simply do not know'; 2. even if there should exist such a problem, it is none of our concern."[219]

director of the Washington Center of the Asia Society, as he explained (in his article entitled "Make an Issue of Human Rights in China? No") why indifference toward human rights in China was the proper course for the U.S. government to follow:

> we should hesitate to condemn them as less moral merely because they are different. . . . Harsh national necessity shapes China's assessment of "human rights." . . . We must respect China's rights to be different or, doing otherwise, expose ourselves to charges of self-righteousness. . . .[220]

If, in many instances, the well-worn clichés of cultural relativism provided encouragement to ignore (or soft-pedal) the repressive policies of the Chinese government, on other occasions compensating factors were discovered balancing the deprivations. Arthur Galston wrote: "Nominally at least they [the Chinese] are not free to change residence or job, but in spite of that and of their restricted political and intellectual freedom, the Chinese masses seem to enjoy a greater measure of control over those agencies that directly affect their daily lives than do most Western city workers."[221]

As always, the context was all-important in evaluating (and redefining) coercion and the state of personal freedoms. Once the social system as a whole was determined to be benevolent and just, few serious questions were raised as to the methods it used to maintain itself in power. Simone de Beauvoir, for example, defended the use of informers:

> Urging people to vigilance the government does indeed exhort them to report the counterrevolutionary activities . . . but we must not forget that these activities consist in arson, the sabotage of bridges and dikes, in assassinations. . . .°

° It will be recalled that an identical case was made for repression in the Soviet Union in the 1930s—indeed few campaigns of terror in our times failed to invoke the justification of self-defense. We still know too little of recent Chinese history to say that the Chinese regime was better justified in making these claims than others. As regards the use of informers, it certainly went far beyond the defensive purposes Simone de Beauvoir envisaged, and its consequences were characteristic of life in totalitarian societies: "M__ who is a teacher from Kwangchow [related Simon Leys] tells me that one never discusses politics with people one does not know well, or even with close friends if those friends belong to one's political unit; one speaks of political matters only with close friends who belong to other units. The reason: within the same unit, people always risk having mutually to accuse each other. Everyone prefers, therefore, not only to reveal as little as possible about himself to potential accusers but, above all, to know as little as possible about friends whom sooner or later he may be led to denounce." We learn from Bao Ruo-Wang (a former inmate of Chinese prisons) about "the omnipresent denunciation boxes which proliferate in every city. A foreigner might mistake them for mail boxes since they

> This cooperation with the police seems more shocking to me in our
> country where law is determined by the interests of a class than where
> justice is made to correspond to the welfare of the people.[223]

Basil Davidson simply disbelieved that the Chinese regime was coercive, perceiving it as "a State which is authoritarian only towards a minority—a minority who are not workers or peasants. This will come
unpleasantly to those who like to fool themselves that China is achieving
her success by dictatorial methods: the truth is that China's successes
are being achieved—and can only be achieved—by the voluntary and
even enthusiastic effort of most of the people of China." Thus it should
not be surprising that he also accepted at face value the official version
of the case of "five foreign nuns . . . placed on trial in Canton for mal-
treating children in their care, and for criminal negligence which was
found to have caused the death of many of these children." He learned
that mortality rates in this orphanage were "astonishingly high" and
that in the nearby common grave "more than one thousand infant skele-
tons were found." He was even "able to question the girl, Wang Yan-
chang . . . who had the task of carrying the corpses of the little children to the common grave . . ." and he was actually shown the common
grave ("deep dark holes").[224]*

As in the case of the Soviet purges, responses such as Davidson's reflected a failure of imagination; even after the experience of the Soviet
Show Trials and false confessions, the idea of staging trials, inventing
lurid crimes, and fabricating evidence in order to discredit particular
groups and individuals had remained a foreign and largely inconceivable possibility for Westerners. Unable to grasp the nature of coercion
in totalitarian societies, Western visitors often fell back on their familiar
experiences and concepts in trying to make sense out of events and institutions in the countries concerned. Thus Kenneth Woodsworth, a
Canadian attorney, after his visit to China in 1960, reported that "There
seems to be a considerable degree of protection against arbitrary arrest
and imprisonment and the impression is that the direction is towards
greater safeguards in this respect. . . ." Lord Boyd Orr and Peter
Townsend, discussing the question of compulsion in the collectivization

---

are painted bright optimistic red, slotted at the top and padlocked closed. Underneath is a shelf space for standard forms and above it a little notice in Chinese character: 'Denunciation Box.' "[222]

* It may be recalled that these (the early 1950s) were the years when the Chinese
government was engaged in the campaign against the Western churches and their
representatives in China, as was also evident from Hewlett Johnson's first book.[225]

of Chinese agriculture, pointed out that there was no legal force applied, but "Inevitably of course, there was a good deal of public pressure. Take the case of the British Agricultural Marketing Boards—when
a plebiscite showed that a certain percentage agreed to join, membership became compulsory. In China when a majority of villagers decided
to form a cooperative, the minority probably found it difficult to remain
outside." John Gittings, the English China scholar (and member of the
Society for Anglo-Chinese Understanding), commented in the same
spirit, "reform through labor, which to a Western visitor has something
of the flavor of the kibbutz combined with the Marxist weekend school
(except that it may last for a couple of years), seemed to be working for the great majority." Professor Fairbank found "Their whole program [of the May 7 Cadre School] . . . very similar to that of basic
training in the U.S. Army, but of course [it] has a much broader perspective and uses more variety of experience."* On his visit to one such
school, his "surprises began with lunch, which turned out to be one of
the best meals we ever had: 7 or 8 courses with several types of steamed
bread and special candies and other products locally produced."[226]

On the whole, Western intellectuals perceived the Chinese penal policies in much the same manner as the Soviet ones were seen in the
1920s and 1930s, but in the light of what has since been learned about
Soviet practices, the Chinese ones were regarded as far superior. In
China there were no bloody purges, no Gulags, no forced confessions,
no show trials. According to Simone de Beauvoir, "the Chinese have
carefully studied that precedent [the Russian Revolution, as a whole]
in order not to repeat its mistakes . . . the dissimilarity to the Stalinist
system is patent, since no administrative internment exists in China."[227]
Bao Ruo-Wang (the former inmate of Chinese prisons and labor camps)
found other differences; he believed that the Soviet camps were "brutally cruel, unsophisticated—and inefficient. . . . What the Russians
never understood, and what the Chinese Communists knew all along,
is that convict labor can never be productive or profitable if it is ex-
tracted only by coercion or torture. The Chinese were the first to grasp
the art of motivating prisoners."[228] Simon Leys shared this view; he regarded the Chinese camps the institution of advanced totalitarianism
par excellence: "In a way the camp represents a model, a projection of
the future, an ideal society. It is what society would be were its man-

---

* Comments and comparisons of this type irresistibly recall Henry Wallace and
Owen Lattimore who found much resemblance between Soviet corrective labor
camps and the TVA and Hudson Bay Company.

agers able to overcome the thousand and one forces of resistance and inertia that everywhere conspire to block the immediate nationwide re- alization of a certain conceptual model, a vision. . . . The camp in- mate . . . is delivered of this lamentable freedom that dooms the ordi- nary mortal. . . ."[229]

The Chinese, like the early Soviet reformers, stressed rehabilitation, work therapy in place of enforced idleness, humaneness over punitive- ness. Both Soviet and Chinese officials fervently claimed that the even- tual reintegration of convicts into society was their ultimate goal, and that the prisons or labor camps did reeducate the inmates. Rhetoric apart, there was some evidence that the Chinese took the goal of re- education more seriously than the Soviet regime had ever done and pursued this objective with determination through group pressure, among other devices, as we learn from the few available accounts of life inside Chinese penal institutions.[230] Corliss Lamont had no difficulty in transferring his benign views of the Soviet correctional system to the Chinese; even more remarkably, he succeeded in professing general ad- miration for both regimes. "In China," he wrote, "even though it re- mains a dictatorship, they don't shoot their dissenters; they 're-educate' them. And that procedure applies also to the highest officials. . . . The same spirit of re-education and rehabilitation governs the treatment of crimes and disputes among the Chinese people."[231]

While most Western visitors entertained a favorable view of the Chi- nese penal system, the majority had no direct experience of even se- lected aspects of it, as the Chinese were not too anxious to display their penal institutions, especially in more recent times. For instance, mem- bers of the Quaker Delegation in 1972 "found the Chinese reticent when we probed into some issues such as crime and punishment." Peter Worsley reported that he "saw no courts or prisons, and a Filipino delegation was told recently that the legal organs are not for sightseeing. Very few first hand reports exist on penal procedures, including prisons. But the general outlines are known and the crucial principle is that of rehabilitation through work."[232] Leon Lipson, a professor of law at Yale University, found it impossible on his visit to arrange meetings with "judges, advocates, prosecutors, police officials or other law officers."[233] On the whole, explorations of the penal system, including and especially prison visits, became more difficult during and after the Cultural Revolu- tion, except for the May 7 schools. Thus the accounts of on-the-spot in- spections of Chinese penal establishments usually date back to the 1950s or early 60s. Simone de Beauvoir's report and commentary is among the most detailed and deserves to be quoted at some length as it also reveals her views of Western prisons:

> I did personally see one prison [in China]. And several years back I visited a model prison in Chicago. This one in Peking was not a model prison;* it was simply the only one in the city area and, for that matter, in the province; and all central prisons are the same in China. What a difference between this and the American system! At Chicago the authorities took custody of my handbag so that I would not be able to pass cigarettes or my lipstick out to the prisoners; corridors and cells were sealed by stoutly locked steel doors. . . . Here, the prison is in the depths of a kind of park; two soldiers are on duty at the outer gate; but once you are inside it you see no wardens, no guards, no guides, only ununiformed and—a fact of some importance— unarmed overseers. They exercise the functions of foremen and political and cultural instructors. The inmates wear no special costume, they are dressed ilke everybody else, and nothing distinguishes them from the employees who supervise their work. The shops are located in the middle of a big garden planted with sunflowers; were it not for the watchtower—unoccupied, furthermore— . . . one would take this for an ordinary factory. . . . the working day being on a nine-hour-shift basis; every man has one day off each week. Eight of the daily twenty-four hours are allotted for sleeping, three for classwork; two hours of ideological instruction, one of general culture. After subtracting the time taken up by meals and the details of personal hygiene, the prisoners are still left with a considerable amount of leisure. They have a field for sports at their disposal, a big courtyard with a theater where a movie is shown or a play presented once every week; the day I was there they were rehearsing a play of their own. There is also a reading room stocked with books and periodicals where they can sit and relax. We visit this library first, then the kitchens, then the laundry. . . . A

---

* This view was disputed by others. Her fellow countryman, Jules Roy, wrote: "It was a model prison. It was shown to all the newspapermen and all the television crews. . . . Eighteen hundred political and common law prisoners were undergoing reeducation here. It seemed scarcely closed in at all. Flowers were carefully cultivated in the courtyards. . . . Some ex-prisoners requested the privilege of continuing to work here for their room and board and a small salary. Everything was scrubbed, polished, shining. Basketball and volley ball teams were working out on the sports field. A rehearsal was going on in the open-air theater . . . hospital attendants studiously corrected the position of patients standing before the X-ray machines. There were no bars on the windows, no locks on the cell doors." Edgar Snow too visited the Peking jail. Bao Ruo-Wang, who had stayed in this notable institution (as well as in many others, unsung by visitors), wrote: ". . . Prison Number One is still one of the best attractions of the standard Peking tour for foreign visitors, and they react predictably. How many pages of emotional praise have I read since my release concerning the wisdom and humanity of the Chinese prison system, all of them due to the good offices of Prison Number One."234

door stands ajar, we peer through it, there are men asleep on cots; they belong to the night shift. The prison was built by the Kuomintang; each cell was then an individual kennel, bars over its little window; since, the in-between partitions have been knocked out, and eight or nine inmates now share relatively spacious, well-lit rooms which on one side give out on the garden and on the other open upon this hall-way that is closed by a grill but only at night."[235]

Trudeau and Hebert were evidently also taken to the same prison, where only one sentry stood guard and within the walls of which "a garden welcomes us, planted with greenery and fine fragrant trees. This is a prison?" They too reported the absence of bars and were informed of the details of the rehabilitation process.[236] Apparently James Cameron, the British journalist, too was taken to the same prison in 1954 in Peking,[237] which he found a "dispiriting establishment" where "the regime claimed to 'treat' its dissidents and 'reform' the unreliable." The prison turned out to be a textile factory "dedicated much more to production than to reform. . . . Everyone appeared to be desperately hard at work." It was explained to Cameron that " 'that is the manner of their redemption . . . reform through production' . . ." and the governor of the prison averred that most of them responded well to such treatment. The few obstinate ones were administered "Social Rebuke," defined as "a critical attitude taken up toward the offender by the more progressive comrades, which manifests itself in an atmosphere of disapproval." But if all else failed, privileges, such as gifts from relatives, could be revoked and sentences could be lengthened. There were no escapes from the prison. " 'As a matter of fact,' said the Governor . . . 'some don't want to leave. They ask to stay when their time is up.' "[238] (As will be recalled, George Bernard Shaw, upon visiting some Soviet prisons, came to believe that inmates enjoyed their stay so much that many of them were reluctant to leave and were granted similar privileges, enabling them to stay "as long as they wished.")

Basil Davidson and his party also visited the jail in Peking and Shanghai in the early 1950s, and he suggested that in China those accused of counter-revolutionary crimes of violence were more leniently treated than violent criminals would be in Britain. "Some of these prisoners were the opium gangsters of yesterday; others were recalcitrant landlords. Little by little they will be drawn back into the everyday life of China,"[239] he wrote. Peter Townsend's account of the Chinese policies of reeducation was largely based on plays performed by the Pure River Corps dramatic group, composed of former Kuomintang secret service agents.* "The Pure River Corps had settled a tract of land between Peking and Tientsin at a place called . . . Pure River. . . . Hundreds of men working eight or nine hours a day gradually turned the wasteland into a garden. . . . There are three meals a day, with plenty of fish and grain, and meat once a fortnight. In season they caught crab: in the irrigation channels. . . . Some of the pleasures of the outside world were brought to them. There was plenty of entertainment. . . . Not all of those freed wanted to leave Pure River Corps. . . . But when a man was released every effort was made to provide him with a job and readjust him to society. . . ."[240]

Felix Greene was another more privileged Western visitor who was allowed some glimpses of Chinese penal institutions in the early 1960s. Like several of his famous compatriots (such as G. B. Shaw, the Webbs, Harold Laski) who had found the Soviet correctional system more successful than the British, Greene felt the same way about the Chinese:

> I went to Peking's only prison . . . having been interested in penal reform in England, and here I found the Chinese doing what we had been trying to get the English authorities to do for years without success. Mainly, of course, to get the stigma, the moral stigma, out of imprisonment.

He too was astonished and pleased to note the virtual absence of guards, the open gates, the low walls, no locks, no window bars and a generally relaxed, genial atmosphere. ("In one workshop . . . I asked where the guard was and was introduced to a smiling youngster in a T shirt. . . .") He did, however, find conditions in the Shanghai prison less appealing, more prisonlike. But even there "The chief warden . . . seemed curiously out of place. . . . a young fellow, wearing a white short-sleeved shirt with an open collar. An open face, firm but likeable. They certainly *use* young people."[241] Audrey Topping was one of the few Western visitors in the 1970s who had a chance to comment on the Chinese penal institutions and policies on the basis of firsthand impressions following a visit to Nanking prison:

> The Chinese fought crime with the same vigorous, politically oriented enthusiasm with which they fought hunger. . . . The Maoist ideology strongly condemns crime as detrimental to the state as a whole, and therefore the potential sinner is confronted not only with a possible prison term if caught but with the disdain of his friends if he is suc-

---

* These plays may remind the reader of the corresponding Soviet fable by Pogodin entitled "Aristocrats" (mentioned in Chapter 4) dealing with the good life and works of assorted political criminals building the White Sea Canal in the 1930s.

cessful. Second, with no organized criminal underground, there is no place to sell stolen wares, no place to escape. . . .

The Chinese attempt to rehabilitate their lawbreakers to become useful members of society. . . . The prison commissioner [in the Nanking prison] said the Chinese do not believe that if a man commits a crime his attitude can be changed by merely locking him up. . . . They feel that the criminal's thinking and his whole approach to life should be changed. This is not done through punishment but through political education and labor. . . .

Occasionally a former prisoner comes back [the warden said] but this is rare. The government gives them jobs and they enjoy equal rights. . . .

". . . what if a prisoner tries to escape" I asked. "Escape!" he answered. "Where would he escape to? If his ideology is no good, the people will turn him in again. There is no place to escape to."[242]

Finally, the varied reactions of members of a Japanese delegation to the Chinese practice of suspended death sentence exemplifies the influence of predisposition on evaluation:

A Japan Socialist Party delegation, feeling themselves very daring, insisted on seeing a reform-through-labour prison. They visited . . . a prison where all the prisoners were under a two-year suspended death sentence, its execution or commutation at the end of that time depending upon the progress of the prisoner's reform. (The right-wingers were shocked, in the same way most Westerners would be; the pacifists were upset by the capital punishment, but relieved that a humane solution was possible; and the left-wingers were delighted at this most intelligent and "advanced" method for dealing with anti-social elements.) . . . the same prison was visited by at least dozens of other foreign visitors.[243]

It is arguable how much of an innovation in regard to the reform-through-labor principle the May 7 schools represented which were introduced during the Cultural Revolution. Their purpose was the reeducation through manual labor of officials, white-collar workers, teachers, managers, and other assorted members of the higher strata of non-manual workers. Professor Fairbank saw them as a device to forestall "the dreaded revival of special privilege for a new ruling class divorced from the people" or a place "to which white-collar personnel . . . regularly repair in rotation for a spell of farm work and Mao study." Bernard Frolic compared them to an "adult Boy Scout Camp, or maybe what the Civilian Conservation Corps was like during the Depression." Harrison

Salisbury described them as "a combination of a YMCA camp and a Catholic retreat."[244] The May 7 schools certainly differed from prisons in that people were sent to them not through judicial or police channels, but through less clear-cut procedures originating at the place of work. Those in "attendance" received their regular salary and could visit their family at certain intervals. The length of stay at these schools was more undefined but generally much shorter than in prison camps: we have reports of two years as well as six months. From the official standpoint, being sent to these schools was not a punishment but an opportunity for self-improvement for those who had lost contact with the masses and were in danger of developing an elitist consciousness based on their superior skills and training. Manual labor was the universal remedy for such tendencies. There was a strong religious streak in the whole enterprise: humility was to be instilled through some pain and suffering. Klaus Mehnert reported how, for example, a woman doctor cleansed herself by immersion in the world of peasants she had earlier despised as a city doctor: "When one of the peasant women was sick she moved in with her in order to give her better care. Here she did some of the dirtiest jobs herself, and so she got rid of her prejudices." Generally speaking, "the most repellent jobs" were considered the most therapeutic, above all the emptying of latrines. One of the officials whose case was described to Mehnert "had come to understand . . . that emptying latrines is not a dirty job, but honorable work."[245] Macchiocchi sensed a "strange fraternity, the unprecedented humanity which permeates this school—where does it come from?"[246]

A more prosaic explanation of attitude change through such methods was proposed by Jules Roy: "Anyone even suspected of a lukewarm attitude toward the party was immediately sent to one of the people's communes for a period of re-education. It seldom required any great length of time, digging in the soil and carrying buckets of excrement, before the recalcitrant no longer thought of anything except returning home and gladly furnished all the required proofs of devotion to the revolution."[247]

Since Mao's death there has been new information coming forth from inside China about the Chinese coercive policies and techniques under Mao—reminiscent of developments in the Soviet Union after the death of Stalin. Like Stalin in the Soviet case, the Gang of Four in China emerged as the source of every abuse of power and the target of blame for every newly acknowledged defect of the system, including its repressive methods and the political violence associated with the Cultural Revolution, the best known and most recent of the various campaigns which periodically raised the level of political violence.* As in the Soviet Union after the death of Stalin, in China Mao's passing led to a break in continuity which resulted in more permissive policies and, in turn, to the rise of some protest, social criticism, and the public airing of grievances, past and present.[249] Contrary to widespread Western beliefs, evidence came to light which suggested striking similarities between Soviet and Chinese penal practices. It turned out after all that not all Chinese methods used to break down and control prisoners were so refined and non-violent. There were now reports of burnings, beatings, kickings, deprivations of food and sleep (even a rule identical to that reported by many Soviet prisoners that "they have to sleep facing the [cell] door" and woken up if not complying); of people who went insane or crippled from being tortured; of people disappearing without trace for years or a decade (or forever); of secret prisons; prolonged solitary confinement; of the most grotesque grounds for imprisonment.[250] There also existed a policy of exile for those released from prison, and there was further similarity in that the Chinese (as the Soviet regime under Stalin) also victimized many of its most dedicated supporters who fell prey to internal power struggles. As one of the wall-posters on political prisoners stated: "The irony is that these usually gifted individuals joined the Communist Party to fight for the freedom and well-being of China and of mankind, and consequently devoted the better part of their lives to obtaining and maintaining the party's political dominance."[251] We have also learned more recently of the permanence of the political stigma once acquired, of peasants (they would be called *kulaks* in Russia) "who 30 years ago lost their property but kept their class enemy status," of "The records revealing class background [which] follow Chinese citizens everywhere,"[252] of people informing on each other not only out of a sense of patriotic duty or fear, but also to settle per-

* Other campaigns taking great human toll occurred between 1949 and 1952, aimed at the liquidation of counter-revolutionaries with estimated executions of 5 million; a 1957 anti-rightist campaign resulted in millions being sent to the countryside for "re-education" and 1.7 million "subjected to police investigation"; between 1966 and 1969 the Cultural Revolution claimed at least hundreds of thousands of victims; during the anti-Lin Pao and anti-Confucius campaign between 1973 and 1975 in Peking alone 1000 workers of the Culture Ministry were "persecuted, jailed, tortured or killed." In attempting to draw this type of balance sheet it must also be recalled that Chinese officials had often referred to the 5 per cent of "bad elements" (about 40 million people) considered to be second-class citizens and treated accordingly.[248]

sonal grievances.[253] Besides the wall-posters, more substantial documents of dissent have also appeared, including the first two works of fiction (rooted in their authors' experience) which convey the suffocating atmosphere of daily life, the group controls, the depredations of the Cultural Revolution, the endemic mistrust, corruption, inequality, and ruthlessness of the political elite.[254]

While it would be premature to conclude that Western visitors were as much deluded in their assessment of Chinese penal institutions and the level of coercion under Mao as they had been about the corresponding Soviet practices under Stalin, such a possibility has considerably increased since the death of Mao.

In conclusion a few clarifying comments should be entered. First, it was not my intention to suggest that China under Mao was very much like the Soviet Union under Stalin, even though I drew attention to a number of similarities, including those between the perceptions and misperceptions of the two political systems by their admirers.

In presenting an extended sampling of the misperceptions of China on the part of intellectuals of various kinds (as well as representatives of the mass media), I did not wish to convey that China scholars and specialists working for the U.S. government were no better informed, or that until Mao's death there was no scholarly data refuting the political pilgrims. There was such information but it was not widely known, or given wide currency by the mass media, as opposed to the enthusiastic reports much publicized after the Cultural Revolution and especially in the early 70s.

I should also note here that the nature of this study as a whole did not permit an effort to organize the perceptions of China according to the different phases of its political development. Rather, it was more congruent with the goals of the enterprise to select and focus on those perceptions and attractions which recurred in different periods.

Lastly, I did not attempt to provide a systematic rebuttal of all misperceptions but preferred to present conflicting views either on those occasions when the misperceptions involved were not self-evidently improbable or absurd, or when there was especially compelling evidence to suggest that the idealized images were untenable.

8

The Techniques of Hospitality: A Summary

. . . his claim to have seen with his own eyes a "real" revolution gave an air of authority to his pronouncements, and it bolstered his image of himself as one who arrived at decisions only on the basis of concrete evidence. GRANVILLE HICKS ON LINCOLN STEFFENS[1]

I had never before travelled in such sumptuous style. In special railway carriages or the best cars, always the best rooms in the best hotels, the most abundant and choicest food. And what welcome! What attentions! What solicitude! Everywhere acclaimed, flattered, made much of, feasted. Nothing seemed too good, too exquisite to offer me. ANDRÉ GIDE[2]

They brought food with a smile. And it was good food. Hot. Chinese. Clean. Eggdrop soup, chicken and green peppers, breaded oysters, pungent pork meatballs and orange pop. The table cloth was clean. The chopsticks clean. I felt myself relaxing. Why, I suddenly thought, it's pleasant to be in this country! HARRISON SALISBURY[3]

(In Havana I kept meeting Communists in the hotels for foreigners who had no idea that the energy and water supply in the working quarters had broken down during the afternoon, that bread was rationed, and that the population had to stand for two hours in line for a slice of pizza; meanwhile the tourists in their hotel rooms were arguing about Lukacs.) HANS MAGNUS ENZENSBERGER[4]

The techniques of hospitality refer to the entire range of measures designed to influence the perception and judgment of the guests; it is a form of attempted persuasion by "evidence," the evidence of the senses. As such, these techniques represent a concentrated effort to maximize control over the experiences of the visitors. Naturally the more centralized and powerful the host governments and the greater their control over the resources of their countries and over their citizens, the more successful they are in controlling the experiences of the visitor. Insofar as each one of the four countries at the times of the visits could be re-

347

garded as totalitarian,[5] the possibilities for shaping the visitor's impressions and experiences were indeed greatly enhanced. Thus there must be certain structural as well as ideological conditions and prerequisites for such a treatment of visitors to become feasible and desirable. From the ideological point of view the hosts must have an extreme concern with the management of the impressions (of selected foreigners), a concern which in turn rests on the belief in the importance of ideas for gaining political advantage. Even relatively poor countries so disposed— i.e., China, Cuba, North Vietnam, and some Soviet Bloc countries—were quite willing to invest considerable resources in the techniques of hospitality (as they were in other prestige-enhancing projects such as public buildings, stadiums, monuments, and the like). Those in control of these regimes believe that since ideas are weapons, the favorable impressions and the hoped-for publicized accounts of influential visitors are political assets to be nurtured carefully. The favorable impressions of distinguished intellectuals, journalists, politicians, specialists, and assorted VIPs from abroad mean good publicity and more. They may also contribute to the development of foreign public opinions more receptive to specific policies—economic, cultural, military—or more favorable foreign elite opinions and attitudes. In regard to the targets of such attentions, the policies of hospitality may fluctuate; they may be aimed at specific elite groups (e.g., scientists, writers, politicians, artists) or some cross-sections of public opinion (e.g., leaders of community organizations or trade unions) or selected key individuals.

The highly developed techniques and policies of hospitality are also linked to certain structural conditions alluded to above. Again, these are most likely to be present in societies which are highly centralized and regimented, in which resources such as public accommodations, travel and tourism, the mass media, cultural activities, and institutions are under strict and complete government control. The government control, or more accurately, monopoly over such resources, tends to go hand in hand with cautious attitudes on the part of the population. Citizens of such societies will at least passively cooperate with the official treatment of foreign visitors; they will not, as a rule, challenge, in personal encounters with foreigners, the official versions of reality, or do so very rarely and if so not forcefully. This is all the more the case since the guides and interpreters accompanying the visitors are more than just guides and interpreters: they are in effect government officials with some authority of which the citizens are well aware. It is in totalitarian societies that the art of such impression-management reaches its fullest fruition as a result of the prevailing official belief in the controllability and interdependence of all aspects of reality and the corresponding policies designed to maximize controls over the most diverse aspects of social existence.

While the Soviet Union pioneered the practices and policies covered by the term "techniques of hospitality" and considered them important enough to divert significant resources to them soon after the regime was established, other political systems, partially or initially modeled after the Soviet, also adopted and pursued the same policies zealously and energetically.[6]

Thus already in 1920 Emma Goldman observed during her stay in the Soviet Union that "The British Mission was entertained royally with theatres, operas, ballets and excursions. Luxury was heaped upon them while the people slaved and went hungry. The Soviet Government left nothing undone to create a good impression and everything of a disturbing nature was kept from the visitors." In the same year Victor Serge, another early supporter of the Soviet regime, wrote: "The only city the foreign delegates did not get to know . . . was the living Moscow with its hunger rations, its arrests. . . . Luxuriously fed amidst general misery . . . led through museums to exemplary kindergartens, the delegates of world socialism gave the impression of being on vacation. . . ."[7]

Of course, all societies prefer to show their brighter side to foreign visitors (as do individual hosts to their guests), but the eagerness and determination to do so increase with the growth of those areas and aspects of life over which the government claims authority and responsibility. As noted above, powerful governments of this type also tend to view ideas and beliefs (including the impressions of foreign visitors) as important political resources. Furthermore, their internal political arrangements facilitate the control over the movements of both their own citizens and of their guests from abroad. Occasionally even technologically and administratively backward police states, such as Uganda under Idi Amin, will attempt, and succeed in, winning the praise of foreign visitors suitably treated. The Pol Pot regime in Cambodia, even after its defeat by the Vietnamese, tried, in the areas remaining under its control, to impress its visitors with what was called "jungle luxury." ("Plates of fruit brought from Bangkok were on each table. New cakes of soap and freshly laundered towels were in the bathrooms. Hammocks were strung among the saplings for siestas." To be sure, such comforts were to benefit the functionaries of the regime as much as the visitors.) And a "highly orchestrated propaganda tour" taken by Andrew Young, the U.N. representative of the United States, at the behest of the Algerian authorities achieved its purpose of persuading him to share the point of view of that government.[8]

The basic premises of the techniques of hospitality are quite uncomplicated. Since generalizing from personal experience is a widespread and almost irresistible impulse—as well as a basic form of learning, understanding, and evaluation—it is imperative to make such experiences pleasant and to select them with a clear purpose. For intellectuals, in particular, generalizing from personal and often limited experience is a major activity. Bearing this in mind, one may understand why, for instance, John Kenneth Galbraith after he was shown the kitchen of a plant in Peking was led to conclude that "if there is any shortage of food, it was not evident in the kitchen."[9] While this was literally true, Galbraith obviously wished to convey that such an example of abundance made a more generalized food shortage unlikely, even absurd. (As will be recalled, G. B. Shaw, looking around in an elegant Moscow restaurant, was also led to scorn reports of famine, and Ramsey Clark, not having personally witnessed any act of repression, was persuaded about the peaceable nature of the North Vietnamese regime.)

The purpose of making the visits pleasant for the travelers is then obvious enough. It is difficult, for most of us, not to have a favorable view of those who treat us nicely. It is also difficult to believe and to imagine that those who are kind to us can be unkind to others. Correspondingly, it is hard to envisage the representatives of a political system allowing their own citizens to lead wretched lives if they are successful in creating the most agreeable living conditions for us (even for only a short time).

Thus it was not surprising that Urie Bronfenbrenner found "their hospitality [in China] . . . really beyond compare . . . they made every effort to grant our every wish." In her hotel in Shanghai, Maria Macciocchi observed: "Everything catered exclusively to our convenience." A delegation of American computer scientists "was received in China with open arms. A greater cordiality and solicitude, a more earnest effort to satisfy our wishes . . . an all-round warmer welcome would be hard to imagine. . . . 'You have brought your wives; next time you must bring your children too,' they said. Egalitarian convictions in no way inhibited them from offering their American guests . . . the choicest foods, accommodations, transportation, amusements and services. . . ." William W. Howells, also an "official guest" and member of the American Paleoanthropology Delegation, recalled that "We were received everywhere with great cordiality, stayed in deluxe hotels (the only kind the Chinese have for foreigners), and were whisked around city and countryside in a cavalcade of cars, feeling embarrassingly like mandarins as we pushed through crowds and red lights." Bernard Pares, in the Soviet Union in the mid-1930s, found in his Moscow hotel "everything both in provision and attention, that could make for the visitor's comfort. . . ."[10]

In the final analysis, it will not be possible to strike a fine balance between the two major determinants of the visitors' evaluation of the societies they had visited: their predispositions on the one hand and what they had actually seen on the other, which in turn was mediated by the techniques of hospitality. As stressed earlier, without the favorable predisposition toward the countries concerned, the sights would have made much less of an impact, as was also illustrated by the euphoric response to objects, sights, or institutions in themselves unremarkable and also to be found in the visitors' own societies. Thus there was a marked congruence between the attitudes of most visiting intellectuals and their hosts: the former wished for the experiential confirmation of the favorable beliefs entertained about the social systems of the countries visited, and the latter were ready to offer just that. (Susan Sontag, for example, believed that ". . . North Vietnam [was] the place, which, in many respects, *deserves* to be idealized.")[11] Rarely did the techniques of hospitality backfire (as happened with André Gide in the 1930s) when they were applied to favorably predisposed visitors. In most instances, the guests succeeded in justifying (or rationalizing) the excellent treatment they had received and overcame whatever unease (a few of them) occasionally felt when they contrasted their comforts with the general conditions of life in the country.

Susan Sontag was among the few who felt occasional misgivings, which however did not interfere with her generally uncritical and enthusiastic reports. She was, for instance, troubled by the elaborate meals given in North Vietnam and also by being taken everywhere, even over short distances, by car. ("Why don't they let us walk . . . ?") For Mary McCarthy "It was [also] obvious that the foreigners . . . lived better than the general population. . . . The knowledge of living much better than others (the meals were very good) and at the expense of an impecunious government . . . produced a certain amount of uneasiness, which, however, wore off." Andrew Salkey in Cuba told his guide about his misgivings: "about the free, all-in, luxurious hotel life for the delegates; hardly what any of us . . . had expected . . . four enormous nightclub dining rooms to choose from, an international cuisine (changed daily), free laundry service, free telephone . . . , free taxi cabs and Congress cars and buses, free (three) daily papers and weekend magazines in three languages, and free entry to the city's theatres and exhibitions . . . added to all that, my return air ticket . . . plus my overweight also paid. . . . Too much, much too much to accept." But in the end he accepted it all, perhaps in part because he was persuaded that "the Cuban hospitality was warmly, affectionately *native* and little inspired by ideological gain. . . ."[12]

In many visitors such generous and attentive treatment created a disarming sense of obligation. They were not "bribed," but they could not help feeling that it is not nice to turn around and be harshly critical of those who showered them with kindness, who took such good care of them. Being critical of one's generous host seems a betrayal both at the individual-social as well as international-political-tourist level. For example, "A 'friend of China' felt constrained from disappointing his host by writing anything critical or unflattering. . . . All the special treatment and effort extended on one's behalf seemed to require repayment. . . . But one fear above all predominated: . . . that if one uttered or wrote 'incorrect' thoughts one would never again be allowed back. And to one degree or another [wrote Orville Schell, whose views on these matters seemed to have undergone considerable change by 1980] . . . most of us who have written about China [one may add Cuba and the Soviet Union] did capitulate to this fear."[13] In turn, some of the political hosts felt genuinely betrayed when, as happened on a few occasions, the lavishly treated guests upon their return (or some time later) failed to restrain their critical sentiments, as was the case with Castro and some Western intellectuals after the Padilla affair. Even when the guests self-consciously tried, as occasionally happened, to be on guard and to fend off the temptation to be disarmed, the techniques of hospitality would in the end contribute to the muting and blunting of criticism, to the giving of every benefit of doubt, and to refraining from "value judgments" unless they were laudatory. It would have been difficult for James Reston, for example, to return from China as a critic of the regime after the excellent medical treatment he had received in an emergency. "A parade of nurses and technicians then slipped quietly into the room. They bathed me with warm towels. They checked everything I had that moved or ticked. They took blood out of the lobe of my ear. They took my temperature constantly, measured pulse beat. They were meticulous, calm and unfailingly gentle and cheerful. . . . I leave with a sense of gratitude and regret."[14] This is not to say that this experience was the prime source of his favorable views of China, but that it had contributed to them and helped him to discard his critical reactions, if he had any.

There were other circumstances too which made it easier for the techniques of hospitality to bring about the results the host-authorities had intended. One of them was the belief—itself a part of the favorable predisposition of the visitors—that their hosts were credible and honest and would not attempt to manipulate the travel experience to impress the visitors by showing them what is exceptional, contrived or conjured up. In short, the guests, as a rule, trusted their hosts. The Webbs, for instance, were free of apprehension not only about the representativeness of what they were shown but also about the reliability of documentary evidence the authorities made available for them ("there is available to the serious student an unusual output of printed documents by the Soviet government through many of its departments . . ." they wrote). If some, like the Webbs and others, had complete trust in the information the host government supplied, Susan Sontag for one confessed that "it was not information (at least in the ordinary sense) that I'd come to find." It did not strain Daniel Berrigan's belief to be told (among other things) by his North Vietnamese informants that former collaborators with the French were reconciled and reformed "through a process of inward change," that the American prisoners displayed by the North Vietnamese declared (in the presence of their captors!) "without prompting" how well fed and well cared for they were, and that the only reason he could not meet any Catholic priests was that they were "very busy." Harry S. Ashmore averred that the constant company of "English speaking escorts who were always on hand . . . was an act of consideration, not of surveillance." Lion Feuchtwanger suggested that both the moral and material defects of the Soviet system were easy to discover, as "they are not concealed."[15] There were visitors who insisted that they could not have been taken to exceptional, pre-selected sights, since they were given choices on their itineraries and often picked particular places or projects at random. They were spared the knowledge that their "choices" were made from carefully pre-selected sights and what appeared "random" was due to artful prearrangement for the most part.[16]

The mystique of personal experience and the belief in the superiority of being-on-the-spot, over any other access to reality or source of information, were also among the factors which made the task of the hosts easier.* We all have a vested interest in the credibility of our own impressions and experiences, sensory or other. It is devastating to entertain the possibility of being reduced to the status of a gullible tourist on a conducted tour who has no way of knowing what is true and false in the narrative of his guides, and who among his genial hosts may be an accomplished liar or trained propagandist.

It is most unwelcome for everybody and especially intellectuals to discover and admit that they were manipulated or deceived on important occasions of their life. Intellectuals have particularly strong defenses against such discoveries, since they take pride in their critical faculties, in their capacity to "explode myths" and see through sham. The possibility that these impulses could let them down and that their assessment of the socio-political realities of a country could be significantly altered by a carefully orchestrated and unrepresentative sampling of experiences and impressions is hard to confront. Hence the issue as such rarely comes up. As a rule, the visiting intellectuals succeed in persuading themselves either that what they had seen was not significantly different from what they did not see, or that they managed to see more than their hosts intended them to see. Galbraith, for example, was, as noted before, reassured that "in all travel one sees much that one is not shown, and Potemkin, whatever his skill, would have had more difficulty dealing with decently experienced economists."[18] Arthur Galston, who had also conceded that his hosts in China "put their best foot forward in every possible instance," was certain that he (and his family) "could not have been completely misled," and "Having applied reasonable mental checks and balances I feel confident that our impressions reflect an accurate picture of society in China today."[19] At times even when the visitor was aware of being taken to something exceptional, it still had a favorable impact. David Caute wrote about a housing project he saw in Cuba: "Admittedly this is a showcase, the familiar trap of the conducted tours, but, on the other hand, it isn't a mirage or a magic lantern and it certainly wasn't erected merely to impress passing clusters of tourists."[20] While the argument has merit, the difficulty lies in assessing *how* unrepresentative are such showcase projects and what sights unseen are to be balanced against them.

---

* This attitude was especially widespread among journalists. As Stanley Karnow noted, "despite obvious news management many journalists who visit China inevitably operate on the old fashioned reporter's principle that seeing is believing. Editors reinforce this tendency *to equate presence and credibility* by attaching enormous importance to datelines."[17]

While we cannot hope to arrive at a precise determination of the relative importance of predisposition versus the techniques of hospitality in the shaping of the judgment of the visitors, a more detailed examination of what these techniques entailed will help to evaluate their relative importance.

The "Ego Massage"

As noted earlier, the techniques of hospitality have two basic ingredients. One is the screening of reality, the attempted control over what the visitor can see and experience. The other one is the way he is treated. The latter can be further separated into material privileges and comforts on the one hand and non-material privileges catering primarily to psychic comforts and ego-gratifications on the other. To be sure, the two often overlap: comfortable accommodations or luxurious means of transportation are not only pleasurable in the physical sense, they also enhance the status and the sense of general well-being and self-image of the travelers. Lavish banquets are addressed both to the stomach and the ego. Nonetheless there is a range of measures or techniques more specifically designed to make the visitors feel important, and they can be distinguished from the provision of physical comforts. The importance of these techniques cannot be overestimated. Even crude flattery is hard to resist and has a disarming effect on the critical faculties. According to Barghoorn, "Soviet* hospitality is likely to be particularly seductive when applied to individuals with above-average susceptibility to flattery. Impecunious intellectuals, ignored or slighted in their home countries, are extraordinarily amenable to calculated flattery."[21] While being impecunious may be among the factors which increase susceptibility to such flattery, most of the visitors dealt with in this study clearly were not. Slighted and ignored some of them might have felt in their own countries, but often such feelings had little objective basis, which however did not make them less intense. Feelings of exclusion from power, or insufficient involvement with it might be closer to reality as far as some of the intellectuals sampled in this study were concerned. In any event, insofar as the regimes in question succeeded in making them feel appreciated and well taken care of, and thus increased their receptivity to the sights to be seen, it mattered relatively little what they were actually shown. When some bond of obligation or gratitude is established be-

---

* We may of course substitute Cuban, Chinese, or North Vietnamese hospitality.

tween guests and host there is likely to be a high degree of responsiveness toward virtually anything that will be displayed. In due course selective perception, contextual redefinition, and the application of double standards will all come into play, and the importance of objective, visually experienced realities becomes reduced. For such reasons the personal treatment of the guests may well be the most important part of the techniques of hospitality, even more important than the selective presentation of various aspects of the social system. Making the visitor feel well liked, important, and good about himself rarely fails to reinforce the favorable predispositions in most cases already present. The process starts right on arrival.

After crossing the border into the Soviet Union, G. B. Shaw and his entourage were provided with a special sleeping car,* and while waiting for the train engine to be refueled "the guide formally introduced him to two waitresses [of the railway restaurant] who were longing to meet the great Bernard Shaw. By an extraordinary coincidence they were intimately acquainted with his works. GBS was sufficiently moved by the remarkable evidence of Russian literacy to express the opinion that waitresses in England were not so well read as their Soviet sisters." Later at the station in Moscow thousands waited for him with cheers and banners. And when he was taken to the theater where his play was to be performed, "Before the show began, the entire company marched on the stage bearing a bright red banner which carried a dedication in English: 'To the brilliant master, Bernard Shaw—a warm welcome to Soviet soil.' "[23] A few decades later and a few thousand miles further to the East in a similar spirit, Simone de Beauvoir was told upon arrival that " 'the Chinese people have been impatiently awaiting [her] arrival.' " At the Hanoi airport Mary McCarthy was met by a delegation from the Vietnamese Peace Committee "with bouquets of snapdragons, pink sweet peas, pale-pink roses, larkspur and little African daisies."[24] (She did not report if she too had been told about the impatient anticipation of her arrival by the Vietnamese people.) "Little girls dressed in colorful uniforms approached [Staughton Lynd and Tom Hayden] hesitantly, with flowers and salutes." A similar "gentle gesture of welcome" also greeted Harry Ashmore and William C. Baggs in Hanoi. Flowers on arrival also impressed Father Berrigan: "the loveliest fact of all was the most elusive and insignificant; we had been received with

---

* According to one source, "The train that meets them [foreign delegations, visitors] at the Soviet border varies in luxury in direct proportion to the importance of the group."[22]

flowers." There were more flowers for him on departure, and he concluded with satisfaction that he measured up to the standards and expectations of his hosts whom he regarded as his "teachers": "We had made it, the smiles of our teachers assured us."[25] Arrival in Cuba was also often colorful and festive: "People were standing on the deck of the ship coming toward us wearing orange sweatshirts with the Brigada Venceremos insignia. The ship circled us. . . . Everywhere along the harbor, people stood watching us come in. The Cubans were smiling, waving and giving us the clenched fist symbol of revolutionary solidarity. We had arrived: revolutionary Cuba, a dream in progress in the Western hemisphere. We were ecstatic." Arrival by air was even more joyous and festive: "Another shout of joy and triumph as the plane touched down safely and we stepped out. The first free soil I had ever known. . . . Smiles everywhere, bright lights as the Cuban newsmen filmed our joy. . . . A trio of singers played Latin music and Che smiled from a portrait on the wall as daiquiris and hors d'oeuvres were offered. Singing, talking, drinking together in Jose Marti Airport in Havana, in Revolutionary Cuba."[26] Ernesto Cardenal "did not go through the customs with the rest. I was taken to a small room where I was greeted by a delegation from the House of the Americas. . . . There were daiquiris and a photographer from *Granma*."[27] Lord Boyd Orr was apprehensive before his arrival in China: "those nagging fears. . . . Would we be met? Was a room booked? Would many speak English? Would we find some English speaking guide, be able to trust him?" There was no basis for apprehension: "Hardly had the door of the plane opened than a blue uniformed figure was bounding toward us . . . [he] beamed and thrust a bouquet into my hands and another into my wife's. 'We have a car.' "[28] Arthur Galston and his party were met at Peking Station by a "large welcoming delegation." Their baggage "once again . . . appeared as if by magic. Then we were whisked away in shiny black Shanghai limousines and settled in comfort at the Hsin Ch'iao Hotel. . . ." At the airport, on a domestic flight, the Chinese were not allowed to board until his party was seated ("we were quite embarrassed by such conspicuously special treatment").[29] Frank Tuohy, an English writer, was led "through a special station entrance for foreigners, full of flowering plants in porcelain pots and on to a double-decker train (more antimacassars, more potted plants) which contains only two other passengers, an elderly Overseas Chinese couple."[30] Needless to say, visiting celebrities were given far more dazzling reception as, for example, Anna Louise Strong reported:

The festivities were tremendous. For weeks we lived in a daze of banquets and banners . . . morning by morning the sound of drums, cymbals and crowds penetrated to the quiet tree-grown compound of the China Peace-Committee where I live. Then I knew that the near-by boulevard was jammed with three hundred thousand people cheering the passing of some chief of state, Prince Sihanouk of Cambodia or President Keita of Mali or President Massamba-Debat of Congo (Brazzaville) or Comrade Choi, President of the Presidium of the Korean People's Democratic Republic. . . . More than 2600 official guests came from over 80 countries. . . . When you add over a thousand tourists on their own tickets, and two or three thousand Overseas Chinese, you admire Peking's capacity for handling guests. Banquets, receptions, ballets were a dozen a day. I settled for six in three days, from the Journalists cocktail party and the state banquet through the big parade and the fireworks. . . .[31]*

While providing visiting heads of state with such treatment is not so unusual, at times important visiting intellectuals (and many other foreigners) were also given elite-privileges, if not hundreds of thousands of cheering crowds lining the streets. Such privileges served not only to increase the sense of well-being and self-importance of the visitors, they also functioned to segregate them from ordinary citizens. Barbara Tuchman, the American author, wrote:

* Simon Leys offers another perspective on such occasions: "The Maoist regime has acquired such skill in handling masses and does it so routinely, that the operators themselves have become quite unconscious of the cynicism underlying their work. . . . The kind of function common people fulfill now is . . . at ceremonies welcoming the arrival of a foreign statesman whom the Maoist authorities wish to impress. . . . For each of them the Peking authorities ration exactly the number of participants—a hundred thousand for this one, two hundred thousand for that one and fifty thousand for the other—as well as the temperature of the 'warm enthusiasm' that must be given. . . . These demonstrations follow an invariable and well-oiled routine. Early in the morning, workers decorate Ch'an-an Avenue . . . the participants . . . arrive by truck and on foot in orderly columns. They take their appointed places. . . . Squatting on the pavement, the gigantic crowds wait—one hour, two hours, three hours—in a state of submissive apathy. . . . Suddenly an order: everyone stands up . . . to take up positions. . . . A whistle sounds: the crowd, tired and listless a moment before, starts shouting: 'Welcome! Welcome!' . . . while thirty limousines roar between the two rows and the foreign visitor has for his memory bank the unforgettable sight of a human sea stirred by a tornado of enthusiasm."

A former participant's recollections bear out Leys' description: "Feverish preparations were made for many weeks before he [Sukarno of Indochina] came . . . I was one of about 500,000 people chosen from schools, government bureaus, factories and other organizations to welcome him. . . . All of us participating were instructed not to wear uniforms, but to put on our best clothes and remove our badges . . . so that Sukarno would not notice that we all came from certain units and therefore suspect that his welcome was not spontaneous. . . ."[32]

Foreigners feel themselves surrounded by the trappings of an elite. They stay in separate hotels, dine in separate dining rooms—or screened off from the Chinese—travel in separate compartments on trains, wait in separate waiting rooms at the station, are cared for on a separate floor of the hospital. During intermission at the theatre we are not left to stand among the crowd but are firmly guided to sit among other foreigners in a private reception room. On the lake at the Summer Palace we can not engage a rowboat to row ourselves . . . but are grandly deposited in a large covered boat provided with tea and tablecoth and poled by two boatmen. In museums our guides push aside Chinese visitors from the exhibit cases to give us unnecessary room; on the bridge at Wuhan traffic is stopped so that we may cross over to view the river . . . at a park our car drives through a pedestrian entrance where the Chinese walk; at a railroad station after imperious horn-blowing we drive through a special gate right up to the tracks. At one of Chairman Mao's former residences in Yenan (all four of which are visited like stages of the Sacred Way in Jerusalem), a group of about fifty students seated on the ground . . . rises on command to move out of our way as we approach.[33]

While Barbara Tuchman (like André Gide almost half a century earlier) felt more an object of manipulation than of friendship, more often, it seems, the flattery and V.I.P. treatment yield the desired result. "A good many foreigners not only get used to being cheered and applauded everywhere they go—there are claques at the entrances to and exits from every school, hospital, factory, even street—but they actually come to enjoy it. . . . They get used to having their tickets taken care of—for trains, theatres, planes; they get used to being picked up, brought back, having their hotel chosen for them; their timetable is filled for them,"[34] Leys wrote.

Further illustrations of this type of treatment were provided by Barbara Tuchman:

"A friend of the Chinese people" is decidedly pampered. We had front row seats—sometimes upholstered armchairs—reserved for us at evening dance performances arranged in the hotels; audiences rose and clapped on our arrival and departure; a special one-car train was put on to take us . . . out of schedule; a former cargo boat, cleaned up for passengers and supplied with tea table and twelve in crew, was summoned to give us alone an hour's cruise on the Yellow River. In Suchow . . . we were ensconced in a separate annex of the hotel with two suites, a private dining room, an attendant butler . . . and besides the usual tea thermos, cigarettes and fruit in the bedroom, a fresh plate of candies every day and fresh arrangement of jasmine buds in the form of a brooch. With everything provided, I, like Queen Victoria, never held a railroad ticket or used a coin.[35]

There were also efficient and cheerful servants placed at the guests' disposal.* As Galbraith noted, "Service is accomplished by inordinately good-natured and obliging waiters. . . ." The waiters were not the only friendly and good-natured people the visitors encountered. Galbraith found "everyone . . . in excellent humor . . ." on the street as in the factory where he and his party "were accorded a good-humored smile from all, literally all, the operatives." David and Nancy Milton also commented on a banquet they attended at which "the flawless food [was] served with dignified informality by white jacketed young men and women . . ." whom they delicately refrained from calling waiters and waitresses.[36]

Meeting the leader (or leaders) was another measure taken to make certain visitors feel important and flattered. In their own countries leading politicians or heads of state rarely took the time to converse earnestly with intellectuals and artists, to seek their advice or share their problems with them. (And in any case they were not the kind of leaders our intellectuals wished to discourse with.) By contrast what made such attentions particularly irresistible was that they were gratuitous: leaders of foreign countries had no obligation to meet with private citizens of other countries. Thus the interest such leaders expressed in meeting the visiting intellectuals seemed untainted by ulterior motives.[37] They seemed merely desirous of an exchange of opinion, a meeting of minds, or to share concerns about the future of mankind. Such meetings often also afforded an opportunity for the leaders to express their appreciation of the visitors' work. To be sure, a private meeting with the supreme leader was a privilege accorded only to the most important and influential among the travelers. (Visitors of lesser importance were sometimes given group interviews or had interviews with other high-ranking officials.) Thus Stalin, for example, had private meetings with Shaw, Feuchtwanger, H. G. Wells, Emil Ludwig, and Hewlett Johnson, among others. Castro even allowed admiring intellectuals such as C. Wright Mills, Sartre, as well as K. S. Karol and Dumont (before their fall from grace), to accompany him on his tours of inspection.[38] He also chauffeured around Senator McGovern, among others. Ho Chi Minh or Pham Van Dong regularly met with important foreign visitors, groups and individuals. The same was the case with Chou En-lai and to a lesser extent with Mao. Simone Signoret and Yves Montand, the French actress and actor, were entertained by Khrushchev and virtually the entire

---

* To be sure, the degree of efficiency varied; doubtless the Chinese services and servants were more efficient than their Soviet or Cuban counterparts.

Politbureau. Simone de Beauvoir, Sartre, Angus Wilson, Magnus Enzensberger, and other European writers were flown "aboard a special plane" to Khrushchev's "country place in Georgia . . . a vast wood, planted with the rarest and most beautiful trees in the whole Union. Khrushchev greeted us pleasantly. . . . He took us to see the swimming-pool he had had made by the shore; it was immense, and all round it had a glass wall that could be made to disappear by pressing a button—he did so several times, with great satisfaction."[39]

Often the purpose and result of such attentions were either to send some specific political message through selected individuals (bypassing regular governmental channels, something the rulers in question often liked to do), or else to make a lasting, favorable impression on individuals who were considered important or potential opinion-makers capable of influencing public opinion in their own countries.

Another obvious route to the heart of intellectuals and artists leads through the appreciation of their work. Arthur Koestler, recalling his treatment in the Soviet Union in 1932, observed: "The people whom [the average visiting foreign author] meets at banquets and parties seem to know his works by heart; he would have to be a masochist, with a touch of persecution mania, to assume that they have been specially briefed for the occasion." G. B. Shaw would have been impressed and moved seeing his play performed in Moscow even without the cast parading on the stage with banners extolling him. It is difficult to see how Picasso could have avoided feeling friendly toward the post–World War II Soviet-sponsored "Peace Movement" which made use (in millions of copies) of the dove image he had designed. Nor could the tens of thousands cheering and applauding the performances of Yves Montand in the Soviet Union have hurt his (and his wife Simone Signoret's) feelings toward the Soviet regime. And it should not be surprising that Lion Feuchtwanger thought highly of the cultural accomplishments of the Soviet regime, having encountered his books in the public libraries and having met "a young man from the land," a peasant, who had informed him that "Four years ago I could neither read nor write, and today I can discuss Feuchtwanger's books with him."[40] G. B. Shaw's running into the waitresses familiar with his work may also be recalled here. Other visitors too "found, to their surprise, that everyone who crossed their path in the Soviet Union was acquainted with their names and work. . . . Everyone on John Dewey's itinerary knew his name, which seemed to be a 'password' for entrance into schools, homes, factories and government bureaus. Writers, whether they had published many noteworthy books or few of mediocre quality, found popular recognition. People whom they met all seemed to know their work by heart, and the literary officials frequently expressed the wish to publish a story by the writer. . . . Adulation was given to painters and sculptors whose art had never been shown outside of independent shows and cafes. . . ."[41] There were also actual offers of publication and large printings of the works of several foreign writers. In Cuba Ernesto Cardenal (who subsequently became the minister of culture in revolutionary Nicaragua) found out that "The edition of ten thousand copies of an anthology of my work published by the House of Americas was sold out in a week." Waldo Frank was commissioned outright by the Cuban government to visit the island and write a book about his trip. More recently the Chinese published Michael Parenti's book on repression in the United States.[42]

What about the psychological effects of the material privileges and comforts? How much difference did the good food, comfortable accommodations, and superior forms of transportation make? On the one hand they were part of the flattery, status symbols, which reflected the importance of the visitor.* At the same time they were calculated to create an agreeable disposition, a sense of contentment, and a rosy outlook on the world. (Just as Harrison Salisbury felt after an excellent and tastefully served meal in China: it must be a fine country where such meals are provided.)

It must be stressed again that it is not any particular form of such hospitality—the food, the lodgings, the limousines, the private entrances and waiting rooms at railroad stations, or being "whisked" through the customs on arrival and departure—that makes the difference, but the totality and cumulative effect of all of them, material as well as psychological. When all these forms of hospitality are combined with the favorable predispositions of the visitors, the result is virtually assured, at least in the short run. (Disillusionment may follow later due to developments and

---

* For instance, in Cuba "Fidel controlled abundant resources that enabled him to regulate the treatment accorded to his guests . . . he used and measured out these resources with his customary skill. I . . . was on the eighteenth floor of the 'Havana Riviera,' where the airconditioning did not work and breakfast took an hour to arrive. Don Balta . . . the short-lived hero of the breaking of the commercial blockade by Chile, and short-lived personal friend of Fidel Castro, had stayed . . . in one of the opulent suites on the twentieth floor. In each of these there was a bar and a small dining room specially for entertaining guests, and the airconditioning worked perfectly. Immediately after these, for selected political leaders, came the Protocol houses, surrounded by gardens and silence in the heart of the most elegant district of Havana."[43]

processes which have just as little to do with the nature of the society admired as the initial infatuation had.)

The importance of the material aspects of hospitality is also reflected
in the frequency with which the visitors themselves commented on its
details. Simone de Beauvoir wrote:

> My room . . . [in the Peking Hotel] was immense: all to myself I had
> two brass double beds covered with bright pink silk. . . . I had a
> mirrored wardrobe, a desk complete with everything needed for writ-
> ing, a vanity table, a couch, armchairs, a low coffee table, two night-
> tables, a radio; on the bedside rug were a pair of bedroom slippers.
> . . . The menu is in English and the service amazingly quick.[44]

Lord Boyd Orr too registered satisfaction with his "fine hotel, six storey
high, with lifts, marble entrance floors and a bathroom to every bedroom." With a touch of resignation and good-natured willingess to accept deprivation, Galbraith conceded that "The Nanking Hotel . . . in
a pleasantly landscaped park, is agreeable and efficient but not palatial.
I have a bedroom, sitting room, bathroom and air conditioning. But that
is sufficient." (Fortunately in the Beautiful River Hotel in Shanghai he
had reason to note that "I occupy a suite, that for its grandeur, causes
my colleagues to call me Chairman.")[45] According to Robert Loh, the
former guide-interpreter in China, "the best hotels were chosen for officials guesthouses" in the cities placed on the tourist circuit. "Local people entered these premises only by special permit. First class attendants,
cooks, hairdressers, and beauty specialists were employed after careful
scrutiny and approval by the Security Bureau."[46]

Sartre in Havana found himself in a "millionaire hotel room," in a
veritable "fortress of luxury." Angela Davis evidently succeeded in calm-
ing her conscience over the luxurious accommodations by recalling that
"the Havana Libre, formerly Havana Hilton, [was] now freed from the
veined fingers of decadent old capitalists. This was the first time I had
stayed in such a fancy hotel. Its elaborateness, however, was quieted by
the guests: workers on vacation . . . and by the *companeros* who staffed
the hotel—men and women with none of the servility usually associated
with bellboys, chambermaids and waiters. . . ." Even in war-torn Hanoi,
accommodation for important visitors was beyond reproach, according
to Mary McCarthy who, "to her stupefaction," found plenty of hot water
in her room. "Other luxuries [she] found at the Thong Nhat Hotel were
sheets of toilet paper laid out on a box in a fan pattern . . . a thermos
of hot water for making tea, a package of tea, cups and saucers, candies,

cigarettes and a mosquito net draped over the bed and tucked in; in Saigon [she] had been tortured by mosquitoes."[47]°

Even as a member of a group tour rather than an honored V.I.P., Jerzy Gliksman reported that he "traveled [in the USSR] in comfortable sleeping cars belonging to an international express train; [he] lived in elegant hotels, each tourist accommodated in single rooms with private bath. In these hotels there were handsome and expensively furnished dining rooms. . . . The food was tasty and plentiful; we lacked neither fine Crimean fruits nor famous Russian fish nor excellent caviar. . . . There was music with every meal and Western dances in the evening. And we could buy whatever our hearts desired in a special store for foreigners."[48]

As far as the transportation of important visitors was concerned in China, Simone de Beauvoir observed that

> The chauffeurs are at it early in the morning: equipped with red, long-handled feather dusters, they whisk every speck of dust from the gleaming cars, inside and out. Two or three times a day we go off for a drive in one of them.

More than a decade later Barbara Tuchman wrote:

> the visitor always has a car at his disposal, not only for the planned program but for whatever purpose at whatever hour: at 6 a.m. if one wants to go out early to watch the city waking, at 10 p.m. to come home from the ballet, or for a private visit or shopping tour that might last several hours. The driver waits like an old-fashioned chauffeur. His convenience is no more consulted, his working hours no more limited than if he were employed by John D. Rockefeller, Sr., in 1920.[49]

Peter Worsley was also somewhat unhappy about privileges of this type ("We go by car. Gates are specially flung open, and I have the unpleasant feeling of being a privileged tourist come to observe the workers on their evening out.") but they did not lead to more far-reaching critical reflections about the nature of the social system he admired. Corliss and Margaret Lamont (met at Leningrad railway station by a "brand new Lincoln Eight") briefly mused about the contrast between the life of the masses and tourists but failed to register any moral discomfort on this account. They explained that "The Russians do not pretend that they have enough Lincolns available for any large number of the population, or that they are able at present to give the masses . . . the same living

---

° It must remain a matter of conjecture in what manner (if any) being bitten or not bitten by mosquitoes influenced her judgment of the respective political systems of North and South Vietnam.

standards as even third class tourists receive. They treat tourists as they do for good and sufficient reasons. . . ." More recently Simone Signoret "crossed Moscow in the back of an enormous Zim with gray satin curtains, wrapped and hatted in pastel mink. [She] had always believed that those curtained cars had been the invention of American film makers who specialized in anti-Soviet pictures."[50] Access to good transportation was an important privilege in Cuba too. Huey Newton (who had stayed longer than most visitors) related that "I was a permanent resident and an honored guest of the government. That included special privileges, like I could always get a driver and a car. Transportation there [in Cuba] is very bad. . . . And I could get reservations in restaurants on the weekends. . . . I had a delegation status so I could get a table in any restaurant. . . ." He also recalled that on his arrival "he had been welcomed with a 'grand tour' of all the provinces."[51]

Luxurious and comfortable transportation was not limited to chauffeured cars; on trains too the guests traveled in comfort and privacy. It was already noted for example that the Dean of Canterbury (Hewlett Johnson) and Edgar Snow traveled on a special train in China (in the company of Chou En-lai). The sharp distinctions between the quality of railway transportation available for foreigners and natives were not readily acknowledged by the hosts. Hebert and Trudeau reported that "We are led to our compartments in a first class sleeping car. 'There are no classes nowadays,' Mr. Hou [the interpreter] explains . . . 'There are different cars, that's all.' " Felix Greene was "led to an observation car at the end of the train . . . our bags already aboard. . . . This was a fancy coach. . . . Leather chairs faced each other set far enough apart for plenty of leg-room. At the rear was a potted tree, and several smaller shrubs, like a conservatory; and there were flowers and ferns on the tables. . . . Two rosy-cheeked, pigtailed girls . . . kept dusting and cleaning, and fetched us tea at frequent intervals."[52]

In the Soviet Union too, "One outstanding privilege given to foreign visitors . . . [was] private transportation sharply differing in quality from that of Soviet citizens. . . . Private sleeping and dining cars were provided for all delegations. . . ." Foreigners were also "allowed to board streetcars at the wrong end . . . [and] the GPU even opened up gasoline stations on holidays or after closing hours for foreigners traveling by automobile." The GPU could also be depended upon to secure a "soft compartment" on the train (at times evidently preferred even by Waldo Frank) and accommodation in more remote locations. The GPU would also assist respected visitors (such as the Lamonts) in other matters ("Intourist tries the special GPU pharmacy. Sure enough, it has the needed ingredient and we receive the medicine").[53]*

The care taken to assure the comfort of visitors extended to every form of transportation. In one instance a special airplane used by the highest leader in the Soviet Union was placed at the disposal of distinguished visitors, such as Simone Signoret and Yves Montand whom Khrushchev wished to befriend. On riverboats too visiting dignitaries (or delegations) were given superior accommodations: "The same delegation was given the entire first and second cabin space on the regular run of a Volga steamer, leaving no decent quarters on the boat for any others." A Soviet citizen grumbled that foreigners consumed their best food and filled their best boats, a resident American noted.[54]

The part played by food in the techniques of hospitality and the travel experience as a whole deserves further comment. There is little necessity to discourse here at length on the basic and profound psychological significance of food and nurturance both as a practical and symbolic matter. Clearly we all appreciate good food in ways which are connected with but also separable from the issues of simple sustenance or physical survival. While good meals by themselves obviously do not change peoples' outlook about the world and particular political systems, or alter the pattern of their moral judgment, they often contribute to a sense of well-being and contentment which, in turn, predisposes to a positive, affirming attitude toward the social environment in which one finds oneself. The often euphoric comments of the visitors about food testify to the significance of eating well and to the subtle and not so subtle links between body and mind.

> It was our introduction to Chinese feasts [wrote Lord Boyd Orr] and thirty officials, most of them from the Ministry of Foreign Trade, helped to induct us. Tiny cups of warm wine for toasts . . . the intricacies of Peking duck . . . soup at the end of the meal. . . . we rose from the meal lighter in heart, for there was Dr. Chi to accompany us for part of our travels. We could not have asked for more.[55]

A Report by the Delegation of the American Association of State Colleges and Universities also included references to the pleasures of Chinese cuisine and hospitality:

* One may suspect that the involvement of the GPU in such benevolent activities as dispensing medication must have been considered by Mr. and Mrs. Lamont as yet another example of the superiority of the socialist system (and its police forces) over the capitalist ones.

Perhaps our outstanding meal was the magnificent banquet hosted by the Director of the China International Travel Service at the Peking Duck #1 Restaurant. The camaraderie, the good fellowship of the sharing of excellent food with our hosts will remain with us.[56]

Harrison Salisbury, already noted for his appreciation of Chinese cuisine, provided many details of his feasts and of his dilemmas in regard to their comparative excellence:

> we had so many remarkable dinners that only an epicure could choose the best among them. The linen was white and gleaming; the waiters silent, quick and efficient; the dishes one surprise after another.
>
> . . . the meal—a triumph of Chinese cuisine. First there were hors d'oeuvres of chicken bits, tomatoes, shrimp, ancient eggs, hardboiled eggs, cucumber slices and fish bits. This was followed by watergreen soup, the greens coming from the Imperial West Lake in Hangchow and found only there. Then, crisp rice with three delicacies—chicken, sea slugs and a third I neglected to note. We then were served crisp fried chicken and duck; French beans with fresh mushrooms; baked shad found only in the Yangtze; a puree of bean soup with crushed almonds; sticky rice cakes; meat patties; bread and butter; plain rice in a bowl; and a watermelon. There were three liquors. . . . enormous prawns and then a Peking fish—mandarin fish I believe—with sweet and sour sauce . . . The dinner [he ate on another occasion] went on and on, from one delight to another. There was Peking duck, some kind of potato salad, several other vegetable dishes, small green pickles, green beans served almost raw but extremely tender, almond milk, eight-treasures pudding . . . and finally Canton oranges, Tientsin apples and delicious pears.[57]

John Kenneth Galbraith, another connoisseur of good food, was also lavish in his praise. His references to the joys of Chinese cooking include a "dinner at an old Chinese restaurant . . . perhaps the most exquisite I ever consumed. It consisted of absolutely nothing but duck. . . ." On another occasion at a textile mill he counted no less than "fifteen dishes on the table. But then some more appeared. Each was irresistible. . . ." This was soon to be followed by a luncheon "which, for munificence rivaled the one yesterday at the textile mill" only to be followed the next day again by a "gargantuan" lunch. There was also a dinner described as "an extravaganza of regional specialties each . . . better than the last." At the end of the tour came "a ceremonial dinner by the Scientific and Technical Association of Shanghai, a most detailed affair featuring napkins shaped like flowers, one dish decorated with a nightingale carved from a pumpkin, soup served from watermelons decorated with elaborately carved friezes and a succession of some fifteen or twenty dishes, each more complex than the last."[58] Everywhere on the visitors' circuit high standards of cooking prevailed. Urie Bronfenbrenner was offered on arrival at the railroad station an "excellent five course lunch" and later "an excellent seven course dinner . . . at a simple table . . . out in a commune." At Tachai the Concerned Asian Scholars feasted on a wide range of food and produce.[59]* At a farewell banquet "every known culinary whim" of Ross Terrill was gratified. There are virtually no accounts of the trips to China without reference to the high quality of the food consumed. While China undoubtedly excelled in offering feasts to the visitors, it was by no means the only country placing emphasis on this form of hospitality. Even in North Vietnam during the war Father Berrigan commented on "a marvelous celebratory banquet," "monumental" breakfasts, and a succession of "delicious" suppers. Janos Radvanyi, a Hungarian diplomat on an official mission, was entertained by food cooked by French trained chefs: "French wines and Napoleon cognacs graced every dinner and at formal banquets we even drank Cordon Rouge champagne."[61] At a province guesthouse in North Vietnam Mary McCarthy dined on "a splendid carp—fished that afternoon from a pond nearby—with dill, tomatoes, rounds of carrots." The Vice-President of the province, who reminded her "of that tough character Stenka Razin, the anarchist hero and brigand leader of the Russian marshes . . ." "poured little glassfuls of mandarin wine . . . very good, though sweetish, and many toasts were exchanged." Susan Sontag had more qualms about being "fed and feted"—as Mary McCarthy put it—at each destination. The "several delicious meat and fish courses" troubled her while "99% of the Vietnamese will have rice and bean curd for dinner tonight."[62] Although Cuba could not compete in culinary achievements with China, many visitors were well enough pleased with the fare offered to them, as we learn, for instance, from Andrew Salkey's refer-

---

* Of the culinary and other appeals of Tachai, Simon Leys wrote: "The lodging house at Tachai had subtle rustic touches: the international capitalists and other tourists who 'do' China are like Marie Antoinette playing at being a shepherdess; the meals are no less delicious or less abundant than in the Peking, Canton or Shanghai palaces for foreigners, but here they are touched with a well-studied primitivism, a shrewd naivete. In the usual vast array of dishes, some dissonant notes are skillfully struck—a dozen hardboiled eggs on a tin plate here, a bowl of gruel there—and added to the usual choice of wines, beers, soft drinks and alcohol is a fearful local spirit. The gourmet brave enough to taste it is suddenly drenched in sweat, giving him the virile and exalting sense that he is somehow communing with the hard task of building socialism."[60]

ences to "delicious criollo pork, rice and wild salad" and other joyous meals with veal cooked to perfection. Ernesto Cardenal mentioned the "sumptuous dining room" of the National Hotel (in Havana) where those assembled were offered, among other things, "lobster thermidor, frogs legs, French wine" and where the "uniformed waiters were not servile but companionable; they didn't call you 'sir' but 'comrade'"—a change in terminology (one cannot resist noting) that was seen by Cardenal as an authentic indicator of the magnitude of social transformations which swept Cuba. The availability of fresh milk in the hotel was connected with the status and concomitant location of the guests, Jorge Edwards observed.[63] Frances Fitzgerald described some of the techniques and their effect on the pampered visitors in Cuba:

> it was embarrassing for us to make demands [in regard to sights and itineraries] since the government insisted on treating us as guests and keeping us in a style to which even Cuban officials are not accustomed. Each of us who stayed behind after the [Anniversary] Celebrations was given a car and driver, and at the Capri we had air-conditioned rooms, meals with beer and wine and as much meat each day as the Cuban rationing system allows an individual for a week.*

Elsewhere she also noted that "foreign visitors were not allowed to pay for anything, even drinks, and from time to time bottles of the finest Cuban rum would appear in every [hotel] room with the compliments of the Communist Party of Oriente Province."[64]

The magnitude of the Cuban effort to envelop important visitors in a web of overwhelming hospitality was illustrated by the arrangements which were made to cater to those invited to a Cultural Congress in 1968. According to a Cuban publication,

> more than 900 service personnel—stenographers, translators, guides, chauffeurs, cooks—were mobilized to attend to the delegates and representatives of the press. Most of the foreign delegates had all their expenses, including travel to and from Cuba, paid for by the Cuban government. The meals were sumptuous. . . . Fidel never scrimped when it came to hospitality on the grand scale. The inhabitants of Havana recall that their food and beverage rations were reduced for three or four weeks before, during and after the congress.[65]...

---

* It may be noted that many of the visitors were not aware of the discrepancy between the provisions placed at their disposal and those of the natives. Most of them certainly preferred not to dwell on such matters; others (such as Salkey) genuinely believed that ordinary people favored the lavish treatment of the visitors out of a simple, traditional sense of hospitality, even if they were deprived as a result.

Even in the jungle hideout of the Pol Pot regime abundant food awaited the visitors:

> The knowledge of the hunger of Cambodia, so painfully visible any-where else on the border, was crowded out by ample supplies of food brought from Bangkok. The meals were French except for the prime minister's banquet, which featured an infinite variety of Cambodian, Chinese and Western dishes. The best Thai beer, American soft drinks, Johnnie Walker, Black Label Scotch, bottled water, soda and ice brought from Bangkok, hundreds of miles away.
>
> The contrast between Cambodian reality and the holiday resort atmo-sphere created . . . by a regime previously known for having imposed a radical and destructive revolution . . . testified to the regime's meed to make itself acceptable to the outside world."[66]

The Soviet government too managed, even at times of great scarcities, to feed lavishly those it regarded as important, that is, the elite groups in its own population and the foreign visitors. There were reports of banquets honoring foreign visitors with "silver plates, cut glass dishes, flowers, fine linen, many courses of excellent food and a table covered with wines and liquors" and of foods provided "at government expense" considered by the proletariat as "long since vanished from the Soviet Union . . . with wines whose original purchaser prided himself in the completeness of his cellar in 1916." Charlotte Haldane recalled that upon her mentioning that she liked caviar she was sent the best grade, and that even during World War II on a visit to the Red Army (with journalists), "Enormous hot meals were produced in the midst of drip-ping forests, the tables laden with vodka, champagne, wines, cigarettes of good quality and chocolate."[67]

Luxurious meals greatly contributed to André Gide's disillusionment with his hosts and the political system they represented—a reaction which, as noted before, was quite atypical. Most visitors, even when they were self-conscious about their privileged treatment, managed to come to terms with it. Gide wrote:

> When, after escaping with great difficulty from official receptions and official supervision, I managed to get into contact with labourers, whose wages were only four or five rubles a day, what could I think of the banquet in my honor which I could not avoid attending? An almost daily banquet at which the abundance of hors d'oeuvres alone was such that one had already eaten three times too much before the beginning of the actual meal; a feast of six courses which used to last two hours and left you completely stupefied. The expense! Never hav-ing seen the bill, I cannot exactly estimate it but one of my com-

panions who was well up in the prices of things calculates that each
banquet with wines and liqueurs, must have come to more than three
hundred rubles a head. Now there were six of us—seven with our
guide; and often as many hosts as guests, sometimes many more.[68]

The privileges of the visitors also included special stores where they
could buy goods at a lower price or articles which were not available to
the ordinary citizens. ("All the stores around the hotels were considered
tourist stores. Cubans can't buy there," Huey Newton reported matter-of-
factly.) Already in the early 1930s stores existed in the Soviet Union that
accepted only foreign currency. (". . . a Russian looks wistfully in those
shop windows with their displays of fine second-hand china, rugs and
silver, assembled from unknown sources, and works of art unavailable
in the open market were sold to visitors at ridiculously low prices.")[69]
At times the visitors were not merely allowed to buy things cheaper but
were given outright gifts. For example, "When the 1929 Ford delegation
left Moscow for Leningrad, all with whom they had been associated
came to say goodby with . . . caviar, cigarettes and wine. This . . .
was repeated when they left Leningrad." Sometimes the gifts were more
"personalized" and less utilitarian and calculated to have an emotional
impact. Thus a pair of simple sandals (similar to those worn by the
Vietnamese) was bound to make a deep impression on Father Berrigan
as did the collected poems of Ho Chi Minh. Staughton Lynd was presented twice with the twenty volumes of the collected writings of Ho
Chi Minh, since he lost them the first time. In addition, he and Tom
Hayden were also given by the director of the Museum of Revolution in
Hanoi a little bronze arrow "approximately one thousand years old, a
reminder of the long Vietnamese tradition of battle against invading
armies." Sontag commented somewhat plaintively on being "plied with
gifts and flowers and . . . seemingly exaggerated kindness. . . ." Andrew Salkey found in his hotel room in Havana "an extraordinary variety of going-away presents from our Congress hosts. . . . They were
lavish and beautiful: ample quantities of books, posters and long-playing
records; an enormous box of cigars with Congress paper rings around
them; a cigarette box made from a mosaic of many Cuban woods; three
large bottles of liqueur rum; and six small ones. All that for each delegate! And one heard that there was more to come. . . . How does one
protest against generosity . . . ?" There was also "a big round box of
liqueur chocolates."[70] Confronted with the gifts, Salkey felt guilty and
helpless, especially since he was aware of the contrast between the
rationing outside his hotel and the luxuries inside provided for the dele-

gates. Yet such feelings did not lead to any reappraisal of his positive view of the Cuban system, to the questioning of the official political morality, or of the authenticity of the hospitality and the purposes behind it. Here one may also note that the distinction between ordinary tourists and the guests of the government was often significant in Cuba: "One man [a bureaucrat] thinking I was a guest of the Cuban government offered me his car," wrote Barry Reckord, "to meet my wife at the airport, told me about his unpublished novel, asked was I happy, was I comfortable, did I want for anything—such total friendliness and humanity. I had to wait quite a long time for a pause in the courtesies to tell him that in fact I was not an invited guest—and he became almost savage. Within five seconds there was no car, no novel, no nothing."[71]

Making the visitor feel pampered and comfortable and enlarging his sense of well-being and importance was the first essential stage in the deployment of the techniques of hospitality. The next one was the actual tour: showing him the carefully selected sights, events, institutions, groups, and individuals and isolating him from others not conducive to a favorable assessment of the social system he was being introduced to.

The Tour: Selective Exposure and Display

The itineraries of the visitors were carefully planned in each country. They usually included construction projects (such as dams, canals, bridges, or factories), new or reconstructed institutions (e.g., nurseries, schools,* hospitals, or collective farms), sights of high aesthetic appeal, either manmade or natural (such as monuments, museums, old palaces, lakes, waterfalls, scenic views), and finally certain groups or individuals symbolizing various aspects of the new social system and conveying specific messages (for example, outstanding workers, old peasants, artists, veterans of the guerilla war, grassroots party workers). In setting up these itineraries the hosts were, in each country, aided by their control of all relevant resources and by the attributes of the economic system they had introduced. As Jorge Edwards said in the Cuban context, "the socialist economy could concentrate its efforts on a small sector and obtain marvelous results, which were visible and highly suitable for im-

---

* Virtually no tour was complete without a visit to a nursery, kindergarten or school. The sight of happy, well-fed, playful and friendly children was among the most irresistible to the visitors. How could a system be bad which displays such solicitude toward children? Exposing the visitors to children was also advantageous because it was easier to make children appear spontaneous than adults.

pressing foreign visitors. . . ."[72] The types of groups or individuals displayed to the visitors depended in part on the background and interest of the visitors. As noted before, meetings with the supreme leaders or high ranking officials were reserved for the more important guests. Since in each country considered the tours were quite standardized, a few examples will suffice to illustrate their character and introduce the reader to the typical sights the visitors were shown.

Corliss and Margaret Lamont's itinerary included the anti-religious museum (in Leningrad), a large clinic (also in Leningrad), the Museum of Revolution (in Moscow), the Park of Culture and Rest (Moscow), a big rubber goods factory, an interview with an official of the Commissariat of Education, St. Basil Cathedral (Moscow), a Marriage Bureau, student housing, a pioneer camp, Anna Louise Strong, an official from the commissariat of heavy industry, headquarters of the Militant Atheist Union, home for reformed prostitutes, an official from the commissariat of finance, a collective farm near Moscow, canning factory and tractor plant (in Stalingrad), experimental farm (near Rostov), workers' housing, the People's Commissar for General Welfare (in Tbilisi), the Artec Pioneer camp (near Yalta), the Dneprostoi Dam, a children's commune for "homeless waifs," and a monastery near Kiev. Julian Huxley saw, among other things, a state farm, a rest-home for workers, a people's court in Moscow, recreational facilities on the Moscow River, the Institute of Plant Industry (an agricultural experimental station), the scientific planning department of the Supreme Economic Council, a children's village, hospitals and children's clinics. In Cuba (as in the USSR), David Caute noted, "the tourist . . . is despatched in pursuit of factories, farms, schools, universities, housing projects and research institutes . . . his holiday is not treated as an escape from the mundane productive world of toil, but as a chance to penetrate the virtues of its socialist model."[73] In regard to the provision of entertainment certain variations may be observed. While Soviet and Chinese hosts pressed on their visitors dance groups, folk artists, or stylized revolutionary operas, the Cubans often regaled them with old-fashioned floor shows in the Tropicana Nightclub of Havana, an institution Soviet ideologues would doubtless describe as a "survival" of the past both in the ideological and chronological sense. To be sure, visitors like Sartre were taken to a "parade and dances of campesinos"[74] more appropriate for their predilections. A combination of entertainment and inspiration was often provided by observing various national holidays and the associated festivities. On these occasions in Moscow, Peking, or Havana the visitors could behold from a reviewing stand the enthusiastic masses parading in front of them. Another category of inspiring, indeed sacred, sights was represented by the birthplace (or various former residences) of Lenin, Stalin, Ho Chi Minh, and Mao (in Lenin's case his bodily remains too), the boat that brought Castro to Cuba, and the monument in the Sierra Maestra mountains dedicated to the guerilla war that culminated in Castro's seizure of power. The museum and monument at the Bay of Pigs were also among such inspirational sights. (The hosts also tried sometimes to impress upon the visitors the wickedness of their own political system. Thus for instance Jonathan Kozol was shown the results of an anti-Castro air attack on a public school, including the blackboard "shredded" by bullets.[75] In North Vietnam American visitors were often shown the damage done by the war planes of their country.)

In Yenan (in China), as in the Sierra Maestra of Cuba, striking landscapes combined with the political significance of the sights embedded in them. Andrew Salkey and his fellow Cultural Congress participants were taken to innumerable exhibits, museums, plays, housing projects, farms, and schools. Father Berrigan in Vietnam was shown (in addition to the American bomb damage) a film on the life of "Uncle Ho," the former prison and cave of Ho (which reminded him of Jesus in the desert and Loyola in Manresa Cave),[76] the Museum of Revolution, a hospital (filled with the victims of American bombing), the head of the union of journalists in Hanoi, a farm commune, many peasants, women soldiers, new rural housing, examples of folk art, a few Catholic laymen, the Hanoi Museum of Art, and centers of supplementary education. The itinerary of the Concerned Asian Scholars included an agricultural commune near Canton and Shanghai, the Canton Deaf-Mute School, the Shanghai Industrial Exhibition, a forum on the nature of the Great Cultural Revolution, the Shanghai Tool Factory, new workers' housing, a woman member of the Central Committee of the Communist party of China, the Soochow Embroidery factory, the Common Man's Garden (built during the Ming dynasty), the East Wind Hospital, the leader of the Soochow Grain Store no. 57 and several other local workers, the Tiger Hill Pagoda and the West Garden, members of the Soochow Revolutionary Committee, the Yangtze River Bridge, performance of "Red Detachment of Women," a primary school in Nanking, maneuvers of the Nanking People's Militia, Sun Yat-sen Mausoleum, Nanking Astronomical Observatory, Summer Palace (Peking), young Cubans visiting Peking, Peking University, Tachai Commune, Taiyuan Heavy

Machinery Factory, archeological site in Sian, production of "White-haired girl," Sian Municipal Red Guard Cultural Troupe, Mao's home in Yenan, delegation from North Korea, Prince Sihanouk, a Peking Middle' School, operations at a hospital attached to Peking Medical College, Peking City Zoo, two Vietnamese films, May 7 Cadre school near Peking, Rolling Stock plant in Peking, a retired worker ("who told stories about his involvement in the great labor strikes which swept China from 1921 to 1923"),[77] Chou En-lai, the Great Wall, the Great Hall of the People, Tsinghua University, etc.

In China certain highly formalized routines accompanied the sight-seeing and the interpretation of the sights for the visitors. The procedures described by Simone de Beauvoir in the 1950s were the same in the 1970s:

> For no matter what factory, school, village anywhere from Peking to Canton, the ritual would never vary an iota. You enter a large room whose walls are covered with red banners bearing gold inscriptions; these are tokens of satisfaction conferred by the government, or messages of friendship. . . . You sit down on a sofa . . . before a low table loaded with cigarettes and cups which an attendant keeps at all times brimful of green tea. . . . Some person of rank, a cadre, sets forth the situation. Next you inspect the premises. After that, it is back to the seats for more tea drinking and question period; the cadre earnestly solicits suggestions and criticisms we are generally altogether incapable of formulating.[78]

Not only the selection of particular sights but their number and pacing too constituted an important part of the techniques of hospitality. The tours were generally overorganized, leaving little time for the visitor to reflect, let alone engage in unscheduled, unsupervised, or random sight-seeing. ". . . the V.I.P.P. [Very Important Potential Propagandist] . . . is hardly ever left to himself," wrote Jacques Marcuse. "He goes on being shepherded and chaperoned about to the point of bodily and intellectual exhaustion. He has to take in all the showplaces, and is made to believe that, could he but stay longer, he would have seen even more, in fact anything he could have asked to see . . . after being politely bowed out of the country by his smiling hosts, his mind is so full of unverifiable facts that he is bound to write something in a postprandial mood."[79] Similar patterns were also noticed in North Vietnam by Susan Sontag: "We are truly seeing and doing a great deal: at least one visit or meeting is planned for every morning and afternoon, and often in the evening as well . . . we are in the hands of skilled bureaucrats specializing in relations with foreigners." She expressed irritation with "the constraint of being reduced to the status of a child: scheduled, led about, explained to, fussed over, pampered, kept under benign surveillance. Not only a child individually, but, even more exasperating, one of a group of children."[80] Magnus Enzensberger, the German radical writer, had similar reactions to the organization of such tours and the excessive solicitude of the hosts:

> The *delegate* is always cared for by an organization. He isn't supposed to—no, he isn't allowed to—worry about anything. Usually he receives a personal guide who functions as translator, nanny, and watchdog. Almost all contact with the host country is mediated through this companion, which makes distinct the *delegate's* segregation from the social realities surrounding him. The companion is responsible for the traveler's *program*. There is no traveling without a program. The guest may express his wishes in this respect; however he remains dependent on the organization that invited him. In this respect he is treated as though he were still under age. The combination of being spoiled and impotent is reminiscent of infantile situations.[81]

Arthur Galston, although appreciative of "the continuing solicitude of Chinese hospitality . . . soon realized that the demands of having our every hour tightly scheduled prevented some of the simpler, more spontaneous pleasures to be found in more direct contact with the Chinese themselves." In Cuba too, a visitor noted, "Most of the time, the Cubans take us around in a tightly arranged schedule, leaving little free time." Edward Luttwak commented on the "ceaseless sequence of action visits from 8 a.m. to 8 p.m." which "In theory . . . still leaves the late evening hours open for individual exploration, but even in Peking this free time is of no consequence, since at night there is absolutely nothing to see or do . . . no open tea houses or shops . . . no restaurants or bars . . . not even street lighting except for a few major boulevards. Soon after 8 p.m. the streets are deserted."[82]

It is of course hardly surprising that in countries in which the authorities exercise tight control over the lives of their citizens, they will be disinclined to leave their foreign guests to their own devices. This is all the more justified from their point of view since the visitors, although sympathetic to the regime, cannot in all instances be fully trusted, as they come from societies which allow more free expression and unorthodox behavior. They may, however inadvertently, provide negative role-models for the natives, which is one reason why they are to be strictly segregated from them. The other obvious but very important point to stress here (in the context of the tight scheduling and careful selection of sights) is that the hosts do not wish to leave it to chance that the visitors acquire favorable impressions. Hence their painstaking and meticulous attention to the details of the itinerary, to questions of what the visitors can or cannot, should or should not, see.

It should also be pointed out that the favorably predisposed visitors (such as Susan Sontag) usually transcended the irritation with the over-planning and overzealous hospitality. Indeed, it is a good reflection of the power of predisposition that the negative reactions to particular aspects of the tour (such as the tight scheduling, little free time, etc.) did not undermine or erode the overwhelmingly favorable attitudes; nor did they lead to the raising of more far-reaching questions about the authenticity of the whole tour and the degree of enlightenment it could provide. Sympathetic visitors also found ways to neutralize negative reactions they might have had on account of the biased and restricted sampling of the points of interest. As Jacques Marcuse put it: "If he [the sympathetic visitor] is at all aware that he has not been shown everything there is to see, he feels that it has been withheld from him for honorable reasons, and it would be disloyal on his part to look further."[83]

The interpreter played a key part in the organization and execution of the tours. He was the most immediate and direct guide in the most literal sense, the crucial mediator between the visitor and the setting, and a "shock-absorber" if there were any discomforts or disappointments the travelers encountered. There was of course practical justification for this, since most visitors did not know the language and because of the underdeveloped state of tourism in the countries concerned. Left to their own devices the guests could not have easily, if at all, made reservations, obtained meals, caught trains, planes, or buses, managed to reach their various destinations. Certainly in countries like the Soviet Union in the 1930s and China at any time since 1949 a helpful interpreter was justifiable even if he or she did not have political tasks to perform. Given the political objectives to be attained, the guides were indispensable. Their main function was to make sure that foreigners were accounted for and to maintain control on communication with the natives. They were also supposed to supervise and channel the activities of the visitors, prevent them from seeing unauthorized sights or meeting citizens who had not been pre-selected for this purpose. They were to interpret reality, broadly speaking, and ensure, as much as possible, that the lessons of the conducted tour would sink in and appropriate political conclusions be drawn. It was a job requiring not only the knowledge of foreign languages and a certified political reliability but also the willingness to engage in political persuasion. Robert Loh provided some inside information about the organization, selection, and official functions of the interpreter-guides:

> [their] qualifications were, in order of importance: 1) membership in the Communist Party or Young Communist League, wholehearted devotion to socialism and political alertness, 2) good presence and manners, 3) knowledge of at least one foreign language.
>
> After they were engaged, they attended frequent political lessons. . . . They had to go early in the morning to receive instructions from the reception committee; each night, after saying good night to the visitors . . . they had to submit a written and verbal report to the committee and discuss any problem which might have arisen during the day, such as unsympathetic attitudes or questions by the foreigners or clumsy behavior by any Chinese.[84]

Sometimes special efforts were made to find congenial guides for particular visitors and thereby increase receptivity to their messages. Thus Simone de Beauvoir on one occasion was "accompanied by a novelist, Madame Cheng; she . . . spent fifteen years of her youth in France and has French literature at her fingertips. . . . Keenly intelligent, exceedingly cultivated, and a remarkable observer, she furnished me with all sorts of precious information on all sorts of subjects. Never a word of nonsense of propaganda from her lips; she is so firmly convinced of the benefits conferred by the regime and of its necessity that she has no need to tell fibs to herself or anyone else . . . she knows nothing of self-censorship. . . ." Jonathan Kozol's interpreter in Cuba was a "remarkable person, who handled the most difficult situations with extreme dexterity. . . ." Lord Boyd Orr described his guide as "a master of detail, efficient manager, ideal secretary . . .". In Communist Hungary Jessica Mitford was "assigned an interpreter, an enthusiastic, energetic young woman who was to be our guide. Whom did we want to meet? What did we want to see? We had but to name it. A tour was quickly mapped out that included a drive into the countryside to inspect a collective farm, a workers' rest home, the new steel town of Stalinvaros [Stalin city] . . . high schools . . . the Pioneer Railway . . . the Hungarian Folk Ballet and other entertainments."[85]

The Western visitors usually failed to grasp the political responsibilities their guides shouldered and the consequent delicacy of their job. Robert Loh relates how, on one occasion, a visitor pressed him to tell whether or not his enthusiasm for the regime was real or feigned. He recalled his feelings at the time:

> I felt real resentment at his naivete or selfishness. He was naive if he thought that I or anyone else could afford to say anything against the Party or Government and if he did not know that cadres minutely questioned every Chinese who talked with foreigners. He was selfish, if, . . . he planned to write when he returned to England that the Chinese Progressive, Mr. Loh, was really bitterly anti-Communist. My job was to save my neck. So I told him emphatically: "I love the Communist Party and Government more than my own life." Our private conversation abruptly ended. He seemed disappointed in me. . . . I do not understand how a really intelligent foreign visitor could expect to have private conversation with anyone on the mainland of China.[86]*

In North Vietnam the war provided special justification for the ceaseless surveillance by the interpreters. Mary McCarthy wrote:

> Your guides are held responsible by the authorities if anything happens to you while you are in their care. This applies particularly to guests invited by North Vietnamese organizations. . . . This of course limited one's bodily freedom, but I accepted it. . . . Whenever we traveled, one of the comrades of the Peace Committee made sure I had my helmet by personally carrying it for me. I was never alone, except in bed or writing in my room. In the provinces . . . each time I went to the outlying toilet, the young woman interpreter went with me as far as the door, bearing my helmet, some sheets of tan toilet paper . . . and at night, the trusty flashlight. She waited outside till I was through and then softly led me back.[88]

An important task of the interpreter was to shield the visitors from aspects of reality which contradicted the claims and messages of the regime. The liquidation of the extreme forms of poverty was among

---

* Simon Leys's observations about political and non-political conversations provide a background for what was quoted above: "Broadly speaking one may say that in China people have now at their disposal two levels of languages: one, human and natural, which allows them to speak in their own voice, and which they use to talk about their health, the weather, food, the latest basketball match, and so forth, and another one, mechanical and shrill, to talk about politics . . . during one conversation, the person you are talking to may well switch several times from his normal voice to a kind of ideologic ventriloquism, according to the topics."

Almost half a century earlier Koestler wrote: "the ordinary Soviet citizen knows that to be seen talking to a foreigner is as unhealthy as touching a leper. Those who did talk to me, in resturants and railway compartments, used the stereotyped cliches of *Pravda* editorials; one might have thought they were reciting conversation pieces from a phrase book."[87]

such claims and consequently the visitors were kept away from sights which suggested the persistence of great poverty. Jacques Marcuse was skeptical of these claims; he also knew where some of the slums of Peking were located:

> And so finally, to Hungjao we drove, and through the most night-marish slum I had ever seen anywhere in China at any time.
>
> . . . In Peking at night, I had seen old people—and children as well—looking for food among the refuse heaps of the *hutungs*. . . . But such squalor as Hungjao Road presented I could not have imagined: the abominable wooden shacks made of old planks, neither rain- nor wind-proof; the emaciated children; the people of all ages in their pitiful rags sitting on their doorsteps (if such a word can be used) or standing idly by, ankle-deep in mud. And, of course, the rubbish piled high and the people going through the filth with the thoroughness and concentration of gold diggers. . . . The stench was pestilential. There were about two miles of this and I had the greatest difficulty in keeping the driver on this course. At every road intersection he would try to turn left, away from this obviously taboo sight, and I had to insist that I would walk if I was not driven where I wanted. This thought—that I might thus see even more of what I had not been supposed to see at all . . . made him finally amenable and we drove straight on, but at a much faster rate than before. . . .
>
> "How do these people live?" I asked Mr. Li [the interpreter]. But Mr. Li had once more been stunned into speechlessness. . . .[89]

A somewhat similar incident was reported by Andrew Smith, a former American communist who had lived in the Soviet Union in the early 1930s as a privileged foreign worker. On a sightseeing boat trip on the Volga, arranged for such foreign workers, the group was to stop and visit a collective farm at one point. "But when we neared the town, the banks were lined with the famished population waiting for the boat to dock. Without a word of explanation to us, the ship suddenly changed its course for the middle of the river. There was no stop at Syzran."[90]

Most visitors were not trying to see unauthorized sights or inclined to defy or antagonize their guides.* Yet it was probably generally true, as Jules Roy observed, that "our guides were happy only when they knew we were safely in our rooms or in the sleeping compartment of a train, with our cameras stowed away for the night. . . ."[92]

* More frequently, they went out of their way to make matters easier for the hosts. Mary McCarthy thought "it would be somehow impolite to express my curiosity in the form of point-blank questions; there are many questions one does not want to ask in Hanoi." She also believed that it would be an "abuse of trust" "To question facts, figures, catch small discrepancies. . . ."[91]

Frequently the visitors were shielded not only from images of stark poverty but also from far more innocent sights which, in the view of the authorities, would detract from the claims of triumphant modernization. Jules Roy, for instance, reported how he and his group were not allowed to film the keeper of picturesque ducks on the grounds that this would have been a violation of his privacy. Since, on many occasions, large groups of tourists were paraded through people's homes or shown hospital patients on the operating table (hardly compatible with the respect for privacy), it was much more likely that, as Roy put it, "To show how he lived in his hut of plaited straw, how he moved his flock from rice field to rice field, and how his ducks fed on grains of rice, tadpoles and tiny fish would have been to attach too much importance to a profession whose continued existence in China they did not want to admit."[93] By not allowing the Western tourists to see or photograph such scenes associated with traditional life, the hosts generally misunderstood the disposition of the visitors. Far from finding the survival of primitive ways of living and making a living undignified or repellent, many Westerners relished and admired the simplicity and authenticity associated with rural life and pre-industrial technology, especially in the 1960s and 70s. The care taken by the interpreter-guide to shield her or his charges from sights and experiences which the visitor might have found unappealing is also illustrated by the recollections of Ruth Epperson Kennell who participated in shepherding around Theodore Dreiser in the Soviet Union as his private secretary. Anxious to keep Dreiser uninformed of the vigorous anti-religious campaigns of the regime, she "was thankful that the Museum of the Godless Society was closed" at the time of his visit. On the other hand, she once "inadvertently remarked that a debate was going on in high government circles over a proposal to tear it [the Cathedral of Christ the Savior] down. He [Dreiser] was aghast. . . . I said that Stalin and his supporters argued that it was not fitting for a church to occupy the loftiest site in the capital. . . ." The approach taken toward Dreiser's tour was further illuminated by the official Soviet interpreter who expressed the hope (to Kennell) that "Between us we ought to be able to manage the old man—right?" As in other cases while every effort was made to shield Dreiser from disagreeable sights, his politically innocuous wishes were promptly gratified, including, for example, his request at the Leningrad public library to be shown the section on witchcraft.[94]

The visitors were also often unmindful of the role of the interpreter in literally "interpreting" reality for them, including the translation (or mistranslation) of conversations with the natives. There were, as a rule, three sets of obstacles in the way of spontaneous conversations between foreign visitors and the natives. The latter were, in the first place, generally pre-selected by the authorities; secondly, contact between them and the visitors was presided over and mediated by the interpreter whose very presence served to squelch spontaneous exchanges even if there were no language barriers;° thirdly, in most cases the communications already predetermined and constricted by these circumstances could, literally, only flow through the interpreter-translator. Margulies offers numerous examples, going back as far as the 1920s, of deliberate mistranslation on the part of Soviet interpreters.[96] Samuel N. Harper, the American historian (among a few others), was able to contrast his experiences as a tourist and non-tourist (in 1934 and 1930 respectively) which highlight the effects of the techniques of hospitality on the contacts between visitors and natives:

> For three weeks [in 1930] I lived like a Soviet citizen. . . . One advantage of living this way [in a dormitory, that is, used by Soviet clerical workers], rather than in one of the hotels, was that my Russian friends could now come around to see me very freely . . . I always realized that the actual conditions of living could not be seen from hotel windows. . . .

By contrast he visited in 1934 under different circumstances:

> The three days in Leningrad I spent, in the main, as an out and out tourist, going on the conducted trips to museums, factories, hospitals, and schools. I did not advertise my knowledge of Russian, and suppressed a smile when the interpreter would water down the translation of the mottoes or banners dealing with world revolution or with atheism which appeared everywhere.

By this time he could "no longer start off on [his] own and drift along; it was impossible to get railway tickets except through the Intourist. . . ."[97]

Even in more recent times highly educated Western visitors thought nothing of entrusting their communications to official interpreters while visiting an incarcerated Soviet dissenter—a scene that brings to mind the fictional version of similar encounters conceived by Solzhenitsyn in his

---

° Sometimes the presence of the interpreter was sufficient to discourage the use of shared foreign language that could have provided a channel for communication between the natives and the foreigner. This was the case in an episode related by Colette Modiano when a group of French-speaking tourists with a French-speaking interpreter met a Chinese who spoke excellent English (as did the author) but refused to use it, evidently because such communications could not have been monitored by the interpreter.[95]

First Circle. Andrei Grigorenko, son of General Grigorenko the well-known Soviet dissenter, wrote:

> Unfortunately, people in the West do not always have a sufficiently clear idea of the Soviet situation and the position of a man behind bars. The fact that the Western psychiatrists who visited Father in the psychiatric hospital did not bother about an impartial translation, but were prepared to conduct a conversation through the official Soviet interpreter, can be explained only as an amazing lack of comprehension. Obviously it did not enter their heads that the translation might not correspond at all to what was said. There is another point. After a conversation in prison conditions, a man remains completely in the power of the administration. . . .[98]

Occasionally the group-guide may be a politically reliable foreigner as was the case with the group that David Caute was a member of. The French guide worked hand in hand with the Cuban interpreter to make sure that visitors acquired the correct political interpretation of everything seen (" 'Cuba has no political prisoners,' Nicole [the French guide] says sharply. 'Terrorists, spies, and counter-revolutionaries are not political prisoners, merely criminals' "). The group was also assured that Cuban workers had the right to strike but—as the venerable official formula has it—" 'In a socialist system,' Nicole says, 'the workers realize that when they strike they strike against themselves.' "[99]

Sometimes the re-interpretation of reality took more extreme forms. In the instance when two reporters (of the United Press International and New York *Times* respectively) observed from a hill in Baku (in the USSR) "six small gray warships docked at seaside, she [the guide] replied 'What warships?' We pointed, drew diagrams, cajoled—but she saw no ships. Her refusal to acknowledge those ships in plain view was matched by the ingenuity of our guide at the Armenian capital of Erivan who, when asked about a tract of rotting, shacklike homes replied: 'The government keeps them there so tourists can see what the slums looked like.' " When Andrew Smith asked his interpreter to explain the presence of "a mass of ragged beggars, mostly women and children" near the railway station in Leningrad, "she explained that they were good-for-nothing drunkards" for whom "the government cannot do anything."[100] The veracity of the guide also appeared problematic to Peter Kenez when on one occasion he and his group "were walking through this factory [and] a guide turned to us and remarked: 'all the machines here were made in China.' This surprised me since in the previous room I had noticed that approximately half of the machines were Czech or Soviet made." Interpreters were not above transparent evasion. Thus when Jules Roy "asked if there were other bridges across the Yangtze [in addition to that which was shown] everyone smiled as they told me they did not know."[101]

Re-interpretation (and denial) of reality apart, a major task of the guide—and a critical aspect of the techniques of hospitality—was the segregation of the visitors from the natives and the forestalling of spontaneous, unplanned, or accidental encounters. It would be incorrect to suggest that the hosts were always successful in achieving this, but it was not for lack of trying. Local conditions, the peculiarities of the countries and the period also made a difference. Obviously it was easier to separate tourists from natives in countries where the population had strikingly different physical attributes from those of Western visitors, notably in China and Vietnam. A lot depended too on the attitudes of the population: Soviet citizens in the 1930s, 40s, and 50s were more apprehensive about meeting foreigners than in the 1960s or 70s. Some Chinese people have become less fearful in this regard since the death of Mao. Yet, on the whole, popular attitudes provided a solid basis for the regime's policy of separating the tourists from the natives. Here again it must be stressed that the interpreter-guides accompanying the visitors were viewed, and justifiably so, as representatives of the authorities and having connections with the state security agencies.[102] Ordinary citizens also knew that the foreigners were either already friends of the regime or were being cultivated to be turned into friends. They were well aware that no effort was spared to make a favorable impression on these visitors and that anything said or shown to them that would detract from this goal would be regarded by the authorities as a form of hostility toward the regime. Moreover, while criticism of the system by the citizens among themselves was regarded as subversive, such criticism expressed in the presence of foreigners was even more severely viewed. The secretiveness of the political systems discussed here also contributed to caution and restraint on the part of their citizens even among themselves, let alone in the company of outsiders. It was better to avoid foreigners, unless explicitly instructed by the authorities not to. Yet here again some differences must be noted. Among the countries concerned (within the specified periods) probably the Chinese were the most apprehensive in their contacts with foreigners, and the Cubans the least, while Soviet citizens of the Stalin era doubtless came close to the Chinese in these matters. Presumably the degree of caution also had to do, within certain limits, with national character and culture. (Frances Fitzgerald remarked that "talk being one of the great commodities of Cuba, people did come up to us from time to time to ask questions or to deliver opinions on various subjects, from the weather to the government.")[103]

The languages the travelers and the natives had in common also influenced the contacts between them. It is reasonable to assume that the proportion of Western visitors who knew some Spanish was greater than those who spoke Russian and, in turn, those capable of conversing in Chinese or Vietnamese represented the smallest contingent among them. There were also more English speakers in Cuba than in the Soviet Union (at least as a percentage of the population) and very few among the Chinese and North Vietnamese.

A cautious or outright intimidated population (with generally limited linguistic skills) provided built-in safeguards, so to speak, against unauthorized contacts (and unorthodox disclosures in the event of contacts) between tourists and natives, and helped to ensure that the two groups will be kept apart. Simon Leys wrote:

> The recurring nightmare of the Maoist bureaucrats is that the foreigners might have fanned out into the countryside and even—this is the worst—managed to make some spontaneous and unsupervised contact with the people. In fact this last fear is groundless: trained by five years of the Cultural Revolution, Chinese people will think twice before speaking to a foreigner. In some provincial cities, it happened to me that people . . . refused even to give me directions. Who could blame them? . . . in six months I had no conversation with any Chinese, except for bureaucrats or people who could justify their contact with me as being part of their jobs—as guides, railroad employees, waiters and so on. . . .[104]

Peter Kenez also commented on the guides' determination "to prevent chance contacts. On one occasion a Chinese who could speak some English engaged us in a conversation on a train, but was quickly and rather rudely removed by our nice and gentle guide." Sometimes even when there was no danger of communicating, "The crowds which surrounded us periodically were chased away by the police or by our guides with unnecessary harshness." Even the most favorably disposed visitors could not deny that the Chinese authorities took great pains to separate foreigners from natives in all public places, including trains, hotels, museums, places of entertainment and restaurants. ("As in other

Chinese restaurants we visited," recalled Staughton Lynd and Tom Hayden, "we were escorted to a separate room, where we could talk easily while eating; but, we were told, the restaurants are open to all, food is the same for everyone, and prices are low.") Contrary to such beliefs, a New York *Times* reporter noted that in the famous Peking Duck restaurant the waitress showed him and another foreigner to "an upstairs dining room, which had a separate, locked entrance. While the local people had bare wooden tables downstairs, the private room upstairs had tablecloths, lace curtains on the windows and a landscape painting on the wall. And in Shanghai a big bookstore on Nanking road has an upstairs section from which local Chinese are barred. . . . Even the wrapping paper upstairs is of a finer quality."[105]

It is a matter of conjecture which were the most important motives for these policies of segregation, or what mixture of motives was present. Certainly the wish to retain control over the experiences of the visitors was a major factor. Flattery ("ego-massage") was another, since—contrary to Messrs. Lynd and Hayden—the establishments involved were not only separate but also unequal. There might have been, in addition, also a desire on the part of the authorities to prevent the natives from knowing the exact dimensions and details of the privileges foreigners enjoyed. But most importantly, the system of segregation functioned to preserve the closed universe in which foreigners moved and was supposed to shape their outlook. Magnus Enzensberger found this system effective, commenting on it in the Cuban context: "contact is limited to designated individuals from the functionary class and to foreigners who live in the same hotels. This umbrella is so effective that most of the political tourists don't have the slightest idea of the working conditions even after weeks or months in the host country."[106]

Although, as noted before, there was probably more unsupervised contact between tourists and natives in Cuba (in part because of a smaller language barrier) than in the other countries discussed, some reports indicate that unanticipated and unplanned contacts were far from welcome on the part of the authorities and their representative, the guide-interpreter. Andrew Salkey described the distress of his guide when they were approached one night near his hotel by a young English-speaking Cuban who finally left them after he was instructed to do so by the militia-guard present. While, on the whole, it was relatively easy for foreigners to move around and have more casual contacts with Cubans in Havana, other parts of the country and its inhabitants were far less accessible. Thus Frances Fitzgerald and other journalists, for example, "could not arrange to take a trip of more than an hour or so outside Havana."[107]

In the Soviet Union too, besides the recurring official association of "foreigner" and "spy" characteristic of the atmosphere of the 1930s, those in charge of hospitality took many steps to make sure that there be no unauthorized contacts or communications between the natives and the tourists. As Margulies related, "Russian citizens were instructed to remain quiet or were told what to say during the visits of foreign guests or delegations" and "Soviet guides accompanying foreign delegations or individual tourists showed annoyance at efforts made by persons under their care to talk with Russians, or even with foreign workers and specialists working in Soviet factories." Not surprisingly, "The presence of GPU agents at social gatherings attended by both foreigners and Soviet citizens further inhibited contacts. . . ."[108]

The interaction between the overseas Chinese and the resident Chinese represented a special case of contact between tourists and natives, and the policies of hospitality extended to this group fluctuated over time. Certainly it was also an important group the regime wanted to win over; yet, it presented problems by virtue of being, looking, and speaking Chinese, and having close personal ties with the citizens. While in the post-Mao period they enjoyed easier access to their relatives and were sometimes even allowed unsupervised visits to rural areas, earlier reports indicate that the officials were, to say the least, uneasy about the contacts between the two groups. Thus we learn that

> Before being allowed to go to the hotel's dining room they have to produce identification with their name, address and employment and state their relationship with the visitor from America. When several members of a family visit together, each has to produce separate identification. This information is recorded by the hotel clerk, who then issues them a pass. This pass, which is collected by the elevator operator, entitles them to visit only one floor of the hotel, such as the dining room floor. After the meal the Chinese are not allowed into their relative's hotel room until another trip to the lobby to fill out more forms after which they are issued another pass.[109]

In the light of such measures perhaps it was not altogether surprising that, as reported by one such visitor from the U.S., "her relatives 'seemed paranoid' [and] fearful of talking to her and seemed to be very upset by her visit."[110]

The most extreme restrictions placed on visitors in recent times were reported from North Korea, and they are a good measure of the un-diluted totalitarianism of that regime. As Harrison Salisbury testified:

> In 16 days of interviews, sightseeing, visits to factories, schools, kin-dergartens, a university, theaters and museums, I only once walked alone on a North Korean street—and then only for about 150 yards—before a panting interpreter, in extreme agitation, ran up to accom-pany me . . . I never spoke to a peasant in the field or in his cottage . . . I never spoke to a worker in a factory with the exception of an occasional group that had been so rehearsed in their performance as to be laughable. . . . I never visited a worker's apartment. I never visited a store. I never ate in a restaurant . . . I was housed in beau-tiful government guest houses . . . surrounded by walls and barbed wire with Tommy gun carrying sentries at the gates. . . .[111]

It may of course be argued that such extremes reflect merely an under-developed stage in the evolution of the techniques of hospitality char-acterized by the shortage of standard show-places or special exhibits, human, material, or institutional.

A new chapter in the application of the techniques of hospitality on a mass scale was written during the 1980 Olympic Games in Moscow. The authorities were especially anxious to separate the visitors from the natives. For instance, "to be doubly sure to keep Russians at bay, the doormen have been reinforced by uniformed policemen and plain-clothesmen, and each hotel honors only its own pass. . . . American tourists reported that their only contact with ordinary Russians had been at the athletic events and amounted to little more than an ex-change of greetings." A Soviet citizen, in a letter smuggled out of the Soviet Union several months before the Olympics, had this to say to the potential foreign visitors and participants:

> Let me explain how the official preparations for your arrival are being carried out. . . . Every free moment has been rigidly scheduled for you in advance. You will be invited to official receptions where vodka and champaign will flow like a river. Your hosts will take you by hand to the theatres, museums and palaces of culture. You will be driven in guided buses to the historic sights. . . .
> . . . you think you'll meet young Russians? Forget it. Our young people have been sent away for the summer to remote construction sites, villages and collective farms. Even the dates of final exams and the entrance exams for institutes and universities were changed to facilitate evacuation.
> Even as I write Moscow is being purged of its "deleterious ele-ments" . . . They are being evicted from the city, hustled out of

sight, swept under the rug. Or arrested. Your hosts are creating a "model city" for you.

The capital of our country has been transformed into a closed city. . . . There is no breaking through the 100-kilometer barrier, not by plane, train, car, bus or boat. Stringent [internal] passport control is everywhere.

. . . any Muscovite will tell you that you will be living not in Olympic villages but in Potemkin villages—false fronts, portable stage sets. All this construction is one gigantic con game as far as the Russian people are concerned. It has nothing to do with the way we actually live.[112]

The selective presentation of social reality came close to but fell short of outright deception. To show the visitors phenomena that were atypical, unusual, and outstanding was misleading but not totally contrived or fabricated. Staged events or displays created solely for the benefit of visitors were fewer in number. They too were part of the techniques of hospitality to which we will turn next.

Rearranging Reality: The Spirit of Potemkin

The deceptions which were part of the techniques of hospitality can be explained by the same motives which account for the policies and techniques of hospitality in general. Political leaders who sincerely believe that ideas are weapons single-mindedly strive to create conditions in which their ideas have a maximum impact, and they also want to ensure that the social system they preside over be seen in the most favorable light. Given such a disposition there will be a sense of urgency about the task of persuading the outsiders of the virtues and accomplishments of their system. Certain of the essential superiority of their regime, the leaders will spare no effort to demonstrate its excellence. They sincerely believe that blemishes and "temporary shortcomings" need not be displayed and may legitimately be denied. They will, in any event, disappear at some future date, so why not anticipate the future, as it were, through the techniques of hospitality? As in socialist realist art, the typical is not the statistical average but the emergent, pregnant with the promise of the future. The visitors should see things the way they are supposed to be, or going to be, not the way they are. And since there are no moral absolutes, no universal moral standards, "truth" and "reality" are relative and everything is moral that hastens the triumph of "socialism," including measures which will help to spread its good reputation to countries where the forces of progress have yet to succeed. Hence there will be no moral scruples in the way of rearranging reality. "Deception" is not an ethical issue when children are dying of hunger in capitalist countries (or so it used to be said), so why not propagandize the achievements and intentions of a superior system with utmost vigor?

Such a highly instrumental approach to truth and morality would not, by itself, have created the deceptions associated with the techniques of hospitality, though it is a major precondition and premise of it. There must also be power and resources at the disposal of the authorities to implement their aspirations and beliefs. More precisely, there has to be a totalitarian sense of omnipotence, and a desire for mastery over the environment, for extending control over as many facets of life as is possible. If so, why not create of whole cloth, as it were, showpieces and showplaces for the delectation of the visitors? One of these days they will cease to be showplaces and will become truly typical. Moreover, there will be no material, organizational, or political problems in rearranging reality. No muckraking journalists will cause embarrassment; no outraged political opposition would protest; indignant citizens will not expose the sham to the foreigners. Nor will there be a shortage of resources with which to implement important projects; there will always be men and material, specialists and equipment, and organizational skills available to build a model prison, a new guesthouse for visitors, an elite kindergarten, an exceptional collective farm, and funds for training competent and politically dependable guide-interpreters.

At last, although difficult to isolate, note must also be taken of the pervasive spirit of un-spontaneity which generally characterizes the political systems in question and is inseparable from the techniques of hospitality. Whatever the origins of this unspontaneity—Lenin's ideas, the mistrust of the masses, the elevation of organization to a supreme principle, the belief in the unity of theory and practice, the desire to hold on to power—it is the single most important factor which explains the techniques of hospitality in general, and the deceptions in particular. Foreigners as a rule simply did not have the experience and imagination to conceive of some of the deceptions they were subject to and of the efforts the regimes were willing to make to create favorable impressions. As Sylvia Margulies put it:

> Just as Hitler recognized the potency of the "big lie," the Soviet regime realized that the more preposterous the façades, the more likelihood that the visitors would be taken in, for they would find it incredible that a country at the stage of development of the Soviet Union would go to such length in attempts to fool foreigners. Who

would believe he was being deceived by GPU men and political officials posing as ordinary workers? Who would imagine that electricity
was temporarily installed in peasant huts solely to impress foreign
visitors?[113]

Lev Navrozov, a former Soviet citizen who had observed such techniques from inside the Soviet Union, recorded the setting up in Moscow
in 1935 of an "Exemplary Fish Store" with "two hundred high quality
fish products" for the benefit of foreigners:

> the price must be high enough to forbid too many Muscovites to con-
> verge on the commodity . . . but low enough to enable the exhibits
> to display a calm yet brisk trade. A foreigner should see that live fish
> is bought well, but not too eagerly. . . .[114]

During the 1980 Olympics types of food and consumer goods ordi-
narily not seen or in short supply suddenly appeared in the shops of
Moscow:

> "During the Olympics it will be wonderful," a grandmother said a
> few months ago. "The stores will be full, they'll keep people from
> other cities from coming in and we'll have it made." Now on the eve
> of the opening ceremony . . . the dream is coming true. . . .
>   On Gorky street . . . it was cheese that had suddenly reappeared
> . . . in bewildering variety. . . .
>   The lines also formed quickly for imported Hungarian duck . . .
> ham and bright red tomatoes from Rumania. . . .
>   Suddenly . . . Moscow was paradise . . .

Such and other improvements in Moscow exacted a price. Again, according to the unofficial Soviet source:

> . . . hundreds of thousands of our population still live in dank base-
> ments or semibasements, or in communal apartments. . . . Our city
> [Moscow, that is] suffers from an acute shortage of the most basic
> medical and sports facilities. In order to erect new luxury hotels and
> special sports structures, the authorities have sharply curtailed housing
> construction. . . .
>   These examples do not scratch the surface. In many Soviet cities,
> ration cards have been required for years to buy meat and butter
> . . . signs are posted in the food stores: "Meat sold by ration card
> only. Allowance 1½ kilos per person per month." That's about three
> pounds or one-tenth of a pound a day. Won't it be a little uncomfort-
> able to put a chunk of shashlik into your mouth if you know it has
> literally been taken out of the mouth of someone living 10 kilometers
> away from an Olympic restaurant?[115]

Jerzy Gliksman (whose unique dual experiences as both privileged visitor to a model prison and inmate in several regular ones were already discussed in Chapter 4) was not the only foreigner who had such contrasting exposures to the Soviet system. Andrew Smith also had opportunities to view Soviet life from different vantage points. On the first occasion he was a member of an American labor delegation to the Soviet Union selected by the U.S. Communist party. The time was 1929:

> On November 1, we arrived at Belo Ostrov, on the Finnish-Russian border. Everything was ready for us on the Soviet side. The finest food and plenty of it was piled high on tables decked with the cleanest of white tablecloths, meats, fish, cake, fruit and wine in abundance. We were greeted as if we were distinguished diplomats representing a foreign power. A squad of Red soldiers saluted us at the border. . . .
>
> The delegation was piloted to the Hotel Europe, which, we were told, was exclusively for the workers. We had everything our hearts desired, free. We had wonderful meals, our suits were pressed and mended, our shoes shined, cigars and cigarettes, shaves and haircuts, laundry service and the use of first-class automobile for transportation. . . . After the evening meal we were taken to the theatre, where we enjoyed a performance of a revolutionary drama. Again speakers greeted us enthusiastically amidst tremendous applause. Fruit and a light lunch was served to us during the intermission. Then back to the hotel again by auto.

Subsequently Smith decided to donate all his savings to the Communist party and settle in the USSR to help build socialism. On this second arrival he was no longer a member of a visiting delegation but one of a group of workers who had committed themselves to live and work in the land of no unemployment. The year was 1932:

> We arrived on the Finnish side of the border in the morning. There was a restaurant at the railroad station which displayed excellent food . . . clean and up-to-date and priced very reasonably. I restrained the group from buying anything, however. "Don't buy here," I said. "On the other side . . . where you see the red flag flying, you will get better food at a much cheaper price." We were all very hungry but we waited until we crossed the border.
>
> There was no delegation to meet us at Belo Ostrov this time. No brass band and no speakers. All we saw were some poor emaciated looking peasants, who passed us with looks that did not appear very friendly. We called to them and cheered in greeting "Long live the Soviet Union. Long live the Red Army." But they passed on with weary steps without answering. . . . We made haste to find the restaurant, near the railroad station. A terrible stench greeted us as we entered. The tables were bare and topped by discolored, dilapidated

boards, spotted with remnants of decayed fish. . . . Some of us were afraid to order anything because of the general appearance of the place. . . . We were told that there was nothing but fish soup. . . .

Subsequently Smith started to work in a large electrical machine factory in Moscow and became a witness from the inside to the displays put on for visiting delegations:

A number of foreign delegations arrived for the May 1st Celebration in 1932. Some of the delegates visited our factory and I had an opportunity to witness from behind the scenes how these people are deceived just as I had been. . . .

We were instructed to give evidence of our enthusiasm and industry. We were to pay attention only to our machines. Above all we were not to talk. This was to be left to the officials. . . .

It took us from four to five hours of arduous labor that day to prepare for the delegation. The workers muttered imprecations under their breath because of this extra labor. . . .

At 10 a.m. next morning the delegation consisting of fifteen workers from Germany, Czechoslovakia, the United States, France and other countries came to the factory. They were headed by Werner, party instructor of the Foreign Bureau and a host of interpreters and propagandists through whom the information about the factory was carefully filtered. . . . After the examination of the factory the delegation was taken to the dining room. Here at last was the only reason for which the workers could be thankful on the occasion of the visit of the delegation. Gone were the filthy aprons of the waiters. . . . The tables were covered with white tablecloths. No sour bread "cutlets," no cabbage soup. Instead there was chicken, vegetables, compote, and other delicacies never seen before. The table was decked with clean plates and, . . . shining knives, forks and spoons to honor the occasion. The workers were unaccustomed to the use of these utensils but they did not let that retard them from doing full justice to this unusual and welcome feast. . . . They knew full well that as soon as the delegation left they would be back to the old regime of cabbage soup. . . .*

One of the delegates, brimming with enthusiasm at the scene urged the interpreter to ask the nearest worker how much he paid for this meal. The worker replied, "two rubles and 30 kopeks." Without winking an eyelash the interpreter turned to the delegate and said "thirty kopeks" . . . "And how much pay does he get?" the delegate asked. In response to the interpreter's question, the worker replied, "Seventy-five rubles a month." The interpreter glibly passed the information to the delegate, "Two hundred and seventy-five rubles."

* More recently in Vietnamese-occupied Cambodia, "According to the refugees the Vietnamese distribute relief supplies of rice by day 'in the presence of international workers, then confiscate (it) after the workers depart the scene,' or replace it with corn."[116]

Following a meeting at which "workers" (actually administrators and party propagandists) answered questions put to them by the delegation, the guests were

> taken to a restaurant used by the directors and high officials, another workers' restaurant they were told, where they were served with a many course repast of fish, soup, roast chicken, all kinds of fresh vegetables, compote and tarts. Wine and cigarettes were at each table. There were even flowers on the table. This was the customary meal of the workers . . . they were told. . . .
>
> After this sumptuous meal the delegates were taken to the factory nursery where the "workers'" children are kept. . . . They were the children of the various rouged and lipsticked women *udarniks* [outstanding workers], whom one could see about the factory, the favorites of the directors and propagandists. But the delegates gazed in open-mouthed enthusiasm as the "workers'" children went through a gymnastic drill for them, some Russian folk-dancing and games. . . . From the nursery, the delegates were taken to the *datchas* near the Ismailov Park. These were beautiful bungalows occupied . . . by the factory bureaucracy. Each . . . contained from four to six rooms. Around each house were beautiful trees, flowers and shaded paths. Each delegate was invited by some "worker" into his home to see how he lived.[117]

Harrison Salisbury, whose views of Soviet society were far less enthusiastic than those he held of China, also came to the conclusion (more recently) that typical factory visits in the USSR were carefully staged affairs for the benefit of the foreigners. He wrote:

> In 25 years of Russian experience, I had probably seen 200 or more plants . . . I knew Soviet visiting procedures . . . I had seen how carefully swept and cleaned the factories were, how well dressed the workers appeared, how efficiently the machines performed. I had listened to the director spiel off his accomplishments. . . . The workers' enthusiasm reached new heights. Their technical innovations could not be equaled. . . .
>
> And when the questioning began, the director would always be edgy and guarded. . . . When he paused at a machine I knew that this had been well rehearsed in advance. It was always a pretty, slightly flustered girl mechanic. . . . Or a veteran worker, his hands horny with toil and honest grease. . . .
>
> Not that the factories were sham. . . . But what went on when a visitor came was a carefully prepared charade. . . . Such a hectic time of washing up, of getting new potted plants for the director's office and the employees' lunchroom; new posters and slogans put up on the walls. . . . The plant and the offices had to be cleaned and swept and sometimes painted. The route of the visit was carefully

worked out so that no obsolete or dismal shops beyond cosmetic treatment would be seen. The workers were briefed on what to say (and, more important, what not to say) and those who were to be interviewed carefully rehearsed the lines. The others were sternly warned against talking to the foreigner (usually an unnecessary precaution since he probably did not know Russian). Those who spoke English or French or German were told that it would be a very serious matter if the foreigner spoke to them in one of those languages and they were caught engaging him in conversation. . . .

In essence, the principles of the visit to the Russian factory had been laid down 200 years ago by Count Potemkin.[118]

While on the occasion of such plant visits the human props or participants were usually the actual workers of the factory (albeit briefed, silenced, or rehearsed), there were at least a few reports of cases when the population belonging to a given institution or area was replaced by others for the benefit of the visitors. One such event was already related earlier, namely, the removal or replacement of some of the prisoners around Magadan by guards or office workers for the benefit of Henry Wallace and his party. A similar event was staged and filmed for Andrew Smith and other foreign workers who were to meet Volga Germans on their collective farms. It turned out that the "German" workers of the Engels collective farm (supposedly part of the German colony in the Volga district) "spoke only a broken German, some with a marked Yiddish accent. They were remarkably well-dressed for agricultural workers, mostly in sport attire. . . ." They were also unfamiliar with German tunes and dances. Smith learned later that "the entire group, consisting of *udarniks* and propagandists, had been shipped from Samara for our enlightenment while the real colonists were kept at a safe distance. . . ."[119] While this incident appears to have been improvised, the more developed techniques of hospitality make provisions for the routinized presentation of (or staged encounters with) groups and individuals who perform particular sociological roles and specialize in conveying certain political messages to the visitors.* A case in point was the reformed capitalist in China. Robert Loh describes this technique and how it evolved:

* The Soviet contribution to the so-called Citizens Exchange Program (headquartered in New York) is made up of such groups and individuals. This program is supposed to bring together typical Soviet and American families, cross sections of each society. On the Soviet side this is a governmental undertaking whereas American participation is voluntary and depends on the individual citizen's interest in Soviet society and his willingness to pay the costs. Interest in the United States as such would be among the least useful qualification for the Soviet participants.

> To meet the request of overseas "friends" for contact with private Chinese individuals, the Reception Committee made arrangements for visitors to call on people in every walk of life. . . . These model homes of scholars, factory workers, peasants and capitalists were the show windows of socialism. . . .

There was particular interest abroad at the time in the treatment and attitude of former capitalists toward the Chinese regime. In response to that interest, "The Communist Party chose about half a dozen big capitalists or directors of large enterprises to serve as typical examples of contented capitalists who had voluntarily given their enterprises to a socialist regime." Those selected were provided with everything, servants and mansions included, required for impressing and entertaining foreign visitors. Loh describes a typical visit as follows:

> At five in the afternoon the two French couples arrived [in Peking, to the house of a certain Chen family] with the usual pig-tailed Communist girl interpreters. When the guests were admitted to the sitting room, they could not hide their amazement at the luxurious standard of living these ex-capitalists were enjoying. Through the French window they could see a large garden full of flowers. A neatly dressed governess was wheeling a child across the lawn, with two dogs frisking about them. In the adjoining room the eldest daughter was practicing the piano. Everything seemed so peaceful and natural that no one could possibly guess that each of these details had been carefully planned and rehearsed. . . . At the guests' request the hosts took them through the house. In their immense garage there were three cars: a Singer, a Buick and a Mercedes Benz. Actually, two of the cars were borrowed for the occasion. The French saw two giant-sized Philco refrigerators in the kitchen and a second piano in another room. In the study there was a fine selection of books. . . . On one wall of the children's room hung a cross (to show that religious freedom existed . . .).
>
> After viewing every room with real admiration, the guests sat on the balcony drinking cocktails. They asked their host: "Mr. Chen, how is it that a great capitalist like you finds it possible to endorse communism and to abandon willingly all your property to the state?"
>
> I had heard the same query from visitors and Mr. Chen's reply more than ten times previously. He had rehearsed it well, and his acting was perfect. He assumed a serious expression, paused for a moment, as though for thought, and answered slowly: "When the Communists first occupied Shanghai, we were very apprehensive. . . ."

The lengthy narrative that followed deepened the good impressions of the two French industrialists. "A banquet followed and [they], completely won over, shook Mr. Chen's hand saying: 'If the French Communists adopt the policy of the Chinese Communists we shall have nothing to say against it.' This phrase was printed in all the newspapers next day."[120]

A similar reformed capitalist was also exhibited for the edification of Jacques Hebert and Pierre Trudeau. He was a former owner and current manager of a textile factory and "a cultivated, pleasant, intelligent man." He too explained the benefits deriving from his position and revealed his deep loyalty to the system. The authors found out subsequently "from cross-checking . . . that he is the same man who told the same story in the same tone to other travelers a few years earlier." Evidently he was also the same person (or very similar) to the one who was presented to the group touring with Colette Modiano, living in a house similarly equipped to that which Robert Loh described and was provided with a Jaguar automobile and "two maids in white aprons." In turn, Lord Boyd Orr and his wife had stumbled upon such a former capitalist by mere chance in the Summer Palace. (They "ran into an old gentleman" who asked him and his wife to have tea with him and his family.) The lord was "intrigued" by the meeting and found "the lunch . . . excellent." Even the wife of this former capitalist spoke "fluent English" and their household was equipped with a cook and two assistant cooks. The "outspokenness" of the host (who was nonetheless a supporter of the government) surprised Lord Boyd Orr. The communist regime in Vietnam also displayed occasionally a privileged model capitalist for visitors. Thus for instance an American television reporter was told by one (the owner of a rug factory) through an interpreter that he still lived in a big house (shown), had two cars, a television set, and money in the bank.[121]

Such model social types were not limited to the upper social scale. Professor J. M. Montias, the Yale economist, reported that on his visit to the Sino-Albanian Friendship Commune (near Peking) his group was "ushered into a peasant's home: (This peasant family, I learn after our return to Yale, is precisely the one Thomas Bernstein of Yale talked to on the occasion of his visit to this commune last summer.)"[122]

The same managed spontaneity characterized the visits to institutions. Frank Tuohy wrote:

> On the steps of Sun Yat-sen's mausoleum, we run into a group of English-speaking students. They are from Nanking University, which we visited yesterday. "We waited in our dormitories all morning but you never came." It is the first direct evidence we have that our visits

are arranged in the smallest detail—from the "discussion" with the questions and answers noted down by a silent, unexplained character in the corner, to the English classes. . . . At Nanking, the periodical room was open and empty. It had a remarkable selection of foreign magazines. A copy of *Encounter* happened to have my name on the cover.[123]

Peter Kenez also felt that he and his group "saw very little which had not been especially prepared and organized for us. In the Shanghai pioneer palace, for example, we had to walk through rather quickly since the next group of foreigners was waiting and we kept on meeting them in the corridors. The children were not at all bashful; I imagine they had seen more foreigners than I saw Chinese children. 'Spontaneity' was organized for our benefit. We visited a commune outside of Sian and our hosts kindly invited us for lunch, dividing us into groups of four and taking us into their houses. Later it transpired that exactly the same rather elaborate meal was served in each house." One is inclined to suspect that similar levels of spontaneity prevailed on the occasion when at a new housing project, Lord Boyd Orr asked his "faithful Mr. Li": "'Can we inspect one of the houses?' 'Anyone you like' he offered. 'Choose!' We chose the nearest and went in and the householders opened their doors to welcome us."[124]

The Peking railway station, which made such an indelible impression on Felix Greene and other visitors, was another interesting case in point. Jacques Marcuse had an opportunity to discuss the matter with Greene:

> I tackled him about the VIPP treatment he had been given on his last trip and about his description of the new Peking railway station. I ventured to suggest that his good faith had been taken advantage of and that what he had written about the station was balderdash: about the station restaurant that stayed open day and night, about the tickets that could be ordered by telephone and were delivered promptly by messenger, about TV rooms, and the "two nurseries for infants, where mothers can leave their children under the care of young trained nurses." He added, "in one of the nurseries I saw rows of little tots fast asleep in their cots."
>
> At the Peking railway station . . . there was only one nursery. It was there alright, there was no denying it—it had glass doors through which one could look in. But no one could *walk* in. Throughout my sojourn in Peking, during which I had gone to that very station at least once or twice a week . . . I had never known this nursery to be in use. Its doors were permanently shut and padlocked. . . .
>
> When I mentioned that to Felix Greene he could not believe it. Others who were present and had been in China for some time bore me out. I asked Greene whether he had been to the station again by

himself and he said he had not. I reminded him that by his own admission in his book his visit had been prearranged and the deputy
stationmaster was there waiting to greet him. I reminded him that the
Chinese were masters at stage management, but that was something
he did not particularly wish to hear.

After that session I saw no more of him, except from a distance
when, for instance, he was filming Wang Fu Ching, which had been
cleared of traffic and down which a sprinkler was operating, a thing
never witnessed before in broad daylight.[125]

More recently an American television crew in Shanghai recalled that
in a "great open square vibrant with pedestrians and bicyclists, . . . In
a matter of minutes we set down a tripod, fixed the camera, plugged in
sound, focused—and the square was empty."[126]

It may be noted that there were no examples in this section of the
"rearrangements of reality" from Cuba. This may be explained in two
ways. It is possible that I have not done an exhaustive enough survey
of the relevant sources and therefore missed the description of such episodes. It is also possible that the Cuban authorities did not resort to
such techniques, feeling more confident about the accomplishments of
their regime and having more authentic showplaces at their disposal to
display.

At the same time there may also be a more indirect connection between the longevity of the Castro regime (and the associated assumptions about the survival of its revolutionary ethos) and the lesser information about its Potemkin Village techniques. Such a continuity in
power may have constrained the articulate expression of the type of
disillusionment—both on the part of citizens and foreign admirers—
which follows the rupture of continuity (and legitimacy) and which
brings in its wake unflattering revelations about the operation of the
political system including its propaganda aimed at foreign visitors.

Everything that had been said earlier about the intellectuals' resistance
to the idea that they can be manipulated and deceived is especially applicable to the techniques which were mentioned in this section. For
those who take pride in their ability to see through sham and prize their
capacity for merciless social criticism, irreverence, and iconoclasm, it is
extremely difficult to entertain the possibility that in certain situations
none of these talents can be relied upon.

9

Conclusions Concerning the Nature of Intellectuals, Estrangement, and Its Consequences

> . . . a society . . . above all is the idea which it forms of itself.
>
> EMILE DURKHEIM[1]

> Thanks to its promises of regeneration . . . Socialism is becoming a belief of a religious character. . . . Hitherto man has been unable to live without divinities. They fall often from their throne, but that throne has never remained empty . . . man possesses the marvellous faculty of transforming things to the liking of his desires . . . which shows us the world as we wish it to be. Each at the bidding of his dreams, his ambitions, his hopes, perceives in Socialism what the founders of the new faith never dreamed of putting into it. . . . It is the sum of all these dreams, all these discontents, all these hopes that endows the new faith with its incontestable power. GUSTAVE LE BON[2]

> Mr. Garry still rhapsodizes about the beauties of the settlement [of Jonestown]. He said the socialist in him was thrilled at people working together and sharing. There was the jungle. Crops. Quiet nights. Happiness. It looked that way to him.   (The New York Times)[3]

> I do not believe in public attacks on socialist countries where violations of human rights may occur.   WILLIAM KUNSTLER[4]

> . . . it is no defense whatever for an intellectual to say that he was duped, since that is what, as an intellectual, he should never allow to happen to him.   GRANVILLE HICKS[5]

The Sources of Estrangement and Social Criticism

Insofar as the concept of estrangement is central to explaining the political pilgrimages and the whole range of attitudes associated with the social role of intellectuals, a final review of its sources is warranted. While earlier, it will be recalled, more attention was paid to the concrete and immediate historical background which led to the rejection of

400

society, at this point I will summarize some of the broader social, cultural, and historical conditions which have given rise to estrangement in our times. They are the same conditions which also produced the political pilgrims and the large reservoir of supportive intellectuals (or quasi-intellectuals) which provided them with a subculture and responsive audience.

We may begin by recalling the traditional social role of intellectuals in Western societies, or, more to the point, the intellectuals' conception of their social role. For well over a century, leading Western intellectuals conceived of themselves as outsiders and critics (especially in the United States), deprived of appropriate recognition, rewards, and power. Although objective social conditions have significantly altered, calling into question the accuracy of such perceptions—resulting from the expansion of higher education, the growth of the mass media and increased governmental reliance on the skills of intellectuals—these perceptions and attitudes have tenaciously persisted. Moreover, "From having felt unwanted and unused intellectuals moved to the . . . conviction of indispensability . . . fully compatible with hostility toward those who seem to deny the rights which come with indispensability."[6]

Secondly, intellectuals, like the rest of the population in Western countries, have experienced the psychological difficulties of living in large-scale, complex, mobile, and bureaucratized urban societies in which the level of social isolation and impersonality has risen and in which communities, as functioning social units, have been undermined. Apparently such isolation, impersonality, and weakened social ties have been especially strongly felt by intellectuals. The reasons for this may lie in their greater mobility, higher expectations (rooted in part in their higher education and occupational involvement with ideas), and presumably also in a selective attraction to the role of intellectuals in terms of personality.[*] Such traits of personality may include a propensity toward certain forms of abstract thinking; idealism; concern with social justice; iconoclastic, debunking, or critical dispositions; the desire for creative self-fulfillment; a degree of perfectionism; high levels of personal aspirations or more generally, expectations geared to non-material goals.

Thirdly, Western societies and Western intellectuals in particular have

---

[*] I did not try to find the answer to the question as to why and how some people become intellectuals and differentiate themselves from others by their peculiar needs, aspirations, and discontents. The issue, who becomes an intellectual, would require a separate and equally lengthy study.

been increasingly affected by the process of secularization in the last decades. Somewhat unexpectedly, intellectuals turned out to be among the least able to confront without pain a world from which "the gods have retreated." For many of them, transient political hopes and certainties have taken the place of religious certainties and comforts.[7] As William Kornhauser has noted, "Those who live for and off symbols—the intellectuals—are least able to suffer a vacuum in the symbolic sphere. . . ."[8]

Although it began centuries ago, the most shattering results of secularization may have been felt in the last decades, manifesting themselves in the weakening of values which made life more or less meaningful or acceptable earlier.[9] These developments have been apparent both at times of economic difficulties and during prolonged periods of prosperity. In the first instance, there were no ideological or philosophical buffers helping to explain or rationalize the hardships; in the second, the satisfaction of the most pressing material needs and the attainment of physical security opened up new opportunities for questioning and contemplating the meaning and meaninglessness of life, bereft both of the diverting struggle for essentials and of well-established myths sustaining the individual.

Fourthly, the relatively privileged and leisured condition of many intellectuals has also contributed to estrangement. The systematic generation and articulation of dissatisfaction and frustration, the nurturing and elaboration of ideals and alternatives require time and freedom from pressing material needs and time-consuming routines.

Fifthly, the level of dissatisfaction with the known society and the familiar social arrangements is also bound to rise, and remain high, when the mass media have a vested (commercial) interest in focusing on and colorfully ventilating the defects of society. Intellectuals themselves employed by the mass media also contribute to muckraking for more disinterested reasons, on ideological grounds.[10]

Sixthly, alienation has also been deepened by the demonstrated decline and weakness of authority in most Western countries and especially in the United States. At first glance, this proposition may seem paradoxical as it could also be argued that it was authority (and especially public or political authority) that was weakened by the spread of alienation which involves the denial of legitimacy to authority. Certainly, the two processes, especially in a longer historical perspective, are difficult to separate. Nevertheless, there may be more merit to the first formulation, since there were concrete and specific events and developments that demonstrated the weakness of authority, particularly at the national political level.

Throughout the 1960s and 70s American political elites in particular showed much wavering, uncertainty, and lack of self-confidence. As Shils has pointed out, "An elite which wavers and abdicates responsibility . . . becomes uncertain of its entitlement to legitimacy. If it cannot claim legitimacy for the actions it undertakes, its actions will be ineffective. Ineffectiveness on the part of an elite breeds disrespect and the refusal of legitimacy."[11] The inconclusiveness of the Vietnam War was certainly among the factors weakening the legitimacy of the American political authorities. A government pursuing an immoral or unjust policy effectively, with determination and sense of purpose, often provokes less hostility and criticism than one that pursues morally questionable policies inefficiently and hesitantly. Successful policies tend to become self-validating no matter how dubious they may be morally. Many historical examples support this proposition. The Vietnam War, in addition to its morally questionable aspects, revealed the ineffectiveness of the government and its supposedly most powerful branch, the military. Likewise, as has often been suggested, the assassination of President Kennedy demonstrated the vulnerability of the figures of the highest authority; it was followed by a spate of assassinations of other public figures. These were specific, discrete events which deepened or inspired alienation and contempt for authority rather than the results of prior alienation or contempt for authority.* There is no doubt that the loss of control is by itself a delegitimating factor.

Let us take a final look at the various dimensions of estrangement and its relationship to the criticism of society.

It has been argued earlier that a strongly critical disposition is among the identifying characteristics of the intellectual as he is generally perceived. At what point does such a disposition and the associated political discontent merit the label of alienation? There is no precise boundary to be crossed. It may be agreed that when social criticism and political discontent amount to the unqualified rejection of society, we enter the realm of alienation or estrangement. The contemporary discourse on

---

* More recently the weakness of American political authority and power has been demonstrated by the helplessness in the face of the taking of American hostages in Teheran (preceded over the years by the murder and kidnapping of many other American diplomats abroad). The inability to control inflation may also be seen as a manifestation of the powerlessness of the government.

alienation is replete with tones of reverence. Being alienated has increasingly come to mean, or be associated with, being free, detached, soaring above a degraded social landscape, leaving behind illusions, seeing things as they are, freed from the need for self-deception. It is widely believed that one should be alienated from a corrupt society and from oppressive social institutions.

Erich Fromm, among others, popularized the notion that it is better to be maladjusted to the wrong kind of social institutions than to adjust to them—that conflict between the individual and society is preferable to harmony and a sign of superior mental health, when society itself is sick.[12] Such views are reminiscent of Rousseau's belief in the superiority of basic human nature over smothering social institutions; they also imply the existence of an ineffable essence, an inner sanctum, threatened, and impinged upon by the outside forces. There is also a presupposition of a previous, non-alienated state in Marxist thought.[13] Thus, paradoxically, the concept of alienation may conjure up, despite its manifestly negative content, a deeply, almost religiously optimistic conception of human nature. It has been shared by many thinkers who have otherwise taken a dim view of the state of society and mankind, here and now. Thus for example, "Marcuse, like Rousseau, Marx, Morris, and other utopians before him, would have us believe in a pure, uncorrupted human essence which will re-emerge like the golden stone of old Oxford colleges once centuries of grime have been washed away."[14] David Caute also noted very aptly that alienation fulfills "in modern ideology the same function as the Fall in Christian mythology."[15]

In recent decades the concept of alienation acquired connotations which seem to be associated with the discontents and difficulties peculiar to life in contemporary Western and especially American society. Let us consider Erich Fromm once more (whose ideas on these matters are also very close to those of Marcuse):

> Today we come across a person who acts and feels like an automaton . . . who experiences himself entirely as the person he thinks he is supposed to be; whose artificial smile has replaced genuine laughter; whose meaningless chatter has replaced communicative speech; whose dulled despair has taken the place of genuine pain. . . . What is modern man's relationship to his fellow man? It is one between two abstractions, two living machines, who use each other. . . . Everybody is to everybody else a commodity, always to be treated with certain friendliness, because even if he is not of use now, he may be later. There is not much love or hate to be found in human relations of our day.[16]

This version of alienation has much in common with unspontaneity, role playing, loss of autonomy, conformity, standardization, and especially, the lack of authenticity. In this elaboration, the idea of the alienated human being also resembles a sociological concept of a more recent vintage, that of the "oversocialized" human being similarly lacking in spontaneity, individuality, autonomy, and authenticity.[17] In anthropological language, "alienation" in recent times has been translated into the theme of "culture against man"[18] which, once more, echoes the ancient belief that there is in human beings buried a core of authentic needs and attributes which certain social arrangements and designs satisfy while others frustrate.

Two conclusions may be drawn from these observations. One is that when a concept such as alienation can embrace such a wide variety of meanings and when it lends itself to the depiction of such diverse human conditions, it will be seized upon and put to many uses some of which may seem contradictory. Secondly, the variations in the meaning and connotation of the concept may depend on to which social groups it is applied. It appears almost as if there was a tacit agreement among those using the concept that alienation will mean something different when applied to intellectuals or artists, as against industrial workers, shop assistants, or traveling salesmen. When used to describe the condition of intellectuals, alienation is compatible with authenticity and other desirable attributes. When applied to the masses, its associations tend to be less favorable. Thus, being alienated may have very different meanings; the positive ones usually ascribed to intellectuals include insights into the social-political process or a raised level of consciousness. By contrast, the undesirable aspects of alienation entail apathy, resignation, acceptance of the status quo, and religious (or other types of) escapism, usually ascribed to the masses. Alienated intellectuals also see themselves as standing apart from the blandishments of the powerholders and the temptations of money, status, and easy integration liable to subvert the principled scrutiny and criticism of the workers of society. "Alienated" may thus also mean uncorrupted, idealistic, and honest.

All the positive conceptions and associations of "alienation" imply that it develops in response to objective social conditions, that it emerges for good reasons. The estranged intellectual is fully justified in ceasing to identify with his society; the social critic is critical because there is much to be critical of. This view of alienation is consonant with both the Marxian and Weberian traditions, which seek to account for it with reference to certain objective characteristics of modern society: either economic factors or bureaucratization and rationalization. Both of these theories and traditions have in common the premise that there is something in the nature of the social setting, institutions, or environment *external to the individual* that creates tension and discontent. In short, intellectuals are not born social critics; they become critic₃ of society because of the nature of the social world they experience.[19] As Joseph Adelson, the social psychologist, described it, "the emphasis is constantly external; radical rage is, for example, largely reactive to the moral disarray out there, in the world."[20]

There is however another, diametrically opposed viewpoint (often associated with hostility to intellectuals). Alienation and social criticism, it is held, exist not because things are wrong with society but because something is wrong with the critics. The latter, it is argued, externalize or project their individual problems and discontents on society, seek scapegoats for personal grievances, and deliberately (or unwittingly) blur the boundaries between the personal and social spheres and problems. In some non-Western societies the latter viewpoint has found institutional expression: what is assumed to be personal discontents or aberrations are not allowed public expression. In the Soviet Union the small number of defiant social critics have officially been defined as mentally unbalanced and in need of psychiatric treatment, or at least confinement in psychiatric institutions or mental hospitals.*

While such attempts to define social critics as mentally unbalanced or neurotic are usually related to the desire to discredit and silence them, legitimate questions may be raised about the more subjective or non-political sources of estrangement and social criticism without ascribing emotional or psychic disturbances to the critics. Explanations of intense social criticism need not be reduced to either the belief that such criticism is a purely rational response to the observable and obvious defects of society, or to the view that social criticism is a product of anguished minds bent on distracting attention from their personal problems. E. J. Hobsbawm, the left-wing British social historian, implies such alternatives in criticizing the view according to which "such [Communist] parties attract only the deviant, the psychologically aberrant, or the seeker after some secular religion, the 'opium of intellectuals.' "[22] These strictures, evidently aimed at writers like Gabriel Almond and Raymond

---

* Solzhenitsyn wrote: "His [the social critic's] very sensitivity to injustice, to stupidity, is presented as a morbid deviation, poor adaptation to the social environment . . . apparently to harbour thoughts other than those which are prescribed means that you are abnormal. . . ."[21]

Aron, unnecessarily limit the ways of explaining the attraction of the Communist parties and related causes. Certainly, as far as the intellectuals are concerned, the appeals of communism or socialism (and the antecedent rejection of their non-socialist society) cannot and need not be forced into patterns of "rational" or "irrational." One may deny that alienation and the associated support for Marxist ideas and regimes are the products of murky psychological forces and suspect emotional needs without claiming that these attitudes are merely the result of applying reason to the social environment, or that it is the flaws of the latter which inexorably elicit them. There is simply no clear correlation between the volume and intensity of social criticism and the magnitude of the ills of society being exposed and condemned.

In trying to better understand the relationship between the quantity and quality of criticism and the observable social-political realities it is directed against, one should not overlook certain attributes of the critics and patterns of their lives. In particular, every attempt to account for the nature of social criticism that ignores the conditions which exist for its expression, or the incentives and rewards associated with it, will be seriously deficient. It is obvious and yet often forgotten that the volume and intensity of social criticism are not merely functions of the evils of society being protested but also the possibilities for the expression of such protest. No matter how evil and unjust a social system and how many potential critics it may harbor, if the critics are intimidated or repressed, if they have no vehicles for the expression of their opinions and beliefs, social criticism is unlikely to surface.

The most vital condition necessary for social criticism to exist is not injustice to be decried but the toleration of public criticism. If people cannot criticize social-political conditions without risking death, injury, incarceration, organized ostracism, the loss of employment or housing; if there are no newspapers or television stations to carry their messages (or not even duplicating machines accessible to them); if public gatherings cannot be addressed by the critics—then, no matter how bad a political regime or social system, its injustices will not be heard of except from those who manage to escape from it or succeed in passing on information to foreigners. Thus while the absence or presence of critical publicity shapes the images of a society, it does not by itself provide much help in determining how defective a social system is.

There is certainly more to the intensification of social criticism in Western countries during the last two decades than the growth of social injustices calling for their vigorous denunciation. In American society in particular, social processes have been at work which not only increasingly permit but encourage the public criticism of social institutions, and create a greater readiness to engage in social criticism. The same processes also encourage a tendency to define certain personal problems as social. This is not to suggest that critics are neurotic malcontents whose criticism is a reflection of their personality rather than the social environment. The argument proposed here is sociological (and social psychological): it takes into account both the condition of social institutions and the patterned circumstances of social criticism. The late David M. Potter has offered a similar interpretation:

> the people of previous centuries were repressed people. . . . But although repressed, people in the past abstained from acts of public defiance of the "system" either because of a conscious awareness that such acts would bring swift and harsh punishment or more likely, because they had internalized their own repression through inhibitions.
> . . . Discontent has many sources. One of these is social injustice, which might be called a public source of discontent. But there are many others, some of which may be called private . . .
> . . . This kind of discontent is emotionally generated; it does not recognize its own source and therefore is not specifically directed toward that source but is a free-floating discontent, ready to be discharged as aggression against any object which is not protected by superior strength or by inviolable psychological sanctions. . . . it follows from the above that the degree of discontent in any society is not necessarily correlated to the degree of injustice or evil in the institutions of the society. . . .

Potter further believes that "the sanctions which gave the American society immunity from attack have diminished and the acceptability of the act of rejecting the society has increased." The same might be said about other Western societies as well—British, German, Italian, French, and others—where similar trends, perhaps less advanced, are evident. Potter suggests that the patterns of upbringing and the intensification of social criticism may be interconnected, especially since the 1960s:

> This matter of the process of identity formation is closely related to the problem of the rejection of society; for it appears that traditional processes of developing social identity have tended to produce a high proportion of men and women who attained their identity by adopting, quite readily, the roles which the society expected of them. . . .
> There is considerable evidence that many people today do not, for whatever reason, adopt expected roles and that they react negatively even to behaving as the role which they have adopted, requires them to behave. If the nature of interpersonal relations has changed in a

way that would somehow impair the capacity of human beings to find and form identities compatible with the society in which they live, it would be one of the most crucial factors in explaining the number of people in America who reject the prevailing society.

Deficient identity formation may also produce problems in authority relations: "the society now produced a much increased number of people who were confused as to their identity and who dislike authority, not wanting either to exercise it themselves or let anyone else exercise it."[23]

Although there is no basis for suggesting that the various social processes which may generally undermine identity formation affect intellectuals with special severity, it may be noted that intellectuals often have a particular aversion to being identified with social roles which they consider constricting, artificial, and antithetical to wholeness and authenticity.

Further connections may also be found between the reluctance to accept socially defined roles, the problems of identity, and the growth of individualism. When large numbers of people find it problematic to answer the question "Who am I?" at least in part by enumerating their social roles, and when society allows and even encourages experimentation with various "identities" (which to some extent replace and confuse social roles), discomfort results. Under such conditions the questioning of society will be followed swiftly by its rejection, for it will be held responsible for the difficulty of answering the question: "Who am I?" Richard Lowenthal, discussing the disaffection of Western intellectuals and the cultural crisis of our times, has also noted "the increasingly defective functioning of the processes of socialization and of the formation of identity." He explained the latter by "the loss of traditional ties . . . [that] leaves a gap in identity. It exposes the uprooted individual to the attraction of fictitious ties—say, to the non-existent 'revolutionary world proletariat,' or to the 'liberation movement' of the former colonial nations."[24] Eric Hansen, an American political scientist, has discerned another link between the intellectual's quest for identity and political attitudes: "His [the intellectual's] very obsession with power as an extension of his own quest for identity tends to transform personal anxiety into political activism . . . the intellectual tends to see the world as a great theatre of morality to which he must bring 'commitment.' . . ."[25]

To sum up: it has been argued that at the present time social conditions in American society (and in other Western societies too) favor the public expressions of discontent and social criticism whatever their sources may be. Under such circumstances, there is a growing tendency to redefine the sources of discontent and frustration by attributing public (or social or political) causes to what was at earlier times viewed as private and personal (and non-political).* These tendencies were especially pronounced since the 1960s among those attracted to radical movements, as for example Christopher Lasch has pointed out: "Radical politics filled empty lives, provided a sense of meaning and purpose . . .", "The left has too often served as a refuge from the terrors of inner life."[26]

One may detect other sources of social criticism and estrangement which have little to do with social injustice or the distribution of good and evil in society. Schumpeter, for example, believes (as has been noted earlier) that capitalist society invites criticism by creating certain spiritual hungers it cannot gratify. He concluded very much like Potter that "it is an error to believe that political attack arises primarily from grievance [meaning political or economic grievance of the more tangible kind] and that it can be turned by justification. Political criticism [of this kind] cannot be met effectively by rational argument."[27] More recently, Irving Kristol argued that capitalist society cannot legitimate itself in psychologically or emotionally satisfactory ways.[28] A similar argument has been made by Daniel Bell in his exploration of "the cultural contradictions of capitalism," which manifest themselves in the clash between the needs of the psyche and those of the place of work and the political arena, or in the disjunction of values which govern personal and cultural life, as against those of the marketplace and the polity.[29]

Such assessments of capitalism are quite venerable even if their consequences have been more momentous of late. Both Marx and Durkheim recognized the subversive nature of the values of capitalism and of the corrosive character of economic rationality, or, more generally, of

---

* For instance, whereas not so long ago marital disputes were usually viewed as primarily personal problems, today we are tempted to consider them reflections of more widespread social, even political, conditions having to do, among other things, with the inequalities of women and their desire to overcome them. Likewise, homosexuality used to be viewed as a sexual preference rather than a political cause. The tendency to depersonalize (or politicize) personal problems and conflicts (note, for example, the feminist term, "the politics of housework") is also related to the contemporary predisposition to invoke social factors, indeed social determinism, in the explanation of an increasingly broad range of personal problems. What is paradoxical in all this is the current combination of belief in social determination *and* the simultaneous affirmation of individualism and individual rights, especially self-expression. What legitimately constitutes self-expression has also been redefined. Self-expression, cousin of individualism, has become, in turn, a new and important justification for many forms of behavior which at other times were reserved for the aristocracy (titled or moneyed), bohemians, and "certified" deviants.

the process of modernization, which leads to the decline of taken-for-granted legitimating myths and beliefs.

Thus capitalist societies engender hostility in intellectuals partly because they cannot meet their needs for meaning and purpose in life—an incentive to hostility quite different from the discernment of exploitation and other forms of social injustice. Thus alienated social criticism is often or in part a reaction to the frustration of the religious (meaning-seeking) impulse for which the critic blames the social environment. Weber's discussion of the intellectual's pursuit of "salvation" further illuminates these roots of political discontent, and of the rejection of society:

> The salvation sought by the intellectual is always based on inner need, and hence it is at once more remote from life, more theoretical and more systematic than salvation from external distress, the quest for which is characteristic of nonprivileged classes. The intellectual seeks in various ways . . . to endow his life with a pervasive meaning. . . . As intellectualism suppresses belief in magic, the world's processes become disenchanted, lose their magical significance. . . . As a consequence there is a growing demand that the world and the total pattern of life be subject to an order that is significant and meaningful.

> That conflict of this requirement of meaningfulness with the empirical realities of the world and its institutions . . . are responsible for the intellectual's characteristic flights from the world.[30]

Developing a critical disposition because society does not meet one's need for meaning in life is not, in the usual sense, politically motivated social criticism. In other words I am again suggesting that the contemporary rejection of Western societies by many intellectuals is one of the delayed fruits of secularization* which has created a predisposition to political-social criticism, even though the social and political factors themselves are not the basic source of these criticisms. The links between secularization and alienation (and the attendant susceptibility to secular religious ideologies) are further illuminated in these comments of Lowenthal:

> the end of the certainty of a value-oriented historical process means more than the mere loss of a great hope. It confronts the individual with a world that has become increasingly incomprehensible and menacing . . . without the support of a simplifying world view.

---

* "Delayed" because, as Lowenthal points out, "secularization did not immediately produce that experience of a loss of meaning because transcendent faith was at first replaced in its function of giving meaning to everyday life by a secular belief in Progress in this world. . . ."[31]

. . . That anxiety is the direct root of the desperate readiness to look for the missing certainty in a doctrine that expresses a belief in secular salvation in a rationally disguised form. . . .[32]

Schumpeter draws attention to another dimension of secularization: "Secular improvement is taken for granted and coupled with individual insecurity that is acutely resented is of course the best recipe for breeding social unrest." In turn, Robert Nisbet has argued that various forms of political alienation (and commitment) had moral rather than material sources: "the typical convert to communism [in the West] is a person for whom the processes of ordinary existence are morally empty and spiritually insupportable. His own alienation is translated into the perceived alienation of the many."[33]

It may be noted here that the apparently insufficient alienation of the Western masses, of ordinary people, and especially the working classes, has for some time been a source of chagrin for alienated social critics (whatever explanation they provided for it), including such figures as Lenin, Sartre, Marcuse, and C. Wright Mills.[34]

While a sense of spiritual emptiness and frustrated quest for purpose in life are undoubtedly associated with the rejection of society by intellectuals, it has also been proposed that less praiseworthy motives play a part. Thus Eric Hoffer has written: "there is a deep-seated craving common to almost all men of words which determines their attitude to the prevailing order. It is a craving for recognition; a craving for a clearly marked status above the common run of humanity."[35] Hoffer suggests that intellectuals evaluate society on the basis of the recognition it bestows on them. It is possible that the frustrated longing for power adds special tone and intensity to the estrangement of the intellectual as it betokens the inability to implement a rich store of ideas and high-minded projects. Hoffer has not been alone in suggesting that intellectuals become alienated when their talents are unrecognized and unrewarded, when they are unattached, unintegrated, marginal, lacking in status, influence, or even decent employment. Social criticism resting on such foundations would be a reasonably rational response to the condition of such intellectuals; through their own status they become sensitized to the other defects of their society, which may or may not be related to their personal fortunes.

Such an explanation will not carry much weight in regard to most of the intellectuals considered in this volume, and many others whose views were not cited. Few of our intellectuals were unattached, marginal, poorly integrated, or deprived in any objective, observable sense.

Most of them were well-known authors, academics, influential journalists, some of them celebrities and recipients of social honors in their own societies. Their work and views were far from ignored, their talents far from unappreciated. If they felt deprived or marginal, this was usually a matter of relative deprivation or perceived marginality. Status deprivation and marginality (of a more objective kind) were not significant factors in the generation of discontent, social criticism, and estrangement among our political pilgrims.[36] On the contrary, sometimes it appears that many critically disposed intellectuals discover an additional source of unease and moral burden in their respectable social status and excellent material conditions for which they try to compensate by redoubled criticism of the social order that "feeds them" so well—as if to make sure that nobody will accuse them of having been "co-opted" or of having "sold out."* Arguments stressing the marginality of intellectuals (as the explanation of their estrangement) have also become undermined by the development in recent decades of large, influential subcultures of alienation (usually in academic settings) which provide a secure basis of solidarity and support for estranged intellectuals in Western societies. Under such conditions it is increasingly difficult to associate and explain their attitudes with reference to social isolation, defensiveness, and marginality. The critics of the status quo in our times (in Western societies at any rate) are at least as influential as the defenders of the established order. Alienation and non-conformity parted company in the course of the 1960s, if not earlier.

Eric Hansen in his discussion of the political attitudes of intellectuals provides further clues for a better understanding of their impatience with the world as it is. He writes: "the life style of the intellectuals is marked by a relative lack of concern (and even contempt) for the immediate, the practical and the concrete. The intellectuals tend to be ends-oriented." Their idealism or "end orientation" leads to a certain lack of balance, to what Hansen calls "the tendency to merge the real and the ideal"—a capacity of particular significance in the perception of the idealized societies. But the tendency to merge the real and ideal is

---

* There is also unease among certain intellectuals on account of the contrast between their self-image as ally of the downtrodden masses and their often privileged and comfortable circumstances of life. This may lead to the type of compensatory behavior observed, for example, in Chapter 2 with reference to Sartre and his urge to prostrate himself, symbolically speaking, before the masses, the proletariat, the peasants of the Third World, minority groups, or The People. (It will also be recalled that "All Power to the People" was a favorite slogan of American middle- and upper-middle-class radicals in the 1960s.)

also consequential in the development of social criticism and alienation. The intellectual's own familiar society becomes, as it were, a negative ideal, the polar opposite of the social and political goodness he is thirsting for. He will project on his own society all the ugliness of the real world and exaggerate its flaws.

These tendencies are also closely related to the rejection of the empirical fragments of life and the capacity, sometimes overdeveloped in intellectuals, to take a "broader view" of things, to integrate—and over-integrate—social realities so that they conform to more orderly and intellectually coherent patterns:

> The quest for the "holy" (wholeness) may be especially marked among those whose lives are lived in the tension between intellect and intelligence, between interiorizing and exteriorizing, between the real and the ideal. The orientation toward the sacred is the imperative of those whose metabolism with reality is most tenuous. . . .[37]

The propensity of intellectuals to synthesize, combine, discern relationships and interdependencies (where none may exist), their dislike of compartmentalization and their desire to take an "organic" view of life (which implies that things hang together, add up to something)—all these are ways of attempting to make sense of the world. Such inclinations reflect revulsion from disorder, fragmentation, and what they imply: meaninglessness. Behind these attitudes there is also the determination to avoid being simple-minded by accepting the world as it appears to be. The overintegrated and "organic" perception of the world expresses the intellectuals' striving not only for meaning but also harmony. These attitudes are exemplified by Daniel Berrigan's insistence (quoted before in another context) that "the American ghetto and the Hanoi 'operation' were a single enterprise . . ."; or by Susan Sontag treating as "self-evident" the "organic connection" between the *Reader's Digest*, Lawrence Welk (a television program), Hilton Hotels, and napalming; or by Norman Mailer conjuring up from a slice of tasteless bread the following vision:

> The sliced loaf half-collapsed in its wax paper was the comic embodiment now of a dozen little ideas, of corporation land which took the taste and crust out of bread and wrapped the remains in wax paper, and was, *at the far extension of this same process, the same mentality* which was out in Asia escalating, defoliating . . . the white bread was also television . . . the white bread was the infiltrated enemy who had a grip on them everywhere . . .[38]

The emphasis on what Hansen has called "ends-orientation" also helps to explain the peculiar hostility of so many intellectuals toward pluralistic, democratic, and capitalist societies—three attributes which have historically hung together. "Democracy is not ends-oriented," and it is incapable of providing the citizen, and the intellectual, with binding recommendations about the meaning of life. "The intellectual distrusts [democratic] politicians and politics because these are concerned with partial solutions, with conflict resolution."[39] By the same token, many intellectuals admire the political leaders of totalitarian societies who offer total solutions, not compromises, bargains, or "options." (G. D. H. Cole, the English economist and social-philosopher, wrote: "Much better to be ruled by Stalin than by a pack of half-witted and half-hearted Social-Democrats.")[40]

Hansen is one of those who perceive a self-liquidating, self-destructive impulse among the non-political (and non-rational) ingredients of the alienation of intellectuals: "the intellectual seems possessed of a death wish: he craves a society where his creative, critical role will have no use . . . intellectuals like Sartre and Picasso sympathize with Communist systems which would be the first to dispense with their particular geniuses."[41] Scott Nearing, the venerable American radical, was described as "a man who welcomed his own executioners," having acknowledged that "if the Communists took control in this country [he] would be one of the first to be executed."[42]

I have tried to make certain distinctions between the sources of estrangement which can be found in the nature of society—and especially in its moral defects—and those which spring from the predispositions and certain attributes of intellectuals. I have argued that the mainsprings of estrangement and the associated social criticism need not invariably arise from the ascertainable shortcomings of social institutions but have also much to do with the ease with which they can be expressed and with the cultural (or subcultural) rewards available for such critical attitudes. I also suggested that the social criticism of intellectuals, for the reasons noted above, differs from those of other, less privileged groups. Finally, I wished to convey that, while the discontents of intellectuals do have social roots, this is not to say that they merely respond to the observable ills of society. The sources of their discontents are deeper and more diffuse than found in other reaches of society. Perhaps Saul Bellow's Herzog put his finger on something important when he noted that "the chief ambiguity that afflicts intellectuals . . . is that civilized individuals hate and resent the civilization that makes their lives possible. What they love is an imaginary human situation invented by their own genius and which they believe is the only true and the only human reality. How odd!"[43] Much of this book could be viewed as an examination of some of the contemporary attempts of intellectuals to overcome this ambiguity.

Revising the Concept of the Intellectual

Have the findings of this study supported the suggestion made early in this book that the conception of the intellectual needs revision? There is little doubt that the accounts of the political pilgrimages, in the 1930s as much as in the 1960s (and 1970s), call into question the widely held belief that being of a critical mind is an essential attribute of intellectuals or, as Edward Shils put it, that they are possessed of an "interior need to penetrate beyond the screen of immediate concrete experience. . . ."[44] On the contrary it was the all too willing suspension of disbelief that characterized many Western intellectuals in these periods, as they quite readily exchanged their more traditional role of hardbitten social critic to that of the trustful admirer, and as their more typical stance of skeptical questioning gave way to zealous affirmation. It should be clear by now that the wish to believe marks the attitudes of intellectuals as much as the need to criticize, negate, or reject. It is the alternation of these two diametrically opposed dispositions that is characteristic of intellectuals rather than a predominance of the critical impulse. There is ample evidence in this study to suggest that the critical component in the make-up of intellectuals has been greatly exaggerated and that its operation is just as dependent on their basic values and predispositions as is the case with other mortals. Certainly in a social setting that they are predisposed to dislike or be suspicious of (usually their own society), intellectuals are intensely and often insightfully critical. But such critical capabilities are not necessarily transferable to other settings, however inviting targets they are for the exercise of the critical faculties.

This study suggests that it is the appeals and values associated with socialism which have provided the most powerful incentive for the suspension of critical thinking among large contingents of Western intellectuals over the last half century.[45] Such intellectuals appear to assume an affirming, supportive stance as soon as a political system (or movement) makes an insistent enough claim to its socialist character.° Philip Rahv asked: "Is it possible that all these years radicals the world over have been imposed upon, ensnared by an elementary plot of mistaken identity? . . . Can it be that it is taken for socialism simply because it represents itself as such and because it seems *different?*"[47] The word "socialism" has retained, despite all historical disappointments associated with regimes calling themselves socialist, a certain magic which rarely fails to disarm or charm these intellectuals and which inspires renewed hopes that its most recent incarnation will be *the* authentic one, or at least more authentic than previous ones had been.[48] (There is little evidence that intellectuals, or for that matter, non-intellectuals, living in countries considered socialist are similarly charmed or disarmed by the idea of socialism.)

The *idea* of socialism continues to capture many discontents today, as it had around the turn of the century when Emile Durkheim wrote: "It is a fervor that has been the inspiration of all these systems [of thought associated with socialism]; what gave them life and strength is a thirst for a more perfect justice. . . . Socialism is not a science . . . it is a cry of grief, sometimes of anger, uttered by men who feel most keenly our collective *malaise*."[49] More recently, Orwell observed in a lighter vein: "One sometimes gets the impression that the mere words 'Socialism' and 'Communism' draw towards them with magnetic force every fruit-juice drinker, nudist, sandal-wearer, sex-maniac, Quaker, 'Nature Cure' quack, pacifist and feminist in England."[50] Certainly every country the appeals of which were examined in this volume laid claim to the title of "socialist," and in each instance intellectuals succumbed to the temptation to project upon these political systems attributes they did not possess but which are associated with the ideals of socialism.

Central to the appeals of socialism is the promise and expectation that it can and will bring about better material living conditions in com-

---

° The appeals of socialism are also among the explanations of the tenaciousness of the sentiments denoted by the term "anti-anti-communism." To the extent that the concepts of socialism and communism are closely linked and to the extent that socialism continues to partake of the notion of the sacred (or selfless—as opposed to the "profaneness" of capitalism), anti-communism is abhorrent. While anti-communism provokes strong moral revulsion, the various incarnations of communism may only elicit the expression of mild distaste or somewhat abstract disavowal. While the juices of moral fervor flow when the specter of anti-communism is raised, communism itself remains something of a dim abstraction saved from total disrepute by the political profiles of those opposing it. Or, as Lionel Trilling put it, although "one need not be actually *for* Communism, one was morally compromised, turned toward evil and away from good, if one was against it."[46]

bination with the maintenance (or renewal) of community and thus provide the blessings of technology, industry, and urban life without the ruptures, conflicts, and disturbances associated with them under capitalism.[51] Peter Clecak, an American social historian, commented of these long-standing appeals of socialism:

> [socialism] was above all a dream *against* boundaries, a recurrent protest against separations, divisions, distinctions. Behind every manifestation lay the wish to restore lost unities, to go beyond painful divisions within the self and conflicts with others. Socialism embodies a wish to return to a condition of wholeness that existed, or was assumed to exist . . . before the Fall, before the plunge into history. Though ultimately psychological and aesthetic in its concern with order, harmony and unity, the socialist dream was made visible most powerfully in theological terms, primarily through Judeo-Christian imagery.

Bernard Henri Levy, one of the French "new philosophers," has also reached the conclusion (as his senior fellow Frenchman, Raymond Aron, had decades earlier) that "Marxism is the religion of our time . . ." and that "it is not enough to say that Marxism is a caricature of Christianity. Marxism, more fundamentally, has become Christianity's current stand-in. . . ."[52]

Even abundant consumption would be free of guilt under socialism (or communism) as the stigma of self-centeredness would be removed from such pleasures in a social context purified of individualism, greed, calculation, and the yearning for material and status gain. The susceptibility to all these promises of socialism suggests a vigorous optimism about the perfectibility of both human nature and social institutions which contrasts sharply with the gloom and pessimism which pervade Western intellectuals when they contemplate human behavior and social institutions in their own societies.

Any belief system, or set of doctrines which lends itself to the interpretations or projections noted above is particularly powerful at times when traditional religions fail to satisfy the need for meaning and purpose. As Gustave Le Bon pointed out almost a century ago, "in order that Socialism . . . might assume so quickly that religious form which constitutes the secret of its power, it was necessary that it should appear at one of these rare moments of history when the old religions lose their might . . . and exist only on sufferance while awaiting the new faith that is to succeed them." The ceaseless theoretical efforts of many contemporary Western intellectuals aimed at revising, rejuvenating, or rehabilitating and applying Marxism, the main doctrinal source of socialism, testify to its powerful and enduring appeals as much as the political pilgrimages to the countries calling themselves socialist. Bernard Henri Levy wrote: "We have a Marxist urbanism, a Marxist psychoanalysis, a Marxist aesthetic, a Marxist numismatics. There is no longer any realm of knowledge that Marxism fails to have a look at, no area off limits, no taboo territory . . . no cultural fronts to which it fails to send cohorts of researchers. . . ."[53]

Thus in our times the wish to believe on the part of intellectuals has found its most characteristic expression in the wish to believe in some variety of Marxism, or embodiment of socialism. Octavio Paz, the well-known Mexican writer, remarked that "Marxism has become an intellectual vice. It is the superstition of the 20th century."[54]

The capacity to cast aside critical faculties in exchange for credulity and unrestrained admiration is not the only trait that has to be entered into the revised conception of the intellectual. There may also be new grounds for wondering about the attributions of idealism and disinterestedness* in the light of the evidence presented in this study and found elsewhere. To be sure, the idealism of intellectuals has been disputed before. In the words of Irving Louis Horowitz, the American sociologist, Western intellectuals engaged in "myopic moral bookkeeping," the roots of which could be traced to self-interest.[56] George Watson, the English literary historian, has expressed still stronger doubts about both the idealism and integrity of many Western intellectuals in his examination of their attitudes toward the outrages connected with Stalinism. He argues that such intellectuals favored Soviet society in the 1930s not out of ignorance of its true character, but well aware of the repression and political violence that prevailed at the time. They were willing to rationalize these policies and events partly because of the instrumental view taken of them and partly because of a deeper attraction to political violence—also discernible in the 1960s when quite a few intellectuals regarded violence as a form of authentic self-expression and the ultimate proof of serious commitment to higher purpose.[57]

Attributions of idealism and disinterestedness also call for re-examination when intellectuals move with lightning speed from vehement moral indignation and moral absolutism (generally reserved for their own

---

* Not infrequently, intellectuals themselves are prone to such flattering self-attributions. Thus, for example, Daniel Berrigan wrote of himself and Howard Zinn, another anti-war activist and professor at Boston University: "Like all resisters, we are afflicted beyond remedy with the idealism of which we read so often in our history." He saw himself and Zinn as "Men of truth, who constantly search their own motivation and hearts. . . ."[55]

society) to a strangely pragmatic moral relativism brought to the assessment of policies of countries they are committed to support. As a character in Lionel Trilling's novel said of Soviet policies: "certain things could not be judged by mere liberal standards."[58] Scott Nearing, "who often left his home in Maine in November rather than watch hunters kill deer, defended Soviet tanks in Budapest [in 1956]. 'Hungarian white guardists, exiled for a decade from their motherland,' he explained, 'were joining the rebels to fight for the restoration of their property. . . .' "[59] Such misjudgments and moral double "bookkeeping" (or double standards) are in part due to the readiness to believe the "other side," in this case the Soviet tales of the white guardists, however implausible they were in the light of all other information about the revolt. Since Nearing wished to rationalize Soviet behavior, his acceptance of the Soviet view of events made it easier to do so. Obviously he felt no need to subject such views to the same scrutiny he would have undertaken of the American reports and interpretations of various political events. Nearing's moral absolutism led him to reject American society, while his moral pragmatism enabled him to temper his judgment of the policies of the regimes he basically approved of. Thus the circle was complete: moral principles and scruples with which he had started out could safely be suspended when seemingly moral objectives were pursued—moral relativism could now be substituted for moral absolutes. Stephen Spender has explained such attitudes by suggesting that "all human beings have an extremely intermittent grasp on reality. Only a few things, which illustrate their own interests and ideas, are real to them; other things, which are in fact equally real, appear to them as abstractions."[60] If so, self-interest may be the key to selective perception.

Another myth to be laid to rest is the belief in the unflinching commitment of intellectuals to freedom, and particularly freedom of expression. The survey of the appeals of the countries discussed in earlier chapters makes it very clear that the absence of freedoms, as commonly understood, hardly concerned the visitors or interfered with the attractions of these societies. To the extent that the lack of free expression was observed—and it is by itself noteworthy how frequently it was overlooked—it was excused or rationalized on the familiar grounds of temporary necessity, amply compensated for by the various achievements of the regimes concerned. As Nicola Chiaromonte, the Italian critic, has put it, "intellectuals in the West either overlook or do not even see the capital importance of the resurgence of the demand for freedom in a situation in which it should theoretically no longer be necessary because of its replacement by 'concrete freedoms.'" Many Western intellectuals prefer such "concrete" or, in the usage of Isaiah Berlin, "positive" freedoms, and minimize the importance of "negative" freedom, including free expression, in societies they admire from a distance—or on the occasion of a visit. This may in part be ascribed to a form of cultural relativism. Yet, Chiaromonte is right in asserting that "the worst insult we can cast on an individual who is poor and oppressed is to presume that all he wants is work, food, clothes, lodging and entertainment."[61] Western intellectuals devalue negative freedoms, including that of expression, partly because it is available for them and thus can be taken for granted and partly because by themselves they fail to satisfy the need for meaning.

Certainly the pursuit of a meaningful life on an *ad hoc*, individual basis, unaided by external agencies or authorities, is difficult and discouraging in a capitalist, commercial, and thoroughly profane society. Evidently intellectuals have an especially strong need to escape the profane. Socialism, or what goes by the name of socialism, still offers, after many historical disappointments, a myth, a way out. The grass seems greener on the other side, in societies which legitimate themselves by high ideals and appeal to (and promise) community, brotherhood, wholeness, social justice, equality, and selflessness; they offer some shared forms of self-transcendence. The attractions of socialism used to be very similar for East European intellectuals:

> A scientifically ordered society held great attractions for the Eastern European intelligentsia [wrote George Konrád and Ivan Szelényi, two Hungarian sociologists], as did the fact that intellectuals were being called upon for their expert knowledge in the construction of the new social order. . . . From now on the people with the requisite professional knowledge would be the ones to make the decisions. It gratified them to think that knowledge not property would legitimize the right to make decisions. . . . The intellectuals hailed their new situation as the realization of their own transcendence. They could finally rise above the service of particular interests . . . their . . . work . . . acquired a transcendent meaning. It was ennobled, elevated from a money-making profession into a calling.[62]

Virtually all the suggested revisions of the concept of the intellectual revolve around the unstable equilibrium between his critical and affirming impulses and activities. It will be recalled that one of the first questions raised in this study and one of its points of departure were related to these contrasts. We must once more return to the concept of double standards which underlies and helps to explain the fluctuation between the critical and uncritical attitudes, belief and disbelief, moral absolutism and moral relativism (or as Ernst Fisher, the German ex-Communist, put it, "the length to which a man can go, who, though neither stupid nor vicious, deliberately ceases to see, to listen, to think critically . . . so as not to doubt the cause he serves . . .").[63]

It is not being suggested here that estranged intellectuals are more prone to use double standards than anyone else. I believe however that their propensity to do so is both more conspicuous and more consequential because they are more vocal, more articulate, and more disposed to the public expression of moral judgments than most other people, and because they have better access to the mass media to disseminate such judgments. Holding double standards is not a singular attribute and failing of liberal-radical intellectuals; however they provide an outstanding contemporary example of a tendency that is deeply ingrained in all of us.

What then are some of the ways in which double standards operate? The variations in the handling of moral indignation or outrage—especially on occasions when their expression would seem highly warranted—allow for a close examination of the techniques employed to defuse or stifle such impulses. Evidently people invest as much effort in suppressing moral indignation or compassion as they do in expressing it. The application of double standards is central to this process.

Probably the most basic technique, or the first line of defense, is disclaiming information.[64] As noted earlier, when people don't wish to be indignant about some atrocity, the first reaction is to deny its existence, minimize it, or cast doubt on the reliability of sources reporting it—as, for example, Noam Chomsky's questioning the reliability of refugee reports of atrocities in Cambodia he would rather not hear of. People also try (and often succeed) in systematically avoiding information that might provoke a sense of outrage and create conflict between their ideological (or value) commitments and the particular incidents or facts undermining such commitments. (E.g., Jane Fonda and Mary McCarthy obviously did not favor torture but were supportive of and sympathetic toward the Vietcong or North Vietnamese; such support would have been more difficult to sustain if atrocities committed by them were fully confronted and acknowledged.)[65] Disclaiming information, strictly speaking, does not involve double standards, since the removal or denial of morally problematic information also removes the necessity to judge similar events by different standards. The only sense in which double standards are used in this context pertains to the evaluation of evidence, which will at times be rigorous and skeptical (as for instance in the case of the Cambodian anti-communist refugees) but relaxed and trusting when the evidence offered is supportive of existing bias or predisposition (when, let us say, other groups of refugees report some brutal military action taken by the armed forces of the United States). Robert Conquest noted this attitude in another historical context when Sartre evidently accepted the reliability of the accounts of the victims of French torture in Algeria but needed official Soviet confirmation of repression under Stalin. An earlier statement of Sartre's may help to clarify his double standard: "As we were neither members of the party nor avowed sympathizers it was not our duty to write about Soviet labour camps; we were free to remain aloof from quarrel over the nature of this system, provided no events of sociological significance had occurred."[66]

The disclaiming of information must be distinguished from plain ignorance. One cannot overestimate the significance of ignorance about the political systems intellectuals evaluated, which has greatly contributed to the massive misapprehension of their actual character. Most of the travelers knew little about the facts of political violence and coercion, of the privileges of elite groups, the oppressive outpouring of propaganda, the enormous and stultifying bureaucracies, of all the large gaps between theory and practice, evidence of which so disturbed them in their own societies. Lack of information and lack of imagination often went hand in hand. It was hard to learn about things which were also hard to imagine—Show Trials, large-scale forced population movements, the pervasiveness of controls in daily life, the elaborate re-creations of reality by propaganda or the possibility of widespread intimidation without overt, observable violence. Even if our intellectuals would have availed themselves of what Koestler has called the "shock therapy of facts,"[67] one may wonder how much of an impression this would have made without the imaginative identification required for their proper appreciation. For the most part, however, there was no such "therapy," and ignorance smoothed the path toward belief and admiration. And few efforts were made to disturb the harmony of belief and "knowledge." Most people, including intellectuals, are not eager to bring about the grinding confrontation (or "dissonance") between established and sustaining beliefs and facts or information which cast doubt upon them.[68]

As was observed earlier, another major technique available to deal

with such difficulties is the contextual redefinition of particular unappealing policies or acts of the otherwise appealing regimes or political
actors.* This technique is sometimes combined with the effort at "understanding" the morally questionable incident—an effort, needless to
say, selectively made. (William M. Kunstler, the radical lawyer, said
"he thinks he can 'understand the reasoning' behind the Vietnamese government's decision to force so-called 'war criminals' to search for mines
left over from the war. 'It's part of a terrible, terrible time,' he added.")[70]

When these mechanisms come into play, the favorably predisposed
observer withholds outright approval but mitigates or neutralizes the
sense of outrage by pointing to the over-all context in which the morally
unsupportable actions have taken place. Expediency and legitimation by
reference to the future typically underlie this type of justification. As
Stephen Spender has described it: "Someday, somewhere, everything
would add up to the happy total. . . . The argument of an abstract sum
held in one's mind, which cancels out all lesser considerations. . . ."[71]
If a political system is "basically" good or "headed in the right direction," that is, if the over-all context is praiseworthy (a circumstance usually deduced from the public expression of its good intentions), dissonant details must be excused and accommodated; denied and dismissed
if possible, reluctantly confronted if unavoidable but put into the "proper
context," that is, deprived of significance in the shaping of moral judgment. Many intellectuals are highly susceptible to the profession of certain types of good intentions which regimes calling themselves "socialist" regularly do. When contextual justifications are resorted to, moral
accountability is reduced not so much by the outright denial of the morally repugnant qualities of the actions or policies involved, but by
stressing the circumstances surrounding them. Similarly, the past or
the future may also provide some form of contextual vindication. Remarkably, many Western intellectuals seem to share the propensity attributed to Lenin and his followers, namely to divorce unsavory means
from the purity of the ends they were supposed to promote.[72]

In our times when so many people, and especially intellectuals, are
haunted by the fear of inauthenticity, moral outrages committed in a
spirit of passion and dedicated sincerity are more readily excused than

---

* Thus, for instance, Staughton Lynd and Tom Hayden explained the North Vietnamese atrocities committed during the collectivization of agriculture (delicately referred to as "The events of 1956"): "We suggest that this episode should be
viewed as an extension of the war against the French and the violence involved
should be assessed in the same context as the terror of the resistance itself."[69]

equally repellent acts carried out with insufficient conviction. Again, good intentions under such circumstances seem more important than unpleasant consequences; idealistic motives provide absolution from harsh moral judgment. In particular, the mystique of revolutionary (or purifying) violence, that is, the violence of the best intentions, has had a great appeal to Western intellectuals and correspondingly had a lesser moral stigma attached to it.[73]

Another venerable and well-known technique of silencing potential moral indignation consists of dehumanizing the victim. In doing so, the morally repugnant acts are not denied but are made irrelevant—they do not count since the victims do not inhabit a moral universe, as it were; therefore, moral considerations or criteria simply do not apply to them, and those committing the moral outrages are freed of responsibility and compassion by the redefinition of their victims as non-human, or negligibly human. Contemporary history and especially the propaganda and terror campaigns of totalitarian states provide an abundance of examples of mass murder preceded by dehumanization. The essence of this technique is the substitution of abstractions for real human beings—a process observed by Aldous Huxley (and others) decades ago. He wrote:

> when particular men and women are thought of merely as representatives of a class, which has previously been defined as evil . . . then the reluctance to hurt or murder disappears. Brown, Jones and Robinson are no longer thought of as Brown, Jones and Robinson, but as heretics, gentiles, Yids, niggers, barbarians, Huns, communists, capitalists, fascists, liberals—whichever the case may be. When they have been called such names and assimilated to the accursed class to which the names apply, Brown, Jones and Robinson cease to be conceived as what they really are—human persons—and become for users of this fatally inappropriate language mere vermin or worse, demons, whom it is right and proper to destroy. . . . Wherever persons are present, questions of morality arise. . . .[74]

(Calling policemen "pigs," popular among many Western radicals in the 1960s, is another example of this phenomenon.)

Finally, there is the mechanism of selective determinism[75] which of late has come to play a prominent part in generating selective moral indignation (and compassion) while exemplifying the use of double standards. Selective social determinism may be viewed as a variant of the contextual justification as it also strives to diminish the responsibility of the wrongdoer (assuming some acknowledgment of "wrongs").

While some degree of the social-cultural (or environmental) determination of human behavior has always been a major theme of the social sciences, what is relatively new in American and other Western societies at present is the extent to which this message has found popular acclaim, the directness with which it has been applied to personal problems, and the selectivity with which it has been used. The determinism popular among many intellectuals in our times proposes (or implies) that only the behavior of the "underdogs" is socially determined and hence *their* responsibility for their actions and attendant moral accountability are reduced. Thus determinism is selectively applied to excuse, mitigate, or condemn morally questionable acts on the part of different groups. Since moral outrage presupposes choice on the part of those who provoke our indignation, a plausible victim-aggressor scheme needs a device, such as selective social determinism, that relieves some groups of responsibility for their behavior but not others, again giving rise to double standards. Not surprisingly, "The rhetoric of oppressed groups is always accepted at face value; their grievances are what they perceive them to be, their motives exactly what they claim." Whereas those not in the underdog-victim category "are always believed to have hidden intentions which need to be ferreted out. . . ."[76]

While selective determinism and the application of double standards may be traced to the way in which the victims or underdogs are identified, there is no longer a broad consensus among Western intellectuals as to the designation of deserving underdogs and authentic victims. Such definitions and designations are not always based on indisputable historical-political evidence but often are rather idiosyncratic, emotional, or dated. One person's underdog is another person's topdog, and disputes attend to the establishment of widely acceptable oppressor-victim hierarchies.

A letter published on the correspondence page of the New York *Times* exemplifies these attitudes in another context:

> Listening to the stories behind each hijacker [of airplanes] points to a recurrent theme of frustration: to the hijacker the hijacking seems to represent a last, desperate effort for personal integrity. . . . It saddens me to hear these frightened, despondent men sentenced to more of the same despondency for 20 years. Perhaps an understanding of the man behind the act will calm our outrage in the hope that a potential hijacker can feel that the people of this nation empathize with him and with his economic and personal frustration and despondency.[77]

Selective determinism is a relatively novel and sophisticated mechanism for neutralizing moral indignation (or enhancing compassion) which emerged from both the popularization of the social sciences and the propensity to social criticism. Social criticism if passionately felt and expressed must clearly focus both on those responsible for the defects of society and those who bear the price of such defects.

A contemplation of double standards may lead one to conclude that the very idea of *moral* outrage and compassion needs re-examination when it can have so many meanings and when on so many occasions the moral impulse can be stifled or inflamed, qualified, rationalized, legitimated or delegitimated in forever more ingenious ways. Certainly this study offers little support for belief in a universal, pure, or impartial moral impulse. On the contrary it appears that the intensity of moral sentiments, and especially of moral indignation and compassion, is far more significantly determined by the identity of the actors engaged in the morally reprehensible acts (and by that of their victims) than by the acts themselves. To the extent that these actors are regarded with sympathy or hatred respectively, similar acts will be perceived and judged differently, defined or redefined as more or less evil. Intellectuals and non-intellectuals alike are prone to these attitudes.[78]

By contrast, Stephen Spender's retrospective soul-searching illustrates what a disinterested moral sensibility may mean:

> When I saw photographs of children murdered by the Fascists, I felt furious pity. When the supporters of Franco talked of Red atrocities, I merely felt indignant that people should tell such lies. In the first case I saw corpses, in the second only words. However . . . I gradually acquired a certain horror of the way in which my own mind worked. It was clear to me that unless I cared about every murdered child impartially, I did not really care about children being murdered at all.[79]

To say that what we are witnessing in connection with the proliferation of double standards is merely a resurgent relativization of secular morality, or that it is all a part of the contemporary fragmentation of values, is a somewhat inadequate explanation of these attitudes. It is inadequate because alongside relativization there may also be observed a determined search for moral absolutes and certainties.[80] It seems as if the moral relativism in the West has given rise to new quests for moral certainties (sometimes through revolutionary politics, sometimes religious cults) which, in turn, breed new forms of moral relativism in all those situations which present the classical dilemma of ends and means.

The proposed revision of the conventional wisdom about intellectuals has been based on three approaches not all of which have been given equal and sufficient attention in the extensive literature on intellectuals.

Much has been written about the marginality, the poor integration or detachment of intellectuals in Western societies. I have noted that these observations are historically dated, representing something of a cultural lag, as intellectuals are no longer marginal or unattached in Western societies, although they often continue to see themselves in such terms.

A certain amount of attention has been given to the alleged power-hunger of intellectuals, or the "philosopher/king syndrome." Certainly a sense of entitlement to influence, if not power, in shaping social institutions and policies has haunted the minds of many Western intellectuals and has influenced the attitudes and beliefs which were dealt with in this book.

At last it is the process of secularization and its consequences for Western intellectuals that have been the least explored and recognized as a source of the attitudes which were the main concern of this study. Perhaps the hitherto prevailing view that intellectuals tend to be rational, skeptical, critical, and detached has led to the underestimation of their need to believe, which apparently is no weaker and possibly stronger than the corresponding needs of "ordinary" people. (This view, in turn, rests on the assumption, elaborated by Karl Mannheim, that since intellectuals are free of class interests—so the argument ran—they have a better grasp of reality since their perceptions and judgments are not distorted by such interests.)[81] The overly rationalistic image of intellectuals has also obscured the sense of loss they had experienced as the fruits of secularization ripened in this century. It was, I believe, the increasing pressure to find purpose and meaning in life that has led intellectuals to the attitudes described in this volume. Politics came to provide new objects of devotion as, in the words of Max Weber, the gods have retreated from the life of Western societies. For a while a large number of Western intellectuals found this object of devotion in the Soviet social system, its leaders, and official beliefs. Their continued devotion to similar "objects" at later times in this century (such as Cuba, China, the Third World) strongly supports the argument that there is a free-floating need in search of gratification and that, although the gratification found was ostensibly political, its pursuit stemmed from deeper, non-political sources.

On Being Anti-Utopian

Unquestionably this study has a basically anti-utopian thrust, even though anti-utopian proselytizing was not its prime objective. Nevertheless, it is among the messages of this book that political regimes which strove for a radical, one might say utopian, and putatively benevolent restructuring of their social institutions and citizens fell far short of their goals, although our knowledge of the details of these shortfalls varies considerably from country to country, and the magnitude of the discrepancies between the ideals and their actualization remains in dispute. Correspondingly, the utopia-seeking intellectuals were the objects of criticism (even occasionally of sarcasm) as it was made fairly clear that their idealization of certain countries and their political systems—which they perceived as being endowed with utopian potentialities—was delusory. Thus, for example, the collectivization of agriculture in the Soviet Union led to starvation in the 1930s and chronic food shortages ever since, while the egalitarian slogans of the October Revolution gave way to hierarchy and new inequalities in the distribution of both power and material privileges. In Cuba under Castro the commitment to moral incentives for work failed to endure. The alleged idealism and anti-bureaucratic goals of the Cultural Revolution in China left behind a debris of economic disruption, cultural disarray and repression. The list of such examples could be lengthened as the passage of time appears to provide more detailed information in support of the assertion that the high hopes inspired by these societies were largely misplaced. Their utopian or quasi-utopian images reflected in the pages of the travelogues were born out of the selective perception of the visitors generously assisted by the techniques of hospitality. The urge to believe was the mainspring of the political misconceptions and misjudgments discussed above. In particular the new forms of coercion, the widespread political regimentation and the rapid rebirth of inequality in combination with the impregnable official self-righteousness extant in each of the countries revered have made it clear that, once more, the realization of utopian ambitions eluded those seeking to implement them. Without taking note of such departures from the utopian claims and stated purposes and their deferred or fictitious attainment, it would have been difficult to argue that the political systems in question were misapprehended by the travelers.

Perhaps most of these observations would provoke little disagreement today; indeed, various historical events and political developments lend support to the viewpoint expressed in this study. Few of the authors quoted in this book would today still persist in affirming their affection for the Soviet Union. Similarly, and more unexpectedly, uncertainty replaced, in the minds of many erstwhile admirers, the reverential attitudes which had been shown toward China and North Vietnam—countries which since the late 1970s became extremely hostile toward each other.° Nor did the emergence of the boat people make it easy to regard Vietnam as an examplar of political virtue, or the Vietnamese invasion of Cambodia allow for viewing the Vietnamese regime as "exercising power in new ways." More recently (in the spring of 1980) Cuba's image suffered too from the unexpected exodus of about 120,000 of its citizens, most of whom grew up under the Castro regime without apparently acquiring the taste for regimentation and deferred material gratification such political systems seek to inculcate. (At the same time Cuban military adventures in Africa and its growing closeness to the Soviet Union did not seem to disturb the die-hard admirers of Cuban socialism. Nor had the release of Hubert Matos, former revolutionary leader, after twenty years of imprisonment, turn the attention of the sympathizers to the less than utopian attributes of the Cuban system.)

It remains to comment more generally on the anti-utopian biases I have entertained. Doubtless these reservations are far from original. They are based on the observation, among others, that large-scale utopian schemes, when politically inspired and implemented, require vast amounts of coercion and a corresponding loss of personal and group freedoms. As a Czech author put it, "You can't build utopia without terror and . . . before long, terror is all that's left." Terror may not be the *only* thing left, but certainly little of what had been intended remains. More recently Bernard Henri Levy observed in a similar vein: "the Gulag [the Soviet camp system under Stalin] is not a blunder or an accident, not a simple wound or after effect of Stalinism, but the necessary corollary of a socialism which . . . can aim for the universal only by confining its rebels, its irreducible individualists, in the outer darkness of a nonsociety. . . . We have to add: . . . *no classless society*

___

° In particular I could not expect when I started writing this book that the Chinese authorities themselves would, after Mao's death, provide counterpoints to the over-enthusiastic travel reports and new bases for skepticism about their validity.

without its terrorist truth."[82] (At the same time it may be possible to build utopia without terror on a communal farm in Vermont or California when such attempts are made by a small number of congenial individuals who are free to disband whenever they wish and who usually have other options should their undertaking fail or sour.)

The rejection of large-scale coercion in the service of elusive and probably unrealizable ends is not the only basis of the reservations here expressed. There is also a deeper misgiving about organized, systematic, self-conscious schemes designed to make individual lives more meaningful and maximize personal happiness by political means. (Needless to say such misgivings do not extend to efforts to make life easier, less materially deprived by political means.) While personal lives can be improved by political means up to a point, political utopias aimed at the ultimate eradication of conflict, frustration, or unhappiness are suspect.[83] I also find the utopian sensibility unappealing because it seems difficult to reconcile it with the regular and vigorous exercise of the critical faculties.

While the suspension of disbelief has its place in human life, it belongs more to the religious (or aesthetic) than the political realm. There is, furthermore, as has been shown by this study, an all too close affinity between high utopian hopes and expectations on the one hand, and credulity, the rationalization of repression, and double standards, on the other.

The Western intellectuals dealt with in this volume (and others similar to them) had no opportunity to initiate or contribute to the realization of contemporary political utopias. They were thus spared the temptations alluded to above, and especially that of sweeping human obstacles from the path of historical progress (as the process is sometimes seen) and of dealing with various aggregations of people as objects to be moved, prodded, and mobilized.

These are then in brief the major grounds for my anti-utopian disposition and for the belief that both the efforts to create utopia by political means and the act of applauding such attempts from a safe distance are questionable at best. At the same time I must also register some reservations about my own position. Being unreservedly anti-utopian is, after all, uncomfortably close to maintaining a prosaic pessimism or corrosive skepticism toward any scheme of far-reaching social improvement. Unqualified anti-utopianism may easily merge into the untroubled acceptance of the status quo, into unmitigated resignation, privatization, and cynicism. Worse yet, it may come close to the insistence that there should be no collective dreams if they can so easily turn into nightmares. The authors of a recent study of Western utopias liken them to dreams without which the psychic health of societies may be as much endangered as that of the individual and they favor the wise cultivation of "the ancient art of wishing."[84] It is hard to argue against the appeal of dreams, against the visions of communal harmony. Whatever their historical consequences, dreams of social perfectibility and human liberation are by themselves attractive, and life without them would be impoverished in some intangible way. Perhaps one may conclude that utopias are harmless until and unless attempts are made to implement them by force.*

The anti-utopian temper need not be denuded of moral concerns as is illustrated by the musings of a Soviet intellectual living in the Soviet Union:

> Then what is important?
>
> It sounds banal. Self-improvement. Individual effort. Study and thought for one's own moral development. The classical liberal virtues. Being honest and loyal and kind to the ten people closest to me rather than professing my good intentions to world history or social movements. And for the country as a whole, tinkering with the economic and social system in small daily ways and stopping to *measure* what works. Measuring real wages instead of mouthing Marxist slogans. Measuring real freedom and well-being instead of talking about class struggles and "socialist" freedom. In other words, *pragmatism*. And an end to Marxism and all other "isms."
>
> We used to assume socialism by itself would produce a better society and better human beings. . . . But this obviously isn't true. Socialism alone doesn't make good men, good buildings, good anything. And certainly not goodwill.[86]

The Consequences

Finally, we must ask what have been the consequences of the attitudes of Western intellectuals examined in this volume? How much does it matter what many Western intellectuals, more and less distinguished, think and feel about certain idealized societies? Are their journeys, their

---

* It is difficult to discuss these matters at the time of this writing without reference to Jonestown (in Guyana), a recent example of how destructive utopian schemes can be and how they may also combine the use of force with voluntary self-surrender, or escape from freedom. Yet even Jonestown was defended as a legitimate response to alienation and discrimination, an attitude based on "willingness to judge a movement (or a policy) entirely by its stated good intentions and noble goals, rather than by a critical evaluation of its methods and consequences."[85]

political pilgrimages, merely transient episodes of contemporary social and intellectual history, or will they have a more enduring effect? Are these pilgrimages evidence of a crisis of values, judgment, and common sense among an important elite group? Should the political (and moral) misperceptions and misjudgments of such intellectuals lead us to conclude that, despite their preoccupation with ideas, superior education, and (allegedly) idealistic disposition, they do not have a better grasp of truth and reality than that which is available to others lacking in such qualifications? And if so, should policy-makers in Western societies give special consideration to their views, exhortations, and advice?

The significance of the phenomenon that has been the main subject of this book—namely, the estrangement of a large number of Western intellectuals—derives, to a great extent, from the premise that these men and women, the political pilgrims, expressed attitudes and predispositions which were shared by many of their lesser known peers and contemporaries. The authors of the travelogues reflected in more extreme, and clearly articulated form more widespread attitudes of disillusionment and confusion and, to a lesser degree, readiness to see virtue in distant societies.

Still, the question remains: what does it all add up to? How much does it matter that Western intellectuals have been enamored at different times with the Soviet Union, China, Cuba, and North Vietnam? Will it matter if the next wave of pilgrims will extol the virtues of Albania or Mozambique or Nicaragua? Clearly, the pilgrimages are more significant as a symptom of estrangement than as reflections of support for particular political systems. It could be argued that the pilgrimages had few enduring results, especially if we consider the Soviet case: the "Red Decade" was followed by the Cold War and an upsurge of hostility toward the Soviet Union and communist movements; the sympathies which prevailed earlier in many circles of intellectual and public opinion were wiped out, especially in the United States in the post–World War II period. With few exceptions, the intellectuals themselves who had earlier favored the Soviet Union repudiated their pro-Soviet fervor or fell silent on the subject; some of them became politically withdrawn (whether or not they had in fact changed their minds).[87]* Likewise, the

* Several of these earlier pro-Soviet or old-left intellectuals emerged into public life in the 1960s lending their support to the student protest and welcoming the new wave of disenchantment with American society which seemed to vindicate their earlier alienation. Most of them, however, did not rekindle their pro-Soviet sentiments.

uncritical fascination with China in the early 1970s gave way after Mao's death to more critical and searching attitudes. It may, however, also be argued that the positive assessments of the early 70s contributed to the more favorable American policies toward China and to the widespread public acceptance of such policies. Certainly the enthusiastic accounts of visits to North Vietnam during the war strengthened the anti-war movement and as such had some practical consequence, although it is clear that the strength of the anti-war movement had more to do with the unfavorable views of the United States and its foreign policies than with the favorable views taken of its enemy. With respect to the attitudes and policies toward Cuba, it is unclear what the impact of the admiring travelogues has been. Cuba still enjoys a reasonably good reputation among many left-wing intellectuals, resulting at least in part from the ardor of its most vocal advocates, which apparently continues to drown out the more critical voices including those of Cuban emigrés. On the other hand, throughout the 1960s and 70s none of these favorable assessments made much of a dent on American foreign policy toward Cuba or on the maintenance of the blockade. And insofar as Castro is sympathetically presented in the Western mass media, it is probably more because of his appearance and colorful personality than the endorsement he has received from estranged intellectuals.

It seems to me that what has been consequential is not the perception or praise of particular countries and their political systems at any given time. What makes a difference in the long run is the cumulative impact of the denigration intellectuals direct at their own society which, as we have seen, almost invariably accompanies the veneration of other societies. Even if one assumes that all or most of the criticism of the Western social systems is thoroughly justified, the cumulative effect of this steady debunking and preoccupation with the ills of society intensifies the sense of malaise and alienation arising out of problems and frustrations, many of which are unlikely to be resolved. These include, above all, the lack of meaning and weak bonds of community in secular, individualistic societies and the sense of powerlessness most citizens experience in such complex mass societies today. The long-range impact of the intellectuals' rejection of their society, their almost instinctive, reflexive disparagement of its major values and their refusal to identify with its established institutions may have another consequence as well. Such attitudes may contribute not only to popular bewilderment but also to the low morale and loss of will of political elites[88]—possibly, in the long run, to the erosion of both popular and elite support for the survival of Western political institutions. It has been said many times that modern societies cannot long survive without the support of intellectuals. Although today the bitter and unqualified rejection of Western societies is less in evidence than it used to be in the 1960s and early 70s, neither is the prevailing ethos supportive; there is little discernible willingness to identify with, support, or legitimate Western values and institutions on the part of Western intellectuals, even among those who are not particularly hostile to their social system. The forms of estrangement scrutinized in this volume are significant even if they do not always betoken clearly articulated hostility but only the passive withdrawal of support; such a withdrawal is one among the many factors which reduce the vitality and capacity for survival of Western societies.*

The attitudes and activities of many present-day Western intellectuals suggest that they believe in the possibility of maintaining their comparatively charmed existence, which enables them to remain at once critical and hostile toward the social system and privileged in their material circumstances, occupational status, and freedom of expression. In short, they seem to believe that "repressive tolerance" will persist and remain quite tolerable. Above all, they persist in taking the freedom of expression for granted. As Nicola Chiaromonte has observed: "we in the West no longer know and want to know what freedom is and are more or less of the opinion that political freedom . . . is a sort of commodity. It is one of the many commodities that our highly advanced society lavishes on us, and we use it because it is there, as we might use a car or a washing machine. But even if it were not there, no great harm would be done."[90] There are many intellectuals who would reject the suggestion that a political system that assures them (and others) the freedom of expression—which is the mainstay of their professional and moral existence—deserves a measure of support. Yet despite their dependence on such freedom, they seem to care surprisingly little about it and have been capable of admiring societies, as was shown earlier, where such freedom does not exist.

The more far-reaching question is whether or not, willingly or inadvertently, Western intellectuals will contribute to the destruction of their relatively free societies, in part because of their illusions about other societies and their recurrent fantasies of new forms of liberation and collective gratification. If, as a Soviet emigré observer of American attitudes

---

* I do not believe that the rise of the so-called neo-conservative intellectuals[89] in the United States or the "New Philosophers" in France has substantially altered the level and kind of estrangement discussed here.

noted, "In the nineteenth century electorates could afford the luxury of not knowing societies different from their own and of electing statesmen who hardly knew anything about them either,"[91] this unfortunately is no longer the case. Ignorance and illusions about other societies (some of which are quite unfriendly)* coupled with the refusal of many Western intellectuals to play a part in the legitimation of their own societies or to give them any moral support, may yet have tangible consequences. It is hard to say how dramatic, since, obviously, the attitudes of intellectuals are not the only factor which affect the health and survival of these societies. One may note, for example, in the United States, the rise of a generation (or more than one) of educated young people unable to conceive of external political threats to their country and some of them ready to revive the old British slogan of "better red than dead," claiming that "there is nothing worth dying for" and, more specifically, that "the consequences of Soviet aggression would be incomparable to those of nuclear war," as a few Amherst College students argued recently.[93] The revival of the anti-draft movement certainly suggests that many members of the younger generation, and especially the more educated among them, are unwilling to take any steps (even registering for a possible future draft) that may in fact remove the alternatives of surrender to Soviet pressures or nuclear war, that is, the choice between "red" and "dead." A slogan of the current opponents of draft registration, "no draft, no war," epitomizes an attitude which puts the blame on the United States for past and future military conflicts and adamantly refuses to acknowledge that there are unfriendly forces out in the world which, Mr. Bernstein's views notwithstanding, have shown little inclination to equate military weakness with either moral or political strength.

If young, privileged Americans are unwilling to register for draft it is not merely because they are selfish or fearful but also because they have few, if any, positive feelings about their society, and its comparative advantages. Since the 1960s such appreciation has been replaced, for many, by vague unease about the historical misdeeds of their country

---

* Mr. Leonard Bernstein, the famous conductor-composer, speculated in an article entitled "Just Suppose We Disarmed": "What would they do with us? [That is, if the U.S. had unilaterally disarmed] Why would they want to assume responsibility for . . . so huge, complex and problematical a society as ours? And in English yet! . . . [and] how can they fight when there is no enemy? The hypothetical enemy has been magically replaced by 200-odd-million smiling, strong, peaceful Americans." He added that if such disarmament took place, the Soviet people would probably "displace their warlike leaders, and transform their Union of Socialist Republics into a truly democratic union."[92]

ranging from the mistreatment of American Indians to the enslavement of blacks, from the bombing of Vietnam to the plundering of under-developed countries by multinational corporations, and the contrasting living standards of Americans with those of much of the rest of the world. The alienation of college professors of the social sciences (or the humanities) filters down to the teachers of social studies in the schools and to their pupils. The mistrust and skepticism of academics, writers, journalists, movie makers, and actresses reach the larger public. Images of American society reflected in the mass media, popular literature, so-cial science texts and courses, and the sermons of "progressive" minis-ters have been largely unfavorable for almost two decades. The tones and manifestations of alienation may have changed in the last few years but not its substance.

As Durkheim said, society is above all the idea it forms of itself. The idea that American society has formed of itself in recent decades—with the assistance of those most systematically involved in the formulation of such ideas, the intellectuals—is not encouraging. If collective self-esteem is as important for the functioning of society as self-respect is for the well-being of the individual, then the outlook is not bright.[94]

It may be objected that this view of the consequences of the attitudes of Western intellectuals discussed in this volume is not only unpleas-antly gloomy but also exaggerates the weight of ideas in social-political affairs. This is not the place to make a last ditch defense of the impor-tance of ideas, either in general terms or with reference to the present undertaking. The reader must judge—and all the evidence is not yet in—how consequential the ideas that were scrutinized in this study have been.

There is no denying that the outlook reflected in these closing pages is far from confident about the survival of values and institutions which used to be held in high esteem in the West. Perhaps such pessimism in-volves an element of magic thinking, a lurking hope that the discour-aging developments envisioned above may be foiled by conjuring them up for anticipatory inspection.

Notes

Preface to Paperback Edition

1. Gladwin Hill, *Los Angeles Times*, November 1, 1981.
2. *New York Times Book Review*, October 11, 1981.
3. *New York Times Book Review*, November 8, 1981.
4. *The New Leader*, November 30, 1981.
5. *Commentary*, December 1981.
6. *The New Republic*, January 27, 1982.
7. See my references in the original Preface to statements of Susan Sontag (concerning Cuba and Vietnam), Mary McCarthy (concerning Vietnam), and those of Jonathan Mirsky and Orville Schell on China. Sontag and McCarthy were among those who cautiously revised their views of the countries concerned, Mirsky and Schell quite radically. John King Fairbank, the famous Sinologist, apparently has not taken the opportunity afforded by his memoirs to revise his views of Mao's China. (See, for example, John Fraser, "The Mandarin of Chinese Studies," *Washington Post*, February 14, 1982; and Miriam and Ivan D. London, "Peking Duck," *The American Spectator*, July 1982.)
8. The attitudes of Corliss Lamont offer a good example of such resistance. See Paul Hollander, "Selective Affinities," *The New Republic*, Oct. 18, 1982.
9. Her original remarks and a few written criticisms to them were published in *The Nation* under the title "Communism and the Left," February 27, 1982. See also Peter Shaw and Seymour Martin Lipset "Two afterthoughts on Susan Sontag," *Encounter*, June–July 1982.
10. Some of the discussion below follows closely points made in a forthcoming collection of my shorter writings entitled *The Faces of Socialism—Essays in Comparative Sociology and Politics* (New Brunswick, 1983).
11. Peter Shaw in *Encounter*, cited p. 40; Walter Goodman, "Hard to digest," *Harper's*, June 1982, p. 67.
12. Quoted in *Political Pilgrims*, p. 271; his statement on Nicaragua was quoted in George F. Will, "Again, the Fact Finders," *Newsweek*, March 1, 1982.
13. As, for example, in Eldon Kenworthy, "Troubled Nicaragua," *The New York Times*, February 18, 1982.
14. *Contentions*, April–May 1982, p. 2; see also "Nicaragua Film on PBS Is Called 'Propaganda,'" *New York Times*, April 9, 1982. For a Berkeley, Calif., publication devoted to the praise of Marxist–Leninist Nicaragua, see *Nicaraguan Perspectives* (e.g., Fall 1981). Since the editors thanked the "Community Project Office of the University of California at Berkeley for the support and encouragement of this project," it may be presumed that once more, as with the program on public television, the taxpayers' money was channeled into pro-Nicaraguan propaganda.
15. Warren Hoge, "Nicaraguan Scene: Fiery Slogans, Designer Jeans," *The New York Times*, January 6, 1982.
16. Warren Hoge, "Nicaragua's Revolution Breaks the Mold," *The New York Times*, December 30, 1981.
17. For example, Ramsey Clark was sympathetic not only to the North Vietnamese regime and that of the Ayatolah Khomeini (as noted on pp. 69, 271, and 479), he

more recently paid friendly visits to the PLO leader Arafat in Beirut. (See Bernard Weintraub, "Israelis Charge Palestinian Use of Mercenaries," *New York Times*, July 11, 1982. The article quoted documents captured by the Israeli forces in which Arafat made numerous references to Clark's visit and empathy.)

18. See also Vladimir Bukovsky, "The Peace Movement and the Soviet Union," *Commentary*, May 1982).

19. Paul Johnson: "Through Pink-Coloured Spectacles," *Times* [London] *Literary Supplement*, December 25, 1981, p. 1486.

20. "New Destinations," *New York Times*, September 21, 1981.

21. Reported in "Washington diarist," *The New Republic*, March 31, 1982.

22. "Cuba Trip Allows One to See for Self," *Massachusetts Daily Collegian*, March 9, 1982.

23. "Mission in Moscow," *The New York Times*, May 17, 1982; "Graham Says Soviet Trip Increased His Crowds," *The New York Times*, May 28, 1982; "Graham Preaches at Church in Moscow," *The New York Times*, May 10, 1982

24. "Graham Offers Positive View of Religion in Soviet," *The New York Times*, May 13, 1982; see also "Billy Graham Rebuffs Criticism of Soviet Trip," *The New York Times*, May 18, 1982; and "Billy Graham, Back Home, Defends Remarks," *The New York Times*, May 20, 1982.

25. See *The New York Times*, May 18, 1982.

Preface

1. Michiko Kakutani, "For Susan Sontag, the Illusions of the 60's Have Been Dissipated," *New York Times*, November 11, 1980, p. C5.

2. Mary McCarthy, "A world out of joint," *The Observer*, October 14, 1979, p. 8. (Her earlier views on Vietnam are discussed in Chapter 6.)

3. Jonathan Mirsky, "Back to the land of little red lies," *The Observer*, October 28, 1979, p. 9. The changed views of Schell are quoted in Chapter 8, p. 352. See also his latest book, *"Watch Out for the Foreign Guests!"* (New York, 1981).

4. Examples of the idealization of Albania and Mozambique will be found at the end of Chapter 6.

5. Christopher Hitchens, "Bukharin could have approved," *The New Statesman*, July 25, 1980. The articles by Anthony Lewis are as follows: "Choices in Angola," *New York Times*, January 22, 1981; "Linkage in Africa," *New York Times*, News of the Week section, January 25, 1981; "Angola Tries Pragmatic Policy," *New York Times*, Business Day, February 2, 1981; "After Mistakes, Angola Turns Toward 'Realism'," *New York Times*, News of the Week section, February 8, 1981.

6. The current appeal of Nicaragua is exemplified by a television program so sympathetic to the new regime that, according to the *New York Times* critic, it "[made] no pretense to 'balance'." See John J. O'Connor, "Oil Rig Thriller, Nicaragua Revolution," *New York Times*, February 20, 1981, p. C26.

7. "New Destinations," *New York Times*, Travel Section, September 21, 1980.

8. The Institute of Policy Studies in Washington is one of the best examples of such an institutionalized and enduring rejection of American society. See Rael Jean Isaac: "America the Enemy—Profile of a Revolutionary Think Tank," *Midstream*, June/July 1980 (reprinted in Ethics and Public Policy Center reprint series, Washington, D.C., July 1980).

9. For a recent summary of such Western attitudes and policies see Arnaud de Borchgrave and Michael Ledeen, "Selling Russia the Rope," *New Republic*, December 12, 1980.

Chapter 1: Themes

1. Norman Cohn, *The Pursuit of Millennium* (New York, 1957), p. 308.

2. Saul Bellow, *To Jerusalem and Back* (New York, 1976), p. 127.

3. This revealing term was applied by Stalin to Soviet writers who were to mold their readers to the official, socialist-realist ideological specifications. There are today left-wing intellectuals in the West who harbor undeclared affinities with socialist realism. Recent demands for "role models" in the arts and mass media in the United States are reminiscent of socialist realism and its positive heroes. The current role models in the West are supposed to benefit and inspire women and blacks, homosexuals, and some other minorities.

4. Edward Shils, "The Burden of 1917," *Survey*, Summer–Autumn 1976, p. 141. Many similar (and more current) beliefs about China and Cuba could also be cited.

5. Hans Magnus Enzensberger, "Tourists of the Revolution," in *The Consciousness Industry* (New York, 1974), p. 140.

6. Leon Festinger's *A Theory of Cognitive Dissonance* (Stanford, 1957) is highly relevant to an understanding of how people deal with such (and other) contradictory or conflicting beliefs and experiences.

7. Staughton Lynd and Tom Hayden, *The Other Side* (New York, 1966), pp. 17–18.

8. James Hitchcock, "Review of G. Lewy: Religion and Revolution," *Commentary*, November 1974, p. 94.

9. "Jean-Paul Sartre: The Marxist Phase," *Ramparts*, March 1967, p. 47. In his quest for a more authentic socialism Sartre also visited and praised the left-wing military regime in Portugal in the mid-1970s (George F. Will, *The Pursuit of Happiness and Other Sobering Thoughts* [New York, 1978], p. 20–21).

10. Hannah Arendt, *On Violence* (New York, 1969), p. 21.

11. Walter Laqueur, "Third World Fantasies," *Commentary*, February 1977, p. 43. For a book-length ode to Albania, see Jan Myrdal and Gun Kessle, *Albania Defiant* (New York and London, 1976).

12. George Urban, "A Conversation with George F. Kennan," *Encounter*, September 1976, pp. 33–34, 35.

13. Norman Birnbaum, *The Crisis of Industrial Society* (New York, 1969), p. viii. The evolution of Castro's Cuba might have contributed to Birnbaum's preference for abortive revolutions. It is doubtful that he held for long to his early assessments of the Cuban regime's commitment to "liberal assumptions" (quoted in Theodore Draper, *Castro's Revolution* [New York, 1962], p. 165).

14. Adam Ulam, " 'The Essential Love' of Simone de Beauvoir," *Problems of Communism*, March–April 1966, p. 63. The persisting "enormous outward self-assurance" of the Castro regime may best explain why it still enjoys a good deal of popularity among Western radicals at a time when China's "façade of self-assurance" has already been punctured.

15. For a further discussion on this topic, see Paul Hollander, "Reflections on Anti-Americanism in Our Times," *Worldview*, June 1978.

16. Arthur Koestler, "On Disbelieving Atrocities," in *The Yogi and the Commissar and Other Essays* (New York, 1961), p. 88.

17. The impact and importance of visual experience is exemplified in the following comment of a critic of American society: "All the Chamber of Commerce pronouncements, the fancy *Fortune Magazine* charts about our progress, the confident State of the Union Addresses fall apart when you take a long walk through any major American city: through Harlem, or Roxbury or Chicago's South Side"

(Howard Zinn, "Marxism and the New Left," in *The New Left*, ed. Priscilla Long [Boston, 1969], p. 65). Needless to say, the corresponding visual experiences in Moscow, Peking, or Havana lend themselves just as well to contrast with ceremonial statements, and would lead to similar conclusions.

18. Bernard Gwertzman, "Human Rights: The Rest of the World Sees Them Differently," *New York Times*, March 6, 1977.

19. *New York Times*, News of the Week section, November 30, 1969, p. 6.

20. Leopold Tyrmand, *Notebooks of a Dilettante* (New York, 1970), p. 70.

21. Paul Hollander, *Soviet and American Society: A Comparison* (New York, 1973), pp. 35–36.

22. Sylvia R. Margulies, *The Pilgrimage to Russia: The Soviet Union and the Treatment of Foreigners, 1924–1937* (Madison, Wisc., 1968), p. 89. This excellent study differs from the present one in three respects: 1. it is limited to the Soviet Union; 2. it is *not* limited to visiting intellectuals; and 3. it is restricted to the period 1924–37. A more recent German volume also containing essays on Western travelers to the Soviet Union is Klaus Kaltenbrunner, ed., *Radikale Touristen* (Munich, 1976).

23. For some further observations on these aspects of modern tourism, especially as it applies to Americans, see Daniel J. Boorstin, *The Image—A Guide to Pseudo-events in America* (New York, 1961).

24. Herbert A. Simon, "Mao's China in 1972," Social Science Research Council *Items* 27, no. 1 (March 1973): 1.

25. Bellow, *To Jerusalem*, p. 44. On the contemporary appeals of Marxism, see Adam Ulam, *The Unfinished Revolution* (New York, 1960); Robert G. Wesson, *Why Marxism? The Continuing Success of a Failed Theory* (New York, 1976); and Raymond Aron, *The Opium of Intellectuals* (London, 1957).

26. Peter Berger, *Pyramids of Sacrifice* (Garden City, N.Y., 1976), p. 17. Susan Sontag too was aware of these aspects of the idealization of Third World countries: "Understandably, one fears succumbing to that cut-rate sympathy for places like Vietnam which, lacking any real historical or psychological understanding, becomes another instance of the ideology of primitivism. The revolutionary politics of many people in capitalist countries is only a new guise for the old conservative culture criticism: posing against overcomplex, hypocritical, devitalized, urban society choking on affluence the idea of a simple people living the simple life in a decentralized, uncoercive, passionate society with modest material means. As the 18th century *philosophes* pictured such a pastoral ideal in the Pacific islands or among the American Indians, and German romantic poets supposed it to have existed in ancient Greece, late 20th century intellectuals in New York and Paris are likely to locate it in the exotic revolutionary societies of the Third World . . ." (*Trip to Hanoi* [New York, 1968], p. 72). As will be seen later, these insights did not prevent her from succumbing to the same attitudes on her visit to North Vietnam.

27. Peter Berger, "The Socialist Myth," *Public Interest*, Summer 1976.

28. Olga Chechetkina, *Andzela v Sovetskom Souze* [Angela in the Soviet Union] (Moscow, 1973). Another curious example of quaint pro-Soviet sentiments in our times was provided by Muhammad Ali, who was deeply moved by his personal meeting with Leonid Brezhnev in Moscow. Full of praise for both Brezhnev and Soviet society on his return to the United States, he observed: "I saw only one policeman. I didn't see no guns. No crime. No prostitute. Not one homosexual" (*New York Times*, editorial, "Sparring with Justice," June 25, 1978). Ralph Abernathy quoted in William F. Buckley, Jr., "A Parable of Our Time," *National Review*, January 19, 1973, p. 110. Stephen J. Whitfield, *Scott Nearing: Apostle of*

American Radicalism (New York, 1974), p. 201. For a survey of similarly startling American scholarly assessments of East Germany, see Norman M. Naimark, "Is It True What They're Saying About East Germany?", *Orbis*, Fall 1979.

29. For a more recent discussion of the concept of alienation see John Torrance, *Estrangement, Alienation and Exploitation* (New York, 1977).

30. Irving Kristol, "About Equality," *Commentary*, November 1972, pp. 42–43.

31. In the 1930s Americans predominated among all the visitors to the USSR. According to Eugene Lyons, 85 percent of them came from the United States (*The Red Decade* [New Rochelle, 1970; first published, New York, 1941] p. 93). Americans might also have been the single largest group among the visitors to China in the 1970s; I know of no figures confirming or refuting this impression.

32. Gabriel A. Almond, *The Appeals of Communism* (Princeton, 1954). See also Sidney Hook, "The Psychology of the Fellow-Travellers," in his *Political Power and Personal Freedom* (New York, 1959); and sections of Philip Selznick, *The Organizational Weapon* (Glencoe, Ill., 1960).

33. David Caute, *The Fellow-Travellers* (New York, 1973).

34. Lewis S. Feuer, "The Fellow-Travellers," *Survey*, Spring 1974, p. 207.

35. For definitions of utopias and utopianism see George Kateb, "Utopianism," in *International Encyclopedia of the Social Sciences* (New York, 1968); Northrop Frye, "Varieties of Literary Utopias," in *Utopias and Utopian Thought*, ed. Frank E. Manuel (Boston, 1966), p. 31; Rosabeth Moss Kanter, *Commitment and Community* (Cambridge, 1972), p. 1; and George Kateb, *Utopia and Its Enemies* (New York, 1972), esp. pp. 7, 9, 17.

36. Adam Ulam, "Socialism and Utopia," in Manuel, *Utopias*, p. 133.

37. Isaiah Berlin, "Two Concepts of Liberty," in *Four Essays on Liberty* (New York, 1969), p. 167.

38. Karl Popper, "Utopia and Violence," in his *Conjectures and Refutations* (London, 1962), p. 361.

39. Crane Brinton, "Utopia and Democracy," in Manuel, *Utopias*, p. 50.

40. Plato is the only major exception to this generalization, as he antedated these periods and developments.

41. Ulam, "Socialism and Utopia," p. 116. See also Frank E. Manuel and Fritzie P. Manuel, *Utopian Thought in the Western World* (Cambridge, 1979), p. 33.

42. Lewis Mumford, *The Story of Utopias* (New York, 1922 and 1962), p. 247.

43. There is a considerable tension in Lenin's thinking about human nature here and now, and its putatively limitless potentials in the future. The associated pessimism is illuminatingly analyzed by Alfred G. Meyer in his *Leninism* (Cambridge, 1967).

44. See Eugene Goodheart, "Utopia and the Irony of History," in his *Culture and Radical Conscience* (Cambridge, 1973).

45. Manes Sperber, "Pilgrims to Utopia," in his *Man and His Deeds* (New York, 1970), p. 1.

46. Henri Baudet, *Paradise on Earth: Some Thoughts on European Images of Non-European Man* (New Haven, 1965), p. vii. See also Gerard Evans, "Paradises lost: or, Where are you, Fidel, when I need you?", *New Society* (London), February 22, 1979. Evans wrote: "Deeply embedded in the concept of paradise is the belief that it is different from our own society precisely in those areas where we feel that society is failing us." And: "It was . . . attractive to believe that elsewhere, in some remote corner of the globe, the conditions might exist for the re-creation of the perfect society" (p. 412).

47. V. G. Kiernan, *The Lords of Human Kind: European Attitudes to the Out-*

side World in the Imperial Age (Harmondsworth, Middlesex, England, 1972), p. 136.

48. Sperber, *Man and His Deeds*, p. 2.

49. Baudet, *Paradise on Earth*, pp. 10–11. For a study that examines such attitudes toward America see Hugh Honor, *The New Golden Land: European Images of America from the Discoveries to the Present Time* (New York, 1976).

50. Baudet, *Paradise on Earth*, p. 51.

51. Kiernan, *Lords of Human Kind*, pp. 22–23.

52. Ignacy Sachs, *The Discovery of the Third World* (Cambridge, Mass., 1976), p. 72.

53. Tocqueville, quoted in Lewis M. Coser, *Men of Ideas* (New York, 1970), p. 227.

54. Quoted ibid., p. 228.

55. Ibid.

56. Ibid.

57. Kiernan, *Lords of Human Kind*, p. 21.

58. Coser, *Men of Ideas*, p. 230. A more recent admirer of autocratic efficiency was moved by similar sentiments as he argued the advantages of the one-party system in the USSR: "The fact that there is one political party which is dominant and which attempts to control every major institution . . . makes for unity of purpose and action throughout the entire societal structure. It is a serious question whether, considering the present level of the public intelligence and the vested interests of present status quo any genuine brand of socialism can be achieved anywhere without dictatorship. . . . a dictatorship . . . makes possible continuity of control over a long period and concrete achievements which might be impossible amidst the turmoil of bitter political conflict" (Jerome Davis, "The Communist Party and the Government," in *The New Russia*, ed. Jerome Davis [New York, 1933], pp. 130–31). The belief in the efficiency of autocracies is one of the unexamined myths of our time. The only area where such efficiency has been clearly established is that of coercive policies directed at opposition, or potential opposition. As to everything else, it is a so-called empirical question whether and when autocracies are efficient.

59. Coser, *Men of Ideas*, p. 231.

60. ". . . I was going to Moscow, a city which has the same symbolic significance for the religious communist as Mecca had for the fanatical Moslem" (Charlotte Haldane, *Truth Will Out* [New York, 1950] p. 192).

61. George Bernard Shaw, *The Rationalization of Russia* (Bloomington, Ind., 1964; first published 1931), p. 31. Of this type of tourist Eugene Lyons wrote: "They guarded their foreign passports like the apple of their eye while sizzling with enthusiasm over this 'new Soviet civilization'" (*Assignment to Utopia* [London, 1938], p. 228). It was also reported that "Another ardent fellow-traveller, Lion Feuchtwanger, was once asked why he didn't move to the country he praised so regularly [i.e. the USSR]; and the novelist replied, 'What do you think I am—a fool?'" (Stephen J. Whitfield: "Muckraking Lincoln Steffens", *The Virginia Quarterly Review*, Winter 1978, No. 1., Vol. 54, p. 90.)

Chapter 2: Intellectuals, Politics, and Morality.

1. Edward Shils, *The Intellectuals and the Powers* (Chicago, 1972), p. 3.

2. Julien Benda, quoted in Lewis A. Coser, "Julien Benda," *Encounter*, April 1973, p. 33.

3. Karl Mannheim, *Ideology and Utopia* (New York: Harvest Book, n.d.; first published in 1929 in Germany, and in 1936 in the United States).

4. Stephen R. Graubard, "Preface to the Issue 'Intellectuals and Tradition,'" *Daedalus*, Spring 1972, p. v; and Arthur Koestler, "The Intelligentsia," in his *Yogi and the Commissar*, pp. 63, 65.

5. Ulam, *Unfinished Revolution*, pp. 195, 200. On intellectuals in power under socialism, see George Konrád and Ivan Szelényi, *The Intellectuals on the Road to Class Power* (New York, 1979).

6. According to the somewhat questionable distinction made by the *Concise Oxford Dictionary*, "the intellectual is a person possessing a good understanding, [an] enlightened person," whereas the intelligentsia is "the part of the nation that aspires to independent thinking." Few of our contemporaries would criticize these definitions today if they were reversed, or even notice the difference.

7. James H. Billington, "The Intelligentsia and the Religion of Humanity," *American Historical Review*, July 1960, pp. 808, 809, 812. According to Nabokov, "The main features of the Russian intelligentsia . . . were: the spirit of self-sacrifice, intense participation in political causes or political thought, intense sympathy for the underdog . . . , fanatical integrity, tragic inability to sink to compromise . . ." (from "Selection: Dear Volodya, Dear Bunny," *New York Times Book Review*, February 4, 1979, p. 26). For a recent assessment of the Russian intelligentsia, see Isaiah Berlin, *Russian Thinkers* (New York, 1978).

8. Julien Benda, *The Treason of Intellectuals* (New York, 1969; first U.S. publication 1928), pp. 43–44.

9. The court jester view of the intellectual is shared by Ralph Dahrendorf: "As the court-jesters of modern society, all intellectuals have the duty to doubt everything that is obvious, to make relative all authority, to ask all those questions that no one else dares to ask" ("The Intellectual and Society," in *On Intellectuals*, ed. Philip Rieff [Garden City, N.Y., 1969], p. 51).

10. Coser, *Men of Ideas*, pp. viii, ix.

11. Edward Shils, "Intellectuals," in *Encyclopedia*, p. 399. Konrád and Szelényi stressed the "culture-creating activity" of intellectuals, noted their transformation from "sacerdotal personage into secular expert" (*Road to Class Power*, pp. 11, 12), and located the qualitative distinctiveness of intellectual knowledge in its concern "with the values which society accepts as part of its culture" (p. 30). Norman Podhoretz defined intellectuals as "specialists in ideological conflict" (*Breaking Ranks* [New York, 1979], p. 83).

12. Robert Nisbet, *Sociology as an Art Form* (New York, 1976), p. 86. For futher definitions of intellectuals stressing the critical, detached, and marginal aspects, see S. M. Lipset, *Political Man* (Garden City, N.Y., 1963), p. 333, and Stanislav Andreski, "Freedom, Influence and the Prestige of Intellectuals," in his *Comparative Sociology* (Berkeley, Cal., 1964), pp. 201, 223.

13. Bennet Berger, "Sociology and the Intellectuals: An Analysis of a Stereo-type," *Antioch Review* 17 (September 1957): p. 283.

14. Richard Hofstadter, *Anti-Intellectualism in American Life* (New York, 1962), pp. 27, 29.

15. Tom Wolfe, *Mauve Gloves and Madmen, Clutter and Vine* (New York, 1977), pp. 105–6. Konrád and Szelényi note other, more sophisticated forms of intellectual status seeking, in which ". . . the concept of intellectual . . . becomes a badge of distinction which individual intellectuals confer on one another . . . a kind of moralizing patent of nobility . . ." (*Road to Class Power*, p. 8).

16. Aron, *Opium of Intellectuals*, pp. 206–9.

17. Lewis Feuer, *Marx and the Intellectuals* (Garden City, N.Y., 1969), p. 2.

18. Lipset, *Political Man*, pp. 333–34. J. P. Nettl went even further, suggesting that "any meaningful concept of intellectual . . . must be free of all forms of institutional attachment" ("Ideas, Intellectuals and Structures of Dissent," in Rieff, *On Intellectuals*, p. 55; see also p. 81). Thomas Molnar argued that the intellectual must not only interpret but also influence the world. See his *The Decline of the Intellectual* (Cleveland and New York, 1961). p. 8.

19. Peter Viereck, *Shame and Glory of the Intellectuals* (Boston, 1953), p. 13.

20. Martin E. Malia, "The Intellectuals: Adversaries or Clerisy?", *Daedalus*, Summer 1972, p. 209.

21. Noam Chomsky, *American Power and the New Mandarins* (New York, 1967).

22. But perhaps the images of guardian of core values and critic of existing society may be reconciled if one accepts Eisenstadt's observation: "Intellectuals were most often conceived as the guardians or would-be guardians of society's conscience—but only when that conscience was thought to be opposed to the established order" ("Intellectuals and Tradition," *Daedalus*, Spring 1972, p. 1).

23. Friedrich Nietzsche, *The Birth of the Tragedy* (Garden City, N.Y., 1956), p. 92. For some explanations of what he calls "the unmasking trend" see Lionel Trilling, *Sincerity and Authenticity* (Cambridge, 1971), pp. 141–42.

24. Alexis de Tocqueville, *The Old Regime and the French Revolution* (New York, 1955), p. 139.

25. Lenin, *State and Revolution* (Moscow, n.d.), p. 163.

26. Tocqueville, *Old Regime*, pp. 140–41, 146, 147.

27. Berlin, *Four Essays*, pp. 150–51.

28. Tocqueville, *Old Regime*, p. 160.

29. Hofstadter, *Anti-Intellectualism*, pp. 417, 423.

30. Robert Conquest, "Intellectuals and Just Causes: A Symposium," *Encounter*, October 1967, p. 47.

31. Lewis Feuer, "The Elite of the Alienated," *New York Times Magazine*, March 26, 1967, pp. 74, 75.

32. Joseph Schumpeter, *Democracy, Capitalism, Socialism* (New York, 1950), p. 144.

33. Karl Marx and Friedrich Engels, *Manifesto of the Communist Party* (Moscow, 1955), pp. 56–57, 58.

34. George Orwell, "Writers and Leviathan," in *The Intellectuals*, ed. George Huszar (Glencoe, Ill., 1960), p. 269. For further discussion of Orwell's attitudes on this subject see Alex Zwerdling, *Orwell and the Left* (New Haven, 1974), esp. chaps. 1 and 2.

35. Arthur Koestler, "The Little Flirts of St. Germain des Prés," *The Trail of the Dinosaur and Other Essays* (London, 1970), p. 62.

36. For a thorough exploration of this phenomenon see "Liberal Anti-Communism Revisited: A Symposium," *Commentary*, September 1967.

37. "The Seven Deadly Fallacies," in Koestler, *Trail of the Dinosaur*, pp. 48–52. For a similar argument about the historical choice of American intellectuals between "endorsing a system of total terror and *critically* supporting our own imperfect democratic culture" see Sidney Hook, "From Alienation to Critical Integrity: The Vocation of the American Intellectuals," in Huszar, *Intellectuals*, p. 528. For another, more wide-ranging criticism (of the same period) of the pro-Soviet attitudes of American intellectuals see also Peter Viereck, " 'Bloody-minded Professors': Shame of the Intellectuals," in Viereck, *Shame and Glory*, pp. 109–26. For a discussion of the political blundering of intellectuals in the 1930s that stresses their failure to understand the threat of Nazism, see Archibald MacLeish, *The Irrespon-*

sibles (New York, 1940). For a Soviet dissenter's critique of Western intellectuals see Andrei Sakharov, *My Country and the World* (New York, 1975), chap. 5. A more recent and rather comprehensive critique of the contemporary versions of fellow-traveling was provided in Jean-François Revel, *The Totalitarian Temptation* (New York, 1977).

38. These views were quoted in George Kateb, "The Political Thought of Herbert Marcuse," *Commentary*, January 1970, p. 57.

39. "The Responsibility of Intellectuals," in Chomsky, *American Power*.

40. Wilhelm Ropke, "National Socialism and Intellectuals," in Huszar, *Intellectuals*, pp. 346, 348.

41. Malcolm Muggeridge, *The Sun Never Sets: The Story of England in the 1930s* (New York, 1940), pp. 281–82.

42. Stephen Spender, Foreword to Alastair Hamilton, *The Appeal of Fascism: A Study of Intellectuals and Fascism, 1919–1945* (London, 1971), pp. x, xi. See also Richard Griffiths, *Fellow Travellers of the Right: British Enthusiasts for Nazi Germany, 1933–1938* (London, 1980).

43. Hamilton, *Appeal of Fascism*, pp. xvi, xvii, xxii, xxi.

44. Andrew Greeley, *Why Can't They Be Like Us? America's White Ethnic Groups* (New York, 1971), p. 123.

45. Lyons, *Assignment*, p. 329 (emphasis added).

46. "Sartre Accuses the Intellectuals of Bad Faith," *New York Times Magazine*, October 17, 1971, pp. 38, 116, 118, 119. For a relevant analysis of Sartre's attitudes, with special reference to his attraction to violence, see Maurice Cranston, "Sartre and Violence," *Encounter*, July 1967. See also Lionel Abel, "Metaphysical Stalinism," *Dissent*, Spring 1961. A part of the explanation of Sartre's attitude toward "the masses" discussed earlier may have to do with the fact that, as one writer put it, "this universal genius of our time was cut off from almost all that is everyday human" (Roland N. Stromberg, *After Everything: Western Intellectual History Since 1945* [New York, 1975], p. 80).

47. Quoted in Barry Reckord, *Does Fidel Eat More Than Your Father?* (London, 1971), p. 119 (emphasis added).

48. C. Eric Hansen, "The Intellectual as a Political Type," *Journal of Politics*, May 1969, p. 324. Probably Sartre and Marcuse are the purest contemporary incarnations of the attitudes sketched by Hansen. On the love of abstractions versus concrete human beings see also Bruce Mazlish, *The Revolutionary Ascetic* (New York, 1976), pp. 23–25.

49. Quoted in Peter G. Filene, *Americans and the Soviet Experiment, 1917–1933* (Cambridge, 1967), p. 146; and Scott Nearing, *The Making of a Radical* (New York, 1972), pp. 209–10.

50. Peter L. Berger, "Are Human Rights Universal?", *Commentary*, September 1977.

51. Gwynn Nettler, "Using Our Heads," *American Sociologist*, August 1968, p. 201.

52. See C. L. Sulzberger, "To Be Obscurely Massacred," *New York Times*, July 2, 1972; William Korey, "The Genocide Convention: Time To Sign," *New York Times*, December 8, 1973; and Roger Morris, "The Triumph of Money and Power," *New York Times*, March 3, 1974.

53. "Nordic Bloc Puts Off Bid for UN Criticism of Uganda," *New York Times*, December 8, 1977. For a more general survey of the dubious record of the United Nations on human rights see Leon Gordenker, "Symbols and Substance in the United Nations," *New Society*, February 1976.

54. "Guineans Are Militant and Suspicious," *New York Times*, June 7, 1972; see also correspondence in *New York Times*, February 19, 1971.

55. Jack Anderson, "Genocide Continues in Asia and Africa," *Daily Hampshire Gazette* (Northampton, Mass.) (reprinted from the *Washington Post*), June 12, 1978; see also Smith Hempstone, "Awakening from a Nightmare: A Bloodbath the World Forgot To Notice," *Daily Hampshire Gazette*, August 11, 1979. Another neglected outrage was the massacre of the Ibos in Nigeria, which involved, according to Simone de Beauvoir, "the extermination of two million people, including a whole generation of children. This indifference makes one suspect the indignation they display when the child-victims of the Vietnamese war are concerned. Scarcely ever, during these last years, have I been so sickened as I was at the magnitude . . . of these massacres—killings encouraged, condoned, or placidly accepted by almost all the 'progressives' in France and the rest of the world" (*All Said and Done* [New York, 1974] p. 417). On some American responses to the sufferings of the Ibos, see "Black Americans Response: Like Whites," *New York Times*, January 14, 1970.

56. "Kurd Chief Asks UN for Aid Against Iraq," *New York Times*, June 8, 1974, p. 18; see also William Safire, "Of Kurds and Conscience," *New York Times*, December 13, 1976.

57. William Safire, "Yellow Rain," *New York Times*, December 13, 1979. For similar developments in Afghanistan see Richard Halloran, "U.S. Told of Soviet Lethal Gas Use," *New York Times*, January 24, 1980; Jack Anderson, "Russians Use Poison Gases in Afghanistan," *Daily Hampshire Gazette*, March 5, 1980; William Safire, "The Other Gas Crisis," *New York Times*, January 28, 1980.

58. Julius Epstein, "A Case for Suppression," *New York Times*, December 18, 1970, p. 39. See also Julius Epstein, *Operation Keelhaul: The Story of Forced Repatriation* (Old Greenwich, Conn., 1973); and Nicholas Bethell, *The Last Secret: The Delivery to Stalin of Over Two Million Russians by Britain and the United States* (London, 1974).

59. Quoted in Joan Colebrook, "Prisoners of War," *Commentary*, January 1974, p. 36.

60. "Activist Lawyer Criticizes U.S. For Violating Human Rights," *Harvard Crimson*, September 28, 1979, pp. 1, 4.

61. Podhoretz, *Breaking Ranks*, p. 234.

62. Noam Chomsky and Edward S. Herman, "Distortions at Fourth Hand," *Nation*, June 25, 1977, pp. 789, 791, 792. Chomsky and Herman also criticized Ponchaud for being "careless" and for "overwhelming" reliance on refugee accounts (p. 792). Of such accounts they wrote: "They [refugees] naturally tend to report what they believe their interlocutors wish to hear. While their reports must be considered seriously, care and caution are necessary. Specifically, refugees questioned by Westerners or Thais have a vested interest in reporting atrocities on the part of Cambodian revolutionaries, an obvious fact that no serious reporter will fail to take into account" (p. 791). Given this assessment of the reliability of refugee accounts, why should they be considered seriously at all? One may also wonder why Chomsky and Herman suggest in the beginning of their discussion of the Ponchaud book that it is "serious and worth reading," since subsequently they have nothing whatsoever to say that would justify either assertion. Why is it worth reading a book whose "veracity is difficult to assess," whose author "plays fast and loose with quotes and numbers," which is "at best careless, sometimes in rather significant ways," which "has an anti-Communist bias and message" and "attained stardom" only by "distortions added to it in an article" (pp. 792, 794)? One can only assume that, as with the refugee accounts, Chomsky and Herman

thought it prudent to add a ritualistic disclaimer to their otherwise unmitigated rejection, a semblance of objectivity to balance their consistently negative assessment of every substantive aspect of both refugee accounts and the Ponchaud book (*Cambodia: Zero Hour* [New York, 1977]).

Chomsky and his coauthor are uncomfortable with the comparison of Cambodia under Pol Pot to Nazi Germany, and prefer a comparison with postwar France, "where many thousands of people were massacred within a few months under far less rigorous conditions than those left by the American war . . ." (in Cambodia, that is) (p. 793).

It is not difficult to understand why Chomsky was anxious to demolish the credibility of Ponchaud's book, which tried neither to reduce the dimensions of the suffering of the Cambodians nor to put the major share of blame for it on the United States. It is the explanation of these sufferings suggested by Ponchaud that might have been most unpalatable for Chomsky: ". . . this total purge was, above all, the translation into action of a particular vision of man. . . ." And while Ponchaud acknowledges that the French and the Americans "bear part of the responsibility for the Cambodian drama," he clearly holds the Cambodian leadership primarily responsible, and in particular "their inflexible ideology [which] has led them to invent a radically new kind of man in a radically new society" (pp. 50, xvi).

Chomsky's polarized world view was also noted by a sympathetic reviewer who called his political writings "maddeningly simple-minded" and found it difficult to read them "without cringing" (Paul Robinson, "The Chomsky Problem," *New York Times Book Review*, February 25, 1979, p. 3). Jean Lacouture, also criticized by Chomsky in the *Nation* article, expressed despair at Chomsky's determined attempts to evade criticism of the Cambodian regime ("The Revolution That Destroyed Itself," *Encounter*, May 1979, esp. p. 57).

Chomsky is the best-known apologist of the now deposed Pol Pot regime, but not the only one. Gareth Porter (whose book Chomsky praised) delicately described the atrocities of the Pol Pot regime as "the policy of self-reliance . . . carried so far that it has imposed unnecessary costs on the population of Cambodia" (*New York Review of Books*, correspondence, July 20, 1978). It may also be noted that at least one member of the American Friends Service Committee (an organization that has consistently given every benefit of doubt to Marxist police states) has also found it necessary to impugn the veracity of refugee accounts ("notoriously unreliable") as they conflicted with his sympathy toward the regime installed by the Vietnamese (see Jerry Elmer, "Food for Cambodians Getting Through," *Daily Hampshire Gazette*, January 11, 1980). For further reports and comments on Cambodia see the columns of Jack Anderson in the *Washington Post* of July 21, 1977, May 2, 3, 4, and 10 and June 1, 1978. See also the famous article by Sydney H. Schanberg entitled, "Old and Sick Included; Economy Is at Standstill—Cambodian Reds Uprooting Millions as They Impose 'Peasant Revolution,'" *New York Times*, May 9, 1974. See also *New York Times*, "Cambodian Refugees Report Growing Hunger and Terror, Even Reaching Ruling Elite," "Refugees Depict Cambodia as Grim, Work-Gang Land," May 13, 1978; *New York Times*, October 31, 1977. For a long review article of three recent books on Cambodia see William Shawcross, "The Third Indochina War," *New York Review of Books*, April 6, 1978.

While the case of Cambodia is of interest not because it became an object of pilgrimages but rather as an example of the stunning selectivity in moral indignation of many Western intellectuals (who could not bring themselves to protest the regularly reported outrages), there was at least one delegation of American leftists who returned with a glowing report. See "U.S. Leftist Editor Says Cambodians Are

Thriving," *New York Times*, May 12, 1978, p. 12. The editor in question, Daniel Burstein, also appeared on a CBS program on Cambodia in June 1978, evidently the only vocal apologist of that regime CBS could round up. See also Joseph J. Zasloff and McAlister Brown, "The Passion of Kampuchea," *Problems of Communism*, January–February 1979.

63. Michael Parenti, "Psychiatry and Politics" (letter), *New York Review of Books*, March 9, 1978; Cora Weiss in "Vietnam War Days Comment on Invasion by China," *New York Times*, February 22, 1979; "Excerpts from Coffin's Sermon at Riverside Church on Trip to Iran," *New York Times*, December 24, 1979; Walter Goodman, "Dissenters and Pornographers," *New York Times*, November 22, 1977. On the questionable equation of American and Soviet noncompliance with the Helsinki human rights agreement, see a letter by Stephen J. Whitfield in the *New York Times*, March 5, 1979; Ramsey Clark, "Treating Iran Fairly," *New York Times*, June 16, 1980. For a contrasting summary of the repressive features of the same political system see Jack Anderson, "What About the Ayatollah's Many Crimes?", *Daily Hampshire Gazette*, June 21, 1980.

64. *Anatomy of Anti-Communism*, Report prepared for the Peace Education Division of the American Friends Service Committee (New York, 1969), p. vi.

65. *Encounter*, December 1972, pp. 59–60. See also Ernst W. Lefever, *Amsterdam to Nairobi: The World Council of Churches and the Third World* (Washington, D. C., 1979).

66. Jonas M. Savimbi, "A Refusal to Become 'Black Russians' or 'African Cubans,'" *New York Times*, December 8, 1976.

67. Julius Lester, *Revolutionary Notes* (New York, 1968), pp. 161–62.

68. *Anatomy of Anti-Communism*, pp. vii, 72. The highly patterned political stances of the Quakers and their selective moral concerns are examined in Marvin Maurer, "Quakers in Politics: Israel, PLO and Social Revolution," *Midstream*, November, 1977.

69. *New York Times*, April 16, 1972, p. 10.

70. Arnold Kettle, Letter in the *Manchester Guardian*, 1958.

71. Such attitudes were not unfamiliar to George Orwell: "Actions are held to be good or bad, not on their own merits but according to who does them, and there is almost no kind of outrage—torture, the use of hostages, forced labour, mass deportations, imprisonment without trial, forgery, assassination, the bombing of civilians—which does not change its moral colour when it is committed by 'our' side." ("Notes on Nationalism," in *The Collected Essays, Journalism and Letters of George Orwell*, ed. Sonia Orwell and Ian Angus (New York, 1968), Vol. 3, p. 369.) This issue—that is, the influence of the identity of political protagonists on the moral responses to their behavior—will be taken up at greater length in Chapter 9.

Chapter 3: The First Wave of Estrangement: The 1930s

1. Cohn, *Pursuit of Millennium*, p. 314.

2. Nearing, *Making of a Radical*, p. 210.

3. Daniel Aaron, *Writers on the Left* (New York, 1965), p. 168. For a detailed and panoramic view of the period see also Daniel Aaron and Robert Bendiner, eds., *The Strenuous Decade* (Garden City, N.Y., 1970).

4. Samuel Hynes, *The Auden Generation: Literature and Politics in England in the 1930's* (London, 1976), p. 66. See also Richard H. Pells, *Radical Visions and*

American Dreams: Culture and Social Thought in the Depression Years (New York, 1973), pp. 97–98, 366.

5. John Dos Passos, *The Theme Is Freedom* (New York, 1956), pp. 2–3.

6. The same point is made in Lyons, *Assignment*, p. 226.

7. Frank A. Warren, *Liberals and Communism: The 'Red' Decade Revisited* (Bloomington, Ind., 1966), p. 65.

8. Filene, *Soviet Experiment*, p. 273.

9. Lyons, *Red Decade*, pp. 101, 111. Lyons also depicted the early enthusiasts as being more "inspired prophets of an embattled revolution" than "press agents of a going, if rather unpleasant business"—the latter description was reserved for the 1930s supporters of the Soviet Union. In my view the distinction was not quite so sharp. Many visitors managed to be just as naively enthusiastic in the 1930s as others were in the 1920s, for better reasons. To be sure, in the 1930s uncritical support for the regime required a greater capacity for faith and self-deception (or, more charitably, selective perception) than earlier.

10. Warren, *Liberals and Communism*, p. 10.

11. Edmund Wilson, quoted in John P. Diggins, *The American Left in the Twentieth Century* (New York, 1973), p. 110.

12. Nearing, *Making of a Radical*, p. 180.

13. Granville Hicks, "How I Came to Communism," *New Masses*, September 1932, p. 8.

14. Neal Wood, *Communism and British Intellectuals* (New York, 1959), p. 38. A further discussion of apolitical aestheticism in the 1920s can be found on pp. 100–105.

15. Pablo Neruda, *Memoirs* (New York, 1977), p. 136.

16. Alfred Kazin, *Starting Out in the Thirties* (Boston, 1965), pp. 85, 138; Muggeridge, *Sun Never Sets*, p. 291.

17. "Text of Statement by Briton Who Spied for Russians," *New York Times*, November 21, 1979; see also Andrew Boyle, "Britain's Establishment Spies," *New York Times Magazine*, December 9, 1979; and Hilton Kramer, "The Blunt Case: A Life Devoted to Beauty and Treachery," *New York Times*, December 2, 1979.

18. Malcolm Cowley, *The Dream of the Golden Mountains: Remembering the 1930s* (New York, 1980), p. 33. See also Kazin, *Starting Out*, p. 87 on the authority of Marxist opinions.

19. Lewis Coser and Irving Howe, *The American Communist Party, 1914–1957* (Boston, 1957), pp. 283–84.

20. Neal Wood wrote: "To understand how the wasteland of the mandarins of the twenties could become the bourgeois decay of the communist intellectuals of the thirties, it is necessary to glance at one of the most significant features of the intellectuals' perspective of the twenties: the lack of interest in politics. *The political sophisticates of the thirties were the political illiterates of the twenties*" (Italics added) (*Communism and British Intellectuals*, p. 103).

21. Hicks, "How I Came to Communism," p. 7.

22. Stuart Samuels, "English Intellectuals and Politics in the 1930's," in Rieff, *On Intellectuals*, p. 244. See also Wood, *Communism and British Intellectuals*, pp. 110–14; Samuels, "English Intellectuals," pp. 208–9.

23. Diggins, *American Left*, pp. 102, 116.

24. Claud Cockburn, *Discord of Trumpets* (New York, 1956), p. 276.

25. Granville Hicks, *Where We Came Out* (New York, 1954), pp. 35, 36. See also Coser and Howe, *American Communist Party*, p. 280. Max Shachtman observed that "for a time it seemed that the Communist Party would gain and main-

tain a monopoly in the realm of intellectuals . . ." (Rita Simon, ed., *As We Saw the Thirties* [Urbana, Ill., 1967], p. 14). Cowley, *Dream of the Golden Mountains*, p. 43.

26. Neruda, *Memoirs*, pp. 319–20.

27. Louis Fischer, *Men and Politics* (New York, 1941), pp. 189–90.

28. Cockburn, *Discord*, pp. 107–8.

29. Hicks, *Where We Came Out*, p. 25.

30. Alan Riding, "For Garcia Marquez, Revolution is a Major Theme," *New York Times*, May 22, 1980.

31. Leon Trotsky, *The Revolution Betrayed* (New York, 1972; first published 1937), p. 305.

32. A. L. Rowse, *Appeasement: A Study in Political Decline, 1933–1939* (New York, 1963), pp. 30, 31.

33. Muggeridge, *Sun Never Sets*, p. 350; Simon, *As We Saw the Thirties*, p. 171.

34. Such was the abundance of the American economy, according to the critics, that "socialism in America might in rather short order provide every family with the equivalent of a $25,000 annual income"; so Corliss and Margaret Lamont believed (see their *Russia Day by Day—A Travel Diary* [New York, 1933], p. 256).

35. Berger, *Pyramids*, is addressed to these issues.

36. An April 1978 CBS television report on child labor in Cambodia (filmed by a Yugoslav crew) provoked few cries of outrage on the part of those who believe that the building of socialism is the decisive context in which matters such as child labor, low wages, or poor working conditions are to be evaluated.

37. Irving Kristol observed that "Bourgeois society seems incapable of explaining and justifying its inequalities . . . how these inequalities contribute to or are consistent with the common good" ("About Equality," p. 45).

38. Waldo Frank, *Dawn in Russia* (New York, 1932), p. 22.

39. Hewlett Johnson, *The Soviet Power* (New York, 1940), pp. xiii, xiv. I debated whether or not clergymen qualified as intellectuals and concluded that some of them do and most of them probably do not, just as some journalists, engineers, or microbiologists may qualify and others may not. The decisive criterion in all such instances is the extent to which the individual transcends the limits of his particular occupational specialization and evinces a minimally creative concern with ideas and broader issues of social existence. "Minimally creative" because if such concerns remain totally passive and private they can never be discovered and evaluated. By the use of such criteria Hewlett Johnson may be considered an intellectual, especially since his social, political, and ethical concerns were expressed in a number of books.

40. Nearing, *Making of a Radical*, p. 202.

41. Ibid., p. 122. Moving between pacifism, vegetarianism, and socialism, Scott Nearing in some ways prefigured the sixties radicals' relentless search for solutions. At the same time, he also resembled Lincoln Steffens, one of the first pilgrims, of whom it was said: "If there is one single pattern in Steffens' thinking, it is his search for a solution . . . he never lost a kind of absolutist impatience . . . [he] eliminated one social solution after another. . . . But there had to be *a* solution" (Granville Hicks, "Lincoln Steffens: He Covered the Future—The Prototype of a Fellow-Traveler," *Commentary*, February 1952, p. 154).

42. Anna Louise Strong, *I Change Worlds: The Remaking of an American* (New York, 1935), pp. 40, 41, 97.

43. Ibid., p. 5.

44. Marx and Engels, *The German Ideology* (New York, 1960), p. 39. The Marxian proposition is also unclear in that it fails to tell us just what these ruling ideas encompass. Beliefs about the purpose and meaning of life? The proper atti-

tude toward work? Conceptions of family life and personal morality? The foundations of the legal system? The nature of the arts? One must presume that Marx and Engels meant all of these.

However, the troublesome fact remains that they did not tell us *how* dominating, preponderant, or influential such ideas and beliefs must be to be called "ruling." To what degree must they exclude and delegitimate all other, nonruling ideas? What degree of coexistence between the ideas of the rulers and nonrulers is compatible with the proposition that the ideas of the rulers are the ruling ones? No matter how hard, in recent times, groups of Western intellectuals have tried to resurrect Marxism by playing down and diluting its economic determinism, it cannot be explained away, as the issue of ruling ideas also suggests. The inclination to see capitalist society as an economically determined monolith interferes with understanding modern pluralistic societies, which have, instead of one clearly defined ruling class, several elites, often working at cross-purposes.

Perhaps the only type of society where these claims of *The German Ideology* would apply are those that are nominally Marxist. In the Soviet Union or China, the ideas of the ruling classes are indeed the ruling ideas, but even there one may find aspects and areas of life where this is not the case.

In the end it comes down to the recognition that those in power cannot always impose their ideas on society, and often they may not even be interested in trying to do so.

45. I have in mind people like Cyrus Eaton, Armand Hammer, and others whose life-long sympathy toward the Soviet Union was not merely an outcome of visions of profitable business ventures or opportunities for trade. For a portrait of Eaton, see *The New Yorker*, October 10 and 17, 1977. Of course, other examples could also be cited in which this type of sentimentality had nothing to do with pro-Soviet attitudes.

46. Malcolm Cowley, *Exile's Return* (New York, 1934), p. 77.

47. Ibid., pp. 216–17.

48. Joseph Freeman, *American Testament: A Narrative of Rebels and Romantics* (New York, 1973; first published 1936), p. 288; Kazin, *Starting Out*, p. 88.

49. Frank, *Dawn in Russia*, p. 112.

50. Cowley, *Dream of the Golden Mountains*, pp. 36–37, 118; quoted in Cowley, *Exile's Return*, p. 77.

51. Frank, *Dawn in Russia*, p. 164.

52. Johnson, *Soviet Power*, p. xiii.

53. Frank, *Dawn in Russia*, p. 42.

54. Julian Huxley, *A Scientist Among the Soviets* (London, 1932), pp. 51, 55, 59, 86, 93.

55. Lion Feuchtwanger, *Moscow 1937* (New York, 1937), pp. 3, 149, 150; Shaw, *Rationalization of Russia*, p. 102; Lamont, *Russia Day by Day*, pp. 257–58; Bernal quoted in Gary Werskey, *The Visible College: The Collective Biography of British Scientific Socialists of the 1930s* (New York, 1979), p. 148; John Strachey, *The Coming Struggle for Power* (New York, 1935), p. 360.

56. Nearing, *Making of a Radical*, p. 253; Riding, "Garcia Marquez."

57. Louis Fischer in Richard Crossman, ed., *The God that Failed* (New York, 1949), p. 203.

58. Stephen Spender, *Forward From Liberalism* (London, 1937), pp. 261–62.

59. Freeman, *American Testament*, p. 570.

60. Arthur Koestler provided an analysis of this mentality and the various techniques used by the diehard defenders of the Soviet system that remains valid and applicable to other totalitarian societies popular with intellectuals. See "The Soviet Myth and Reality" in *Yogi and the Commissar*, pp. 111–75.

61. E. J. Hobsbawm, "Intellectuals and Communism," in his *Revolutionaries* (New York, 1973), p. 27.

62. Crossman, *God that Failed.*

63. For a powerful critique of social and historical determinism see Isaiah Berlin, "Historical Inevitability," in *Four Essays.*

64. Rosa Luxemburg, *The Russian Revolution and Leninism or Marxism* (Ann Arbor, 1961), pp. 62, 77. More recently a well-known American sociologist commented on the same issues: "Where power is monopolized by a tiny elite as it is in all one-party or other authoritarian systems, whether they describe themselves as leftist or rightist . . . the great mass will have little or no way to prevent those who control the economy from dictating the way they shall live. Hence . . . any movement, regardless of its manifest objectives, which undermines existing institutions which facilitate opposition to power-holders, however inadequately is a force for authoritarian rule, and for increased rather than reduced inequality. Wherever small elites command the resources of society and polity . . . they can only be restrained from . . . exploiting the non-elite by the ability of the segments of the latter to bring pressure to bear on those in power." S. M. Lipset, "Ideology and Mythology: Reply to Coleman Romalis (and other critics)," in *Perspectives in Political Sociology*, ed. Andrew Effrat (Indianapolis, 1973), p. 254. These issues are further clarified in "The Two Concepts of Liberty" in Berlin, *Four Essays.*

65. Henry T. Hodgkin, ed., *Seeing Ourselves Through Russia* (New York, 1932), pp. 3, 92, 54.

66. Daniel Boorstin, *The Americans: The Colonial Experience* (New York, 1958), p. 63. Boorstin added that "whenever tested the Quakers chose the solution which kept themselves pure, even though others might have to pay the price"; Cowley, *Dream of the Golden Mountains*, p. 41.

67. On the long tradition and many variations (aesthetic, moral, patrician, bohemian, socialist) of alienation among American intellectuals see Edward Shils, "Intellectuals and the Center of Society in the United States," in *Intellectuals and the Powers*, esp. pp. 178–79.

Chapter 4: The Appeals of Soviet Society: The First Pilgrimage

1. Edmund Wilson, *Travels in Two Democracies* (New York, 1936), p. 242.

2. Owen Lattimore, "Letter to the Editor," *New Statesman*, October 11, 1968, p. 461.

3. Malcolm Muggeridge, *Chronicles of Wasted Time* (New York, 1973), p. 244; Muggeridge, *Sun Never Sets*, p. 79.

4. M. Zhivov ed., *Glazami Inostrancev: Inostrannie Pisateli o Sovetskom Souze* [Through the Eyes of Foreigners: Foreign Writers on the Soviet Union] (Moscow, 1932).

5. Huxley, *A Scientist Among the Soviets*, pp. 4–5. See also Feuchtwanger, *Moscow 1937*, pp. 145–46 for a similar argument.

6. Muggeridge, *Chronicles of Wasted Time*, pp. 211, 212–13; for other depictions of similar shipboard moods and anticipations see also Wilson, *Travels in Two Democracies*, pp. 150–52; and Violet Conolly, *Soviet Tempo: A Journal of Travel in Russia* (New York, 1937). Of her fellow travelers she wrote: "Most of the Americans were travelling in a group under the auspices of 'Universal Travel.' They plastered the ship's Log Book with effusive salutations to their Soviet fatherland (where they have never been) as soon as they got on board . . ." (p. 8). As far as the "English comrades on board" were concerned, "none of them has been in Russia before, and yet they fixed you with a glassy and uncomprehending eye if

you attempted any criticism of the USSR. . . . Everything on the boat was perfect because it was a Soviet boat . . ." (p. 12).

7. William C. White, "Americans in Soviet Russia," *Scribner's Magazine* 89 (February 1931): 171.

8. Ibid.

9. Lewis Feuer, "American Travelers to the Soviet Union, 1917–1932: The Formation of a Component of New Deal Ideology," *American Quarterly*, Summer 1962, p. 121.

10. Lyons, *Assignment* p. 329.

11. White, "Americans in Soviet Russia," p. 173.

12. Pells, *Radical Visions*, p. 355.

13. Margulies, *The Pilgrimage to Russia*, p. 16. A similar observation was made in Frederick C. Barghoorn, *The Soviet Cultural Offensive* (Princeton, 1960), p. 333.

14. Coser, *Men of Ideas*, pp. 239–40.

15. Meno Lowenstein, *American Opinion of Soviet Russia* (Washington, D.C., 1941), p. 157. For further discussions of the background of the trips and the upsurge of interest in the Soviet Union see also "Soviet Russia: Lodestone of the American Liberal," in Warren, *Liberals and Communism;* Daniel Aaron, "American Writers in Russia: The Three Faces of Lenin," *Survey*, April 1962; Lewis Coser, "Riding the Waves of the Future in the Thirties" in Coser, *Men of Ideas.* For portraits of distinguished Western visitors at the time, see Louis Fischer, "The Revolution Comes Into Its Own," chap. 10 in his *Men and Politics.*

16. Gyula Illyés, "Oroszország 1934" [Russia 1934] in *Szives Kalauz: Utijegyzetek, Külföld* [The Cordial Guide: Travel Notes Abroad] Budapest, 1966, pp. 21–22. The peculiarities of selective and wishful perception were also noted by two other Hungarian writers who visited the Soviet Union in 1951 with a delegation of writers: "The writers crossed the border in a spirit of devotion and a wide-open heart; they got off the train deeply moved. Here was at last the realization of their fondest dream: they set foot on the soil of the most advanced socialist society. . . . They were taken to art galleries and factories, museums and schools, but regrettably—though they requested it—not to the homes of ordinary citizens of Moscow. It did not matter; whatever was wanting, or whatever requests were unmet were quickly passed over—whatever was good and attractive was discussed at length and with enthusiasm. They inspected department stores full of low-quality goods, and subsequently they told each other of the wonderful displays they had seen. No, they did not lie. They were dedicated party members who were determined to view the Soviet Union as the country of wonders, and they had succeeded" (Aczel Tamas and Meray Tibor, *Tisztito Vihar* [The Cleansing Storm] [Munich, 1978], pp. 128–29).

17. Lyons, *Assignment*, p. 54. Or, as another visitor put it, "Every detail had special significance" (Peggy Dennis, *The Autobiography of an American Communist* [Berkeley, 1977], p. 58).

18. Strong, *I Change Worlds*, p. 91.

19. Huxley, *Scientist*, p. 26.

20. Committee of Concerned Asian Scholars, *China! Inside the People's Republic* (New York, 1972), p. 9; LeRoi Jones, *Home: Social Essays* (New York, 1966), p. 41.

21. Frank, *Dawn in Russia*, pp. 121, 127, 135.

22. Lyons, *Assignment*, p. 329.

23. Lamont, *Russia Day by Day*, p. 72.

24. Feuchtwanger, *Moscow 1937*, p. 8.

25. Dos Passos, *Theme is Freedom*, pp. 67–68. Enzensberger's disclosure was

reported in Richard Eder, "The Literati Discuss Censorship," *New York Times*, February 14, 1980, p. C-19.

26. Fischer, *Men and Politics*, p. 530.

27. Hodgkin, *Seeing Ourselves*, p. 55.

28. Trips to Spain or border areas in the same period represented another combination of business and pleasure, or edification and enjoyment. In these instances exhilaration was heightened by the hostilities taking place due to the civil war. The participants in such tours were mostly British and French, one may surmise from a report of Malcolm Muggeridge: "Fashionable parties were organized to visit the Franco-Spanish frontier and watch hostilities take place in that area; and men-of-letters, or of politics, or of both, weary of reviewing books, turning over thoughts often turned over; of dining in restaurants where cooking was excellent . . . and of meeting one another in rooms soon crowded and stuffy, sherry steadily consumed and conversation incessant—were exhilarated and spiritually refreshed by a stay in Barcelona. It was real, it was earnest, it was lively" (*Sun Never Sets*, pp. 295–96). It should be noted that visits to Spain during this period often differed sharply from the type depicted by Muggeridge, involving genuine hardship and exposure to danger. The "pilgrimages" to Spain remain outside the purview of this study, since, among other reasons, the Loyalist regime did not have the wherewithal for the techniques of hospitality.

29. Edmund Wilson, *Travels in Two Democracies*, pp. 207, 197.

30. Theodore Dreiser, *Dreiser Looks at Russia* (London, 1928), p. 26. Waldo Frank reacted in a similar spirit to the "Volga muzhiks . . . their rags, their feet sweating in bast or straw, their greasy caps and shawls, the mire of their roads, the grime of their izbas . . ." (*Dawn in Russia*, p. 229).

31. D. F. Buxton, *The Challenge of Bolshevism: A New Social Ideal* (London, 1928), p. 71.

32. Ibid., pp. 29, 30, 76.

33. Dreiser, *Looks at Russia*, pp. 48, 78. Sherwood Eddy reached virtually identical conclusions: "Here, for almost the first time in history . . . we have the leaders of a whole nation . . . sharing wellnigh all that they have with the people. . . . Instead of asking special privileges, they impose upon themselves unusual sacrifices . . . the sons of the poor peasants and workers are often admitted to the universities and to other privileges before those of Party members and officials. Even the President, Kalinin, must live the simple life in his flannel shirt. Stories of luxury and extravagance on the part of the leaders are for the most part grossly false" (*The Challenge of Russia* [New York, 1931], pp. 220–21).

34. Freeman, *American Testament*, p. 456.

35. Hewlett Johnson, *Soviet Russia Since the War* (New York, 1947), pp. 176–77.

36. Feuchtwanger, *Moscow 1937*, p. 35.

37. Harry F. Ward, *The Soviet Spirit* (New York, 1944), pp. 113, 115, 117, 116 (my emphasis). For other comments on this topic see also pp. 44, 107.

38. Huxley, *Scientist*, p. 97.

39. Freeman, *American Testament*, p. 461.

40. Wilson, *Travel in Two Democracies*, pp. 163, 204–5.

41. Alexander Wicksteed, *Life Under the Soviets* (London, 1928), p. 189.

42. Ward, *Soviet Spirit*, p. 42.

43. Lamont, *Russia Day by Day*, p. 115.

44. Feuchtwanger, *Moscow 1937*, p. 13.

45. Ward, *Soviet Spirit*, pp. 20, 24.

46. Dyson Carter, *Russia's Secret Weapon* (Winnipeg, Manitoba, 1942), pp. 87, 110; see also John A. Kingsbury, "Russian Medicine: A Social Challenge," *New Republic*, April 5, 1933.

47. Johnson, *Soviet Power*, pp. xiii, xiv.

48. Sherwood Eddy was one of those ready to dispel such misinformation and "wild rumors." See *Russia Today—What Can We Learn From It?* (New York, 1934), p. xiv. It should be noted that in this volume he made more critical comments about the Soviet system than in the previous one cited in n. 33.

49. Shaw, *Rationalization of Russia*, p. 26.

50. Lyons, *Assignment*, p. 430.

51. Huxley, *Scientist*, p. 67.

52. Feuchtwanger, *Moscow 1937*, p. 5.

53. Fischer, *Men and Politics*, pp. 9, 10.

54. Homer Smith, *Black Man in Russia* (Chicago, 1964), pp. 19–21.

55. Muggeridge, *Chronicles*, pp. 257, 258.

56. Maurice Hindus, *The Great Offensive* (New York, 1933), p. v.

57. Strong, *I Change Worlds*, p. 373.

58. Ruth Epperson Kennell, *Theodore Dreiser and the Soviet Union, 1927–1945* (New York, 1969), p. 11.

59. Coser, *Men of Ideas*, p. 236.

60. Gertrude Himmelfarb, "The Intellectual in Politics: The Case of the Webbs," *Journal of Contemporary History*, no. 3., 1971, p. 11.

61. *Stalin–Wells Talk. The Verbatim Report and a Discussion by G. B. Shaw, H. G. Wells, J. M. Keynes, Ernst Toller and Others* (London, 1934), pp. 35–36.

62. John Dewey, *John Dewey's Impressions of Soviet Russia and the Revolutionary World: Mexico, China, Turkey, 1929* (New York, 1964), pp. 100, 104, 105.

63. Eddy, *Russia Today*, p. 177.

64. Wilson, *Travel in Two Democracies*, p. 321.

65. Beatrice Webb, Introduction to Wicksteed, *Life Under the Soviets*, pp. x, xi. See also Francis A. Hanson, "What the Soviets Live By," in Davis, *New Russia*. Hanson was identified in the list of contributors to this volume as "an executive secretary of the National Religion and Labor Foundation" at New Haven (p. xi).

66. Ralph Lord Roy, *Communism and the Churches* (New York, 1960), pp. 70, 424.

67. Dreiser, *Looks at Russia*, p. 87.

68. Buxton, *Challenge of Bolshevism*, pp. 7, 27, 28, 81, 82, 85.

69. Hodgkin, *Seeing Ourselves*, p. 27.

70. Quoted in Roy, *Communism and Churches*, p. 69.

71. Feuchtwanger, *Moscow 1937*, p. 151.

72. Wilson, *Travel in Two Democracies*, p. 235–36.

73. Davis, *New Russia*, p. xii.

74. Frankwood E. Williams, "The Psychologic Bases of Soviet Successes," in Davis, *New Russia*, pp. 26–27. For a similar assessment of Soviet mental health and social problems see E. C. Lindeman, "Is Human Nature Changing in Russia?", *New Republic*, March 8, 1933. Lindeman believed that it was indeed changing. He also reported a drastic decline of prostitution and homosexuality and averred that suicide had "all but disappeared" (p. 96). The author was a social worker.

75. Albert Rhys Williams, for example, commented on the gaps between the principle enshrined in *both* the American and Soviet constitutions and their faulty implementation. See *The Russians* (New York, 1943), p. 235.

76. Johnson, *Soviet Power*, pp. 63, 4, 5; Johnson, *Russia Since the War*, p. 89.

77. Hindus, *Great Offensive*, p. 20.

78. Bernard Pares, *Moscow Admits a Critic* (London, 1936), p. 42.

79. Feuchtwanger, *Moscow 1937*, pp. 15, 23.

80. Quoted in *William · Du Bois: Scholar, Humanitarian, Freedom Fighter* (Moscow, 1971), p. 24.

81. Strong, *I Change Worlds*, pp. 126, 226.

82. Lamont, *Russia Day by Day*, p. 258.

83. Dewey, *Impressions*, p. 45, 46.

84. *New York Times*, February 27, 1967, p. 47. It has been noted elsewhere that "otherwise intelligent Americans . . . sometimes are moved to find in the lands of the godless that children play in the parks and pedestrians go about their affairs unimpeded by iron balls and chains" (Lawrence Nevins, "Politics Through Tinted Glass (Brightly)," *Worldview*, November, 1977, p. 25).

85. Joseph E. Davies, *Mission to Moscow* (New York, 1943), p. 9.

86. Henry A. Wallace, *Soviet Asia Mission* (New York, 1946), p. 21.

87. Ella Winter, *I Saw the Russian People* (Boston, 1947), p. 294.

88. Pablo Neruda, *Memoirs*, p. 194.

89. Daniel Berrigan, *Night Flight to Hanoi* (New York, 1968), p. 45.

90. Frank, *Dawn in Russia*, pp. 10, 98, 99, 230, 113, 121, 111.

91. Lamont, *Russia Day by Day*, pp. 185, 186.

92. Huxley, *Scientist*, pp. 16–17.

93. Freeman, *American Testament*, p. 461.

94. Pares, *Moscow Admits a Critic*, pp. 35, 36, 91, 41.

95. Feuchtwanger, *Moscow 1937*, pp. 3–4.

96. Frankwood E. Williams in Davis, *New Russia*, pp. 17, 19–20, 11, 28.

97. Quoted in Barbara Drake, "The Webbs and Soviet Communism" in *The Webbs and Their Work*, ed. Margaret Cole (London, 1949), p. 226.

98. Huxley, *Scientist*, pp. 11–12.

99. Hindus, *Great Offensive*, p. 15.

100. Wilson, *Travel in Two Democracies*, p. 200.

101. Frankwood Williams in Davis, *New Russia*, p. 23.

102. Frank, *Dawn in Russia*, pp. 51, 52, 186.

103. Winter, *I Saw the Russian People*, pp. 294, 298.

104. Wilson, *Travel in Two Democracies*, p. 211.

105. David Caute's argument in *Fellow-Travellers* applies to these appeals of Soviet society. He did, however, overemphasize them, to the virtual exclusion of others.

106. Huxley, *Scientist*, pp. 77, 2, 52.

107. Feuchtwanger, *Moscow 1937*, p. viii.

108. "To All Active Supporters of Democracy and Peace" (letter to the editor), *The Nation*, August 19, 1939. Approximately four hundred American intellectuals and artists signed this letter, including Waldo Frank, Dashiell Hammet, Granville Hicks, Rockwell Kent, Corliss Lamont, Max Lerner, Clifford Odets, S. J. Perelman, Frederick L. Schuman, Vincent Shean, Louis Untermeyer, James Thurber, Harry F. Ward, William Carlos Williams, and many other prominent academics and men and women of letters. Ironically, the publication of this statement, designed to reaffirm the differences between the Soviet Union and Nazi Germany, preceded by less than a week the signing of the Nazi-Soviet Pact on August 24, 1939.

109. Neruda, *Memoirs*, p. 242. Arthur Koestler's observations apply to Neruda's attitudes: "The Dnieper Dam, the Turk-Sib railroad, the White Sea canal and the Moscow underground, etc., were thus seen not as respectable technical achievements comparable to similar achievements in England and America, but as something unique the world has never seen, the very essence and flower and fulfillment of socialism itself" ("Soviet Myth and Reality" in *Yogi and the Commissar*, p. 130).

110. Fischer, *Men and Politics*, p. 189.

111. *Stalin-Wells Talk*, p. 4.

112. Frank, *Dawn in Russia*, pp. 134, 139, 136.

113. Lamont, *Russia Day by Day*, pp. 43, 44.

114. Aneurin Bevan, E. J. Strachey, and George Straus, *What We Saw in Russia* (London, 1931), p. 18.

115. Shaw, *Rationalization of Russia*, p. 21.

116. Bertrand Russell, *Portraits from Memory* (New York, 1956), p. 79.

117. Carter, *Russia's Secret Weapon*, pp. 91, 6, 94. Bernal quoted in Werskey, *Visible College*, p. 193.

118. Dewey, *Impressions*, p. 58.

119. Lamont, *Russia Day by Day*, p. 39.

120. Carter, *Russia's Secret Weapon*, pp. 92–93.

121. Lyons, *Assignment*, p. 63.

122. Winter, *I Saw the Russian People*, p. 119.

123. Cf. for example Margaret I. Cole, "Women and Children," in *Twelve Studies in Russia*, ed. Margaret I. Cole (London, 1933).

124. Anna Louise Strong, *This Soviet World* (New York, 1936), p. 250.

125. J. L. Gillin, "The Prison System," in Davis, *New Russia*, pp. xi, 220, 227.

126. Ella Winter, *Red Virtue* (New York, 1933), p. 206. OGPU is the acronym of the Soviet State Security Organs, or political police. In a later account of a trip taken in 1944, Winter returned to the same theme, observing that "the Soviet Union, I felt, is interested in cures, not in convictions; in rehabilitation, not in punishment. It is not the proud record of a politically ambitious prosecuting attorney which is at stake, but the long future of the little erring Soviet citizen" (*I Saw the Russian People*, p. 203). Bernard Pares also found correction rather than punishment the objective of Soviet penal policies; see his *Moscow Admits a Critic*, p. 91. Sherwood Eddy insisted that "it will probably be found on careful study that its [the Soviet] penal system is one of the most advanced, the most modern and redemptive in the world. . . . The man whom a capitalistic society brands as criminal they count a little brother who has gone wrong, perhaps through no fault of his own, because of poverty, ignorance, neglect or social injustice. He is never called a criminal . . ." (*Challenge of Russia*, pp. 104, 147). In all fairness to Eddy, it should be pointed out that he was aware of the difference between the treatment of "class enemies which is often cruelly unjust" (p. 147) and "the nine-tenth of the population."

127. D. N. Pritt, "The Russian Legal System," in Cole, *Twelve Studies*, p. 161.

128. Harold J. Laski, *Law and Justice in Soviet Russia* (London, 1935), p. 25.

129. Strong, *This Soviet World*, p. 254.

130. Mary Stevenson Callcott, *Russian Justice* (New York, 1935), pp. 161, 236–37.

131. Wicksteed, *Life Under the Soviets*, p. 78.

132. Sidney and Beatrice Webb, *Soviet Communism: A New Civilization?* (New York, 1936), pp. 587, 588. For favorable comments on Bolshevo see also Pares, *Moscow Admits a Critic*, p. 50, and Gillin, "Prison System," p. 228.

133. Hindus, *Great Offensive*, pp. 305, 306.

134. Strong, *Soviet World*, p. 256.

135. Callcott, *Russian Justice*, p. 35.

136. Shaw, *Rationalization of Russia*, p. 91.

137. Strong, *Soviet World*, p. 262.

138. Pritt, "Russian Legal System," pp. 161, 162, 163, 164.

139. Quoted in Strong, *Soviet World*, p. 258.

140. Shaw, *Rationalization of Russia*, pp. 92, 73.

141. Lamont, *Russia Day by Day*, p. 142.

142. Lenka von Koerber, *Soviet Russia Fights Crime* (London, 1934), p. 179.

143. Callcott noted that "while he is at his labor, the convict works under the

same conditions and with the same protections that he would enjoy in outside labor" (*Russian Justice*, p. 165; see also p. ix).

144. Laski, *Law and Justice*, p. 28.

145. Callcott, *Russian Justice*, pp. 186–87, 189–90, 190–91, 192, 201, 221, 224.

146. Koerber, *Russia Fights Crime*, pp. 17, 19, 197.

147. Laski, *Law and Justice*, pp. 27, 28.

148. Koerber, *Russia Fights Crime*, pp. 40, 43, 44–45.

149. Laski, *Law and Justice*, p. 28.

150. Callcott, *Russian Justice*, p. 173.

151. Strong, *Soviet World*, pp. 264–65.

152. As Alexander Solzhenitsyn, among others, has documented, the mistreatment of political prisoners did not begin under Stalin; see his *Gulag Archipelago* (New York, 1973, 1975, 1976). For further information on political imprisonment in the early 1920s see also International Committee for Political Prisoners, *Letters from Russian Prisons*, with introduction by Roger N. Baldwin (London, 1925).

153. See, for example, Strong, *Soviet World*, p. 257.

154. N. F. Pogodin, *Aristocrats* [in Russian] (Moscow, 1936); Edmund Wilson, in *Travels in Two Democracies*, reported seeing it in Moscow (p. 245). André Malraux was also impressed by the rehabilitation of prisoners at the Belomor project; see his "Literature in Two Worlds," *Partisan Review*, January 1935, p. 18.

155. *Belomor: An Account of the Construction of the New Canal Between the White Sea and the Baltic Sea* (New York, 1935), pp. vii, vi. Since Alexander Solzhenitsyn devoted a lengthy section of his study of Soviet penal institutions to the Belomor project, the reader may find it morbidly fascinating to consult his *Gulag Archipelago II* (New York, 1975), pp. 80–102 for a contrasting view of the enterprise.

156. Webb, *Soviet Communism*, pp. 589, 590, 591.

157. Muggeridge, *Chronicles*, pp. 234–35.

158. Webb, *Soviet Communism*, pp. 579, 585, 586, 591, 594.

159. Vladimir Dedijer, *The Battle Stalin Lost* (New York, 1970), p. 38.

160. Muggeridge, *Chronicles*, pp. 206–10, 141, 146–51. Bertrand Russell wrote: "Both of them were fundamentally undemocratic and regarded it as a function of a statesman to bamboozle or terrorize the populace" (*Portraits from Memory*, p. 109). Trotsky too was both contemptuous and scornful of them; see *Revolution Betrayed*, pp. 302–5.

161. Shaw, *Rationalization of Russia*, p. 112.

162. Jerome Davis, *Behind Soviet Power: Stalin and the Russians* (New York, 1946), p. 41.

163. In his *The First Circle* (New York, 1968), Solzhenitsyn presents a fictionalized satire of the extreme gullibility of Westerners on a prison tour and the Soviet techniques designed to exploit them; see pp. 327–37.

164. Jerzy Gliksman, *Tell the West* (New York, 1948), pp. 163–78.

165. For discussions of camps and conditions in this (and other) regions, see Robert Conquest, *Kolyma: The Arctic Death Camp* (New York, 1978); Alexander Solzhenitsyn, *Gulag Archipelago I and II* (New York, 1974, 1975); and David J. Dallin and B. N. Nicolaevsky, *Forced Labor in Soviet Russia* (New Haven, 1947).

166. Conquest, *Kolyma*, p. 204.

167. Wallace, *Soviet Asia Mission*, pp. 33–35, 217, 84.

168. Owen Lattimore, "New Road to Asia," *National Geographic Magazine*, December 1944, p. 657.

169. Elinor Lipper, *Eleven Years in Soviet Prison Camps* (Chicago, 1951), pp. 111–12, 113, 115.

170. Lattimore, "Letter," p. 461.

171. Lipper, *Eleven Years*, pp. 266–69.

172. Frank, *Dawn in Russia*, p. 37, 41. Similar observations were made by the Lamonts, *Russia Day by Day*, p. 124–25.

173. Jerome Davis, *Behind Soviet Power*, p. 30.

174. Quoted in Jean Lacouture, *André Malraux* (New York, 1975), p. 230.

175. Max Shachtman wrote: "The traditional journals of American liberalism, *The Nation* and *The New Republic*, endorsed the Moscow Trials with only slightly less vigor and tenacity than did the Stalinists themselves. They endorsed them with arguments that are to be the unexpungeable shame of the American liberals." Even the world of entertainment, or a large part of it, was politicized and supportive of the trials: "The movie colony was at the time virtually inundated by Stalinist radicalism. . . . Like their counterparts throughout the country, they were ready at every moment to speak out against an injustice in the United States and everywhere in the world. . . . For the victims of Stalinist injustice not a soul could be found to say a word." As far as the radical intellectuals were concerned, "the bulk of them went along slavishly and uncritically, some of them disgracefully, with the persecutors. . . . In the prevailing climate it took a great deal of integrity, intelligence and courage to come out in Trotsky's defense or even in favor of a fair and impartial hearing of the Russian defendant" (Max Shachtman, "Radicalism in the Thirties: The Trotskyist View," in Simon, *As We Saw the Thirties* (pp. 39, 41–42). For further discussions of Western attitudes toward the Purge Trials, see "Western Images of the Soviet Union," *Survey*, April 1962, esp. pp. 86–95; also Robert Conquest, *The Great Terror* (New York, 1968), pp. 499–513. According to George Watson, "Between 1933 and 1939 many (and perhaps most) British intellectuals under the age of fifty, and a good many in other Western lands, knowingly supported the greatest act of mass murder in human history" ("Were the Intellectuals Duped?", *Encounter*, December 1973, p. 30). My own interpretation of these attitudes, conveyed in the text, is somewhat different.

176. Upton Sinclair and Eugene Lyons, *Terror in Russia? Two Views* (New York, 1938), pp. 60–61.

177. Sinclair in Sinclair and Lyons, *Terror in Russia*, pp. 11, 12.

178. Davis, *Behind Soviet Power*, p. 31.

179. Henri Barbusse, quoted in Davis, *Behind Soviet Power*, p. 28. Romain Rolland also believed in the authenticity of the Moscow Trials and the guilt of the accused. Cf. Walter Laqueur and George L. Mosse, eds., *Literature and Politics in the Twentieth Century* (New York, 1967), p. 209.

180. Davis, *Behind Soviet Power*, p. 30.

181. Quoted by Sidney Hook in "Bert Brecht, Sidney Hook and Stalin" (letter), *Encounter*, March 1978, p. 93. Stephen Spender too was persuaded of the existence of "a gigantic plot against the Soviet government"; see his *The Thirties and After* (New York, 1978), p. 59.

182. Feuchtwanger, *Moscow 1937*, pp. 114, 121, 122–23, 132–33.

183. Walter Duranty, *The Kremlin and the People* (New York, 1941), p. 49, 65.

184. Davies, *Mission to Moscow*, pp. 29, 163, 168, 169, 46, 26, 25. The belief that the purges forestalled the activities of fifth columnists was also shared by Albert Rhys Williams. See his *The Russians*, p. 72, and Davis, *Behind Soviet Power*, p. 30. Dyson Carter went so far as to claim that "Russia is the only country in Europe where the Quislings were caught [that is, during the purges of the Red Army] and shot before they could carry out their vile treachery," *Russia's Secret Weapon*, p. 56.

185. Neruda, *Memoirs*, p. 197. Harold Laski was also impressed by Vishinski: "I found a man whose passion was law reform. . . . He was doing what an ideal Minister of Justice would do if we had such a person in Great Britain. . . . He

brought to the study of the law . . . an energy which we have not seen in this country since the days of Jeremy Bentham" (*Law and Justice*, p. 24).

186. Jerome Davis, quoted by Sinclair in Sinclair and Lyons, *Terror in Russia*, pp. 40–41; Lattimore, quoted in Conquest, *Kolyma*, p. 212.

187. Sidney and Beatrice Webb, *The Truth About Soviet Russia* (London, 1942), p. 19.

188. Jerome Davis, *Behind Soviet Power*, p. 29.

189. Barghoorn, *Soviet Cultural Offensive*, p. 324; see also "Dr. Jerome Davis Is Dead at 87; Educator Espoused World Peace" (obituary), *New York Times*, October 24, 1979. Corliss Lamont, who displayed a similar perseverance in "espousing" pro-Soviet causes up to our time, entitled a collection of his essays *The Independent Mind*. This and other aspects of his political profile are discussed in Hicks, *Where We Came Out*, pp. 166–69.

190. Cf. Vivian Gornick, *The Romance of American Communism* (New York, 1977); Jessica Mitford, *A Fine Old Conflict* (New York, 1977); and Peggy Dennis, *The Autobiography of an American Communist*. Claud Cockburn and Lillian Hellman also belong to these categories.

191. "Editorial: The USSR," *Life*, March 29, 1943, p. 20.

192. Lamont, *Russia Day by Day*, p. 63.

193. Wilson, *Travels in Two Democracies*, p. 322.

194. Shaw, *Rationalization of Russia*, p. 18.

195. Neruda, *Memoirs*, p. 250.

196. Quoted in Davis, *Behind Soviet Power*, p. 13.

197. Quoted in *Stalin-Wells Talk*, p. 47.

198. Bertrand Russell wrote: "The worship of the state . . . had led both the Webbs and also Shaw into what I thought an undue tolerance of Mussolini and Hitler, and ultimately into a rather absurd adulation of the Soviet government" (*Portraits from Memory*, pp. 107–8). John Reed's admiration for Mussolini was noted in Bertram D. Wolfe, *Strange Communists I Have Known* (New York, 1965), p. 30.

199. Webb, *Truth About Soviet Russia*, pp. 16, 18.

200. Johnson, *Soviet Power*, p. 309.

201. Feuchtwanger, *Moscow 1937*, p. 78.

202. Davies, *Mission to Moscow*, pp. 72, 82.

203. I. F. Stone, "1937 Is Not 1914," in Aaron and Bendiner, *Strenuous Decade*, p. 465.

204. Williams, *The Russians*, p. 78.

205. Davis, *Behind Soviet Power*, p. 12; Julius Lester, ed., *The Seventh Son— The Thought and Writings of W. E. B. Du Bois*, 2 vols. (New York, 1971), Vol. II, p. 619.

206. Davies, *Mission to Moscow*, p. 208.

207. Emil Ludwig, *Nine Etched From Life* (Freeport, 1969; first published New York, 1934), p. 348.

208. Feuchtwanger, *Moscow 1937*, pp. 76, ii, xi.

209. Davies, *Mission to Moscow*, p. 217. To be the object of the visible affections of children and animals seems the ultimate proof of authenticity and a much-used technique of legitimation, as evidenced by the predilection of dictators (and other political leaders) to be photographed with children or dogs. The intended message is that those who love and are loved by children or certain pets cannot be bad people. Moreover, power acquires a new glow by its juxtaposition with the innocence and comparative helplessness of children.

210. Ludwig, *Nine Etched From Life*, p. 346–47.

211. Webb, *Soviet Communism*, p. 804. This oft-cited homily makes one wonder

about the frame of mind in which it was made. Possibly it was a totally cynical remark, even a form of black humor. On the other hand it might have been genuine, but intended to apply only to those who deserved and were to benefit from such care, as opposed to those resembling weeds, and poisonous ones at that, who were to be destroyed without compassion.

212. Williams, *The Russians*, p. 72.

213. Fischer, *Men and Politics*, pp. 89–90; Bernal quoted in Werskey, *Visible College*, p. 318.

214. Davis, *Behind Soviet Power*, p. 15.

215. Johnson, *Russia Since the War*, pp. 65, 66–67, 71.

216. Neruda, *Memoirs*, p. 319. Neruda goes to some length to disavow any personal link with or admiration for Stalin, whom he saw only "at a distance." Yet he notes with apparent satisfaction how anxious Stalin was to make sure that he, Neruda, got the Stalin prize. Of all his poems, he tells us, only one was dedicated to Stalin! (pp. 316, 319).

217. See for example N. S. Khrushchev, "Report to the 20th Party Congress," in *The Anti-Stalin Campaign and International Communism: A Selection of Documents* (New York, 1956); and Milovan Djilas, *Conversations with Stalin* (New York, 1962).

218. John Strachey, *The Coming Struggle for Power* (New York, 1935), p. 358. André Malraux expressed similar views in his article in *Partisan Review* cited in n. 154.

219. Frank, *Dawn in Russia*, pp. 173–74, 177.

220. Wilson, *Travels in Two Democracies*, p. 212.

221. Feuchtwanger, *Moscow 1937*, pp. 45, 46; similar appreciative comments were also made by Upton Sinclair whose books also were published in large editions in the Soviet Union (see Sinclair and Lyons, *Terror in Russia*, p. 21). The Hungarian writer Gyula Illyés, another visitor in the early 1930s (quoted earlier), had a somewhat more critical reaction to the treatment of writers: "These days the Soviet [system] wins over the writers in other ways. First, their remuneration is remarkably good. Elsewhere it is upsetting to contemplate the poverty of writers, here their good fortunes make one apprehensive. The writers and artists, together with the scientists, occupy the highest rungs in the hierarchy, sometimes they take precedence over the party leaders.

"The poet can live well for a month from a poem of his. It will first be printed in the factory newspaper, then in a daily, monthly, and in a book; subsequently it will be translated into several languages of the Soviet nationalities . . ." (Illyés, "Oroszország 1934," pp. 237–38).

222. See for example Ilya Ehrenburg's account of Stalin's interest in one of his novels in *Eve of War, 1933–1941* (London, 1963), p. 274.

223. Arthur Koestler in Crossman, *God that Failed*, p. 57. Such techniques are more fully discussed on pp. 56–59 of the same volume.

224. *Memoirs of Waldo Frank*, ed. Alan Trachtenberg (Amherst, 1973), pp. 186–87.

225. Coser, *Men of Ideas*, p. 230.

226. Vladimir Nabokov, *Speak, Memory* (New York, 1966), pp. 262–63.

Chapter 5: The Rejection of Western Society in the 1960s and 70s

1. Howard Bruce Franklin, *Back Where You Came From: A Life in the Death of the Empire* (New York, 1975), p. 219. Franklin displayed several attributes of

the archetypal convert. Prior to becoming a leading campus radical at Stanford and a late admirer of Stalin (he edited *The Essential Stalin* [Garden City, N.Y., 1972]), he attended Amherst College, studied American literature, belonged to the ROTC, and flew bombers for the Strategic Air Command. (He also considered himself a white working-class aristocrat for a while because he had worked on a tugboat.) Thus he moved from early years of darkness, as it were, to a new enlightenment, and in particular to the realization that the United States embodied all the interconnected forces of darkness in this world.

2. Michael P. Lerner, *The New Socialist Revolution* (New York, 1973), pp. 310, 311, 245.

3. Jerry Rubin, *Do It* (New York, 1970), p. 24.

4. According to Joseph Adelson, "Even in the sunny, sleepy 1950s a now familiar critique of American society was already well established. The seminal ideas . . . of current radical thought had been set down in the writings of C. Wright Mills, Marcuse, Goodman and others, and from another flank, in the work of Norman O. Brown, Mailer and Allen Ginsberg" ("What Generation Gap?", *New York Times Magazine,* January 18, 1970, p. 36). In a similar vein, Charles Kadushin observed that the American intellectual elite's disapproval of the foreign policy of the United States dated back to the late 1950s and was linked to the changing perceptions of the Cold War, and more generally to that of the Soviet Communist threat; see his *The American Intellectual Elite* (Boston, 1974), pp. 214–15. In the same book he noted that "the [Vietnam] war merely served as a catalyst in moving intellectuals to the left" (p. 124).

5. Quoted in Carl Gershman, "New Left–New Face," *Freedom at Issue,* March–April, 1979, p. 3.

6. Bertrand Russell, *A History of Western Philosophy* (London, 1946), p. 703.

7. John K. Galbraith, *The Affluent Society* (New York, 1958).

8. Hobsbawm, *Revolutionaries,* p. 254.

9. Kenneth Keniston, "You Have to Grow Up in Scarsdale to Know How Bad Things Really Are," *New York Times Magazine,* April 27, 1969, pp. 130, 124. For a fuller discussion of such attitudes (and of the period as a whole) see Stanislav Andreski, *Prospects of a Revolution in the U.S.A.* (New York, 1973).

10. Jan Myrdal, *Confessions of a Disloyal European* (New York, 1968), p. 20. Myrdal was a rather typical European representative of the radical counter-culture, as his autobiography reveals. It appears that while growing up in Sweden he saw little of his liberal parents, who were busy at the UN and with other organizations and causes. In turn, the young Myrdal seemed to average one visit with his own son every two to three years, since he traveled a great deal. His "confessions" include many references to bouts of drinking and coupling. He hitchhiked a lot and was several times down and out with no place to stay except police stations. He felt guilty primarily for being a European. (His American counterparts felt guilty for being American, but also for being white and middle-class.) He was an idealist, uninterested in money or power, and a champion of what he perceived to be the underdog (e.g. China, Albania, and the Pol Pot regime after its defeat).

11. Rubin, *Do It,* p. 57.

12. Susan Stern, *With the Weathermen* (New York, 1975), pp. 142, 143, 145, 291. For other glimpses of the nonthreatening perception of authority in the United States see also Abbie Hoffman [or Free], *Revolution for the Hell of It* (New York, 1968), pp. 19–20 and p. 46 ("Jail is a goof"). For jolly and nostalgic recollections of the famous Chicago Conspiracy Trial (on the part of the defendants), see J. Anthony Lukas, "Bobby Seale's Birthday Cake (Oh, Far Out!)," *New York Times Magazine,* October 31, 1971. Angela Davis, notwithstanding her grim views of political repression in the United States, confidently observed, "I knew they could not

hold me for any period of time without allowing me to contact a lawyer" (*Autobiography* [New York, 1974], p. 16).

13. Susan Sontag, "Some Thoughts on the Right Way (for Us) To Love the Cuban Revolution," *Ramparts*, April 1969, p. 16.

14. For an interesting discussion of the dropout as a "successful failure" and of the cultivation of such status, see Stephen Spender, "Anti-Americanism," *New York Times*, June 11, 1972.

15. George Orwell, "Inside the Whale," in *Collected Essays, Journalism and Letters 1920–1940* (New York, 1968), vol. 1, pp. 515–16.

16. Rubin, *Do It*, p. 87. For a rather different assessment of the motives of American policymakers, see Guenter Lewy, *America in Vietnam* (New York, 1978), especially chap. 1 and Epilogues.

17. Stromberg, *After Everything*, p. 77.

18. John W. Aldridge, *In the Country of the Young* (New York, 1969), pp. 79–80.

19. Rubin, *Do It*, p. 87.

20. *New York Review of Books*, February 24, 1972, p. 47.

21. See also Peter L. Berger and Richard John Neuhaus, *Movement and Revolution* (New York, 1970), p. 60.

22. Henry Fairlie, *The Spoiled Child of the Western World* (Garden City, N.Y., 1976), p. 23. Abbie Hoffman wrote: "You want to get a glimpse what it feels like to be a nigger? Let your hair grow long." And: "A fifteen-year-old kid who takes off from middle-class American life is an escaped slave crossing the Mason-Dixon line" (*Revolution for the Hell of It*, pp. 71, 74). For another example of the quest for victim status, see Jerry Farber, *The Student as Nigger* (North Hollywood, 1969).

23. See also David Zane Mairowitz, *The Radical Soap Opera: An Impression of the American Left from 1917 to the Present* (London, 1974), p. 227. Such attempted identification with authentic heroes was also reflected in Jerry Rubin's admiring remarks about Che Guevara and his attendant fantasies of "going into the hills as guerillas" (*Do It*, p. 20). Abbie Hoffman too admired the Cuban revolutionaries. Also symptomatic of these attitudes, and of the spirit of the times, was that even the pacific Dr. Spock was, according to the *New York Times*, "wearing—at a Black Panther trial—a badge showing a hand clutching a rifle" (Mairowitz, *Radical Soap Opera*, p. 255).

24. David M. Potter, *History and American Society* (New York, 1973), p. 381.

25. For critical discussions of such tactics, see Irving Howe, "The New 'Confrontation Politics' Is A Dangerous Game," *New York Times Magazine*, October 20, 1968; and by the same author, "Political Terrorism: Hysteria on the Left," *New York Times Magazine*, April 12, 1970; see also George F. Kennan, "Rebels Without a Program," *New York Times Magazine*, January 21, 1968. For a more detailed discussion of confrontation politics and the associated attitudes see "Desperadoes in Wargasm" (chap. 6) in Mairowitz, pp. 239–81.

26. Stern, *With the Weathermen*, pp. 76–79. A conversation between Robert Cole and a policeman reflected another view of such occasions. Said the officer: "Have you ever seen those college kids shouting at the police? I've never seen anything like them for meanness and cheapness. The language that comes out of their mouths . . . those kids go crazy when they see us. The uniform seems to trigger something in them. They become dirty, plain dirty. They use the worst language I've ever heard. They make insulting gestures at us. They talk about killing us . . . I can't believe it's what they *say* it is, that they're just upset about injustice." Robert Coles, "A Policeman Complains: Between gangsters and hoodlums, the Negroes and drunks, the college crowd and the crazy ones, it's a miracle more of us don't get killed," *New York Times Magazine*, June 13, 1971, pp. 11, 75.

27. Rubin, *Do It*, p. 125.

28. *New York Times*, August 30, 1971, p. 5.

29. *New York Times*, November 21, 1971 p. 48. In the same spirit, an advertisement for *Glamour Magazine* proclaimed, "Commitment and Involvement Is In" in the *New York Times*, February 6, 1968. An outfit in Kansas advertised "beautiful movement jackets . . . for instant recognition" (*Massachusetts Daily Collegian*, November 23, 1970, p. 10); Cowley, *Dream of the Golden Mountains*, p. 42.

30. Rubin, *Do It*, p. 169. Abbie Hoffman's message was similar: "Do what you want. Take chances. Extend your boundaries. Break the rules. Protest is anything you can get away with. . . . We are a gang of theatrical cheerleaders . . ." (Hoffman, *Revolution for the Hell of It*, p. 157).

31. Edward Shils's observations further explain these developments: "New methods of pedagogy and exclusion from the labor market—as far as middle-class young persons are concerned—have reduced the amount of experience with severely hierarchical and repressive institutions. They are thereby spared direct contact with the very painful features of the conditions of scarcity . . ." ("Plenitude and Scarcity" in *Intellectuals and the Powers*, p. 278).

32. A somewhat similar point was made by Stromberg: "The young militants do not really want socialism at all, whatever they may say, but the wildest individualism; not security but danger; not the rational organization of society but a regaining of mystery and adventure" (*After Everything*, p. 239).

33. Russell, *History of Western Philosophy*, pp. 707, 709.

34. Shils, *Intellectuals and the Powers*, p. 275; see also his comments on p. 278. Stromberg also observed that "people have learned that their wants are sacred and of right ought to be satisfied. They have learned to consider any obstacle to personal fulfillment an intolerable affront. . . . They no longer accept sharp limitations on individual desires in the name of the group" (*After Everything*, p. 240). See also Daniel Bell, *The Cultural Contradictions of Capitalism* (New York, 1976), pp. 14–17, among many others.

35. Andrew Hacker, *The End of the American Era* (New York, 1972), pp. 167–68.

36. See for instance Robert J. Ringer (author also of *Winning Through Intimidation*), *Looking Out for Number One* (Beverly Hills, 1977) and its full-page advertisement in the *New York Times*, June 16, 1977, p. 7.

37. Wolfe, *Mauve Gloves*, pp. 126, 128, 129.

38. Paul Hollander, "Sociology, Selective Determinism, and the Rise of Expectations," *American Sociologist*, November 1973; for a related discussion see Gwynn Nettler, "Shifting the Load," *American Behavioral Scientist*, January–February 1972.

39. For example Harold Taylor, "We Need Radicals," *New York Times*, February 27, 1971, p. 27; also George Wald, "The Cure for Student Unrest Is *Adult* Unrest," *New York Times*, April 26, 1969. For other highly idealized images of the radical young, see Kenneth Keniston, *Young Radicals* (New York, 1968); Robert Jay Lifton, "Protean Man," *Partisan Review*, Winter 1968. For a critique of such views see Stanley Rothman et al., "Ethnic Variations in Student Radicalism: Some New Perspectives" in *Radicalism in the Contemporary Age*, ed. Severyn Bialer and Sophia Sluzar (Boulder, Colo., 1977) vol. 1; by the same author, "Intellectuals and the Student Movement: A Post Mortem," *Journal of Psychohistory*, Spring 1978; and S. M. Lipset and Gerald M. Schaflander, *Passion and Politics* (Boston, 1971). See also "The Crisis of Authority in American Education and Society," in Hollander, *Soviet and American Society*, pp. 173–78.

40. Quoted in Ethel Grodzins Romm, *The Open Conspiracy: What America's Angry Generation is Saying* (Harrisburg, Pa., 1970), p. 195. Edward Shils wrote:

"The students' hostility against authority . . . was reinforced by their elders' chorus of denunciation of authority, including their own. . . . Elites now quail before the charges of 'elitism' . . ." ("Intellectuals and the Center of Society in the United States," in *Intellectuals and the Powers*, pp. 182, 184).

41. Peter Berger further observed: "As the individual becomes uncertain about the world, he necessarily becomes uncertain about his own self, since that self can be subjectively real only as it is continually confirmed by others. Put differently, as the social identification processes become increasingly fragmented, the subjective experience of identity becomes increasingly precarious" ("'Sincerity' and 'Authenticity' in Modern Society," *Public Interest*, Spring 1973, p. 8).

42. Rothman et al., "Ethnic Variations"; Adelson, "What Generation Gap?"; Podhoretz, *Breaking Ranks*, p. 288. For another incisive discussion of various myths concerning the young see also Joseph Adelson, "Inventing the Young," *Commentary*, May 1971; and James Hitchcock, "Comes the Cultural Revolution," *New York Times Magazine*, July 27, 1969.

43. Diana Trilling, *We Must March My Darlings* (New York, 1977), pp. 113–14. The references are to the 1968 student occupation and demonstrations at Columbia University in New York. At the end of the same academic year a countercommencement was held, where the dissident radicals received the benediction of such adult authority figures as Dwight Macdonald, Erich Fromm, Harold Taylor (former president of Sarah Lawrence College), and Robert Lowell (pp. 139, 144–53).

44. Paul Wilkes, "Leonard Boudin: The Left's Lawyer's Lawyer," *New York Times Magazine*, November 14, 1971, p. 48. For a more general discussion of this phenomenon see Midge Decter, *Liberal Parents, Radical Children* (New York, 1975).

45. James Hitchcock wrote: "Although like most professors, radicals do not generally believe that the rewards of their calling are adequate, they also feel a certain guilt at the privileges of their status—leisure, the right to think and speak critically, freedom from constant need to 'produce' on the job. . . . The older intellectual performs for the adolescent rebel the service of systematizing his often incoherent feelings . . . and justifying them under a moral and political rubric. . . . He also gives them a certain respectability by demonstrating that they are actually more rational than the beliefs of apparently 'sane' liberals and moderates. (This is done by ignoring the often random character of social reality and postulating a gigantic and highly coordinated 'system' in which everything fits, from the Vietnam war to the teaching of poetry.)

"The students' deep and perhaps ineradicable cynicism about the entire culture (not only of America but of the whole West) . . . is continually fed by their awareness that so many of the most attractive people of the older generation—intelligent, sympathetic, morally concerned parents, professors, and clergy—are ridden with self-doubt often bordering on contempt. . . . Young people who regularly encounter adults of this kind would be hard pressed to believe anything good about the 'system' even if they were so inclined . . . since the most apparently concerned people of the older generation are more than eager to confess to any charge leveled at them" ("A Short Course in the Three Types of Radical Professors," *New York Times Magazine*, February 21, 1971, pp. 34–35, 44).

46. Berger and Neuhaus, *Movement and Revolution*, pp. 35, 37. See also Robert Nisbet, "Who Killed the Student Movement?", *Encounter*, February 1970, pp. 11–12. Henry Fairlie compared the anger of the young in the 1960s to "the longings of the child in a mood of angry defiance at its own limitations in a world that is intractable" (*Spoiled Child*, p. 174). As far as the contributions of the family to these attitudes was concerned, Richard Flack, a sympathizer, was in basic agreement with

the critics: "The combined result of these ideas [psychoanalysis, progressive education, etc.], plus feminism and the rising status of women, was to create a new kind of middle class family—less authoritarian, less hierarchical, more child-centered, more democratic, more self-conscious in its treatment of children" ("Revolt of the Young Intelligentsia," in *The New American Revolution*, ed. Roderick Aya and Norman Miller [New York, 1971], p. 229). See also Aldridge, *Country of the Young*, pp. 66–67.

47. See Robert Brustein, *Revolution as Theatre* (New York, 1971).

48. Rubin, *Do It*, pp. 106–7; see also Boorstin, *The Image*.

49. Renata Adler, *Toward a Radical Middle* (New York, 1971), p. xxi.

50. Stern, *With the Weathermen*, p. 155.

51. See for example Stanley Rothman, "Intellectuals and the American Political System," in *Emerging Coalitions in American Politics*, ed. S. M. Lipset (San Francisco, 1978), p. 343–45.

52. For example, Marie Winn, *The Plug-In Drug* (New York, 1978), pp. 15–16, 102–16.

53. Adler, *Radical Middle*, p. xxii.

54. Robert Brustein, "If An Artist Wants To Be Serious and Respected *and* Rich, Famous and Popular, He Is Suffering from Cultural Schizophrenia," *New York Times Magazine*, September 26, 1971, pp. 85, 12, 85.

55. See for example *New York Times Magazine*, November 21, 1976.

56. Bell, *Cultural Contradictions*, pp. 34, 35.

57. Stromberg, *After Everything*, p. 116; see also his chap. 4, "The Disease of Modernism."

58. William V. Shannon, "The Death of Time," *New York Times*, July 8, 1971.

59. On how socialist realism provides "role models" (or models of behaviors) see Paul Hollander, "Models of Behavior in Stalinist Literature," *American Sociological Review*, June 1966.

60. "Offensive to Gay Liberation: TV Mailbag," *New York Times*, November 19, 1972.

61. John Leo, "Styron's Turner Irks Negroes Who Call It Racist, Distorted," *New York Times*, February 1, 1968. For a criticism of a play on Lumumba written in a similar spirit see Clayton Riley, "A 'Murderous' Portrait of a Black Patriot?", *New York Times*, January 2, 1972.

62. "Black Panelists Link Art to Politics," *New York Times*, May 29, 1972, p. 29.

63. Kevin Philips, "Networks Are Under Fire for Racism, Sexism and Ageism," *TV Guide*, September 3–9, 1977; see also Grace and Fred M. Hechinger, "There Are No Sexists on 'Sesame Street,'" *New York Times*, January 30, 1972. For a critique of an example of feminist socialist realism replete with "tone[s] of didactic uplift" and "ideological ecstasy" see Pearl K. Bell, "Her Life as a Rebel" (review of Alix Kates Shulman, *Burning Questions*), *New York Times*, Book Review Section, March 26, 1978; for a discussion of a work conceived in the same spirit see John Leonard, "Shirley MacLaine—Revisited," *New York Times*, November 6, 1970.

64. Grace Glueck, "Art Group Disrupts Museum Parley," *New York Times*, June 20, 1970.

65. Louis Kampf, "Notes Toward a Radical Culture," in Long, *New Left*, p. 426. Kampf also confessed in the same essay that he found "it difficult not to gag on the word 'culture'" (p. 420). The essay abounds in expressions of guilt over his earlier (unenlightened) enjoyment of culture (e.g., p. 424).

66. Robert Brustein, "New Fads, Ancient Truths," *New York Times*, August 17, 1969. For another report on the ultimate absurdities of the living theater movement

see Frank Moses, "Freedom? Boredom? Fascism?", *New York Times*, March 30, 1969.

67. This title was quoted in David Caute, *The Illusion* (London, 1971), p. 45.

68. Nancy Moran, "Scarsdale Course Teaches Guerrilla War Tactics," *New York Times*, August 15, 1969; see also the editorial "Vietnam in Scarsdale" in the *New York Times*, August 16, 1969.

69. Sontag, *Trip to Hanoi*, p. 87; see also Stromberg, *After Everything*, p. 55 and Rubin, *Do It*, p. 105. Irving Howe wrote: "There is a feeling abroad, which I partly share, that even if the Vietnam war were to end, our cities to be rebuilt, and our racial conflicts to be eased, we would still be left with a heavy burden of trouble, a trouble not merely personal or social but having to do with some deep if ill-located regions of experience" (Irving Howe and Michael Harrington, eds., *The Seventies* [New York, 1973] p. 53). For a lucid analysis of the attitudes associated with the protest against the war and some of the lessons of the protest, see Peter L. Berger, "Indochina and the American Conscience," *Commentary*, February 1980.

70. In the course of the 1960s the new and somewhat peculiar position of anti-anticommunism solidified and was embraced by many intellectuals who were not communist themselves yet strongly opposed anticommunist attitudes and policies. This was, above all, a reaction against McCarthyism and, more generally, against extreme right-wing domestic anticommunism. At the same time it was also a reaction against the Vietnam war, which was considered the most deplorable demonstration of the consequences of anticommunist attitudes and policies. The vigor of anti-anticommunism signified a renewal of old leftist sentiments that abhorred "red-baiting" and could see "no enemy on the left." Finally, anti-anticommunism, insofar as it was related to the new spirit of social criticism and estrangement, also represented a protest against the belief (a part of the anticommunist position) that Western societies were superior to communist ones. For various comments on the vicissitudes of "liberal anticommunism" see "Liberal Anti-Communism Revisited. Symposium." Lillian Hellman's *Scoundrel Time* (New York, 1976) is a characteristic and popular expression of anti-anticommunism. For two criticisms of the book (and the associated attitudes) see Alfred Kazin, "The Legend of Lillian Hellman," *Esquire*, August 1977, and Irving Howe, "Lillian Hellman and The McCarthy Years," *Dissent*, Fall 1976.

71. Frank Parkin, *Middle Class Radicalism: The Social Basis of the British Campaign for Nuclear Disarmament* (Manchester, England, 1968), pp. 5, 32 (my emphasis). He also noted that "protest against the Bomb was often a thinly-veiled protest at certain other aspects of the social order . . ." (p. 108).

72. Berrigan, *Night Flight to Hanoi*, p. xiv. Similar hyperbole proliferated during these years. A remarkable document of the period, a compendium by the members of the Venceremos Brigade, spoke of "total fascism that daily grips us inside the U.S." See Sandra Levinson and Carol Brightman, eds., *Venceremos Brigade: Young Americans Sharing the Life and Work of Revolutionary Cuba* (New York, 1971), p. 219.

73. For example, it was found that "cities which had riots were more likely to be those in which (1) the black occupational structure was most similar to that of whites, (2) black unemployment levels declined to levels similar to those for whites, (3) black income approached white levels . . ." (James A. Geschwender, ed., *The Black Revolt* [Englewood Cliffs, N.J., 1971], p. 321).

74. "Indians Ripped Up Federal Building," *New York Times*, November 10, 1972, p. 17.

75. See for example Walter Goodman, "When Black Power Runs the New Left,"

New York Times Magazine, September 24, 1967; Renata Adler, "Radicalism in Debacle: The Palmer House," in *Radical Middle;* Martin Peretz, "The American Left and Israel," *Commentary*, November 1967. The temporary flow of white radicals into black slums to do "community organizing" was another activity undertaken to expiate guilt. Thus, for instance, Tom Hayden had "an overwhelming sense of the sinfulness of the affluent, 'quasi-fascist' society; for him to organize the outcasts of Newark is the equivalent of a religious fast—penance for the sins of status committed in Sodom" (Jack Newfield, *The Prophetic Minority* [New York, 1967], p. 89).

76. For a critical survey of such practices see Nathan Glazer, *Affirmative Discrimination* (New York, 1975).

77. For some comments on this phenomenon see Ronald Berman, *America in the Sixties* (New York, 1968), pp. 281–82. Norman Mailer's essay on *The White Negro* (San Francisco, 1957) is a forerunner of the cult being discussed here.

78. This photo was published in (among other places) the *New York Times*, February 5, 1968, p. 70. It was also suggested that "Huey Newton, a luminous man, is in prison because he is black, compassionate, sensitive, courageous and unprepared to cooperate with his would-be assassins" (Carl Oglesby, ed., *The New Left Reader* [New York, 1969], p. 223).

79. For example, Howard Bruce Franklin, *The Victim As Criminal and Artist* (New York, 1978). For various views of George Jackson, much admired black prison inmate who was killed during his attempted escape, see Tad Szulc, "George Jackson Radicalizes the Brothers in Soledad and San Quentin," *New York Times Magazine*, August 1, 1971; Roger Wilkins, "My Brother, George," *New York Times*, August 21, 1971, p. 31. For dissenting views of George Jackson's status as a political prisoner see Malcolm Braly, "They're Not Political Prisoners," *New York Times*, October 11, 1971, p. 35; on the correspondence page, "George Jackson: A Hero-Victim?", *New York Times*, September 15, 1971; "Political Prisoners or Criminals," *New York Times*, October 26, 1971. Jessica Mitford was among his admirers; see her "A Talk with George Jackson," in *Poison Penmanship* (New York, 1979).

80. Referred to in "On Prisoners' Nobility," *New York Times* (correspondence), January 25, 1972.

81. Quoted in Victor Navasky, "Right On! With Lawyer William Kunstler," *New York Times Magazine*, April 19, 1970. For a more comprehensive discussion of such "punitive moralism" see Oscar Glantz, "The New Left Radicalism and Punitive Moralism," *Polity*, Spring 1975.

82. See, for example, Alex Thio, "Class Bias in the Sociology of Deviance," *American Sociologist*, February 1973. For a rebuttal see Kurt Tausky, "Comment on 'Class Bias in the Sociology of Deviance,'" *American Sociologist*, February 1974.

83. Quoted in Paul Johnson, *Enemies of Society* (New York, 1977), pp. 203–4.

84. Sontag, "Some Thoughts," p. 16.

85. C. Wright Mills, *The Power Elite* (New York, 1956); William G. Domhoff, *Who Rules America?* (Englewood Cliffs, N.J., 1967); and by same author, *Higher Circles: The Governing Class in America* (New York, 1970).

86. Robert Paul Wolff, Barrington Moore, Jr., and Herbert Marcuse, *Critique of Pure Tolerance* (Boston, 1965). As recently as 1980 Noam Chomsky entertained similar views on the more subtle ways of repression in the United States. See George de Stefano, Jr., "Brainwashing under Freedom," *Valley Advocate*, February 13, 1980, p. 16A.

87. This also applied to children: "The only children who have the slightest chance of escape from this supervised nightmare . . . are the children of the ghettos and the working class where the medieval conception of open community—living

on the street—still lingers. . . . Individual children are barely noticed, let alone supervised; children are often allowed to roam far from home or play out on the street until all hours. . . . In class they are wild and unruly, as indeed they ought to be. . . ." Such was the entrancing vision of lower-class childhood for Shulamith Firestone. See her *Dialectic of Sex* (New York, 1971), pp. 100–101.

88. See also Podhoretz, *Breaking Ranks*, p. 74. For satirical treatments of such attitudes, see Wolfe, *Mauve Gloves*, and Cyra McFadden, *The Serial* (New York, 1978). For major statements on the values of the counterculture see Theodore Roszak, *The Making of a Counterculture* (Garden City, N.Y., 1969); and Charles Reich, *The Greening of America* (New York, 1970). For a critical discussion of the new radicalism and aspects of the counterculture see Irving Louis Horowitz, *Radicalism and the Revolt Against Reason; the Social Theories of George Sorel* (Carbondale, Ill., 1968). On the spread of increasingly irrational attitudes and pursuits see also George Steiner, "The Lollipopping of the West," *New York Times*, December 9, 1977. It was also a sign of the times that at its 1978 meetings the American Anthropological Association "gave top priority to symposiums on witchcraft, shamanism, abnormal phenomena and extrasensory perception" (Marvin Harris, "No End to Messiahs," *New York Times*, November 26, 1978).

89. Morris Dickstein, *Gates of Eden* (New York, 1977), p. vii.

90. Philip Slater, *The Pursuit of Loneliness* (Boston, 1970), p. 150.

91. Firestone, *Dialectic of Sex*, pp. 208, 209.

92. Quoted in Newfield, *Prophetic Minority*, p. 90.

93. Nearing, *Making of a Radical*, pp. 262, 193. Joseph Freeman, who knew Nearing personally, wrote of him: "The flannel shirt he wore on his body was a symbol of the hair shirt he wore on his soul. Behind many of his political beliefs was the anterior conviction that wealth, luxury, riches, surplus destroyed a man's initiative. . . . Nearing approached the revolutionary movement from the moral presupposition that the psychology of many possessions was bad. . . . He believed both in the Tolstoyan gospel of doing everything with your own hands and in Lenin's idea of a great organized, planned industrial society administered collectively by its members. He was opposed to shedding the blood of cows and chickens and so ate raw lettuce, carrots and apples; but he wanted socialism, and so cheered the victories of the Red Army over the White Guards and approved the dictatorship of the proletariat" (*American Testament*, pp. 332–33).

94. Nearing, *Making of a Radical*, p. 199.

95. Tocqueville wrote: "By this means, a kind of virtuous materialism may ultimately be established in the world which would not corrupt, but enervate the soul, and noiselessly unbend its springs of action." Quoted in Richard Hoggart, *The Uses of Literacy* (Boston, 1961), p. 141.

96. Herbert Marcuse, *One-Dimensional Man* (Boston, 1964), p. 50.

97. Ibid., p. 241.

98. "Marcuse Defines His New Left Line," *New York Times Magazine*, October 27, 1968, p. 92.

99. Marcuse, *One-Dimensional Man*, pp. 245–46.

100. Ibid. pp. 244–45 (my emphasis). It is not too difficult to visualize situations and personal experiences which could have provoked such critiques of life in America, where people let their radios and television sets blare, decorate their dwellings much as they please, in total ignorance of the canons of good taste, where policemen or cab drivers may call a professor "Mac" and the cashier at the supermarket may ask "How are you today?", "oozing unwanted familiarity."

Given such sentiments, one may wonder how Marcuse developed his appreciation of the youth culture and its raucous "new sensibility," which produced much noise and undecorous public behavior. And yet Marcuse noted approvingly the "mixing of the barricade and the dance floor, love play and heroism" (*An Essay on Liberation* [Boston, 1969], p. 26). (But two pages later he pleaded for "a modicum of protection from noise and dirt.") Other critiques of Marcuse may be found in Maurice Cranston, "Herbert Marcuse," *Encounter*, March 1969; and Alasdair MacIntyre, *Herbert Marcuse: An Exposition and Polemic* (New York, 1970).

101. Roy Reed, "Back to Land Movement Seeks Self-Sufficiency," *New York Times*, June 9, 1975, p. 19.

102. Freeman, *American Testament*, p. 276.

103. Quoted in Russell, *Portraits from Memory*, p. 113.

104. Rubin, *Do It*, p. 127. For a more theoretical discussion of the rejection of role relations see Richard Lowenthal, "Unreason and Revolution," *Encounter*, November 1969, esp. p. 31.

105. Levinson and Brightman, *Venceremos Brigade*, pp. 311, 373.

106. Norman Mailer, *The Presidential Papers* (New York, 1963), pp. 69–70. Almost identical feelings were expressed by LeRoi Jones on the corruption of the mind in the United States in *Home: Social Essays*, p. 61.

107. Slater, *Pursuit of Loneliness*, pp. 3, 18.

108. Ibid., p. 103. More recently Slater rediscovered (in his *Wealth Addiction* [New York, 1980]) that, in the words of a reviewer, "the root of all evil, at least in America, is a love of money" (Christopher Lehmann-Haupt, *New York Times*, March 14, 1980).

109. Firestone, *Dialectic of Sex*, pp. 198–99, 226.

110. Slater, *Pursuit of Loneliness*, p. 88.

111. Michael Lewis, *The Culture of Inequality* (Amherst, 1978), pp. 88, 192.

112. Ibid. This is a debatable proposition, since crime exists in all contemporary societies including those without "the individual-as-central-sensibility." Moreover, American society has become decreasingly punitive, and increasingly relativistic and socially deterministic. In fact, less and less moral indignation is occasioned by crime as it has become more and more commonplace. One must also ask, *just how much* crime is needed to make the noncriminal population feel self-righteously decent?

113. Quoted in Nigel Young, *An Infantile Disorder? The Crisis and the Decline of the New Left* (London, 1977), p. 309; Arthur Liebman, *Jews and the Left* (New York, 1979), p. 563.

114. For example, Stokely Carmichael said that "the 'real' reason the United States was fighting the Vietnam war was to 'serve the economic interests of American businessmen who are in Vietnam solely to exploit the tungsten, tin and oil . . .'" (quoted in "Carmichael To Take Part in War Protest April 15th," *New York Times*, March 30, 1967).

115. Sontag, *Trip to Hanoi*, p. 18.

116. Davis, *Autobiography*, pp. 109, 110, 111.

117. Evidently such attitudes had something to do with the early influence of Bettina Aptheker, daughter of Herbert Aptheker, a long-time party functionary of unswerving loyalty. Angela Davis wrote: "I had first met Bettina in New York when we were both high school age. . . . At that time Bettina was in the leadership of Advance, the youth organization I joined, which had fraternal ties with the Communist Party. What subsequently remained most vividly in my mind about Bettina was the way she had described a trip to the Soviet Union. I had been enormously impressed by the egalitarianism she said she witnessed. She had visited

the apartment of a worker and the apartment of a doctor; the doctor's, she said, was no more luxurious than the worker's" (Ibid., p. 304). These recollections show that even the *second-hand experience of the conducted tour* can serve to confirm the predisposition of the believer.

The case of Angela Davis and the Apthekers was one among many that showed that, in the words of Arthur Liebman, "the New Left did not represent an abrupt break with the past or with the Old Left" (Liebman, *Jews and the Left*, p. 539).

118. Parkin, *Middle Class Radicalism*, p. 36 (my emphasis); on the "politics of gesture" see also Mairowitz, *Radical Soap Opera*, p. 261.

119. Newfield, *Prophetic Minority*, pp. 87–88. Another notable (if basically unconvincing) expression of the anti-intellectualism of the period was Susan Sontag's essay *Against Interpretation* (New York, 1966).

120. The works of Abbie Hoffman and Jerry Rubin were the best examples of this genre.

121. For a study of recent forms of alienation stressing the role of expectations and perceptions see David C. Schwartz, *Political Alienation and Political Behavior* (Chicago, 1973), esp. pp. 3–21, 233–46.

122. Quentin Anderson, "On the Middle of the Journey," in *Art, Politics and Will: Essays in Honor of Lionel Trilling*, ed. Quentin Anderson, Stephen Donadio and Steven Marcus (New York, 1977), p. 254. For corresponding references to radical politics as forms of "self-dramatization" see Christopher Lasch, *The Culture of Narcissism* (New York, 1978), pp. 81–83.

123. Slater, *Pursuit of Loneliness*, p. 83.

124. For a British view of such contemporary agonies see Robert Conquest, "The American Psychodrama Called 'Everyone Hates Us,'" *New York Times Magazine*, May 10, 1970.

125. Almond, *Appeals of Communism*, p. 103.

126. Levinson and Brightman, *Venceremos Brigade*, pp. 2, 50, 69, 125–27, 170, 219, 317, 328, 392, 388, 385. Angela Davis too felt inferior to the Cubans: "Being North Americans, we all felt we had to constantly demonstrate our worth" (*Autobiography*, p. 204).

The use of the recollections of members of the Venceremos Brigade may seem to contradict the description of the present study as based on the writings of intellectuals. Rather than being creative writers, artists, or scientists, the Brigaders were mostly college students, graduate students, or college dropouts. Only two justifications might be offered for designating them as marginal intellectuals. One is their obvious concern with ideas, ideologies, and social criticism; the other, their student roles. Even if they were not creative or competent intellectuals they certainly exemplify the quasi-intellectual subculture of which they were a part and which is inseparable from the academic setting.

127. Firestone, *Dialectic of Sex*, p. 103.

128. For instance, a popular textbook on social problems included among its major topics the following: inequality, racism, corporate power, militarization, education, health, welfare, the police, criminal law and corrections. See Jerome H. Skolnick and Elliot Currie, eds., *Crisis in American Institutions* (Boston, 1970). During the 1960s and early 1970s sociology courses on race relations and social problems reached their peak popularity, and probably hundreds of textbooks (if not more) were published on these issues.

129. Aldridge, *Country of the Young*, p. 115.

130. Shils, *Intellectuals and the Powers*, p. 190.

Chapter 6: New Horizons: Revolutionary Cuba and the Discovery of the Third World

1. Huey P. Newton, "Sanctuary in Cuba?", *CoEvolution Quarterly*, Fall 1977, p. 28.

2. Saul Landau, "Cuba: The Present Reality," *New Left Review*, May–June 1961, p. 22.

3. Warren Miller, *Ninety Miles from Home* (Boston, 1961), p. 8.

4. Susan Sontag, "Some Thoughts," p. 10.

5. Jonathan Kozol, *Children of the Revolution: A Yankee Teacher in the Cuban Schools* (New York, 1978), p. xx.

6. LeRoi Jones, "Cuba Libre," in *Home: Social Essays*, p. 39.

7. Paul Baran quoted in Peter Clecak, *Radical Paradoxes* (New York, 1973), p. 93. Kingsley Martin, the editor of *New Statesman*, was also convinced that Castro "will never deprive the present generation of pleasure for the theoretical benefit of future generations" ("Fidel Castro's Cuba," *New Statesman*, April 21, 1961, p. 614).

8. For a more recent report on such inequities see Jon Nordheimer, "Reporter's Notebook: How Willing Are Cuba's Volunteers?", *New York Times*, June 27, 1978. The graffiti and recent economic difficulties were reported in "Castro's Sea of Troubles," *Newsweek*, March 3, 1980, p. 39–40.

9. Quoted in Clecak, *Radical Paradoxes*, p. 152.

10. For an example of such a negative assessment see Norman Birnbaum, "America, A Partial View," *Commentary*, July 1958.

11. Dennis Wrong, "The American Left and Cuba," *Commentary*, February 1962, p. 95.

12. Philip Abbot Luce, *The New Left Today* (Washington, D. C., 1971), p. 51.

13. Beauvoir, *All Said and Done*, pp. 409–10. For a detailed account of the Padilla affair see Jose Yglesias, "The Case of Herberto Padilla," *New York Review of Books*, June 3, 1971. In 1978 a number of famous Western intellectuals and early admirers of Castro expressed their disapproval of the twenty-nine-year prison sentence meted out for alleged espionage to Doctor Martha Frayde, described in their letter as "a revolutionary idealist" who disagreed with Castro's pro-Soviet policies. Those signing the letter included Simone de Beauvoir, Michel Foucault, Juan Goytisolo, Norman Mailer, Octavio Paz, Jean-Paul Sartre, and William Styron (see *New York Review of Books*, December 7, 1978). Padilla emigrated to the United States in 1980 ("Havana Permits a Censured Poet to Move to U.S.," *New York Times*, March 17, 1980).

14. Jorge Edwards, *Persona Non Grata* (New York, 1977), p. 44.

15. See, for example, Saul Landau, "The U.S. Cannot Dictate Terms," *In These Times* ["The Independent Socialist Newspaper"], April 6–12, 1977. Stephen Bingham, the radical lawyer who visited Cuba in 1969, remained a steadfast admirer as of 1974 (see "Bingham, Lawyer Hunted in Six Prison Killings, Is Active in Hiding," *New York Times*, September 22, 1974). The Quakers were also sympathetic, and produced *Ten Years After: A Quaker Visit to the* [Cuban] *Revolution* (See Maurer, "Quakers in Politics," (p. 42).

16. Such as Kozol. Jim Jones was also among the more recent enthusiasts who visited Cuba; he was there in 1977. See Robert Levering, "Rev. Jim Jones," *Valley Advocate*, December 6, 1978, p. 8A. It was also reported that shortly before the mass suicides he contemplated the relocation of the group to Cuba (or the Soviet

Union). See Joseph B. Treaser, "Jim Jones' 1960 Visit to Cuba Recounted," *New York Times,* March 25, 1979.

17. Venceremos Brigade pamphlet, no date; see also *Venceremos* ["A Publication of the Venceremos Brigade"], February 1976, on recruitment and the motivation of the participants.

18. Harry Maurer, "With the Venceremos in Cuba," *Nation,* July 2, 1977, p. 8.

19. Venceremos pamphlet.

20. Levinson and Brightman, *Venceremos Brigade.*

21. E. J. Dionne, Jr., "City University Teachers Union Assails a Travel Course for Barring Cuban-born," *New York Times,* October 9, 1977.

22. Irving Louis Horowitz, "The Cuba Lobby," *Washington Review of Strategic and International Studies,* July 1978, pp. 66, 60, 61, 67, 66.

23. See, for example, Louis Wolf Goodman, "The Social Sciences in Cuba," Social Science Research Council *Items,* December 1976, and "Lowell U. president says Cuba relaxed," *Massachusetts Teacher,* January–February, 1979, p. 23.

24. Andrew Salkey, *Havana Journal* (Harmondsworth, U.K., 1971), pp. 81, 91, 140, 150, 151, 194.

25. Ronald Radosh, "The Cuban Revolution and Western Intellectuals," in Radosh, ed., *The New Cuba: Paradoxes and Potentials* (New York, 1976), pp. 40, 41, 42. Juan Goytisolo noted similar attitudes among European and Latin American intellectuals ("20 Years of Castro's Revolution," *New York Review of Books,* March 22, 1979, p. 17).

26. Frances Fitzgerald in Radosh, p. 171.

27. Edwards, *Persona Non Grata,* pp. 48–49.

28. Draper, *Castro's Revolution,* p. 48. For a more recent assessment of Cuban socialism and its increasing resemblance to the Soviet model see Carmelo Mesa-Lago, *Cuba in the 1970s: Pragmatism and Institutionalization* (Albuquerque, 1978).

29. Horowitz, "Cuba Lobby," p. 61.

30. Davis, *Autobiography,* pp. 208, 203. Cardenal, the Nicaraguan monk-poet, had very similar reactions to the contrast between commercial and political advertisements on his visit to Cuba. See Ernesto Cardenal, *In Cuba* (New York, 1974), p. 37.

31. Davis, *Autobiography,* p. 141.

32. See, for example, Jo Thomas, "10,000 Cubans Said To Be Crowded into Peruvian Embassy in Havana," *New York Times,* April 7, 1980; "230 Cuban Refugees Arrive in Costa Rica," *New York Times,* April 17, 1980; Jo Thomas, "Amid Tension of Exodus to U.S., Havana Attacks Vast Social Ills," *New York Times,* June 8, 1980.

33. Philip Brenner made these remarks on television, in an interview on the *MacNeil/Lehrer Report,* and was quoted in Joseph Sobran, "Communism can't stifle yen for freedom," *Daily Hampshire Gazette,* April 18, 1980; the views of Zimbalist were also quoted in the *Daily Hampshire Gazette,* May 13, 1980, under the title, "Scholars here assess the exodus from Cuba." Among those interviewed, Johnetta Cole, an anthropologist at the University of Massachusetts, Amherst, also subscribed to the theory that it was the antisocial element that was anxious to leave Cuba, people "who have been unwilling to work and would want to live off crime and prostitution."

34. See also Boorstin, *The Image.*

35. Hans Speier, "Risk, Security and Modern Hero Worship," in *Social Order and the Risk of War* (New York, 1952), pp. 125, 126.

36. Robert Nisbet, *Twilight of Authority* (New York, 1975), pp. 102, 109.

37. Hannah Arendt, *Eichmann in Jerusalem* (New York, 1964). For a critique of her main thesis see Norman Podhoretz, "On the Banality of Evil," *Commentary,* September 1963.

38. Stanley Milgram, *Obedience to Authority* (New York, 1974).

39. Norman Mailer, "The Letter to Castro," from *Presidential Papers,* pp. 67, 68, 75.

40. Jean-Paul Sartre, *Sartre on Cuba* (New York, 1961), pp. 44, 99, 102, 103; see also James Higgins, "Episodes in Revolutionary Cuba," *Liberation,* March 1968, p. 20, on how little Castro sleeps.

41. Speier, "Risk, Security and Modern Hero Worship," pp. 126, 127–28.

42. Hoffman, *Revolution for the Hell of It,* p. 13; see also Luce, *New Left Today,* p. 52.

43. Cardenal, *In Cuba,* p. 131.

44. Draper, *Castro's Revolution,* p. 27.

45. Elizabeth Sutherland, "Cubans' Faith in Castro," *Manchester Guardian Weekly,* December 7, 1961.

46. Kirby Jones and Frank Mankiewicz, *With Fidel: A Portrait of Castro and Cuba* (Chicago, 1975), pp. 9, 10.

47. Lester, *Revolutionary Notes,* p. 177.

48. Landau, "Cuba: The Present Reality," p. 15.

49. Leo Huberman and Paul Sweezy, *Cuba: Anatomy of a Revolution* (New York, 1961), p. 176.

50. Davis, *Autobiography,* p. 207.

51. David Caute, *Cuba, Yes?* (New York, 1974), p. 138; K. S. Karol, *Guerillas in Power* (New York, 1970), pp. 451, 459; René Dumont, *Is Cuba Socialist?* (New York, 1974), p. 57.

52. George McGovern, "A Talk with Castro," *New York Times Magazine,* March 13, 1977, p. 20. For excerpts of McGovern's interview with a Cuban official publication see "McGovern's Mission to Havana," *New America,* December 1977, p. 5. Julian Bond's remark was made in an interview published in the *Daily Hampshire Gazette,* October 23, 1979, p. 9.

53. Karol, *Guerillas in Power,* p. 58.

54. Ibid., p. 342.

55. George McGovern, *Grassroots: The Autobiography of George McGovern* (New York, 1977), pp. 276–77.

56. Caute, *Cuba, Yes?,* p. 134.

57. Elizabeth Sutherland, *The Youngest Revolution: Personal Report on Cuba* (New York, 1969), p. 112.

58. Dumont, *Is Cuba Socialist,* p. 106; see also Cardenal, *In Cuba,* p. 112, on the ubiquitousness of Castro.

59. Jones and Mankiewicz, *With Fidel,* pp. 217–18.

60. Karol, *Guerillas in Power,* p. 459; Dumont, *Is Cuba Socialist,* p. 133.

61. Levinson and Brightman, *Venceremos Brigade,* p. 113; also Cardenal, *In Cuba,* p. 170.

62. Wrong, "American Left and Cuba," p. 99. For a further discussion of Castro as culture hero see Berman, *America in the Sixties,* pp. 267–72.

63. Quoted in Malcolm Muggeridge, "The Protesters' Pin-up," *Observer,* August 18, 1968.

64. Richard Lowenthal, "Unreason and Revolution," *Encounter,* November 1969, p. 32. Renee Winegarten also commented on the Christ-like perceptions of Guevara in *Writers and Revolution* (New York, 1974), pp. 324–25.

65. David Dellinger, "Cuba: The Revolutionary Society," *Liberation*, March 1968, pp. 11, 9.

66. Levinson and Brightman, *Venceremos Brigade*, p. 375.

67. Michael Parenti, quoted in Radosh, ed., *The New Cuba*, p. 41.

68. Cardenal, *In Cuba*, p. 6. In a similar vein Andrew Salkey wrote of the people on the streets of Havana: "People's faces without a trace of that sullen, dispossessed look . . . No dumb insolence. No peevish nonsense. No self-pitying attention-drawing shrugs and grimaces. Society planned on their behalf . . ." (*Havana Journal*, p. 24).

69. Newton, "Sanctuary in Cuba?", p. 28. David Dellinger likewise discerned "a whole new sense of priorities and attitudes in which the welfare of one is indistinguishable from the welfare of all" ("Cuba: Revolutionary Society," p. 12).

70. Levinson and Brightman, *Venceremos Brigade*, p. 398.

71. Sontag, "Some Thoughts," pp. 14, 10.

72. Todd Gitlin, "Cuba and the American Movement," *Liberation*, March 1968, p. 13.

73. Levinson and Brightman, *Venceremos Brigade*, p. 318.

74. Ibid., pp. 308, 310, 318–19.

75. Waldo Frank, *Cuba: Prophetic Island* (New York, 1961), p. 163. Waldo Frank was not the only one who transferred his earlier, pro-Soviet sympathies to Cuba. Scott Nearing, the venerable social critic of the 1930s, also made trips to Cuba in 1960–61 and was "duly impressed" (see his *Making of a Radical*, pp. 240–41).

76. Caute, *Cuba, Yes?*, pp. 84, 85.

77. LeRoi Jones, *Home*, p. 44; for further reference to the carnival atmosphere see also Luce, *New Left Today*, p. 54.

78. Ronald Radosh, "On the Cuban Revolution," *Dissent*, Summer 1976, p. 315.

79. Conn Nugent (holder of a history and law degree from Harvard, former Peace Corps Volunteer, and director of two private foundations in Boston) made this observation in *CoEvolution*, Fall 1977, p. 30.

80. Gitlin, "Cuba and the American Movement," p. 16. In a similar spirit Johnetta Cole, the black anthropologist, was thrilled to report that in Cuba "universities are open to all those who can pass the entrance exam" ("Cole Reports on Cuba," *Massachusetts Daily Collegian*, March 8, 1973). It is doubtful that she would have found similar measures sufficient to assure the adequate representation of blacks at universities in the United States.

81. Salkey, *Havana Journal*, p. 52.

82. Radosh, ed., *The New Cuba*, pp. 64, 65.

83. Cardenal, *In Cuba*, p. 125.

84. Dellinger, "Revolutionary Society," p. 12.

85. C. Wright Mills, *Listen Yankee* (New York, 1960), p. 182; see also p. 183.

86. Frank, *Prophetic Island*, p. 149. Maurice Zeitlin and Robert Scheer also went to considerable lengths to explain sympathetically why no elections were held in Cuba; see their *Cuba: Tragedy in Our Hemisphere* (New York, 1963), pp. 186–87. See also Sidney Lens, "The Birth Pangs of Revolution," *Progressive*, December 1961.

87. LeRoi Jones, *Home*, p. 43; see also p. 55.

88. Ibid., pp. 61–62.

89. Joseph A. Kahl, "The Moral Economy of a Revolutionary Society," in *Cuban Communism*, ed. I. L. Horowitz, 3d ed. (New Brunswick, 1977), p. 111.

90. Davis, *Autobiography*, p. 204.

91. Levinson and Brightman, *Venceremos Brigade*, p. 399.

92. Sontag, "Some Thoughts," pp. 6, 14.

93. Gitlin, "Cuba and the American Movement," p. 13.

94. Jose Yglesias, *In the Fist of the Revolution* (New York, 1969), p. 307.

95. For a summary of some of its characteristics see Zeitlin and Scheer, *Tragedy in Our Hemisphere*, pp. 15–19.

96. According to Draper, "Cuba before Castro was, indeed, a country with serious social problems, but it was far from being a peasant country or even a typically 'underdeveloped' one. Its population was more urban than rural: 57 per cent lived in the urban areas and 43 per cent in rural. . . . The people dependent on agriculture for a living made up about 40 per cent, and of these over one-quarter were classified as farmers and ranchers" (*Castro's Revolution*, p. 21; see also pp. 22, 23 for further data on this topic). On improvements in public health in prerevolutionary Cuba see Jorge I. Dominguez, *Cuba: Order and Revolution* (Cambridge, 1978), pp. 75–76.

97. Davis, *Autobiography*, p. 204.

98. Reckord, *Does Fidel Eat More*, p. 25.

99. Salkey, *Havana Journal*, p. 48.

100. John Clytus, *Black Man in Red Cuba* (Coral Gables, 1970), p. 53; Victor Franco, *The Morning After* (New York, 1963), p. 180.

101. Levinson and Brightman, *Venceremos Brigade*, p. 160.

102. Cardenal, *In Cuba*, p. 14.

103. For example, in Salkey, *Havana Journal*, pp. 94, 204.

104. Ann Crittenden, "The Cuban Economy: How It Works," *New York Times Business & Finance*, December 18, 1977, p. 9.

105. Karol, *Guerillas in Power*, p. 429.

106. Kozol, *Children of the Revolution*, p. 102.

107. Levinson and Brightman, *Venceremos Brigade*, p. 143.

108. George Volsky, "And Cuba Tightens Its Belt," *New York Times International Economic Survey*, January 30, 1977, p. 30; and Cardenal, *In Cuba*, pp. 135–36.

109. Clytus, *Black Man*, p. 48; on shortages, pp. 45–47; Karol, *Guerillas in Power*, p. 338.

110. Dumont, *Is Cuba Socialist*, pp. 58, 127, 128. For further references to Alfa Romeos and other status privileges see also Fred Ward, *Inside Cuba Today* (New York, 1978), p. 4; Joe Nicholson, Jr., *Inside Cuba* (New York, 1974), p. 116; and Jon Nordheimer, "20 Years With Fidel!", *New York Times Magazine*, December 31, 1978, pp. 28, 29. Alfa Romeos (and other privileges) as status symbols of the new class were also mentioned in Gunter Maschke, "Kubanischer Taschenkalender," *Kursbuch* (West Berlin), December 1972, p. 143.

111. Dominguez, *Order and Revolution*, p. 229.

112. Kozol, *Children of the Revolution*, p. 196–97; see also Salkey, *Havana Journal*, p. 65; Samuel Bowles, "Cuban Education and the Revolutionary Ideology," *Harvard Educational Review*, November 1971.

113. Sartre, quoted in Axel Madsen, *Hearts and Minds: The Common Journey of Simone de Beauvoir and Jean Paul Sartre* (New York, 1977), p. 213.

114. Jose Yglesias, *Down There* (New York, 1970), pp. 42, 46, 47, 33.

115. See also Radosh, ed., *The New Cuba*, pp. 226, 227.

116. Hoggart, *Uses of Literacy*.

117. Nicholson, *Inside Cuba*, p. 223. For some visitors such accomplishments represented the essence of true religious values. Cardenal wrote: "I said that true religion . . . comes to the aid of widows and orphans and . . . in Latin America

that . . . was the religion Fidel practised: daycare centers, polyclinics, schools . . ." (*In Cuba*, p. 327). It may be recalled that the Soviet system was seen in a similar light a few decades ago, as realizing the most authentic values of Christianity.

118. Reckord, *Does Fidel Eat More*, p. 24.

119. Ibid., p. 61.

120. Jones and Mankiewicz, *With Fidel*, p. 241.

121. Salkey, for instance (*Havana Journal*, pp. 166–70), made a special visit to "the only surviving Cuban runaway slave" (p. 166).

122. Jeffrey Levi, "Political Prisoner in Cuba," *Dissent*, Summer 1978, p. 284.

123. Joshua Muravchik, "Kennedy's Foreign Policy: What the Record Shows," *Commentary*, December 1979, p. 38.

124. See Cardenal, *In Cuba*, pp. 49–50, 20, 78–79 (where reference is made to the so-called "social disgrace units"), and pp. 292–94. Yglesias wrote: "UMAP are the initials for work-prison camps called Military Units for Aid to Production; they were begun in 1965 presumably to rehabilitate young men of military service age whose ways made them unsuitable for integration in the regular army" (*Fist of the Revolution*, p. 6; see also pp. 161, 275–80).

125. Ward, *Inside Cuba Today*, p. 290.

126. Edwards, *Persona Non Grata*, p. 90.

127. Levi, "Political Prisoner," p. 284.

128. See John Martino, *I Was Castro's Prisoner* (New York, 1963), esp. pp. 133–39; Frank Calzon, "How Many Prisoners Does Castro Hold?", *Dissent*, Summer 1976; Levi, "Political Prisoner"; Frank Emmick, "An American's Fourteen Years in Cuban Prisons," *New York Times*, April 12, 1978.

129. Richard Eder, "Prisoner of Castro: The Huber Matos Story," *New York Times*, February 4, 1980, and Jo Thomas, "Freed Cuban Tells of Years Spent in 'Concrete Boxes' Underground," *New York Times*, October 24, 1979. A former political prisoner said: "Solzhenitsyn described it far better than I can in 'One Day in the Life of Ivan Denisovich.' The only difference was the climate" (Jo Thomas, "Freed American Talks Calmly of Cuba," *New York Times*, September 21, 1979).

130. Calzon, "How Many Prisoners," p. 241.

131. Dominguez, *Order and Revolution*, p. 253–54.

132. Calzon, "How Many Prisoners," p. 242.

133. Nicholson, *Inside Cuba*, p. 111; see also Caute, *Cuba, Yes?*, p. 73.

134. Nicholson, *Inside Cuba*, pp. 119, 120, 121.

135. Yglesias, *Fist of the Revolution*, pp. 6, 275; Cardenal, *In Cuba*, pp. 21, 85. UMAP was disbanded in 1967 (see Dominguez, *Order and Revolution*, p. 367).

136. Calzon, "How Many Prisoners," p. 243.

137. Karol, *Guerillas in Power*, p. 45. Evidently belonging to the CDR can in some instances also bring material advantages, as in the case of the family that reportedly owned two cars and two TV sets, yet, to the surprise and anger of neighbors, decided to leave Cuba (Jo Thomas, "Behind Barred Doors in Havana, Would-Be Exiles Wait Fearfully," *New York Times*, May 2, 1980).

138. Yglesias, *Fist of the Revolution*, p. 283. For further comments on the repressive function of the CDR see Dumont, *Is Cuba Socialist?*, p. 119.

139. Reckord, *Does Fidel Eat More*, p. 60.

140. Draper, *Castro's Revolution*, p. 151. Castro's capacity for impulsive vindictiveness is illustrated by the following story: "A young sentinel guarding some new rice plantings had one night let cows graze amidst them, and Castro wanted to have him shot. He was restrained with difficulty by being reminded that the grazing would in fact encourage the plant growth. Once over his rage, he agreed to have

the sentence changed to fifteen years on a prison farm" (Dumont, *Is Cuba Socialist?*, p. 115).

141. Hugh Thomas, "Castro plus Twenty," *Encounter*, October 1978, p. 115.
142. Cardenal, *In Cuba*, p. 23.
143. Frank, *Prophetic Island*, p. 18.
144. Cardenal, *In Cuba*, p. 68.
145. LeRoi Jones, *Home*, pp. 33, 38.
146. Kozol, *Children of the Revolution*, pp. 104, 92.
147. Sontag, "Some Thoughts," pp. 16.
148. Salkey, *Havana Journal*, pp. 36, 37.
149. Cardenal, *In Cuba*, p. 22. Subsequently Cardenal came to the conclusion that his Cuban informant was wrong in this matter (pp. 34–36).
150. Salkey, *Havana Journal*, pp. 272, 27, 57. The naiveté of the visitors was illustrated by a question of Salkey's companion, who wondered if the Cuban government financed "perhaps wholly" the publication whose editorial freedom was being discussed (p. 57).
151. Sontag, "Some Thoughts," p. 16. Subsequently her confidence in the Cuban regime was shaken when the poet Padilla was jailed, humiliated, and forced to confess. She joined other famous Western intellectuals in protesting his treatment.
152. Carlos Ripoll, "Dissent in Cuba," *New York Times Book Review*, November 11, 1979, pp. 11, 31.
153. Kahl, "Moral Economy," p. 113. Mary McCarthy expressed similar beliefs on her journey to North Vietnam: "The license to criticize was just another capitalist luxury, a waste product of the system. This of course is true" (*Hanoi* [New York, 1968], p. 126). The decline of intellectual freedom in the Cuban academic setting is graphically illustrated in a conversation between David Caute and the dean of a provincial university who assured him that there were no differences of opinion on political questions among the faculty or students, and who considered it "antisocial" for a poet to "write simply to please himself" (Caute, *Cuba, Yes?*, pp. 155–59, provides a full account of this conversation).
154. Sontag, *Trip to Hanoi*, p. 86. The seeming strength of America was also an important factor in the development of pro-Vietnamese sentiments. Thus William Sloan Coffin, Jr. believed that "a David was warring against a Goliath" (*Once to Every Man* [New York, 1977], p. 314).
155. McCarthy, *Hanoi*, p. 34. Referring to various trips she took from Hanoi, she wrote: "Each departure, smacking of danger, was an adventure" (p. 36).
156. Coffin, *Once to Every Man*, pp. 308, 309.
157. Harry S. Ashmore and William C. Baggs, *Mission to Hanoi* (New York, 1968), p. 13. McCarthy, *Hanoi*, p. 16; she has also written that "no normal person set down in a North Vietnamese rice field beside an anti-aircraft unit manned by excited boys and girls, could help being thrilled . . ." (pp. 89–90).
158. In several instances, the purposes of the hosts were very specific: for example, they suggested that the visitors address American troops on Radio Hanoi, which Jane Fonda, among others, agreed to do. Coffin, Cora Weiss, and others agreed to play a part in the American prisoner release. Mary McCarthy was asked by Premier Phan Van Dong to write a book about the North (*Hanoi*, p. 130). Ashmore and Baggs were given messages to deliver to the United States government.
159. Falk, a professor of international law at Princeton University, believed that the Ayatollah Khomeini was "defamed" by the American news media and erroneously "associated with religious fanaticism," and that "the depiction of him as a fanatical reactionary and the bearer of crude prejudices seems certainly and happily false." Moreover, Falk also found "encouraging" the fact that Khomeini's "entourage

of close advisers is uniformly composed of moderate, progressive individuals." See Richard Falk, "Trusting Khomeini," *New York Times,* February 16, 1979. See also Anthony Lewis, "Trusting in Illusions," *New York Times,* March 12, 1979, in which the author reflected on the readiness of American intellectuals to fall prey to political illusions, as exemplified by Falk's attitudes. Apparently Falk idealized the ayatollah because he represented the alternative to the shah, who had been supported by and identified with the U.S. government. It was once more a bizarre case of "my enemies' enemies are my friends." Falk paid a reverential visit to the ayatollah in Paris, shortly before Khomeini's return to Iran, in the company of Ramsey Clark.

160. "Vietnam: A Time for Healing and Compassion," advertisement, *New York Times,* January 30, 1977. For a critical discussion of those unwilling to reexamine their commitment to the North Vietnamese regime even in the light of recent events see Stephen Miller, "Vietnam and the Responsibility of Intellectuals," *American Spectator,* November 1977. Miller wrote: "The last thing these critics [of American policies] were interested in was the plight of particular Vietnamese. The people of Vietnam, one might say, were only grist for their mill—less real persons than characters in an allegory, in which the hero, suffering from the stain of having been born in a wasteland, undergoes purification by visiting the good 'enemy' " (p. 14).

161. "The Truth About Vietnam," *New York Times,* June 24, 1979. The advertisement published by Joan Baez was entitled, "An Open Letter to the Socialist Republic of Vietnam," *New York Times,* May 30, 1979.

162. Kathleen Teltsch, "Visitors to Vietnam Report Farming Gain," *New York Times,* March 11, 1977, p. 9.

163. "Clark's Hanoi Comments," *New York Times,* October 25, 1974. Reportedly Clark also observed while in Hanoi in 1972 "that U.S. prisoners of war in North Vietnam were healthier than he was" (Will, *Pursuit of Happiness,* p. 158).

164. Sontag, *Trip to Hanoi,* pp. 69, 77.

165. Lynd and Hayden, *Other Side,* p. 57.

166. Berrigan, *Night Flight to Hanoi,* pp. 45, 48, 79.

167. Thus Coffin was "struck" by the "complete assurance" of his guides that he was "in no danger from any North Vietnamese" (*Once to Every Man,* p. 319). Ashmore and Baggs were impressed by the "unfailing courtesy everywhere we went despite our conspicuous foreign look" (*Mission to Hanoi,* p. 30), and by the fact that "in no case was there a display of personal animosity against us as loyal citizens of the country that was spreading death and destruction across their homeland" (p. 33). See also Berrigan, *Night Flight to Hanoi,* p. 41.

168. Sontag, *Trip to Hanoi,* pp. 25, 29, 70.

169. Coffin, *Once to Every Man,* p. 316.

170. Levinson and Brightman, *Venceremos Brigade,* p. 327.

171. Berrigan, *Night Flight to Hanoi,* pp. 32, 106, 105, 107.

172. Lynd and Hayden, *Other Side,* p. 164.

173. Sontag, *Trip to Hanoi,* p. 71.

174. Coffin, *Once to Evrey Man,* pp. 312, 314, 315, 325.

175. Berrigan, *Night Flight to Hanoi,* pp. 125, 130.

176. McCarthy, *Hanoi,* pp. 115–16.

177. Lynd and Hayden, *Other Side,* pp. 58, 62.

178. Sontag, *Trip to Hanoi,* p. 75.

179. Berrigan, *Night Flight to Hanoi,* p. 191. Lynd and Hayden also praised the new style of the North Vietnamese leadership, contrasting it favorably with "Western or stable Communism" (*Other Side,* p. 33).

180. Walter Goodman, "The False Art of the Propaganda Film," *New York Times Arts and Leisure,* March 23, 1975.

181. Berrigan, *Night Flight to Hanoi,* p. 110.

182. Ibid., p. 121.

183. Ibid., pp. 99, 107, 123. Ashmore and Baggs, *Mission to Hanoi,* p. 32; Lynd and Hayden, *Other Side,* pp. 68, 69, 71.

184. McCarthy, *Hanoi,* p. 50.

185. Berrigan, *Night Flight to Hanoi,* pp. 106, 60.

186. McCarthy, *Hanoi,* pp. 27, 50, 51.

187. Sontag, *Trip to Hanoi,* p. 66, also pp. 63–64; and McCarthy, *Hanoi,* pp. 121, 126.

188. McCarthy, *Hanoi,* pp. 49–50.

189. See, as one of the rare examples of such attitudes, "U.S. Leftist Editor Says Cambodians Are Thriving," *New York Times,* May 12, 1978, p. 7: "Challenging refugee accounts of forced labor and repressions, Mr. Burstein said his group traveled along more than 700 miles of Cambodian highways, visited numerous work sites and conducted random interviews without finding any evidence of coercion." For another favorable view of the Pol Pot regime see Chomsky and Herman, "Distortions at Fourth Hand" (discussed in more detail in n. 62, Chapter Two). The "distortions" referred to are those of the Western press accusatory of the Cambodian regime. For a recent examination of Chomsky's views on Cambodia see Leopold Labedz, "Chomsky Revisited," *Encounter,* July 1980.

190. Myrdal and Kessle, *Albania Defiant,* pp. 184–85.

191. Ibid., pp. 15, 30, 170.

192. Ibid., pp. 146, 173.

193. Ibid., pp. 175, 184.

194. Ibid., pp. 154, 144, 174, 183, 181, 182, 155, 178, 156, 129.

195. Ibid., pp. 183–84, 184.

196. Ibid., p. 179.

197. Nearing, quoted in Whitfield, *Scott Nearing,* p. 201–2.

198. Serge Thion, "Africa: War and Revolution," *Dissent,* Spring 1979, p. 212.

199. Tom Wicker, "Hope and Discipline," *New York Times,* November 12, 1978.

200. Michael T. Kaufman, "Mozambique Is Viewed as Africa's Best Hope for the Flowering of Socialism's 'New Man'," *New York Times,* November 14, 1977. For other examples of such positive attitudes toward Mozambique (and other left-wing dictatorships) see Stephen Chapman, " 'Shot from Guns'—The Lost Pacifism of the American Quakers", *New Republic,* June 9, 1979. In it the author observed a "pattern of selective moralism" and a "double standard for human rights [that] has made the American Friends Service Committee practically indistinguishable from any number of leftist groups that propagandize against right-wing governments and for left-wing ones." (p. 17). He also pointed out that "When the AFSC deals directly with conditions in communist countries, it averts its eyes from the sort of shortcomings it cites elsewhere," (p. 16.) Besides Mozambique the countries qualified for such benign treatment included communist Vietnam and even North Korea.

201. Falk, "Trusting Khomeini." Falk and Ramsey Clark were not the only sympathizers of the new Iranian regime. Others included George Wald, noted war critic and Harvard professor of biology; Leonard Weinglass, defender of the Chicago Seven; Mary Anderson, a lecturer at the Massachusetts Institute of Technology who worked for the American Society of Friends (Quakers); John Gerassi, an admirer of Cuba and member of Bertrand Russell's War Crimes Tribunal; and Lennox Hinds, a professor at Rutgers University who sought the help of the United Nations

in 1978 against the mistreatment of blacks and Indians in American prisons. All those mentioned attended the anti-American conference in Teheran in June 1980 (see "Sketches of Americans at Iran's Conference on U.S.," *New York Times*, June 4, 1980).

Chapter 7: The Pilgrimage to China

1. Urie Bronfenbrenner, "From Another Planet," *Human Ecology Extra*, (East Asia Research Center Files, Harvard University, n.d.), p. 6. (Hereafter cited as EARC Files.)

2. Maria Antonietta Macciocchi, *Daily Life in Revolutionary China* (New York, 1972), p. 466.

3. Simone de Beauvoir, *The Long March* (Cleveland, 1958), p. 10.

4. John K. Fairbank, "The New China and the American Connection," *Foreign Affairs*, October 1972, pp. 31, 36.

5. Hans Konigsberger, *Love and Hate in China* (New York, 1966), p. 26.

6. Lucian W. Pye, "Building a Relationship on the Sands of Cultural Exchanges," in William J. Barnds, ed., *China and America: The Search for a New Relationship* (New York, 1977), p. 118.

7. Concerned Asian Scholars, *China!*, p. 1; Felix Greene, *China: The Country Americans Are Not Allowed to Know* (New York, 1961), p. 19.

8. Even Field Marshal Viscount Montgomery wanted to do his share in removing misconceptions: "One hears it said that children in the communes are removed from their parents. I investigated this and found it to be totally untrue. There are great misconceptions in the Western world about this new China, particularly in the United States . . ." (quoted in Greene, *China*, p. 147).

9. Konigsberger, *Love and Hate in China*, p. 25.

10. Quoted in Frank Ching, "China: It's the Latest American Thing," *New York Times*, February 16, 1972. There was even a "Summit Meeting Medal" minted to commemorate Nixon's meeting with Chou En-lai in February 1972, made of gold and silver sterling and showing Nixon and Chou shaking hands and smiling at one another (see advertisement, *New York Times*, February 20, 1972). The volatility of American public opinion toward China was also reflected in a public opinion poll: e.g., "Mainland Chinese Have Risen in Favor in U.S., Poll Finds" *New York Times*, March 12, 1972, p. 5 (the reported shift came after the Nixon visit).

11. David K. Shipler, "Alsop Looks Back on China Stories," *New York Times*, February 4, 1973.

12. Harrison E. Salisbury, *To Peking—and Beyond* (New York, 1973), p. 12.

13. Evelyn Wiener, published in *Rehabilitation World*, Winter 1976.

14. Peter Worsley, *Inside China* (London, 1975), pp. 12–13.

15. David Kolodney, "Et tu China?", *Ramparts*, May 1972, pp. 8, 10, 12.

16. Macciocchi, *Daily Life*, p. 2.

17. Quoted in Martin Bernal, "Puritanism Chinese-Style," *New York Review of Books*, October 26, 1967, p. 23.

18. Bernard Frolic, "Comparing China and the Soviet Union," *Contemporary China*, Summer 1978, pp. 31, 37.

19. Peter Kenez, "A Sense of Deja Vu: Traveling in China," *New Leader*, November 1973, p. 9.

20. Bernard Frolic, "Reflections on the Chinese Model of Development," *Social Forces*, December 1978, pp. 384–85, 386.

21. Macciocchi, *Daily Life*, pp. 29–30.

22. *Experience Without Precedent: Some Quaker Observations on China Today,* Report of an American Friends Service Committee delegation's visit to China (Philadelphia, May 1972), p. 7, v. (Hereafter cited as *Quaker Report.*)

23. David Selbourne, *An Eye to China* (London, 1975), p. iv.

24. John K. Fairbank, "The New China Tourism of the 1970s," in his *China Perceived* (New York, 1974), p. 165. A similar view was expressed in Philip A. Kuhn, "China: Excerpts from a Historian's Journal," *University of Chicago Magaine,* Spring 1975, p. 29.

25. E. H. Johnson, "Notes on the Church in China," mimeographed (EARC Files, March–April 1973), p. 1.

26. Stanley Karnow, "China Through Rose-Tinted Glasses," *Atlantic,* October 1973, p. 75. Edward N. Luttwak believed that "it is only the rare newspaperman who makes his own prior decision that he will seek no second visa who can be counted upon to serve us, and not the Chinese" ("Seeing China Plain," *Commentary,* December 1976, p. 33).

27. Greene, *China,* pp. 7–8.

28. Ruth Sidel, *Women and Child Care in China: A Firsthand Report* (Baltimore, 1973), p. xiii.

29. Pye, "Building a Relationship," p. 14.

30. Simon Leys, "Human Rights in China," *Quadrant,* November 1978, p. 74.

31. Herbert Passin, *China's Cultural Diplomacy* (New York, 1963), pp. 9, 12, 119, 120, 121, 122.

32. Quoted ibid., p. 117.

33. Lorenz Stucki, *Behind the Great Wall* (New York, 1965), pp. 16, 18, 19.

34. Jacques Marcuse, *The Peking Papers* (New York, 1967), pp. 8, 19.

35. Jules Roy, *Journey Through China* (New York, 1967), p. 282.

36. Alfred Fabre-Luce, "Chinese Journey," *Atlantic,* December 1959, p. 44.

37. Robert Loh, "Setting the Stage for Foreigners," *Atlantic,* December 1959, p. 81. See also by the same author, *Escape from Red China* (New York, 1962).

38. In Sperber, *Man and His Deeds.*

39. For instance, the Committee of Concerned Asian Scholars wrote: " 'Book learning' was never quite convincing enough. Now, finally, we could see for ourselves" (*China!,* p. 3).

40. Adam Ulam, "USA: Some Critical Reflections," *Survey,* January 1964, p. 53.

41. Greene, *China,* p. 23.

42. Macciocchi, *Daily Life,* p. 106; Concerned Asian Scholars, *China!,* p. 165.

43. Carol Tavris, "Field Report: Women in China," *Psychology Today,* May 1974, p. 43.

44. Lynd and Hayden, *Other Side,* pp. 39, 40. The descriptions of Peking in this book reminded Christopher Lasch of "earlier accounts, by American radicals in the twenties and thirties, of the sentimental journey to the Soviet Union" (*New York Times Book Review,* April 23, 1967, p. 18).

45. Ross Terrill, *800 Million: The Real China* (Boston, 1971), p. 2.

46. Barbara Wooton, "A Journey to China," *Encounter,* June 1973, p. 26.

47. Shirley MacLaine, *You Can Get There From Here* (New York, 1975), pp. 126–27. Dr. Benjamin Spock was "also impressed by the serenity of the people, their smiling and relaxed appearance . . ." and he "never saw children fighting . . . grabbing . . . even whining or complaining" "Dr. Spock in China," *New China,* 1974 [first issue, n.d.]).

48. David Rockefeller, "From a China Traveler," *New York Times,* August 10, 1973.

49. Jay Matthews, "Sabbatical in China," *Washington Post,* March 1974; C. K.

Jen, "Mao's 'Serve the People's Ethic,'" *Science and Public Affairs: Bulletin of the Atomic Scientists,* March 1974, p. 18.

50. "Churchmen Find a Lesson in China," *New York Times,* September 19, 1974, p. 13.

51. Hewlett Johnson, *The Upsurge of China* (Peking, 1961), p. 368. Getting his book published by the Chinese government puts Johnson in a special category, conferring on him the recognition of the Chinese authorities as a truly important friend. Anna Louise Strong also perceived an affinity between the policies of the Chinese regime and the true principles of Christianity. By coincidence, she found herself "supported by the comments made by Dr. Chao Fu-sam, eminent leader of Protestantism in China," who "admitted that the Church membership was much reduced [in China] but he thought the spirit was better" (Anna Louise Strong, *Letters from China,* numbers 21–30 [Peking, 1965], p. 172).

52. Hewlett Johnson, *China's New Creative Age* (London, 1953), pp. 106, 110, 112. Meray's articles were published in the French newspaper *Franc Tireur* in 1957.

53. Johnson, *China's New Creative Age,* p. 184.

54. James Reston, "Letters from China: II," *New York Times,* July 30, 1971.

55. Simon Leys, *Chinese Shadows* (New York, 1977), p. 45.

56. Konigsberger, *Love and Hate in China,* pp. 118–19.

57. Johnson, *Upsurge of China,* p. 256; Arthur Galston, *Daily Life in People's China* (New York, 1973), p. 130.

58. Greene, *China,* p. 157.

59. Orville Schell, *In the People's Republic: An American's First Hand View of Living and Working in China* (New York, 1977), p. 94.

60. Claudie Broyelle, *Women's Liberation in China* (Atlantic Highlands, N.J., 1977), p. 150; for examples of the way in which the sense of purpose permeates the upbringing of children see p. 74; and on the irrelevance of good looks for women, pp. 151–53.

61. Sidel, *Women and Child Care,* p. 43; also Schell, *In the People's Republic,* pp. 161–62, 243–44.

62. MacLaine, *You Can Get There,* p. 183; Macciocchi, *Daily Life,* p. 106.

63. Bao Ruo-Wang, *Prisoner of Mao* (Harmondsworth, U.K., 1976), p. 190.

64. "'Human nature' is being changed," in Jan Mydral and Gun Kessle, *The Revolution Continued* (New York, 1970), p. 192.

65. Worsley, *Inside China,* p. 20.

66. Ibid., p. 129.

67. Basil Davidson, *Daybreak in China* (London, 1953), p. 139.

68. James Reston, "Letters from China: I," *New York Times,* July 28, 1971.

69. *Quaker Report,* p. 35.

70. Pierre Elliot Trudeau and Jacques Hebert, *Two Innocents in Red China* (Toronto, New York, London, 1968), p. 54.

71. Sidel, *Women and Child Care,* pp. xii, 186.

72. Chun-tu Hsueh, "Journey to China," mimeographed (EARC Files, n.d.).

73. Concerned Asian Scholars, *China!,* p. 284. Felix Greene too had "come to believe that the Chinese derive their deepest emotional satisfactions . . . from sharing in activities which have aims beyond the individual" (*China,* p. 106).

74. Beauvoir, *Long March,* p. 164.

75. Beauvoir, *All Said and Done,* p. 415.

76. Davidson, *Daybreak in China,* pp. 96, 97.

77. Fairbank, "The New China," pp. 36–37, 41.

78. Macciocchi, *Daily Life,* p. 107.

79. Greene, *China*, p. 7.

80. Concerned Asian Scholars, *China!*, pp. 2, 126.

81. Joshua Horn, *Away with All Pests* . . . (London, 1969), pp. 182–83.

82. "The Making of a Red Guard," *New York Times Magazine*, January 4, 1970, p. 58. Leys, "Human Rights," p. 73. According to a Chinese author, the popular practices of the Cultural Revolution also included tying people to long poles and spinning them around, a technique called "flying an airplane." "Anyone who had experienced this routine would suffer irregularities in blood pressure or malfunction of the heart" (Hsia Chih-yen, *The Coldest Winter in Peking* [Garden City, N.Y., 1978], p. 106).

83. MacLaine, *You Can Get There*, p. 245; see also Macciocchi, *Daily Life*, p. 107 concerning the "reeducation" process foreigners unwittingly undergo in China.

84. Worsley, *Inside China*, p. 13.

85. Galston, *Daily Life*, p. 240.

86. Ibid., p. 233.

87. Beauvoir, *Long March*, p. 49. The Concerned Asian Scholars were also apparently reassured by the official explanation of the survival of such forms of manual labor (*China!*, p. 125).

88. Concerned Asian Scholars, *China!*, pp. 278–79. A similar attitude to work was exemplified by the story related by another group of visiting Americans: "Although crippled since infancy . . . he was determined to contribute to production. . . . He gathered scraps of metal around the village and made them into turnip graters in the cave where he lived . . . he has become a model of initiative and self-reliance." More generally, "The thorough integration of the handicapped into this vast and still poor society is another impressive indication that present-day China is a country in which the concept of refuse, human or material, is being overcome: everyone and everything is considered useful" (Report from Science for the People, *China: Science Walks on Two Legs* [New York, 1974], pp. 90, 108).

89. See Jacques Marcuse on some of the official efforts to make night soil collection more appealing, and the persisting popular distaste toward those engaged in it (*Peking Papers*, pp. 216–23).

90. Macciocchi, *Daily Life*, pp. 97, 88–89.

91. Joseph Kraft, *The Chinese Difference* (New York, 1973), pp. 82–83.

92. According to one visitor, commenting on such assignments, "It became clear that the point of physical work was not to contribute to production but to improve character" (Kenez, "Sense of Deja Vu," p. 9).

93. Myrdal and Kessle, *Revolution Continued*, pp. 139, 168, 171.

94. Concerned Asian Scholars, *China!*, p. 171.

95. Claudie and Jacques Broyelle, "Everyday Life in the People's Republic," *Quadrant*, November 1978, p. 15. This article was written after the authors' disillusionment with Communist China, where they spent several years; see p. 14. There are also many references to similar practices, and to the hardships of rural assignments, in Hsia, *Coldest Winter in Peking*.

96. Macciocchi, *Daily Life*, p. 34; Beauvoir, *Long March*, pp. 53, 54.

97. Schell, *In the People's Republic*, pp. 21–22.

98. Leys, *Chinese Shadows*, p. 117. The number of pockets as an indicator of status (and rank) was also noted by William Safire in his "China: The New Mysteries," *New York Times Magazine*, June 19, 1977, p. 48.

99. Luttwak, "Seeing China Plain," p. 30.

100. Lucian Pye, *China Revisited*, Center for International Studies, M.I.T., (Cambridge, 1973), p. 153.

101. Macciocchi, *Daily Life,* p. 314.

102. John S. Service, "Life in China Is 'Obviously Better,'" *New York Times,* January 26, 1972.

103. Leys, *Chinese Shadows,* pp. 113, 115–116; "Top China Aides Enjoy Luxuries Others Can't Get," *New York Times,* November 27, 1977; "The Rise and Fall of Mao's Empress," *Time Magazine,* March 21, 1977 (see also Roxane Witke, *Comrade Chiang Ching* [Boston, 1977]); Colette Modiano, *Twenty Snobs and Mao: Travelling de Luxe in Communist China* (London, 1969), pp. 154, 155. On corruption and nepotism see also Fox Butterfield, "In China, Austerity Is Less Austere If One Has Friends in Right Places," *New York Times,* December 11, 1977; and by the same author, "Peking Presses Campaign Against Official Corruption and High Living," *New York Times,* May 7, 1978; "Discipline, Favoritism Are Problems for Peking," *New York Times,* June 24, 1979; and "Peking Preparing Drive Against Corrupt Officials," *New York Times,* August 1, 1979.

104. Concerned Asian Scholars, *China!,* pp. 195, 102, 253, 257; see also p. 265. According to Sophia Delza, the dance arts were also flourishing ("The Dance-Arts in the People's Republic of China: The Contemporary Scene," *Asian Music,* March 1974, p. 39).

105. Greene, *China,* p. 221.

106. Concerned Asian Scholars, *China!,* p. 133.

107. Science for the People, *Science Walks on Two Legs,* p. 5. The authors of this book included a graduate of the Experimental College of the University of Minnesota (interested in political theory and movements), a medical student, a computer programmer, a graduate student in social psychology, a former director of a feminist studies program, a registered nurse, a nuclear chemist working for "an innovative admissions program," a "juvenile justice planner," and others whose connection with the sciences was equally tenuous. "The organization grew out of a campus-based group formed to oppose classified war research but later expanded its concern to such areas as the deprofessionalization of science . . . providing critiques of present science curricula . . . and raising crucial women's issues within the scientific community" (front page, unnumbered).

108. Ibid., pp. 6, 11.

109. *Quaker Report,* p. 23.

110. John Kenneth Galbraith, *A China Passage* (Boston, 1973), p. 120.

111. Martin King Whyte, "Inequality and Stratification in China," *China Quarterly,* December 1975, pp. 685, 692.

112. Donald S. Zagoria, "China by Daylight," *Dissent,* Spring 1975, pp. 138–39. Michael Frolic reported tenfold income differences in 1971; see "What the Cultural Revolution Was All About," *New York Times Magazine,* October 24, 1971, p. 123. Following the general reassessment of conditions in China since Mao's death there have been more analyses of inequality. See, for example, Nick Eberstadt, "China: How Much Success?", *New York Review of Books,* May 3, 1979. In this article Eberstadt concluded that "income differences in China may be quite a bit greater than in a number of countries commonly associated with 'fascist' elites and exploited masses" (p. 41). Hsia, *Coldest Winter in Peking* is also full of references to inequalities and elite privileges; see, for example, pp. 22, 52, 64, 67 (on those of the military), 72–74 (in rural settlements), 88 (foreigners), 132–33 (malnutrition among the poor and surfeit among the elite), 134, 159 (access to different brands of cigarettes), 164, 172.

113. Edgar Snow, *Red China Today* (New York, 1970), p. 285.

114. Terrill, *800 Million,* p. 9.

115. MacLaine, *You Can Get There,* p. 130.

116. Audrey Topping, *Dawn Wakes in the East* (New York, 1973), p. 3. It might be noted here that, in the words of Sheila K. Johnson, "the current enthusiasm for China also draws on a much older, religious strand in American thought which dates back to the missionary movement of the 19th century. . . . This missionary-inspired idealization of the Chinese peasant . . . can once again be found in much of the current writing" ("To China With Love," *Commentary*, June 1973, p. 45).

117. Concerned Asian Scholars, *China!*, p. 107.

118. Norma Lundholm Djerassi, *Glimpses of China from a Galloping Horse* (New York, 1974), pp. 14, 17, 15. E. H. Johnson, the Canadian Presbyterian, who was anxious not to offend his hosts by inquiries about religion (cf. p. 285), found that "everywhere the people . . . radiated exuberant good health . . . were well fed, showed few signs of minor ailments like colds and open sores, and the women, who used no makeup, needed none because of their pink cheeks and general radiant health. . . . I came away with the impression of a people who are happy and at peace with themselves" ("Challenge of the New China," 2, mimeographed [EARC File], p. 3).

119. Horn, *Away with All Pests*, p. 26; Galston, *Daily Life*, p. 14.

120. A related observation concerning recent American perceptions of China was made by Frederic Wakeman, Jr.: "Our own kind of social idealism was almost instantly projected upon the Chinese, exotic though they remained . . ." ("The Real China," *New York Review of Books*, July 20, 1978, p. 9).

121. Davidson, *Daybreak in China*, p. 125.

122. Peter Townsend, *China Phoenix: The Revolution in China*, (London, 1955), p. 202.

123. Frank, *Dawn in Russia*, pp. 121, 127.

124. Concerned Asian Scholars, *China!*, p. 9; MacLaine, *You Can Get There*, p. 127; Galston, *Daily Life*, p. 32. Orville Schell also commented favorably on Chinese trains (*In the People's Republic*, p. 199), as did Hewlett Johnson (*China's New Creative Age*, chap. 8).

125. Beauvoir, *Long March*, p. 459.

126. Greene, *China*, pp. 21–22.

127. Davidson, *Daybreak in China*, p. 51; Galbraith, *China Passage*, p. 71. Djerassi, a poet, confessed that "the touch of nature here in Hangchow fills me with nostalgia. . . . I feel a serenity here . . ." (*Glimpses of China*, p. 104).

128. Jan Myrdal, *Report from a Chinese Village* (New York, 1972), p. xvi.

129. Salisbury, *To Peking*, p. 73–74. Similar comments were made about Russia by Waldo Frank and Pablo Neruda, among others.

130. James Reston, "Letters from China: I."

131. Paul Dudley White, "China's Heart Is in the Right Place," *New York Times*, December 5, 1971.

132. MacLaine, *You Can Get There*, p. 206; Leys, *Chinese Shadows*, p. 47; Galston, *Daily Life*, p. 64.

133. Sidel, *Women and Child Care*, p. xii.

134. Horn, *Away with All Pests*, pp. 31–32.

135. Urie Bronfenbrenner, "Child-Watching in a Chinese Classroom," *New York Times*, Education Abroad Supplement, January 15, 1975, p. 95; Trudeau and Hebert, *Two Innocents*, p. 105.

136. Passin, *China's Cultural Diplomacy*, p. 4.

137. Horn, *Away with All Pests*, pp. 27, 28; see also Townsend, *China Phoenix*, pp. 217–18.

138. David and Nancy Dall Milton, *The Wind Will Not Subside* (New York, 1976), p. 12.

139. Beauvoir, *Long March*, p. 428.

140. Irene Dawson, "Lifelong Learning in China," *Ontario Library Review*, September 1974, p. 170.

141. MacLaine, *You Can Get There*, p. 245.

142. Fairbank, "New China," p. 40.

143. Macciocchi, *Daily Life*, p. 372.

144. Alberto Jacoviello, "A Communist Looks at China," *New York Times*, January 25, 1971.

145. Concerned Asian Scholars, *China!*, p. 194.

146. Chester Ronning, "China's 700 Million Are On the Way," *New York Times*, June 7, 1971.

147. Andrew L. March, "China: Image and Reality," *New York Times*, September 12, 1975; Seymour Topping, "China: Economic Policy Stresses Local Self-Help," *New York Times*, June 27, 1971, p. 20.

148. Science for the People, *Science Walks on Two Legs*, p. 16.

149. Corliss Lamont, *Trip to Communist China* (New York, Basic Pamphlets, 1976), p. 13.

150. Leys, *Chinese Shadows*, p. 76; Macciocchi, *Daily Life*, p. 230.

151. Bronfenbrenner, "From Another Planet," pp. 4–5; Lynd and Hayden, *Other Side*, p. 45.

152. Berger, "Socialist Myth," pp. 8–9.

153. Quoted in Greene, *China*, pp. 102–3.

154. Hewlett Johnson, *Upsurge of China*, p. 369; Fairbank, "New China," p. 38.

155. *Quaker Report*, p. 21.

156. Nearing, *Making of a Radical*, pp. 247–48.

157. Horn, *Away with All Pests*, pp. 18–19, 32.

158. "Report of the Delegation of the American Association of State Colleges and Universities," mimeographed (EARC Files, April 1975), p. 3.

159. Tavris, "Field Report," p. 98.

160. Concerned Asian Scholars, *China!*, p. 122.

161. Dudley White, "China's Heart."

162. Leys, *Chinese Shadows*, p. 201.

163. Lamont, *Trip to Communist China*, p. 21.

164. Worsley, *Inside China*, p. 185.

165. Concerned Asian Scholars, *China!*, p. 155.

166. Edward P. Morgan, "Smokestacks and Pagodas: One Man's Impressions of China," *Sierra Club Bulletin*, October 1977, p. 21. See also Fox Butterfield, "China Wakes up to Dangers of Industrial Pollution," *New York Times*, April 6, 1980.

167. Harrison Salisbury, "Once Arid Region of China Blooms," *New York Times*, June 27, 1972.

168. Joseph Lelyveld, " 'Everything Was Green and Nice,' U.S. Crop Expert Says of China's Farms," *New York Times*, September 24, 1974.

169. Beauvoir, *Long March*, p. 108; Galston, *Daily Life*, pp. 129–30. Djerassi also praised "the immaculate cleanliness of the streets" (*Glimpses of China*, p. 44). On these campaigns see, for example, Johnson, *China's New Creative Age*, pp. 78–79; Davidson, *Daybreak in China*, pp. 76–77.

170. Galbraith, *China Passage*, pp. 104, 115.

171. Terrill, *800 Million*, p. 233. Peter Berger's *Pyramids of Sacrifice* discusses the legitimation of political repression by economic advances.

172. See, for example, UPI, "China Says Mao's Errors Resulted in Vast Hunger," October 7, 1979, Fox Butterfield, "Official in Peking Concedes 60's Moves Led to Catastrophe: Yeh Describes Cultural Revolution as 'Appalling' . . . ," *New York*

Times, September 30, 1979; by the same author, "In Peking Two Miles of Botched New Housing," *New York Times,* August 14, 1979. Not even the famed Dazhai (Tachai in earlier transliteration) model communal farm—a standard sight on most itineraries—escaped criticism (UPI, "Farm Unit Praised by Mao Is Assailed by Chinese Party," *New York Times,* October 4, 1979). There was also a new realization that the United States can learn little from Chinese medical practices (cf. M. J. Halberstam, "Suggestions for the Reorientation of American Physicians," *Modern Medicine,* November–December 1979).

173. Broyelle and Broyelle, "Everyday Life," p. 15. The Cultural Revolution was also blamed by the Chinese authorities themselves for juvenile crime and the decline of the educational system. See, for example, James P. Sterba, "China Says Its Rising Juvenile Crime Stems from Cultural Revolution," *New York Times,* December 26, 1979; Fox Butterfield, "Schools in China Still Lag," *New York Times,* February 12, 1980; and Fred M. Hechinger, "In China the Pendulum Is Swinging," *New York Times,* July 17, 1979.

174. Fox Butterfield, "China's Road to Progress Is Mostly Uphill," *New York Times,* February 4, 1979; Malcolm W. Browne, "Visitors' Views of China's Gains Seen as Overstated," *New York Times,* March 27, 1979.

175. Broyelle and Broyelle, "Everyday Life," p. 15.

176. Nick Eberstadt, "Has China Failed?" *New York Review of Books,* April 5, 1979, pp. 39, 36, 34; and by the same author, "Women and Education in China: How Much Progress?", *New York Review of Books,* April 19, 1979, p. 39.

177. Broyelle and Broyelle, "Everyday Life," p. 16.

178. Fox Butterfield, "Tree Loss in China Affecting Climate," *New York Times,* April 18, 1979; and by the same author, "Chinese Ecology Upset by Food Drive," *New York Times,* April 7, 1980.

179. Galbraith, *China Passage,* p. 104; Padmai Desai, "China and India: Development During the Last 25 Years," *American Economic Review,* May 1975, p. 367.

180. Zagoria, "China by Daylight," p. 138. For further comments on comparative rates of modernization and regimentation see also Ben J. Wattenberg, "Mao's Funeral," *Harper's,* February 1977, pp. 32–33.

181. Peter L. Berger, "Good News from India?" *Worldview,* October 1976, p. 27. Since Mao's death the Chinese authorities admitted that the press has been systematically exaggerating economic progress ("Press in China Admits to Lies, Boasts and Puffery," *New York Times,* August 29, 1979).

182. For instance, he accompanied the Dean of Canterbury, Hewlett Johnson, in a special train to inspect the Miyun Dam (see Johnson, *Upsurge of China,* p. 336). Edgar Snow was given the same treatment (Snow, *Red China Today,* p. 102).

183. Evidently Mao used to be more accessible and informal before his rise to power. In the later 1930s and early 40s he was described as "a correspondent's delight, casual in his manner, generous with his time, and masterful in his conversation . . . [he] normally scheduled his interviews . . . conducted in . . . a loess cave, for late in the evening. They continued until two or three in the morning, when a bleary-eyed . . . newsman would take leave of his unwearied host" (Kenneth E. Shewmaker, *Americans and Chinese Communists, 1927–1945,* [Ithaca, N.Y., 1971], p. 184). Such images of Mao are more reminiscent of Castro in his revolutionary period than of Stalin, to whom he was later compared (p. 188).

184. Here again the impression of the early visitors was quite different from the image that was created after the conquest of power: "The charismatic force of Mao Tse-tung is truly astonishing. Through the writings of Americans and Euro-

peans, Mao became a legend in his own time. To Edgar Snow, Mao was the prophet in a cave. . . . Snow felt a 'certain force of destiny . . . a kind of elemental vitality.' . . . Helen Snow emerged from Mao's darkened cavern with memories of an 'Olympian figure' who made pronouncements like a 'Delphian Oracle'" (ibid., p. 186).

185. Klaus Mehnert, *China Returns* (New York, 1972), p. 241. See, for example, Richard L. Walker, "Chinese Supermen," *New York Times Book Review*, February 18, 1962. According to Walker, Mao's cult only abated briefly after Khrushchev's "secret" speech in 1956, and then intensified again after 1957.

186. Science for the People, *Science Walks on Two Legs*, p. 21. Dick Wilson, ed., *Mao Tse-Tung in the Scales of History* (Cambridge, 1977), p. 8; Myrdal and Kessle, *Revolution Continued*, p. 191.

187. Michel Oksenberg in Wilson, *Mao Tse-tung*, p. 70; Snow, *Red China Today*, p. 177.

188. Han Suyin, *China in the Year 2001* (New York, 1967), pp. 186, 199. For a highly critical review of Suyin's work see Orville Schell, "A Friend of China," *New York Times Book Review*, July 20, 1980.

189. Quoted in Whitfield, *Scott Nearing*, p. 185.

190. Edward Friedman in Wilson, *Mao Tse-tung*, p. 300.

191. Greene, *China*, pp. 143–44. More recently Professor Fairbank expressed similar views and ridiculed the idea that the Chinese leaders might engage in a power struggle after Mao's death. He wrote that by calling it a power struggle, "we impose our self-image on the distant Chinese scene," and also expressed the belief that "Ford vs. Carter is a more naked power struggle than anything going on in Peking." He stressed that the Chinese had disagreements over principles and policies rather than personalities, in short, that the sordid scramble for power had little place in Chinese politics (*New York Review of Books*, October 14, 1976, p. 3).

192. See for example Davidson, *Daybreak in China*, p. 138.

193. Schell, *In the People's Republic*, pp. vii-viii. In a similar spirit Leonov, a Soviet writer, observed that Stalin "inculcated a small particle of his will into every single Soviet man and woman—he 'divided himself among them'" (quoted in Paul Hollander, "The New Man and His Enemies," (Ph. D. dissertation, Princeton, 1963), p. 171).

194. Myrdal and Kessle, *Revolution Continued*, p. 187; Fairbank, "New China," p. 41.

195. Johnson, *China's New Creative Age*, p. 153; see also Concerned Asian Scholars, *China!*, pp. 46, 48.

196. The most comprehensive documentation of this cult may be found in George Urban, ed., *The Miracles of Chairman Mao: A Compendium of Devotional Literature, 1966–1970* (London, 1971); see also Mehnert, *China Returns*, p. 113 for a few other "miracles."

197. See, for example, William Hinton, *Fanshen* (New York, 1966), p. 183.

198. Lord Boyd Orr and Peter Townsend, *What Is Happening in China?* (London, 1959), pp. 57, 58.

199. Robert Jay Lifton, *Revolutionary Immortality: Mao Tse-Tung and the Chinese Cultural Revolution* (New York, 1968), p. 91.

200. Wilson, *Mao Tse-tung*, p. 2; Concerned Asian Scholars, *China!*, p. 46.

201. E.g., Julie Nixon Eisenhower, "Chairman Mao Says Good-Bye," *Ladies' Home Journal*, January 1977, p. 67; Djerassi, *Glimpses of China*, p. 21; Concerned Asian Scholars, *China!*, p. 21.

202. Johnson, *China's New Creative Age*, p. 153; Milton and Milton, *Wind Will Not Subside*, pp. 103, 108.

203. Beauvoir, *Long March*, p. 429.

204. Topping, *Dawn Wakes in the East*, p. 42.

205. Salisbury, *To Peking*, p. 250.

206. Johnson, *China's New Creative Age*, pp. 145–46; Djerassi, *Glimpses of China*, p. 22.

207. Harrison E. Salisbury, "Now It's China's Cultural Thaw," *New York Times Magazine*, December 4, 1977, p. 108; and Edward Friedman, "McCarthyism in China," *New York Times*, February 21, 1979.

208. Salisbury, "Now It's China's Cultural Thaw," p. 24.

209. This was quoted from a Chinese official publication by Simon Leys in the introduction to Chen Jo-hsi, *The Execution of Mayor Yin*, (Bloomington, Ind., 1978), p. xxvii. For further comments on Chinese socialist realism see also Paul Hollander, "Socialist Realism in a Comparative and Historical Perspective," *Studies in Comparative Communism*, Autumn 1976.

210. Leys, *Chinese Shadows*, pp. 136, 134, 129.

211. Robert Guillain, *The Blue Ants* (London, 1957), p. 99. See also Charles Mohr, "Peking Propagating Contempt for Intellectuals and Experts," *New York Times*, November 3, 1968.

212. Nearing, *Making of a Radical*, p. 141. Rewi Alley co-authored with Wilfred Burchett, *China: The Quality of Life* (Harmondsworth, U.K., 1976). Hewlett Johnson, the Miltons, and Anna Louise Strong are among the foreigners who make reference to Alley.

213. Greene, *China*, p. 241.

214. Beauvoir, *Long March*, pp. 310-11, 313, 311.

215. Johnson, *China's New Creative Age*, pp. 94–95; Davidson, *Daybreak in China*, pp. 134–35, 148; Myrdal and Kessle, *Revolution Continued*, pp. 139, 168, 171; Concerned Asian Scholars, *China!*, pp. 170–71.

216. Robert Guillain, *When China Wakes* (New York, 1966), p. 224.

217. Jacoviello, "Communist Looks at China."

218. Boyd Orr and Townsend, *What Is Happening*, p. vi.

219. Leys, "Human Rights," p. 70.

220. Robert W. Barnett, "Make An Issue of Human Rights? No," *New York Times*, April 2, 1978.

221. Galston, *Daily Life*, p. 160.

222. Simon Leys, "Broken Images," *Dissent*, Fall 1976, p. 361; Bao Ruo-Wang, *Prisoner of Mao*, p. 61.

223. Beauvoir, *Long March*, pp. 388–89.

224. Davidson, *Daybreak in China*, pp. 98, 176, 177.

225. It will also be recalled that several of the victims described in Robert Jay Lifton, *Thought Reform and the Psychology of Totalism: A Study of 'Brainwashing' in China* (New York, 1961), were missionaries and priests.

226. Quoted in Greene, *China*, p. 192; Boyd Orr and Townsend, *What Is Happening*, p. 73; John Gittings, "Pine and Willow," *Manchester Guardian Weekly*, May 3, 1971; John K. Fairbank, "Travel Notes," mimeographed (EARC Files, May 30, 1972), pp. 2, 3. There were also comparisons made of the young Chinese dispatched to the rural areas during the Cultural Revolution and the young people joining the Peace Corps in the United States. "As the Peace Corps demonstrated, young people are capable of volunteering for service that calls for sacrifice. Much as young Americans volunteered for service in remote areas . . . in response to a call from President Kennedy, so young Chinese have volunteered to help bring a higher educational and cultural level to the less-developed areas of China in response to a call from Chairman Mao," wrote Frank F. Wong, an associate professor

of history from Antioch College (Letter to the editor, *New York Times Magazine*, September 15, 1974).

227. Beauvoir, *Long March*, p. 388.

228. Bao Ruo-Wang, *Prisoner of Mao*, p. 10. Similar comments were made about the difference between the Chinese and Soviet approaches to political controls in David Erdal, "I Worked in Mao's China," *Worldview*, November 1977, esp. p. 7. For an older but valuable account of informal (or semiformal) social controls in everyday life and especially in school, see Sansan and Bette Lord, *Eighth Moon* (New York, 1964), esp. pp. 54, 56, 59, 63, 65, 71, 95–96, 98, 114, 132, 134–35.

229. Leys, "Broken Images," pp. 374–75.

230. Not that other methods were neglected; food deprivation too was generously used. Bao Ruo-Wang wrote: "Rationing had been introduced as a formal part of the interrogation process. No greater weapon exists for inducing cooperation. . . . After a year of this diet I was prepared to admit virtually anything to get more food" (*Prisoner of Mao*, p. 46).

231. Lamont, *Trip to Communist China*, pp. 20–21.

232. *Quaker Report*, pp. iv–v; Worsley, *Inside China*, p. 214.

233. Leon Lipson, "Impressions of China: Law," *Yale Alumni Magazine*, October 1974. Jerome Alan Cohen of Harvard reported similar difficulties ("Chinese Justice: It's a Puzzlement," *Washington Post*, July 4, 1972).

234. Roy, *Journey Through China*, p. 53; Bao Ruo-Wang, *Prisoner of Mao*, p. 99. Edgar Snow had also visited the Peking jail (*Red China Today*, pp. 357–60).

235. Beauvoir, *Long March*, p. 385.

236. Trudeau and Hebert, *Two Innocents*, pp. 21, 21–23.

237. This is suggested not only by Beauvoir's claim (*Long March*, p. 386) that there was only one prison in Peking but also by the similar figures given to Cameron, Beauvoir, and Jules Roy about the prison population. Such similarities, however, do not explain the different physical appearance reported by Cameron. There might have been renovations since Cameron's visit.

238. James Cameron, *Mandarin Red: A Journey Behind the "Bamboo Curtain"* (London, 1955), pp. 95, 96, 97, 99.

239. Davidson, *Daybreak in China*, p. 183.

240. Townsend, *China Phoenix*, pp. 318, 319, 320, 321. As to the efforts to facilitate the readjustment of the newly released prisoner: Bao Ruo-Wang reported the case of a prisoner—one does not know how typical—who after his release found himself so ostracized and badly treated by his family and village that he begged readmission to the jail (*Prisoner of Mao*, p. 308).

241. Greene, *China*, pp. 55–56, 208–9.

242. Audrey Topping, *Dawn Wakes in the East*, pp. 66–67.

243. Passin, *China's Cultural Diplomacy*, pp. 119–20.

244. Fairbank, "New China," p. 40; Michael Frolic, "Wide-eyed in Peking: A Diplomat's Diary" *New York Times Magazine*, January 11, 1976, p. 32; quoted in Sheila Johnson, "To China with Love," p. 44. Martin Whyte called the May 7 schools "quasi-penal institutions"; see "Corrective Labor Camps in China," *Asian Survey*, March 1973, p. 256. His article also examines some similarities and differences between the Chinese and Soviet camps.

245. Mehnert, *China Returns*, p. 63.

246. Macchiocchi, *Daily Life*, p. 96.

247. Roy, *Journey Through China*, p. 164.

248. Leys, "Human Rights," p. 73; Safire, "China: New Mysteries," p. 34, Professor Richard L. Walker estimated that the Chinese Communist regime was responsible for the death of at least 34 and probably close to 50 million of its citizens

("Death of 34 Million Laid to Chinese Reds," *New York Times*, August 13, 1971).

249. See for instance Harold C. Schonberg, "Shanghai Youth Use Boston Symphony Visit for Protest," *New York Times*, March 16, 1979.

250. Fox Butterfield, "Peking Dissident in Rare Account Tells of Political Prisoners' Torture," *New York Times*, May 7, 1979; also in the same issue, "Excerpts from the Wall Poster Describing How Detainees Are Treated" (see p. 10 for regulation quoted on required sleeping position). Subsequently the author of this "rare account" and of the wall poster referred to, Wei Jigsheng, was given a fifteen-year prison sentence (Fox Butterfield, "Leading Chinese Dissident Gets Fifteen-Year Prison Term," *New York Times*, October 17, 1979; for excerpts of the transcript of his trial see "Excerpts from Peking Trial Transcript," *New York Times*, November 15, 1979).

For a more general discussion of political imprisonment see *Political Imprisonment in the People's Republic of China* (London, Amnesty International Publications, 1978). On the fate of those released and "rehabilitated" (some of them posthumously) in the post-Mao years, see Fox Butterfield, "China's Purge Victims Don't Exactly Get a Warm Welcome," *New York Times*, July 15, 1979. In this article an official Chinese source was quoted to the effect that 40 to 70 percent of those accused of being counterrevolutionaries were found to be innocent. On the mistreatment of a woman writer, see Fox Butterfield, "Peking Honors Mao's Second Wife, Long in Eclipse," *New York Times*, June 7, 1979. For further examples of prison conditions, see Broyelle and Broyelle, "Everyday Life," p. 17.

251. "Excerpts from the Wall Poster," p. 10.

252. Ross H. Munro, "China is Still Stigmatizing 'Rich Peasants' of the 1940s," *New York Times*, October 13, 1977, p. 10.

253. Ross H. Munro, "In China, Tight Curbs Woven into Social Fabric Limit Rights," *New York Times*, October 11, 1977.

254. Hsia, *Coldest Winter in Peking* and Chen, *Execution of Mayor Yin.*

Chapter 8: Techniques of Hospitality: A Summary

1. Hicks, "Lincoln Steffens," p. 152.

2. Andre Gide, *Afterthoughts on the USSR* (New York, 1938), p. 60.

3. Salisbury, *To Peking*, p. 17.

4. Enzensberger, "Tourists of the Revolution," p. 152.

5. A recent definition of totalitarianism offered by Barrington Moore, Jr. recaptures the essentials of the concept that other authors have increasingly discarded as insufficiently scientific: "A totalitarian society is one where a small ruling elite controls the means of coercion and persuasion and in the name of some ideal uses police and propaganda to stamp out dissent and reduce social and cultural space to a minimum" (*Injustice: The Social Bases of Obedience and Revolt*, [White Plains, N.Y., 1978], p. 483).

6. See Passin, *China's Cultural Diplomacy*; also Hebert and Trudeau, *Two Innocents*, pp. 65–66. Richard L. Walker noted that the Chinese regime under Mao "has applied the same techniques developed by the Soviet communists over the past four decades" ("Guided Tourism in China," *Problems of Communism*, September–October 1957, p. 31). Caute observed that for the Cuban regime "tourism is primarily a weapon of propaganda. They believe that they have something admirable to show and they want to show it" (*Cuba, Yes?*, p. 48).

7. Emma Goldman, *My Disillusionment in Russia* (New York, 1970), p. 59; Victor Serge quoted in Enzensberger, "Tourists of the Revolution," p. 137.

8. Roy Innis, an American black activist, and some black journalists were favorably impressed after their trip to Uganda, as was the Rev. Ralph Wilkerson, a California evangelist (see Jack Anderson, "Amin's Newest Ploys," *Daily Hampshire Gazette*, July 26, 1978, p. 6); Henry Kamm, "Pol Pot Living in Jungle Luxury In Midst of Deprived Cambodia," *New York Times*, March 4, 1980; "Andrew Young's Wrong Algerian Tour" (correspondence), *New York Times*, February 21, 1980.

9. Galbraith, *China Passage*, p. 54.

10. Bronfenbrenner, "From Another Planet," p. 1; Macciocchi, *Daily Life*, p. 305; "Computing in China: A Travel Report" (EARC Files, July 1972), p. 2; William W. Howells, "A Visit to China," *News About Peabody Museum*, Autumn 1975; Pares, *Moscow Admits a Critic*, p. 27.

11. Sontag, *Trip to Hanoi*, p. 72.

12. Ibid., p. 33; McCarthy, *Hanoi*, p. 14; Salkey, *Havana Journal*, p. 25.

13. Schell, "Friend of China," p. 10. David Caute's interpreter in Cuba also linked criticism to the betrayal of hospitality (*Cuba, Yes?*, p. 161).

14. James Reston, "Now, About My Operation in Peking," *New York Times*, July 26, 1971, p. 6. Daniel Berrigan's reaction to the assignment of a doctor to his group in North Vietnam was similar: "It was another experience of anonymous kindness during this long week of courtesy and revelation" (*Night Flight to Hanoi*, pp. 109–10).

15. Webb, *Soviet Communism*, p. x; Sontag, *Trip to Hanoi*, p. 6; Berrigan, *Night Flight to Hanoi*, pp. 78–79, 86, 111; Ashmore and Baggs, *Mission to Hanoi*, Feuchtwanger, *Moscow 1937*, p. 147.

16. Huxley, *Scientist*, p. 72; Margulies, *Pilgrimage to Russia*, p. 116; see also Walker, "Guided Tourism in China," p. 34.

17. Karnow, "China Through Rose-Tinted Glasses," p. 76. See also *Accuracy in Media Report* (Washington, D.C., January 11, 1979), p. 3.

18. Galbraith, *China Passage*, p. 104.

19. Galston, *Daily Life*, p. 8.

20. Caute, *Cuba, Yes?*, p. 121.

21. Barghoorn, *Soviet Cultural Offensive*, p. 127. For a further discussion of the impact of flattery see Sperber, *Man and His Deeds*, p. 9, and Margulies, *Pilgrimages to Russia*, p. 89.

22. White, "Americans in Soviet Russia," p. 173.

23. Shaw, *Rationalization of Russia*, pp. 16, 17, 19.

24. Beauvoir, *Long March*, p. 12; McCarthy, *Hanoi*, p. 4.

25. Lynd and Hayden, *Other Side*, p. 57; Ashmore and Baggs, *Mission to Hanoi*, p. 14; Berrigan, *Night Flight to Hanoi*, pp. 38, 134.

26. Levinson and Brightman, *Venceremos Brigade*, pp. 74–75, 90.

27. Cardenal, *In Cuba*, p. 2.

28. Boyd Orr and Townsend, *What Is Happening*, p. 32.

29. Galston, *Daily Life*, pp. 32, 13.

30. Frank Tuohy, "From a China Diary," *Encounter*, December 1966, p. 8.

31. Strong, *Letters from China*, nos. 21–30, pp. 2–3.

32. Leys, *Chinese Shadows*, pp. 185–86; Loh, "Setting the Stage for Foreigners," pp. 80–81.

33. Barbara Tuchman, *Notes from China* (New York, 1972), pp. 58–59, 62.

34. Leys, *Chinese Shadows*, p. 21.

35. Tuchman, *Notes from China*, pp. 61–62.

36. Galbraith, *China Passage*, pp. 32, 29, 53; Milton and Milton, *Wind Will Not Subside*, p. 10.

37. The reactions of Jonathan Kozol to being taken on an inspection of Cuban schools by the minister of education exemplifies these techniques and their impact: "At last I started to get hold of the idea that the whirlwind visit which I was about to make into Cuban public schools would take place in the company of the man who had the job of making sure that every need and possible precondition for the operation of these schools had been fulfilled. I was, in short, with one of the three or four true leaders of the Cuban revolution" (*Children of the Revolution*, pp. 130–31).

38. Ernesto Cardenal also met Castro and discussed with him the affinities between Christianity and Marxism as the latter was practiced in Cuba (*In Cuba*, pp. 326–27). In regard to Castro's ability to charm women and businessmen, see, for example, "Castro Regales New Englanders," *New York Times*, October 28, 1977, p. 2; and "Castro Dazzles Visitors", *Daily Hampshire Gazette*, October 31, 1977 (both, Associated Press dispatches). Earlier in 1977 Castro also enchanted Mrs. Ernest Hemingway: "Castro looks 'so much like Ernest—the beard, the way his head sits on his shoulders, the height. Fidel is just the type of man who appeals to me,' she said" (AP, *Daily Hampshire Gazette*, July 19, 1977).

39. Simone Signoret, *Nostalgia Is Not What It Used to Be* (New York, 1978), pp. 166–69; Beauvoir, *All Said and Done*, p. 290. Robert Frost also had a meeting with Khrushchev. (F. D. Reeve: *Robert Frost in Russia* Boston, 1963 p. 110).

40. Koestler in Crossman, *God that Failed*, p. 58; Feuchtwanger, *Moscow 1937*, p. 17, 15–16. While on his visit Frost's "poems were cropping up almost daily in the [Soviet] papers." (Reeve *cited* p. 30).

41. Margulies, *Pilgrimage to Russia*, pp. 86–87, 88.

42. Cardenal, *In Cuba*, p. 76; Frank, *Prophetic Island*, p. 1. The publication of Parenti's book was reported in Fox Butterfield, "Peking Surveys Students and Find They Lack Zeal for Communism," *New York Times*, May 6, 1979. Cardenal's position as minister of culture in Nicaragua was reported in the *New York Times*, August 1, 1980, p. 2.

43. Edwards, *Persona Non Grata*, pp. 210–11.

44. Beauvoir, *Long March*, pp. 16, 17.

45. Boyd Orr and Townsend, *What Is Happening*, p. 34; Galbraith, *China Passage*, pp. 76, 85.

46. Loh, "Setting the Stage," p. 81.

47. Sartre, *Sartre on Cuba*, p. 7; Davis, *Autobiography*, p. 203; McCarthy, *Hanoi*, pp. 13–14.

48. Gliksman, *Tell the West*, pp. 163–64.

49. Beauvoir, *Long March*, p. 18; Tuchman, *Notes from China*, pp. 57–58.

50. Worsley, *Inside China*, p. 62; Lamont, *Russia Day by Day*, pp. 24, 25; Signoret, *Nostalgia*, p. 163. As early as in 1931 William C. White reported that "the Soviet trusts put their new Rolls-Royces and expensive American cars at the disposal of visitors . . ." ("Americans in Soviet Russia," p. 175).

51. Newton, "Sanctuary in Cuba?", p. 27; and Robert Trumbull, "Newton Plans to Resume Control of Black Panthers," *New York Times*, June 28, 1977.

52. Hebert and Trudeau, *Two Innocents*, p. 34; Greene, *China*, p. 21. Lord Boyd Orr and Peter Townsend were also among those satisfied with the railways: "The Peking-Nanking night express was warm and comfortable, and long before we passed through Tientsin we were asleep in our first class berths" (*What Is Happening*, p. 109).

53. Margulies, *Pilgrimage to Russia*, pp. 94, 95; Frank, *Dawn in Russia*, p. 120; Lamont, *Russia Day by Day*, p. 238.

54. Signoret, *Nostalgia*, pp. 186–87; White, "Americans in Soviet Russia," p. 171.

The OGPU was also asked for assistance when Dreiser was unwell; see Kennell, *Dreiser and the Soviet Union*, p. 150.

55. Boyd Orr and Townsend, *What Is Happening*, pp. 34, 35.

56. "Report by the Delegation of American Association of State Colleges and Universities," p. 1.

57. Salisbury, *To Peking*, pp. 41, 255–56, 284.

58. Galbraith, *China Passage*, pp. 40, 55, 60, 61, 75, 101.

59. Bronfenbrenner, "From Another Planet," p. 2; Concerned Asian Scholars, *China!*, pp. 158, 160.

60. Leys, *Chinese Shadows*, p. 75.

61. Terrill, *800 Million*, p. 116; Berrigan, *Night Flight to Hanoi*, pp. 108, 100, 132; Janos Radvanyi, *Delusion and Reality* (South Bend, Ind., 1978), p. 16.

62. McCarthy, *Hanoi*, p. 60; more on being "fed and feted" on p. 35. Sontag, *Trip to Hanoi*, p. 33.

63. Salkey, *Havana Journal*, pp. 195, 218; Cardenal, *In Cuba*, p. 4; Edwards, *Persona Non Grata*, p. 188.

64. Frances Fitzgerald, "A Reporter at Large: Slightly Exaggerated Enthusiasm," in Radosh, ed., *New Cuba*, p. 144; also in *New Yorker*, February 18, 1974, p. 41. For another example of similar techniques (and pressures) of hospitality, see Victor Franco, *Morning After*, p. 29.

65. Quoted in Radosh, ed., *New Cuba*, pp. 201–2. Attention to the welfare of the foreign guests at the 1979 non-aligned nations conference in Havana included fleets of new Soviet cars and 115 new Mercedeses, it was reported (Flora Lewis, "Havana Parley: Long on Oratory," *New York Times*, September 5, 1979).

66. Kamm, "Pol Pot."

67. Margulies, *Pilgrimage to Russia*, p. 84; White, "Americans in Soviet Russia," p. 174; Haldane, *Truth Will Out*, pp. 42, 215.

68. Gide, *Afterthoughts*, pp. 60–61.

69. Newton, "Sanctuary in Cuba?", p. 28; White, "Americans in Soviet Russia," p. 173.

70. Margulies, *Pilgrimage to Russia*, p. 84; Berrigan, *Night Flight to Hanoi*, pp. 40, 46; Lynd and Hayden, *Other Side*, pp. 64, 67; Sontag, *Trip to Hanoi*, p. 6; Salkey, *Havana Journal*, p. 210.

71. Reckord, *Does Fidel Eat More*, pp. 45–46.

72. Edwards, *Persona Non Grata*, p. 198.

73. Caute, *Cuba, Yes?*, p. 49. For a recent summary of standard sights in Cuba see John Womack, Jr., "The Regime Tightens Its Belt," *New Republic*, May 31, 1980, p. 20.

74. Sartre, *Sartre on Cuba*, p. 120.

75. Kozol, *Children of the Revolution*, p. 44. Kozol was also shown the "school of the Martyrs of Kent," named after the four American students killed by the National Guard during a demonstration in the late 1960s. Kozol was informed that "at the last moment, at the request of pupils, faculty and staff, Fidel agreed to change the name of the first new school *en campo* as a symbol of respect for those in the United states who had been working to attempt to stop the war in Vietnam" (p. 164).

76. Berrigan, *Night Flight to Hanoi*, p. 46.

77. Concerned Asian Scholars, *China!*, p. 21.

78. Beauvoir, *Long March*, pp. 20–21.

79. Marcuse, *Peking Papers*, p. 9; see also Walker, "Guided Tourism in China," p. 34. For a discussion of the same techniques in the Soviet context see Margulies, *Pilgrimage to Russia*, pp. 123–24.

80. Sontag, *Trip to Hanoi*, p. 12.

81. Enzensberger, "Tourists of the Revolution," pp. 135–36.

82. Galston, *Daily Life*, p. 6; Radosh, ed., *New Cuba*, p. 66; Luttwak, "Seeing China Plain," p. 29. For another report of techniques of hospitality in Cuba see Marjorie Hunter, "A Programmed Look at Cuba: Fascinating and Frustrating," *New York Times*, February 26, 1978.

83. Marcuse, *Peking Papers*, p. 118.

84. Loh, "Setting the Stage," p. 80. For an inside view of the political functions and operating procedures of Soviet interpreters in the late 1920s and early 1930s see Tamara Solonevich, *Zapiski Sovetskoi Perevodchitsy* [The Memoirs of a Soviet Interpreter], (Sofia, 1937).

85. Beauvoir, *Long March*, p. 26. Sperber regarded her comments on this interpreter as an example of "unfaltering self-delusion" (*Man and his Deeds*, pp. 3–4). Kozol, *Children of the Revolution*, p. xviii; Boyd Orr and Townsend, *What Is Happening*, p. 149; Mitford, *Fine Old Conflict*, p. 241.

86. Loh, "Setting the Stage," p. 84.

87. Leys, *Chinese Shadows*, p. 168, Koestler in Crossman, *God that Failed*, p. 60.

88. McCarthy, *Hanoi*, pp. 7–8.

89. Marcuse, *Peking Papers*, p. 204 .

90. Andrew Smith, *I Was a Soviet Worker* (New York, 1936), p. 146.

91. McCarthy, *Hanoi*, pp. 6, 124.

92. Roy, *Journey Through China*, p. 282.

93. Ibid., p. 242. The elderly and poorly dressed were also hidden from the camera crew of Antonioni (see John J. O'Connor, "Whose China Is Nearer the Truth?", *New York Times*, January 28, 1973).

94. Kennell, *Dreiser and the Soviet Union*, pp. 81, 82, 88, 107.

95. Modiano, *Twenty Snobs and Mao*, p. 155.

96. Margulies, *Pilgrimage to Russia*, pp. 142–44.

97. Samuel N. Harper, *The Russia I Believe In: Memoirs*, ed. Paul V. Harper (Chicago, 1945), pp. 176, 209, 213.

98. Andrei Grigorenko, "In Time of Trouble: The Life of P. G. Grigorenko's Family During his Persecution," in *The Grigorenko Papers: Writings by General P. G. Grigorenko and Documents on his Case* (Boulder, Colo. 1976). The parts referred to in Solzhenitsyn's *First Circle* (pp. 327–37) encompass some of the most extreme and comic rearrangements of reality in a prison for the benefit of American visitors.

99. Caute, *Cuba, Yes?*, pp. 50, 155.

100. Gail Gregg and A. O. Sulzberger, "The Long Way Home," *New York Times Magazine*, July 1, 1979, p. 26. Smith, *Soviet Worker*, p. 35; see also p. 151 for a similar episode.

101. Kenez, "Sense of Deja Vu," p. 8; Roy, *Journey Through China*, p. 120.

102. Even some of the visitors were aware of the connection between the guides and the political police; see, for example, Waldo Frank, *Dawn in Russia*, p. 63.

103. Fitzgerald, *New Yorker*, February 18, 1974, p. 41.

104. Leys, *Chinese Shadows*, 1977, p. 19. Jerome Alan Cohen, the American expert on Chinese law, reported the refusal of a Chinese citizen to tell him even the name of a soup in a restaurant when, unaccompanied by a guide, he attempted to strike up a conversation ("Up Against the Great Wall," *Pacific/The Traveler's Magazine* 4, no. 4 (1975): 22.

105. Kenez, "Travel Notes from China", mimeographed, p. 11.; Kenez, "Sense of Deja Vu," p. 9. Frank Ching, "For Some U.S. Chinese in China, the Best of Everything is a Bit Much," *New York Times*, August 18, 1973.

106. Enzensberger, "Tourists of the Revolution," p. 110.

107. Salkey, *Havana Journal*, pp. 42–43. Fitzgerald, *New Yorker*, February 18, 1974, p. 41. Jessica Mitford was also discouraged from making "chance contacts" with the natives in Hungary (*Fine Old Conflict*, p. 244).

108. Margulies, *Pilgrimage to Russia*, pp. 124, 127, 129.

109. Ching, "U.S. Chinese in China."

110. Harrison E. Salisbury, "Student Visitors Learn That In China Boy Meets Girl Shoulder-to-Shoulder," *New York Times*, June 26, 1976.

111. Salisbury, *To Peking*, p. 192.

112. Anthony Austin, "U.S. Tourists' View: Impressive but Grim," *New York Times*, July 23, 1980, p. B-9; "The Potemkin Olympics," *New York Times*, July 17, 1980.

113. Margulies, *Pilgrimage to Russia*, p. 155.

114. Lev Navrozov, *The Education of Lev Navrozov* (New York, 1975), p. 519.

115. Craig R. Whitney, "For Olympics, Deprived Moscow Gets Taste of Consumer Paradise," *New York Times*, July 17, 1980, p. 5; "Potemkin Olympics."

116. Jack Anderson, "Viets Take Rescue Food of Victims," *Daily Hampshire Gazette*, April 4, 1980.

117. Smith, *Soviet Worker*, pp. 19–20, 31–32, 74–78; see also p. 21 for yet another example of deception concerning housing. The exchange between the Soviet worker and the foreign delegates on the subject of the worker's salary (reported above) had its Chinese variant in Boyd Orr and Townsend's narrative. When they inquired about the earnings of laborers at a reservoir construction, "those whom we asked 'on the job' reported that they were reasonably paid . . ." (*What Is Happening*, p. 104).

118. Salisbury, *To Peking*, p. 101. The rearrangements of reality were also palpable on his short visit to North Korea: "My visits often seemed a bit like a poor scenario out of an old Keystone Cop comedy, with security men racing around corners to prepare the workers in the next shop for the oncoming visitors; . . . plants in which hasty placards had been lettered and painted to make certain that the American visitors would get the optimum dose of anti-American propaganda; and where little work teams (often composed entirely of plain-clothesmen hastily dressed in painfully new coveralls) approached the visitors to hector them about the sins of American imperialism" (p. 202).

119. Smith, *Soviet Worker*, pp. 183, 184, 186.

120. Loh, "Setting the Stage," pp. 82, 83, 84.

121. Hebert and Trudeau, *Two Innocents*, pp. 99, 100; Modiano, *Twenty Snobs and Mao*, pp. 154–58, 155; Boyd Orr and Townsend, *What Is Happening*, pp. 141–42. Cf. "Vietnam: Picking Up the Pieces," Public Television, Hartford, Conn., April 11, 1978, 9 p.m.

122. J. M. Montias, "Travel Notes From China," mimeographed (1973), p. 54.

123. Tuohy, "China Diary," p. 10. Rearrangements of reality in China were also the subject of two recent short stories, one dealing with the sudden arrival of unusually abundant but not-for-sale food supplies at a local market in anticipation of a visit by foreigners, the other with the demand by party functionaries that residents in a city to be visited by American journalists remove not only their clotheslines but the contraptions supporting them. See "The Big Fish" and "Nixon's Press Corps" in Chen, *Execution of Mayor Yin*.

124. Kenez, "Sense of Deja Vu," p. 8; Boyd Orr and Townsend, *What Is Happening*, p. 133.

125. Marcuse, *Peking Papers*, pp. 106–7.

126. Irv Drasnin, "The Welcome Mat Was Slippery," *TV Guide*, November 12, 1977, p. 14.

Chapter 9: Conclusions

1. Emile Durkheim, *The Elementary Forms of Religious Life* (New York, 1961), p. 470.

2. Gustave Le Bon, *The Psychology of Socialism* (Wells, Vt., 1965; first published in English 1899), pp. ix–x, xi–xii.

3. Wallace Turner, "Sect Lawyer Explains Role in Custody Fight over Boy," *New York Times*, November 27, 1978.

4. William Kunstler quoted by Nat Hentoff, *Village Voice*, May 28, 1979.

5. Hicks, *Where We Came Out*, p. 66.

6. Shils, *Intellectuals and the Powers*, p. 183. It has, however, also been argued that, at least as far as a small sample of elite intellectuals were concerned, their way of life constrained their alienation: "Despite their apparent alienation in the sixties, most of the elite American intellectuals were simply too well off and too enmeshed in the daily routines of bureaucratic life to qualify as highly alienated . . ." (Kadushin, *American Intellectual Elite*, p. 355–56).

7. As Nicola Chiaromonte puts it: "Modern man cannot conceive of any other absolute than the political absolute . . ."; thus political faith becomes the substitute for religious (*The Worms of Consciousness and Other Essays* [New York, 1976], p. 232).

8. William Kornhauser, *The Politics of Mass Society* (Glencoe, Ill., 1959), p. 184.

9. According to Lipset and the data cited by him, "No other country can come close to the U.S. in commitments to religious beliefs," a finding that seems to contradict the argument being made here (Seymour Martin Lipset, "Introduction to the Norton Edition," *The First New Nation* [New York, 1979], pp. xxxvi–xxxvii). Lipset's conclusion was based on survey research and in particular on statements made by respondents when asked about the importance of religious beliefs in their lives, frequency of church attendance, and belief in God. For a critical analysis of such findings see Jay N. Demerath and Richard Levinson, "Baiting the Dissident Hook," *Sociometry* 34, no. 3 (1971). It is doubtful that the extent to which religious values inform peoples' lives and lend them meaning can be established from such indicators. It could be further argued that religious values, practices, and institutions themselves have become significantly secularized in the United States, thus making it easier to embrace them. There is also the perennial problem of survey research, namely that people report beliefs and attitudes that they consider appropriate or correct but that have little to do with their actual conduct.

Notwithstanding the professions of religious belief, there is little to indicate that religious values provide much assistance to most Americans on occasions when important choices or decisions are to be made. Neither work, nor mate selection, nor leisure time activities, nor sexual morality, nor patterns of consumption, nor the familiar grapplings with identity problems bear the imprint of religious values as far as the majority seem to be concerned.

Andrew Greeley also maintains that religious beliefs and practices are as widespread today as at any time in history (*Unsecular Man* [New York, 1972]). I am in agreement with him about the persistence of religious *needs*, but I think that the available forms of religious beliefs and practices have become unsatisfactory for an increasing number of people in Western societies—and therein lies the meaning of secularization.

10. Shils has written: "There is . . . a very strong representation of aggrieved intellectuals within the institutions of public opinion. In television there is a similar

situation. The professional tradition of muckraking, the tradition of reportorial vigor, the tradition of sensationalism and of the maxim that 'good news is no news' all mean that disorder, failure, catastrophe are given the greatest prominence. Delight in disorder, occasional sympathy with its perpetrators and the cause which it purportedly serves, cause disorder to be much attended to in the mass media." (*Intellectuals and the Powers*, p. 186).

Further evidence of this type of "demystification" can be found in the recent publication of a muckracking exposé of the Supreme Court of the United States, until now the most respected secular institution in American society and virtually immune to criticism. The book completes, symbolically speaking, the total profanization of all American institutions (Robert Woodward and Scott Armstrong, *The Brethren* [New York, 1979]).

11. Shils, *Intellectuals and the Powers*, p. 189; see also pp. 180, 190.

12. Erich Fromm, *The Sane Society* (New York, 1955), chap. 2: "Can a Society Be Sick? The Pathology of Normalcy."

13. "The notion of a 'fall' from a state of perfection was retained in the concept of an anterior stage when men were not yet subject to that 'alienation' which the division of labor under capitalist exploitation later imposed upon them" (George Lichtheim, "Alienation," in *Encyclopedia*, p. 264).

14. David Caute, "Two Types of Alienation," in *Illusion*, p. 169.

15. Ibid., p. 172.

16. Fromm, *Sane Society*, pp. 16, 139. Norman Mailer expressed similar sentiments in his "Letter to Castro," *Presidential Papers*.

17. Dennis Wrong, "The Oversocialized Image of Man in Sociology," in *Skeptical Sociology* (New York, 1977; first published 1961).

18. Jules Henry, *Culture Against Man* (New York, 1963).

19. Alienation that is expressed in intense social criticism falls into the category of "alienation from dominant social values," which defines "middle class radicalism" in Frank Parkin's scheme. He distinguished three major types: alienation as social isolation, alienation as powerlessness, and alienation from dominant social values. The intellectuals being discussed here were neither isolated nor powerless; they might have *felt* powerless, but certainly not isolated, in the periods that were our concern. Frank Parkin, *Middle Class Radicalism*, pp. 11–32.

20. Adelson, "Inventing the Young," p. 46.

21. Quoted in Zhores Medvedev, *A Question of Madness* (New York, 1971), pp. 135–36.

22. Hobsbawm, *Revolutionaries*, p. 26.

23. Potter, *History and American Society*, pp. 343, 358, 360, 361, 362, 363–64, 385.

24. Richard Lowenthal, "On the Disaffection of Western Intellectuals," *Encounter*, July 1977, pp. 10, 12, 11.

25. C. Eric Hansen, "Intellect and Power: Some Notes on the Intellectual as a Political Type," *The Journal of Politics*, May 1969, p. 325.

26. Lasch, *Culture of Narcissism*, pp. 7, 15. There were precedents from other times. Carey McWilliams, in the early 1930s, gravitated toward radical political activism in part out of boredom and "personal dissatisfactions," he reported in his autobiography (*The Education of Carey McWilliams* [New York, 1978], p. 66).

27. Schumpeter, *Democracy, Capitalism, Socialism*, p. 144.

28. Kristol, "About Equality."

29. Bell, *Cultural Contradictions of Capitalism*.

30. Max Weber, *The Sociology of Religion* (Boston, 1963), pp. 124–25.

31. Lowenthal, "Disaffection of Western Intellectuals," p. 11.

32. Ibid.

33. Schumpeter, *Democracy, Capitalism, Socialism*, p. 145; Robert Nisbet, *The Quest for Community* (New York, 1953), p. 34.

34. For a discussion of this issue see Milovan Djilas, "On Alienation—Thoughts on a Marxist Myth," *Encounter*, May 1971, esp. p. 13.

35. Eric Hoffer, *The True Believer* (New York, 1951), p. 131; see also p. 132. A character in an American novel has also made some suggestive remarks about the intellectuals' attitude toward power and some of its sources: *"Democracy and freedom . . . in the most secret heart of every intellectual . . . there lies hidden the real hope that these words hide. It is the hope of power, the desire to bring his ideas to reality by imposing them on his fellow man. We are all of us . . . the little children of the Grand Inquisitor . . . How can we possibly be guilty when we have in mind the welfare of others, and of so many others?"* (Lionel Trilling, *The Middle of the Journey* [New York, 1976], p. 219).

36. By contrast, survey research suggests that political disaffection and withdrawal (defined as alienation) *is* the characteristic response to various tangible deprivations. Thus, for example, black people in the U.S. are more alienated in this sense than whites. However, research of this type does not differentiate intellectuals from the rest of the population and hence has little to say about their estrangement. See, for example, James Wright, "Political Disaffection," in *The Handbook of Political Behavior*, ed. Samuel Long (New York, 1980).

37. Hansen, "Intellect and Power," pp. 316, 319; see also Frank Parkin, *Middle Class Radicalism*, p. 96.

38. Berrigan, *Night Flight to Hanoi*, p. xiv; Sontag, "Some Thoughts," p. 16; and Norman Mailer, *The Armies of the Night* (New York, 1968), p. 77 (my emphasis).

39. Hansen, "Intellect and Power," p. 322. Sartre exemplified many of these attitudes with a special clarity, as has been increasingly recognized. Various French intellectuals assessing his significance after his recent death had this to say:

"He said you always have to be for the revolution. . . . He said, If it turns out badly, if I've been cuckolded, I'll change my mind."—Geismar

"Sartre didn't adjust his ideas to facts. It was just the opposite: he only accepted facts that fit his ideas. He had no tolerance for anyone who disagreed, no sense of measure."—Manent

"In his theses he was against all established powers, but he really disdained democracy and practiced the lowest form of bootlicking toward dictators. . . ."—Gauchet

"Sartre didn't try to understand totalitarians. He was just against the bourgeois spirit. . . . Really, Sartre lived in an ivory tower. His involvement wasn't with the real world. . . ."—Manent

"He eulogized Palestinian terrorism. We were against the massacre at the Munich Olympics and he was for it. He said terrorism is the weapon of the poor."—Geismar

Quoted in Flora Lewis, "Sartre Tradition: Role of the Master and the Void He Left," *New York Times*, June 14, 1980.

40. Quoted in Watson, "Were the Intellectuals Duped?", p. 29.

41. Hansen, "Intellect and Power," p. 324.

42. Whitfield, *Scott Nearing*, p. 192.

43. Saul Bellow, *Herzog* (New York, 1965), p. 370.

44. Shils, *Intellectuals and the Powers*, p. 3.

45. As Zygmunt Bauman has observed: "Socialism has been, and to some extent still is, *the* utopia of the modern epoch" (*Socialism: The Active Utopia* [London, 1976], p. 36). See also Eugéne Ionesco, "Of Utopianism and Intellectuals," *Encounter*, February 1978.

46. Quoted in Arthur Schlesinger, Jr., "The Making of a Social Conscience," *New York Times Book Review,* June 24, 1979.

47. Philip Rahv, *Essays on Literature and Politics, 1932–1972* (Boston, 1978), p. 288.

48. Peter Berger wrote: "The basic formula for coping with the various disappointments is always the same (after, that is, the customarily prior denial that there is anything to be disappointed about): The disappointing country does not embody 'true socialism'; therefore it does not falsify the socialist vision; 'true socialism' is either still in the future, or must be looked for elsewhere—if not in Russia then in China, if not in China then in Vietnam, and so on *ad infinitum*" ("Socialist Myth," p. 11).

49. Emile Durkheim, *Socialism* (New York, 1962), p. 41.

50. George Orwell, *The Road to Wigan Pier* (New York, 1958; first published 1937), p. 206. More recently, a similar cluster of traits has been observed in another group of alienated English people: "To take a trivial example, the wearing of beards did appear to me more common among Campaign for Nuclear Disarmament supporters . . . also many respondents indicated they were vegetarian . . . 8% of female respondents were divorced (and an additional 4% separated), a figure which compares with less than 1% for women in the general population. This does suggest that estrangement from certain central values may be conducive to deviance in a wide range of social behaviour" (Parkin, *Middle Class Radicalism,* p. 29).

51. Both Peter Berger ("Socialist Myth") and Adam Ulam (in his *Unfinished Revolution*) emphasize these dual appeals and promises of socialism.

52. Peter Clecak, *Crooked Paths* (New York, 1977), p. 26; Bernard Henri Levy, *Barbarism with a Human Face* (New York, 1979), pp. 168, 170.

53. LeBon, *Psychology of Socialism,* p. xii; Levy, *Barbarism with a Human Face,* p. 172.

54. Quoted in Alan Riding, "For Octavio Paz, A Solitude of His Own as a Political Rebel," *New York Times,* May 3, 1979; see also Raymond Aron, *In Defense of Decadent Europe* (South Bend, Ind., 1977), p. xiii. Aron's *Opium of Intellectuals,* first published in 1955, remains the major work on this topic.

55. Berrigan, *Night Flight to Hanoi,* p. 136. With reference to the Berrigans, it has been suggested that there may be a connection between the sense of moral superiority and feelings of guilt: "Guilt aches for release, and release is achieved through self-flagellation . . . the result of which is atonement . . . one catapults oneself from a status of moral depravity to a status of moral superiority . . . those who victimize themselves transfigure themselves into new people, into an ethical elite. . . . The ultimate dividend of such an investment of religious energies in politics is arrogant self-exaltation. . . . Self-abasement is indeed a precondition of self-righteousness . . ." (Dale Vree, " 'Stripped Clean': The Berrigans and the Politics of Guilt and Martyrdom," *Ethics,* July 1975, pp. 285, 286, 287).

56. For example, Horowitz wrote: "There was nothing asked about the disruption of Russian society until 1938, because the intelligentsia was not directly involved as a victim. When it was the peasantry there was no outcry. When it was the urban proletariat it was perfectly acceptable that they go to the rack. When it was one ethnic minority after another it was perfectly rationalized in terms of development and nationalism. But when the intelligentsia felt the lash in 1938, questions about Soviet genocide arose. Genocide becomes a problem only when the intellectuals are affected; until then they are incredibly capable of myopic moral bookkeeping" (Irving Louis Horowitz, *Genocide: State Power and Mass Murder,* [New Brunswick, N.J., 1977], p. 82).

57. Watson, "Were the Intellectuals Duped?" With respect to the appeals of violence for intellectuals, Peter Berger has noted the contrast between their life

style of "pacific tranquility" and dreams of violence. (*Pyramids of Sacrifice*, p. 77). Koestler offers another explanation of the appeals of revolutionary violence: "The fulfillment of the promise should be preceded by violent upheavals; the Last Judgment, the advent of the comet, etc. Hence the instinctive rejection by full-blooded communists of all reformist ideas about a smooth transition of Socialism. The revolutionary apocalypse is necessary to fulfill the pattern of the Advent" (*Yogi and the Commissar*, p. 118).

58. Trilling, *Middle of the Journey*, p. 227. Renee Winegarten also commented on such transformations of moral absolutism into moral relativism in *Writers and Revolution*, p. 319.

59. Whitfield, *Scott Nearing*, p. 199.

60. Stephen Spender in Crossman, *God that Failed*, p. 253. A similar point was made in a recent article about devotees of Stalin "incapable of assimilating information incompatible with their political mindset." The author also noted that "a truly critical posture . . . is uncomfortable" (Nevins, "Politics Through Tinted Glass (Brightly)," pp. 24, 35).

61. Chiaromonte, *Worms of Consciousness*, pp. 217, 224.

62. Konrád and Szelényi, *Road to Class Power*, pp. 204–5. A further interpretation of the attractions of socialism has been offered by George Orwell: "The underlying motive of many socialists, I believe, is simply a hypertrophied sense of order. The present state of affairs offends them not because it causes misery, still less because it makes freedom impossible, but because it is untidy; what they desire basically is to reduce the world to something resembling a chessboard" (*Road to Wigan Pier*, p. 211).

63. Quoted in Sidney Hook, "Will to Illusion," *New Republic*, November 16, 1974, p. 27.

64. For a detailed discussion of such techniques in the Soviet context see Arthur Koestler, "Soviet Myth and Reality," in *Yogi and the Commissar*.

65. Mary McCarthy *preferred* to believe (as was noted in Chapter 2) that the United States and not North Vietnam was responsible for the Hue massacre.

66. Conquest, *Great Terror*, p. 513. Sartre was quoted in Laqueur and Mosse, *Literature and Politics*, p. 25.

67. Koestler used this expression in an essay suggesting that those enamored with the Soviet system might be cured if sentenced to one year of forced reading of assorted Soviet materials produced for home consumption ("The Candles of Truth," in *Trail of the Dinosaur*).

68. The concept of cognitive dissonance helps to explain this phenomenon (see Festinger, *A Theory of Cognitive Dissonance*). Koestler's observations are also pertinent: "Such unconditional surrender of the critical faculties always indicates the presence of a factor which is *a priori* beyond the reach of reasoning. . . . Deep-rooted, archetypal beliefs lead only to neurosis when doubt provokes conflict. To keep doubt away, a system of elastic defenses is established" (*Yogi and the Commissar*, p. 120).

69. Lynd and Hayden, *Other Side*, p. 179. See also pp. 169, 176–77, 183 for further examples of contextual rationalization of repression.

70. "Activist Lawyer Criticizes U.S. for Violating Human Rights," pp. 1, 4.

71. Spender, in Crossman, *God that Failed*, pp. 255, 256.

72. Nathan Leites, the American political scientist, wrote of this mentality: "Bolsheviks do not consider the chance of attaining certain goals lessened by the . . . protracted and large-scale use of means which are at extreme variance to them; in fact the problem is not posed" (*A Study of Bolshevism* [Glencoe, Ill., 1953], p. 105; see also pp. 109, 141). In a similar spirit Sartre suggested that evidence of Soviet forced labor camps should be ignored lest the French proletariat "might be thrown

into despair," presumably upon discovering that the Soviet alternative is not noticeably superior to conditions prevailing in their own society (Conquest, *Great Terror*, p. 509). The connection between expedience and belief in one's cause was also pronounced in past conflicts that had a religious component: "A justification of the Puritan barbarities might also be based on the assumption that the Puritans were fighting for a just cause against the unrighteous Cavaliers. Of course that was what the Puritans actually believed, and on this ground they might consider themselves justified in doing many things which they condemned as outrageous misdeeds in the Cavaliers, without being guilty of any inconsistency. . . . They thought themselves perfectly entitled to the true belief that their cause was just and therefore favored by God, although they resented every expression of a corresponding but false belief of their adversaries" (Svend Ranulf, *Moral Indignation and Middle Class Psychology* [New York, 1964; first published 1938], p. 91).

73. Winegarten wrote: "Today not only young hotheads but distinguished novelists and critics of mature years are among those drawn to the most potent myth of the religion of revolution, the dream of a total human transformation to follow general destruction. . . . During the last two centuries . . . many aesthetic, heroic, and religious currents have converged to help to make the words 'revolution' and 'revolutionary' sacred . . ." (*Writers and Revolution*, p. 322, 325).

74. Aldous Huxley, "Words and Behavior," *Collected Essays* (New York, 1953), pp. 254–55.

75. For a more extended discussion of this concept see Hollander, "Sociology, Selective Determinism and the Rise of Expectations."

76. James Hitchcock, "The Intellectuals and the People," *Commentary*, March 1973, p. 66. For a discussion of what I called selective determinism (and moral double standards) in the writings of the Berrigan brothers see Vree, " 'Stripped Clean,' " pp. 280–81.

77. Correspondence, *New York Times*, July 16, 1972.

78. Similarly, concern with human rights "is determined not by what happens but by who does it," as exemplified by the indifference to such violations in China as against the concern with far lesser violations in the Philippines (Robert B. Goldman, letter, *Commentary*, September 1979, p. 32). See also Jeanne Kirkpatrick, "Dictatorship and Double Standards," *Commentary*, November 1979. Michael Parenti, mentioned earlier as one who insisted that the political abuse of psychiatry in the United States was no different from that in the Soviet Union, argued on another occasion that there was too much concern in the American press with the victims of the Iranian revolution and not enough with those of the shah (Letter, *New York Times*, May 10, 1979). And an unnamed columnist in the *New York Times*, commenting on Richard Falk's advocacy of the Khomeini regime in Iran, wrote: "Excuses can always be found for repression if the desire to find them is strong enough" ("Comedians," *New York Times*, April 1, 1979). The application of political double standards was also revealed by the study by Glantz ("New Left Radicalism and Punitive Moralism").

79. Spender in Crossman, *God that Failed*, p. 253–254.

80. Barrington Moore, Jr., has made a somewhat similar observation: "During the twentieth century there has been both a rapid disintegration of traditional moral standards and a sharp increase in conflicts that have a powerful moral component" (*Injustice*, pp. 435–36).

81. Mannheim, *Ideology and Utopia*, pp. 155–58.

82. Erazim V. Kohak, "Requiem for Utopia," *Dissent*, January 1969, p. 41; Levy, *Barbarism with a Human Face*, p. 158. On the difficulties and unintended consequences of creating utopia by institutional means see Leszek Kolakowski,

"Marxist Roots of Stalinism," in *Stalinism*, ed. Robert C. Tucker (New York, 1977), p. 297.

83. These objections focus largely on what George Kateb has called "a world of . . . effortless virtue." He notes that a society of peace, abundance, and effortless virtue, if ever achieved, would also be an impoverished one. In particular, it would be without "the struggle against great odds, against scarcity, against infirmity of will, the chance to do a great deal with very little, the occasion to display certain virtues or habits or characteristics which only a dark world gives, are all, in theory, eliminated from a utopian society" (*Utopia and Its Enemies*, p. 230).

84. Manuel and Manuel, *Utopian Thought*, p. 814.

85. Bernard D. Davis, "Of Jonestown and the Search for Utopias," Letter, *New York Times*, December 17, 1978.

86. An Observer, *Message from Moscow* (New York, 1968), pp. 238–39.

87. This was less true in Western Europe and especially France, where more pro-Soviet and pro-communist intellectuals retained such loyalties and even Communist party affiliations. See David Caute, *The French Left* (New York, 1964), p. 361.

88. Loss of will and the quality of leadership are probably also related. The declining global assertiveness of the United States in the post-Vietnam era reflects not only the trauma of that experience and the caution it has bred, but also an uncertainty as to which values are worthy of defending and what, if anything, in American (and Western) social systems deserves strong, determined support. The current problems of leadership may also be connected with the impassioned egalitarianism that swept the country in the 1960s. Such connections, in the broader, historical context, were also discovered by the sociologist Digby Baltzell, who commented on the effects of Quaker egalitarianism on elites in Philadelphia: "To understand the problems of American leadership today just look at Philadelphia . . . Philadelphia's Quakers believed that all men were equal and discouraged the emergence of 'great men'. . . . Egalitarian societies tend to lose pride in themselves. . . . Our society has never been as egalitarian as it is today and consequently, it is losing its pride" ("Leadership Culture in Boston Praised in Contrast to Philadelphia's," *New York Times*, November 25, 1979). See also his book, *Puritan Boston and Quaker Philadelphia: Two Protestant Ethics and the Spirit of Class Authority and Leadership* (New York, 1979).

89. For a study of American neo-conservative intellectuals see Peter Steinfels, *The Neo-conservatives* (New York, 1979).

90. Chiaromonte, *Worm of Consciousness*, p. 213.

91. Navrozov, *Education of Lev Navrozov*, p. 366.

92. Leonard Bernstein, "Just Suppose We Disarmed," *New York Times*, June 10, 1980.

93. Tod Buchanan (and five other unnamed Amherst College students), "Draft registration: Some student views," *Daily Hampshire Gazette*, March 14, 1980; see also Steven V. Roberts, "Students Opposed to Carter Intensify Campaign in New England," *New York Times*, February 17, 1980; and "Confidence of Students in Government Down," *New York Times*, December 23, 1979 (this last was a national poll of high school seniors).

94. One may perhaps also see some significance in the fact that the considerable ($80,000 worth) damage to the Statue of Liberty—probably the best-known national monument and most symbolic of collective self-esteem and national pride—aroused no discernible public indignation, and the charges against the political protestors responsible for it were "reduced to a misdemeanor—by definition, damage of less than $100. . . ." "Follow-up on the News: Statue Climbing," *New York Times*, July 13, 1980.

Selected Bibliography

The following represents a compromise between a full bibliography and none at all. A full bibliography would have added significantly to the costs of producing an already long book and would have represented an extensive and unnecessary duplication of the source references found in the Notes. The Selected Bibliography aims at providing the reader with an easy access to the more important sources upon which this volume was based or which were consulted. The works included are mostly primary sources, either important for the substantive information contained in this volume or theoretically significant for its arguments. The Selected Bibliography contains probably no more than one third of all source materials used. I omitted from it most of the references dealing primarily with the social history of the 1930s and 1960s, many general discussions of intellectuals, all newspaper articles cited, and other works tangential to the main body of the book or infrequently referred to even if valuable in their own right.

The sources are grouped under four substantive headings which partially follow the structure of the book: the literature dealing with 1. *The Soviet Union*, 2. *Cuba and the Third World*, and 3. *China*, respectively; and works relevant to the relationship between 4. *Intellectuals, Politics, and Morality*. Most of the works listed under *Intellectuals, Politics, and Morality* pertain primarily to Chapters 1, 2, and 9, and secondarily to Chapters 3 and 5. (The bibliography does not separate the writings of "pilgrims" from other, more detached discussions of the countries concerned.)

Undoubtedly there are several sources which could have been listed in more than one of the subdivisions of the bibliography; I placed each item in only one subdivision where it seemed to fit best. Books written or edited by several authors are listed only once under the name of the first author.

The Soviet Union

Books

Barbusse, Henri. *Stalin*. New York: 1929.

Barghoorn, Frederick C. *The Soviet Cultural Offensive*. Princeton: 1960.

Belomor—An Account of the Construction of the New Canal Between the White Sea and the Baltic Sea. New York: 1935.

Bevan, A.; Stratchey, E. J.; and Strauss, A. *What We Saw in Russia*. London: 1931.

Buxton, D. F. *The Challenge of Bolshevism: A New Social Ideal*. London: 1928.

Callcott, Mary Stevenson. *Russian Justice*. New York: 1935.

Caute, David. *The Fellow-Travellers*. New York: 1973.

Cole, Margaret I., ed. *Twelve Studies in Soviet Russia*. London: 1933.

Conolly, Violet. *Soviet Tempo: A Journal of Travel in Russia*. London: 1937.

Davies, Joseph E. *Mission to Moscow*. New York: 1943.

Davis, Jerome, ed. *The New Russia*. New York: 1933.

Davis, Jerome. *Behind Soviet Power: Stalin and the Russians*. New York: 1946.

Dennis, Peggy. *The Autobiography of an American Communist*. Berkeley, 1977.

Dewey, John. *Impressions of Soviet Russia and the Revolutionary World: Mexico-China-Turkey*. New York: 1964; first published New York: 1929.

Dos Passos, John. *The Theme Is Freedom*. New York: 1956.

Dreiser, Theodore. *Dreiser Looks at Russia*. New York: 1928.

Duranty, Walter. *The Kremlin and the People*. New York: 1941.

Eastman, Max. *Love and Revolution: My Journey Through an Epoch*. New York: 1965.

Eddy, Sherwood. *The Challenge of Russia*. New York: 1931.

———. *Russia Today—What Can We Learn From It?* New York: 1934.

Feuchtwanger, Lion. *Moscow 1937*. London: 1937.

Filene, Peter A. *Americans and the Soviet Experiment, 1917–1933*. Cambridge: 1967.

Fischer, Louis. *Machines and Men in Russia*. New York: 1932.

———. *Men and Politics*. New York: 1941.

Frank, Waldo. *Dawn in Russia*. New York: 1932.

Freeman, Joseph. *An American Testament*. New York: 1973; first published, 1936.

Gide, André. *Afterthoughts on the USSR*. New York: 1938.

Gliksman, Jerzy. *Tell the West*. New York: 1948.

Goldman, Emma. *My Disillusionment in Russia*. New York: 1970; first published, 1923.

Haldane, Charlotte. *Truth Will Out*. New York: 1950.

Hindus, Maurice. *The Great Offensive*. New York: 1933.

Hodgkin, H. T., ed. *Seeing Ourselves Through Russia: A Book for Private and Group Study*. New York: 1932.

Huxley, Julian. *A Scientist Among the Soviets*. London: 1932.

Johnson, Hewlett. *The Soviet Power*. New York: 1940.

———. *Soviet Russia Since the War*. New York: 1947.

Kennell, Ruth Epperson. *Theodore Dreiser and the Soviet Union 1927–1945*. New York: 1969.

Koerber, Lenka von. *Soviet Russia Fights Crime*. London: 1934.

Lamont, Corliss and Margaret. *Russia Day by Day*. New York: 1933.

Laski, Harold J. *Law and Justice in Soviet Russia*. London: 1935.

Lipper, Elinor. *Eleven Years in Soviet Prison Camps*. Chicago: 1951.

Lovenstein, Meno. *American Opinion of Soviet Russia*. Washington, D. C.: 1941.

Ludwig, Emil. *Nine Etched From Life*. Freeport, N.Y.: 1969; first published, New York: 1934.

Lyons, Eugene. *Assignment in Utopia*. London: 1938.
————. *The Red Decade*. New Rochelle, N.Y.: 1970; first published New York: 1941.
Margulies, Sylvia R. *The Pilgrimage to Russia: The Soviet Union and the Treatment of Foreigners, 1924–1937*. Madison: 1968.
Muggeridge, Malcolm. *Chronicle of Wasted Time*. New York: 1940.
Neruda, Pablo. *Memoirs*. New York: 1977.
Pares, Bernard. *Moscow Admits a Critic*. London: 1936.
Shalamov, Varlam. *Kolyma Tales*. New York: 1980.
Shaw, George Bernard. *The Rationalization of Russia*. Bloomington, Ind.: 1964; first published, 1931.
Shaw, G. B.; Wells, H. G.; Keynes, J. M.; Toller, Ernst; and others. *Stalin–Wells Talk. The Verbatim Report and a Discussion*. London: 1934.
Sinclair, Upton, and Lyons, Eugene. *Terror in Russia? Two Views*. New York: 1938.
Smith, Andrew. *I Was a Soviet Worker*. New York: 1936.
Smith, Homer. *Black Man in Red Russia: A Memoir*. Chicago: 1964.
Solonevich, Tamara. *Zapiski Sovetskoi Perevodchitsy*. (Memoirs of a Soviet Interpreter.) Sofia: 1937.
Spender, Stephen. *Forward from Liberalism*. London: 1937.
Strachey, John. *The Coming Struggle for Power*. New York: 1935.
Strong, Anna Louise. *I Change Worlds: The Remaking of an American*. New York: 1935.
————. *This Soviet World*. New York: 1936.
Trachtenberg, Alan, ed. Memoirs of Waldo Frank, Amherst: 1973.
Wallace, Henry A. *Soviet Asia Mission*. New York: 1946.
Ward, Harry F. *The Soviet Spirit*. New York: 1944.
Warren, Frank A. *Liberals and Communism: The "Red Decade" Revisited*. Bloomington, Ind., and London: 1966.
Webb, Sidney and Beatrice. *Soviet Communism: A New Civilization?* New York: 1936.
————. *The Truth About Russia*. London: 1942.
Werskey, Gary. *The Visible College: The Collective Biography of British Scientific Socialists of the 1930s*. London: 1978; New York: 1979.
Wicksteed, Alexander. *Life Under the Soviets*. London: 1928.
Williams, Albert Rhys. *The Soviets*. New York: 1937.
————. *The Russians: The Land, the People and Why They Fight*. New York: 1943.
Wilson, Edmund. *Travels in Two Democracies*. New York: 1936.
Winter, Ella. *I Saw the Russian People*. Boston: 1947.
Zhivov, M., ed. *Glazami Inostrantsev: Inostrannie Pisateli o Sovetskom Souze*. (Through the Eyes of Foreigners: Foreign Writers on the Soviet Union.) Moscow: 1932.

Articles and Shorter Pieces

Drake, Barbara. "The Webbs and Soviet Communism." In Margaret I. Cole, ed., *The Webbs and Their Work*. London: 1949.

Feuer, Lewis. "American Travelers to the Soviet Union, 1917–1932: The Formation of a Component of New Deal Ideology." *American Quarterly,* Summer 1962.

Himmelfarb, Gertrude. "The Intellectual in Politics: The Case of the Webbs." *Journal of Contemporary History,* No. 3, 1971.

Knox, James. "Diary of a Soviet Guide." *Contemporary Russia,* Vol. 2, Autumn 1937, pp. 44–55.

Koestler, Arthur. "Soviet Myth and Reality." In *Yogi and the Commissar.* New York: 1961.

Lattimore, Owen. "New Road to Asia." *National Geographic Magazine,* December 1944.

Malraux, André. "Literature in Two Worlds." *Partisan Review,* January–February, 1935.

White, William C. "Americans in Soviet Russia." *Scribner's Magazine,* Vol. 89, February 1931.

"How I Came to Communism—A Symposium." *New Masses,* Vol. VIII, September 1932.

Cuba and the Third World

Books

Ashmore, Harry S., and Baggs, William C. *Mission to Hanoi.* New York: 1968.

Baudet, Henri. *Paradise on Earth: Some Thoughts on European Images of Non-European Man.* New Haven: 1965.

Berger, Peter L. *Pyramids of Sacrifice: Political Ethics and Social Change.* Garden City, N.Y.: 1976.

Berrigan, Daniel. *Night Flight to Hanoi.* New York: 1969.

Cardenal, Ernesto. *In Cuba.* New York: 1974.

Caute, David. *Cuba, Yes?* New York: 1974.

Clytus, John. *Black Man in Red Cuba.* Coral Gables, Fla.: 1969.

Coffin, William Sloan, Jr. *Once to Every Man—A Memoir.* New York: 1977.

Davis, Angela. *An Autobiography.* New York: 1974.

Dominguez, Jorge I. *Cuba: Order and Revolution.* Cambridge: 1978.

Draper, Theodore. *Castro's Revolution: Myths and Realities.* New York: 1962.

Dumont, René. *Is Cuba Socialist?* New York: 1974.

Edwards, Jorge. *Persona Non Grata.* New York: 1977.

Franco, Victor. *The Morning After: A French Journalist's Impression of Cuba Under Castro.* New York: 1963.

Frank, Waldo. *Cuba: Prophetic Island.* New York: 1961.

Huberman, Leo, and Sweezy, Paul M. *Cuba: Anatomy of a Revolution.* New York: 1960.

———. *Socialism in Cuba.* New York: 1968.

Jones, Kirby, and Mankiewicz, Frank. *With Fidel: A Portrait of Castro and Cuba.* Chicago: 1975.

Karol, K. S. *Guerrillas in Power: The Course of the Cuban Revolution.* New York: 1970.

Kozol, Jonathan. *Children of the Revolution: A Yankee Teacher in Cuban Schools*. New York: 1978.

Lefever, Ernest W. *Amsterdam to Nairobi: The World Council of Churches and the Third World*. Washington, D.C.: 1979.

Levinson, Sandra, and Brightman, Carol, eds. *Venceremos Brigade*. New York: 1971.

Lewis, Oscar; Lewis, Ruth M.; and Rigdon, Susan M. *Four Men: Living the Revolution: An Oral History of Contemporary Cuba*. Urbana, Ill.: 1977.

Lockwood, Lee. *Castro's Cuba, Cuba's Fidel*. New York: 1967.

Lynd, Staughton, and Hayden, Tom. *The Other Side*. New York: 1966.

McCarthy, Mary. *Hanoi*. New York: 1968.

Mesa-Lago, Carmelo. *Cuba in the 1970s: Pragmatism and Institutionalization*. Albuquerque: 1978.

Miller, Warren. *Ninety Miles From Home*. Boston: 1961.

Mills, C. Wright. *Listen Yankee*. New York: 1960.

Myrdal, Jan, and Kessle, Gun. *Albania Defiant*. New York: 1976.

Nicholson, Joe, Jr. *Inside Cuba*. New York: 1974.

Radosh, Ronald, ed. *The New Cuba: Paradoxes and Potentials*. New York: 1976.

Reckord, Barry. *Does Fidel Eat More Than Your Father?* New York: 1971.

Sachs, Ignacy. *The Discovery of the Third World*. Cambridge: 1976.

Salkey, Andrew. *Havana Journal*. Harmondsworth, U.K.: 1971.

Sartre, Jean-Paul. *Sartre on Cuba*. New York: 1961.

Silverman, Bertram, ed. *Man and Socialism in Cuba: The Great Debate*. New York: 1971.

Sontag, Susan. *Trip to Hanoi*. New York: 1968.

Sutherland, Elizabeth. *The Youngest Revolution: Personal Report on Cuba*. New York: 1969.

Ward, Fred. *Inside Cuba Today*. New York: 1978.

Zeitlin, Maurice, and Scheer, Robert. *Cuba: Tragedy in Our Hemisphere*. New York: 1963.

Yglesias, Jose. *In the Fist of the Revolution*. New York: 1969.

———. *Down There*. New York: 1970.

Articles and Shorter Pieces

Berger, Peter L. "Are Human Rights Universal?" *Commentary*, September 1977.

Bowles, Samuel. "Cuban Education and the Revolutionary Ideology." *Harvard Educational Review*, November 1971.

Calzon, Frank. "How Many Prisoners Does Castro Hold?" *Dissent*, Summer 1976.

Dellinger, David. "Cuba: The Revolutionary Society." *Liberation*, March 1968.

Gitlin, Todd. "Cuba and the American Movement." *Liberation*, March 1968.

Goytisolo, Juan. "Twenty Years of Castro's Revolution." *New York Review of Books*, March 22, 1979.

Horowitz, Irving Louis. "The Cuba Lobby." *The Washington Review of Strategic and International Studies*, July 1978.

Jones, LeRoi. "Cuba Libre." In *Home: Social Essays*. New York: 1966.

Kahl, Joseph A. "The Moral Economy of a Revolutionary Society." In Irving Louis Horowitz, ed., *Cuban Communism*. New Brunswick: 1977.

Landau, Saul. "Cuba: The Present Reality." *New Left Review*, May–June 1961.

Laqueur, Walter. "Third World Fantasies." *Commentary*, February 1977.

Lens, Sidney. "The Birth Pangs of Revolution." *Progressive*, December 1961.

Levi, Jeffrey. "Political Prisoner in Cuba." *Dissent*, Summer 1978.

Mailer, Norman. "The Letter to Castro" from his *The Presidential Papers*. New York: 1963.

Martin, Kingsley. "Fidel Castro's Cuba." *New Statesman*, April 21, 1961.

Maurer, Harry. "With the Venceremos in Cuba." *The Nation*, July 2, 1977.

McGovern, George. "A Talk with Castro." *New York Times Magazine*, March 13, 1977.

Miller, Stephen. "Vietnam and the Responsibility of Intellectuals." *The American Spectator*, November 1977.

Newton, Huey P. "Sanctuary in Cuba?" *Co-Evolution Quarterly*, Autumn 1977.

Radosh, Ronald. "The Cuban Revolution and Western Intellectuals." In R. Radosh, ed., *The New Cuba: Paradoxes and Potentials*. New York: 1976.

———. "On the Cuban Revolution." *Dissent*, Summer 1976.

Ripoll, Carlos. "Dissent in Cuba." *New York Times Book Review*, November 11, 1979.

Sontag, Susan. "Some Thoughts on the Right Way (for Us) To Love the Cuban Revolution." *Ramparts*, April 1969.

Thion, Serge. "Africa: War and Revolution." *Dissent*, Spring 1979.

Wrong, Dennis. "The American Left and Cuba." *Commentary*, February 1962.

China

Books

Bao Ruo-Wang. *Prisoner of Mao*. Harmondsworth, U.K.: 1976.

Beauvoir, Simone de. *The Long March*. Cleveland and New York: 1958.

Lord Boyd Orr, John, and Townsend, Peter. *What Is Happening in China?* London: 1959.

Broyelle, Claudie. *Women's Liberation in China*. Atlantic Highlands, N.J.: 1977.

Burchett, Wilfred, with Alley, Rewi. *China: The Quality of Life*. Harmondsworth, U.K.: 1976.

Cameron, James. *Mandarin Red: A Journey Behind the 'Bamboo Curtain.'* London: 1955.

Chen, Jo-hsi. *Execution of Mayor Yin*. Bloomington, Ind.: 1978.

Davidson, Basil. *Daybreak in China*. London: 1953.

Galbraith, John K. *China Passage*. Boston: 1973.

Galston, Arthur W. *Daily Life in People's China*. New York: 1973.

Greene, Felix. *China: The Country Americans Are Not Allowed To Know*. New York: 1961.

Guillain, Robert. *The Blue Ants*. London: 1957.

Hebert, Jacques, and Trudeau, Pierre Elliot. *Two Innocents in Red China*. Toronto, New York, London: 1968.

Hevi, Emmanuel John. *An African Student in China*. New York: 1962.

Horn, Dr. Joshua S. *Away with All Pests: An English Surgeon in People's China, 1954–1969*. London: 1969.

Hsia, Chih-yen. *Coldest Winter in Peking*. Garden City: 1978.

Johnson, Hewlett. *China's New Creative Age*. London: 1953.

————. *The Upsurge of China*. Peking: 1961.

Konigsberger, Hans. *Love and Hate in China*. New York: 1966.

Kraft, Joseph. *The Chinese Difference*. New York: 1973.

Leys, Simon. *Chinese Shadows*. New York: 1977.

Loh, Robert. *Escape From Red China*. New York: 1962.

Macciocchi, Maria Antonietta. *Daily Life in Revolutionary China*. New York: 1972.

Mehnert, Klaus. *China Returns*. New York: 1972.

Marcuse, Jacques. *The Peking Papers*. New York: 1967.

Milton, David, and Milton, Nancy Dale. *The Wind Will Not Subside*. New York: 1976.

Modiano, Colette. *Twenty Snobs and Mao: Travelling Deluxe in Communist China*. London: 1969.

Moravia, Alberto. *The Red Book and the Great Wall*. New York: 1968.

Myrdal, Jan. *Report From a Chinese Village*. New York: 1965.

Myrdal, Jan, and Kessle, Gun. *China: The Revolution Continued*. New York: 1970.

Passin, Herbert. *China's Cultural Diplomacy*. New York: 1962.

Portisch, Hugo. *Red China Today*. Chicago: 1966.

Roy, Jules. *Journey Through China*. New York: 1966.

Salisbury, Harrison E. *To Peking—and Beyond. A Report on the New Asia*. New York: 1973.

Schell, Orville. *In the People's Republic: An American's First-Hand View of Living and Working in China*. New York: 1977.

Selbourne, David *et al*. *An Eye to China*. London: 1975.

Shewmaker, Kenneth E. *Americans and Chinese Communists, 1927–1945*. Ithaca, N.Y.: 1971.

Sidel, Ruth. *Women and Child Care in China—A Firsthand Report*. New York: 1972.

Snow, Edgar. *Red China Today*. New York: 1970.

Strong, Anna Louise. *Letters From China*. Peking: 1965.

Stucki, Lorenz. *Behind the Great Wall*. New York: 1965.

Suyin, Han. *China in the Year 2001*. New York: 1967.

Terrill, Ross. *800,000,000—The Real China*. Boston: 1971.

Topping, Audrey. *Dawn Wakes in the East*. New York: 1973.

Townsend, Peter. *China Phoenix: The Revolution in China.* London: 1955.

Tuchman, Barbara W. *Notes From China.* New York: 1972.

Urban, George, ed. *The Miracles of Chairman Mao. A Compendium of Devotional Literature 1966–1970.* London: 1971.

Wilson, Dick, ed. *Mao Tse-Tung in the Scales of History.* Cambridge, U.K.: 1977.

Worsley, Peter. *Inside China.* London: 1975.

China! Inside The Peoples Republic. By the Committee of Concerned Asian Scholars. New York: 1972.

China—Science Walks on Two Legs. A Report from Science for the People. New York: 1974.

Experience Without Precedent: Some Quaker Observations on China Today. Report of an American Friends Service Committee Delegation's Visit to China. Philadelphia: 1972.

Political Imprisonment in the People's Republic of China. London: 1978.

Articles and Shorter Pieces

Broyelle, Claudie and Jacques. "Everyday Life in The People's Republic." *Quadrant* (Sydney, Australia), November 1978.

Desai, Padma. "China and India: Development During the Last 25 Years. Discussion." *American Economic Review,* May 1975.

Eberstadt, Nick. "Has China Failed?" *New York Review of Books,* April 5, 1979.

———. "China: How Much Success?" *New York Review of Books,* May 3, 1979.

Fabre-Luce, Alfred. "Chinese Journey." *The Atlantic,* December 1959.

Fairbank, John K. "The New China and the American Connection." *Foreign Affairs,* October 1972.

———. "The New China Tourism of the 1970s." In his *China Perceived.* New York: 1974.

———. "On the Death of Mao." *New York Review of Books,* October 14, 1976.

Frolic, Bernard. "Comparing China and the Soviet Union." *Contemporary China,* Summer 1978.

———. "Reflections on the Chinese Model of Development." *Social Forces,* December 1978.

Johnson, Sheila K. "To China with Love." *Commentary,* June 1973.

Karnow, Stanley. "China Through Rose-Tinted Glasses." *The Atlantic,* October 1973.

Kenez, Peter. "A Sense of Déjà Vu—Traveling in China." *New Leader,* November 1973.

Kolodney, David. "Et Tu China?" *Ramparts,* May 1972.

Lamont, Corliss. *Trip to Communist China: An Informal Report.* (Pamphlet.) New York: 1976.

Leys, Simon. "Human Rights in China." *Quadrant* (Sydney, Australia), November 1978.

Loh, Robert. "Setting the Stage for Foreigners." *The Atlantic*, December 1959.

Luttwak, Edward N. "Seeing China Plain." *Commentary*, December 1976.

Pye, Lucian W. "Building a Relationship on the Sands of Cultural Exchanges." In William J. Barnds, ed., *China and America: The Search for a New Relationship*. New York: 1977.

———. *China Revisited*. (Monograph.) Center for International Studies, Massachusetts Institute of Technology. Cambridge: 1973.

"Dr. Spock in China." *New China*, Issue 1, 1974.

Tavris, Carol. "Field Report: Women in China." *Psychology Today*, May 1974.

Walker, Richard L. "Guided Tourism in China." *Problems of Communism*, September–October 1957.

Whyte, Martin King. "Inequality and Stratification in China." *The China Quarterly*, December 1975.

———. "Corrective Labor Camps in China." *Asian Survey*, March 1973.

Wooton, Barbara. "A Journey to China." *Encounter*, June 1973.

Zagoria, Donald S. "China by Daylight." *Dissent*, Spring 1975.

Intellectuals, Politics, and Morality

Books

Aaron, Daniel. *Writers on the Left: Episodes in American Literary Communism*. New York: 1961.

Aaron, Daniel, and Bendiner, R., eds. *The Strenuous Decade: A Social and Intellectual Record of the 1930s*. Garden City, N.Y.: 1970.

Aldridge, John W. *In the Country of the Young*. New York: 1969.

Almond, Gabriel A. *The Appeals of Communism*. Princeton: 1954.

Aron, Raymond. *The Opium of Intellectuals*. London: 1957.

Bauman, Zygmunt. *Socialism: The Active Utopia*. London: 1976.

Beauvoir, Simone de. *Force of Circumstance*. New York: 1965.

———. *All Said and Done*. New York: 1974.

Bell, Daniel. *The Cultural Contradictions of Capitalism*. New York: 1976.

Berman, Ronald. *America in the Sixties*. New York: 1968.

Brustein, Robert. *Revolution as Theatre*. New York: 1971.

Chomsky, Noam. *American Power and the New Mandarins*. New York: 1967.

Clecak, Peter. *Radical Paradoxes; Dilemmas of the American Left: 1945–1970*. New York: 1973.

Cockburn, Claud. *Discord of Trumpets*. New York: 1956.

———. *Crossing the Line*. London: 1958.

Coser, Lewis A. *Men of Ideas*. New York: 1965.

Cowley, Malcolm. *The Dream of the Golden Mountains: Remembering the 1930s*. New York: 1980.

Crossman, Richard, ed. *The God That Failed*. New York: 1949.

Diggins, John P. *The American Left in the Twentieth Century*. New York: 1973.

Feuer, Lewis. *Marx and the Intellectuals*. Garden City, N.Y.: 1969.

Franklin, Howard Bruce. *Back Where You Came From: A Life in the Death of the Empire*. New York: 1975.

Glazer, Nathan. *The Social Basis of American Communism*. New York: 1961.

Hamilton, Alastair. *The Appeal of Fascism: A Study of Intellectuals and Fascism 1919–1945*. London: 1971.

Hicks, Granville. *Where We Came Out*. New York: 1954.

Howe, Irving, and Coser, Lewis A. *The American Communist Party: A Critical History 1919–1957*. Boston: 1957.

Hynes, Samuel. *The Auden Generation: Literature and Politics in England in the 1930s*. London: 1976.

Kadushin, Charles. *The American Intellectual Elite*. Boston: 1974.

Kazin, Alfred. *Starting Out in the Thirties*. New York: 1965.

Koestler, Arthur. *The Trail of the Dinosaur and Other Essays*. London: 1970.

Konrád, George, and Szelényi, Iván. *The Intellectuals on the Road to Class Power*. New York: 1979.

Laqueur, Walter, and Mosse, George L., eds. *The Left-Wing Intellectuals Between the Wars, 1919–1939*. New York: 1966.

———. *Literature and Politics in the Twentieth Century*. New York: 1967.

Madsen, Axel. *Hearts and Minds: The Common Journey of Simone de Beauvoir and Jean-Paul Sartre*. New York: 1977.

Manuel, Frank E., and Manuel, Fritzie P. *Utopian Thought in the Western World*. Cambridge: 1979.

Marcuse, Herbert. *One-Dimensional Man*. Boston: 1964.

———. *An Essay on Liberation*. Boston: 1969.

Milosz, Czeslav. *The Captive Mind*. New York: 1955.

Myrdal, Jan. *Confessions of a Disloyal European*. New York: 1968.

Nearing, Scott. *The Making of a Radical*. New York: 1972.

Newfield, Jack. *The Prophetic Minority*. New York: 1967.

Parkin, Frank. *Middle Class Radicalism: The Social Bases of the British Campaign for Nuclear Disarmament*. Manchester, U.K.: 1968.

Pells, Richard H. *Radical Visions and American Dreams: Culture and Social Thought in the Depression Years*. New York: 1973.

Revel, Jean François. *The Totalitarian Temptation*. New York: 1977.

Rieff, Philip, ed. *On Intellectuals*. Garden City, N.Y.: 1969.

Schwartz, David C. *Political Alienation and Political Behavior*. Chicago: 1973.

Shils, Edward. *The Intellectuals and the Powers and Other Essays*. Chicago: 1972.

Steinfels, Peter. *The Neo-Conservatives*. New York: 1979.

Stromberg, Roland N. *After Everything: Western Intellectual History Since 1945*. New York: 1975.

Wesson, Robert A. *Why Marxism? The Continuing Success of a Failed Theory*. New York: 1976.

Whitfield, Stephen J. *Scott Nearing: Apostle of American Radicalism*. New York: 1974.

Winegarten, Renee. *Writers and Revolution: The Fatal Lure of Action*. New York: 1974.

Wood, Neal. *Communism and British Intellectuals*. New York: 1959.
Young, Nigel. *An Infantile Disorder? The Crisis and Decline of the New Left*. London: 1977.
Anatomy of Anti-Communism. A Report Prepared for the Peace Education Division of the American Friends Service Committee. New York: 1969.

Articles and Shorter Pieces
Adelson, Joseph. "Inventing the Young." *Commentary*, May 1971.
Berger, Peter L. "The Socialist Myth." *Public Interest*, Summer 1976.
Billington, James H. "The Intelligentsia and the Religion of Humanity." *The American Historical Review*, July 1960.
Caute, David. "Two Types of Alienation." In *The Illusion*. London: 1971.
Chomsky, Noam, and Herman, Edward S. "Distortions at Fourth Hand." *The Nation*, June 25, 1977.
Conquest, Robert. In "The Intellectuals and Just Causes—A Symposium." *Encounter*, October 1967.
Enzensberger, Hans Magnus. "Tourists of the Revolution." In *Consciousness Industry*. New York: 1974.
Evans, Gerard. "Paradises Lost: Or Where Are You, Fidel, When I Need You?" *New Society* (London), February 22, 1979.
Glantz, Oscar. "The New Left Radicalism and Punitive Moralism." *Polity*, Spring 1975.
Hansen, A. Eric. "Intellect and Power: Notes on the Intellectual as a Political Type." *Journal of Politics*, Vol. 31, May 1969.
Hicks, Granville. "How I Came to Communism." *New Masses*, September 1932.
Hobsbawm, E. J. "Intellectuals and Communism." In *Revolutionaries*. New York: 1973.
Hollander, Paul. "Sociology, Selective Determinism and the Rise of Expectations." *The American Sociologist*, November 1973.
————. "Reflections on Anti-Americanism in Our Times." *Worldview*, June 1978.
Koestler, Arthur. "On Disbelieving Atrocities." In *Yogi and the Commissar*. New York: 1961.
————. "The Intelligentsia." In *Yogi and the Commissar*.
Kohak, Erazim V. "Requiem for Utopia." *Dissent*, Winter 1969.
Kolakowski, Leszek. "Intellectuals Against Intellect." *Daedalus*, Summer 1972.
Labedz, Leopold. "Chomsky Revisited." *Encounter*, July 1980.
"Liberal Anti-Communism Revisited." Symposium, *Commentary*, September 1967.
Lowenthal, Richard. "On the Disaffection of Western Intellectuals." *Encounter*, July 1977.
Maurer, Marvin. "Quakers in Politics: Israel, PLO and Social Revolution." *Midstream*, November 1977.

Morris, Stephen. "Chomsky on U.S. Foreign Policy." *Harvard International Review,* December–January 1981.

Nettler, Gwynn. "Shifting the Load." *American Behavioral Scientist,* January–February 1972.

Paz, Octavio. "Sartre in Our Time." *Dissent,* Autumn 1980.

Potter, David M. "The Roots of American Alienation" and "Rejection of the Prevailing American Society." In *History and American Society.* New York: 1973.

"Sartre Accuses the Intellectuals of Bad Faith." *New York Times Magazine,* October 17, 1971.

"The Last Words of Jean-Paul Sartre." *Dissent,* Autumn 1980.

Sperber, Manes. "Pilgrims to Utopia." In *Man and His Deeds.* New York: 1970.

Ulam, Adam. "Socialism and Utopia." In Frank E. Manuel, ed., *Utopias and Utopian Thought.* Boston: 1966.

Vree, Dale. " 'Stripped Clean': The Berrigans and the Politics of Guilt and Martyrdom." *Ethics,* July 1975.

Watson, George. "Were the Intellectuals Duped? The 1930s Revisited." *Encounter,* December 1973.

Index

Page numbers followed by the letter "n" refer to names to be found in the note section of the book. All other names appear in the text.